Writers on the Left

WRITERS
ON THE LEFT

Daniel Aaron

OXFORD UNIVERSITY PRESS

OXFORD   NEW YORK

© 1961, 1977 by Daniel Aaron

Preface to the Galaxy Book edition, copyright © 1973 by the American Studies Research Center

First published by Harcourt, Brace & World, Inc., 1961, in the Communism in American Life series, Clinton Rossiter, General Editor

First issued in a paperback edition by Avon Books, 1965

First issued as an Oxford University Press paperback, with a new Preface, 1977

Reprinted by arrangement with Harcourt Brace Jovanovich, Inc.

Library of Congress Cataloging in Publication Data

Aaron, Daniel, 1912-
   Writers on the left.

   Includes bibliographical references and index.
   1. American literature—20th century—History and criticism. 2. Communism and literature. 3. Authors, American—20th century—Political and social views.
I. Title.
PS228.C6A2 1977   810'.9'3   77-2792
ISBN 0-19-519970-7

Printed in the United States of America

To Howard Mumford Jones

Many people find their way to the general *through the* personal. *In that sense biographies have their right. And, that being so, better they should be written without great distortions (small ones are quite unavoidable).*

LEON TROTSKY

. . . at the beginning of a revolution, the vividness of emotions always exceeds the importance of events, as at their close the very opposite is sadly true.

ALEXIS DE TOCQUEVILLE

It is not the business of writers to accuse or prosecute, but to take the part even of guilty men once they have been condemned and are undergoing punishment. You will say: what about politics? what about the interests of the State? But great writers and artists must engage in politics only as far as it is necessary to defend oneself against it. There are plenty of accusers, prosecutors and gendarmes without them; and, anyway, the role of Paul suits them better than that of Saul.

ANTON CHEKHOV

Forbearance—good word.

F. SCOTT FITZGERALD

PREFACE TO THE GALAXY BOOK EDITION

LET'S ASSUME from the outset that it is presumptuous for an author —especially an academic author—to undertake a post-mortem of his book even if he does so for the purposes of scholarly discussion. On such occasions he is likely to become self-conscious or self-defensive or overly apologetic. But if he submits himself to such an exercise, what is the safest approach he can take? Perhaps to view the writing and reception of his book as a discrete historical 'event' and to offer his reconsiderations almost as if he were *amicus curiae* rather than party to an action.

Writers on the Left was commissioned. It had never occurred to the author to write a book on Communism and American writers until he was invited in 1955 to contribute to a series of studies of Communist influence in American life sponsored by the Ford Foundation. Some of his friends warned him that it was premature to write such a book, that he was opening up a can of worms, and the first public response to the Foundation announcement seemed to bear out these apprehensions. J.B. Matthews, "garrulous and unstable" (according to Arthur Schlesinger) and ideological aide for Senator Joseph McCarthy, roasted the Ford scholars in the *American Mercury* as crypto-Reds or at best as biased and incompetent and predicted the Ford project would

Paper delivered before the American Literature Section of the Modern Language Association in December 1972, at the invitation of the program chairman, Professor Michael Millgate. Each participant was asked to review one of his own books and indicate what further work in the same general area seemed most interesting. First published in the *Indian Journal of American Studies*, III (June 1973).

be "the largest pile of mis-educational printed matter on Communism ever to roll from the presses in this country." Most of the writers involved conducted their researches in what might be called a 'below-board' way—sneaking interviews, submitting to inspections by their suspicious subjects, taking measures to protect their informants.

The author never really finished his book. He just stopped writing, knowing how much he had left undone. Probably every author discerns a good many weaknesses in his book before he submits it to the publisher. He secretly hopes that the flaws so apparent to him will not be as obvious to his readers. This feeling may be less intense, though not altogether absent, if his subject is unprovocative; but if he is breaking new ground, if his scope is large, if the topics introduced are the kind that arouse intense feelings and highly partisan responses—then his uneasiness is likely to be great. This is especially so when he is trying to justify an excursion into the 'visitable past,' when he knows that many of the persons who figure in the book (as well as their friends and enemies) will be around to read it.

Writers on the Left got a friendly and, at the same time, a critical reception, partly owing to its subject matter and partly to the timing of its publication. After two decades, the 30's—the memories of which had been forgotten, or, more likely, suppressed in intellectual and cultural circles—were about to be activated. By 1961 the fears and animosities engendered by Senator McCarthy and his inquisitors had largely if not entirely diminished. The timid 50's had come to a close. All the same, many of the men and women once active in radical affairs hardly relished the prospect of seeing their pasts dredged up— even in the interest of social history. A number of them had become prominent in academic life, in publishing, films. Some held government office. Some were writers, art dealers, labor officials, businessmen.

But what fears they may have had proved groundless. Neither his book (nor any other book in the Ford series) 'named names' or touched off any investigations. The book was widely reviewed; it inspired a considerable amount of unpublished commentary as well— some of it in the form of crank mail but more of it from people who had lived through the period covered in the book and who knew at first hand the episodes and people discussed. In addition to communications from strangers, the author had the criticisms of friends and the supplementary reflections of informants to ponder.

Now after more than a decade, he is pondering this book again. The blemishes immediately spotted by both friendly and unfriendly critics in 1961 stand out more plainly than ever. The spate of monographs, biographies, memoirs, letters, and articles about the 1930's—if they don't invalidate the facts and interpretations of *Writers on the Left*— certainly complement them, amplify them, show them in different contexts. This was bound to happen given the quickened interest in the decade and the fact that many of the writers mentioned in the book— Matthew Josephson, Malcolm Cowley, John Dos Passos, Edward Dahlberg, Mike Gold, Max Eastman, Josephine Herbst, Jack Conroy and others—had reached that stage in their lives when they wanted to set the record straight in their own terms. In some instances the author was directly responsible for these revelations. He urged Mike Gold to return to the days of *Jews Without Money* and to re-see these times in a less tendentious way. Gold strongly resisted the idea at first but then began a series of reminiscences in the *Peoples' World*—a sort of unlugubrious sequel to his best known work. He also encouraged Max Eastman to complete the second volume of his autobiography and served as an unofficial literary agent for its publication.

In short, apart from its intrinsic merits and defects, *Writers on the Left* helped to loosen the social and political constraints that for twenty years had inhibited the writing of a frank and objective history of what the book not very precisely called literary communism. Of course it was not his book alone that opened up the subject to candid examination, but with few exceptions, most previous studies (Eugène Lyons, *The Red Decade,* is only one example) might be described as historical diatribes. His own book (he makes this claim on the basis of the letters he received after the book came out) made it possible for a good many people to turn their hitherto averted eyes and thoughts to the forbidden past. Many of his correspondents (some of whom had participated in the events he described) seemed eager to pass on their own recollections, to correct as well as to criticize. If nothing else,

Writers on the Left had a therapeutic value. It dissolved feelings of shame and guilt, mitigated anxieties, and started people remembering.

So much for one of its happier consequences. When one turns to the book itself, its sins of omission and commission are clearer than they were a decade ago. It does not seem too important today that the author was accused of being 'sentimental' and 'soft' in his treatment of political nincompoops and bad writers and of suffering knaves and fools too gladly; that the picture of the 30's he presented was less gaudy, ferocious, and melodramatic than the reality. But one can't pass over criticisms about imperfect structure, misplaced emphases, and curious lacunae.

In devising the form of *Writers on the Left,* the author took a few cues from John Dos Passos's *U.S.A.*—a collective novel that covered approximately the same period he was attempting to encompass. From Dos Passos he borrowed the trick of passing back and forth from what might be called 'group narratives' (that is to say, narratives about organizations, magazines, coteries and the like) to stories of 'representative men' and to inter-chapters of literary history that might be likened in a very loose sort of way to Dos Passos's "News Reels." What he failed to do (it was Henry Nash Smith who first called this failure to his attention—only too late for him to do anything about it) was to introduce a counterpart to *U.S.A.'s* "Camera Eye." He didn't suffuse sufficiently enough or critically enough his own point of view into the book as a whole.

The author's excuse seemed more valid to him in 1961 than it does now. His assignment, he decided then, required him to write a chronicle, a book of annals. Since others had judged and condemned before the evidence had been gathered, he thought his responsibility was to narrate and describe without trying to play the role of Rhadamanthus. However (as he knew they would), biases, preconceptions, creep willy-nilly into the strictest reports. What the literary historian elects to write about, what he considers of major or lesser importance, the reliance he places on certain kinds of information and his rejection (whether deliberate or unconscious) of other sources—all conspire against objectivity.

In this instance, the author paid a penalty for his close association with a man without whom he would have been unable to see the Communist literary movement from the inside and without whom he would never have obtained an introduction into closed circles. He was a good man and a brillant man; he became the author's close friend and mentor while assisting and 'educating' him—but he was far from being an unprejudiced informant. Any historian whose subject is the recent past must weigh the advantages and disadvantages of working with the principal actors in the events he is relating—people who have their own axes to grind; and this is especially true when the activities in which these actors participated have more than a passing historical interest—when his readers may include not only scholars but government investigators with the power of subpoena. The advantages are obvious, the disadvantages perhaps less apparent. It may turn out that what the historian interprets as cooperation may inadvertently be metamorphosed into collaboration.

Several of the author's reviewers entertained such a possibility or at least implied that he had lent his ear too readily and too uncritically to certain voices. Floyd Dell gently said as much in a letter filled with reminiscences; James T. Farrell made the charge more bluntly in a series of letters, and the same implication is carried in William Phillips's thoughtful and trenchant essay, "What Happened in the 30's," in which he addressed himself, along with other matters, to *Writers on the Left*. The essay is worth mentioning not only because Phillips discussed the book at considerable length, but also because he himself served in some of the literary campaigns of the Depression decade and was sensitive to its incongruities and contradictions.

Phillips found *Writers on the Left* freer of the more egregious faults that in his opinion disfigured most of the 30's scholarship—especially that spurious objectivity which is an outgrowth of ignorance, the kind that "means an inability to make discriminating judgments," but he criticized the book for reliving rather than re-examining or re-thinking the period. It supplied the facts; it was balanced and fair; it served "as an antidote to the notion of Communism as nothing but a 'conspiracy' bandied about by reactionaries and obsessive anti-Communists—a notion which absolves people from thinking about history." But the author's "scholarly neutrality," he went on to say, made it difficult for him "to separate independent ideas from orthodoxies or from free-lance nonsense that was officially tolerated."

The charge is over-stated. The author had no trouble in separating the ideas of talented artists and independent thinkers from those of partisan idiots, but Phillips is by no means off the mark. The author might have drawn sharper distinctions between the statements and opinions of original minds and those of the rank-and-file practi-tioners of Left rhetoric. His failure to do so can be attributed partly to his expository method, his trick of paraphrasing the views of his sub-jects, major and minor, as if he had entered into their minds and was speaking in their behalf. Hence ideological and literary fatuities were set down most of the time without explicit authorial comment.

Again (another failure of commission) it was not enough for the author simply to record the struggle between the Party people and the anti-Stalin dissidents over the control of the *Partisan Review*; the lit-erary implications of that fight needed to be spelled out. Phillips's com-ment—that he and his friends who took over the magazine stood for "purity in politics and impurity in literature" would certainly have been disputed at the time—and not only by the Stalinist hacks. It was the 'impurity' of their Trotskyist politics that made editors of the new *Partisan Review* persona non grata with the CP leadership—not their admiration for Eliot and Kafka and Yeats. He is right, however, in underscoring the anti-intellectual biases that pervaded the radical lit-erary movement in the 30's and in linking these biases with the "free-wheeling grass roots tradition." *Writers on the Left* did not ignore what Phillips calls "the conflict between a free floating radical spirit and a historical force that both channeled it and throttled it," but the book did less than justice to the influence and literary importance of such anti-Stalinists as Sidney Hook, Meyer Schapiro, James T. Farrell, Edmund Wilson, Dwight Macdonald, and Mary McCarthy. It stopped short of tracing the literary implications of Trotsky's dismissal of pro-letarian art and his concessions to Bohemia. It passed over too cavalierly those writers-on-the-left who were never Communist, perhaps not even socialist, but who considered themselves on the left side of the political spectrum.

It could be argued, in fact, that some of the political nomenclature used in the book is inexact even while conceding that radical terminology in the 30's was never very precise. Take the key word—Communist—that meant and still means different things to different people. An accurate history of the literary left, as Joseph Freeman cautioned the author, ought to define 'Communism' at every "crucial *point of change* in at least three ways. It should show what Moscow meant by 'communism,' what the Party meant by it and what various WRITERS meant by it." The same is true for the word 'left' or the word 'revolutionist.'

Floyd Dell considered himself a revolutionist even after he had repudiated the Communist Party. "I was always interested in movements (feminist, educational, Freudian) which had revolutionary implications," he wrote to the author; "and these were none the less truly revolutionary if Communist politicians were unable to understand the value of them. . . . The question can be raised of how truly revolutionary any professional (or practical) revolutionist can be." To extend Dell's point, the clash between radical politics and radical avantgarde art was discernible in the United States, as Meyer Schapiro has shown, at least as early as the Armory Show. For Phillips, the most portentous consequence of the radical movement in the 1930's was the fact that it "broke the radical spirit of literature by lowering its sights and making it more palatable for popular consumption." The process by which the Party seized upon this audience and the reasons for doing so can be found in *Writers on the Left,* but it is not evaluated.

Some of the objections to the merely descriptive treatment of this literary chronicle might have been obviated had the author devoted more space to the description and analysis of literary examples. Interchapters placed at strategic intervals and recording the changes in literary fashions would have swelled an already lengthy book. But the discussion of key works of fiction or poems or plays or critical articles —representative books of both the radical establishment *and* its opposition—would have dramatized, made concrete, sharpened some of the generalizations and *implied* judgments that fill *Writers on the Left*. Such moments would have provided the author with an occasion to speak out more boldly than he did and declare explicitly his own point of view.

As it stands, *Writers on the Left* is a useful book, a book to cite, still readable and informative but incomplete. While writing it, the author had its sequel in mind, a book that would describe the writing of the original, the bizarre adventures and embarrassments experienced while researching it, the stories told to him off the record. The sequel would have enabled him to prepare a candid and opinionated conclusion in which his antipathies and prejudices and unacknowledged convictions would be given full vent. He also thought of writing a purely literary review of 30's literature to complement the social and political record of the literary left.

He did neither partly because the first would have been a betrayal of confidences and the second an ordeal he wasn't ready at the time to undergo.

Hence he can understand the animadversions of his friends and well-wishers and his less amiable critics. *Writers on the Left* turned out to be a scenario—pretty detailed, full of hints, stocked with literary lore, sometimes amusing—but a scenario. The full-fledged exploration of the 30's is now more than ever a collective enterprise.

D. A.

This book is a social chronicle of the Left Wing writer from 1912 to the early 1940's. More specifically, it describes the response of a selected group of American writers to the idea of communism and deals with particular issues and events during the first forty years of this century which helped to shape their opinions. I have paid only the slightest attention to the literary Left after 1940; by this time it was already separated from the main currents of American intellectual life and had acquired a sociological rather than a literary interest.

A very small fraction of the Left Wing writers were once members of the Communist Party. A considerably larger number might better be designated "fellow travelers." I apply this slippery and inexact phrase to those who were in the "movement," who sympathized with the objectives of the party, wrote for the party press, or knowingly affiliated with associations sponsored by the party. Without including the fellow travelers or liberals or nonparty radicals, the story of literary communism would be very thin indeed, for the Communist Party had far less influence on writers than the *idea* of communism or the image of Soviet Russia.

It is of less importance now to know who was in the movement than to understand why so many writers were once affected by the current radicalisms and were angrily opposed to what they felt to be the cruelty and stupidity of the standing order. What caused the alienation of artists and intellectuals? Why did so many well-intentioned, sensitive, and gifted men and women turn to communism or support Communist-inspired causes? Why did most of them remain in the movement for such a short time? And why did they finally break away?

In order to provide some answers to these questions, I have tried to place the story of the literary radicals in the context of our cultural history. I have consulted the participants whenever possible—right, left, and center—and have written their experiences as a series of episodes, each of which reveals something significant about the movement and about the men and women who were active in it. Although most of the writers who had anything to do with what I call literary communism are at least mentioned, the book focuses on a relatively small number of people who represented, in my opinion, the prevailing attitudes among a cross section of the literary Left Wing.

My account is necessarily incomplete. Nevertheless, I hope it will serve a threefold purpose: first, to help the younger reader, for whom the events described here are as remote as the Peloponnesian War, to learn why it was that so many writers and intellectuals were once willing to embrace a revolutionary cause; second, to explain the writers to those who lived through the radical decades without ever coming into contact with the literary Left Wing; and third, to remind the veterans who actually participated in a few literary skirmishes what they may have forgotten or never have known about the campaign as a whole. To the world, and perhaps to them, the story of their political and literary adventures between two world wars may seem unimportant, certainly not worth retelling in any great detail, "yet unto us," as Cotton Mather said of some skirmishes in his own day, "it hath been considerable enough to make an history."

It was to discover more about the impact of communism on American life that the Fund for the Republic set up a project under the direction of Professor Clinton Rossiter and generously provided me with funds to write this book. During the course of my research, I consulted many of the writers mentioned in the following pages. Almost without exception, they were candid and friendly in their response, and I have come to know and admire them as people even when I have disagreed with their past or present convictions. Almost all have revised wholly or in part the political and economic opinions they once embraced, but I have not written this book either to castigate them for their former beliefs or to "clear" them. My evaluation of the meaning of their collective experience can be found in my concluding chapter.

I am especially indebted to Michael Blankfort, Malcolm Cowley, Jack Conroy, Leon Dennen, Theodore Draper, Max Eastman, Joseph Freeman, Michael Gold, Josephine Herbst, Granville Hicks, Joshua Kunitz, Albert Maltz, Nina Melville, William Phillips, George Sklar, Herbert Solow, Tiba Wilner, and Edmund Wilson.

Bruce Bliven, Kenneth Burke, E. E. Cummings, Robert Gorham Davis, John Dos Passos, Waldo Frank, Henry Hazlitt, Alfred Kazin, Joseph Wood Krutch, John Howard Lawson, Harry Levin, Lewis Mumford, Upton Sinclair, Allen Tate, and Thornton Wilder have also supplied me with pertinent facts.

I have profited from my discussions with my colleagues in this series: Daniel Bell, Donald Egbert, Moshe Decter, Theodore Draper, Nathan Glazer, Robert Iversen, William Goldsmith, David Shannon, Ralph Roy, and Clinton Rossiter.

The first draft of the book was written at the Center for Advanced Study in the Behavioral Sciences. I wish to thank the officers of the Center and Ralph Tyler, the director, for enabling me to spend a year of research and writing at Stanford, California.

My thanks go also to Mr. Stanley Pargellis, the director of the Newberry Library, Kenneth S. Davis, former editor of the *Newberry Library Bulletin,* and the twenty-one scholars who attended the Tenth Library Conference in American Studies for their helpful if sometimes rough comments on my paper "Communism and the American Writer." I am also indebted to David A. Randall, Director of Rare Books at the Indiana University Library, for permitting me to use the Upton Sinclair collection.

A number of friends read portions of my manuscript and made helpful suggestions, among them my brother, Benjamin Aaron, Newton Arvin, Lee Benson, Mrs. Hollis Chenery, Theodore Draper, Max Eastman, Donald Egbert, Joseph Freeman, Granville Hicks, Richard Hofstadter, Arthur Mann, Henry F. May, Jacqueline Miller, Norman

Holmes Pearson, Sylvan Schendler, Edward Shils, Mark Schorer, Henry Nash Smith, and George Sklar.

Finally, I should like to express my gratitude to my students Peggy Gilder, Arlene Hirst, Margaret Sheffield, Nan Darling, Beverly Black, Leila Wilson, Diane Scharfeld.

CONTENTS

Contents

Writers on the Left

PART ONE

·

PATTERNS

OF

REBELLION

American literature, for all of its affirmative spirit, is the most searching and unabashed criticism of our national limitations that exists, the product of one hundred and fifty years of quarreling between the writer and his society. The social criticism of writers, both the open and the veiled kind, has usually sprung from an extreme sensitiveness to the disparity between ideals and practices, but it has also reflected the hostility of the artist to a world that slights his needs and holds his values in contempt.

The American writer, of course, has shared many of the convictions of his audience and, like the members of other minority groups, has shown signs of self-hatred and guilt for his failure to measure up to the national ideal. Reared in a society honoring action rather than contemplation, a society distrusting any effort, intellectual or physical, that served no obviously useful purpose, the writer was sometimes hard-pressed to justify his occupation.* He had not only to

* According to Van Wyck Brooks, American writers began as disinterested searchers for truth and ended by succumbing to the American tradition of "getting things done, of definite accomplishment. . . . The natural temper of the country is horribly evangelical, and it is only by trying to get some new ideas 'across,' that the intellectual comes to feel that he has a respectable place in our contemporary social life. When thought is despised and feared, one must make action and verbiage do duty for thought; one must 'show results.'" "Where Are Our Intellectuals?" *The Freeman*, II (Sept. 29, 1920), pp. 53-54.

reckon with the indifference of the average man, engrossed in the problems of everyday living; he had also to face the clerical and religious bias against the unsanctified imagination.

Hence the nineteenth-century American writer sermonized in his poetry and fiction. Lest his public condemn him as frivolous if not subversive, he presented himself in the role of secular priest and often chose literary forms (the religious treatise, the humorous dialogue, the educational essay, the political tract, among others) best suited for inspiration and instruction as well as for entertainment.

From its beginnings, American literature has been hortatory and didactic, a literature of "exposure," of the first person, and although the moral tone becomes less obvious and persistent after the mid-nineteenth century, it never disappears. The didactic note sounds not only in the angry "protest" novels that have periodically aroused a lethargic public since the days of *Uncle Tom's Cabin,* but also in the less evangelical and more truly dangerous novels like *Huckleberry Finn* where the moral burden is masked in genial humor.

Paradoxically, the American writer's running quarrel with his society, his natural inclination to admonish and to castigate in the guise of entertainment, may have sprung as much or more from his identity with that society as from his alienation. He has never been easy during his rebellious moods, never able to divorce himself from the cowards, scoundrels, and vulgarians he attacks. Indeed, the very intensity with which insurgent generations of rebels have assaulted the unkillable beliefs of the bourgeoisie suggests an attachment to their enemy the rebels themselves have hardly been aware of. Made bitter by rejection, and despising a milieu so uncongenial for the creative artist, the aberrant or misfit writer still yearns to be reabsorbed into his society, to speak for it, to celebrate it. And the history of rebellious literary generations, which is in one sense the history of the writer in America, is a record of ambivalence, of divided loyalties, of uneasy revolt.

These revolts seem to have occurred periodically from the early nineteenth century to the present, and although each displays unique features, a recurring pattern seems to run through them all.

In act one, which might be called the preparatory stage, the new generation of writers comes of age. Usually the beneficiaries of a culture that has nourished and educated them, they are often precious and censorious, impatient of traditional literary or aesthetic conventions, and frequently unaware or neglectful of the accomplishments (and blunders) of their predecessors. That is why some critics have seen the history of American letters as a succession of new starts, as "momentary efforts by solitary writers or by intellectual groups to differentiate themselves and to set a new current in motion, with the inevitable petering out, and the necessity of a fresh start over again." That is why we have "a new generation of writers every five years" and why American literary movements, unlike those abroad, seem to move back and forth without ever incorporating what has already been accomplished.[1]

Each new generation has its prophet, sometimes more than one, who articulates its aspirations and directs the assault against the Philistines.* The period of preparation is usually marked by the pursuit and discovery of a philosophical system, sometimes of a domestic but more often of a foreign origin, to sanction the movement. American intellectuals, like American technicians, have always been great borrowers; Europe has traditionally provided the theory, America the application. Molded by American conditions and preoccupied by American problems, the artist or intellectual "reaches out for the results of an older and more complex culture . . . reworks them and refashions them to suit his own needs, and . . . perturbs and enriches the life of America."[2] Coleridge, Carlyle, Fourier, Taine, Spencer, Tolstoy, Nietzsche, Freud, Shaw, and Marx are only a few of the European prophets who have been domesticated and sometimes vulgarized to serve American intellectual purposes.

Act two, the flood tide of the movement, is customarily heralded by a manifesto of some kind. Then what begins as philosophical

---

* By literary "generation," I do not mean necessarily an age group, but, rather, a *cluster* of writers bound together by shared assumptions and attitudes and by a common program. The "Philistines" appear under a number of guises: as the "Men of Understanding" in Emerson's day; as the "Plutocrats" in the Gilded Age; as "Puritans" in the half-dozen years before 1918; as the "Booboisie" or "Babbitts" in the Menckenian twenties; as the "Bourgeoisie" in the Marxist thirties; as the "Middlebrows" in the fifties; and perhaps the "Squares" today.

criticism soon turns into social criticism, from the false ideas of the dominant class to its false and ridiculous practices. In sermons, essays, poems, and plays, in fully realized works of art and in thinly concealed tracts, the artist conveys his vision of society. Sometimes he remains a party of one; sometimes he is associated with other literary or quasi-literary alliances. Usually in each literary period, economic or social events or "causes" break through the artist's isolation: economic depressions; Negro slavery; the plight of labor, the urban poor, the farmer; trials and miscarriages of justice; corruption and graft; civil-rights issues; foreign revolutions; imperialism and wars. For short periods, the engaged writer takes a stand on public issues.

In act three, the movement declines, for literary radicalism never seems to be sustained over a long period, and the writer is gradually absorbed again into the society he has rejected. The aftermath of his revolt is sometimes tragic, sometimes pathetic or ludicrous. Often the disenthralled writer becomes embittered or ashamed after his adventure in nonconformity, or he becomes tired as his idealism flags and the prison-house of the world closes upon him.

But even as the old revolution is expiring, a new one is flickering into life and a new generation, equally brash, confident, or angry will announce itself with the customary flourish.

The history of American literary communism is the story of one more turn in the cycle of revolt. Like the earlier experiments in rebellion, it has its ancestors and founders, its foreign prophets, its manifestoes, its saints and renegades. It also begins in joy and ends in disenchantment. And growing amidst its monuments and ruins are the shoots of the rebellions to come.

ONE · THE REBELS

A LEAGUE OF YOUTH

THE FIRST MOVEMENT of literary insurgency in the twentieth century began between 1910 and 1912 and ended in 1919, one of the grimmest years in American history. Historians have called it the "joyous season," the "confident years," the "little renaissance." Such phrases suggest its gaiety and rebelliousness, if not its complexities and contradictions, but they perpetuate a misconception: that this interlude of creativeness had nothing or little to do with what preceded or followed it.

Actually, the young rebels who heaved and struggled and effervesced during the early years of Wilson's administration were at once the inheritors, practitioners, and enemies of a traditional culture and the forerunners of new fashions in thought and literature. To understand the "lost generation" of the twenties and the "depression generation" of the thirties, to measure the distance that the American intellectual traveled between 1912 and 1929, we must look hard at the still-inhibited but happy anarchists who flourished just before the outbreak of World War I and the Russian revolution.

Like the hopeful young contemporaries of Emerson, they made their appearance at a time of general economic and social stability when no war seemed imminent and the country was receptive to change. As in Emerson's day, too, the young rebels challenged the hostile guardians of traditional culture without differing from them so widely as to make all communication impossible. The "League of Youth" appeared to be tough and irreverent; at bottom it was religious and idealistic. One suspects that even the most ardent pleasure-seekers among them did not advocate an irresponsible hedonism, but made the pursuit of pleasure an almost holy cause, another way of yielding to divine impulses. They also resembled their nineteenth-century transcendental counterparts in their extreme individualism—an individualism that in no way contradicted a vaguely socialist or utopian aspiration.

Floyd Dell, one of the principal spokesmen for the artist-rebels, acknowledged somewhat belatedly the kinship between his group and the Emersonians. Perhaps they were cranks, he wrote in 1921,

but certainly not the cautious modern reformers. They were engaged in trying to see the world anew—to see in imagination, and with the help of reason, what it might become. Their views represented a fairly undifferentiated mass of anarchism, communism, feminism, and republicanism—but all of an extreme kind, and hence entitled to our respect.[1]

Another young rebel observed many years later that "fifty years after the first publication of *Leaves of Grass,* the words of Whitman— and of Emerson—were the neutral air we breathed, whether we had read them or not. . . . It is really hard to overestimate how much we depended upon transcendental optimism, how much we were under the spell, politically, of Lincoln, Thoreau, Emerson, Jefferson, Rousseau, and the German sentimental poets of a century earlier, and correspondingly in for disillusionment." [2] And Art Young, the genial cartoonist of *The Masses,* testified in his autobiography that he found "enough of revelation to satisfy me" in any page of Emerson. "This pioneer against Puritanism told us young men of forty years ago to 'stun and astonish the intruding rabble of men and books and institutions by a simpler declaration of the divine fact.' Emerson knew that everybody had something divine in him. But, alas, how many of us succumb to the 'intruding rabble' of books and men and institutions? Taken page by page, Emerson reads like serene lightning." [3]

Of all their literary forebears, Whitman alone spoke most directly to them, not only because of his idealism and his contagious democratic gospel, but "because," as Louis Untermeyer surmised in 1917, "of his words":

. . . it was this love and sublimation of the colloquial and racy that made him so great an artistic influence—an influence that was not only liberal but liberating. It was Whitman, more than any single element, unless one includes the indirect force of a wider social feeling, that broke the fetters of the poet and opened the doors of America to him.

Ezra Pound agreed, and so did Max Eastman, who confessed that "we have drunk of the universe in Walt Whitman's poetry." James Oppenheim, editor of *The Seven Arts,* saw Whitman as an ally "of those of us who are in revolt against the New England tradition." [4] Van Wyck Brooks proclaimed him the first major American writer to challenge "the abnormal dignity of American letters" and the precipitator of the American character who blended action and theory, idealism and business. Although he regretted the older Whitman's fondness for pompous pronouncements, no better ancestor, he believed, could be found for the League of Youth than this pagan democrat-radical who possessed "rude feeling and a faculty of gathering humane experience," who "retrieved our civilization" and "released personality." [5]

Whitman's friend and unofficial secretary, Horace Traubel, was a familiar figure in the offices of *The Masses* and contributed to its successor, *The Liberator*—a direct link with the Camden poet. Young radicals must have read with approval a remark of Whitman's that Traubel recorded for *The Seven Arts* in 1917:

The trouble is that writers are too literary—too damned literary. There has grown up—Swinburne I think an apostle of it—the doctrine (you have heard of it? it is dinned everywhere), art for art's sake: think of it— art for art's sake. Let a man really accept that—let that really be his ruling—and he is lost. . . . Instead of regarding literature as only a weapon, an instrument, in the service of something larger than itself, it looks upon itself as an end—as a fact to be finally worshipped, adored. To me that's all a horrible blasphemy—a bad smelling apostasy.[6]

WHAT THEY BELIEVED

"Released personality," "expression of self," "emotion," "intuition," "liberation," "experiment," "freedom," "rebellion"—these phrases and words connote the prevailing spirit of the "new" magazines, books, and plays as well as the manifestoes, art exhibitions, and political rallies between 1912 and 1917. The Young Intellectuals were not indiscriminately rebellious. Although the more extreme made disagreement with any vested opinion a point of honor, they did not reject completely the entire battery of cultural, political, and economic assumptions that had sustained an older America. But they irritably brushed aside the "frigidly academic," the sweetened, mollified, but still-restraining "Puritanism" of the genteel custodians of the old culture, who were frightened by the uncontrolled veerings and yawings of the new.

By Puritanism, they meant "repression," "bigotry," "prudishness," "Comstockery," attitudes which they attributed to a dry and arid New England, and they detected its confining influence in politics, economics, religion, education, and art. Mencken was only the most violent and articulate of a whole host of Puritan-baiters. In fact, the indiscriminate and uninformed attack by the rebels against Puritans and Puritan culture prompted a *New Republic* reviewer to observe in 1918: "the whole younger set, including Mr. Dreiser, never see the word 'puritan' without getting out their axes, refreshing their memories of Freud and Forel, remembering bitterly the small towns they were brought up in, thanking God they can find the way to Greenwich Village, even if they do not live there—and taking another whirl at the long-suffering men whose manners and customs, distorted and unillumined by that unearthly light in which they lived, have yet been the mold in which our country's laws, literature, education, religions, economics, morals, and points of view have become petrified." [7]

The Young Intellectuals felt no piety toward these formulators of the American mold and even less for the genteel men of letters, with their white, Protestant, Anglo-Saxon, "schoolmarm" culture, who applied their absolute moral values as rigorously to poetry as they did to politics. In contrast, the Young Intellectuals intended to be "freely experimental, skeptical of inherited values, ready to examine old dogmas, and to submit afresh its sanctions to the test of experience." [8]

This was the program of a generation trained in the pragmatism of William James, with its sympathetic receptivity to emotion and innovation, and in the instrumentalism of John Dewey, which provided a basis for "social and intellectual reconstruction." [9] The Young Intellectual loved "change" for its own sake, because it dissolved rigidities, and agreed with the Dreiser of 1916 who wrote: "Not to cling too pathetically to a religion or a system of government, or a theory of morals or a method of living but to be ready to abandon at a moment's notice the apparent teachings of the ages, and to step out free and willing to accept new and radically different conditions is the ideal state of the human mind." [10]

After a diet of Ibsen, Nietzsche, Bergson, Wells, Shaw, Dostoevsky, and Freud, how could one accept bourgeois moralities uncritically? Intuition, as Bergson demonstrated, was a more reliable guide than the Puritan conscience, and the American undergraduates of 1913 no longer shilly-shallied, but spoke "with manly and womanly directness, even when the most delicate, or indelicate subjects are broached." Boldly they declared, "We will spare no man and no institution, we will revere nothing, but look the facts in the eye and speak out what we think." They took seriously the credo of Louis Dubedat in Shaw's *The Doctor's Dilemma:* "I believe in Michelangelo, Velasquez and Rembrandt, in the might of design, the mystery of color, the redemption of all things by beauty everlasting, and the message of Art that has made these hands blessed, amen." [11]

Young America had welcomed the "liberating gods" from abroad, and by 1918, thanks to enthusiastic popularizers like James Gibbons Huneker, had become familiar with such un-Anglo-Saxon names as Stirner, Schnitzler, Wedekind, Nexö, Sudermann, Hauptman, Maeterlinck, D'Annunzio, Strindberg, Gorky, Baudelaire, Huysmans, Laforgue, writers never studied in American universities. Whether or not the Americans quite took in the violent import of their message was another matter. Van Wyck Brooks felt at the time that their ideas and subject matter were still too remote from the American experience to be properly savored, and that, transplanted, they had "at once the pleasing remoteness of literature and the stir of an only half-apprehended actuality." Huneker's indiscriminate enthusiasm for anything European was itself, Brooks thought, a product of Puritan repression, an outpouring of senses too long restrained. He incarnated "the banked-up appetite of all America for the color and flavor, the gaiety and romance, the sound and smell of continental Europe." [12]

It was, of course, Brooks himself who made the most celebrated attack against the sterile theorist and the vulgar Philistine. He blamed the failure of American culture on the absence of a "collective spiritual life" and on the materialistic social pressures that transformed talented artists into vulgarians or cranks. Because American writers had to serve "ulterior and impersonal ends," Brooks concluded, they fell into the abstract, the nonhuman, the impersonal, or they became social reformers, thus enabling themselves "to do so much good by writing badly that they often came to think of artistic truth itself as an enemy of progress." [13] Brooks's observation, as will be shown, applied even more aptly to the thirties, when "social consciousness" became for some revolutionary enthusiasts a legitimate reason to abnegate literary responsibilities, than it did to Wilsonian America. The contentions of Brooks were seconded and amplified by Waldo Frank, James Oppenheim, and others. In the 1920's, the charges against the inhospitable American milieu became even more common.

THE "VILLAGE"

One way to challenge the inertia of the social system was to establish enclaves of rebellion or little Bohemias within it, as the innocent and high-minded Brook Farmers had done before the Civil War.

The very word "Bohemia," traditionally anathema to Protestant middle-class America, suggested strolling players, tipsy artists, free thought, free love—everything hostile to religion and business. Some kind of underground Bohemia had existed since the early nineteenth century, but it was never publicized and rarely escaped beyond the narrow confines of a few of the larger cities. But by 1912, "Bohemias" were exhibited without apologies and almost defiantly. "Bohemia" might be a little circle of artists and writers in Chicago or St. Louis or Davenport, Iowa, but its Mecca was a few blocks in downtown New York known as Greenwich Village. Here, in effect, the intellectual and cultural and even political revolution was brooded over, if not hatched, and here came young rebels from all over

America to be free, to flout convention, to live vibrantly and indecorously.

The scores of reminiscences of these Greenwich Village years are probably tinged with the poignancy and bittersweetness that inevitably steal into recollections of "dear, dead days." Yet enough of these participant-historians have testified to the enchantment of the prewar Village to give their memories at least an apocryphal validity. Floyd Dell, the most painstaking of the Village chroniclers, converted it into a Forest of Arden where "vagabond youth . . . ignored the codes invented by those who have settled down and have a property-stake in the world." [14] There, if we are to trust his memory, the play spirit prevailed, "secrecy and hypocrisy were unnecessary," and joys were cheap.

If, to Floyd Dell, the Village was a paradise for carefree artists, a less sympathetic observer regarded the Villagers as overgrown children and compared their Bohemian collective to the undergraduate societies they sneered at as irremediably bourgeois. Both provided refuges from middle-class Philistinism and permitted the same freedom of dress and speech; both were studiedly critical of authority and contemptuous of the powers that be. If the undergraduate had his football hero, the Villager had his "Big Bill" Haywood, the I.W.W. chieftain, to worship. The board meetings of the "little magazines" resembled those of the college magazines, and the Village rebels offended the authorities with a characteristically undergraduate intent. The Village was diverting, in short, but it was no place for mature people.[15] This was a conservative response, of course, but the analogy was not preposterous. It was the former Harvard cheerleader John Reed who led the Paterson strikers in militant song fests, and it was this same Reed (with two other Americans) who embarrassed Lenin before a crowd at the Moscow Opera House by raising him on their shoulders as though he had scored a touchdown against Yale.[16]

Even in those unspoiled times before the Village had grown fashionable and an inundation of "bourgeois pigs" had raised the rents, many hard-working professional people—Lincoln Steffens, Theodore Dreiser, young Sinclair Lewis, among others—lived among the Bohemians, and many serious-minded outsiders like Walter Lippmann came to Village parties and discussions. By 1916, even those who sympathized with the rebellion demanded something more than license and chaos and revolt. "It is our hope . . . that the end has come to this fledgling stage," Waldo Frank declared in *The Seven Arts*. "Judgment is entering and torturing the blandness of our life. Alternatives of interest dull the edge of our promiscuous enthusiasm. The fact of our vociferousness no longer passes as a sign of health. We are, in fact, struggling beyond the imitative morning into the ruthless noon of self-exploration." [17] According to Joseph Freeman, there had always been a serious purpose behind the Bohemian frivolity. Village play in itself was a gesture of rebellion. "It was at once a post-graduate school, a playground and a clinic for those who had broken with an old culture and had not yet found a new one, or had not yet discovered and accepted the fact that they were irrevocably committed to the old." Most of the rebels ultimately submitted again to the old authorities after their brief moment of intransigency; a small minority, more deeply moved by a social vision, became committed to revolution. But during this period of radical incubation— for all its childishness, theatricality, irresponsibility—the origins of the more serious rebellion to come can be discovered. Not merely nostalgia is suggested in the comment of the radical cartoonist Art Young:

But for all that, the Village remains more like a home to me than any other sections of New York. I like it for the enmity it once aroused and the friends it brought together. In this atmosphere a man felt something like his raw self, though he knew well that he had been cooked to a turn by the world's conventions. Here a woman could say damn right out loud and still be respected.[18]

CONFUSION OF TONGUES

Much of the charm and much of the tumult of the postwar Bohemia can be attributed to the frenzied experimentation in literature, the arts, and education that struck the conservative taste makers as a kind of perpetual Chardon Street Convention. Contributing to the intellectual hullabaloo were the famous "evenings" at the Fifth

Avenue house of Mabel Dodge (a wealthy avant-gardist, the friend of Leo and Gertrude Stein, Bernard Berenson, and Hutchins Hapgood and the inamorata of many writers and artists), who had reestablished herself in the United States after a protracted stay in Italy. This remarkable woman, a latter-day reincarnation of Ann Hutchinson and the transcendental conversationalist and "comeouter," Margaret Fuller, also suggested Henry James's intelligent, sensitive, and destructive Princess Casamassima, who flirted with the anarchists of London. To Mabel Dodge's "evenings," burlesqued in Carl Van Vechten's *Peter Whiffle* (1922) and romantically treated in Max Eastman's *Venture* (1927), came a troop of socialists, anarchists, cubists, feminists, reformers, syndicalists, labor leaders, poets, and journalists. Here they heard or delivered disquisitions on sex, penology, anarchism, birth control, poetry, and modern art—anything, in short, that came under the heading of opinion. And here young men and women of the middle-class could consort with notorious radicals who were happily subverting the social order by word and deed.

Among the contending radical philosophies, anarchism and syndicalism appealed more to young artist-rebels than the more staid versions of socialism, and the activists in the revolutionary movement—Gene Debs, Big Bill Haywood, Emma Goldman, Mother Jones, for example—seemed closer to the spirit of the artist's rebellion than the white-collar bread-and-butter theorists. Middle-class socialism of the Ruskinian sort or the bureaucratic practical business-socialism of Victor Berger and Morris Hillquit were tame compared to flamboyant programs of direct action and dynamite or proclamations announcing the supremacy of the individual and voluntary co-operation. When Victor Berger declared in 1912: "In the past we often had to fight against Utopianism and fanaticism, now it is anarchism again that is eating away at the vitals of our party," he was unconsciously allying himself with the Philistines the friends of Mabel Dodge hoped to embarrass, or shake up. When Bill Haywood in the same year announced:

. . . no Socialist can be a law-abiding citizen. When we come together and are of a common mind, and the purpose of our minds is to overthrow the capitalist system, we become conspirators then against the

United States government. . . . I again want to justify direct action and sabotage. . . .

he was expressing the artistic credo of the Greenwich Village Bohemians in political terms.* It was not simply coincidence that Haywood and Alexander Berkman and Emma Goldman attended Mabel Dodge's evenings with representatives of the "angry, idealistic college-student generation," or that the rebel artists displayed equal enthusiasm for two important events of 1913: the exhibition of international art held in the New York Armory and the strike of the textile workers in Paterson, New Jersey.[19]

Each in its way signified revolutionary protest and combined politics and art. The radicals who projected the Armory show and defended it against abuse and ridicule made the new art a symbol of individuality, freedom, the impulsive. The stodgy academicians who opposed them seemed to reek with death. Many of the legion against old-fogyism disliked the European moderns almost as much as the outraged classicists, and probably felt as the puzzled but amused Theodore Roosevelt did. Max Eastman, for example, enjoyed it as an anarchist "free-for-all," as "a wild and sumptuous blossoming-place for all old lunatics and new geniuses and a glorious butt of ridicule and good-humored hilarity for the newspapers." [20] Louis Fraina, later to become one of the founders of the Communist Party, attacked the conceptions of modern art held by both the radicals and the conservatives. To say that futurism or cubism are degenerate

---

* After the Right Wing elements at the 1912 Socialist Party convention adopted an antisabotage plank and in 1913 expelled Haywood from the executive committee, New York intellectuals (including Max Eastman and Walter Lippmann) defended him. "This Polyphemous from the raw mining camps of the West had dedicated himself to the organization of the unskilled, the poverty-stricken and forgotten workers." Daniel Bell, "Marxian Socialism in the United States," in Donald Egbert *et al., Socialism and American Life,* Princeton, 1952, I, p. 290. Hence his appeal to the guilt-ridden youth of the middle-class, characterized as follows in a *New Republic* editorial of 1914: "Then suddenly, perhaps for reasons too intimate for analysis, the idea of what poverty means begins to burn into them, they are tortured with the thought of it. The feeling goes deeper than their reason, draws upon desire within them that is stronger than theory, and makes the war on poverty the central passion of their lives." (Dec. 26, 1914, p. 6.) Socialism provides the only answer in a society that offers silence or platitudes, the editorial continues, and the radical is likely to become "that terrible nuisance, a man with a fixed idea."

is fallacious, he wrote, but even if they were, "they express a cultural urge conditioned by the social *milieu.*" Byron, Wagner, Nietzsche, Strauss have all been called "decadent," but all "vital art expresses the vital urge of its age." The new art does not represent a decadent capitalism but "capitalism dominant (Cubism) and capitalism ascending (Futurism). The aggressive brutal power of Cubism and Futurism is identical with the new power and audacity of capitalism, of our machine civilization. The New Art is typical of capitalism as the architecture of the skyscraper. . . . The Cubists paint as if there were nothing but mechanism in the universe," and the Futurists, trying to catch the "spirit of machinery,—energy, motion, aggression," are also trying to mechanize man. No socialist, he concluded, could support futurism, which so superbly illustrates the capitalist spirit. Socialist art had to forge its own tools to express its own culture.[21]

Most radicals were ready to accept an art that "hurts the optic nerves" so long as it exuberantly cut through the sweetness, sentimentality, and drabness of an allegedly dying culture. As the sculptor Jo Davidson put it: "War is the only way to keep from stagnation and decay," and Mabel Dodge, who helped to launch the show, took a positive pleasure in contemplating the fragmentation of the old and the emergence of the new. "Life at birth is always painful, never beautiful," she wrote, but "only death is ugly."

Nearly every thinking person is in revolt against something, because the craving of the individual is for further consciousness, and because consciousness is expanding and is bursting through the molds that have held it up to now; and so let every man whose private truth is too great for his existing condition pause before he turns away from Picasso's painting or from Gertrude Stein's writing, for their case is his case.[22]

Her radicalism derived more from the vitalism of Bergson than from the anarchist seers, but it helps to explain why the color and drama of the I.W.W. strike leaders, romantic and reckless, should appeal so strongly to her and her circle.[23]

The subverters of good taste who met in Mabel Dodge's studio and planned to "upset America" by demolishing "the old order of things" naturally sympathized with the political individualists who wished to throw some bombs of their own. And when the one-eyed

Wobbly leader, Big Bill Haywood, debated with other socialists in her drawing room, and openly advocated sabotage, "no matter what the risk might be to human life," [24] he made a deep impression. "He sits upright and perfectly motionless with his hands resting on his thighs," says the young hero of Max Eastman's novel, *Venture,* who envisages him as a kind of proletarian priest. "Bill's hands are very small, as the hands of a mountain would be. When he gets up he brings them together for a moment in front of him, passing one slowly over the other. All of his motions are slow, and his presence, in spite of a certain torn and coarse look of reckless will, is majestic. He has only one eye, and he peers about with it like a tame eagle." [25]

In the same novel Eastman reports Haywood's remarks about proletarian art which Mabel Dodge also alluded to in her memoirs. Addressing his audience as "Fellow workers and folks," Haywood explains why there is no proletarian art for the Pittsburgh steelworker and what workers' art will be like:

"Not only is art impossible to such a man," he said, "but life is impossible. He does not live. He just works. He does the work that enables you to live. He does the work that enables you to enjoy art, and to make it, and to have a nice meeting like this and talk it over."

Bill used "nice" without irony; he meant it.

"The only problem, then, about proletarian art," he continued, "is how to make it possible, how to make life possible to the proletariat. In solving that problem we should be glad of your understanding, but we don't ask your help. We are going to solve it at your expense. Since you have got life, and we have got nothing but work, we are going to take our share of life away from you, and put you to work."

"I suppose you will want to know what my ideal of proletarian art is," he continued, "what I think it will be like, when a revolution brings it into existence. I think it will be very much kindlier than your art. There will be a social spirit in it. Not so much boasting about personality. Artists won't be so egotistical. The highest ideal of an artist will be to write a song which the workers sing, to compose a drama which great throngs of workers can perform out of doors. When we stop fighting each other—for wages of existence on one side, and for unnecessary luxury on the other—then perhaps we shall all become human beings and surprise ourselves with the beautiful things we do and make on the earth. Then perhaps there will be civilization and a civilized art. But there is no use putting up pretenses now. The important thing . . . is that our side, the workers, should fight without mercy and win. There is no hope for humanity anywhere else." [26]

Eastman's account may be tricked up a little, but his novel, written more than a decade after Haywood's talk, still explains why Jack Reed and others formed a kind of literary auxiliary to help Haywood and his lieutenants, Elizabeth Gurley Flynn and Carlo Tresca, publicize the plight of the Paterson silk workers. Reed's arrest and incarceration made sensational news in the New York press. Moved by the dogged heroism of the workers and the passion of their leaders, Reed and his friends (including Mabel Dodge, Hutchins Hapgood, Walter Lippmann, Ernest Poole, and Robert Edmond Jones) planned and produced a pageant in Madison Square Garden in which the workers themselves dramatized their fight. Presented in scenes, the pageant, according to the program, enacted the "battle between the working class and the capitalist class conducted by the Industrial Workers of the World." It portrayed police brutality, the murder of a strike leader, and worker solidarity and ended with the cast calling for an eight-hour day and singing "The Internationale." To one spectator in the audience, it seemed

that the machinery was grinding those workers to pieces. We thought of industrial accidents and diseases, of how the terrible toil sucked all life, all initiative out of the workers. They were dying inside that mill and worse than dying, and it was the same all over the world. We held our breath. And then—something happened. The machinery stopped grinding. A faint free cry rises slowly to deafening hozannas from a thousand throats as the workers rush from the mill. They wave their hands, they shout, they dance, they embrace each other in a social passion that pales individual feeling to nothing. They are a mad mob, glad and beautiful in their madness. They sing the Marseillaise. The strike is on! It is the carmagnole of oppression lifting itself at last to the heights. Here and there, from the balcony, the boxes, and the great main floor, the sound of sobbing that was drowned in singing proved that the audience had "got" Paterson.

To the intellectuals, the pageant, like the Armory show, was passionate and colorful, presaging the time, in Hutchins Hapgood's words, when "self-expression in industry and art among the masses may become a rich reality, spreading a human glow over the whole of humanity." To the strikers, the pageant was an exciting but disappointing fiasco.[27]

The Masses

The Madison Square pageant failed in its primary purpose—to raise money for the strikers—but it was one important episode in the pilgrimage of John Reed from Bohemian to revolutionary, and it brought the reality of the "war in Paterson" to impressionable young radicals who had already devoured Reed's exciting reports of the strike in *The Masses,* soon to become the Bible of the radical avant-garde.

Before *The Masses* (that spectacular organ of socialism, anarchism, paganism, and rebellion) hit the newsstands in January 1913, most socialist magazines gave only perfunctory attention to literary or aesthetic matters. Reports from abroad, labor news, articles on the theory and tactics of socialism filled the pages of the socialist papers published in 1912. Book reviews, occasional poems and short stories, and infrequently a serialized novel like Upton Sinclair's *The Jungle* might be published in weeklies like *The Appeal to Reason* (1895-1929), *The International Socialist Review* (1900-1918), and *Wilshire's Magazine* (1900-1915). Only one magazine, *The Comrade,* founded in 1901, devoted itself expressly to socialist art and literature. Serving on its editorial board were several future leaders of the Socialist party, John Spargo and Algernon Lee among them. Its editors declared:

While we firmly believe in the importance of the economic factor, in the development of society—while indeed we recognize in it the basic human fact—yet we shall not directly deal with the economic. Other Socialist papers do that, and do it well. Our mission is rather to present to our readers such literary and artistic productions as reflect the soundness of the Socialist philosophy. *The Comrade* will endeavor to mirror Socialist thought as it finds expression in Art and Literature. Its function will be to develop the aesthetic impulse in the Socialist movement, to utilize the talent we already have, and to quicken into being aspirations that are latent.[28]

With its Pre-Raphaelite genteel personifications of socialism, its utopian fantasies, its evangelical calls for "the love of comrades" and
"the high-in'brothering of men," *The Comrade* was closer to Whitman and Edward Bellamy than to Karl Marx. Any critic of the social
order, from the vaguest reformers to the most revolutionary, could
express himself in its pages. Hence Thomas Nast, Richard Le Gal-
lienne, Ella Wheeler Wilcox, Mary Wilkins Freeman, and Edward
Markham were printed side by side with Jack London, Maxim Gorky,
Clarence Darrow, Upton Sinclair, Eugene Debs, and Mother Jones.

Although the literary standards of *The Comrade* were tepidly bourgeois, the editors did try to apply socialist theory to their evaluations
of books and writers and to criticize Tolstoyan deviants like Ernest
Crosby, head of the Anti-Imperialist League, for his anarchistic
notions "toward the ballot and majority rule." Far removed from
the proletariat themselves, a few contributors like Robert Rives La
Monte entertained misty notions about the "proletarian poet," and
Edward Markham, whose populist poem "The Man with the Hoe"
had created a stir in the nineties, anticipated in 1901 the proletarian
literature of the future. He wrote:

I believe we stand at the threshold of a great revival of literature, not
in this country especially, but also in other countries as well, that will
have a broader basis and deeper note than anything the world has ever
seen.

In the past, the great movements of mankind have always gone in
waves, and the literature of different periods was the outcome of these
mental and political upheavals . . . the problem of the present age is
the emancipation of labor, and before that is accomplished the world is
likely to see such a struggle as it has never before witnessed. . . . You
and I may not live to see the end of this movement, although it may
perhaps come much sooner than we expect; but it is sure to bring in its
train a literary renaissance which will have humanity entirely as its
study.[29]

The Comrade, whose circulation never amounted to more than a
few thousand, was soon absorbed into Charles H. Kerr's more tough-
minded *The International Socialist Review,* and socialist artists had
to wait until 1913 before a magazine devoted principally to art and
the class struggle appeared.

Before *The Masses,* socialist art and criticism had been a very serious business. Socialist novelists and poets tended to brood over the miseries of mankind, to document the squalor of industrial life, or to project hopefully decorous visions of the co-operative commonwealth. To write gaily and humorously implied that the writer had no quarrel with his hideous society; a preoccupation with the sordid, on the other hand, suggested a dedication to the cause of "the great economic revolt to which the name of socialism is commonly narrowed." [30]

But was socialism irrevocably committed to mean austerity, vegetarianism, anemic Puritanism, gloom, sobriety, and plain food? On the contrary, a socialist observed in 1913, "Capitalism itself is essentially Puritan for the worker. . . . There is, indeed, a very close alliance between capitalism and religious Puritanism." In Catholic Spain and Ireland, capitalism languished. Socialism, he concluded, stands for a "wise, healthy paganism." [31] As Jack London made clear, its program to restore Hellenic harmony would bring forth a race of supermen.

The Masses, founded by Piet Vlag in 1911, was to become the voice of this "wise, healthy paganism" after young Max Eastman, a recent Columbia graduate student and pupil of John Dewey, took over the editorship of the magazine in December 1912, and made it unabashedly "red." Vlag, who managed a co-operative restaurant in the basement of the Rand School of Social Science, intended *The Masses* "to speak for the cooperative side of the socialist movement." [32] Financial support came from a socialist vice-president of New York Life Insurance Company. Under the editorship of Thomas Seltzer, *The Masses* ("a general ILLUSTRATED magazine of art, literature, politics, and science" co-operatively owned by a group of artists and writers) featured the fiction of Tolstoy, Björkman, Sudermann, and other European authors as well as articles by socialists and former muckrakers. Gustavus Myers, John Spargo, W. J. Ghent, Charles Winter handled the art work. By the summer of 1912, after another editor, Horatio Winslow, had failed to increase circulation, the discouraged Vlag suggested that *The Masses* merge with a Chicago feminist paper, but the original founders aided by other young militants decided to resuscitate the magazine. Art Young recommended Max Eastman as the new editor, to serve without pay.

The resurrected *Masses* was a noisier and more flamboyant bird than its lackluster predecessor which was "indifferent to economic and political struggles, and even in literature . . . a long way from the vanguard." Whereas Vlag's *Masses* had been against the I.W.W., Eastman's *Masses* was direct-actionist in its socialism and given to impertinent assaults against capitalism and its culture. John Reed, who came on the editorial staff in 1914, typified one aspect of its insurgency in his proposed "statement of purpose." What *The Masses* chose to print, Reed wrote, depended upon the whim of the editors. "We don't even intend to conciliate our readers."

The broad purpose of the *Masses* is a social one: to everlastingly attack old systems, old morals, old prejudices—the whole weight of outworn thought that dead men have saddled upon us—and to set up new ones in their places. Standing on the common sidewalk, we intend to lunge at spectres—with a rapier rather than a broad-axe, with frankness rather than innuendo. We intend to be arrogant, impertinent, in bad taste, but not vulgar. We will be bound by no one creed or theory of social reform, but will express them all, providing they be radical. . . . Sensitive to all new winds that blow, never rigid in a single view or phase of life, such is our ideal for the *Masses*.[33]

Eastman borrowed some of Reed's phrases in preparing his own draft for the masthead of *The Masses,* but he confessed later in his autobiography that Reed's version "prickled with notions I could not endure." As a "revolutionary experimentalist," Eastman had already editorialized on the difference between reform and revolution and he did not want the magazine given over to rebellious talk. His own statement, which appeared henceforth in every issue, read as follows:

THIS MAGAZINE IS OWNED AND PUBLISHED COOPERATIVELY BY ITS EDITORS. IT HAS NO DIVIDENDS TO PAY, AND NOBODY IS TRYING TO MAKE MONEY OUT OF IT. A REVOLUTIONARY AND NOT A REFORM MAGAZINE; A MAGAZINE WITH A SENSE OF HUMOR AND NO RESPECT FOR THE RESPECTABLE: FRANK, ARROGANT, IMPERTINENT, SEARCHING FOR THE TRUE CAUSES; A MAGAZINE DIRECTED AGAINST RIGIDITY AND DOGMA WHEREVER IT IS FOUND; PRINTING WHAT IS TOO NAKED

OR TRUE FOR A MONEY-MAKING PRESS; A MAGAZINE WHOSE FINAL
POLICY IS TO DO AS IT PLEASES AND CONCILIATE NOBODY, NOT EVEN
ITS READERS—THERE IS A FIELD FOR THIS PUBLICATION IN AMERICA.[34]

Yet Reed's ebullient rebelliousness better expressed, perhaps, the
feelings of the associated editors than Eastman's sterner and more
disciplined approach to revolution. Eastman gave William English
Walling the assignment of keeping *The Masses'* readers up-to-date
on world socialism in a monthly column called "The International
Battle Line," and he himself editorialized in his own department,
"Knowledge and Revolution," but most of the other contributors [35]
devoted themselves somewhat indiscriminately (and joyously) to private and public causes. Suffragism, free love, the single tax, birth
control, anarchism found their way into the pages of *The Masses*
along with the Paterson strike and the "Ludlow massacre" in Colorado, which Eastman covered with Frank Bohn. The artists in what
Floyd Dell called the "little republic" of *The Masses,* especially those
who placed a high premium on self-expression, resented editorial
direction.

Eastman, as he put it later, wanted "everybody to express his own
individuality to the limit, so long as he did not transgress the principles of socialism," but he was irritated by the vagaries of anarchism
and Christian socialism and even more annoyed by what he called
"Greenwich Village Studio Art." To Eastman, Art Young, Dell,
Mary Heaton Vorse, and a few others, *The Masses* was primarily
a socialist organ, not a medium for artistic self-expression. As the
anarchist poet Arturo Giovannitti grandiloquently put it:

It is the recording secretary of the Revolution in the making. It is NOT
meant as a foray of unruly truant children trying to sneak into the rich
orchards of literature and art. It is an earnest and living thing, a battle
call, a shout of defiance, a blazing torch running madly through the
night to set afire the powder magazines of the world.

To George Bellows, John Sloan, and some of the other contributing
artists, personal freedom, not "scientific procedure toward a goal,"
was the chief consideration. As it turned out, these two emphases
were certainly not antithetical, and Eastman himself did not condemn
Bohemianism as such. "I do think you might feel a little differently

about *The Masses,*" he told Norman Thomas, "if you got a deeper taste of its mood. I think there is an Elizabethan gusto and candor in the strong taste for life which must be won back over the last relics of Puritanism." But he deplored the substitution of *mere* Bohemianism "in place of serious social thought and effort . . . the substitution of this personal revolt, and this practical communication of qualities, for the practical scientific work of mind or hand that the revolution demands of every free man in its desperate hour— it is that which is to be condemned." From the beginning, he fought "the puny, artificial, sex-conscious simmering in perpetual puberty of the grey-haired Bacchantes of Greenwich Village." [36]

Most readers of *The Masses* (and they could be found among the rebel spirits in many American small towns as well as in New York) cherished both its artistic obstreperousness and its revolutionary zeal. It was "objectionable" to the genteel not so much because of its anti-capitalistic doctrines as because its manner (as Eastman noted) "outraged patriotic, religious, and matrimonial, to say nothing of ethical and aesthetic tastes and conventions. The state, the church, the press, marriage, organized charity, the liberals, the philanthropists, the Progressive Party—they were all game for our guns and always in season." [37] To young radicals like Joseph Freeman, Michael Gold, and other future Left Wing writers still in their teens, the matter and the manner of *The Masses* were irresistibly appealing. They drank in Max Eastman's fervent words: "Your place . . . is with the working people in their fight for more life than it will benefit capital to give them; your place is in the working-class struggle; your word is Revolution." "These words," Joseph Freeman recalled later, "were not merely an expression of opinion; they were absolute truth. We remembered them for years, and cited them verbatim to convert others." [38]

THE SPECTRUM OF REBELLION

The Masses expressed the distinctive mood or attitude of the prewar insurgency; it also expressed its contradictions and uncertainty, and, to some extent, its vagueness. Contributors wrote in defense of industry and the machine and against them; some were fiercely unconventional about politics or marriage or religion and some were Puritans like Upton Sinclair or unconscious Victorians, impiously idealistic but, as Max Eastman described himself, "excessively squeamish about risqué or ribald jokes." He was something of a prude in those days, and his magazine, "while bold in its serious views on sex . . . was delicately modest in its laughter. It did not add 'obscenity' to 'blasphemy,' and might have come to a quick end, I suspect, if it had." Hutchins Hapgood, after reading Floyd Dell's autobiography, *Homecoming,* decided that Dell had always been a conformist despite his Bohemian fringe. From bourgeois conventionalities he moved to socialist ones, but in all his actions Hapgood sensed the "instinct to conform." The same poet or painter who condoned sabotage might hate imagism or free verse or cubism. Neither Floyd Dell nor Eastman, for example, were drawn to experimentation in the arts and, later, remained hostile to Eliot and his poetic posterity, to "obscurity," and to modish European importations. Eastman probably expressed his own views when his hero observes in *Venture:* "But those futuristical artists most of them haven't any driving force that I can see. None of their art contains either a great passion or a great idea—just painter's ideas and studio-feelings, and then that great passion to be an artist. They are not living life, they are living art. That's the trouble with them. Life is creative, life is inherently futuristic. . . ." [39]

These differences hardly mattered when most writers were united against the minions of gentility. Menckenians, socialists, anarchists, Bohemians appeared in the same magazines. They agreed on many of their antipathies and honored in common a certain number of spiritual ancestors if they differed in their aesthetic standards and in their political and social goals. But as the war approached, class and political affiliations began to count for more. A shorthand summary of the literary groups or coteries may suggest why some literary rebels became more revolutionary after 1917 and why most did not.

"The Masses" group: It continued the Protestant-evangelical radical tradition, purveying the "glad tidings" and a refurbished social gospel irreverently; it was more pragmatic and scientific-minded than the nineteenth-century Utopians. Although influenced particularly by

"liberating gods" of Europe, especially Shaw, Wells, Rolland, and Nexö, it found "in the literature of our own country . . . a mass of libertarian eloquence—the speeches of Wendell Phillips, the fiery Abolitionist poems of Whittier, the dithyrambs of Walt Whitman in celebration of the individual, the burning advice of Emerson to be uncompromising, the invective of Thoreau upon the spirit of social conformity—a veritable arsenal of swordlike thoughts with which to fit youth out for its first struggles with whatever tyrannies of traditional society it might meet." [40] Negroes, Jews, and the foreign-born belonged to the *Masses* group, but the leadership was primarily lower to upper middle-class. Eastman, the leader, was a confident amateur who could move in and out of radical causes, speak to strikers and strike leaders one day and obtain funds from a Vanderbilt the next or tap the bankers for money to protect anarchists. He could write inflammatory editorials with his left hand and pure poetry with his right.

These were not "party" people. What distinguished them from the "hard" Communists of the twenties and thirties was their refusal to subordinate their art to politics. Not that Eastman was averse to publishing revolutionary poetry whenever possible. "I was joyous," he remembered later, "when a genuinely revolutionary poem like Ralph Chaplin's 'Hi Buddy, how I'm longing for the spring!' came in, as that did during the West Virginia strike. When Giovannitti wrote those exquisite brief lines about the Red Army coming home I was so happy I set them in ten-point type, as I remember, in the middle of a page. No, there just *wasn't any* blending of poetry with revolution. Nobody wrote revolutionary poetry that was any good." [41] Yet eager as he and Floyd Dell were to print good revolutionary verse, neither of them for a moment would have judged a writer by his political affiliations. The artist as artist was beyond social criticism. It took World War I and the Russian revolution to induce some of them, like the cartoonist Robert Minor, the reporter Jack Reed, and (to a lesser extent) the poets Eastman and Dell to renounce poetry for revolution. As Reed put it, "This class struggle plays hell with your poetry."

The Apostolic "Student Movement," or, the Priests of Young America: This is a facetious designation but not an inaccurate one.

It refers to the "League of Youth" led by Van Wyck Brooks and Randolph Bourne but including Lewis Mumford, Waldo Frank, James Oppenheim, Paul Rosenfeld, and (marginally) Walter Lippmann. The leaders of the "ASM" came largely from eastern seaboard universities and the environs of Boston, Cambridge, New York. They were more academic than the *Masses* group, less heterogeneous, more middle class. Representing them completely or in part were *The Seven Arts, The Nation, The New Republic, The Dial.* They opposed the business civilization with its money culture; the "brutal burden of the pioneering West," [42] and the expatriate, repulsed by the rawness of his country "and so withdrawn to a magnificent introversion." Whistler, the painter, and James, the novelist, served as antimodels for Waldo Frank: "I suspect that the true reason for their *ivory tower,*" he wrote, "was lack of strength to venture forth and not be overwhelmed . . . our artists have been of two extremes: those who gained an almost unbelievable purity of expression by the very violence of their self-isolation, and those who, plunging into the American maelstrom, were submerged in it, lost their vision altogether, and gave forth a gross chronicle and a blind cult of the American Fact." [43]

They wanted a socialist society that would provide a hospitable milieu for the artist, writer, scientist, and "a collective spiritual life"; [44] a literature, neither highbrow nor lowbrow, authentically American, that might inspire a "true social revolution." Their distinguishing characteristics were: a strong penchant for the hortatory and a tendency (as one of the group noted later) to overrationalize "the process of artistic creation. Literature, painting and music were going to be produced . . . out of the impulse to rectify American life; and the summons to youth was couched too frequently in the shape of moral exhortations and appeals to the conscious will"; [45] a sense that life is a struggle and that "the happiest excitement in life is to be convinced that one is fighting for all one is worth on behalf of some clearly seen and deeply felt good and against some greatly scorned evil." [46]

Nevertheless, they did not carry on the struggle with the gaiety of *The Masses.* A tone of high seriousness prevailed in their work. Francis Hackett was not far off when he detected something harsh and humorless about Brooks: "He is drably eager for rude reality and gloomily earnest for joy." [47] The same was true of Walter Lippmann, impatient with the play spirit, and of Randolph Bourne.

The Literary Experimenters or the Priests of Art: These writers were primarily preoccupied with technique. Whereas the Eastman-Dell-*Masses* group was rather conservative in its literary tastes and radical in social beliefs, this group had little interest in political or economic questions and was revolutionist only in literary matters. It was European-minded, but in a different sense from the Brooksians, who were cultural nationalists and who considered Europe a leavening agency, not a spiritual homeland. The Experimenters were closer in spirit to James and Whistler, who made Europe the base of their literary and artistic operations. They included artists as widely separated as Pound, John Gould Fletcher, Amy Lowell, Robert Frost, Maxwell Bodenheim, T. S. Eliot, the contributors to "little magazines" with small circulations. Pound and Gertrude Stein were two obvious leaders, but the founders of *Poetry* (Harriet Munroe) and of *The Little Review* (Margaret Anderson) probably belonged with them, especially the latter, who fought in the vanguard of the "revolution of esthetic curiosity." According to the Bohemian poet Maxwell Bodenheim, *"The Little Review continued to be an unhonored grandmother until the last gasp of its breath. The circulation never extended beyond 1500. Under the control of Margaret Anderson and later Jane Heap, the magazine continued to be unpopular with all the subsidized literary middles and extremes of its time and country. The radical and conservative chambers of commerce headed respectively by The Dial and The Atlantic Monthly, ignored it as an uncertified, untrammeled, sharp-faced wanderer through the maze and effluvia of literary politics. The social-radical forces regarded it as an irresponsible, precious nuisance. The remainder of the field was unaware of its existence."* [48]

The Experimenters seemed to share some of the enthusiasm for what Pound called in *Patria Mia* the American *"resorgimento,"* and many of them were America-minded, but at the same time, they were less optimistic than the Brooksians or the *Masses* people, less confident in the "promise of American life," more aristocratic, more radically subjective, more indifferent to public response. In their aggressive nonsocial individualism, their preoccupation with aesthetic questions, and technique, they resembled the detached artists of the twenties.

The Journalistic Shockers: These iconoclasts were at war with Academia, skeptical of socialism, derisively antigenteel, and against the "Puritanical" in all of its manifestations. They believed it was necessary to conduct a campaign of indiscriminate destruction before American culture could come of age. Their spiritual ancestors were the bourgeois Bohemians of the turn of the century: Edgar Saltus, James Gibbons Huneker, Frank Harris. To them, Nietzsche was the patron saint, Mencken (assisted by Willard H. Wright, George Jean Nathan, and others) his prophet and oracle. The principal organ of the Journalistic Shockers was *Smart Set,* forerunner of *The American Mercury.*

As impertinent and (almost) as irreverent as the *Masses* group, the Menckenians retained vestiges of middle-class propriety; although truculent foes of Comstockery, they were hostile to feminism, free love, and eccentric economics. Like the *Masses* group, they were aggressively antirural and naïvely pagan. They were the least likely, however, to become political radicals, even though Mencken himself kept on good terms with the livelier socialists. With Mencken they deplored the "democratic trend in thinking—that is, a trend toward short cuts, easy answers, glittering theories," and were not exhilarated by the sight of the "Hindenburg" of the American novel, Theodore Dreiser, becoming, in Mencken's words,

a professional revolutionary, spouting stale perunas for all the sorrows of the world. Here Greenwich Village pulls as Chatauqua pushes; already, indeed, the passionate skepticism that was his original philosophy begins to show signs of being contaminated by various so-called "radical" purposes. The danger is not one to be sniffed in. Dreiser, after all, is an American like the rest of us, and to be an American is to be burdened by an ethical prepossession, to lean toward causes and remedies.[49]

The Unclassifiables: Belonging to this group are the writers who had no strong group affiliations, who formed a part of the "freedom movement" but who floated between them all. One example would be a "sport" like Vachel Lindsay, an inhabitant of the ur-Greenwich Village before the arrival of Dell, a contributor to *Poetry, The New*

Republic, The Masses. Dreiser, who wrote for Bohemian little magazines, the friend and protégé of Mencken, admired by Bourne and Brooks, sympathetic to the program of *The Masses* and *The Liberator,* associate of Eastman and Dell, would be another. Upton Sinclair was completely *sui generis:* a faddist, a Puritan, and a socialist. Sherwood Anderson, the pet of the Chicago literati, mystagogue of *Middlewesternismus,* the admirer of Gertrude Stein, the friend of Waldo Frank and Brooks, is another unclassifiable whose writing appeared in all of the coterie magazines.

These are very inexact classifications, to be sure, and perhaps the shared assumptions of the prewar "camps" were more important than their differences. But the response of these writers and intellectuals to the stunning events that ended the "joyous season" may have been foreshadowed in their early affiliations. We shall see how America's decision to enter the war against Germany and the seizure of power in Russia by the Bolsheviks converted a small number of them into Communists dedicated to the radical reconstruction of American society and forced the majority to "put aside with a kind of shame its broken and shattered ideals." [50]

TWO · FOUR RADICALS

YOUNG EASTMAN

IN 1917, Max Eastman was thirty-four years old and probably the best-known literary radical in the United States. His career up to then had been "a long war of independence," and an entry in his notebook of that year, "My life began in January, 1917!" [1] had a symbolic if not literal truth.

Born in Canandaigua, New York, in 1883, he had changed from a rollicking, spunky baby into a fearful and sensitive child. After his clergyman-father's breakdown, the family moved to West Bloomfield, New York, and when Max was six years old his mother (strong, witty, and imaginative) was ordained and became the best-known woman minister in America.

In 1894, the family settled down in Elmira, New York, where Max Eastman came under the influence of an unconventional congregationalist minister, Thomas K. Beecher, a far more appealing figure than his more famous brother, Henry Ward Beecher. An activist, jack-of-all-trades, and antisectarian, a friend of prostitutes, an organizer of baseball games who installed a pool table in the church parlor and who kept his private beer mug in the local saloon, here was the proper guide for the future editor of *The Masses*. Mark Twain, whom young Eastman met and admired, fitted well into this liberal atmosphere; in fact, aside from the sexual inhibitions that prevailed everywhere in middle-class America, there was nothing intellectual in the Elmira experience that Eastman had to repudiate. "Conformity is beautiful until it requires a sacrifice of principle," his mother wrote to him when he was at prep school, "—then it is disfiguring." And again: *"Live out of yourself persistently*. Become interested in all that is going on in the world and train yourself to think about it. It's better to have your own thought, even if it is a mistaken one, than to be always repeating other people's better thoughts." [2]

As a Williams College student, as a philosophy instructor at Columbia from 1907 to 1911, and as a poet-editor, Eastman followed these injunctions. He came out for woman suffrage, sided with rebels of every persuasion, and ratified his rebellion in 1912 by announcing his affiliation with the Socialist Party in a militant letter to the New York *Call* in which he declared his scorn "of the good or bad opinion of everybody in the world but the whole fighting proletariat." [3] Then, as later, however, a strain of skepticism in him (partly sustained, perhaps, by his exposure to Dewey at Columbia as well as by his stubbornly speculative mind) made him suspicious of revolt for its own sake and inclined him to what he termed a "hardheaded idealism."

Did Eastman ever reconcile these divided impulses in his nature, the unregenerate, seditious side of him, the impulsive, self-indulgent, and egotistical side with the cool and dispassionate analyst of ideas political and aesthetic? Never completely. But for the most part he confined his Bohemian predilections to his private affairs and tempered his evangelistic bias, his yearnings for earthly salvation, with a dry recognition of the actual.

In 1912, the "red" Wobblies attracted him, the "yellow" reformist wing of the Socialist Party did not. The contempt he felt for the middle-class Socialists eating their four-course dinners while advocating peaceful and legally conducted strikes and reprehending any form of violence made him side somewhat emotionally with the swashbuckling syndicalists of the I.W.W. [4] But the anarchists, Eastman thought, belonged to the "kindergartners in the school of revolutionary thinking" and he consistently opposed their "sentimental leftism," possibly because he sensed a touch of it in himself, and possibly, too, because of their unreticent discussions of sex and physiol-

ogy. When Emma Goldman, who went to jail for recommending
that women "keep their minds open and their wombs closed," was
released, Eastman refused to preside at a Carnegie Hall meeting
celebrating her return largely because of one of the speakers "who
thought it radical to shock people with crude allusions to their sexual
physiology." [5]

He felt even a closer attachment to a group he labeled the "Sentimental Rebels," men like Hutchins Hapgood, Clarence Darrow,
Fremont Older, Lincoln Steffens. They were Americans, first of all,
whose anarchism simply meant "an irresponsible distaste for politics." They were latter-day antinomians without a personal God, and
by siding with social outcasts, they exhibited their defiant if secular
Christianity. Against them also Eastman posed his own brand of
"hard" socialism:

By hard I meant objective; I meant ruthless in confronting the facts,
whether they be tough or tender, and clear in conceiving the ideal,
whether it prove easy or arduous to attain. I meant employing thoughts
in order to better the real world, the world of all men, not in order to
attain a comfortable equilibrium in your own mind.[6]

Marxism satisfied Eastman's hunger for a secular religion ("I need
no longer extinguish my dreams with my knowledge. I need never
again cry out: 'I wish I believed in the Son of God and his second
coming.' "), but it appealed just as strongly to his respect for facts.
He played down the dogmatic and determinist aspects of Marxism
at the same time that he exalted its revolutionary imperatives.

The end we have in view [he wrote in *The Masses*] is an economic and
social revolution, and by revolution we do not mean the journey of the
earth around the sun, or any other thing that is bound to happen whether
we direct our wills to it or not. We mean a radical democratization of
industry and society, made possible by the growth of capitalism, but to
be accomplished only when and if the spirit of liberty and rebellion is
sufficiently awakened in the classes which are now oppressed. A revolution is a sweeping change accomplished through the conquest of power
by a subjected class. . . .

Eastman was speculating in the early years of *The Masses* about the
possibility of applying the methods of experimental science to social
change. Marx and Engels, he thought, had been correct in turning

off the path of Utopianism, but they had no true conception of science and "they had no suspicion of the limitations which the discipline of genetic and experimental psychology must impose upon their economics." Without the aid of experimental science, man's ancient dreams of justice and brotherhood would remain unrealized. "If we can master and possess, towards our extraordinary ends, a method of procedure that at every point accords with current science," he concluded, "and renew it with each fresh conclusion or discovery, and hold it more important than our dream, then it is not impossible that, though we are so few, we shall profoundly touch the course of evolution." [7]

But as Eastman wrote these words events were shaping up that made it difficult to maintain a dispassionate attitude toward social change or to convince his fellow radicals that the experimental method might go hand in hand with revolution. The 1913 strike of the coal miners in West Virginia (deliberately blotted out of the news, the editors of *The Masses* angrily charged, by the biased Associated Press) [8] heaped fuel on radical emotions. A more shocking event, the "Ludlow massacre" of 1914, turned the cool pragmatist himself into a raging partisan. On April 20, the Colorado state militia opened fire on a tent colony housing the families of striking coal miners who had been evicted from their homes by the owners. The militia then set fire to the camp and shot down a strike leader who tried to save the 120 women and 273 children trapped in the blaze. Twelve women and children died. This incident inspired Eastman to write two articles ("Class War in Colorado" and "The Nice Ladies of Trinidad") that were "as proletarian-revolutionary as anything that had appeared in the United States." [9]

Yet even the "Ludlow massacre" did not shake Eastman's confidence in the scientific approach to industrial conflict. "A little more verification," he suggested, "a little less assertion, would be so much to the health of socialist hypotheses," and he much preferred Thorstein Veblen's controlled anger, his cool critiques of social problems, to undirected humanitarian protest.

Every full-blooded young person [he wrote at this time] has in his arteries a certain amount of scorn. Literary young persons have usually directed this scorn against philistinism, the middle class monotonies, and any provincial obtuseness to those finer values discriminated by the cultured and by those who possess Art. But in our day the full-blooded young persons have got their scorn directed against a more important evil—against the ground-plan of money-competition built on industrial slavery which orders our civilization and makes all our judgments of value, even the most cultured, impure. Indeed, we suspect everything that is called culture—we suspect it of the taint of pecuniary elegance. We have armed our critical judgment with Thorstein Veblen's "Theory of the Leisure Class"—perhaps the greatest book of our day, for it combines a new flavor in literature with a new and great truth in science. This theory has taught us how to see through "culture." We know something about knowledge. We have been "put wise" to sophistication.[10]

While violence flared in factory and mining camp, the sparks from a larger conflagration abroad were beginning to drift across the ocean to America. Eastman and his fellow editors on *The Masses* were no longer quite so certain of socialism's imminent success or even that the gains in social progress could be held. A short trip to Europe in 1915 gave him a sobering picture of the hideousness and monotony of war and "tamed the revolutionary part of my socialist passion." Upon his return, he changed the banner of his column in *The Masses* from "Knowledge and Revolution" to "Revolutionary Progress," as if to suggest by the milder caption an approval "of any event or measure which narrows the gulf between the owning and laboring classes." [11] The realities of the war had made him chary about the use of violence, more concerned, as were the Socialist Party and the I.W.W., with keeping America out of war than with the smashing of capitalism.

Eastman's essays on the war were collected and published in 1916 as *Understanding Germany: The Only Way to End the War and Other Essays.* They trace his thinking from 1914, when he hoped for a German defeat as a way of hastening a long-delayed revolution in that country, to a strict antiwar position. He did not openly advocate the turning of an imperialist war into a class war, but he declared his preference for the latter. "A class war," he wrote, "is not beautiful. It does not trail after it the glamours of poetry and art. It is not aristocratic, not noble in the feudal character of the word. It is, indeed, a stern, desperate, dirty, inglorious and therefore extremely heroic struggle toward a real end." [12] These essays were shot through with Veblen's ideas and manner, even though Veblen had taken a pro-Ally position.

By May 1916, Eastman and his sister, Crystal, the leading spirit of the American Union Against Militarism, were working hard to combat the mounting drive toward American participation in the war. With such people as Paul V. Kellogg, Amos Pinchot, Winthrop D. Lane, and Randolph Bourne, Eastman spoke at mass meetings in various parts of the country, telling his audiences that nothing was to be gained by joining in on the kill, that all chance of appealing to Germany's liberal elements would be lost with America's entrance against it. After April 1917, Eastman's tone hardened. He knew now that the brief interlude of fun and freedom had ended, that the New Freedom was finished and the New Intolerance had begun. "You can't even collect your thoughts," he told an audience on July 18, 1917, "without getting arrested for unlawful assemblage. They give you ninety days for quoting the Declaration of Independence, six months for quoting the Bible, and pretty soon somebody is going to get a life sentence for quoting Woodrow Wilson in the wrong connection." [13]

FLOYD DELL COMES TO *The Masses*

The associate editor on *The Masses,* Floyd Dell, had never been so revolutionary in his socialism as Eastman although he had come earlier to it as a sensitive young poet in Davenport, Iowa. In Chicago, where Dell had gone in 1908 to seek his literary fortunes, he had quickly drawn attention to himself as a poet and literary critic, and his articles in *The Friday Review* (a literary supplement of the Chicago *Evening Post*) were praised by readers as diverse as Ezra Pound, Gordon Craig, Upton Sinclair, Vachel Lindsay, and Carl Van Doren. Dell left Chicago in 1913. At the outbreak of World War I, he was helping Eastman edit *The Masses,* and for the next few years, the battles in Europe seemed too remote from parties in the Village and Provincetown to count for much. Like other editors, Dell favored the Allies, but he remained a pacifist, if an uncertain one, and shrank from committing himself to a war that did not advance the cause of revolution.

In 1915, Anthony Comstock, the symbol of Puritan inhibition and snooping pruriency, died after his lifelong battle against sin, unlamented by Dell and his friends. To Emma Goldman, Comstock was "the autocrat of American morals," the modern Torquemada: "he dictates the standard of good and evil, of purity and vice. Like a thief in the night he sneaks into the private lives of the people, into their most intimate relations. The system of espionage established by this man Comstock puts to shame the infamous Third Division of the Russian secret police." [14] Both Emma Goldman and Floyd Dell considered the fight for political freedom and sexual freedom the same, and so it must have seemed ironically appropriate that the Woodrow Wilson who had appointed their enemy Comstock as United States delegate to the International Purity Congress in 1915 should betray the Greenwich Village radicals in his second administration. He had won a second term on the slogan "He kept us out of war." Six months later America was fighting Germany.

In April 1917, Dell wrote on his draft card, "Conscientious objector against this war," discovered Edna St. Vincent Millay, and continued to write for *The Masses* until the government banned it from the mails and indicted its editors for conspiring to obstruct the draft. By the time they came to trial in April 1918, the February and November revolutions in Russia had already taken place and radicals who had previously denounced all the World War imperialist powers now considered fighting against Germany, Russia's (so it appeared) implacable foe. After Brest-Litovsk, Dell wrote, "Germany seemed to some of us, to me certainly, an enemy, because German militarism threatened the existence of Soviet Russia." [15]

The case of the government against *The Masses* rested on some editorials and cartoons and one poem, a free verse celebration of Emma Goldman and Alexander Berkman,[16] which, taken together (so the government alleged), promoted mutiny in the armed forces and obstructed enlistment. Indicted with Eastman, Dell, and John Reed (en route from Russia when the trial opened) were Josephine Bell, two cartoonists, Art Young and H. J. Glintenkamp, and Merrill Rogers, the business manager of *The Masses*.

Dell wrote later that he "felt a certain pride as an author in having my own writings, among others, thus treated as matters of social and political importance; and I reflected that even if during the rest of my political career my work should receive no other public testimonial, I should never complain that it had been permitted to languish neglected." Three decades later, writers and intellectuals subpoenaed by congressional committees and compelled to testify about their past or present radical associations and opinions found the experience less exhilarating than Floyd Dell did in 1918. "There are some laws that the individual feels he cannot obey," he had written in *The Masses*, "and he will suffer any punishment, even that of death, rather than recognize them as having authority over him. The fundamental stubbornness of the free soul, against which all the powers of the State are helpless, constitutes a conscientious objection, whatever its sources may be in political or social opinion." When the government cited this passage as a violation of the espionage law, Dell regarded the opportunity of developing his ideas before judge and jury as a "spiritual adventure," and he took the stand "with pleasure." The cross-examination had the air of a Socratic dialogue, and the whole affair seemed "a strange, stimulating, and—or so I found it—an agreeable experience." The trial ended with a hung jury, and the defendants were temporarily dismissed.[17]

THE TRANSFORMATION OF JOHN REED

John Reed had arrived in New York one day after the end of the first *Masses* trial, but he was on hand as one of the defendants for the second, which began in late September of 1918.

For Floyd Dell, Reed had stepped into the shoes of Jack London —that "modern Rover boy of socialism" whose last acts before his death in 1916 had angered and saddened his friends. Reed shared London's gusto for life and his romantic-rebellious attitude toward revolution, but he had never put any stock in the racial nonsense that beguiled London's primitive fancies. At a time when London, as Floyd Dell put it, was "singing the tunes that had been taught to him by the American oil-men who were engaged in looting Mexico," and preaching "Nordic supremacy, and the manifest destiny of American exploiters," Reed was riding with Pancho Villa and writing sympathetic reports of the uprising. Whereas Reed opposed the European war from the start, London hailed it as "a Pentacostal cleansing that can only result in good for humankind," and London's resignation from the Socialist Party in 1916 because of "its lack of fire and fight" occurred a year before Reed officially joined.[18]

Reed's transformation from a college boy who was at times obnoxiously aggressive and hell-bent for extracurricular success to a dedicated revolutionist and posthumous Communist Party saint has been commented upon at length by his friends and critics. Yet despite the close attention he has received, it is not at all clear why this well-bred, well-fed boy from Portland, Oregon, should have become, in Earl Browder's words, "the passionate partisan of a great cause." Poet, adventurer, romanticist, collegian, he had an impulsiveness and deep-seated need to stand out boldly from the multitude that had made him suspect both in Cambridge and, later on, in Moscow. "He was a composite," Louis Untermeyer thought, "of Peck's bad boy, Don Giovanni, Don Quixote, Jack London, and the Playboy of the Western World." Walter Lippmann, in a patronizing but perceptive portrait written in 1914, made him an amiable exemplar of *The Masses'* view of life:

He assumed that all capitalists were fat, bald, and unctuous, that reformers were cowardly or scheming, that all newspapers are corrupt, that Victor Berger and the Socialist party and Samuel Gompers and the trade unions are a fraud on labor. He made an effort to believe that the working class is not composed of miners, plumbers and working men generally, but is a fine, statuesque giant who stands on a high hill facing the sun. He wrote stories about the night court and plays about ladies in kimonos. He talked with intelligent tolerance about dynamite, and thought he saw the intimate connection between the cubists and the I.W.W. He even read a few pages of Bergson.[19]

Reed never matured into a poet or thinker of power, and he remained, at twenty-nine, as he confessed, a "romanticist."

Some men seem to get their direction early, to grow naturally and with little change to the thing they are to be. I have no idea what I shall be or do one month from now. Whenever I have tried to become some one thing, I have failed; it is only by drifting with the wind that I have found myself, and plunged joyously into a new role. I have discovered that I am only happy when I am working hard at something I like.[20]

But for all his drifting, Reed was moving away from "the well-fed smug" to the side of workingmen and strikers and the people who hoped to lead them in what Reed believed to be the inevitable class struggle. By 1917, he was farther left than his guide and mentor, Lincoln Steffens, through whom he had met the radical intelligentsia of New York. The strikes he observed and reported, the dramatic excursion into Mexico, and the brief but ugly interlude when he covered the war on the eastern front with the artist Boardman Robinson in 1915 not only made him one of the best-known newspapermen of his time; they also deepened his revolutionary convictions and his antagonism to the war. "Wherever his sympathies marched with the facts," Lippmann had noted, "Reed was superb." [21]

His sketches and stories written between 1913 and 1918—scenes from the Mexican revolution, New York Bowery life, the war in the Balkans—are sharply observed (he had a wide-ranging and retentive reporter's eye) and set down in the impressionistic or expressionistic manner of Stephen Crane.[22] If they lack Crane's precision, his "long logic" and sad irony, and if they are sentimental and romantic where Crane is not, they reveal a sensitive and generously impulsive young man who sympathizes with the down-and-out. A touch of O. Henry can be detected here, a touch of the young Dos Passos. Reed, the gifted and upper-class young man has not yet identified himself completely or unself-consciously with the proletariat. He is still luxuriating in the colors and the paradoxes of the big city. His bums, prostitutes, revolutionaries, capitalists, Mexicans, Serbs are still "materials" to be exploited for their journalistic possibilities.[23]

Between 1915, when he returned from the Balkans, and September 1917, when he went to Russia, already emotionally committed to the Bolshevik cause, Reed lectured, took on minor magazine assignments, wrote some verse, drew up plans for a workers' theater along the lines of the Paterson pageant, and agitated against the preparedness program that was sweeping America into the war. Offers came to report Pershing's expedition into Mexico, to cover the European war, but Reed felt his place was in America. Believing the re-election of Wilson was the best way to ensure American neutrality, he joined a committee of writers organized by George Creel in Wilson's behalf and wrote articles warning the voters "against sinister influences at work to plunge them into war." Reed's campaign against the war did not stop with America's entrance on the side of the Allies. He attacked conscription and lashed out in *The Masses* at the superpatriots and profiteers. "With a sort of hideous apathy," he wrote, "the country has acquiesced in a regime of judicial tyranny, bureaucratic suppression, and industrial barbarism, which followed inevitably the first fine careless rapture of militarism." [24]

Discouraged and depressed by wartime America and without sufficient outlets for his writing, Reed decided to take a closer look at what he had first dismissed as "a bourgeois revolution" in Russia and especially at the revolutionary Soviet of Workers' and Soldiers' Deputies. His *Masses* friends managed to raise enough money for the trip (no newspaper or press syndicate would have anything to do with him at this time), and Reed arrived at St. Petersburg on the eve of the Bolshevik seizure of power. For the next six months, he watched the revolution unfold and described it as if he himself were a participant. In a certain sense he was. He did some work for the Bureau of International Revolutionary Propaganda and addressed the All-Russian Soviets. At Trotsky's suggestion, Reed was even appointed Bolshevik Consul General in New York, a gesture hailed by Max Eastman as "the most beautiful and astute expression they have yet given to the international character of the class struggle and the social revolution." Lenin's decision to cancel the appointment did not diminish Reed's revolutionary fervor. [25]

The stories he cabled to *The Masses* were not published until March 1918, for the government had banned the November-December issue from the mails, and its successor, *The Liberator,* did not appear until February 1918. But when Reed got back to New York in the spring of that year, he lectured on the revolution, wrote articles, and finally compressed his Russian experience into *Ten Days That Shook the World* (1919), unreservedly recommended by Nikolai Lenin "to the workers of the world."

To some of Reed's contemporaries, especially the younger ones, he was a one-man personification of the revolution. "He seemed to me a creative force rather than a great intelligence," one of them recalled. "He loved to be where things were going on and could report what he saw through a powerful and candid lens. The things that stood out about him were his big lunging youth, his audacity, speed, and his wide and sensitive human sympathies. I remember no thoughtful conversations in which he went to the bare bones of the logic of things, as men like Steffens, Minor and Dreiser would do." An older and more knowledgeable Marxist regarded Reed at this time as a bourgeois intellectual "who came to hate present society out of sheer ennui." He remembered a debate between Reed and a Menshevist, well trained in Marxian theory. Reed was asked if Bolshevism were not the opposite of Marxism, and he replied: "Oh, you fellows are not living beings; at best you are bookworms always thinking about what Marx said or meant to say. What we want is a revolution, and we are going to make it—not with books, but with rifles." [26]

The Masses TRIALS

John Reed had come back to stand trial, much to Trotsky's amusement. Presumably a Marxist revolutionist did not "play the game" according to the rules of capitalist sportsmanship, but Reed retained at least this vestige of bourgeois loyalties. Max Eastman, who had explained the class struggle to him and who had been studied in turn by Reed, found his pupil and friend strengthened and toughened by his experiences. The revolution, Reed reported to the readers of *The Liberator,* had taught him three things:

That in the last analysis the property-owning class is loyal only to its property.

That the property-owning class will never readily compromise with the working class.

That the masses of the workers are capable not only of great dreams, but they have in them the power to make dreams come true.[27]

He no longer seemed so gay, however, and his seriousness somewhat affected Eastman's own revolutionary zeal. Reed's chief job was to write *Ten Days That Shook the World,* but Lenin and Trotsky also expected him to help organize a Bolshevist Marxist movement in the United States. Would a skeptical and humorous America be receptive to a mystical creed from medieval Russia? Eastman wasn't sure, but he strongly felt the change in Reed from a gay, daredevil journalist to the tough and lonely professional revolutionist.

Eastman at this time considered socialism neither a philosophy of life nor a religion; it was *"an experiment that ought to be tried."* He did not believe in 1916 that a proletarian revolution was inevitable. Marx's system was "a rationalization of his wish," and he proposed to remodel it "and make of it, and of what else our recent science offers, a doctrine that shall clearly have the nature of hypothesis." When the Bolsheviks succeeded in Russia, Eastman was more pleased than surprised. He likened the Parliament of Proletarian Deputies to "an American Federation of Labor convention with the majority of I.W.W.'s." How dazzling "to have one's ideas one had been loving in a kind of Platonic-super-world fly down and alight casually, still shining with celestial exactitude, right here on earth." Now such phrases as "class struggle," "expropriation of the capitalist," "international solidarity," "dictatorship of the proletariat," "resistance of bourgeoisie" ("that last word we didn't even know how to spell in America")—phrases only heard in discussions at the Rand School, and usually in foreign accents—would come into common parlance. It would no longer be possible for a reporter to translate the motto hanging from a façade in Petrograd as "Proletarians of every country, join yourselves together!" [28]

In 1912, Eastman had joined the Socialist Party as the one that most clearly embodied his views, but he had always been an activist who espoused the class-struggle side of the movement and he preferred the direct-action tactics of the I.W.W. to the fabianism of the Socialists. As a social scientist, he disdained dogma, "the bigotry of the Marxian religion," and distinguished between the class struggle, which he accepted as "inevitable," and class hate, which he did not. His position might be summed up in the greeting of Mother Jones to the Warden at San Quentin: "Poor boy, God damn your soul, ye can't help it!" [29]

Eastman's discovery of Lenin's *Program Address to the Soviets,*

poorly translated in a Rand School pamphlet as *The Soviets at Work,*
brought him closer to the revolution, for it suggested to him that the
first socialist republic was in the hands of an astute, flexible, and undoctrinaire leader, "an all-powerful union of will and intelligence
consecrated to the highest aims of man." Five years later, while
reading through Lenin's untranslated writings in Moscow, he detected a religious animus behind Lenin's scientific manner; he was to
conclude, finally, that Lenin believed with "an iron faith" in the
inevitable logic of history, and that when reality did not seem to
co-operate, he instilled an autocratic party dictatorship "which made
a farce of its great purpose." But in 1918, Lenin seemed the world's
greatest statesman, a superscientist who could think "in a concrete
situation."

He was glad to publish Lenin's *Letter to American Workingmen,*
smuggled in by Carl Sandburg at the request of the Russian propagandist Michael Borodin, and he stoutly defended the Soviets in *The
Liberator* against misconceptions and slander. To Lippmann's charge
in *The New Republic* that the Bolsheviks were "repudiating all authority and obligations" and his description of the Russian government as "a complete dissolution of centralized organization into local
atoms of self-government," Eastman replied that "there is growing
into maturity in that country the most just and wise and humane and
democratic government that ever existed in the world." [30]

Eastman's defense of Russia did not seem inconsistent early in
1918 with a qualified support of Wilson's war policies. The President's plans for a postwar peace, his refusal to permit the Japanese
to invade Siberia, and his warning to the Allied powers to stay out of
Russia seemed to presage a revival of his liberalism. Trotsky himself
held an interview on March 5, 1918, in which he suggested that the
U.S. and the U.S.S.R. might march together as "Fellow-travelers,"
and Eastman accepted that line for *The Liberator.* Reed demurred.
Eastman's policy, he thought, smacked too much of Menshevism,
and he resigned from *The Liberator* staff, although he stayed on good
terms with Eastman and continued to send him articles.[31]

When *The Masses'* editors came to trial in the spring of 1918,
the then new periodical *The Liberator* was supporting the war. By
the fall of that year, when the second *Masses'* trial began, the de-

fendants no longer felt conciliatory toward the government. American troops had been sent to Siberia, and at home, even though the war was over, the persecution of the radicals hardly slackened. During the trial, Reed under cross-examination gave the jury a stomach-turning account of trench warfare, and not one of the defendants, he noted later, dissembled what he believed:

This had its effect on the jury, and on the Judge. When Max Eastman defended the St. Louis declaration of the Socialist Party, when Floyd Dell defended the conscientious objectors, when Art Young made it clear that he disapproved of this war and all wars on social and economic grounds . . . a new but perfectly consistent point of view was presented.

But Eastman's summing up, Reed believed, was "the one great factor in our victory." He "boldly took up the Russian question, and made it part of our defense. The jury was held tense by his eloquence; the Judge listened with all his energy. In the courtroom there was utter silence." [32]

Max Eastman's Address to the Jury in the Second Masses Trial, issued as a pamphlet in 1919, was more than an artful summing up of a law case or a defense of free speech. Eastman had no difficulty in proving *The Masses* editors did not "intend" or "conspire" to obstruct recruitment, but it took courage in 1918 to affirm the socialist position toward war, the domestic economy, and Russia. How can a socialist opposition operate in wartime and still remain within the law? After sketching the background of the two *Masses* trials, he concluded:

We came into this court because the United States Government—the Postmaster General—has hopelessly bungled a job of handling in a business-like and courteous way the people who are opposed to the war on political grounds, but who want to conform to the regulations and don't want to impede the military operations of the government.

He lucidly explained the Socialist Party program, denied that Russia was a pro-German, terroristic government, and exalted socialism "as one of the heroic ideas and ardent beliefs of humanity's history."

It is a faith which possesses more adherents all over the surface of the earth who acknowledge its name and subscribe to its principles, than any other faith ever had, except those private and mysterious ones that we call religious. It is either the most beautiful and courageous mistake that hundreds of millions of mankind ever made, or else it is really the truth that will lead us out of our misery, and anxiety, and poverty, and war, and strife and hatred between classes, into a free and happy world. In either case, it deserves your respect.[33]

As in the first trial, the jury split—this time eight to four. "We await the third with equanimity," Jack Reed wrote.[34]

RANDOLPH BOURNE

Three months after the second *Masses* trial, Randolph Bourne, the friend of Eastman, Dell, and Reed, died of pneumonia in New York City. Unlike most of the radicals and liberals who had wavered in their attitude toward the war, Bourne remained an unrelenting oppositionist—so much so that by 1918, he had come close to renouncing the country that seemed in 1913 to stand on the threshold of a new era. Because Bourne had expected so much from America, he furiously resented "this irrelevance of war" that had "slammed the door" on his hopes. "It will be a thousand years," he remarked to a friend, "before it opens again." [35]

In 1913, when Bourne went to Europe on a Columbia University fellowship, it was the culmination of a long and hard struggle over enormous handicaps. His misshapen dwarf's body and twisted face deprived him of many of the normal experiences of childhood and adolescence, but he had somehow managed to rise above his handicap, even though his adjustment was probably less complete than some commentators have claimed. Bourne accepted his crippled body as a fact to be analyzed and understood, just as another person might analyze a personal trait. Yet his anguished reply to an incredibly tactless letter from a friend describing a love affair in great detail shows how starved he was for intimate female companionship and his failure, despite his brave efforts, to sublimate completely his handicap: "You make me feel suddenly very old and bitterly handicapped and foolish to have any dreams left of the perfect comrade who is, I suppose, the deepest craving of my soul. It is to her I write to, meet casually in strange faces on the street, touch in novels, feel beside me in serene landscapes and city vistas, grasp in my dreams. She wears a thousand different masks, and eludes me ever. In half a dozen warm friends the mask is very thin but it is always a mask." To a close woman friend he confessed in 1916: "Love, fame, joy in work, would bring, perhaps, the resources for the freedom that I want to move about and yet have a centre and a hearth. All my problems are interwoven; if I had one solved, it seems as if they should all be solved. Of course, it seems to me the key to all of them is love, and the deprivation the one impediment to blossoming." [36]

Financial difficulties postponed Bourne's higher education, but when he was graduated from Columbia University in 1913, he was already, at twenty-seven, an accomplished writer, with a volume of essays to his credit, and a self-proclaimed defender of "Youth" against the "Older Generation." He had written a Whitmanesque hymn to "Sabotage," proclaimed the I.W.W. as the harbinger of industrial democracy, and had attended the Paterson pageant in Madison Square Garden.

Already a socialist of sorts, the year he spent in Europe following his graduation hastened the change from a religiously inspired to a more practical, if still idealistic, radicalism. England, with its ideals of militarism and imperialism, its snobberies and prejudices, under-scored (he wrote home) "my own incorrigibly plebeian nature." Bourne acknowledged the surface placidity of English life but sus-pected "an enormous amount of subterranean connection between big business and government which would perfectly scandalize our American conscience." He found no analogy in the United States to the public-spirited English aristocracy, but he felt impelled "to ad-mire our naive, youthful traits, which make us notice everything and ask pointed and embarrassing questions about our political and so-cial life." [37]

His English sojourn also gave him a deeper appreciation of Ameri-can writers, especially Emerson, Thoreau, Henry and William James, Royce, and Santayana, whose merits now forcibly impressed him. "Why can't we get patriotic and recognize our great men?" he asked his friend Alyse Gregory. "The first six express the American genius and those ideals of adventurous democracy that we are beginning to lose, partly through having filled our heads with admiration of English rubbish, and partly through having formed a stupid canon of our own with Poe and Cooper and lifeless Hawthorne and bourgeois Longfellow and silly Lowell." Oddly enough it was Henry James who made the deepest impression upon him:

And Henry James, too, though it sounds surprising to say so, was perhaps the most thoroughly American, with that wonderful sensitiveness to the spiritual differences between ourselves and the Older World, and the subtle misunderstandings that follow our contact with it. I found him one of the best guides to Europe. I read him in London with the keenest glow and appreciation, feeling constantly how impossible it would have been for any English person to have seen or felt the things that he pictures so delicately and truthfully. To be sure, where the English writer usually caricatures the American, he always makes the Englishman far too charming; but then his Americans are apt to be charming, too, so I suppose the proportion is kept right.

Bourne found the French more congenial than the English, more free and democratic in their social relations. Jules Romains, already a kind of oracle for young radical Americans, interested him although he felt Romains' *La Vie Unanime* would strike an American as bizarre, for "he is not used to feeling so keenly the social reverberations, the power of the group, and the intoxication of camaraderie." A quick trip through Italy and a briefer stay in Switzerland were too short for him to gather more than superficial impressions. In Germany, already mobilizing for war, he was impressed by the efficiency of the people and "the clear massive lines of the new German architecture," but was disturbed by "something in the soul of the people . . . a sort of thickness and sentimentality and a lack of critical sense. . . ." [38]

He left a civilization "about to be torn to shreds" and returned home believing more than ever in the importance of a national culture and in what Van Wyck Brooks called *"the apostolic role of the young student class."* He had some disagreeable truths to tell his countrymen about their literature, art, and education, their business ideals, their false gentility and fondness for cant. News of the "Ludlow massacre" had reached him in Rome ("Rockefeller," he wrote to a friend, "has the psychology of a twelfth century baron") and made him more certain than ever that America needed socialists in

Congress who could protest against such outrages. But the possibility seemed remote: "with our deep-seated distrust of social equality, our incapacity for political life, our genius for race-prejudice, our inarticulateness and short-sightedness, it seems highly probable that we shall evolve *away* from democracy instead of towards it." [39]

Until America entered the war, Bourne conducted a literary war of his own for a democratic collectivism and an art thoroughly involved "with religion and politics and the affairs of men." Between 1914 and 1916, he wrote for *The New Republic* and worked closely with his young contemporaries who were trying to fulfill "the promise of American life." Bourne, like Lippmann, Eastman, and others, still espoused a Deweyan instrumentalism which he valued for its sharp edge "that would slash up the habits of thought, the customs and institutions in which society had been living for centuries." It was only when Dewey, arguing instrumentally, repudiated pacifism as a lack of "faith in constructive, inventive, intelligence," and supported American participation in the name of "creative intelligence," that Bourne turned bitterly against his teacher. Dewey's philosophy "worked" during times of placidity and prosperity, when men could think tranquilly; it failed during crises. "The motley crew of socialists, and labor radicals, and liberals and pragmatist philosophers" who now lent their energies and minds to the war effort had no program; their blazing patriotism only served to conceal "the feebleness of their intellectual light." Bourne condemned *The New Republic* liberals, he told Brooks, for trying to retain their high goals while submitting to military necessity that made their achievement impossible. They were victimized by their "intellectualism," more concerned with system than with freedom. Everywhere, on all levels, he found "an insensate scramble for action, a positive delight in throwing off the responsibility of thought." [40]

Bourne was well aware from the start that his war views would make him unpopular, and as early as October 1915, he sensed a growing hostility against him. "I have become an impious, ungrateful, pro-German venomous viper," he wrote a friend; two years later, he felt his ostracism even more keenly.

I feel very much secluded from the world, very much out of touch with my times, except perhaps with the Bolsheviki. The magazines I write for die violent deaths, and all my thoughts seem unprintable. If I start to write on public matters I discover that my ideas are seditious, and if I start to write a novel I discover that my outlook is immoral if not obscene. What then is a literary man to do if he has to make his living by his pen?

Bourne's death on December 22, 1918, at age thirty-two, removed the one man, Waldo Frank wrote in 1919, who had managed to join "the political and cultural currents of advance." Most American artists, Frank thought, fled from the machine; most radical propagandists withdrew from life. "Bourne almost alone embraced the two. . . . Now, the political field is once more clearer to the pat materialist, the shallow liberal, the isolated radical whom he despised, and whom, eventually, his power of irony must have shamed." But Frank saw some hope in the handful of "well-equipped and intellectual athletes, schooled and traveled" who would "take the lead in the stern and ugly business of social welfare." There was the poet Max Eastman, who "turns his lyricism to propaganda," the romantic John Reed, friend of Lenin, who "returns to New York with the vision of transfiguration in his eyes," and the critic Floyd Dell, who "interprets the social impulse of aesthetic work to minds that are eager but are still not aesthetically quickened." None of these, however, succeeded in ending the "dualism between poetry and politics which affected the pre-war radical intelligentsia." [41]

ART AND POLITICS

The December 1918 issue of *The Liberator* carried Floyd Dell's review of Eastman's *Colors of Life,* a volume of poems prefaced by the author's apologetic introduction in which he explained that he had dedicated his energies but not his heart to revolution. Rather, he had found his "undivided being . . . in those moments of energetic idleness when the life of universal nature seemed to come to its bloom of realization in my consciousness." Life, Eastman declared, is "older than liberty . . . greater than revolution," and while he fought against the cruel system that denied life to others, he wanted life "also for myself." In commenting upon his friend's one-man manifesto, Dell observed that Eastman might prefer poetry to politics, but now there was no choice for the artist. Not only did the public need truth and candor in a world of lies; it was also "more *interesting* to talk truth than to create beauty," if one were an artist in 1918. "Other things are so damnably interesting—and promise to remain so! How can one be an artist in a time when the morning paper may tell of another Bolshevik revolution somewhere?" [42] The only salvation for the ivory-tower artists, he suggested, would be to plot the course of history for the next fifteen years so that they would not have to keep shifting their opinions.

In both Dell and Eastman, the "bourgeois heart" struggled privately with the "socialist head." Eastman, in particular, had difficulty managing what he called his three-horse chariot: earning his living, working for mankind, and thinking and writing creatively.* The triumph of the Bolsheviks had strengthened his faith in the coming socialism, but it had also (so he wrote to a friend) "taken all of the compelling anguish out of the temptation to sacrifice my creative life to the revolution." With all well in the practical world, it would now be possible, he hoped, to "live in the world of my thoughts." [43]

But the world continued to intrude, and Eastman continued to vacillate in his ideas about the poet and politics. As a good Bolshevik, he believed that the artist ought to accept the intellectual guidance of the revolutionary party and yet retain his creative autonomy. Two incidents—one occurring in 1919, the other in 1920-21—forced him to think through a little more systematically than he had done before the problem of art and politics.

In the December 1919 issue of *The Liberator* appeared "A Declaration of Intellectual Independence," written by Romain Rolland

---

* "It just happens that political emotions did not move me to write poetry. Were they less profound, less organic, less *clear* perhaps, less wholly myself? I don't know. I really don't like politics. I'd like to abolish it altogether! I've never thought this overmuch, and it would take quite a self-examination to explain it, but I think my sonnet *To the Twelfth Juror* at least lays bare this unfortunate split in my nature. However, far from being a policy that I wanted to put over in the magazine, it was a limitation of my nature that I would occasionally try to overpass. But there's no use *trying* to write poetry. (I tried, by the way, a 'Ballad of Wat Tyler' that appeared under a *nom de plume* in one of the early numbers of the *Masses*.)" Max Eastman to author, April 3, 1957.

and signed by a number of other internationally known artists and intellectuals including Jane Addams, Selma Lagerlöf, Andreas Latzko, Stefan Zweig, Ellen Key, Bertrand Russell, Hermann Hesse, Henri Barbusse, Benedetto Croce, and Israel Zangwill. Rolland invited the intellectuals of the world, who so recently had degraded themselves in behalf of narrow nationalisms, to write for *"the whole of Humanity*. The declaration concluded:

We do not know peoples. We know *the* People—one universal—the People which suffers, struggles, falls to rise again, and which ever marches onward on the rough road drenched with its sweat and blood—the People of all men, all equally our brothers. And it is that they shall become conscious with us of this brotherhood, that we raise above their blind battles the Ark of the Covenant—the unshackled Mind, one and manifold, eternal.

Replying in the same issue of the magazine, Eastman politely repudiated the whole philosophy of the declaration with its misty abstractions of "the Mind" and what Eastman took to be its snobbish distinction between a "superior cult" of intellectuals representing "higher thought" and the lower orders. The intellectuals, he said, needed only to affiliate with the class-conscious proletariat, not to work independently of it:

For there exists a science, consisting of a series of hypotheses as to the method by which this choice of ours may be carried out in the actual world, and that science is one of the clearest and most ardent achievements of the human mind. It is the science that was founded in the Communist Manifesto of 1848—the science of revolution based upon the Economic Interpretation of History. And almost the first postulate of that science so far as it applies to the present times, is that if we wish to achieve liberty and democracy for the world we must place ourselves and all our powers unreservedly upon the side of the working class in its conflict with the owners of capital. We must adopt—at least so far as we are engaged upon this social quest—a fighting mentality and we must engage in a conscious class struggle. That is, I believe, the supreme edict which mind at its best—that is, its most scientific—now delivers to those who choose freedom and democracy as their goal for the world.

To which Rolland replied: "The disagreement between us is certainly complete. So complete that I will not attempt to discuss it here." [44]

Four months after Eastman had read Rolland a lesson in what might be called revolutionary scientism, he replied in somewhat the same fashion to the French novelist Henri Barbusse, the celebrated author of *Under Fire,* who in 1919 had organized an international group of intellectuals in the Clarté movement. Its official name was "A League of Intellectual Solidarity for the Triumph of the International Cause," and its self-declared purpose was "to exercise in complete independence the activities designated by its title." The Clarté group was more openly revolutionary than the Rolland group, more vigorously committed to the Third International. "There are but two nations in the world," Barbusse told the French war veterans, "—that of the exploiters and that of the exploited. The more powerful is the prisoner of the other, and we all belong, proletarians of battles, to the one that is vanquished. Such is the tragic, made, shameful reality. All the rest is but foul superannuated sophisms which will bring the world's end by mere force of absurdity—if slaves remain slaves."

Eastman approved of this revolutionary fervor, but he found in Clarté the same unscientific thinking and bourgeois sentimentality that he had complained of in Rolland's group. The Clarté manifesto assumed that "a conflict of beliefs and abstract ideas" produced social change, and it seemed "to be entirely ignorant of those deeper-lying and more pervading motives, those currents of material interest, which Marx so long ago declared and which recent events have so abundantly proven, to be the real motor forces in social evolution." Intellectuals could never rise above their class interests to form a revolutionary army of thought, Eastman lectured.

The task at hand is the overthrow of a master class by the workers of the world. It is just as simple as that. In this operation the humanitarian intellectuals will function up to the critical moment as obscurers of the issue, and when the critical moment comes they will function as apostles of compromise and apologists of the masters.

Barbusse's phrase from his address to the soldiers—"There are but two nations"—Eastman concluded, was worth all the rest of his misty platitudes. So long as Clarté contained within its membership "bourgeois liberals like H. G. Wells and Blasco Ibanez" and "proletarian revolutionaries like Steinlen and Anatole France and Raymond Le Febvre," it would either split in two or expire.[45]

Eastman's rebuff may or may not have influenced Barbusse, but in the spring of 1921, Clarté redefined itself as "A Center of International Revolutionary Education" instead of "an international of intellect." In order to purge itself of "those internationalists—reformists and sentimental pacifists—who resist all destruction, indispensable as it is to the construction of mankind," the new manifesto expressly endorsed "the absolute principles of International Communism," and dedicated itself to "the radical destruction of the capitalist system" by contributing intellectually "to the task of the Communist Socialist Party." At the same time, it wished to remain "aside and apart from all polemic, political or doctrinaire organs and organizations." [46]

Eastman approved of the new line. He could recognize the similarity between the cultural program of Clarté and that of *The Liberator;* but still he had deep reservations about affiliating with the French group.

The Clarté correspondent had written to him: "Our program . . . is very simple—we are undertaking the task of prolet-culture (in so far as such can be attempted in a capitalist regime) which the communist party, now entirely occupied with questions of propaganda, organization, etc., has not the leisure to attempt." Eastman gagged on the term "prolet-culture," which sounded "so dull, busy, self-conscious, ugly and uninspiring a name for any creative occupation" that he could scarcely bring himself to use it. But other overtones in the new manifesto disturbed him even more. Why make a distinction between "revolutionary education" and "propaganda"? Did the literary people of Clarté think themselves more "intellectual" than the party leaders? Anyone who wanted information about communism would do better to read the party press than the Clarté writers or *The Liberator*. If artists could contribute "neither theoretical education, nor a more circumspect and authentic practical information," as Eastman believed, what was their proper function? His answer was "poetry."

We are distinguished, we literary and artistic people, by our ability to realize—to feel and express the qualities of things. We experience vividly the existing facts, and the revolutionary ideal, and the bitterly wonderful long days of the struggle that lies between these two. All the way along we are dealing as experts in experience. Experience is our trade. We receive it vividly and we convey it vividly to others. And this faculty of vivid living—besides the ultimate and absolute value that it has in itself—contributes something indispensable to the practical movement. It contributes something that we might call *inspiration.*

But if artists could inspire, even the most revolutionary among them sometimes made political asses of themselves—like Gorky and Barbusse himself. Hence writers and artists, more than any other group, needed party discipline:

Is it wise for these people whose service to the revolution is inspiration—the poets, artists, humorists, musicians, reporters, story tellers, and discursive philosophers—to form a distinct and autonomous organization of their own? To me it seems unwise. These particular people, I should say, are more in need of guidance and careful watching by the practical and theoretical workers of the movement than the members of any other trade. There is so strong an admixture of play in their work—that is the reason. Their work has to be playful in order to be creative. It has to be very free and irresponsible. It cannot, I think, submit to the official control of a party. And for that very reason the task of making it circumspect enough never to injure practically while it is aiding poetically, the work of the party, is a very delicate one. It is one which can best be accomplished . . . if the party is the only *organization,* the only corporate source of intellectual guidance.[47]

No better evidence could be found to illustrate the dualism, if not the contradictions, in Eastman's conception of the revolutionary artist who was at once free and not free, and who ought not to submit to party control but who must yet turn to the party for intellectual guidance.

Barbusse, replying in the fall of 1921, denied that Clarté was trying to maintain false distinctions between manual and intellectual workers, but he continued to insist that intellectuals and artists had an obligation to overcome the inertia of the "ignorant and intoxicated masses" who did not understand their own rational interests. They could better perform this duty if they stayed clear of party ties and stuck to principles. The ceremonials of party, Barbusse thought, often turned people away before they had even listened to party doctrine. It was enough for the intellectuals to present the truth, correct falsehood, and then let people come to communism in their own way. Barbusse disagreed with Eastman's idea that the poet must be at once free and under discipline. Poets, he said, as non-politicals, should organize as poets but place their talents at the disposal of the revolution, explain what communism is to other intellectuals, and write poetry that would inspire their readers to change the world.[48]

Eastman's rejection of Clarté inspired other rejoinders besides that of Barbusse. Writing in *The Freeman,* Van Wyck Brooks took Eastman to task for declaring that intellectuals could not lead a revolutionary movement, that art is play, that there was no difference between education and propaganda, and that artists must follow in the wake of the working class. His stand, Brooks thought, explained what was wrong with the feeble revolutionary movement in the United States. Intellectuals in Europe had given the masses "enlightened desire," but America had no Ibsen or William Morris, no Nietzsche or Anatole France; it still fed on the dry husks of old rebels whose ideas were "fantastically unrelated to the America of 1921! . . . and on the mere spectacle of Soviet Russia; and on air and emotion." The task for American writers, Brooks concluded, was not to fan emotions but to write good books.[49]

DELL ON THE POET AND SOCIETY

At the same moment that Max Eastman was laying down the law on the poet as politician to Romain Rolland, his associate editor, Floyd Dell, was grappling with the problem in a less doctrinaire spirit. Like Eastman, Dell felt simultaneously the conflicting impulses to dream and to act, to be a self-centered artist and the self-immolating servant of society. There were moments in history, he thought, when life became so unbearable that people turned to dreams, "the long periods of discouragement or disillusion or despair that lie between one revolution and the next." There were also intoxicating interludes, "the brief periods of great social hope—popularly called Revolutions," when action and dream became one.* Poets, as the

---

* "We can tell by the poetry of Milton that people believed for a brief period that life had a sublime purpose; and by the poetry of Pope that they had concluded that life was a pretty prosy affair after all. And we have there the history of English republicanism. We can tell from the poetry of "seismographs of social disturbance," delicately responded to these popular tremors; they alternated between accepting the world or rejecting it. Unfortunately, the former response was often a prelude to tired resignation, the latter to futile despair. Dell wanted poetry to take "the leadership in not merely the acceptance but the evaluation of life, and with the purpose of making it possible for us not only to face the present but to create the future."

The critic might assist in this effort by explaining "just why Vachel Lindsay can never be expected to salute with verbal cannonades the Dictatorship of the Proletariat in Springfield, Illinois" or answering the question whether "under the Soviet Arturo Giovannitti would stop, and whether Max Eastman will begin, writing Bolshevik poetry; and if not, why not?" He might speculate on what Louis Untermeyer would do if he were "elected head of a Special Commission to Suppress Counter-Revolutionary Tendencies in the All-American Poetry Soviet?" The critic might ask, in short: "Do these poets as poets understand the Present, and can they help us shape the Future?" [50]

So much for what poets and critics ought to do. But could they reconcile the warring tendencies that contested within them, the struggle between the public and the private self so persistently exhibited in the pages of *The Masses* and *The Liberator?*

Dell himself had discovered socialism when he was a youth in Quincy, Ill. "It was a glorious evening," he recalled in 1918, "in which I heard from the lips of a streetsweeper in broken English that my dreams and I were a part of a living movement that was preparing to take the world into its hands to shape anew. . . ." But he also realized that individualism was in "the very fabric of our lives," that he was deeply rooted in the very America which had

---

Blake that wild purposes were forming under the suave exterior of eighteenth century civilization; and from the poetry of Byron that these purposes had come to some tragi-comedy and ironically unexpected success. And there we have the history of the French revolution—and Napoleon. Nineteenth century English poetry confronted the result of the French revolution—a triumphant bourgeoisie. The poets reflected in their songs the attitude of society at large toward this new regime. They turned their minds away from it—toward the middle ages." *The Liberator*, II, Dec. 1919, pp. 39-40. Dell was to develop these ideas more specifically in later articles and most completely in his best book, *Intellectual Vagabondage* (1927).

hurt and offended him, and detached, like most of his contemporaries, from the American tradition of radical protest:

We do not even know that the literature of America is above everything else a literature of protest and of rebellion. We actually know, most of us, no more of American literature than a European knows. . . . We do not guess how many of our "experiments" merely reproduce the efforts of the generation of Longfellow to escape from an unfriendly milieu; and, not knowing the past, we cannot learn by its mistakes—we must go ahead enthusiastically and make them on our own account. We only slowly come to learn that what we sometimes contemptuously call "American" is not American at all; that it is, astonishingly enough, we who are American: that Debs and Haywood are as American as Franklin and Lincoln, and that the Loyal Legions are no more American than the Ku-Klux-Klan.[51]

Dell dramatized the conflict between his socialist conscious self and his anarchist Unconscious in an amusingly frank essay entitled "A Psycho-Analytic Confession." Dell's conscious self unequivocally holds on to sound socialist doctrine but it cannot repress the nagging inquiries of the subversive Unconscious, who is all for the Co-operative Commonwealth so long as it is far away, but who finds the goals of the Soviet Republic too materialistic and mundane. "If man remains the slave of the machine under Communism," it observes, "I do not see that he is much better off than he was under Capitalism."

Dell denounces his Unconscious for being selfish and depraved, for having lingering "bourgeois tendencies," for speaking "utopian nonsense," but the Unconscious, who prefers Veblen's *The Instinct of Workmanship* to the *Communist Manifesto* and poetry to economics, will not be silenced. It admits it is utopian, but retorts:

And between us, I think you are, too. I think you are a Socialist simply because you want a different kind of world, one you can be happy in. And you work for the social revolution just as other people work to make a fortune. You want to see your dream come true. But the dream which you want to see come true is my dream—not Lenin's seven hundred million electric bulbs, but a houseboat and a happy family living in a state of moderately advanced and semi-nude savagery!

Finally Dell scornfully challenges his Unconscious. Does this mean, he asks, that "you are lacking in sympathy for the great experiment in common ownership of the machinery of production in Russia?" Are you going to refuse me your assistance, which I need, in order to make people understand communism? The Unconscious does not answer for a moment, but, then, after humming "a silly old warsong," it replies: "I have gone through a long period of barbarism, too, you know, and I understand that better than you do. Fighting for the sake of victory! You would be shocked if you really knew me." [52]

THE APOSTATES

In this debate, the Unconscious, spokesman for an untamed and semibarbarous individualism, had the best of the argument,[53] but Dell, like Eastman, was not prepared to give up the socialist reality for the poet's "houseboat" or to permit the detractor of the Russian experiment to go unanswered. And when Dell's idol, Bertrand Russell, suddenly repudiated his pro-Communist position in the fall of 1920, both Dell and Eastman condemned his apostasy in *The Liberator*.

Famed before the war as a mathematician and logician, Russell had won additional respect from the American radicals for his resolute pacifism. Cambridge University had expelled him, and the British government had kept him in jail for six months. As late as the spring of 1920, Russell had written an article for *The Liberator* in which he not only defended Russian Communism, but also justified some of the repressive policies of the Soviet Government:

The regime of international socialism [Russell wrote then] would have to be, in many regions, a regime of armed force, backed by rigid control of the press and schools. There is no reason to suppose that, when the time comes, the Bolsheviks will shrink from such a course, however little imperialism there may be in their present purposes. Their outlook on the world, like that of the early Mohammedans, is at once realistic and fanatical. Believing, as they do, in the Marxian formula of inevitable economic development, they feel their ultimate victory fatalistically assured. What they regard as of most importance is that the guns should be in the hands of the class-conscious proletariat. This once secured, they feel convinced that propaganda can bring to their side the part of the proletariat which is still misled by "bourgeois catchwords," such as religion and patriotism.[54]

Russell had come out for the "victory of international Socialism" and "a thorough-going, root and branch transformation such as Lenin attempted" just before he visited the Soviet Union with a British trade-union delegation. A cursory glimpse at dictatorship of the proletariat destroyed his Communist fervor, and he concluded that "kindliness and tolerance are worth all the creeds in the world." [55]

Because Russell's apostasy so dismayed his American admirers and because some of his most irate critics later denounced the Soviet Union with more emotion and rage than Russell did, his measured comments deserve closer attention.

He had gone to Russia, he said, believing himself to be a Communist, and he left with his anticapitalist opinions unchanged. "My objection," he wrote then, "is not that capitalism is less bad than the Bolsheviki believe, but that socialism is less good, at any rate in the form which can be brought about by war." Russian Communism, Russell said, had concentrated "immense power in the hands of a few men," and although he saw the enormous tasks that plagued the Bolshevik leaders and although he paid tribute to their unselfish heroism, he saw no reason why the West should abandon their "slower methods of democracy and popular agitation" for the Bolshevik methods of violent revolution:

In Russia, the methods . . . are probably more or less unavoidable; at any rate, I am not prepared to criticize them in their broad lines. But they are not the methods appropriate to more advanced countries, and our socialists will be unnecessarily retrograde if they allow the prestige of the Bolsheviki to lead them into slavish imitation. It will be a far less excusable error in our reactionaries if, by their unteachableness, they compel the adoption of violent methods. We have a heritage of civilization and mutual tolerance which is important to ourselves and to the world. Life in Russia has always been fierce and cruel to a far greater degree than with us, and out of the war has come a danger that this fierceness and cruelty may become universal . . . it is essential to a happy issue that melodrama should no longer determine our views of the

Bolsheviki; they are neither angels to be worshiped nor devils to be exterminated, but merely bold and able men attempting, with great skill, what is an almost impossible task.[56]

The very certainty of the Bolshevik leaders, their unwillingness to consider the "psychological imagination" and their insistence that everything in politics derived from purely material causes, seemed only to intensify his own doubts. For all these reasons, and others as well, Russell broke with the Third International.

To the young Bolsheviks on *The Liberator,* Russell's unenthusiastic appraisal of New Russia and his preference for an England that had failed him during the war, that exploited its colonial population and ground down its proletariat was contradictory and sentimental. How could Russell, Floyd Dell asked, describe Lenin's regime as a kind of Asiatic despotism buttressed by a secret police and still concede that he would support it if he were a Russian? How could this ruthless tyranny enlist the ablest men? Why did Russell predict that the Soviets, given peace and trade, might soon surpass the United States? Why did Russell admit that Russia needed a hard government and then deplore the concentration of power in the hands of a minority? Russell's confused thinking, said Dell, might puzzle his American friends but he was a familiar type to the Russians:

The political woods in Russia are full of people like that. Under the label Menshevik, Right Social Revolutionist, Left Social Revolutionist, and Anarchist, they have been cluttering up the progress of Russian history for the past three years. His opinions are an old story to the Russians. Every one of his complicated idealistic attitudes is well known. All his arguments have been learned by heart—and answered over and over again until the Communists are sick and tired of answering them.

Only two of Russell's observations disturbed Dell: the proliferation of the Soviet bureaucracy and the growing spirit of nationalism, but he found evidence to suggest that neither trend was likely to endure. Russell, he concluded, behaved like the class-prejudiced, naïve English gentleman that he was; he had visited Russia hoping to have his doubts confirmed.[57]

Eastman's comments on Russell's change of heart were no less critical than Dell's, but he rejected the class explanation of his proletarian friends as too simple. To be sure, Russell was "by birth a member of the ruling class, and by profession a fellow of the ancient society of its ideologists and apologizers," but he was also an idealist of the "soft," who had not mastered the lesson of Nietzsche. Nietzsche, Eastman said, failed to acknowledge the "ultimate sovereignty" of science; he ignored biology and economics and scorned Marx. Yet he "advocated the creation of a *genuine* aristocracy. And we may as well agree with him, I think, that that is what we want—not a morass of mediocrity, but an eminence, and also a lively dominance through sheer natural force and influence of the people of real ability and value." The reading of Nietzsche should be required for any student of communism, Eastman recommended, for until "we have got purged of the contagion of softness, we are not even ready to begin to search for a true theory of progress." Russell never purged himself of this contagion; hence he returned "wounded and shocked by the hard vigor of the Bolshevik leaders." [58]

But Russell's failure to see that the Bolsheviki were "Nietzschean *free spirits,*" not "Christianical *saints*" did not mean that all bourgeois intellectuals would revert to old class affiliations. One might still distinguish "these revolutionary cherubs" from the "thinking revolutionists." "It *is* possible," he affirmed, "for persons of drastic and pure intellect, or militantly sympathetic emotion, to abstract from their own economic or social situation . . . the process of revolutionary struggle scientifically, and put their personal force in upon the side where lie the ultimate hopes of human life." [59]

THE IMAGE OF RUSSIA

Ostensibly, Eastman's defense of Lenin and his compatriots against the canards of the anti-Communists was a rational one. He favored the Bolsheviki because they were good instrumentalists (neither fanatical nor dogmatic, as Russell alleged) who were testing a still-undisproved hypothesis. He acknowledged "that the fanatical dogmatizing, religion-making tendency is at work among revolutionists, as it is everywhere else—the attempt to shift off upon some God or rigid set of ideas the burden and responsibility of the daily exercise of intelligent judgment." But he felt all "lovers of liberty" would struggle against this tendency.[60]

Yet before he wrote these words, some American literary radicals had already converted Soviet Russia into a bastion of liberty islanded in a churning ocean of reaction. They had deified its leaders from Lenin to Radek and announced their unshakable belief in the laws of Marx. Arturo Giovannitti, *The Liberator*'s bard of revolution, chanted an ode "On Lenin's Birthday":

Victory, lightning-faced, flame-winged, has come
Just on the day it was told by your prophets and seers,
The harbingers of your great day; the builders of your highway,
The blazers of your world-trails!
Holah; ye the axmen of truth, blasters of lies and wrongs,
Torch-bearers of the sun, incendiaries, petroleers,
Marshallers of the storms, thinkers and pioneers,
Hurlers of proclamations, bomb-throwers of song,
Raisers of mobs and altars, knights of the mad crusade,
Arise! Break from your chains, burst through your jails.
Tear through the noose of the gibbets—the day of days has come!!
For lo! the Red Army has broken through the blockade,
And Russia that spoke with the bible, now speaks through the cannonade
And her spokesmen that were in the dungeon are now on the barricade
In Berlin and Dublin and Rome!
. . . .
Your teachers enlighten the people without any rest or stint,
And they give them one good rifle with every good book they print;
And the workers now own everything, even their right to be born,
And the peasants have taken in the full flax and the wheat and the corn,
And in Moscow it is high noon, and in Europe it is the morn,
And the Soviets are everywhere! [61]

Rose Pastor Stokes, the fiery soapboxer who had worked in a sweated cigar factory before she married the wealthy and aristocratic J. G. Phelps Stokes, rhapsodized in dithyrambic free verse about her comrades, the peasants and proletarians of Russia:

O, Russian Proletariat, my Comrades!
I long to share your meager bowl of Kasha,
For the sweet touch to my lips of a wooden spoon
Whittled with Liberty's new pocket knife.
. . . .

O, Mass! O, laughing, starving, challenging Mass!
What would I not give to laugh and starve with you,
And with you to fling my challenge in the face of the foredoomed enemy;
To hear your Red Standard laughing in the wind! . . .
Flaming kisses would I kiss you, O wind that bore its laughter,
Though your breath should be icy as the frozen Steppe.[62]

Even the pragmatic Eastman, the foe of dogmatizing, said it was
"much better to have the dogmatism of communism than the hypocrisy of capitalism enthroned and deified," and he saw more hope
"in a 'bureaucracy' of seven hundred thousand trained and consecrated communists, as compared to a plutocracy of seven thousand
ruthless exploiters of labor!" [63]

Russia had come to symbolize for the radical young intellectuals
of 1919 what Italy had symbolized to the young Victorians. It stood
for struggle, for joy, for the new day, and it evoked, as Rebecca West
observed, the poetry of Turgenev and Tolstoy, the scenes and episodes from Dostoevsky, Chekhov, Gorky. Czarist Russia was Russia
corrupt and somnolent, "the reek of drunkenness through a fog of
ignorance." Soviet Russia was the Red Army sweeping across "the
steppes and the tundras," the dedicated Bolshevik leader, the holy
revolutionary, martyrs, the "Comrades of the Crimson Cause of the
People!" Through the articles and books of Albert Rhys Williams
and Arthur Ransome, one could meet Lenin and Trotsky and share
vicariously in the agonies and triumphs of the revolution. Here was
a great country achieving remarkable gains under impossible conditions. Standing behind the *Communist Manifesto* were 160,000,000
people inhabiting one sixth of the globe. Russia was chaotic, James
Oppenheim acknowledged in 1917, but it was a

hopeful chaos, that confusion of the nebula, out of which a new world
shapes itself. The Russians of all people are seen now as the appropriate
beginners and pioneers—for nowhere else is there a people who are so
intuitively profound, so emotionally quick. They are not held back
by cleverness, and success, and organization, and intellectualism. . . .
Whether they go through the dark periods of reaction or destruction—
it does not matter. In them the fire leaps which may finally fuse us . . .
beyond the curtain of fire, a little beyond the wall of battle-smoke, there
stands waiting and radiant, Revolution. And in her arms is a little child:
an inarticulate infant: the new Humanity.

It both reassured and astonished the sympathetic American spectators, moreover, that the beleaguered and blockaded Russian Government still devoted care and attention to the task of bringing culture to the masses. Albert Rhys Williams reported that the Commissioner of Education, Lunacharsky, spoke "insistently upon the creative force of the proletariat as far as art and literature is concerned" and disclosed plans to publish all the classics in cheap editions. Floyd Dell enthusiastically announced that the Bolsheviks were concerned with art "to a degree that would seem incredible to an American politician." What is more, he said, they had *"turned over the artistic destinies of Russia to her artists"* and laid *"the foundations of a genuine proletarian socialist art."* He quoted with approval a Soviet document urging that the proletariat not only learn to appreciate the culture of the past, but create a new and superior art, and he assumed that the books and plays chosen for the Russian masses

will not merely acquaint the worker of Russia with the art of storytelling and the characteristics of human nature in many lands, but will above all teach him courage and confidence in his destiny, teach him with their satire to scorn the ideals of bourgeois and capitalist society, deepen his sense of community with his fellow-workers in their worldwide struggle for freedom, and make him face the future with a clear and unshakable resolution, an indomitable will to victory and freedom.[64]

The documentary reports on the cultural plans of the Soviet state cited by Dell were collected and published in New York City under the title *Education and Art in Soviet Russia* by the Socialist Publication Society. In his introduction to the volume, Eastman likened Lunacharsky and his fellows to the philosopher kings of Plato. "These documents," he wrote, "reveal not only a determination to make the schools of the New Russia 'revolutionary,' but to make them wise. . . . To me, at least, much as I have believed in the possibility of ideal developments once the capitalist obstacle was removed, the degree in which such a development appears already in these fragments of the most vital news from Moscow, is astonishing." [65]

REED THE MARTYR

Floyd Dell, Max Eastman, and others had merely celebrated the Russian revolution; the activist, John Reed, who had made the strenuous months of 1917 come alive for his American comrades, "died at his revolutionary post, October 17, 1920" (as *The Liberator* put it), and his burial in the Kremlin seemed to confer a new dignity on the cause of revolution in the United States.

Ten Days That Shook the World was more than a history to Floyd Dell. It made him see and hear the Bolsheviks who had once been merely unknown names. The book was "lighted with those flashes of interpretation and description which make history when it is well done the most fascinating kind of imaginative literature." Its "emotional reach," for another reader, came from a "blend of conviction and prophecy and belief in the fundamental justness of the claims of the masses." [66] On this single occasion, Reed had found a subject grand and real enough to sustain his rapturous poetic impulse. Russia was not an experiment for him, and he did not try to envisage its leaders as coolheaded engineers. It was the embodiment of a social truth and a clue to the future.

For Upton Sinclair, disturbed by the course taken by the Russian revolution and fearful of a German victory, Reed, in the fall of 1918, set down his credo.

The Bolshevik dictatorship, whose excesses Sinclair deplored, had to deal sternly with the bourgeois moderates, because these old leaders were disappointed with the revolution and because they proposed to establish "capitalism in its most malignant form" in Russia. Even the mildest socialist program would not have deterred the French and English Governments from conspiring with the counterrevolutionaries. It was time, Reed said, for the Socialist movement to get rid of all conscious or unconscious advocates of parliamentarianism and the so-called intellectuals still loyal to the class which trained them. "Bolshevism is not for the intellectuals; it is for the people."

Reed roughly brushed aside Sinclair's distinction between "west-

ern" and "German" capitalism. Sinclair had described German capitalism as "The Beast with the Brains of an Engineer." All capitalist
states were "beasts," Reed declared, "the quality of their brains im-
material." And then Reed warmed up to his conclusion:

> You say that in the western democracies, whenever the people are
> ready to change the Government, they can change it. You do not and
> will not see that the ruling classes everywhere, whether bound by consti-
> tutions or not, will not permit the change of Governments when it touches
> their property, will resist this change with arms. If you think that what
> happened to the I.W.W. in this country, what is happening to the Socialist
> party, is because they opposed the war, you are simply fooled. . . .
> Even in Russia, in full flux of Revolution, with universal freedom of
> speech, assembly and vote, the democratic elements of the population
> could not assure a single one of the petty reforms they wanted without
> overthrowing the Ministry by force. Five times they did it, and finally
> got tired of such infinitesimal progress, and went the only way.
> You describe us as a bunch of musicians sitting down to play a sym-
> phony-concert in a forest where there is a man-eating tiger. One man-
> eating tiger, Germany! This tiger must be shot before you, for one, can
> enjoy the concert. . . .
> This is like that other hoary parable of the house on fire, and the
> primal necessity of putting out the fire. The house doesn't belong to us.
> If we put out the fire we will be slammed back in the cellar with hand-
> cuffs on our feet, where we were before. No sir. If you want me to put
> out the fire in your house, you get out; I'll put out the fire only when
> it's my house. Otherwise, it were better that the house burned to the
> ground; then I, being a worker, can rebuild the house—and you, being
> an owner, will have to go to work with me or sleep on the ground.
> To you, Upton, there is only one tiger in the forest. To me there is a
> whole flock of tigers—the tiger who eats me and the tigers who eat other
> people. These tigers are fighting, and whichever side wins, I get eaten
> just the same. Under these circumstances it is a bit heartless to imagine
> any of us, at any time, playing symphony concerts. I have been around
> a bit, like you, in Colorado, Bayonne, Lawrence, and on the battlefields
> of Europe. I have yet to see the world's working-class playing symphony-
> concerts—but I hope to see them, sitting on the carcases of those tigers.[67]

Reed's last days were as dramatic in their way as the rides with
Pancho Villa. Leaving in September 1919 for Russia as a delegate
of the newly formed Communist Labor Party, he worked his passage
to Norway as a stoker, crossed to Finland as a stowaway, nearly

missed his Finnish contacts at Åbo, and finally was smuggled through the Finnish lines to Russia by sympathizers. There he talked with Lenin and Trotsky, and despite his unconcealed disagreement with certain Comintern policies, he was appointed to the Executive Committee of the Communist International in preference to Louis Fraina, the American delegate of the rival Communist Party. In September 1920, after returning to Moscow from a Congress of Oriental Nations held in Baku, he came down with typhus and died the next month.

The charge that Reed had already become disenchanted with communism before his death has been made and contradicted, but whether his intransigent "Wobbly" spirit made or would have made him a rebel in the Soviet Union is beside the point for our purposes.[68] If he was troubled with self-doubts, none of his friends in America suspected it, and some of them envied his hard faith. "You see," said his old friend and counselor, Lincoln Steffens, after Reed's death,

in Moscow, in Soviet Russia, where there are lice and hunger and discipline and death; where it is hell now; they see—even a non-communist can see something to live or to die for. They can see that life isn't always going to be as it is now. The future is coming; it is in sight; it is coming, really and truly coming, and soon. And it is good. They can see this with their naked eyes, common men can; I did, for example. So, to a poet, to a spirit like Jack Reed, the communist, death in Moscow must have been a vision of the resurrection and life of Man.[69]

THREE · EXPATRIATES AND RADICALS

JOSEPH FREEMAN

THE JULY 1922 issue of *The Liberator* announced that "Joseph Freeman, poet, trade union professor of history and economics and book reviewer extraordinary" would join the staff of the magazine. Freeman, who was to become an almost ubiquitous figure in the Left Wing cultural organizations of the twenties and thirties, had returned in the fall of 1921 from a two-year stay abroad. His history before he took up his new duties on the magazine is worth sketching for several reasons: it is a fascinating record of the Americanizing of a Russian-Jewish immigrant boy, and it suggests some explanations why young intellectuals with similar backgrounds and experiences embraced socialism. He also represents the less-publicized "red" section of the "Lost Generation" who viewed the huckstering American society with the same distaste as his politically uncommitted contemporaries but who arrived at revolutionary conclusions when most of them did not.*

* Much of the information about Freeman's formative years and his career down to 1936 is brilliantly assembled in his autobiography, *An American Testament: A Narrative of Rebels and Romantics* (1936). Numerous conversations and over a thousand pages of private correspondence have provided me with supplementary material about Mr. Freeman's activities and opinions and furnished invaluable insights into the history and meaning of the Communist movement. Mr. Freeman is thus not only one of the principal actors in the story of writers and Communism, but also one of its most perceptive interpreters.

Freeman's family had left the Ukrainian village of his birth when he was seven years old, and he spent his childhood and early adolescence in a poverty-stricken Brooklyn ghetto. Speaking only Yiddish and feeling very alien in the crowded slums of Williamsburg, Freeman slowly and painfully made his adjustment to the new life. He attended Hebrew school every afternoon (he read his first American novel, *The Last of the Mohicans,* in a Hebrew translation),[1] but the public school opened to him vistas of a new culture utterly remote from a world of bearded patriarchs, pushcarts, and street fights. He discovered the *Boy's Life of Napoleon* in the public library, bought his first book, Samuel Smiles's *Life and Work,* from a pushcart pedlar for five cents; and these and other books he read "on the top floor of a putrid sunless tenement."[2] By the time he entered high school in 1912—he was then fifteen years old—he and his precocious comrades were already socialists, familiar with the revelations of Upton Sinclair, Ida Tarbell, and Lincoln Steffens and already making plans to become professional men, teachers, and artists.

Freeman's Americanization and radicalization continued simultaneously through the next four years. Anti-Semitism kept his Jewish nationalist feelings alive and he accepted uncritically the idea of class war at the same time that he worshiped Theodore Roosevelt. His desire "to reconcile the warring cultures which struggled within me for dominance"[3] made him susceptible to the most diverse influences: Theodore Herzl and Karl Marx, Napoleon and Eugene Debs, Shelley and Byron and Bernard Shaw. In *The Masses,* he found the Justice and Beauty, that moral and aesthetic fusion, which he craved. The articles of Eastman, Reed, and Dell united politics and poetry. If they dealt with love and sex "in the spirit of lofty romanticism," they also reported the violence in the West Virginia coal fields and the industrial war in Paterson. *The Masses* helped Freeman to distinguish between liberalism and revolution, but it offered no convincing solution to a problem that already began to plague him: how to reconcile the romantic poetry he loved with the wage cuts and strikes and unemployment of the real world.

When he enrolled at Columbia in 1916, his father's real-estate business had begun to pick up. Soon he would be a rich man. Freeman's radicalism, however, only increased during the war years, and he had nothing but contempt for moneyed success. He and his Columbia friends (among them Matthew Josephson, Louis Hacker, Richard McKeon, Louis Gottschalk, and Kenneth Burke) were still remote from the realities they professed to understand, but the noise of the industrial violence erupting around them and the angry disputes of the friends and foes of the mounting preparedness campaign broke into the classrooms. The campus was divided. One contingent, Freeman among them, acted upon Max Eastman's diagnosis—that the President not only wanted to keep the United States out of the war but also to organize the nations in a permanent league to enforce peace—and supported Wilson. Events of the next month, the passage of the Espionage Act and the mounting patriotic hysteria, changed his views. He got himself elected as a delegate to the People's Council of America, organized by the radical economist Scott Nearing and supported by a cross-section of liberals and radicals in an effort to force the Allied powers to formulate their war demands and to work out a peace policy along the lines recommended by the newly formed revolutionary government in Russia. After attending a People's Council meeting at Chicago in the summer of 1917, where he saw and met many of his boyhood heroes, he was warned by the bursar of Columbia that he would be expelled from the university if his name appeared again "in connection with any such subversive activity." [4]

That fall, Columbia expelled two professors. One was J. M. Cattell, a psychologist and a pacifist; the other, Henry Wadsworth Longfellow Dana, who taught literature and who later became a familiar figure in Communist intellectual circles. In Dana's rooms, where Freeman had gone to say good-by, he met Frank Tannenbaum, sentenced in 1914 to a two-year jail term for leading a crowd of unemployed into a church and now a Columbia student, and Randolph Bourne. "Swinging his child's legs from the desk on which he sat," [5] Bourne mockingly deplored Dana's refusal to kick up a fuss and blamed him for treating the affair "as a gentleman's quarrel." The same could not be said, however, about Dana's colleague Charles Beard. Although he supported the war as firmly as Dana opposed it, he regarded the dismissal of Dana and Cattell as a violation of academic freedom and resigned in protest.

Freeman and his radical friends bitterly fought the war spirit on the campus, but the November revolution in Russia changed the meaning of the war for them, and the Treaty of Brest-Litovsk seemed to indicate that the survival of the revolution depended on the defeat of Germany. He joined the R.O.T.C., and in the summer of 1918, after reading some letters from William Slater Brown describing the work of the ambulance corps on the western front, he decided that driving an ambulance was "the best way to avoid killing without being accused of cowardice." Dean Kepple persuaded him to wait and sign up with the Student Army Training Corps. As it turned out, the war ended before he fired a shot, but he had "acquiesced in becoming a soldier" [6] even while opposing the objective of the war, because he felt that he had no moral right to desert his friends and country.

Freeman had worked out a solution of private action insofar as the war was concerned, but a knottier problem still remained unsolved. How could one be a poet and a revolutionist, or, as Freeman phrased it, how could the claims of the proletariat, "with which we had grown up and with which we identified ourselves," be reconciled with the achievements of the bourgeoisie, "whose culture we were absorbing at the university" and who "monopolized the treasure house of art." The socialists themselves had no answer, as the examples of Eastman and Dell proved. A poet could write a lyric about a butterfly or compose an agitational poem on the lynching of Frank Little, the Wobbly organizer, as Giovannitti did. Each would appear in *The Liberator*. Lincoln, Debs, Shelley, Jack London, Goethe; pure art and pure propaganda; the Puritan and the vagabond free lover— all blended chaotically with the program of the new society. Having discovered no way of reconciling art and socialist reality, Freeman and other radical young collegians developed what he called "the cult of the Universal Man."

The cult held up the ideal of the intellectual doer who combined "imaginative with practical pursuits, art with the life of action." Its ancestors were Sir Philip Sidney, Goethe, Dante, Cervantes, Hugo; its contemporary models were Reed, Eastman, Dell, Giovannitti, Robert Minor. If these latter-day renaissance youths slighted the physical for the intellectual and approximated the aestheticism of

Pater more than the versatility of Leonardo, the "mirage of the Universal Man" sustained them in their distaste for specialization—that curse of the bourgeois world—and strengthened their conviction to become "physically, mentally and spiritually, active in politics and creative in literature."

As a preparation for his announced role, Freeman sailed for Europe in the summer of 1920, a year after his graduation from Columbia. Neither art nor revolution was "a paying proposition" in the United States, now in the high tide of postwar reaction. America condoned the Mitchell Palmer raids against anarchists, "the unseating of the five socialist assemblymen in New York," the deportation of "undesirable" aliens on the steamship *Buford,* the "massacre" of strikers in Centralia, Washington. In Europe, he reflected, and especially in Paris, you could help the proletariat overthrow the old order. He looked forward to his "partly heroic, partly sinful" adventure.[7]

THE MIDDLE-CLASS EXPATRIATES

Freeman left for Paris and the pagan life one year before the general exodus chronicled by Malcolm Cowley in his *Exile's Return.* The crowd of young middle-class writers, however, who acknowledged to each other that "they do things better in Europe; let's go there," justified their departure by a different set of rationalizations from those that operated for Freeman's set. "My own circle," Freeman wrote, "could neither explain nor justify its conduct without taking socialism into consideration. Our most private acts could appear rational only as we related them to the most general laws of history. . . ." Cowley and his friends had no such unifying commitment. They did not even constitute a "group." What linked these disparate young men was their conviction that America offered no rewards to the talented and their desire "to recover the good life and the traditions of art, to free themselves from organized stupidity, to win their deserved place in the hierarchy of talent." [8]

In 1921, thirty "intellectuals" considerably older than the generation of Freeman and Cowley [9] set about to disparage systematically almost every vestige of American life. Their joint denunciation appeared in 1922 as *Civilization in the United States,* edited by Harold Stearns, and although it contained attitudes and assumptions already considered obsolete by their juniors, it did corroborate their belief that America was no place for the would-be artist. Stearns himself had already grimly set down in 1920 the disadvantages of life in America, where institutions conspired "for the common purpose of blackjacking our youth" not merely with the acceptance but also the glorification of the *status quo.*[10] Now the symposium of disgusted intellectuals—"men on the edge of middle age or over it who seem to be the shrillest and most violent in their disaffection and hark back most regretfully to the forgotten standards of their youth," as Horace Kallen put it—inadvertently encouraged the expatriates.[11]

In a shrewd review of *Civilization in the United States,* George Santayana offered some generalizations about the contributors that seemed to separate them quite sharply from the migratory artists en route to the Continent. Americans, he said, were likely to be either complacent or shamefaced, but both attitudes sprang from the need to have the best or be the biggest, "or else you must blush for it." Hence they had never learned to accept what they have, hence they sounded querulous and outraged not so much because of their affronted ideals, but because society had failed to approximate the scale of greatness they had set up. The intelligentsia, Santayana said, were no different from the majority they pretended to defy: "The instinct and the ideal of uniformity are very profound in them; if they are compelled to be rebels, they become propagandists, like the authors of this book, and if they cannot conform to the majority they are not happy until they make the majority conform to them. Why this passion?"[12]

Cowley contended in *Exile's Return* that his generation did not feel this passion; unlike their rebellious elders, they avoided issues, smashed no idols. Or as he phrased it:

"They" had been rebels: they wanted to change the world, be leaders in the fight for justice and art, help to create a society in which individuals could express themselves. "We" were convinced that society could never be changed by any effort of the will.[13]

But if Cowley and his friends spurned "causes" and cynically included themselves among the "fools and scoundrels" of the world, they were not nearly so detached from the moral imperatives of their fathers and their class as they imagined. His group could admire Eliot's *The Waste Land* without responding to its mood of disillusionment; life was simply too exciting, too much of an adventure.

Nor did the expatriate years turn out to be a feckless and purposeless experience for all these allegedly "illusionless" artists. Living abroad gave many of them a new respect for their country and a new optimism about its possibilities. America might be hostile to artists; it might lack a rich and dense culture. But it had stability and power, and its rebels, seen from the Parisian outpost, acquired a special dignity.

Writing home to the readers of *The New Republic* in 1922, Edmund Wilson paid tribute to the Felix Fays and Carol Kennicotts who read Shaw "in remote farms and dreary towns of the vast deserts of the West," who left their Gopher Prairies for Greenwich Village. Wilson jocosely continued:

When I think of Greenwich Village, it is almost with tears. For there this battered battalion dress their guns against a whole nation. Where the traffic, gnashing iron teeth, no longer oppresses the pavement, where the toned red bricks of low houses still front an open square . . . from the darkest corners of the country they have fled for comfort and asylum. You may think them feeble and ridiculous—but feebleness is always relative. It may require as much force of character and as much independent thought for one of these to leave his Kansas home and espouse the opinions of Freud as for Wagner to achieve new harmonies or Einstein to conceive a finite universe. . . . Let me return: I shall not cease from mental fight nor shall my sword rest in my hand till intolerance has been stricken from the laws, till the time-clock has been beaten to a punch-bowl! [14]

America, he felt, was going to produce something better than breakfast foods.

Even those who retained their distaste for things American expressed their opinions with a picturesque violence that belied indifference, and in faraway places could not, as a commentator in *The Freeman* wrote, escape from the sense of "sharing the guilt and the responsibility" of the society to which, in their hearts, they belong; and for this reason we may expect, as more and more of our enlightened spirits drift about the earth, a running fire of criticism directed upon us from the outside by those who know us best and who know also a world of things that have never been dreamt of in the American philosophy.[15]

They might admire Paul Valéry's "intellectual man" refusing to "be anything whatsoever," the pure and dehumanized intellect "almost completely cut off from society," [16] but they were too enamored with life to model their conduct after him.

Expatriates like Cowley and Matthew Josephson (both of whom swerved sharply leftward at the end of the decade) were moral even in their antimorality, and their momentary espousal of Dadaism was an act of protest rather than one of renunciation and indifference. Ostensibly, the Dadaist movement that flared up between 1916 and 1924 meant a withdrawal into the freedom and privacy of the completely detached personality. Yet its adherents were passionately involved with the society they so furiously rejected. Far from being ignored, the world, as Cowley said, was "to be fought, insulted, or mystified." [17] Perhaps Dada, as an American critic argued in 1922, "deserved to die." Perhaps it was only a stunt to gain notoriety. But the young Americans who defended it were expressing, if somewhat obliquely, a critique of their society and a program for its rehabilitation.

The prescient Edmund Wilson caught the significance as well as the humor of the American Dadaist attitude in his imaginary conversation between Paul Rosenfeld, who was still dedicated to the ideals of the prewar *Seven Arts* magazine, and the bumptious expatriate Matthew Josephson, who spoke for his associates on *Broom.* The literature of the past is dead and stinking, Josephson declares, and only Dadaists like Tristan Tzara, the high priest of Dadaism, can "appreciate the gigantic, the gorgeous, the fantastic world of the twentieth century." American genius, he continues, is not embodied in its fine art, but in its advertising, its screeching taxicabs, screaming sirens, electric signs; Irving Berlin, Gershwin, Krazy Kat, prize fighting, the movies, and Wall Street are more interesting and important that Eliot, Joyce, and Schönberg.

To this tirade of Josephson's on the modern aesthetic, Rosenfeld replies that advertisers do not write out of joy (consider the experience of Sherwood Anderson); the true artist will attack the machine and glorify the human spirit. Then Josephson snorts:

The honor of the human spirit . . . the principles of justice and humanity . . . Liberty, Fraternity, Equality . . . the dawn of a new day . . . Workers of the world, arise! you have nothing to lose but your chains! . . . E. E. Cummings could make a very amusing poem by mixing them all up together and sticking in the Paris urinal and the venereal affiches. My dear fellow, you take it all too seriously. In Europe no one takes those things seriously. Those old illusions, old campaign cries, old political catchwords and shibboleths are as stale and as lifeless now as old newspapers of the war.

No, he concludes, Europe wants to be entertained, and Dada is the answer, "For Dada is the spirit of play, of the delightful idiocy of things. It shows the lack of connection between everything with a dazzling quickness of mind." It's all right for Rosenfeld to brood over artists who were killed, who were denied hearings, who sold out. Very noble. And yet Rosenfeld in sneering at jazz and lowbrow culture is denying the only positive artistic forces in American life.[18]

The debate imagined by Edmund Wilson was carried on in real life by Rosenfeld's friend and associate, Waldo Frank, and Josephson's Parisian ally and Dadaist *extraordinaire,* Malcolm Cowley. Dada, Frank observed, might suit a tired Europe; it was "a salutary burst of laughter in a world that felt itself too old," but America, said Frank, *is* Dada. Dada is the Ku Klux Klan and revival preaching and the aesthetics of William Jennings Bryan and Hollywood. "It is in the medley of strutting precepts and low deeds that make America. We are a hodgepodge, a boil. We are a maze of infernos and nirvanas. Our brew of nigger-strut, of wailing Jew, of cantankerous Celt, of nostalgic Anglo-Saxon is a brew of Dada. No wonder they imported our essential chaos to lighten the regularities of France."

Frank's diagnosis of Dada angered Cowley, in 1924 no longer an expatriate, and he declared himself to be the "American Dada." Frank then proceeded to read him a lesson. Cowley's poetry proved that he was destined for better things than Dada:

When you achieve the moral courage to confront the reality of the world, and the spiritual energy to make issue with it; instead of permitting yourself to be flung off by its centrifugal action, in the fond belief that because you fly off to nothing in a graceful pirouette and with a foreign oath upon your lips you are being any the less booted about and beshat and befooled by the very elements of life which you profess to despise.

To be Dada in the United States, Frank said, was "to be platitudinous and banal." [19]

THE QUARREL BETWEEN THE GENERATIONS RESTATED

Frank's interchange with Cowley underscored the not very acrimonious debate, unorganized and barely conscious, carried on from 1920 to 1925 between the generation that had come of age just before the outbreak of World War I and those who had reached their majority early in the next decade. The former generation, rebellious and romantic, still retained much of the optimism and idealism of "Old America," and its spokesmen did not accommodate themselves easily to the self-proclaimed cynicism of their jazz-age juniors. The war had sobered them, and they no longer "called for 'Life! More Life!' " [20] so passionately. But intellectuals like Frank, Van Wyck Brooks, Paul Rosenfeld, James Oppenheim still believed that the artist was not merely the residue of an event, and that he could—indeed, that he had obligation to—shape the world.

Brooks was particularly disturbed by the decline in the faith in progress and the abandonment by the young writers of the heritage of Schopenhauer, Nietzsche, Ibsen, Strindberg, Tolstoy, and Dostoevsky. "A strange, brittle, cerebral artistocratism has succeeded the robust democratism of the last age," he complained in 1923, and he blamed the fear of life and the divorce of art and science from humanity on the Great War. "The great currents of thought and feeling that sprang from Germany, Russia, and Scandinavia and had begun to change the face of European literature were defeated as effectually in 1918 as the arms of the North; and Paris became once more for literature what it had long justly been for painting, the center of all attention."

Brooks deplored this "unholy alliance" between literature and the plastic arts and attributed the "learned spoofing" and the freakish experimentation to its influence.

[The new writers] fetch up the tags and tatters of a badly assimilated erudition; they match unfamiliar quotations, they no longer seek to shock the grocer, they are satisfied if they can dazzle one another. These are the fruits of a parvenu intellectuality; and indeed the fashionable pedant. . . . What serious aim dignifies these activities? . . . However it may be in the plastic arts, in literature, the subject, the content *dictates* the form. The form is an inevitable consequence of the thing that is to be said and rises out of it as naturally as the flower rises out of the seed. To seek forms, therefore, is to confess that one lacks things. It is the frankest sort of acknowledgement of a complete literary insolvency.

The compulsion to become ingeniously individualistic, he thought, might be expected in a disunited society in which the national will and the individual will clash. Defiant individualism would last so long as "the life of the individual is destined to be subjected to the steamroller of the majority." [21]

What Brooks proposed in the early twenties, and what he continued to advocate, was the necessity for the writer to risk poverty, to chance public indifference, but not to secede from bourgeois society. The writer (as he paraphrased Wordsworth somewhat later) must "create the taste by which he is understood." [22]

The young men for whom this message was intended, however, did not find Brooks's views very convincing. What is more, his evangelical manner seemed to embody precisely the sort of emotionalism they found embarrassing in their elders. A later generation would call it "corny."

To Kenneth Burke, for example, Brooks blamed the sorry conditions of American culture on the hostile social environment and at the same time criticized American writers for failing to express this environment. Edmund Wilson wrote a brilliant imaginary conversation between a serious Brooks and a very funny and very brash F. Scott Fitzgerald which in effect accused Brooks of being so concerned with the failure of American letters that he ignored its current vitality; the more he burrowed into the past, the bleaker seemed the present. Like most of the others in the *Seven Arts* group (the exceptions were Randolph Bourne, its organizing genius, and Paul

Rosenfeld, who saw and heard what he wrote about), Brooks was interested "too exclusively in the soul." W. C. Blum (James Sibley Watson), who made this observation, pointed out that Brooks declared Margaret Fuller a better literary critic than Poe because for her the technical aspects of literature were less important than the "spiritual." Such nonsense might be defended, but not the willingness of the Brooksians "to disregard and despise as un-American very admirable and very American poets like Ezra Pound, Marianne Moore, and William Carlos Williams." In short, as Malcolm Cowley retrospectively noted, Brooks, Frank, Oppenheim and company impressed their younger associates as literary man-midwives: "They gathered about the great unhappy body of the nation, they laid their spells upon it and adjured it to labor intellectually and bring forth a native American literature. When the baby was born, many of the doctors were looking the other way." [23]

What Brooks denounced as the "unholy alliance" between literature and the plastic arts, the young aestheticians hailed as a hopeful sign. Modern artists had repudiated hazy emotion for pure sensation. They had returned to "geometrical conflicts" and employed devices "less likely to lead the spectator away from the primary aesthetic intention." The new writers did not hold with Brooks that literature was a branch of morality, that art was "an inconsiderable afterthought." [24] On the contrary, Louis Untermeyer declared,

They are all—or at least their manifestoes are—for a new intellectual discipline, for severity of structure, for the subjection of the material to the design. Form is the word most often on the lips of these younger writers; they speak of mathematics, the architecture of literature, of mass and planes, of suspensions and modulations—of an abstract form, as a musician, despising the theatricalism of opera, might speak of absolute music.

The "New Patricians," as he called them, shared no common program. Kenneth Burke was a "candid and complete cerebralist"; Josephson "straight dada, accepting the dadaists' denial of logic and their glorification of incoherence"; Cowley experimental in poetry but critical and definite; Gorham Munson accepted Dada's "exploitation of the materials created by the machine's impact on human life" but rejected "its arbitrary symbols"; Cummings attempted "a primitive simplification of visual as well as tangential sensations";

Dos Passos, Foster Damon, Hart Crane moved in different directions.[25] But they were all self-disciplinarians who, acknowledging their inability to shape the kind of society desired by Brooks, tried at least to shape and control their art.

The controversy between the Brooksians and the "New Patricians" did not mean that only two literary roads lay open to the writer in the twenties: the hortatory sociocritical one and the apolitical aesthetic. Some writers, like Edmund Wilson and John Dos Passos, kept their curiosity about American social and intellectual life and at the same time sympathized with the program of the formalists. And to their left were the socialist intellectuals (still small in number and not very intellectual), who were trying to convert literature into a revolutionary weapon. In the socialist camp, too, one could distinguish between the romantics and the disciplinarians.

FREEMAN AS EXPATRIATE

During Freeman's stay abroad, half of it spent in Paris, the other half in London, he worked on the Paris *Herald* and then on the Chicago *Tribune,* wrote verses, searched for the idealized "free" woman "among the art models and midinettes of Paris" [26] and, in contradistinction to his less revolutionary contemporaries, read the *Communist Manifesto* as well as Baudelaire in his dim and chilly hotel room. Like Cowley and his friends, Freeman also rediscovered America, and the more aggressively American he became, the more at home he felt in Europe. He felt at home because he was an "internationalist." His "sense of internationalism," in turn, derived from his socialism— his identification with the striking workers in England and the Continent, the Red battalions everywhere. Cowley and his friends had not yet added to their hatred of "bourgeois philistinism" a hatred of "capitalist oppression." Freeman and his friends had.

But if they were not Dadaists, if they were not tempted by "the anodynes of alcohol and sex," not everyone in Freeman's circle was dedicated to revolution, and Freeman himself hovered between the world of imagination and that of fact. Like the torn hero of James's novel *The Princess Casamassima,* he was both revolted by the cruelty of privileged society and charmed by its culture, and there were moments when he felt drawn to a "heartless aestheticism." When his Communist friends in New York remonstrated, he assured them that his "frail verses and shrill encomiums of Paris" had not dulled his awareness of "the brutal march of events." He felt he was serving the revolution in his own way. If his poems spoke of the problems of modern love, the beauty of the modern city, the message of Nijinsky, Picasso, and Stravinsky, they also dealt with themes that obsessed him then and for years to come: politics and friendship, history's intolerance of failure, mankind's idolatry of its destroyers, poetry and revolution.

In England, where he continued to report for the Chicago *Tribune*, he wrote to his correspondents in New York that merely to write poetry was sterile, and he asked his friend and former teacher Irwin Edman not to call him a "professional poet," the "most contemptible of creatures." The whole "art for art's sake twaddle" began to revolt him. Since childhood, he had committed himself to "social justice"; this concern had made him a Communist. He was ready now to cast away "the intellectual and emotional debris" which stood in the way of his becoming a useful and active worker for the cause.

Freeman knew perfectly well what Gorham Munson meant when he wrote in the early twenties: "It is difficult to be a social revolutionary and escape Puritanism, to condemn a social scheme and perceive the beauties thrown off by it. Yet to do both is the business of living men." [27] Irwin Edman had said as much in a letter to Freeman in which he observed: "We're both Puritans at heart . . . but I feel as you do that nothing of any serious or permanent attraction as art can be empty." Then why did Freeman bridle when a friend accused him of losing his grasp of the impending revolution and of being attached to a past "that binds you to restraining activity and antiquated ideals"? He could counter that in Russia, the nursery of the revolution, the government was sponsoring the publication of the classics, art exhibitions, theater productions, concerts. He was not yet ready, however, to face the implications of Van Wyck Brooks's shrewd remark: "Radical artists as a rule cannot understand that their work becomes effective precisely in the degree in which they enter, impersonally, as artists, into the world of their adversaries." [28]

In the fall of 1921, having decided to become more actively engaged in the revolutionary movement, he returned to New York and soon began to work for the party press.

FREEMAN JOINS *The Liberator*

Since March 1918, *The Liberator* had continued the battle for art and socialism and had opened its columns to some of the best writers and artists in the country. More studiedly political than *The Masses* and devoting more space to economic and social affairs, it still retained much of the old Bohemian intransigence and charming inconsistency that aroused the delight and the irritation of its well-wishers. Max Eastman, with his sister, Crystal, owned 51 per cent of the shares of *The Liberator*. As editor, he no longer deferred so amiably to the whims of his editorial associates, but his pro-Bolshevik harangues contrasted oddly with Floyd Dell's praise of G. K. Chesterton's war against the servile state; the hymns to Lenin clashed with lyrics to absent lovers and poetic celebrations of pagan rites. *The Liberator* quickly doubled the circulation of *The Masses* (it reached 60,000 at its peak), and Henry Mencken pronounced it the best magazine in the United States. But there were others asking why Eastman and Dell were not complete socialists. Why did they juxtapose good revolutionary articles with bourgeois poetry and contradict their own true insights? The magazine, in short, was not integrated or complete; it suffered "from being given over to phrases and contradictions." [29]

Eastman concluded later that for all *The Liberator* did for art and literature, it made hardly a "dent on the cultural history of the United States. Few now can imagine what an insular, irrelevant, hole-in-the-corner thing socialism was in the America of those days." [30] Whatever its ultimate significance, to young radicals like Freeman, *The Liberator* in 1920-21 spoke for all the right causes: for political prisoners, for the recently arrested anarchists Nicola Sacco and Bartolomeo Vanzetti, for the working-class victims of the class war. And it was to *The Liberator* office on West Thirteenth Street that Freeman went in 1922, not to *The Dial* a few doors away, where his nonpolitical contemporaries were editing a magazine frankly and avowedly "aesthetic."

Max Eastman, already preparing for his long and momentous expatriation, welcomed this young man whose verse he had already printed. To Freeman, who had written to Eastman from Italy thanking him for solving the "tormenting problem" of how "to combine a love of poetry with a passion for revolution," [31] Eastman in the flesh seemed a god incarnate. The following rhapsodic extract to his girl suggests the idolatry that Eastman evoked not only in Freeman but in many other young writers.

The most exciting thing that's happened to me since we discussed life and labor under a dark midnight rain has been meeting *Max Eastman*.

What a man! I ought to say what a god—because it seems to me that he is very much like Apollo must have been both in appearance and in temper. In him you have wisdom without timidity, strength without insolence, and beauty without vanity.

And to his broad humanity I can testify because he flattered me into helpless intoxication by telling me how much he liked my poems, by calling me his friend in the inscription on a copy of his new book which he gave me, by inviting me to his house, but most of all by seeming to agree with me on most of the things I care about.

You may be particularly interested to know that he agreed with me when I complained of those radicals who think revolution is synonymous with puritanism—that we all ought to stop writing poetry and ought to join the executive committee of a labor union.

The object of revolution, as he sees it, is to make the world consist of live people; most people today are dead, and therefore those of us who are now alive are doubly precious.

Of Max's miraculous personality you have probably heard too much already; what struck me most in our conversation yesterday afternoon was his shining smile, his melodious voice and his remark that those who expect the revolution to come tomorrow are fools.

My plans are to hitch up with some radical or liberal periodical, newspaper or school; if I fail, the loss won't be entirely mine. [32]

At Eastman's house in St. Luke's Place, he met the Negro poet Claude McKay, who had joined *The Liberator* staff several years before. McKay had come to America from Jamaica in 1911. After attending Kansas State College for a few years, he worked as a diningcar waiter. Before Frank Harris discovered him in 1918, he had published a volume of poems, *Songs of Jamaica* (1912), and had contributed two sonnets to *The Seven Arts* under the pseudonym Eli Edwards. Eastman accepted a group of his poems for the July 1919 issue of *The Liberator*. "I think his conscience," Eastman wrote then, "is a little more austere in matters of social conduct than in matters of art." McKay spent the years 1919 and 1920 in England. There he met George Bernard Shaw, frequented Marxist circles, met some of the leading English radicals, and as a writer for Sylvia Pankhurst's *Worker's Dreadnaught* got himself involved in the anti-Red drive that ended with her arrest and imprisonment. Returning to New York in 1920, he worked on *The Liberator* staff until his departure for Russia in 1922. McKay some years before his death in 1948 became Roman Catholic and repudiated his Left Wing ties. It is doubtful whether Winston Churchill knew McKay's radical past when he recited McKay's militant poem to the Negro people, "If We Must Die," to the beleaguered British after Dunkirk.

Shortly after meeting McKay, Freeman introduced himself to Floyd Dell, subsequently his close friend and mentor, whom he discovered dining alone in a dimly lit Village restaurant. At this time he also began his long association with the "outstanding 'proletarian' of the group," Mike Gold. Off and on for the next seventeen years, Freeman and Gold were to work together on a number of cultural enterprises for the Communist movement and in time were regarded as the leading literary lights of the party.

MIKE GOLD

Irwin Granich (Gold's real name) grew up in the East Side slums so redolently described in his best book, *Jews Without Money*. The memories of the ill-smelling world of his boyhood stayed with him: a world of summers so hot that the "asphalt bubbled underfoot," of flies, bedbugs, litter, of saloons, whores, gangsters, swarming immigrants, and poor Jews suffocating in their rattletrap tenements. He remembered the sweatshops,

dark sinks of all the evil in the world. Filthy, opaque windows that were never washed from one end of the year to the other shut out the blessed sunlight. The floors were knee-high in rubbish and lint; there was a stench from the putrid toilet; a fog of steam and sweat hung in the room and made it ghastly and dim as an inferno. The whirling of the machines sickened the heart like an endless dirge. There, in the gloom, in the stench, under the wavering gaslight, pale, melancholy men and women labored and suffered and died.

These childhood experiences did not sour him or destroy his zest for new ones, but they help to explain his compulsion to "change the world" (as he was to call his column in the *Daily Worker*) and his contempt for the bourgeois defenders of what he believed to be a rotten social order.

Gold quit school at twelve, and for the next ten years he worked for the Adams Express Company. His initiation into the radical movement occurred in 1914 when he blundered into an unemployment demonstration in Union Square, listened to the "rebel girl" Elizabeth Gurley Flynn, and bought a copy of *The Masses*. Between 1915, when he contributed his first poem to Eastman's magazine, and 1921, when he joined the editorial staff of *The Liberator,* Gold lived the wandering and exciting life of the Bohemian-anarchist artist. He wrote three one-act plays for the Provincetown Players and spent a summer with the happy and hard-drinking group at the Cape. In New York, after attending rehearsals at the Provincetown Playhouse, he would join Eugene O'Neill and anarchist friends at a saloon on the corner of Fourth Street and Sixth Avenue, the "Hell Hole," and listen to O'Neill recite "The Hound of Heaven." Dorothy Day, a "rebel girl" of the Village and, later, the much-admired and selfless editor of the *Catholic Worker,* remembers at this time that she and Gold were reading Tolstoy together. "He used to make fun of my religious spirit," she wrote later, "but he himself was in sympathy with the Christianity expressed by Tolstoi, a religion without churches or a priesthood. Mike had a religious upbringing in his home on the East Side and liked to sing Yiddish folksongs and Hebrew hymns." [33]

In 1916 (although he afterward disclaimed it) [34] he spent a few painful months at Harvard College as a special student, but soon moved to Boston, where he lived in an anarchist home and reported a strike at the Plymouth cordage factory for Hippolyte Havel's *Blast*.

On this assignment, the first labor story he wrote, he met Bartolomeo Vanzetti.

Gold left the United States for Mexico sometime in 1917 in order to escape the draft. His entrance into that country with a fellow refugee from New York had a dreamlike casualness. He and his friend had holed up in a cheap hotel in El Paso. One hot summer night, Gold put down a novel by Dostoevsky he was reading and walked with his companion to the Rio Grande. Without thinking, they started to wade across the river, and continued until they reached the Mexican side.

During his almost two years below the border, Gold wrote for an English paper in Mexico City, worked for about eight months in the Tampico oil fields and for about half a year on a ranch. The journalist Carleton Beals remembers him in 1918 as a "rough-hewn, dark chap, earthy, elemental, brooding but devil-may-care, full of flame-like seriousness lightened by a whimsical sneer." The Mexicans liked his "gipsy nonchalance toward time, tide and food." Beals himself was drawn to the tough poet with his "tousled hair and dark eyes, his rough corduroy trousers and heavy shoes" who at this time "was fluctuating between literature and Marxianism, Bohemia and the class-struggle." [35]

In January 1921, when Gold took up his job as a contributing editor to *The Liberator,* he was "a dark-eyed, handsome-featured social mutineer, with wide, lush lips, uncombed hair, and a habit of chewing tobacco and keeping himself a little dirty." So Eastman saw him, and he attributed this dress and manner to Gold's way of showing his proletarian leanings. Like Walt Whitman, whom Gold adored and whose style he emulated, Gold had a proletarian imago. "He affected dirty shirts," Freeman wrote, "a big, black, uncleaned Stetson with the brim of a sombrero; smoked stinking, twisted, Italian three-cent cigars, and spat frequently and vigorously on the floor—whether that floor was covered by an expensive carpet in a rich aesthete's studio or was the bare wooden floor of the small office where Gold's desk was littered with disorderly papers. These 'proletarian' props were as much a costume as the bohemian's side-burns and opera cape. They enhanced Gold's loveable qualities; his assumed naiveté, dark animated face and deep laughter, and his ironic mode of speech won people easily." [36]

Gold not only acted the "proletarian"; he also preached "proletarianism." In the passionate, flamboyant and inchoate essays he wrote for *The Liberator,* he broke away from the liberal-individualist tradition that still animated Eastman and Dell and called for "a continuation and development of the revolutionary tradition in *art itself."* [37] This was the tradition of Upton Sinclair and Jack London, not the tradition of Shaw and Wells.

"Towards Proletarian Art," published in February 1921 in *The Liberator,* is a kind of prose poem very similar in spirit and style to the rhapsodies of Arturo Giovannitti. "In blood, in tears, in chaos and wild thunderous clouds of fear the old economic order is dying," Gold begins.

We are not appalled or startled by that giant apocalypse before us. We know the horror that is passing away with this long winter of the world. We know, too, the bright forms that stir at the heart of all this confusion, and that shall rise out of the debris and cover the ruins of capitalism with beauty. We are prepared for the economic revolution of the world, but what shakes us with terror and doubt is the cultural upheaval that must come. We rebel instinctively against that change. We have been bred in the old capitalist planet, and its stuff is in our very bones. Its ideals, mutilated and poor, were yet the precious stays of our lives. Its art, its science, its philosophy and metaphysics are deeper in us than logic or will. They are deeper than the reach of the knife of our social passion. We cannot consent to the suicide of our souls. We cling to the old culture, and fight for it against ourselves. But it must die. The old ideals must die. But let us not fear. Let us fling all we are into the cauldron of the Revolution. For out of our death shall arise glories, and out of the final corruption of this old civilization we have loved shall spring the new race—the Supermen.

He did not condemn the artist who hesitated to sink his culture in the maelstrom of revolution. As an apostle of Nietzsche and Whitman, all art was sacred to him: "to stifle the meanest of Life's moods taking form in the artist would be death," and he would not wish "to speak a word against their holy passion." But Gold nevertheless felt obliged to express the experiences of the poor—his own experiences. "I was born in a tenement. . . . There, in suffering youth, I feverishly sought God and found Man . . . Man, who is Life speaking. . . . All that I know of Life I learned in the tenement. . . . The tenement is in my blood. When I think it is the tenement thinking. When I hope it is the tenement hoping. I am not an individual; I am all that the tenement group poured into me during those early years of my spiritual travail." [38]

Having proclaimed the right of artists "sprung from the workers" to "express in art that manifestation of Life which is so exclusively ours," Gold contrasted the "baffled solitaries" of capitalist society, compelled to "be lonely beasts of prey—competitive and unsocial," with proletarian artists. The former, lacking faith or will, spiritually sterile, cultivating a sick aestheticism, had "lost everything in the vacuum of logic where they dwell." The latter had found sanity "through solidarity with the people." And in a Tolstoyan passage, Gold affirmed:

Masses are never pessimistic. Masses are never sterile. Masses are never far from the earth. Masses are never far from heaven. Masses go on— they are the eternal truth. Masses are simple, strong and sure. They are never lost long; they have always a goal in each age.

Hence, the "boy in the tenement" must cling to the masses and must "create a new and truer art" that derives from the social revolution:

The Social Revolution of to-day is not the mere political movement artists despise it as. It is Life at its fullest and noblest. It is the religion of the masses, articulate at last. It is that religion which says that Life is one, that Men are one, through all their flow of change and differentiation; that the destiny of Man is a common one, and that no individual need bear on his weak shoulders alone the crushing weight of the eternal riddle. . . . The Revolution, in its secular manifestations of strike, boycott, mass-meeting, imprisonment, sacrifice, agitation, martyrdom, organization, is thereby worthy of the religious devotion of the artist. If he records the humblest moment of that drama in poem, story or picture or symphony, he is realizing Life more profoundly than if he had concerned himself with some transient personal mood. The ocean is greater than the tiny streams that trickle down to be lost in its godhood.

This was Walt Whitman's dream, that "giant with his cosmic intuitions and comprehensions," but Whitman erred in supposing political democracy could achieve it, and his successors turned away from the "earthy groundwork" that had prompted his unfulfilled expectations.

But the Russian revolution proved Whitman's contention "that the spiritual cement of a literature and art is needed to bind together a society," and in Russia, declared Gold, "the proletarian culture has begun forming its grand outlines against the sky." The "Prolet-Kult" of the Bolsheviks, he said, is "not an artificial theory evolved in the brains of a few phrase-intoxicated intellectuals, and foisted by them on the masses," but "Russia's organized attempt to remove the economic barriers and social degradation that repressed the proletarian instinct during the centuries." Out of this revolution would come "strange and beautiful things," and resurrection of the mass-soul.

And America? Nothing comparable could emerge so long as leisure-class artists with their *Little Review* and their *Seven Arts* tried to "set in motion the sluggish current of vital American art." No "great lusty tree" could flourish in "that hot-house air."

When there is singing and music rising in every American street, when in every American factory there is a drama-group of workers, when mechanics paint in their leisure, and farmers write sonnets, the greater art will grow and only then.[39]

So Michael Gold felt in 1921. In subsequent articles he explored further the decadent philosophers of art that held back the aesthetic rehabilitation of America, the plutocratic and the superrefined.

Representing the first was *The Saturday Evening Post,* whose manufacture involved the exploitation of hundreds of lumberjacks standing "knee-high in icy water to send the logs down for pulp," kept "hundreds of office-girls round shouldered at typewriters," and "hundreds of pale, nervous authors who plough their brains for this magazine." It poured out "spiritual opium" for the masses and corrupted readers and writers alike. "Oh! The filthy lackeyrag, so fat, shiny, gorged with advertisements, putrid with prosperity like the bulky, diamonded duenna of a bawdy house." [40]

The second was exemplified by "the mad solitary priests of Dada," the sterile pessimists of "pure art" isolated from the working men and women of America, disgusted with the world and using art as a refuge.[41]

Bolshevik art, he concluded, would be neither vulgar and bloated nor etiolated and effete, but would fuse "the dualism of flesh and spirit." And he painted a vision of New York five hundred years hence that incorporates the visions of Ruskin, Bellamy, Whitman, and Fourier:

It is the week of the spring festival in May, when all the world stops to celebrate the anniversary of the universal revolution, and the growing of the corn and the wheat, the lilac and the rose. All day in a hundred amphitheatres of the city, there have been tragedies and comedies, followed by prize-fights, wrestling contests, foot races, poetry readings and song recitals. They have baseball games, too, football games, pageants and gymnastic evolutions in which thousands of athletes join. No one can any longer see any discord in such a programme; and there is no division in this audience between brutalized worker and over-refined idealist.

In the dusk the crowds go to great common eating-halls and eat simple, good food and drink wine, and speeches like those of Pericles are made to them, and they are happy and exalted.

It is night, the stars are out; the crowds come back to immense fields in different parts of the city, and on each of these fields a great drama is played, in which there are hundreds of thousands of actors.

The multitudes of men and women are in darkness, deep, bitter darkness. They lie on the ground and weep, remembering the eons of oppression. They moan in a low key, like the sweep of a vast wind. They remember the slavery in which their forefathers lived—they remember poverty, lynching, war. It is good for them to remember this—it keeps them humble and it makes them stern in the conviction that such things not come again.

The darkness is slowly invaded by a faint red glow from a color organ. The moaning changes to a more hopeful key. Tremendous batteries around the field have cast a wider and more brilliant scarlet light on the mob. It is an illumination that makes the heart leap with hope; the people rise to their feet and move about singing a new song.

A thousand great mechanical orchestras, more wonderful than anything we know, break into mighty strains. The people chant a marvellous cantata that rises to the stars like the hymn of life. Now the color-organs have burst into full flower. They throw strange patterns on the sky; the sky is filled with a thousand clashing beautiful colors; the earth is filled with powerful singing; not a man, woman, child or dog is outside the communion of this night; the world is wonderful; it is the drama of the proletarian revolution; it is the proletarian art.[42]

FOUR · FROM BOHEMIA TO REVOLUTION

The Liberator: DECLINE AND FALL

GOLD'S DREAM of a proletarian New Jerusalem must have seemed touchingly old-fashioned and evangelical to the literary sophisticates who happened to read it, but was their own brand of romantic rebelliousness any more down to earth? Certainly not to the generation of Eastman, Frank, Dell, and Brooks, and, increasingly, as the decade drew to a close, not to themselves.

Since 1912, a polarizing process had been under way which divided the Bohemian from the revolutionary. The rebel could no longer encompass all varieties of intransigence, conduct simultaneously a private and a public war against the established order. The time was near at hand when he would feel impelled to choose between gratifying his personal compulsions or serving "the party of humanity."

The dedicated socialists who wrote for *The Liberator* had to make a decision in the early twenties. Not many years would pass, however, before a group of young writers, hitherto apolitical or antipolitical, would conclude that anarchist defiance, "ivory towers," and escape from responsibility—what Floyd Dell called "intellectual vagabondage"—offered no permanent satisfactions. Gradually the mood of gay and sometimes desperate hedonism passed away to be replaced by a new attitude of social seriousness. The exiles were becoming partisans.

A windfall had come to *The Liberator* late in 1921 when Postmaster General Will H. Hays refunded $11,000 to the magazine and restored second-class mailing privileges, which had illegally been denied by Wilson's administration. Unfortunately, this timely restitution was offset when the bookkeeper ran off with $4,000. By 1922, the overworked staff, finding it hard to pay themselves or their contributors, was issuing appeals for assistance to the friends and subscribers of the magazine.

On the surface, *The Liberator* reflected the "amiable and pointless life" of the Village. Each issue continued to be put together as casually and as haphazardly as ever. Famous and talented people like Charlie Chaplin or H. G. Wells were constantly dropping in. E. E. Cummings came once to discuss his poetry with Claude McKay, and Elinor Wylie, enigmatic and elegant, also chatted with McKay in his office. A more frequent and less predictable visitor was the futurist poet Baroness von Freytag-Loringhoven, "gaudily accoutred in rainbow raiment, festooned with barbaric beads and spangles and bangles, and toting her inevitable poodle in gilded harness," who would read her bizarre poems to any available listener.

And yet the magazine began to show a toughness and militancy in its social attitudes that bore out Michael Gold's revolutionary convictions. "Socialists," he said, "are being asked to take over the management of the world's muddled affairs, and they must train themselves for the task." His own fiery reports of the Pennsylvania coal strikes and the bloody battles between scabs and striking coal miners in Herrin, Illinois, illustrated this trend, as did the stories from Russia sent in by John Dos Passos and Anna Louise Strong. McKay and Jean Toomer dramatized the humiliations of the Negro, and a writer who signed himself Edmund Wilson, Jr., contributed a brutal story of a veteran whose dreams of revenge against his captain are turned against the "red agitators." Among all the literary magazines, only *The Liberator* spoke up in behalf of Sacco and Vanzetti. If it "made the mistake," as Freeman put it, "of ignoring T. S. Eliot's *The Waste Land,* which appeared at this time but which we did not review," it tried to deal with the larger social issues that mattered little to most of the other literary magazines—wage cuts, revolutions, crusades.[1]

The Liberator, in short, was doing a good job, and yet by the fall of 1922, it was already beginning to lose its momentum and to reflect the uncertainties and divisions in the minds of its editors. Working against its success were the times and the temperaments of artists and writers who created it.

The new postwar prosperity and the "normalcy" installed by the Harding administration withdrew attention from the outrages chronicled in the pages of *The Liberator,* and the radicals themselves, who in 1919 and 1920 had confidently expected the spread of socialism throughout Europe, now abandoned their revolutionary hopes. Even in Russia, the period of militant Communism had given way to the New Economic Policy, a program that seemed less an adjustment to economic realities than a capitulation. What middle-class support the magazine had enjoyed fell away as Eastman, the chief fund raiser, left for Europe in the spring of 1922, as Floyd Dell retired to Croton, as Boardman Robinson consigned the art work to youngsters like William Gropper, as Robert Minor left the drawing board for practical radical politics.

What Freeman described as the "arguments, compromises, postponements" that had always kept the editorial staff in a turmoil now deepened into real rifts. Gold and McKay, appointed by Eastman as joint executive editors in 1921, had never liked each other. McKay felt that his colleague wanted to turn *The Liberator* into "a popular proletarian magazine, printing doggerel from lumberjacks and stevedores and true revelations from chambermaids." Although not against getting "material out of the forgotten members of the working class," he wanted to preserve the old literary standards. Their differences almost ended in a fist fight, and McKay, deciding he could never cope with "Gold's social revolutionary passion," resigned.[2]

Gold, as McKay noted, "was still battling up from the depths of proletarian starvation and misery," and he particularly resented Floyd Dell's allegation that he, and indeed all *The Liberator* editors, were middle-class. "Comrade Mike," Dell said, "is a literary man, an intellectual, and a member of the salaried middle class." This was nothing to be ashamed of. "But Comrade Mike is for some obscure reason ashamed of not being a workingman. At least, I deduce that from his conversation and writings. And so he is in awe of the workingman when he meets him, and says extravagant things in praise of him." What Gold did not understand, Dell said, was that workers are "properly envious" of the middle class and wanted to join it. Dell could understand this desire because he wanted the workers to have more leisure. But Gold, who worked as hard as any proletarian, was subject "to a peculiar middle-class emotion. I mean the shame at enjoying the leisure thus provided by somebody's hard work. . . . He falls down in prayerful awe before Steam and Steel and Mother Earth, and Mud, and Heat, and Noise, and such things." Like Eugene O'Neill, who in *The Hairy Ape* mistook "a minor poet" for a "typical working-man," Gold, Dell concluded, "has come back from the stoke-hold talking about how beautiful Strength and Steam and Steel and Noise and Dirt are. If so, I say, why abolish capitalism?" [3]

Dell humorously exaggerated and was not being quite fair to Gold, but there was enough truth behind his joking to hurt. The term "middle-class" was a "fighting phrase" to Gold, and he never concealed his disgust for "aesthetes" in the habit "of sitting around and talking" or his admiration for hard-fisted miners or steelworkers, who took on the proportions of the proletarian demigods pictured in the cartoons of Fred Ellis, Robert Minor, Boardman Robinson, and William Gropper.

Gold might well have been influenced by Eden and Cedar Paul's *Proletcult* (1921), the first extensive discussion of this portmanteau word meaning "proletarian culture." The authors defined it "as a fighting culture . . . based upon the conception of the class struggle . . . its fundamental aim, in the pre-revolutionary phase, is to render the workers class-conscious, and thus to give them both the knowledge and the fighting impetus which will enable them to achieve their historic mission. . . ." Gold's "proletarianism" seems to have been in 1920-22 a composite of the humanist view of culture as propounded by Lenin's Commissar for Education, Lunacharsky, and the more explicitly Marxist proletcult views of Poliansky, Director of Advanced Education in 1921, who wished to purge the minds of masses of "petty bourgeois and anarchistic sentiments" and of "capitalistic bourgeois culture." It also reflected the extreme views of A. A. Bogdanov, who demanded a distinctive proletarian culture constructed upon an entirely new ideological foundation.[4]

It was not, at bottom, the personal frictions among the literary staff that finally killed *The Liberator,* but the still-unsettled war between art and revolution, between the free, undisciplined writer and the disciplined, responsible party member. The magazine's commitment to Bolshevism meant that pure art, pure poetry had less justification than ever. Proletcult in its prerevolutionary phase was intended to be primarily "a fighting culture," a means of helping the proletariat to tear down the old order.[5] The conception left no room for bourgeois nostalgia or aestheticism, and the party writer was expected to subordinate himself to the class war.*

One way to solve the dilemma was to follow the path of John Reed, already fading into legend, or of Robert Minor, the cartoonist-turned-organizer: to renounce art for practical politics. Communist Party functionaries felt rather contemptuous of "intellectuals" and their creative work. Their disdain mattered less to the editors of *The Liberator,* however, than the feeling that they were "cut off," as Freeman said, "by political differences from the official literary world." That is why they decided to turn *The Liberator* over to the Communist Party in the fall of 1922. Max Eastman had urged this move, rather than allow the magazine to disappear. The request to do so came from Robert Minor, but the decision was the combined staff's (minus Mike Gold, who had left for California), and until 1924, two editorial staffs, one political, the other artistic, managed the magazine.[6]

The split was symbolic. Whereas Eastman, Dell, and Reed had combined political commentary with poetry and happily quarreled in public, each proud of his idiosyncrasies, the less important artists, under party direction, had to leave editorial policy to the politicos. In *The Masses* and the old *Liberator,* art and politics were fused; now they were mechanically joined. Party leaders acknowledged, of course, that creative writers like Upton Sinclair and Jack London helped the movement. Had not Karl Radek and Trotsky hailed *The Iron Heel?* But the radical literati lamented the growing politicizing

---

* As Freeman confided in his notebook at this time: "If one wishes to voice his private opinions all the time, if one insists on doing this even after a majority has adopted a policy, one should stay out of politics." He subsequently decided that this is precisely what artists should do.

of the magazine even though they blamed themselves for clinging to their petty-bourgeois loyalties. Writing from California in the spring of 1923, Gold begged Freeman not to stop fighting for the artists and to keep *The Liberator*'s columns open to the poets. At the same time, he was berating California writers for taking it easy in "the fattest, laziest, hungriest, richest, cheeriest, reactionary state in the Union" and writing nothing worth reading:

There are epic events here [he told them], as everywhere. They are not genteel; life is never genteel. There is the epic of the Wobblies, the migratory workers and their vast, violent, dramatic life; a story yet to be written. There is the Chinese population, the Mexicans, the old life of the Barbary Coast that the genteel writers could not touch. There are the mining camps, lumber camps, fishing fleets in this state.

Someday, he said, somebody would write a true story of California: "God help him, too; for the Vigilantes will surely hang him for his genius, or teach him it is safer to be genteel." [7]

LAUNCHING *The New Masses*

After *The Liberator* had been turned over to the Workers' Party in 1922, the executive editors, Robert Minor and Joseph Freeman, moved the magazine over to the headquarters of the party on East Eleventh Street, to the un-Bohemian section east of the Village where the trade-union workers lived.

The transfer, as Freeman belatedly recognized, was "a turning point of the utmost importance in the history of the radical and liberal writer in America." Hitherto, the radical magazines of literature and art (including *The Comrade, The Masses,* and *The Liberator*) had been managed and directed by the artists themselves. As independent radicals, they did not hesitate to criticize Socialist or Communist policy when it offended them. Now for the first time, "a radical magazine of arts, letters and politics was owned and directed by a radical party"; and this party itself differed from previous radical parties because of its relation to the Communist International. At the time, the artists and writers had no quarrel with the party line. But having no interest in a purely political magazine, they gradually withdrew.[8]

Many of the former contributors to *The Masses* and *The Liberator,* however, still hoped to revive the old *Masses* in a new form, or at least to provide a substitute for the older publications.

Upton Sinclair as early as 1923 had considered starting a radical magazine and had asked Mike Gold if he would like to assist him. Gold had already given some thought "to a literary magazine of the revolution," but he hesitated to collaborate with his ascetic friend:

It is like being asked by a pure young girl in marriage [he wrote to Sinclair] when one is a battered old roue with five or six affairs on hand. I am immoral, Upton, I drink, smoke, swear, loaf, sneer, shoot pool, dance jazz, shake the shimmy, ride box-cars, and do most everything. I would rather take a long walk into the country with a bunch of rough-necks than write a novel. I cannot be pious and love Jesus. I used to, but I don't anymore. After I have been with good people, formal people, however revolutionary, for more than a month or two, I want to bust loose and do something wild. Etc. I am not boasting about all this; I just don't want you to labor under any misapprehensions. I am a good Red, etc. and take that seriously enough, but it might get on your nerves if you found me smoking six or seven cigars a day, and hanging out in bootlegging joints with a bunch of wobblies. I can't be as pure, fervent and puritanical as yourself, Upton, and I would not want to be. The mass of humanity, stupid or intellectual, is fond of any kind of fun, sensuality, relaxation, sport and frivolity, and I am one of them.

Gold also raised some practical questions about the prospects of radical journalism in the early twenties. What audience did Sinclair have in mind? Did he want to compete with the Socialist Party pietists? They had their organ, as did the Communists and the Wobblies. It took large amounts of money to support a nonpartisan Left magazine, and Gold saw no point in Sinclair's trying to duplicate *The Nation,* a strongly backed and effective journal of opinion. Nor did he want to have anything to do with a "personal magazine" in which Sinclair would play "the solo of a single virtuoso." Such a notion clashed with his idea of revolution. He could see a powerful editor dominating a magazine, "but when he gets mistaking himself for a public movement I want to kick him in the pants."

What sort of magazine, then, did Gold have in mind? He would like to think of Sinclair and himself as editors of a "group paper" whose duty it would be to nurse and to bring forth "something fine and big into life out of the materials of the world around us." Since

The Masses, no experiment of this kind had been tried "to develop revolutionary artists—poets, fictioneers and draughtsmen." There was hardly a place, in fact, "where a fiction story with a strong revolutionary or workingclass implications" could be printed in America. *The Liberator* had become a party organ. No magazine except Mencken's *American Mercury* reached the college boys and the young intellectuals. Here was Sinclair's chance "to make a bright, artistic, brilliant magazine that would captivate the imagination of the younger generation and rally them around something real—not the sterile mockeries and gibings at the boobs that Mencken has taught them."

No one else, said Gold, had such influence with young thinkers as Sinclair; no one else combined the artist and the revolutionary so admirably. If Sinclair pitched his appeal to those people who wanted to feel, to laugh, to live colorfully, his magazine "would be more a possible success than the independent Marxian sheet I fear you are planning." Did this sound like Greenwich Village talk? He hoped not. He was simply "reflecting much of what is going on in Germany, Russia and other countries," simply insisting that "artists are a vital part of a revolution, and the intellectuals." Only American Marxists considered poetry a vice.

What Gold had in mind, as he made clear in "a supplementary word" to Sinclair, was a periodical "to conduct a cultural defense of the revolution" and to establish a haven for young artists and intellectuals "wanting to do and say something to solve the bloody mess we all are in." For them, the sneers of the Menckenians, the "mystical withdrawals from life" of the Sherwood Andersons, and the "pattern-makers escape" of the Amy Lowells and other poets were no solutions at all. They hungered for a program based "on reason, social life and struggle, mass art." At present they shied away from the capitalist realities, because they were afraid to sound like propagandists. The new magazine would give them a home, would hail, as *The Masses* had done, "every new star on the horizon— every sight and portent."

Nothing came of Sinclair's magazine project, as Gold must have expected. He loved and admired him as a fighter who stuck to his guns, whose life had purpose, who wasn't "a lousy dilatante," but deplored his puritanism; he admired his splendid indignation, but accused him of loving "some ideal you have formed" of the working class, not the workers themselves. Sinclair's revolutionary magazine would have been juiceless and joyless; Gold's ideal magazine gay and tolerant. And so he could say to his crusading friend,

Attack the filthy, the blood-stained luxuries of rich all you want to, but don't moralize against the poor little jug of wine and hopeful song of the worker. It helps him to live and fight. The little pleasure I get out of this wretched world helps me to live and fight. I love humor, joy and happy people; I love big groups at play, and friends sitting about a table, talking, smoking, and laughing. I love song and athletics and a lot of other things. I wish the world were all play and everybody happy and creative as children. That is Communism; the communism of the future. Meanwhile there is a lot of dirty work to do and a dirty world to live in. Let's do it as communistically as we can.

The magazine Gold had so exuberantly outlined for Sinclair began to seem less remote in the late spring of 1924. Writing to Sinclair from New York, Gold spoke of the old veterans of *The Masses* and *The Liberator* who were "crazy to be talking out again" and who were convinced that an audience was "waiting for the stuff." Hugo Gellert, Scott Nearing, and Gold, it appeared, might get "a big bunch of money to start a new free non-partisan revolutionary Masses in New York." This time, Gold told Sinclair, they wanted to go after a mass circulation, to print the sheet "in newspaper style like the old Appeal to Reason. . . . This fooling around with a 15,000 circulation among extremists and 'tired radicals' and intelligentsia is the bunk." [9]

Gold had no desire to edit the paper. At this time his heart was set on becoming a playwright and producer, but he and his friends continued to agitate for a new magazine, and by February of 1925, the projectors had received hearty encouragement from scattered and isolated radicals of all persuasions. "I am absolutely with you," wrote John Dos Passos, "and would gladly do anything to help. *The Masses* was the only magazine I ever had any use for." "There are many of us," wrote Susan Glaspell, "who have never ceased to mourn the Masses, and I see no reason why your venture should not be to this time what the Masses was to those good old fighting days." Eugene

O'Neill and Carl Sandburg sent their best wishes, as did Sherwood
Anderson, John Howard Lawson, Elmer Rice, and Stuart Chase.
"Perhaps the old Masses hasn't been killed yet!" wrote Lewis Mum-
ford.[10]

The magazine owed its materialization indirectly to a young graduate of Harvard College, Charles Garland, "who celebrated his majority by dedicating his paternal inheritance to the service of the
radical cause." [11] In the fall of 1925, the American Fund for Public
Service, which administered the Garland bequest, released the first
installment of a $17,000 grant to the Executive Committee of *The
New Masses* after months of delicate negotiations.

These negotiations began in March when a group of writers and
artists approached the Garland Fund and requested "a one year
endowment for a magazine to be known, tentatively, as 'Dynamo.' "
With this request they submitted a prospectus, an itemized budget
of $50,000, and a collection of letters from well-known artists and
writers who favored the project. More than half of the backers belonged to the *Masses-Liberator* group. In the light of subsequent
charges that the Communist Party controlled the magazine from the
start,[12] the following facts cannot be too strongly emphasized: 1) the
overwhelming majority of the organizing committee were liberals or
independent radicals; 2) the sponsors of the magazine clearly intended to keep it free of any party label; 3) the directors of the
Garland Fund knew this when they granted the appropriation.

The prospectus, written by Joseph Freeman after "repeated discussions" with his colleagues, affirmed in less rhapsodic language
what Michael Gold had written to Upton Sinclair several years earlier.
But it also revived the spirit of cultural nationalism; it spoke of
"new creative forces" at work in America which were quite as fundamental in their way as the vast economic and political changes.
Echoing the manifestoes of Emerson and Whitman, of Bourne and
Van Wyck Brooks, it called upon American artists and writers to
face up to America's "potential riches" and its problems:

This country is fast becoming the greatest empire in the world and
with this development are appearing modes of life which have no prece-
dent in history or art. The stockyards of Chicago, the steel mills of
Pittsburgh, the mines of West Virginia, the lumber camps of Wash-

ington and California, the lynching of Negroes in the South, the clothing industries in the East, the Klan, tabloid newspapers, automobiles, and the private life of average citizens; the national political conventions, the nation-wide fetish of big business, the adventures of American imperialism south of the Rio Grande, the life in skyscraper, factory and subway—these have still to find expression in imaginative, essential and permanent forms.

To express these neglected aspects of the American scene did not imply adherence to a single party or program. All parties and all programs, the prospectus continued, would get a fair hearing if they presented their ideas vividly. As for the magazine itself, it must avoid propaganda. It "must never take itself too seriously. It must be interesting above everything else; fresh, vivid, youthful, satirical, brave and gay; an expression of intelligent American youth." While maintaining the highest standards, "it must also be sympathetic to any crudeness which is the expression of something young, vital and as yet groping and undeveloped."

The new magazine, in short, would share certain points of view with news weeklies critical of "the present social order" (*The Nation, The New Republic, The New Leader, The Survey*), but it would be livelier, funnier, more satirical. It would be less negative than *The American Mercury,* more national-minded than *The Dial,* more concerned with "that larger America" than *The Little Review* was or *Vanity Fair* and *The New Yorker* ("mere intellectual fashion journals") were. The planners promised to fill half the pages with cartoons and drawings, to keep the articles and stories short, to publish poetry "favoring vigorous expression of positive ideas and ideals," and to reserve ample space "for the type of discussion of spiritual values for the younger generation of which Waldo Frank has been the exponent." Of course controversies would never be one-sided. If Robert Minor had something to say about "the spiritual values of Communism," he would be heard, and Gorham Munson, and others.[13]

The twenty-three associate editors elected Waldo Frank editor in chief, Edwin Seaver associate editor, Helen Black business manager, and John Sloan and Hugo Gellert art editors. Then they waited for the decision of the Garland Fund.

The directors of the fund were cautiously receptive. They agreed to supply $17,000 if the friends of the magazine raised $8,500 and set up a businesslike working staff. But over the summer, Waldo Frank and Edwin Seaver resigned, and the planners dropped the name "Dynamo" for "The New Masses." The whole enterprise seemed vaguer than it had appeared to be in the spring, and the fund at first hesitated to release the $1,500 promised for promotional purposes. Thanks to friendly board members like Freda Kirchwey, who worried about "the poor things . . . clamoring for their money," the fund accepted Gold and Freeman as substitute editors, and in October, Elizabeth Gurley Flynn, the fund secretary and at this time an anarchosyndicalist, notified Freeman that the $1,500 had been released.

Although news of the grant and the proposed magazine was announced amid considerable fanfare in December, with well-publicized hosannas from Eugene O'Neill, Sherwood Anderson, John Haynes Holmes, Alfred Kreymborg, Waldo Frank, Bernard Shaw, H. L. Mencken, William Allen White, Max Eastman, Clarence Darrow, Edwin Arlington Robinson, and other notables, the $8,500 to be raised by the friends of the magazine was not collected until February of 1926. Rex Stout, not yet the famous author of detective stories, pledged $4,000 of that sum and donated the office furniture. A new slate of editors, Freeman, James Rorty, and Egmont Arens prepared the first issue. In May 1926, *The New Masses,* as big and almost as gaudy as its illustrious namesake, reached the newsstands of New York.[14]

DELL'S CRITIQUE OF VAGABONDIA

Mike Gold's call for a literature neither aridly political nor detached from the lives of the working class went largely unanswered simply because most American writers, even the rebellious ones, had pretty much lost interest in Russia and Communism and in proletarian culture by 1923. The New Economic Policy (NEP) seemed to them a betrayal of Communism, although they had not lifted a finger in its behalf.[15] For them, as Floyd Dell remarked in 1922, the revolution had passed into its prose period after its period of poetry, from "wonderful dreams" to "dull realities."

So say many of our friends, who shared with us here as dazzled on-lookers the poetry and the glory and the dream of that revolutionary dawn. . . . And now, when we ask them to share with us, again as on-lookers only, for that as yet is all the part assigned us by destiny, the sober, realistic, everyday triumphs of the revolution in its prose period, they turn to us and ask: "Is this reality enough to satisfy you, after those great dreams? Don't you feel a little fooled? Was it worth while? Is this what you wanted? Or—speak candidly now!—is the Revolution, after all, a failure? Inevitably so—nobody's fault—the best that could be expected—nothing to cry about—but still, different from what we all did expect—in short, pretty small potatoes, after such tremendous hopes! How about it? [16]

Yes, Dell said, the prose was worth the dreams, but what Joseph Freeman called "the bourgeois cult of the ego" seemed to fascinate the rebels more than the prose of revolution. What is more, Freeman complained to Dell, they were not even aware of their own radical literary traditions.

Dell responded with a series of articles beginning in the October 1923 issue of *The Liberator* in which he put the tradition in historical perspective and trenchantly analyzed the recurring patterns of literary rebellion.[17] He wrote as the loving yet stern critic of the fallible intelligentsia, and in defending them felt obliged "to uncover our idiosyncratic follies to whatever ridicule they deserve" even though such disclosures confirmed the prejudices of the Philistines.

Dell's underlying thesis was the interaction of literature and life. Every writer reflected in some way his response to his environment, his rejection or acceptance of its culture and institutions. And between the two titanic events of modern times, the French and Russian revolutions, the writer's attitude toward his society had alternated between hope and disenchantment. The splendid promise of 1791 had ended in the despair of 1816, when the romantics fled from the butcheries of the terror to "those far and solitary peaks, glaciers, caverns, seas, deserts, which constitute the favorite milieu of early nineteenth-century poetry." Byronic cynicism supplanted Rousseauian confidence. After Darwin's revelations ended the myth of "the re-

bellious and untamed purity of Nature," or, rather, exposed nature
for the bloody thing it was, some writers retreated to the medievalism
from which the eighteenth-century intellectuals had so recently escaped, while others, disheartened and appalled by "the dreary and
horrible realities of nineteenth-century capitalism," sought refuge in
"the last frontier of literature, the stepping-off place into the realm
of madness—of private and incommunicable dream."

Addressing himself directly to his own contemporaries, Dell
warned of the consequences of such alienation and the dangers of
becoming cozily and smugly habituated to life on this spiritual
frontier.

It is the final renunciation of relations with a world felt to be intolerable; a spiritual divorce from reality. In this mood, the artist does not
quarrel with the world, nor laugh at it, nor least of all, seek to persuade
it that its realities are poorer than his own dreams; in this mood, the
unhappy one does not even leave the world, and seek refuge in cave or
garret or "ivory tower"; he remains in but not of the world, utterly
content with the realm of his own dreaming.

The prewar American literary radicals were the beneficiaries of nineteenth-century romanticism, but they were also heirs of American
libertarianism and sharers of a middle-class socialist vision that kept
them, Dell saw, in touch with the world about them. Bellamy's
beautiful Boston epitomized Utopia to these tender socialists, although
"it was too good to be true," and so sure were they that "Capitalism
must produce Socialism," that they watched the "trustification" of
America "with a jealous and parental eye." Even when the anarchists
convinced them that parliamentarianism was a fraud and politics a
delusion, they kept their confidence in themselves and found consola-
tion, Dell wrote, "in an increasing number of imaginative writings
which served to help reconcile us to our situation, which deepened
our cynicism with regard to violent social change, which enabled us
to think very well of ourselves and even to regard our laissez-faire,
do-nothing selfishness as a pattern of social heroism." Nightmarish
prognostications like Ignatius Donnelly's *Caesar's Column,* Dell
noted, failed to interest them, "because Donnelly had pictured Revolution in such romantic and absurd terms. What! violent revolution
and bloody counter-revolution, with an accompaniment of famine and

massacre! No—such things could not happen. We were too civilized."

It was possible in the early 1900's to cast one's lot emotionally with the working class "as the protagonist of the Future" and still espouse the gospel of Vagabondia, "divorced utterly from any form of political idealism, and reunited with the romantic tradition of homeless but happy poets and artists." To be supremely disinterested and detached, to be sublimely indifferent to the compelling responsibilities of the bourgeoisie became part of the artistic code.[18] But it was never more than a play theory. Dell and his friends, who "really preferred ice-cream soda to absinthe, were content to be secretly tame and conventional so long as we have a public reputation for hieratic wickednesses." Hence they were immensely pleased when H. G. Wells and Bernard Shaw gave them a preview of the new order and convinced them that they might become the "Samurai" of the future.

Wells was the more reassuring of the two, for his heroes seemed "to throw the glamour of righteousness" over our impulsive follies: "Nobody in any of Mr. Wells' novels ever achieves anything with the help of any organized body, scientific, political, or economic—he does it all by himself. And we were thereby confirmed in our disposition to rebuild the world by means of that sacred bundle of egotisms and impulses which constituted our individual personalities." He prepared them for the Future, but not the Present. Shaw's heroes were also as individualist and cranky as could be wished, but his plays satirized the attackers of institutions more than the institutions themselves, and he raised a disturbing question: *"Can you create a new civilization upon the ruins of the old? Can you even get along in such a new civilization if some one else creates it for you?"*

World War I discredited "the schemes and instruments" of human idealism, and Dell eloquently expressed the despair of the young minds "trained in disillusion."

Humanity appears to have climbed painfully up from the primeval slime and reached out its hands toward the stars in vain. Its arts and sciences, its religion and politics, its braveries and prides, have provided it with the full means of self-destruction, and there seems to be nothing to stay its hand. There are evidently flaws in our human nature which make our idealism a tragic joke. . . . Facing an ironic doom which it feels powerless to avert, the intelligentsia of our time has for the most part put aside with a kind of shame its broken and shattered ideals, and has confessed its hopelessness by the very nature of its new esthetic and intellectual interests. Some, indeed, refusing to face at all so black a reality, have retired into a sort of new Ivory Tower hastily jerry-built according to some fantastic futurist blue-print, and occupy themselves with such harmlessly esthetical pastimes and intellectual cross-word puzzles as will serve to pass the time. But others, perhaps more deeply hurt, have expressed their pain and disillusion in enthusiasms for such new imaginative works as reflect, indirectly but impressively, this shattering of their hopes.

Dell saw the postwar writer's preoccupation with form, his cultish conception of literature as an "esoteric mystery of the elect," and his "celebration of the ugliness and chaos of life" as a symptom of infantile regression. It might be argued, he admitted, that our willingness to write and to read books that remind us of our miserable state is a sign of our "psychic health," but he volunteered a less consoling explanation. Aren't we trying to read our own befuddlement into the cosmos, he asked. Doesn't the obvious pleasure we take in mucking around in the *"disjecta membra* of psycho-analytic research" suggest "that we, at this moment of history, do *not* want life to seem capable of being interpreted and understood, because that would be a reproach to us for our own failure to undertake the task of reconstructing our social, political and economic theories, and in general, and in consonance with these, our ideals of a good life"?

Spiritual "vagabondage," the culmination of this "disillusioning process," Dell concluded, resulted finally in an "inverted sentimentality" that indiscriminately transposed every good thing into its unattractive antitype. The intelligentsia spurned political commitment after the momentary excitement kindled by the Russian revolution, not because of their indifference, but because of "a secret temperamental antipathy." They resented any imposition of order on chaos, whether it be imposed by the Bolsheviks or the American capitalists. "The introduction of machinery into Russia, and eventually throughout Asia, is not the sort of change to warm our hearts. . . . Far from it. The American intelligentsia has a deep sentimental attachment to barbarism and savagery, preferably of a nomadic sort." The threat to their precious "freedom," which the Russians have proved is only a "bourgeois myth," made them resent the rehabilitation of the conventional virtues, "including such dull matters as honesty, sobriety, responsibility, and even a sense of duty." *

Yes, Dell said, their refusal as artists to perform their responsibility—the interpreting of life for those without the opportunity or ability to do it as well—and the leaving of that task to comic strips, films, jazz, and the other "lively arts" was at once a capitulation and a betrayal. The time will come, he predicted rather grimly, when a younger generation will take its duties more seriously and salvage the ideals junked by its predecessors: ". . . it may well feel called upon to liquidate the liberal-and-radical 'freedom' movement which has so obviously reached the point of bankruptcy." A new conception of literature may result, neither cultish nor irresponsible, that will help the new generation "to love generously, to work honestly, to think clearly, to fight bravely, to live nobly. . . ."

MENCKEN AND THE EXPATRIATES

It can be imagined what E. E. Cummings—a devotee of Krazy Kat, burlesque shows, circuses, love, and freedom, and a spoofer of "the great American mentality"—would have thought of Dell's reflections had he read them.[19] But would any of the writers Dell was alluding to have recognized themselves in the portrait of the Vagabond? Did they hate civilization as ferociously and as unselectively as Dell charged?[20] Was he writing history or autobiography?

* Freeman was later to develop this thought. Speaking of the Bohemians in the twenties, he wrote: "The prosperous middle classes needed a little bohemianism to spend their money in ways not sanctioned by the puritan tradition; the bohemians needed a little puritanism to go with their newly acquired money. Indeed, bohemianism requires a certain amount of social stability. The bohemian wishes to 'shock' the bourgeois. For this purpose, the bourgeois must be well entrenched, secure financially, able and willing to be shocked; and the bohemian himself must feel that the road back to the world he is 'shocking' is not entirely closed. In the depths of his heart he not only fears but hopes that his eccentricities, which are part of his stock in trade, will earn him a fatted calf as the returning prodigal. It is not capitalism that he hates, as a rule, but the responsibilities which any highly developed social system imposes upon its members." *An American Testament,* p. 285.

Consider H. L. Mencken, not specifically mentioned in Dell's book but obviously included among "the users of words" who, far from trying to prop up "a decaying order . . . about to collapse," were helping to undermine it. When Dell began to write his history of literary vagabondage in 1923, Mencken had already been cast aside by *The Liberator* editors for his sarcastic essay on one of the radical patron saints, Thorstein Veblen. Dell had reviewed *Prejudices: Third Series,* in which the Veblen essay appeared, and was so annoyed that he consigned Mencken to the popular magazines and conferred upon him the mantle of Elbert Hubbard and Dr. Frank Crane.[21] Another *Liberator* reviewer, Paul Simon, carried on the anti-Mencken crusade by making him the spokesman of "Manufacturers and Bankers" and by presenting his doctrine as follows:

I, Henry Louis Mencken, belong to a superior caste in America, that of the liberated intelligences, those capable of living with gusto and without any labor that trespasses upon the expression of their personalities. Duties and obligations are for the lesser breeds *within* the law. As for the classes beneath us, they are clowning politicians, foreign cattle, Presbyterian elders, damned radicals, emasculated professors and cowardly witch-hunters. Most of them serve to amuse me and I like to watch the show. As for the police, the lawyers, and the politicians, they also are useful in that they hold back the have-nots from the haves, and thus help make my position so much more secure, since I ally myself with the haves against the have-nots.[22]

A third reviewer in the next year numbered Mencken among the "literary apostles" attacking "the theory of Americanism," but underscored his limitations: "H. L. Mencken, while undoubtedly sincere in his criticisms, does not propose to be cheated of his fun; after setting fire to the rubbish-heap of present-day standards, he is content to stand aside, happily fiddling his own praises while his flames consume both reputation and reason."[23]

The radicals' annoyance with Mencken was understandable enough, but he was in no sense a renegade who had gone over to the enemy. Mencken had never tried to conceal his antidemocratic bias, even if his iconoclasm had strengthened the common assault against Philistia, and he had always regarded "the army of uplifters and world-savers" as mountebanks. But the socialists in the early twenties could not decide when he was serious and when he was joking. He described himself as a minor capitalist, a lover of order and property who believed it was easier to bamboozle the boobs than to shoot them; he professed to dislike radicals and liberals but encouraged them because they encouraged him to make phrases; and although he favored one uniformed mob to keep down the other mob in overalls, he despised the bounders who ran America and who would be ruined by their own hoggishness. Temperamentally and politically, he was a Tory, but there were no authentic Tories to vote for in the United States.[24] This, at any rate, was the public pose. Did it reveal the authentic Mencken?

Edmund Wilson, reviewing Mencken's career in 1921, suspected another Mencken beneath the arrogant Tory exterior. His Nietzscheanism, Wilson thought, and his long-maintained conception of a master-slave society forced him to repudiate radicalism and liberalism and "the idea of human rights to freedom and justice" even though he hated "repression and injustice." The Palmer raids of 1919-20, however, shattered his pose of indifference, and his love of America shone through his disgust. Thus he could make poetry out of the "democratic life which absorbs and infuriates him," for, Wilson concluded, "Mencken is the civilized consciousness of modern America, its learning, its intelligence and its taste, realizing the grossness of its manners and mind and crying out in horror and chagrin." [25]

Mencken's subsequent career belies this theory, for his conservatism became at last merely shrill and vindictive. Yet up to the 1930's, there is much in Mencken's writing to support the thesis that his self-publicized role of the American Thersites masked the moralist, and that his practice of heaving dead cats into sanctuaries had a serious purport. He served a country he pretended to despise as a kind of reactionary liberator who cut through the undergrowth of provincialism and prejudice and cleared a path for finer minds. Finally, he outlived his usefulness. His once-formidable rhetoric turned stale. But his irreverence and iconoclasm made him far more hated and feared than the "saccharine liberals," with their "preposterous dreams," and he did a good deal to convince future leftists in the twenties that capitalist culture was decadent. By espousing boldly (and getting away with it) ideas considered un-American, by assailing "the general stupidity" of the business classes, he helped to destroy the popular faith in their invulnerability. Although the Communists hated him in the 1930's and thereafter, one suspects that their success with the intelligentsia during the Roosevelt era may have been undeliberately assisted by Mencken's abrasive philosophy. The cynicism of the twenties, which he did so much to promote, created an ideological vacuum which Communism, with its revolutionary fervor, rushed in to fill.[26]

Dell saw nothing salvageable in Mencken, and he feared that his other "shell-shocked" contemporaries were too deeply immersed in "their private vagaries to desert their jerry-built ivory towers." More might be expected from "a younger generation of sensitive and creative-minded men and women." [27] But who were they and where were they? We have seen that Van Wyck Brooks and his *Seven Arts'* cronies, who shared many of Dell's literary dislikes and ideals, regretted that the new generation seemed to be hopelessly sunk in aestheticism. They meant, of course, the young writers on *The Dial* and the expatriates and former expatriates of Paris, the publishers of the audacious and ephemeral "little magazines" like *Broom, Secession,* and *S4N,* and their contributors. Was Dell also referring to this literary avant-garde? It is hard to say.

At any rate, he was not alone in his thinking. Gilbert Seldes, for example, declared that experimental American writing as represented by *The First American Caravan* in 1926 was wanting in satire and rebelliousness. The contributors were unconcerned "with American business and intellectual life" (the work of Mencken and Sinclair Lewis had apparently no influence upon them, and the middle class hardly figured in their writing); instead, they preferred to deal with the Negro, both in the South and in Harlem, with "the peasant, the alien, and the outcast." With few exceptions, the tone of the poetry and prose was brooding, melancholy, languid. "What most of the authors care about, obviously, is an intense expression of some private emotion." [28]

But if we consider the intellectual gropings of these writers between the time when Dell began his pieces on the "vagabonds" and 1929, usually designated as the year of the great swing leftward, we find that collectively they were less detached or apathetic than their social-minded accusers made them out to be and that most generalizations about their social indifference must be qualified. This could be said not only of the few authentic literary radicals like Paxton Hibben [29] and John Dos Passos but also of others whose intransigence was less under control or less purposely directed.

One is struck, first of all, by the rage and bitterness that emanates from their attack against "Americanism" and its products. According to William Carlos Williams in 1924, America had

become "the most lawless country in the civilized world" a panorama of murders, perversions, a terrific ungoverned strength excusable only because of the horrid beauty of its great machines. Today it is a generation of gross knownothingism, of blackened churches where hymns groan like chants from stupified jungles, a generation universally eager to barter permanent values (the hope of an aristocracy) in return for opportunist material advantage, a generation hating those it obeys.

In the same year, Glenway Westcott confessed that an "indignant population" surrounded American writers and that "all writers are spiritual expatriates. Their position in this commonwealth is that of a band of revolutionaries or a cult of immoralists. They exist by sufferance, by their willingness to endure poverty, or by 'protective coloration.' " Ludwig Lewisohn described America as a haven for "fat-paunched" magnates, fundamentalist preachers, and baseball players, a country inhabited by a "duped and stupified populace." [30]

When Eugene Jolas, editor of *transition* (published in Paris), asked a number of American expatriates in 1928 why they preferred to live outside America, some of them voiced the familiar complaints against American prudishness, the tyranny of the machine, and the tastelessness of mass culture. Kay Boyle wrote:

Americans I would permit to serve me, to conduct me rapidly and competently wherever I was going, but not for one moment to impose their achievements upon what is going on in my heart and in my soul. I am too proud and too young to need the grandeur of physical America which one accepts only at the price of one's own dignity. I am making a voyage into poverty because I am too proud to find nourishment in a situation that is more successful than myself.

Other comments were less personal if equally explicit. America, said Gertrude Stein, was the best country to have been born in, but

not the best country to live in. It was much better to live in a country
that had already attained civilization than in one which had not yet
attained it. E. E. Cummings put it more succinctly: "France has
happened more than she is happening, whereas America is happening more than she has happened." Another complained that in
America there were "no facilities for the enjoyment of leisure or
apparatuses for reflection. . . . Considerable time must be wasted
in self-justification both verbally and introspectively and many questions settled which are otherwheres taken for granted." [31] In sum:
writers preferred Europe because they could live in a leisurely way
and not feel guilty, because Europe had not accepted the spirit of
the machine, because Europe was cheaper, because it was easier and
cheaper in Europe to see and hear and produce art, and because if
Europe was rotten and decadent, the United States had the "blight
and decay" of green fruit. An American contributor summed up
these opinions in the following poem:

> Why wasn't I born with a different face,
> In a different age and a different place?
> I'd much rather have been the bastard
> of Dante and Beatrice
> Than the legitimate son of
> Whittier and Barbara Frietchie.

But replies to some other questions of Jolas suggested a more
serious concern for the artist and his society. "How do you envisage,"
he asked, "the spiritual future of America in the face of a dying
Europe and in the face of a Russia that is adopting the American
economic vision? . . . What is your feeling about the revolutionary
spirit of your age, as expressed, for instance, in such movements as
communism, surrealism, anarchism? . . . What particular vision do
you have of yourself in relation to twentieth century reality?" [32]

What is interesting and characteristic about these questions raised
by Jolas was his juxtaposing of Communism and surrealism (the
latter signifying "freedom," the former "authority") and his implication that a dying Europe was flanked by two dynamic cultures guided
by the same economic vision. He himself believed social conditions
determined art, that the artist could not escape from the collective
influence, but he opposed any industrial system, capitalist or commu-

nist, that flattened individuality under the pretext of making life more hygienic and comfortable. Let the artist, he said, express his sympathies for the working class but not at the expense of his individuality: "What determines the inspirational and conceptual development of a vision is the individual impulse. It is for this reason that the great artist is in advance of his age, since he works instinctively against mass impulsions and mass psychoses." [33]

THE COLLECTIVE AND THE "INDIVIDUAL"

By 1928 Jolas and some of his American contributors no longer felt immune to the appeal or the threat of Bolshevism (depending upon how they looked on Russia), and the same could be said for other American writers in and out of the United States. Perhaps a few of them closely resembled the sick and self-absorbed irresponsibles described by Dell, but the evidence contained in the books and magazines of the period suggests that the rebellious avant-garde were excited and disturbed by the challenge of events in America and Russia even though they contemplated Russia without rapture. The execution of Sacco and Vanzetti in 1927 seemed to illustrate, said Matthew Josephson, "the perfect impotence of Individualists in the face of mass-realities," [34] and yet not many writers were ready to accept the revolutionary program of Michael Gold, who, with Joseph Freeman and others, had founded the radical but not yet Communist literary magazine *The New Masses* in 1926.

Josephson by this time had lost some of his Dadaist jauntiness but reflected the political uncertainty of the still-uncommitted writer out of sorts with capitalism yet very suspicious of the Russian state. Reporting from America in 1928, he pointed out that prosperity had undercut the Reds ("the people vote for General Motors!") and that in the "vast Coney Island" of America the artist was the chief casualty. He likened the artists to soldiers in the front lines or aliens never absorbed into mass life. "Under the more bitter effort to survive, envying luxury or power, the problems of the individual, of the human identity in fact, assume a more immediate and absolute character. Whether through self-defense or opposition, the artist finds himself by natural stages led to nourishing and cultivating his specific differences at all costs." But Josephson saw the American situation as the result of "social collectivism," and he suspected the sufferers "from moral uniformity and regimentation" would find life as unpleasant in Russia as in the United States.[35] The detached and the disinterested, "all in short to whom the derisive term 'intellectuals' is applied," simply could not function in a mass society. Confronted by this standardized world given over to Economics and the Machine, the artist retreated into a cul-de-sac of "pure art" or "aesthetic mysticism" or lost his soul in the vast collectivity of Demos. Neither course was inevitable nor desirable; it was time, Josephson concluded, for the artist to cease being the "pariah" and to essay more ambitious roles. "Childish to think of 'fighting the machine!' He must compete." [36]

What course, then, was open to the writer? A number of volunteer guides were ready to point in different directions. It was the poet's function, Jolas preached, to subvert the existing order or overthrow the capitalist system. He recommended revolt in its most "terrible" form, the expression of individual vision "through the word." Addressing himself to his Communist correspondent in America, he wrote: "You demand of me that I vow myself to activism, that I oppose the life of contemplation, that I plunge headlong into a struggle for the humanity." No, he answered, politics led only to sterility. The only job the poet has is to create. "I shall oppose mass-action, mass-feeling, mass-ideas with all my power, as long as there is breath in me." [37]

Ezra Pound, no longer expecting the *risorgimento* he had so confidently predicted in 1913, still maintained that art had no place in a mechanized culture. But he had never countenanced the cult of the artist-against-the-world nor advised the writer to avoid social themes. "A work of art," he wrote in *Patria Mia,* "need not contain any statement of a political or of a social or of a philosophical conviction, but it nearly always implies one." Only minor artists, he said on another occasion, do not see the importance of "social problems"; it was the virtue of the classics, he continued, that people could interpret the symbols in them "as equivalent of some current struggle which they are unable to treat more directly." [38]

He had warned the writer, nevertheless, not to embroil himself in "civic campaigns" or "dilutions of controversy"—advice, unfortunately, he later failed to heed—and he had never ceased his campaign against the centralized state. "The problem of civilization," he wrote in 1922, "is to keep alive a sufficient number of individuals who can and will not be subjected to machines, or to the clichés of tyranny; a non-exploitable minimum of men who give, but who cannot be milked, who are neither afraid, nor yoked under ideas." The artist had to resist the state:

> One ought *almost* to say it is the job of a great art to keep government in its place, i.e., to kick it out of life, and reduce it to its proper, and wholly mechanical functions: street cars, water-mains, et cetera, a convenience, as your gas range is a convenience.
>
> This is not a cry for propagandist art, which means a touting one form of government in opposition to some other. It means an exclusion of politics, fads, crankisms from art; a driving them out of the minds of the few individuals who can, in their excess of natural energy, combine and form a civilization, in the midst of the unconscious and semiconscious gehenna. . . .
>
> The present plague of democracy is that we have lost the sense of demarcation between Res Public, the public business, and the affairs of the individual.[39]

Now in 1928, as tyrannies, institutions, restraints seemed to be closing in on the freethinking, mobile, and heterodox individualist "in the name of frothy social theories or the deplorable slave morals of the gospels," Pound delivered a series of pronouncements to the young writer. First, he must get out of himself and begin to study the world around him:

> The young American writer (as apparent in mss. rejected by this office) suffers from lack of perception. Concern with his own, often quite uninteresting interior, cd. be with advantage replaced by observation of his milieu, not merely its otiose factors but the members of it having organic social function . . . no undergrad need lack a subject-matter while we still have congressmen. I strongly suggest our "fiction" writers occupy themselves with portraits of the *types* of humanity now permitted to govern America, congressmen, members of state assemblies, lobbyists, etc.
>
> As in Greek tragedy, the fate of kings was of more import than the

fate of a slave, so now the type of critter whose stupidity or lucidity functions in the social organism to the benefit, but more usually the malefit of his milieu is better literary matter than affairs of a few tired bar-flies and bar flutter-boys.[40]

Lenin, for example, ought to be of interest to the serious writer apart from his social importance: "He never wrote a sentence that has any interest in itself, but he evolved almost a new medium, a sort of expression halfway between writing and action. This was a definite creation, as the Napoleonic code was creation." [41] Second, the writer must work to eradicate the stupidities in governmental administration. He must oppose censorship, passports, State Department officials, and major parties as well as bad prose. All bureaucrats, especially, were to be dispensed with; in fact, "all bureaucrats ought to be drowned. All interference in human affairs by people paid to interfere ought to be stopped." [42]

Pound never explained how the writer was to escape political entanglement by engaging in a private war against the state. The writer simply had to be politically antipolitical or antipolitically political. But in the opinion of Michael Gold, who had begun to carp at *transition* about this time as a magazine "full of furious anarchistic spirit which has too few roots in world realities," the young writers had no such choice. Not only did he agree with Josephson that the writers must drop their aesthetic poses and abandon Bohemia; he also called upon them "to aspire to strength and discipline, in a world rapidly dividing into two great camps of Fascism and Communism!" [43]

To this invitation, few responded in 1927 and 1928. Why, he was asked, must we assume that only Communists can achieve strength and discipline, and not Bohemians and aesthetes? Any old mountebank, for that matter, might "turn from wealth, acclaim, and affection, and suffer untold agonies in order to foist upon the world a profitless nostrum." Gold was merely offering one pulpit gospel for another, "a political doctrine supported, like the political doctrines of Plato, Jesus, the Stoics, Judge Gary . . . by a profound faith in the value of individual rectitude . . . the doctrine of general wellbeing through personal salvation." [44] Josephine Herbst, who would soon switch to Gold's camp and then depart again, sardonically rejected his utopia as well as Josephson's as late as 1929:

All in all, I find the position of Mr. Josephson singularly like that of Mr. Gold. Both are hell bent toward a banalium, one communistic, the other mechanistic. Both utter hoarse cries to loyal cohorts, both point the finger of derision at other Pathfinders or rather deny that there is more than one Path. Pathfinder Josephson and Pathfinder Gold both paint enviable pictures of the promised land. Both have such jolly cohorts, such enthusiastic, robustious, forward looking companions in their steady tread toward the Soullenium. I can't make up my mind which gent is the better bet. Both are undoubtedly sound. There's not a question in my mind but that we're all headed toward some sort of bolognyum. Yours for the Aluminium.[45]

Another cynic, Robert Sage, pretended to see Gold's Communism as merely the latest literary fashion, and mockingly sketched the passage of the artist from the "Wildian esthete . . . with the silk knee britches, chrysanthemum and package of paradoxes" to the proletarian writer. His was a less serious history of intellectual vagabondage.

The Bohemian, said Sage, "wore a big black *chapeau d'artiste,* a flowing tie, a corduroy suit with pegtop pants, and a cape. He always froze in the winter, he lived on breadcrusts and coffee all the year around. . . . But how that boy could turn out masterpieces that were worth a million after he was dead!" Unfortunately, this type did not fit very well into practical America, and "with no other adequate model, the potential American artist was in a bad way for a while." Then Floyd Dell came. "Here was an article that was at the same time hot stuff and perfectly practical."

Dress didn't matter so much, as long as it was careless: the important thing was to be out of tune with the environment. One revolted against parents, religion, morals, the movies, the newspapers—anything that the simple-minded burghers held in respect. One saw strange powerful beauties in the things the other folks thought were ugly. One flirted with intellectual girls and discussed with them suffragism, birth control, the single moral standard and the outworn institution of marriage. One read a great deal of poetry and studied Marx and Freud. And one wrote about the intimate complaints of one's soul.

Now, said Sage, a new model has been unveiled: the artist as Communist.

Mr. Gold reveals to young men that if they want to be artists they must be workingmen. Anyone who reads the *New Masses* already knows, of course, that all workingmen have hearts of gold and are just so many diamonds in the rough, while the hypocrites who wear white collars are a pack of scoundrels. Therefore it follows that one has to go Left before one can have any serious hope of being an artist. One must have both feet on the ground, his shoulder to the wheel, his nose on the grindstone and his head anywhere but in the clouds.

This new artist of Mr. Gold's is going to hop out of his cot in the morning, full of vigor, don his work-stained clothes and dash off to the job to work shoulder to shoulder with other Reds who are doing big vital things, things that count. At night he will return reeking with sweat, heavy with fatigue, but happily drunk with inspiration. He will sit down at his bare table and, writing at top speed, turn out page after page of virile lyric literature—the real stuff. His works will come straight from the guts and he will scorn that attention to form and polish that those dilettantes over in Paris think so important. Here, says Mr. Gold, is the future artist of America, the coming Jack London or Walt Whitman!

Abandoning his jocular tone, Sage concluded with an admonition of his own. The real artist, he said, will ignore any orders "to go left, right, forwards, backwards, up or down." [46]

And so it turned out even for the writers who became Communists or Communist sympathizers. The majority, the talented and the untalented alike, never goose-stepped to party orders, but in the next decade a good many accepted uncritically and emotionally the party's diagnosis of society and world politics and were led, if not driven, by the party gods into red pastures.

FIVE · RUSSIA WITH (WITHOUT) RAPTURE

EASTMAN IN RUSSIA

EDITORIALIZING in *The Liberator* in the early winter of 1920 on the anarchist deportations, Max Eastman concluded that "our boast of superior liberty and regard for human rights is hollow and absurd." This "deliberate shipping back to Russia of a boatload of unsubmissive slaves," he wrote,

> explodes the romance that has hypnotized Europe for a hundred years, and that made Woodrow Wilson's great sanctimonious international swindle possible. It will never be possible again. The dreamers and revolters against tyranny are travelling East instead of West, and the eyes of all true lovers of liberty in all the world are turning in the same direction as they go.[1]

Eastman was referring to the culmination of A. Mitchell Palmer's campaign against "Bolsheviks" and "Red Bombers" in December 21, 1919, when the government deported 249 foreign-born "undesirables" on the steamship *Buford*. Some 199 of them were members of the allegedly subversive Union of Russian Workers. Of the remaining, forty-three were anarchists and seven were "public charges, criminals, or misfits." The two most notorious of the deportees were Emma Goldman and Alexander Berkman, anarchists with criminal records, but the overwhelming majority had never broken any laws or advocated terroristic measures. In general, the expulsion of the 249 met with an almost unqualified approval in the American press, and more "Soviet arks" were called for to preserve America from the Red pestilence.²

The liberal and radical magazines bitterly opposed the policy of deporting radicals, but by this time the minority who had spoken out against the formidable federal apparatus set up during the war to stifle dissenting thought exercised little influence. The Espionage Act of June 1917 and the Sedition Act of May 1918 practically guaranteed that any opposition to the *status quo* could be interpreted as traitorous. Far from protesting such acts, the majority of American intellectuals, teachers, and writers either held their tongues or worked with George Creel's Committee on Public Information to teach patriotism, conscript public opinion, and mobilize thought. "Never before in history," wrote Charles and Mary Beard, "had such a campaign of education been organized; never before had American citizens realized how thoroughly, how irresistibly a modern government could impose its ideas upon the whole nation and, under a barrage of publicity, stifle dissent with declarations, assertions, official versions, and re-iteration." ³

Eastman and his *Masses* staff, as well as his young protégés on *The Liberator,* reported the details of the wartime and postwar persecutions at their peril. The government had silenced *The Masses;* the Department of Justice raided *The Liberator* offices in 1922. The appeal of Communism to the young idealists of the early twenties can never be appreciated unless these hysterical days of official lawlessness are recalled.

This was the America Eastman was leaving in 1922 when he turned eastward in order to find out what was going on in the workers' republic.

Eastman by this time had completely repudiated his qualified support of Wilson, the man who he had once thought might become the militant leader "of the labor parties of the world," but he had never renounced Soviet Russia or the Communist movement. In 1919 he had supported the "hard" side of the socialists against the "soft" leadership of Morris Hillquit and Eugene Debs and took his stand with the Workers' Party of America, the extreme Left Wing of the American Communist movement. *The Liberator* endorsed the Third International and likened Marxism and Leninism to the discoveries of Copernicus, Kepler, and Newton. It dismissed phrases like "political democracy," "liberty," "suffrage," "responsible government," "free speech," "right of assembly," "the people," as liberal catchwords or "plausible ideologies" or "moralistic disguises" of a ruinous capitalism.[4]

By 1919 Eastman stood behind the faction of the Communist movement who wanted to form, in Eastman's words, "a revolutionary party adapted to American conditions, and capable of taking root in the American working class." This did not mean, as he insisted on many occasions, that the Americans should repeat Soviet methods or maintain an underground party, as many of the non-English-speaking Communists wished to do. He favored an independent party and an independent press.[5]

But while he minced no words with the American comrades, he was less than critical when he wrote of the great experiment beyond the ocean and rebuked the Right Wing Socialists who accused the Communists of trying to attach the Socialist Party to the Russian dictatorship. Authoritarian excesses in Russia he attributed to the accidents of Russian history and conditions, and he predicted that the temporary deprivation of civil liberties over there would ultimately mean a "more democratic world." He did caution the Russians against exerting undue discipline. The revolution would succeed, he felt, only if the leaders respected "the conditions of production" and "the hereditary instincts of men," if it were truly *scientific,* in short; yet he still saw Soviet Communism as a "scientific hypothesis in process of verification." [6]

The U.S.S.R., Eastman decided in 1922, had weathered its crisis, and he no longer felt obliged to devote all of his energies to the salvation of mankind. The "victory of Soviet Russia," he wrote to a friend, "has taken all the compelling anguish out of the temptation to sacrifice my creative life to the revolution. The whole scene is changed. It is well with the practical world, and I can live in the world of my thoughts." Now he could go to Russia and see if what he had been saying was true.

On board the S.S. *Olympic,* where he immediately began to write a series of what he hoped would be "simple and spontaneous" letters to his friends on *The Liberator,* Eastman entertained a few "counterrevolutionary" thoughts about the dangers of bigness, the tendency "to measure everything by extent and quantity." And he went on: "I feel sometimes as though the whole modern world of capitalism and communism and all, were rushing toward some enormous nervous efficient machine-made doom of the true values of life." [7] This outburst sounded more like the complaint of a Paris expatriate than the view of Lenin's American champion, but Eastman quickly resumed his role of Bolshevik commentator as he prepared to cover the international economic and financial conference to be held at Genoa in April 1922. Convened at the suggestion of the Russian Government to discuss the possible repayment of the Czarist debt as a way of obtaining recognition by the world powers, the conference also coincided with an Allied project to create an international consortium whose purpose it would be to develop Russian resources, stimulate European recovery, and enable Germany to meet her reparations payments. [8]

At Genoa, Eastman was charmed by the professional demeanor of the Soviet representatives and by their "Emersonian serenity," but he gave more space in his "letter" to a visit he made with Ernest Hemingway and an English correspondent to the home of Max Beerbohm in Rapallo. At almost the same moment, German and Russian representatives were clinching a treaty which effectively undermined the Genoa Conference, but Rapallo, Eastman wrote, "recalled us from our political to our literary selves." For the time being, Beerbohm interested him more than the Bolsheviks, and he found him "a serene and undisturbed aristocrat" untroubled "by the restless thought of democracy—the sense of the multitudes of authentic values that their wills create." Beerbohm refused an invitation to see the Russian delegates. They were men with "diagrammatic minds," he said, according to Eastman, and they had made a "mess" in Russia by ignoring the "obvious facts of human nature." Eastman's comment to his *Liberator* readers discloses how firmly he believed in Russia and her leaders in the spring of 1922. Beerbohm would be vexed by the delegates, he wrote, not because of their failures or their ignoring of facts, but

because they have minds equal to his own in point of humane culture, and superior in the scope of facts their science comprehends. It is because in order fully to understand what they are doing in Russia he would have to make a very youthful effort of intelligence. He would have to lift himself forward over a good span of years. He would have to put himself to school a little to those Bolshevik teachers.

For Eastman, the collapse of the Genoa Conference and the Russian-German Treaty of Rapallo proved once again the "instrumental intelligence" of the Russian dictatorship and the "hard-headed idealism" that had been his theme song in *The Masses*. The Soviet delegates were ready to make concessions, but not at the risk of jeopardizing their economy. To end business stagnation, they proposed the cancellation of Czarist debts and the "mutual limitation of armaments." And how did the bourgeois statesmen respond to this "clear drive of will and intellect into the future"?

. . . with neurotic denunciation, sentimental scolding, moralistic reminiscence, hypocritical concession, homiletical bombast, legal evasion, general fuss, fume, and bewilderment, and final complete impotence and inability to decide anything at all—except that the Russians must sit on the other side of the table.[9]

Eastman left Genoa more devoted than ever to the Bolshevist cause. He stayed in Italy for a while and ran into Albert Rhys Williams, on his way to Moscow, and Josephine Herbst, headed for Berlin. He joined them, and in Berlin, after some delay, he obtained his visa, which opened the gates to Russia and plunged him into the "future." The July issue of *The Liberator* announced that its readers could look forward to a "first-hand interpretation of the situation in Russia" by "the finest equipped reporter and travelling philosopher America could have sent there." [10]

Passing through Lithuania to Latvia, Eastman waited briefly in Riga and then crossed the boundary into Russia in September. His first impressions confirmed his high expectations. He saw a people's army whose purpose, he happily concluded, was to defend the working class, not the rich. He saw "a people brimful of energy and health." [11] He found Big Bill Haywood, who had jumped bail two years before and had fled to Russia, and the American Communist officials James P. Cannon and Max Bedacht. Rather plushly housed by Moscow standards and enjoying the life of a city still unplagued by spies and informers, Eastman, well received as editor of *The*

Liberator, proceeded to ingratiate himself with the Russian leaders by his speechmaking and poetry. He heard Lenin speak and was vastly impressed; and he urged Trotsky in bad French not to allow the American Communist Party to be directed by foreigners.

That fall and in the winter of 1923, Eastman perfected his Russian, read the Russian classics, and for the first time began to study Marx seriously. Now it occurred to him to write a biographical portrait of Trotsky, whose dynamism and brilliance had already captivated him. Anna Louise Strong, another American radical in Moscow, had made the same proposal, but Trotsky agreed to allow Eastman to do the book. For the next months, Eastman visited the War Office at intervals and conversed with his hero. A "portentous document" signed by Trotsky enabled him to travel wherever he wanted to go and interview anyone he wished to see.[12]

During the year and nine months Eastman stayed in Russia, much of the time spent in the reading room of the Marx-Engels Institute in Moscow, he resumed his study of Marxism and the scientific method. He had not come to Russia expecting the millennium, nor did he believe that revolution automatically produced "liberty." Revolution only allowed the idealists "to take the mockery out of the word, and enable those who love liberty to strive with sincerity and sound reason to produce the conditions which will make it possible." The dictatorship of the proletariat merely cleared away the barriers.

Yet one thing seemed to him "calamitously bad" about the Soviet experiment. The "sacred scriptures of Marxism" were taken as holy writ, not as science, and the Bolshevik theorist had only to apply the given theory to each new situation. "Instead of liberating the mind of man, the Bolshevik Revolution locked it into a state's prison tighter than ever before. No flight of thought was conceivable, no poetic promenade even, no sneak through the doors or peep out of a window in this pre-Darwinian dungeon called Dialectic Materialism." As Eastman put it later, "cerebral automatism" had taken the place of "reasoned inquiry." [13]

Trotsky's failure to act decisively and courageously following the death of Lenin in January 1924 was another disenchanting experience for Eastman. In May, a month before he left Russia, he attended the

party congress and observed how Stalin seized control of the bureaucratic machinery while the paralyzed Trotsky stood by and made no
fight to preserve "Lenin's trampled policies." It was at this convention that Trotsky told him of Lenin's last message to the party, his
"Testament," which Stalin and his henchmen had withheld from the
Central Committee. Eastman later told of his response to this dis-
closure:

"In God's name," I said, or words to that effect, "why don't you peel
off your coat and roll up your sleeves and sail in and clean them up?
Read the 'Testament' yourself. Don't *let* Stalin lock it up. Expose the
whole conspiracy. Expose it and attack it head on. It isn't your fight, it's
the fight for the revolution. If you don't make it now, you'll never make
it. It's your last chance." [14]

In the short time left before his departure, Eastman collected the
documents incorporated in *Since Lenin Died,* published the next year
in London. For the first time, Eastman wrote later, the outside world
was made privy to the quarrels within the Comintern and learned
how Trotsky, lacking Lenin's guile and strength, had been out-
maneuvered by the crafty Stalin. The issue between Trotsky and
Stalin, Eastman said then, was not whether or not the revolution
should go on in the capitalist countries or in Russia alone (both
men agreed that the revolution should continue simultaneously within
and without); rather, their mortal dispute hinged on the issue of
bureaucratic centralism. Trotsky tried and failed to carry on Lenin's
program for an increasing participation of proletarian groups in governmental affairs.[15]

But Trotsky disavowed Eastman's exposé of the Stalin "conspiracy," with its evidence that Lenin had designated Trotsky as his
successor and warned the party against Stalin, not because he hoped
to ingratiate himself with Stalin, but because he felt obliged to defend the workers' state even though his archenemy directed its destiny. Although Trotsky, at the request of his own supporters, soon
"disavowed his disavowal," for a time Eastman became the villain
of the Stalinist International. He still considered himself a Communist defending "the science of communism" against "the mystic
religion of the communist party," but on his arrival from Europe in

1927, his old political friends snubbed him on the streets. "I was a traitor, a renegade, a pariah, a veritable untouchable, so far as the communists were concerned." [16]

THE RED MOSES

A curious response to *Since Lenin Died* came from an old friend who had passed the mid-point in his life of "unlearning" and who had already decided that Soviet Russia represented the Future. His name was Lincoln Steffens, the mentor of Jack Reed, and he had spent some time in Russia on three separate occasions: in the spring of 1917, again in March 1918, when he served as an unofficial member of the unofficial Bullitt commission, and for the third and last time in the summer of 1923, when he traveled with Senator Robert La Follette, Robert La Follette, Jr., and the sculptor Jo Davidson.[17]

Steffens, vacationing in Switzerland with his new wife and infant son, gratefully acknowledged Eastman's book as "a fine example of clean reporting, clear thinking, and extraordinarily simple writing." He professed to be absolutely convinced by Eastman's revelations and felt that Communists on the outside would be no less persuaded. He himself had received letters from Moscow corroborating Eastman's testimony. But he was by no means sure that these facts should be made public in Russia, and he approved of Trotsky's tactic of repudiating his American disciple lest the revolutionary cause be discredited. "The fight," he wrote Eastman, "must be fought out within the party—the machine, as we used to call it—has to be supported, even as against Trotsky. It is liberalism to resent the injustice done to Trotsky, it is liberalism to feel as strongly as you do, I think, the crookedness of the methods of the bosses of the machine. These things are not worse, morally, than the red terror, which we have learned to understand." Steffens did not intend this comment as criticism. He merely wanted Eastman to answer a question that had been bothering him.

Would it not be better to assassinate Zinoviev and Stalin than to write this book of yours? How are men to deal with a situation like this, which rises in every such movement (and therefore is "natural" and typical), and yet hang on to the party as a weapon and tool of the revolution? . . . Trotsky is clearer than you are in his evident view that nothing must jar our perfect loyalty to the party and its leaders. Even as it stands, a menace not only to him and to the best of the followers of Lenin, but to revolution, it is the mainspring of the revolution and has to be identified with it—always. Or doesn't it? That is my question. How are we to beat Paul and keep from beating Jesus? [18]

This was not the first time such a question had been raised, and it continued to trouble a good many subsequent believers in the Cause, who worried from time to time whether or not the organizers truly spoke in the name of the Master. Good Communists, like good Democrats and good Republicans, prized party loyalty and supported the machine. But supposing the party no longer stood for apostolic principles? Renegades from the allegedly corrupted church risked the same obloquy they met when they renounced the corrupt world and followed Marx and Engels and Lenin.

Steffens, the seeker, was still too dazzled by his vision of the New Jerusalem to question the legitimacy of its hierarchy. His later references to the Trotsky-Stalin feud were a little vague, if not misleading. In his autobiography, he implicitly condoned the expulsion of Trotsky on the ground "that he broke the Bolshevik law against open debate" and said nothing about Stalin's ruthless quashing of the opposition, about which he presumably knew in 1925. He spoke of Eastman and his young Russian wife coming "direct from Russia with news and with light on the dark spots there." But the *Autobiography* appeared in 1931, when his convictions had hardened, and he was even less inclined than he had been in 1925 to worry over the misgivings of sentimental liberals. Because Steffens's book became "almost a textbook of revolution" and apparently helped to swing many writers and intellectuals to a pro-Communist or pro-Soviet position, the progress and development of his revolutionary convictions are worth looking at.[19]

Before 1917, Steffens had already paid his disrespects to the "good men" and "reformers" who blamed the failures of democratic society on the crooked politician. But the Russian revolution crystallized his case against the "righteous" and loosened his old ideas. In the process of becoming "de-educated," he cast aside liberalism for good.

He had become disillusioned, he wrote to an old reformer, Brand Whitlock, "but I am working along in a leisurely, unimportant way, upon my discovery that whenever I lose an illusion I can find in the facts that destroyed it a better, or at any rate another—illusion." What Steffens spoke of as his "discovery" (he liked to think of himself as the cool detached observer), another might describe as a conversion—an experience preceded by a period of brooding after the discarding of the liberal faith; the sudden "flash as I 'saw' it . . . of the wreck of my political philosophy in the war and the revolution, AND the threads of the new, and better, conceptions which lay mangled but traceable in the debris"; and then the thrilling awareness that he had traveled into the future, that at last he *knew*.[20]

Secure in his faith, Steffens could look unmoved at the boils and carbuncles on the Soviet body politic that sickened the squeamish liberals. These were temporary blemishes and would disappear. He had it on Lenin's own authority that the dictatorship did not carry with it "much risk of tyranny, as we know it," because the unavoidable terror was only a passing phase. "Don't minimize any of the evils of a revolution," Lenin told him. "They occur. They must be counted upon. If we have to have a revolution, we have to pay the price of revolution." [21] Yet beyond the curve of this revolution lay the Promised Land.

It was a pity, Steffens thought, that the architects and makers of the revolution were never permitted to enter the land of Canaan. History reserved that right only to the children untainted by associations with the past. A few who did catch a glimpse of the Promised Land, like Bertrand Russell and Emma Goldman, only saw it as "uncomfortable, illiberal and state socialism," instead of as a stage through which all revolutions must travel. What does it matter, Steffens would ask, if Emma Goldman or I get liberty? "An important thing is that Bolshevik Russia shall go through its tyranny patiently and arrive at liberty for the whole Russian people and perhaps for the world." [22] Revolutions, he concluded, were like storms that could be plotted; their movements and results could be predicted. The point was to study them and learn to mitigate their terrors.

Steffens declared that he hadn't the "organizing power" or the "sense of literary order" to write a book on the science of revolution, but he conveyed his vision in a historical parable which he called *Moses in Red* (1926), told, he wrote to a friend, in the light of the revolution, as a classic example of how a revolt of a people goes. Jehovah symbolizes Nature; Moses, the reformer and leader; Pharaoh, the king or the employer-capitalist; Aaron, the orator; and the Jews, the people.[23]

The Jewish revolution closely followed the pattern of the Russian revolution, or, for that matter, Steffens thought, all revolutions. Mob violence did not produce it; it was made by the unyielding masters, the obstinate Pharaohs. And the Jews themselves, these uneager instruments of God's work, were hardly prepared for their divine role. Imbued with the (wage) slave consciousness, they could not take to Moses' new laws until forty years of wandering had killed off the adults and left the children (who had "not learned the ethics of slavery but the fresh morals of the desert") [24] to enter the Promised Land. God wisely excluded even the old radicals and liberals of the Egyptian days and struck down Moses before he could cross the River Jordan. They, too, bore the Egyptian stamp.

Steffens wrote this book for the liberal reformers whose superstitious commitment to the old moralities brought on the revolutions they so desperately sought to prevent. He contrasted them with the Russians who thought scientifically and "big." Not, he hastened to add, that he relished their hardness and intolerance or enjoyed their company. They were self-righteous and unkind, "the damnedest set of stinkers I ever met," but they were also heroes, the vanguard of the Future, and he believed Russia would "win out" and "save the world." Steffens felt obliged to admire from the outside, corrupted as he was by "the easy life of the old culture." Like Moses, he was not fit for the Promised Land, but he pointed eastward and showed the way to idealistic young Americans tough enough to serve in the Communist legions. By the beginning of the thirties, he had stopped "thinking" about Communism and simply accepted it; Communism in Russia was something you either "got" or you didn't. "A big superficial survey is what I advise you to take now," he wrote to his young wife, Ella Winter. "Don't," he cautioned her, "fuss with such subjects as Trotsky and his fate and Stalin and his policies. Russia is not like that. Get at the policies and ideas of the government, of the

Communist Party." Russia was an elixir, a tonic which the "Youth
School" of writers (Hemingway and Dos Passos) would find more
exhilarating than alcohol. "You can take it, as it is, in the living form
of a people on the job, in a religion. Faith, hope, liberty, a living—
Russia doesn't need to drink." [25]

Several decades later, Max Eastman attributed Steffens's whole-
hog support of the U.S.S.R. to his wife, Ella Winter, "unmellowed
by experience" and "excessively positive." It was she, he explained,
who "captured" him and transformed him "during the decade left to
him, from a sentimental rebel preaching Jesus to both sides of the
class struggle to a hard-cut propagandist of the party line." Steffens's
letters, however, suggest that Eastman erred, for it was Steffens who
educated his young wife and taught her what to look for, and it was
she who sent back reports that confirmed what he already believed.

FREEMAN IN THE PROMISED LAND

In his *American Testament,* Joseph Freeman reported the following conversation with his then prosperous father. *Time:* the early
months of 1926. *Topic:* Freeman's dedication to radicalism, his inglorious future, and the present squabbles in Russia. (Freeman has
just argued that the new civilization will be "based on cooperative
effort.")

[Father]   "Nonsense, my boy. Every man looks out for Number One.
             I read in the papers that Trotsky is having a fight with his
             pals, who should play first fiddle in Russia. What's the dif-
             ference between that and Morgan?"
[Freeman] "The aim. The bolsheviks don't fill their pockets with the
             people's money. Their fight for leadership is a fight for prin-
             ciples, for policy. The personal ambition is secondary."
[Father]   "I read in the papers that your friend Max Eastman claims
             the Soviet government has fallen into the hands of crooks.
             You see, human nature doesn't change. When people get
             power, they lose their ideals."
[Freeman] "Trotsky says Eastman lies."
[Father]   "How do you know he lies?"

[Freeman] "Even if what he says is true, it makes little difference. The revolution is bigger than the man. The leaders of the French Revolution guillotined each other—but that revolution was later called by everybody the most progressive historic event since the rise of Christianity. The Russian Revolution is an even greater event—and the Russian leaders will not guillotine each other. The quarrels are part of the vast growing pains of a vast social transformation. What is our alternative? Capitalism, war, unemployment, poverty for the mass of the people. We live in an inferno. Think of what life has meant for most people in our times. The bolsheviks may be hard, they may make mistakes—but they are building a better world."

[Father] "All right, son. Go ahead with these noble fantasies. You're old enough to know what you're doing. Everyone in America is making money and living a normal life—and you are wasting your life on a wild-goose chase." [26]

Twenty-two years after the father had emigrated to America, the son was en route, not to Russia, but to the Union of Soviet Socialist Republics, to the first socialist republic in history. The distinction is important. Czarist Russia represented imperialism, autocracy, reaction, and (to hundreds of thousands of Jews) officially sponsored pogroms. The U.S.S.R. stood, Freeman felt in 1926, as "part of that international brotherhood which we were going to join sooner or later." [27] Although he had collaborated with Scott Nearing on *Dollar Diplomacy* (1925), a bristlingly documented exposé of American imperialism, and had thereby raised his stock among his party comrades, he failed to acquire a delight in statistics. The party leaders who distinguished "serious" work like *Dollar Diplomacy* from the trivialities of art had never read Clausewitz, but they instinctively followed his recommendation that a commander directing a battle must pay no attention to the sensuous beauty of the landscape. [28] Freeman remained covertly hostile to this dictum. For the moment, however, the never-ending struggle between poetry and politics was only smoldering, and Freeman waited impatiently for his visit to the transformed country of his birth.

A number of his friends had recently preceded him. Besides Eastman, Robert Minor, and Scott Nearing, there were Mike Gold, who had spent an intoxicating summer in Leningrad with some friendly anarchists; and Ruth Stout, editorial secretary for the recently founded *New Masses*. Freeman borrowed $600 from a trusting friend, quit his job on a news agency, "signed up as supercargo with a small freighter bound for Batum," and took off for Russia. He left a faction-ridden radical movement, and he himself was torn by doubts and contradictions. Russia, he hoped, would bring him into contact once more "with revolutionary reality." [29]

The very sight of "the first socialist republic" in May 1926 relaxed him. He no longer belonged to a despised and persecuted sect, or the "queer" and the "abnormal." Here, he was a part of a great army who were going to change the world. Here, there was no irreconcilable conflict between poetry and fact, and one could feel lyrical about oil cans, paint, leather factories, steel production, tea plantations, and cement. Traveling in stages from Batum to Tiflis, then on to Moscow via Baku, Nizhni Novgorod, and Stalingrad, Freeman began to get some perspective on himself and "our bright young literati at home" and came to the same conclusion as had Floyd Dell. The bourgeois intellectuals ridiculed or feared the machine because it seemed inimical to traditional literary themes, but it was capitalism, not the machine, that was at fault. The Soviets, he decided, had permanently solved the Jewish problem, eliminated ghettos and the possibility of pogroms.* Everywhere he saw polite

---

* An important consideration for the American Communists, who were trying to recruit membership among the Jewish working class and lower middle classes. Privately, Jewish party leaders and intellectuals were by no means so confident. Joshua Kunitz's monograph, *Russian Literature and the Jew* (N.Y., 1929), noted sadly how the vicious Jewish stereotype present in Russian literature from Pushkin on reappeared as the Jewish businessman or fake revolutionist in the twenties. Freeman's review of Kunitz's book in *The New Masses* (June 1929) noted that the prejudiced representations of the Jew after 1917 were confined to writers "with a Kulak viewpoint" and regretted that Kunitz did not make more of the Soviet removal of all civil disabilities against the Jew. Yet twenty-five years later, Freeman remarked in a letter that Stalin fought Trotsky, Zinoviev, Kamenev, and Radek "by an undercover anti-semitic campaign which roused the latent antisemitism of the mass not only against those old Bolos but against all Jews." In America, the Foster group attacked the Lovestone group during the twenties on the ground that "Lovestone, Bert Wolfe, Willie Weinstone were COLLEGE MEN—bourgeois!" and "that they were JEWS . . . this slimy campaign was conducted by word of mouth." Freeman to author, June 8, 1958.

policemen, comradely soldiers, idealistic young workers, wise old peasants. The villains he met occasionally turned out to be kulaks, dispossessed nobility, shifty relics of the bourgeoisie. To be sure, Freeman acknowledged in the thirties, he had come to the Soviet Union as a Communist sympathizer, but he had also come as an intellectual who retained deep in his heart an allegiance to the art and the values of the bourgeois world.

An American Testament is an unconvincing record of how Freeman exorcised these bourgeois demons, unconvincing because he could not, even as he told of his transformation into a good Bolshevik, be acceptably doctrinaire about the officially prescribed enemies of the U.S.S.R. or suppress his affection for ideologically tainted artists. But it shows the methods by which writers and intellectuals, once enamored with the socialist dream, were willingly disciplined by its interpreters.

Thanks to strong, assured, and sane comrades, the prototypes of the idealized party leaders and organizers who were celebrated in the Left Wing fiction of the thirties, Freeman learned not to talk "like a Greenwich Village poet," or to interpret the crimes and peccadilloes of comrades as a sign of Communism's failure. Communists were not all noble men, and it was sentimental liberalism to suppose so. Yet the party transcended its individual parts and ultimately resolved all disharmonies. "If you are a good bolshevik," an American representative to the Comintern told him, "no man, however highly placed, can hurt you for merely personal reasons. Don't you think," he continued, "that's something of an advance in the barbarous history of mankind?" Mistakes or "miscarriages," to be sure, could and did occur; people erred. But the party and the system of justice it stood for remained immaculate: "for *its* objective, as distinguished from bourgeois justice, was to destroy the exploitation of man by man, and to establish the classless co-operative society."

So Freeman apparently felt in 1926 (although he noted disquieting episodes that suggested a misplaced faith) and so he wrote a decade later during the high point of Communist influence in the United States. He was passing through the phase of the radical's intellectual pilgrimage in which he was still "bound to the humanism of the past" yet drawn to "the socialist society of the future." This precarious dualism, he told himself, could not be permanently sustained. Past and future could be fused only in the fire of the class struggle. John Reed had shown how the sincere idealist could be transformed by a courageous acceptance of reality and change from a protesting member of the bourgeois class into a full-fledged revolutionist, but most men of letters found it very hard "to shake off the old intellectual and moral prejudices." Even Mayakovski, whom Freeman had often seen and talked to, had not succeeded in becoming the "integrated communist," and the artists whose function it was to "refashion the souls of men" were still "poisoned by impure longings" for the "old and rotten."

If Freeman had been able to discover more examples of the "integrated" Communist among the writers he associated with at the Lux Hotel in Moscow, his doubts might have been more quickly assuaged and he might actually have become as sturdily untroubled as he appeared to be in his autobiography. But what he heard and observed at the offices of the Communist International, where he worked as a translator, and at the often "undisciplined" parties held at the Lux did not reassure him or lay his lingering doubts. Attending the funeral of F. E. Dzerzhinski, organizer of the Cheka, in Red Square, he saw Stalin and his close associates clustered on the top step of the speakers' stand and, below him, isolated from the rest, "Trotsky, also in a white rubashka, very pale, stiff, immobile, his leonine head proudly thrown back, straight as a soldier." Freeman did not miss the portentous implication. He was present, also, at social gatherings where Trotsky's adherents quarreled angrily with the supporters of the Central Committee, and although he favored the latter group, he disliked its steam-roller methods. Admitting the party is right and Trotsky is wrong, he argued then, isn't it dangerous to use Stalin's tactics? "Aren't we making it possible some day for those who are *wrong* to use the same tactics against those who are right?" [30]

He was witnessing other things in 1926 and 1927 that made him "wonder about the future of the vision." [31] His acquaintances were pretty well confined to Russian writers and critics and to an international radical Bohemian set who had not completely succeeded in changing themselves "into real communists" or transcending "their past in the aggressive present and luminous future." The writers he met through May O'Donnell—an Irishwoman in charge of his department at the Comintern—introduced him to contemporary Russian writing while he initiated them into the mysteries of H. L. Mencken, Carl Sandburg, James Branch Cabell, and Ernest Hemingway.* Through these literary contacts, Freeman collected material on Soviet writers (Isaac Babel, Boris Pasternak, Vladimir Mayakovski, Sergei Eisenstein, Boris Pilnyak, Vsevolod Meyerhold among them) later published in *Voices of October* (1930). Freeman gravitated to a circle of proletarian writers whose ideals and program seemed closest to that of *The Masses* and *The Liberator,* but he mingled with other literary coteries as well and had no feeling that Soviet writers in 1926 were being hounded by the authorities. And an even greater degree of spontaneous abandon seemed to obtain among his more intimate friends in the Lux.

In many respects, they reminded him of Hemingway's worldlings in *The Sun Also Rises,* "the lost generation of the revolutionary movement, corrupted by the war and by their bohemian heritage." There was something comic and poignant about this group, so temperamentally unsuited to the grimness of Russian politics and so unlike the wholesome proletarians prominently featured in the re-

---

* Among those whom he came to know very well were Ossip Beskin, a novelist and director of the foreign department of the State Publishing House; Ivan Anissimov, film critic; Nikolai Asseyev, a futurist poet; and, especially, a young critic, Serge Dinamov, and a professor of literature named Ivan Kashkin. The last two were American literature specialists. Freeman's friendship with Kashkin incidentally resulted in the introduction of Hemingway into Russia. Hemingway had contributed a couple of short pieces to *The Liberator* in 1922, one of them the sketch of the shooting of the Greek ministers in the rain. At that time, he was a Paris reporter and a friend of Max Eastman; the famous fight that ended with Hemingway punching Eastman in the jaw was more than a decade away. The publication of *In Our Time* made him famous almost overnight. Freeman admired the book enormously (he had spent an afternoon drinking with Hemingway at the Brevoort Hotel shortly after it came out), and loaned his copy to Kashkin, who quietly appropriated it. Kashkin's translation, which appeared in the bilingual magazine *Nash Put* (Our Way) introduced Hemingway for the first time to a Russian audience. The two men corresponded afterward. Hemingway commemorated the friendship in *For Whom the Bell Tolls,* in which one of the few sympathetic Russian characters is named Kashkin. (Freeman to author, June 18, 1958.) For an account of Hemingway's continuing popularity in the Soviet Union, see Columbia dissertation, *American Writing in Soviet Russia: 1917-1941* (1952), by Deming B. Brown.

ports sent home by enraptured Americans. To Floyd Dell, curious about the customs of love in the new society, Freeman communicated his impressions in verse and prose and entertained his cynical international companions with poetic reflections on the unchanging character of women, whether in capitalist America or in Communist Russia. H. G. Wells's epigram "I will not say that all women can be bought, but I do say that all women must be paid for" was accepted as an obvious truth by a number of already prominent and soon to be even more prominent Communists of the Lux. "For we all understood by this time," Freeman wrote many years later, "that nine years after the revolution there was *no equality*—and that just as 'bourgeois' girls preferred men with money so communist girls preferred men with power (we did not have the sense yet to see that money is, among other things, power and power is, among other things, money)." Freeman himself was half amused and half disgusted by the efforts of his girl to get him to "amount to something" in the movement. He was also bewildered. Did such motives operate in "the non-competitive, classless, skeleton society of human equals"? On the strength of his coauthorship of *Dollar Diplomacy,* she had him appointed without his consent to the Comintern's Commission on Imperialism.

Freeman never permitted the full import of his reveries to seep into his consciousness. It was enough to write verse in the style of Pound and Eliot as a kind of play, to joke about the opportunism and place-seeking of comrades, of Left Wing Madame Pompadours, of evenings when

> Tobacco smoke and vodka fumes
> float like mist across the table,

of hypocrites nodding and hopping "at Lenin's back." These sardonic poems, some of which appeared in *The New Masses* during its gay and undoctrinaire early phase, contained truths which Freeman at this time did not care to face. "In this way," he concluded later, "doubt dissipated itself in irony"—not in "the deliberate irony of the man who sees the truth frankly and without flinching, who is aware of what is what and who is who, and who uses irony as a device, necessary in this time and place, for uttering a truth." Rather, it was "the irony of the man who is confused by what is going on, who cannot tell the false and the true apart—and who says true things with a laugh and does so as much to placate his own doubts as to placate the piety of others." The corruption would sink and "the children of a wiser age than ours" would see the vision fulfilled.

One could believe this in 1926-27, for the great struggle between Stalin and Trotsky had not yet been resolved, "and no one dreamed, least of all Stalin's allies, that the Georgian who modestly styled himself Lenin's disciple" would destroy his enemies and "totally alter the course of the revolution and the nature of the vision." A few years later, by 1929 and 1930, no one dared to write irreverently about love in the U.S.S.R., and by the middle thirties, writers lost their lives by stepping out of line either deliberately or accidentally. In 1926, however, Freeman assured his American correspondents that the revolution would never devour its children. He could see the leaders of the opposition, reported executed in the bourgeois press, walking around in the Moscow streets, and the clash between Stalin and Trotsky (as he explained it a decade afterward in *An American Testament*) was not "the two 'elder sons' of the bolshevik family . . . fighting for the mantle of the dead leader" but "the collision of principles and social classes." [32]

Late in 1926, Freeman, in his capacity as one of the translators for the American delegation, attended the plenum of the Executive Committee of the Communist International. He heard Stalin state the case for constructing socialism in one country and listened to Trotsky, that "magnificent narcissist" (as he described him in 1936), drive himself "politically into a blind alley dank with counterrevolutionary spleen." This was Freeman's official view when he came to write his memoirs, but in 1926 he privately disbelieved the official interpretation of the inner-party crisis:

During that plenum in the Throne Room of the Kremlin at which I translated the last debate which Stalin and Trotsky were to have in the Comintern, I sensed with all my being that the conflict had little to do with the economic statistics and the quotations from Marx, Engels and Lenin with which the two great opponents belabored each other;

I felt this was a *personal* war; yes, our fate, the fate of the Movement, the Revolution and the world was being determined by the furious, implacable battle of two men, diametrically opposed by nature in every possible way, fighting for "executive power." . . . But this was heresy! When I returned to the news agency in New York in the summer of '27 and said that Stalin and Trotsky envied each other and that the conflict between them was a personal conflict for priority, for dominion, I was ridiculed—and seriously condemned, too—as a "petit bourgeois" intellectual and a "Freudian"; for every good "Marxist" knew that personal factors play no role in history whatsoever; everything is determined by economics. They talked me down and, without giving up my thoughts, I kept them to myself and put them in my poems; but if I had had the courage of my convictions—and if I had known and understood more, I would have foreseen there and then that the dogma that personality counts for nothing in history would lead to the cult of personality; and what that dogma really meant, as it turned out, is that *you* don't count and *I* don't count and *our neighbors* don't count and most of us must be content to be as they had not been—but HE, the great, brilliant, genial Leader, the most colossal thinker and hero of all times, HE counts all the time in everything.[33]

Freeman bottled up his reservations when he returned to the United States and took his place in the Communist movement. He wrote about himself, and he believed it, that he could transcend his private aims, that he was reacting violently "against the lyricism and romanticism of my past life." But the inward struggle between his literary loyalties and the claims of the "selfless, incorruptible" party had already been tacitly resolved.

One could be an artist and a revolutionary, he decided, without violating artistic integrity. The epic films of Eisenstein, the productions of Meyerhold, the poetry of Mayakovski projected the socialist vision in images that Freeman could accept. And these Russian friends, unlike his New York comrades, urged him to write poetry, to make literature his career. They did not think he was cut out for politics, and having seen politics in its most naked form in the Throne Room of the Kremlin, he was convinced that his friends were right. His decision not to rejoin the Communist Party when he returned to New York in the summer of 1927 was his way of announcing his new position. Henceforth he would serve the Cause but in his own way and on his own terms.

SCOFFERS AND SKEPTICS

By 1928 only a tiny percentage of American intellectuals looked to the U.S.S.R. for guidance and salvation, although an increasing number regarded it as an unprepossessing or encouraging harbinger of the future. Spengler's prediction (noted by Freeman in a letter to Irwin Edman in 1920) that a great new civilization, embodied by Russia, would arise in the East was being repeated with even greater insistence in the early and middle twenties. Writing to *The Dial* in 1923, Hugo von Hofmannsthal spoke of the mingled thrill and terror with which the Germans contemplated "the spectre of Bolshevism" and the birth of a new and terrible world. The American, he predicted, would soon feel the same way:

In some day not far off, with the keenness of a besetting fever, with the poignancy of a dream, and the oppression of a nightmare, he will become conscious that all these European matters are by no means things of an unrelated past, but the living and fermenting present, a ferment in which so tremendously much of the past is a factor. He will see that this European present is also his American future, from which there is so little chance of his withdrawing himself or withdrawing his great young sea-encircled continent.

And Thomas Mann, four years later, suggested in his letters to the same magazine that a new society was emerging of which the bourgeois world with its cult of "art" and "poetry" had no knowledge. Almost every day during the twenties, an article or essay appeared in the American newspaper and periodical press attacking, defending, analyzing, or describing the U.S.S.R.[34]

Most of these reports and comments were prejudiced and misinformed or uncritically enthusiastic, but some of them were intelligently hostile, like John Maynard Keynes's reflections on the new Russia that appeared in *The New Republic* in 1925. Leninism, he said, combined two things that the West had kept distinct: religion and business. The Soviet leaders, moreover, a group of ruthless idealists, subordinated the latter to the former. "To say that Leninism is the faith of a persecuting and propagating minority of fanatics led by hypocrites," he continued, "is, after all, to say no more nor less than that it *is* a religion and not merely a party, and Lenin a Mahomet, not a Bismarck." But for a man brought up free of religion, Russia was detestable. He could sympathize with those seeking to find "something good in Soviet Russia"; he could put up with the physical discomforts. But he opposed a society that suborned spies and set up as a Bible an obsolete economic textbook that exalted a boorish proletariat over the intelligentsia. Communism as an economic system, he concluded, had nothing to contribute, but as a religion it possessed an elation and confidence that modern capitalism—"absolutely irreligious, without internal union, without much public spirit"—no longer had. To defeat Communism, capitalism would have to be many times more efficient and perhaps more religious. In Russia, despite its oppressiveness and stupidity, the people really believed they could solve their problems, and Keynes did not rule out the possibility that they would succeed.[35]

This note of hope for Russia's future on which Keynes ended his unfavorable appraisal could be detected in the writing of American intellectuals who commented on the Great Experiment from time to time. The avant-garde found little that was exhilarating on the Russian cultural front * but, as one of them observed, the Bolsheviks might atone for the crimes of Czarist imperialism and the Soviet experiment might prove "to be a tonic-purgative for an over-sophisticated, cynical, senescent, cunningly complicated world of individualistic enterprise, a world which has long since solved the problem of adequately producing wealth, but falters at the task of finding satisfactory methods for controlling and justly equalizing its distribution."[36] What if the Bolsheviks did idealize Western technology and

---

* A contributor to *transition* wrote in 1928: "Russia interests me but little. I think that it will become a sort of fat, complaisant, second-rate United States. It is rapidly adopting the American economic vision because the revolution cleared a way for it. When the country becomes properly Americanized, say in fifty years, it will be producing hoards and hoards of Russian Harold Bell Wrights and Edgar Guests, while the one time Dostoievskys will have become merely classical legends, like Shakespeare in England today. I do not expect to live long enough to see anything but trash out of the metamorphosis. The country will become industrialized, radioized, movieized, and standardized, the huge population of illiterate peasants will be taught how to read advertisements, newspapers, and bibles, the country will placidly settle down to the preoccupation of money grubbing" (pp. 100-01).

worship Lenin, Lewis Mumford asked. They had "created a society which endeavors to maintain the rigorous justice of the shipwreck, even if it lacks the easier egalitarianism of a picnic," and the idealization of mechanical labor was preferable to idealizing the Romanovs. The Bolshevik mind was not un-Western, Mumford declared, nor could he take seriously the bogy of the new collective man. "The human mind is capable of projecting all sorts of false notions— demons, archangels, witches, pain-and-pleasure personalities, Gradgrinds, Robots, Babbitts and mechanized non-individuals; but in the long run these ideas and projections lose their efficacy, and the richer, organic personality which belongs to all of us emerges at last, and modifies or destroys these false notions." [37]

Doubtless few if any of the American literary "exiles" still residing in France by the late twenties would have cared to exchange Paris for Moscow, but they could see as early as 1926 that the onetime Dadaists had "given their allegiance to Moscow" and that, in Paul Morand's words, "the most abstract, individualistic, and egocentric of writers can be brought sooner or later to emerge from his isolation and enter the fray." Expatriates and former expatriates no longer sympathized quite so unqualifiedly with Pound's obstinate clinging "to an obsolete political idealism" or felt the same nostalgia for the "romantic looking-backwards to medievalism" that informed the *Cantos* of Pound. They now began to write approvingly of the tough young Soviet novelists and poets, tempered by "war, revolution, counter-revolution, starvation," who had dispensed with "dreamers" and "decadence." These strong men, Bernard Smith explained in *transition,* were not "tough" in the manner of "the American middle-class playboys." They indulged in no fantasies, nor did they set down the brutality and selfishness of life in order to appear hard-boiled. As yet, he conceded, the Soviets had produced no master, but they had energy, humanity, and ideas. [38]

In America, the old skeptic, Theodore Dreiser, published his impressions of Russia gained from an eleven-week trip through the Soviet Union that he took in the late fall of 1927. At a farewell dinner tendered to him shortly before his departure, Dreiser publicly regretted the fall of the Romanovs and expressed a nostalgia for monarchy. His well-wishers laughed this off as an amiable weakness, but they must have been a little relieved when his book, stuffed with unanalyzed documents thoughtfully provided by the Soviet authorities, appeared in 1928.[39]

Although a self-declared "incorrigible individualist—therefore opposed to Communism," Dreiser in general approved of the regime and its program. He deplored the absence of creature comforts, the execrable cooking, the Muscovite's inexhaustible tolerance of dirt and disorder, and, most of all, "the inescapable atmosphere of espionage and mental as well as social regulation which now pervades every part of that great land." Yet despite the government's incessant propaganda and terroristic practices, Dreiser was convinced that it enjoyed the allegiance of the majority and he sympathized unreservedly with the goals of its leaders. Here was a government, he wrote, that is "actually awake to and enthused by the possibilities of the human mind as a creative instrument that, freed from dogma and slavery of every kind, is likely to lead man away from ignorance and misery to knowledge and happiness." He approved of the easy divorce laws—"merely a declaration of intention to separate . . . no shyster lawyers, nor overcrowded courts with sociologically uninspired judges, nor priests with ceremonies and sacraments that cost and bring money into the exchequer of a fat loafing hierarchy of religious sooth-sayers." (Dreiser's vehement anti-Catholicism made the Communist position on the church very congenial to him and may very well have been one of the principal inducements that ultimately drew him into the party.) He had only praise for Soviet theories on education and the family.[40]

In short, Dreiser was astounded and touched by the audacity of the Russian experiment from which would come, he felt, certain great practical and intellectual experiments. "I wouldn't trade my trip here for any previous experience," he wrote home in November, 1927. "It is new and I have gotten a light on certain things which are not visible in America. The difference in the two lands and temperaments make them invisible there." [41]

John Dos Passos, the "Amerikanski Peesatyel," reporting from Moscow in December 1928, shared Dreiser's doubts and hopes about the society beginning to take shape in the seething chaos of the people's republic. Seven years earlier, he had visited Tiflis, when the "communists in Moscow" were "still struggling ahead on the thorny path to Utopia." This was the period of the NEP. The government was tending, he felt, "more and more towards a confused and un-theoretical attempt to conserve what's left of the old civilization. My impression is that communism in Russia is a dead shell in which new broader creeds are germinating; new births stirring are making themselves felt, as always, in people's minds by paroxysms of despair. Communism and the old hierarchy of the Little Father both belong to the last generation, not to the men who have come of age in the midst of turmoil. It is they who will re-create Russia." Dos Passos in 1921 did not conceal his concern over the terroristic methods of the Cheka and the brutalities of Soviet justice, but, like Dreiser, he declared that "in spite of the new sort of tyranny," it was plain that "the mass of the people have infinitely more opportunities for lead-ing vigorous and unstagnant lives than before the revolution." [42]

In 1928 events occurring in his own country had toughened his revolutionary socialism, but a second look at the U.S.S.R. had not resolved all his misgivings about Soviet Communism. The woman, a theater director, who had come to see him off had one question to ask him on behalf of the young performers in her company. "They want you to show your face," she said. "They want to know where you stand politically. Are you with us?" He could not give a straightforward reply. The new and the old still jostled each other in his mind. He caught the despair and the nostalgia of the old, the youth and force of the new, and wondered if a mere writer, a gatherer of impressions, could ever do any more than to set down "picture postcards" without the knowledge and feelings "that have been trained into the muscles, sights, sounds, tastes, shudders that have been driven down into your bones by grim repetition, the modula-tions of the language you were raised to talk." The promise was still there, and so was the terror: the lesson of Kronstadt, the grinding down of the Trotskyists, the whispered stories of night arrests. Russia meant pigsties and icons and assembly lines and singing soldiers of the Red Army and "any untrampled unfenced section of the earth's surface where men, tortured by the teasing stings of hope, can strain every apprehension of the mind, every muscle of the body to lay the foundations of a new order." [43]

"HAIL! RED YOUTHFUL GIANT"

To the small body of convinced Communists in the United States, the Soviet republic by 1926 was no longer an experiment, but an unqualified success in social planning, "as fresh, as new and beautiful," wrote the enraptured Mike Gold, "as first love." [44]

He had made his first pilgrimage in 1924 and had come back to New York enormously refreshed. He had not expected Utopia, but he found he could relax in a place "so primitive, so easy going, so goodnatured." He went on to explain to Upton Sinclair, then planning to visit Russia himself, that "one sheds one's years there."

You will get a royal reception there, and it will heal many of the sore places that America produces in all rebels. One feels so normal and strong in Russia; and all things one only theorizes about here and feels a little bitter and savage in defending, are so simple and real in Russia. It's a great new amazing place, everything beginning, life young and hopeful and strong . . . it is the earth and not heaven; the earth in the throes of the birth of a new race of giants.

Nothing had ever stirred him so deeply, nothing in America or Europe or Mexico, "as hum-drum Russia at its business of bringing in Communism." [45]

Hailing the ninth anniversary of the Soviet republic two years later, Gold compared it to the Athens of Pericles, the England of Shakespeare, the France of Danton, and the America of Whitman. To be sure, there were the "heartburnings, defeats, defeats." The Russians were fighting "a realistic battle with ignorance, greed, imperialism, and conservatism," but after nine years it had become the nation of artists, scientists, and workers, and was "the greatest victory in world history."

Hail! red youthful giant, as you go marching and singing out of the tragic present into the glorious future! Our deepest hopes are centered in you, our right arms are yours to command, our life is your life. You have killed the dogma of capitalism as surely as the French revolution killed monarchism. Hail! [46]

Convinced himself that the U.S.S.R. had built the Co-operative Commonwealth, but that Americans, and especially American writers, were deplorably ignorant of its heroic achievements, Gold tried to tell Young America how it could learn far more from the dynamic laboratory of Russia than it could from the "café-culture" of France. The French revolution, he pointed out, ushered in not only a political revolution, but a cultural revolution as well. It had inspired Wordsworth, Shelley, Byron, Blake, Leigh Hunt, and Hazlitt. So also would the Russian revolution metamorphose the writer and shame him out of his introspective morbidities.[47]

Until Stalin converted the literary practitioners into a public information army of the Soviet state, a kind of perpetual Creel Committee, the American defenders of Communist culture had every reason to be optimistic. The "Resolution on Literature" adopted by the Political Bureau in July 1925, just four months after Lenin's death, announced a hands-off policy toward the rival literary groups then contending among themselves. To be sure, the party brooked no overt attacks against the regime, nor could it condone "neutral art in a class society," but it spoke out strongly against "all pretentious and semi-illiterate 'Communist conceit' " and denied itself the right to grant one literary faction a monopoly of publication. "The Party," read the resolution which Stalin signed with the others, "should declare itself in favor of the free competition of various groups and tendencies in the field of literature. Any other solution to the question would be quasi-bureaucratic." [48]

Gold's emphasis on the "titan artists" in the Soviet Union who were "grappling with the Machine Age" implicitly contradicted a trend of thought emanating from Berlin and Paris: that Russia acted as "the advance guard" of "a bolshevized Asia" soon destined to envelop the West. Anatol Lunacharsky, the Commissar of Education in Soviet Russia, had persuasively attacked this widespread notion, entertained by both the friends and enemies of the U.S.S.R., as a "faddish craze" akin to Negrophilism in the United States. The Russian revolution, despite the Spenglers and the "blatant and noisy crowd of Orientophiles," did not signify "the decline of the West," Lunacharsky declared, and "flirting with the mystic idea of Asia" ill became the "friends of the proletariat and the Russian revolution."

The Russians were "first of all Europeans," and the aim of the U.S.S.R. was "not to Orientalize Europe, but rather to Europeanize Asia," first by emancipating the colonial peoples from capitalist domination and then incorporating all peoples into a humane international order.[49]

To Gold and his associates, the symbol of the cultured Europeanized Russian artist-leader, "almost as universal as Leonardo da Vinci," was Leon Trotsky. His remarkable *Literature and Revolution,* published in 1926 (just after what Joseph Freeman hopefully but inaccurately described as the "political rumpus raised by the Opposition" [50] had publicly subsided), was the manifesto of a sophisticated revolutionist. Trotsky was the ideal mediator between the intelligentsia and the party, the artists and the people. Learned, sophisticated, satirical, arrogant, his polemical manner suggested the literary hooliganism of Ezra Pound and the lyricism of a poet-prophet. If he readily and sarcastically rebuked the romantics and individualists who still hankered for the defunct past, he understood the reasons for their "servile" self-preoccupations and wrote even more sardonically about the sentimental propagandists of proletarian art who wanted to dispense with bourgeois art while the masses were still culturally immature.

What distinguished men like Lenin, Trotsky, and Lunacharsky from Stalin and his intellectual praetorians was their belief that the revolutionary government ought to condone all artistic groups not actively counterrevolutionary. Trotsky's contempt for the individualist "who wishes to replace the whole world with himself" did not signify a denial of personal uniqueness. He simply meant that individuality was less a matter of self-assertion than it was the expression of self through a blending of personal and institutional elements.[51]

Here was a great military leader, an industrial organizer and financial expert, Gold noted admiringly, who spoke six languages, wrote intelligently about Freud, published articles and books on international politics, the Einstein theory, and Chinese history, and who kept up with the literary avant-garde. Of most importance to Americans, Gold thought, was Trotsky's scientific approach to literature and his dexterous use of the "tools of the Marxian methodology." Whereas American critics engaged in literary conversation and resorted to the "bouquet of criticism" or "kick in the rear" school of criticism, Trotsky's masterly literary survey of the postrevolutionary years exposed the class roots of the various literary coteries and the progressive or reactionary tendencies of their respective programs. "It is strange and amusing," Gold said, "to meet all the familiar slogans and evasions of American literary specialists in Trotsky's pages." Like their American prototypes, some of the Russian writers were "the priests of the esthetic God" or "servants of a divine class-less mystery," who reverted to their class origins when confronted by the class struggle.[52]

The Left writers in America during the late twenties derived a double benefit from the Soviet articles on art and literature. They quoted and discussed the literary opinions of influential Soviet leaders in order to correct the Philistine attitudes they discovered in the American Communist Party and as proof to the skeptical middle-class intellectuals that socialism distinguished between Bohemian deca-dence and the genuinely creative. When Joseph Freeman quoted Bukharin's warning that proletarian poets must not become "organ-izers and politicians *at the cost of studying life,* at the cost of *self-development,*" that the party did not want "walking saints even of the proletarian type who think it is their duty to kiss machines," he was tacitly criticizing the literary zealots in his own camp and telling the unaffiliated writer that he need not immolate his individuality in the Cause or stop having fun.[53] Russian writers drank, a *New Masses* editor wrote back from Moscow in 1928, but they drank better liquor than the Prohibition brew available to American writers. They also danced ("in spite of counter-revolutionary rumors to the contrary") the fox trot and the Charleston ("rather more vigorously and jerkily than we do").[54]

A relatively small number of Americans were tempted to see for themselves or to follow the direction of Gold and Freeman, but a refined and classically pessimistic professor of literature, Joseph Wood Krutch, mournfully conceded in 1929 that perhaps the future did lie in Russia. *The Modern Temper* summed up the doubts and despair of a generation that, according to Krutch, had rejected abstract con-ceptions of patriotism, love, self-sacrifice, respectability, and honor, and had lost its belief in the greatness of man and the tragedy of life.

Russia, Krutch believed, had not yet passed through the "debilitating stages of culture"; its people had a terrible but simple optimism and could bypass the problems that plagued the West: individual salvation and the psychology of the soul.

The image of a raw vibrant nation teeming with a vigorous happy people who were, excepting some unimportant physical discomforts, free from the economic and spiritual malaise afflicting the capitalist countries was to become a familiar stereotype in the decade to come.

PART TWO

·

THE

APPEAL

OF

COMMUNISM

In his epilogue to *Exile's Return,*
Malcolm Cowley described the joyless and desperate New Year's Eve
parties that ushered in the Depression decade. One of his friends,
after a night of party-going, "found himself in a strange sub-cellar
joint in Harlem. The room was smoky and sweaty and ill-ventilated;
all the lights were tinted green or red, and, as the smoke drifted
across them, nothing had its own shape or color; the cellar was
likely somebody's crazy vision of Hell; it was as if he was caught
there and condemned to live in a perpetual nightmare." Out of this
Tartarus, this capitalist nightmare, his friend stumbled into the harsh,
cold, ugly, but clear light of a new day and a new era.

Cowley did not say that he and his friends were "reborn" in the
religious sense, but their change in attitude, their exhilarating insights, their resolving of plaguy contradictions, followed the classical
formula of the conversion experience. For one thing, it meant the
end of romantic dichotomies: art and life, intellectual and Philistine,
poetry and science, contemplation and action, literature and propaganda. The collapsing world and the new faith made such distinctions
impertinent. Now Cowley demanded a humanistic art that would
transform the rapidly changing world into myth without neglecting
"the splendor and decay of capitalism and the growing self-awareness

of the proletariat." No longer could the artist hold aloof from the class struggle. To do so involved the risk of "blinding and benumbing" himself. Embracing the cause of the workers might cut him off from his culture and his class; yet an alliance with the untutored and the dispossessed would put an end "to the desperate feeling of solitude and uniqueness that has been oppressing artists for the last two centuries." [1] He had come, in the words William James used to describe Tolstoy's conversion, "to the settled conviction . . . that his trouble had not been with life in general, not with the common life of common men, but with the life of the upper, intellectual, artistic classes, the life which he had personally always led, the cerebral life, the life of conventionality, artificiality, and personal ambition. He had been living wrongly and must change." [2] Cowley predicted "great days ahead for artists" if they survived the struggle, kept "their honesty and vision," and learned "to measure themselves by the stature of their times." [3]

Conservatives interpreted the literary turn to the Left as a new fad or as a conversion to "the Gospel of St. Marx." Radicals attributed the politicizing of the writer to economic necessity. Neither was wholly wrong, although each simplified the process. Personal inadequacy, the need to conform, the disease of careerism also drew writers into the radical movement. But the radical impulse before and after 1930 sprang from the motives that had prompted good men in all ages to denounce, in Hawthorne's words, "the false and cruel principles on which human society has always been based."

The elation and hope that stirred Cowley and his friends did not outlast the decade. They learned, like the narrator of *The Blithedale Romance,* "the most awful truth in Bunyan's book;—from the very gate of heaven is a by-way to the pit!" Yet after they had resigned from the Party of Hope, they might also have said with Hawthorne's disenchanted poet and would-be Utopian, "Whatever else I may repent of, therefore let it be reckoned neither among my sins nor follies that I once had faith and force enough to form generous hopes of the world's destiny." [4]

It is not hard to understand why many writers who were once fascinated by Soviet Communism but who ultimately became disenchanted should now feel the need to divulge the "baser drives" that made the "Soviet myth" so appealing and to play down the objective reasons for their temporary aberration.[5] The apostate must confess his delinquencies if he sincerely wishes to be readmitted into the American Establishment, and many liberal intellectuals felt obliged to seek absolution, to explain to the world and to themselves why they had been deluded into excusing the deceptions and cruelties of a false faith.

Unquestionably, a number of them entered the movement for less high-minded reasons than they supposed. No man, as Jonathan Edwards knew, is immune to "the labyrinthine deceits of the human heart." Yet who in retrospect can deny that the situation at home and abroad during the thirties justified a critical appraisal of the social and the political order? Who can question the sincerity and magnanimity of those hundreds of artists and intellectuals who took upon themselves the task of saving mankind from poverty and war? Communism's appeal can never be understood if it is considered merely an escape for the sick, the frustrated, and the incompetent or a movement of fools and knaves. Not the "aberrations of individuals" drew men to Communism in the 1930's, but the "aberrations of society." [6]

The Great Depression, with its hunger marches, its Hoovervilles, its demoralized farmers, its nomads and park sleepers, its angry workers, its joyless youth and bankrupt entrepreneurs was not the projection of sick personalities. The writers who wrote about bread lines, for whom evictions were "an every-day occurrence" and the furniture of the dispossessed "a common sight in the streets," [7] and who described in novels, poems, and plays the economic and moral breakdown of middle-class families did not get their instructions from Moscow. As might be expected, they dramatized their private difficulties and expressed, often with more passion than felicity, their feelings of outrage at what they saw with their own eyes.

Other writers before them had made literary capital out of the sordidness and violence in American life. Stephen Crane's sketches of human misery, Frank Norris's unclinical studies in degeneration, Upton Sinclair's stomach-turning descriptions of the Chicago stockyards, and Jack London's catastrophic visions of revolution had already documented some of the unsmiling realities. This was the first time, however, an entire literary generation explored so relentlessly those areas hitherto ignored by the majority of their predecessors. After 1929 it was hardly necessary for the social writer to work up his subject matter in libraries; history collaborated with his designs, and every day's newspapers furnished him with a thousand themes.

For this, as Edward Newhouse explained in his novel *You Can't Sleep Here* (1934), was not the "lost generation," but the "crisis generation," disburdened of some of the moral problems that had obsessed their elders but just as troubled and guilty as the generation of Hemingway and Faulkner. It consisted of the young people who had to live with their parents because they "had never been absorbed into industry or the professions"; of recent college and high-school graduates who knew with painful certainty that the economy had no place for most of them.[8]

Whether the writer chose for his subject the lives of the "Bottom Dogs," the adventures of young Irish delinquents, the "Neon Wilderness" of Chicago's North Side Poles, the Negro slum dwellers, the poor East Side Jews, Georgia "crackers," California fruit pickers, toilers on the Detroit assembly lines, Gastonia's textile workers, decaying Southern families, rebellious farmers, department-store wage slaves, or "boxcar" hoboes, it was the Depression itself, impersonal and ubiquitous, that gave meaning to their specific documentations. If much of the so-called "proletarian" writing violated almost every literary canon and if to many it positively reeked with the Depression, the best of it managed to objectify the social forces as they operated in the lives of real people.[9]

In contrast to the dreary scenes of capitalism in decline, Russia during the early thirties seemed a hive of happy industry—not only to its well-wishers, but also to a large number of unideological observers. Confronted with what appeared to be a social and economic breakdown in their own country, a good many Americans were powerfully affected by the well-publicized achievements of the U.S.S.R., where history "was acting like a fellow-traveler." They contrasted the unemployment, the labor violence, the social disorders, the widespread despair in the United States with the energy and hopefulness of the Soviets. "The contrast," wrote Arthur Koestler, "between the downward trend of capitalism and the simultaneous steep rise of planned Soviet economy was so striking and obvious that it led to the equally obvious conclusion: They are the future— we, the past." [10]

Joshua Kunitz found it impossible to communicate his deep feelings of joy and excitement in beholding busy bustling Moscow in the summer of 1930. The hardships persisted, the food shortages, the dearth of consumers' goods, but at least there was no unemployment, and the people were heroic.[11] Five years later, he could scarcely find words to describe the miraculous transformation that had occurred between his first and last visits:

> The entire trip has been one continuous gasp of wonderment. The excellent shops, splendid window displays, asphalted streets, cars, trucks, buses, glittering new trams and trolley buses—noise, movement, snappy traffic cops, innumerable parks of culture and rest—young trees, flowers all along the main streets in all cities I visited—cars, ties, felt hats, European clothes, dance halls, cafes, new schools, new sanitoria and the universal spirit of song, joy and creative effort—these all one must see and experience really to believe.
>
> The Moscow subway is not an isolated phenomenon: it is merely a superb symbol of the beautification of life that is proceeding at an inconceivable rate all over the USSR. The Soviet peoples are reaping the results of their superhuman labor and great initial sacrifices in industrializing and collectivizing the country. And this is just beginning.[12]

Other friendly visitors to the Soviet Union, as well as Kunitz himself, were by no means oblivious of the blights and blemishes in the Socialist Eden. Waldo Frank, for example, worried a little about "intellectual absolutism" in Russia, but he went on to say, "perhaps the want of flabby relativism which goes by the name of liberalism in the West and which is so often nothing but a want of conviction, is not an unmixed evil." [13] So far as he was concerned, the West was culturally finished, and many "friends" of the U.S.S.R., enraptured by the poetry of Soviet statistics and depressed by the inability of the American Government to cope with the crisis at home, were ready to agree that the future might belong to the "greasy muzhiks" and their canny leaders.

In America, the government turned its troops against the Washington bonus marchers. Had three thousand bourgeois marchers descended on the Kremlin, Malcolm Cowley wrote in 1933, "They would be efficiently suppressed (not executed; the day of mass executions has passed in Russia). What would happen if 3,000 proletarians marched on the Kremlin? They wouldn't do so, because the Soviets are their own government. But if they ever did march, the government would yield to them, or cease to be communist." [14]

Just as the Russian worker entered joyously into the mighty schemes of the new socialist commonwealth, so the Russian writers, the literary "shock troops," were also pictured as eager participants in the task of socialist reconstruction. Unlike their unemployed and unhonored equivalents in America, they were valued by the state and closely tied to their vast readership. Faced with the bewildering changes in daily life, they found, according to Kunitz, the newspaper incomparably more fascinating than the fairy story. They discovered the poetry of fact, the magic of collective farms and tractor factories. It was not enough for them to reflect life; they had to mold it as well. [15]

Amidst these "cultural crusaders in the service of the Revolution," American writers sometimes felt a little apologetic, a little humiliated to be introduced as mere students of literature. So Isidor Schneider felt when he "admitted shamefacedly" to a machinist in a Moscow park "that I was a writer." As Americans, they could not share the intoxication that came with the knowledge that one was a part of a gigantic idealistic enterprise. Commenting on the literary life of Moscow in 1935, Matthew Josephson described it as "the *ville lumière* which was Paris," a center of activity, creation, and joy. The exiles who crowded the city joined with people instead of "festering idly" as foreigners. Although Josephson regretted the excessive attention to reportage, the unremitting revolutionary tempo which allowed no place for a "genial disinterested and prophetic vision," he felt the excitement of the great projects in which all the Russian writers were involved. He noted, too, how comfortably they lived. [16]

To many American writers, then—the eminent and the obscure—

Russia in the thirties was both a reproach to America and a hope of the world. Its totalitarian features were not ignored, its curtailing of civil and intellectual liberties regretted, but its gains and its ultimate goals appeared to overbalance its failures. Were it not for its enemies, waiting for a chance to destroy it, the Russian leaders would not have had to devote the bulk of their country's resources to national defense or to limit personal freedom. Even so, according to Upton Sinclair, who sent his revolutionary greetings to the U.S.S.R. in 1937, the Russians had followed the advice of Emerson and hitched their wagon to a star. They had solved the problem of national minorities, raised a degraded peasantry "from superstition and drunkenness," introduced modern machinery, ended racial discrimination, and established a workers' government.[17] Finally, and perhaps most important for a large number of American intellectuals after 1932, they had assumed the leadership in the world struggle against the menacing power of international fascism.

Before Hitler seized power in January 1933, the American Communist Party, following the lead of the Comintern, had made no effort to mobilize all antifascist opinion in the United States. Not until late March did the *Daily Worker* call for "A United Front to fight Fascism." Meanwhile, Joseph Freeman, on his own authority, wrote a manifesto against the Nazis in *The New Masses*,[18] and on March 3, a number of writers and journalists were invited by the editors to send in their protests against German fascism.

The statements from Newton Arvin, Roger N. Baldwin, Heywood Broun, Lewis Corey (Fraina), Waldo Frank, Michael Gold, Horace Gregory, Granville Hicks, Sidney Hook, Horace M. Kallen, Scott Nearing, James Rorty, Isidor Schneider, and Edwin Seaver, while differing in emphasis, agreed on fundamental points: 1) Hitlerism was a brutish doctrine, "pitilessly hostile to every impulse of the intellectual or the creative life"; 2) the Nazis represented the last murderous impulse of a dying capitalism; 3) the victory of National Socialism in Germany would encourage and strengthen America's native fascists; 4) the Nazi threat compelled a "grim rallying together of all progressive groups throughout the world"; and 5) the American intellectuals had to politicize themselves and to take the lead in setting up "an anti-Fascist front of intellectual workers in America." [19]

Until the Nazi-Soviet pact in 1939, hatred of world fascism brought writers and intellectuals into the Left orbit who otherwise might never have affiliated with the movement. The New Deal was at least beginning to grapple with the problems of the Depression; undoubtedly the Roosevelt administration won over a good many incipient radicals. Even those who were not prepared to junk capitalist democracy, however, unhesitatingly supported any antifascist organization no matter what group or party was sponsoring it. Their antifascism was subsequently judged in some quarters as "premature," but throughout the thirties, fascism and Nazism were hardly phantom movements. There is no need to ask why so many writers, prompted by the age-old vision of the just society, should have believed their joint resistance to Hitlerism was at once moral and practical.[20]

The revulsion inspired by the Nazis in American liberals and radicals antedated the revelations of Belsen and Auschwitz; to them, Hitler was a forerunner of a "new and bloody 'dark ages.' " The reports, official and unofficial, flowing out of Germany after his triumph, the stories of pogroms and book burnings and concentration camps, enforced the image of the Third Reich as a medieval hell. It is impossible to understand why so many writers and artists flocked into the movement unless one can begin to sense the violent loathing, rage, and fear provoked by the Nazis. Any group, in or out of the United States, that condoned or aided fascism took on its gruesome aspect, whether it was the Ku Klux Klan, the Black Legion, or the Croix de Feu; any group persecuted by the Nazis, whether Communist or Socialist or Catholic or Jewish, met with approbation. The majority of writers during the thirties agreed with Mike Gold's assertion: "Every anti-fascist is needed in this united front. There must be no base factional quarrels." [21]

The culmination of antifascist sentiment among the American writers came at the point when many of them had become skeptical of Stalin's grandfatherly mask and disturbed by some of the party tactics. The event that aroused them more powerfully than any other episode during the entire violent decade, and which distracted them from the Moscow trials his managers had already begun to stage, was the Spanish Civil War and the armed intervention of Germany and Italy.

We shall see later how the party benefited from this sentiment and why some of the volunteers who literally crawled on their hands and knees to cross the border into Spain became disillusioned. It is enough to say now that between 1936 and 1939, an overwhelming majority of the American intelligentsia—artists, teachers, writers, men and women of all the professions—regarded the Spanish war as "a testing ground for war with fascism in general." [22] The writers and artists who spoke for the Spanish Loyalists, who raised money for medical aid, or who smuggled themselves into Spain as volunteers were not consciously furthering party interests, nor was there anything ulterior or sinister in their devotion to the Spanish peasantry. The issues appeared clear-cut, the cause of Spain the cause of democracy and morality. Sectarian bickerings seemed contemptible in the light of such awesome events, and for more than a few, the nobility of the Spaniards engendered a comparable nobility in themselves.

The writers beguiled by "the colossal attraction" of Bolshevism's "ultimate vision" [23] did not consider their acceptance of Marxism as a departure from traditional progressive values. They conceived of it, rather, in Arthur Koestler's words, "as the logical extension of the progressive humanistic trend . . . the continuation and fulfilment of the great Judeo-Christian tradition—a new fresh branch on the tree of Europe's progress through Renaissance and Reformation, through the French Revolution and the Liberalism of the nineteenth century, toward the Socialist millennium." If the rebel's quarrel with society had neurotic roots, as Koestler profoundly believes, he observes nonetheless "that in the presence of revolting injustice the only honorable attitude is revolt." The perversion of noble ideals that marks the end of most revolutions signifies both human fallibility and the melancholy truism "that a polluted society pollutes even its revolutionary offspring." [24]

The writers subsequently identified with the Communist Party, either as converts or as sympathizers, made up a most diverse group and one not easy to classify. A few were dedicated socialists, spiritually thirsting for community. For them the party was the beneficent agency through which the good society would be inaugurated and mankind released from its long bondage, and they felt strengthened as writers, less weak and vulnerable and useless, when they gave themselves to the revolutionary cause. It was not a decision lightly taken; as Meridel Le Sueur described it:

It is difficult because you are stepping into a dark chaotic passional world of another class, the proletariat, which is still perhaps unconscious of itself, like a great body sleeping, stirring, strange and outside the calculated, expedient world of the bourgeoisie. It is a hard road to leave your own class and you cannot leave it by pieces or parts; it is a birth and you have to be born whole out of it. In a complete new body. None of the old ideology is any good in it. The creative artist will create no new forms of art or literature for the new hour out of that darkness unless he is willing to go all the way, with full belief, into that darkness.[25]

For others, agreement with Communist interpretations and solutions involved no such trauma or rapture. Communism appealed to them because it seemed a science as well as an ethic, because it explained and foretold as well as inspired, and because it had become incarnate in a dynamic country directed by a hardheaded elite. Contemptuous of their own "politicians" and impatient with the government's failure to cope with the Depression at home or to recognize the menace of fascism abroad, American intellectuals uncritically accepted the Bolshevik self-portrait. Soviet propaganda pictured a society where unemployment and racial discrimination had been permanently abolished, where artists and writers were honored and made use of, a country resolutely opposed to imperialistic ventures and staunchly antifascist.

In America, tirades against the "Reds" by reactionaries and Right Wing crackpots, the frenetic anti-Communist editorials in the Hearst newspapers, seemed to confirm the party's cartoon image of its enemies and amounted almost to an endorsement. According to Isidor Schneider, the Communist Party had "ideas and a program, unlike the intellectually-dead 'regular' parties," which concealed their programs. "That is why," he wrote, "although numerically at any given moment the Communists may be vastly outnumbered by sporadic and amorphous movements like the Townsend Plan and Coughlin's League for Social Justice, Communists make the strongest and most enduring impression; why the hatred of the bourgeoisie is concentrated against them; why unorganized elements within the masses turn to 'red' organizations in spite of the bitter propaganda against them; and, finally, why there is so great curiosity about them." No other party, he might have added, sponsored such an array of cultural and political organizations, bookshops, theatrical companies, dance groups, and films, or such well-publicized and carefully staged mass meetings. "The Communist calendar," Orrick Johns discovered after he had joined the party, was "as full of dates as *festas* in Italy, all of which must be prepared for and exploited in one way or another: the anniversary of Marx, of Lenin, of the Sacco-Vanzetti execution, of May Day, of the October Revolution and so on." The tens of thousands who attended mass meetings in the San Francisco Civic Auditorium to hear Dreiser speak on behalf of Tom Mooney never suspected the weeks of preparation that preceded it. Although jointly sponsored by trade-unionists, socialists, anarchists, and liberals, the "moves of the hostile colleagues were anticipated at 'fraction' meetings, and district meetings. The best way to work with this opposition was worked out, and speakers were planted to deal with the controversial points. As a result the Communists usually carried the argument." [26]

The comments of neither Schneider nor Johns, however, begin to make clear why the party attracted the relatively small number of writers who became bona fide members in the 1930's. Nor does the published and unpublished testimony of converts really give the literary historian much to go on. Retrospective explanations may be illuminating, but not completely trustworthy. With some writers, the reading of a book initiated the impulse; Malraux's *Man's Fate,* Lenin's *The State and Revolution,* John Strachey's *The Coming Struggle for Power,* and Lincoln Steffens's *Autobiography* each demanded in its own way that the reader make a choice for or against humanity. Others were drawn into the movement by their friends, or because a solicitous editor of *The New Masses* had invited them to contribute to the magazine, or because they had visited the U.S.S.R., or because they wanted the chance to mingle with real proletarians.[27]

It was also reassuring to feel that one belonged to an international movement whose ultimate triumph no temporary setbacks could avert, that one was working for mankind. At the same time, the party might solve racial, sexual, social, or economic anxieties as well as satisfy spiritual yearnings. The dances in Webster Hall, the unit socials, benefits, picnics, and forums guaranteed that no good Bolshevik need be lonely.

Yet for the majority of writers who were associated in some way or another with the movement, it was the times, not the party, that made them radicals. The party attracted them because it alone seemed to have a correct diagnosis of America's social sickness and a remedy for it. The overwhelming majority never joined the party, but they put on "red shirts" as an emblem of revolt, as a way of showing their repudiation of the "stuffed shirts." Few were ready to make the sacrifices demanded by the party in the early thirties, but the issues that preoccupied the party during the first half of the thirties— the plight of the hungry and the evicted, the exploitation of the Negro, the miseries of the unemployed, the persecutions in Germany, the struggles of labor—became their preoccupations. For a short time, American writers wrote novels, poems, plays, criticism, and reports that dealt rudely and sometimes powerfully with the most pressing issues of American life.

If the thirties ended in disenchantment, and if passionate men with passionate convictions sometimes deceived others and more often were self-deceived, in no other decade did writers take their social roles more devotionally. As in all periods of great revivals, whether religious or political, the majority of the converts lapsed into their old ways, unable to maintain the enthusiasm that momentarily overcame them. Only a few held on to the vision after its earthly prophets had been discredited.

SIX · "GO LEFT, YOUNG WRITERS"

ON THE EVE

"THERE is no revolutionary situation in America," Robert Wolf, one of the contributing editors to *The New Masses,* told the Communist Academy in Moscow in December of 1927. "Factory girls in America wear silk stockings but have no class consciousness—capitalism is in blacker and more complete control than anywhere else on earth." [1]

Out of the 20,000 members of the Communist Party in the United States, said Wolf to his Russian audience, only 3,000 spoke English. [2] Each successive immigrant group—German, Italian, Polish, Russian Jewish—had been corrupted by bourgeois ideas as it acquired a knowledge of English. Proletarian literature had never developed in America because "there was no one to write it for, and so it didn't get written at all." The workers now, he said, were bribed by radios and Ford cars, "and for all practical purposes, these workers, the only American-speaking workers in heavy industries, are at present ideologically a part of the bourgeois class." When they did read, it was the kind of tripe manufactured by *The Saturday Evening Post.*

Left Wing writers were not usually so openly pessimistic about the prospects of a working-class audience, especially after 1930, but *The New Masses* editors, while encouraging young proletarian hopefuls and envisaging a culture-hungry populace eagerly waiting for the new class-conscious literature that would at last tell the truth about their lives, were more directly concerned with winning over the skit-

tish intelligentsia. Admittedly, most of the intellectuals were hopelessly corrupted by past associations and were "the most ancient and
venerable of prostitutes." [3] Cowardly, unreliable, vacillating, cynical,
and, above all, "confused," they were perhaps more of a handicap
than a help to the revolutionary movement, yet a salvageable remnant might come to see that their future as writers lay with the militant working class for whom and about whom they were to write in
order to win salvation. From the mid-twenties on, they were alternately scolded and wooed in the leftist press, and their progress
through the ideological jungles was watched with interest and solici-
tude.

In 1926, the year *The New Masses* was launched, the stereotype
of the apolitical bourgeois writer began to take shape in the radical
imagination. He was likely to be a man who cried " 'pooh' at every
sentiment and every generalization," who distrusted all convictions
and ideals, whose chief foe was dullness, who insulated himself from
the currents of life ("Greenwich Village is worse than Wall Street"),
who despised the yokels and morons but was much farther from reality than they. "Caught between the upper and nether millstones of
big capital and organized labor," he squirmed in confusion, "cursing
the lies of this civilization" when times were bad and behaving like
an aristocrat during periods of prosperity. The intelligentsia (professional people, writers, artists) formed no distinct class but took their
character and opinions from the class upon whom they depended for
their living.[4]

GOLD AND THE INTELLECTUALS

No writer in the Left movement at this time fussed and worried
over, exhorted, and admonished the uncommitted liberal artist more
passionately than Mike Gold. With Freeman and a few others, he had
agitated for Communism when few were willing to listen, when a
Communist was "less tolerable to the literary authorities than the
feeblest fairy of Greenwich Village," and when the American Communists themselves considered "all forms of literary activity . . . a
childish self-indulgence, not useful, not functional." [5] Toward the

end of the decade it began to look as if Communist ideas were about to have a wider currency, and Gold eagerly noted any sign of the impending change.

Sympathetic as he was to the "young writers with the adolescent flair for rebellion," Gold sternly condemned them for becoming the cultured hired hands of the *nouveaux riches,* and tried to make them understand why their "bitter work" would never satisfy the "crap-shooting bourgeoisie," the "new culture audience" who swarmed "like blue-arsed flies around the world's sugar bowl." To succeed in this market, the writer had to remove all bitterness from his work, amuse at all costs, and reassure his readers that they were immune from any social catastrophe. Gold deplored the susceptibility of the "intellectual mob" to cultish enthusiasms and kidded them for their preposterous theorizing:

You can read essays by American intellectuals to prove . . . that a man can live with three wives; that it is sorrowful to be a Lesbian; that mental telepathy really works; that the soul of America is to be found in Walt Whitman; that the soul of America is to be found in Henry Ford; that Prohibition will ruin the arts and sciences; that there is a fourth dimension; that sex should be free; that music ennobles the soul; that liquor ennobles the soul; that there is "pure" poetry; that when a bridge breaks, God is Love; that Poe was sexually impotent; that Henry Clay was oversexed; that Carrie Nation, Bryan, Sidney Lanier, Buffalo Bill and Bob Fitzsimmons all suffered from the inferiority complexes, that Martha Washington suffered from an Oedipus complex . . . that since Plato every philosophy has been the product of a bad liver, a complex, or an unhappy marriage; that Henry the VIIIth made British history because he was over-sexed; that Abraham Lincoln made the Civil War because he was undersexed; that history is sex; that America is sex; that sex is soul; that soul is all; Oom, Oom; *pfui!* [6]

What drew him to the "politically imbecile" writers who had grown up during World War I, what made them worth salvaging, was their rejection of the "false democracy" and "false patriotism" and all of the "capitalist lies" that were "legally cheered" by their elders. They wrote out of a "desperate honesty that seems pathological in a world built on lies"; they wrote "like soldiers who have been betrayed by their commanders." Therefore a magazine like *transition,* although it reflected their despair and "the undisciplined chaos of the subconscious," the "horror-dreams of world catastrophe, disgust, and corruption," also displayed an honesty that set it apart from the hireling bourgeois magazines. Its aesthetic contributors, the former disciples of Dada, were "groping from the dead Socialist-liberal spirit in writing, into the Communist or Fascist discipline," [7] and Gold tried to explain to them why he had chosen the harder course of being a Communist writer. His reasons were at once moral and aesthetic.

Communism, Gold wrote, did not impose a barracks discipline upon the writer, but induced a "creative self-discipline." Whereas fascism required its supporters to refurbish decadent institutions, "to re-write the stale hymns to the old fatherland," Communism demanded that the writer be a life-bringing Prometheus, a daring experimenter, a smasher of idols. Put in literary terms, Mussolini, the ham actor, wrote like a "male Elinor Glyn in medals and riding boots"; Lenin's style curiously resembled Hemingway's. The Communist writer avoided rhetorical flourishes, having no need for prayers and pieties, and embraced unshrinkingly the hard facts of his times and culture. There was no need, Gold insisted, to seek for strange themes in exotic places. Working-class America was virtually undiscovered, a lost continent that could provide the young writer with "all the primitive material he needs. . . ." [8]

Nor would the writer clip the wings of his genius by submitting himself to the collectivity. American intellectuals mistakenly thought that individualism was indispensable to their "Art," but their kind of individualism led "only to little cafe cliques and minor eccentrics." The great artists, the great scientists, were never individualists in the narrow "escapist" sense; rather, they were titans who "shared in the world vision of their times." Bourgois-baiting intellectuals might describe America as a hideous collectivism in order to justify their running away, but individualism, not collectivism, produced anarchic competitive capitalism. In the coming struggle between the retrogressive and progressive collective forces—Big Business and the Social Revolution—each knowing what it wanted and attuned to social realities, the poor intellectual who now wandered "in a kind of twilit no-man's land" would be potted by both sides. To save himself, he would have to stand his ground and make the choice.[9]

THE INTELLECTUALS' RESPONSE

Gold and his *New Masses* colleagues supplemented their challenging pronunciamentos to the liberal bourgeois writers from time to time by polling a selected number of them [10] on certain social and artistic questions, a practice they may have borrowed from the *transition* questionnaires. "Are artists people?" *The New Masses* asked in 1927. "If you prick an artist, does he bleed? If you starve him, does he faint? Is heaven his home or can he properly take an active part in our mundane struggle for the fact of bread and the concepts of liberty, justice, etc.? As a social critic and evaluator, can he not merely say what's wrong, but also and by more than negative implication, declare what's right?" [11]

In order to get some specific information on these matters, the magazine asked fourteen writers why they wrote and for what audience; their definition of literary prostitution; their opinion of American culture; their attitude toward the machine; how the artist should adapt himself to the machine age; the feasibility of writers uniting to secure artistic and economic advancement; whether society had the right to make social demands on the writer; and what attitude, if any, the writer should take toward the revolutionary labor movement.

The replies, as might be expected from such sweeping questions, were not always illuminating, but in general they might be summarized as follows:

1. Most of them agreed that they wrote for personal satisfaction and out of some deep-seated need as well as for economic reasons. Although a few protested that appreciation by an audience was a secondary concern, most confessed feeling pleasure from outside recognition—but not at the price of betraying their convictions for money.

2. Was contemporary American culture decadent? The more militantly Left writers like Edwin Seaver thought so, but the majority described it as unfulfilled and immature rather than decadent. "American culture has never flourished," Edmund Wilson declared; "how

can it decay?" Van Wyck Brooks said it was "decadent" in that it
reflected life rather than created it, but he attributed this failure to
cultural infantilism.

3. Did the "advent of the machine mean the death of art and
culture" or "the birth of a new culture"? This question, much discussed during the twenties, evoked a variety of responses. Fewer
than might be expected took a positive stand for or against the machine, and most advised the writer to accept the machine (since he
had to willy-nilly). The more revolutionary-minded laughed at the
Ruskinians, who bewailed its advent; no one—not even Genevieve
Taggard, who shortly was to reprimand the aesthetes for "talking
about the evils of present-day life-standardization, and the robot
crowds in the subway"— [12] agreed with Mike Gold that a person was
likely to become a better artist by accepting the Machine Age and
the proletarian cause. Genevieve Taggard disapproved of this line,
because it seemed to promise the writer "proletarian stocks and
bonds, glories and goodies." One simply did not become a machine
artist by willing it. "The *New Masses*," she concluded, "is making a
great mistake if it tries to convert bourgeois artists into proletarian
ones." Its job was to help "the artist to take hold of the spectacle of
modern life by printing the work of those who have begun to make
inroads upon it."

4. No great aversion was shown to unions or guilds of writers
combining for economic or artistic reasons, although only Edmund
Wilson thought that artists "can benefit by coming together in groups
in which they can work at their problems together and profit by each
other's experience."

5. "May society properly demand of the artist, not merely good
craftsmanship and good reporting but the 'transvaluation of values'—
the creation of new social values?" Yes, said Upton Sinclair and
Edwin Seaver. No, said practically everyone else. Society had no
right to "demand" anything except honest work. Artists, it was conceded, do change values, but not designedly or under compulsion.

6. The answers to the question about the writer's attitude to the
revolutionary labor movement and the kind of world culture that
might eventually emerge through the rise of the working class varied
considerably. Dedicated radicals like Sinclair, Harbor Allen (who

wrote under the name of Paul Peters), and Edwin Seaver had no doubt about the imminence of the new society and of its certain superiority over the old. "The artist," Seaver said, "must accept the revolutionary labor movement as one of the most vital activities of our time." The "social revolution," said Allen, "will be the torch for a new flame of art, hopeful where it is now frustrated, lusty where now it is anemic, bold and gleeful where now it is bound and surly." Most of the others, while conceding that a workers' state might ultimately be best for the artist if it produced more freedom, went no further than expressing a sympathetic interest in the revolutionary labor movement. Edmund Wilson acknowledged that it might strike fire from one sort of artist as "plutocratic drinking parties" might for another, but despite the important changes in the arts and sciences produced by a social upheaval, the essential character of culture would not change. There could be no proletarian literature any more than there could be proletarian chemistry or proletarian engineering:

All the talk about "class" literature and art seems to me, rather pointless. The arts and sciences produce classes of their own which cut across the social classes. When the proletariat learn to appreciate art and to understand science, they will appreciate and understand them in the same way as anyone else, and, when they make contributions to them, their contributions will be valuable, if they are valuable, in exactly the same way as those of the capitalist Proust and the aristocrat Bertrand Russell. There are already great proletarian names among the arts and sciences; but they are the great names of artists and scientists, not of proletarians.[13]

The answers to *The New Masses* questionnaire can hardly be said to express a representative cross section of literary opinion about literature and society in 1927. They do support, however, the impression borne out by other evidence that the period of random rebelliousness was drawing to a close and that politics and economics were supplanting sex in the literary consciousness.*

* After Floyd Dell, V. F. Calverton (see pp. 322-33) and Upton Sinclair expressed their views on sex and politics in *The New Masses* (III, Mar. 1927, pp. 11-12; June 1927, p. 27), the subject pretty well died down in the radical press.

Communism's apparent indifference to the sex question disturbed Dell. He still considered psychosexual themes no less serious than the class struggle, and he was not yet prepared to "propose a proletarian revolution as the perfect and obvious solution to a hero's problems." Was Freudian science,

The liberal writer was by no means ready to yield his independence; he was still detached, still proudly isolated. But the self-contempt of radical intellectuals, particularly noticeable in the early thirties, was already present in 1927. Genevieve Taggard's soft hardboiled confession is a good illustration of this mood:

Practical men run revolutions, and there's nothing more irritating than a person with a long vague look in his eye to have around, when you're trying to bang an army into shape, or put over a N.E.P. If I were in charge of a revolution, I'd get rid of every single artist immediately; and trust to luck that the fecundity of the earth would produce another crop when I had got some of the hard work done. Being an artist, I have the sense that a small child has when its mother is in the middle of house-work. I don't intend to get in the way, and I hope that there'll be an unmolested spot for me when things have quieted down.[14]

Things did not quiet down, as it turned out. Events occurred and reoccurred that made the writer abandon his aloofness and enter, often hesitantly and without confidence, the conflicts of his day. None had more explosive consequences than the execution of Sacco and Vanzetti on August 22, 1927.

---

he asked, counterrevolutionary? Did it divert "the interest and energies of rebellious and intelligent youth from revolutionary mass-movements of a political and economic nature . . . ?" Even if true, "must Freudian science be denounced by the critical watchdogs of the Revolution as a pernicious bourgeois fad?—or on the other hand (and simply on the ground that it happens to be a true science), should it be studied by revolutionists, and made use of, like any other kind of knowledge . . . mathematics for instance?"

V. F. Calverton, whose interest in sex was no less intense than Dell's, lashed out at the "radical who is enthusiastic about revolution in economic life but timid about revolution in sexual life." The proletarian-revolutionary not only fought for shorter hours and higher wages; he also rejected "monogamy, or sex-possession" as "one of the basic property relations in our bourgeois world."

Sinclair, who shared none of Calverton's anarcho-pagan theories about sex, declared that worker-revolutionaries never let sex interfere with their real work. Some wished to have children and to train them to "take part in the workers' struggle." For others, sex life contributed "comradeship and understanding to the cause" and made the partners better workers. "That rules out any sex life," he serenely concluded, "that exposes either party to disease and any that is merely trifling and waste of time, that involves one or both lovers in a tangle of futile and distracting emotions."

The questions raised by Dell, Calverton, and Sinclair continued to disturb some of the radical intellectuals during the next decade, but the party probably thought it had enough to handle without launching a sexual revolution. Besides, the whole issue smacked of Village Bohemianism.

"A GOOD SHOEMAKER AND A POOR FISH PEDDLER"

The arrest of Nicola Sacco and Bartolomeo Vanzetti in Brockton, Massachusetts, on May 5, 1920—they were charged with the robbing and murder of a shoe-factory paymaster and his guard—and their trial and death sentence in July 1921 did not immediately bring American writers to their defense. To be sure, *The Liberator* editors gave some attention to the case, and a Sacco and Vanzetti Defense Committee, headed by Joseph Ettor and Arturo Giovannitti, was formed shortly before the July trial, but save for the anarchists, few others seemed to know or care about these unimportant immigrants.

Ettor and Giovannitti had been framed on a murder charge in 1913 in the midst of a fierce textile strike in Lawrence, Massachusetts, which, as hot I.W.W. agitators, they had helped to organize. Ten years later, in an appeal to the readers of *The Liberator,* "Would You Like To Be Electrocuted?" they warned that no radical could get a fair trial in Massachusetts.

We know it. We have been there. Ten years ago we were arrested in that State, charged with what cannot be described otherwise than psychic murder. We were kept in jail for eight months. . . . But it was not at all necessary for the prosecution to prove that we had committed or desired murder. Apparently it was not necessary to prove anything at all, save that we did not approve of private ownership and that we were alive at the time when some unknown individual had killed another.

We learned how charges are built up, how "evidence" is gathered, how "expert testimony" is obtained. . . . And we know how hard it is to prove that you are an honorable man when the State of Massachusetts contends and affirms that you are a scoundrel—especially if you are an Italian.

They were acquitted, but it took "ten months of national agitation, an international protest, the resignation of a Socialist member of the Italian parliament, a threatened boycott of American ships by the Scandinavian workers, an assault on the American consulates in Berne, Barcelona, and Milan, the diplomatic intervention of the Italian Government, eight lawyers, fifteen investigators, several thousand mass meetings and some 200,000 dollars." Sacco and Vanzetti, the appeal concluded, needed a few thousand dollars for their trial or they would be electrocuted.[15]

Ettor and Giovannitti did not know how closely the struggle to free Sacco and Vanzetti would parallel their own, nor could they measure then the power and authority that would prevent another acquittal.

In a few years, the case began to attract the attention of internationally known figures, but as late as 1924, H. L. Mencken was the only American writer of wide reputation mentioned by the Defense Committee. John Dos Passos became deeply involved in December 1926, and Upton Sinclair in the next spring, but the massive support from American artists and intellectuals came only after an appeal sent out by the Defense Committee on August 8, 1927, two days before the original date of the execution. A twelve-day reprieve permitted a last rallying of the writers, but their appeals and petitions could not halt "the almost automatic clicking of the machinery of government spelling out death for two men with the utmost serenity." [16]

To the Communists, the Sacco-Vanzetti affair was merely another episode in the conspiracy of capitalism to single out its most dangerous foes in the class war and to eliminate them. Vanzetti's anarchism made him extremely critical of Soviet Communism, but the Russians and the American Communist Party nonetheless saw him and his less articulate friend as symbols of the oppressed proletariat. Eight days before the execution, Michael Gold described a respectable Boston "possessed with the lust to kill. The frock-coat mob is howling for blood—it is in the lynching mood." It was dangerous for anyone to walk through the police-cordoned streets if he wore a beard, had "dark foreign hair or eyes," or acted in any way like a man who had not graduated from Harvard. Gold and Dorothy Parker, along with such other "unwashed, ill-clad, bewhiskered desperadoes" as Dos Passos, Katharine Anne Porter, Edna St. Vincent Millay, John Howard Lawson, Grace Lumpkin, Ruth Hale, and Lola Ridge, had been arrested for picketing the State House on August 10. Four days later, Gold was convinced that only a world strike could prevent the legal murder of the condemned men by degenerate New England blue bloods "flamed up into a last orgy of revenge," and "insane with fear and hatred of new America." [17]

On execution night, Gold, Millay, Dos Passos, Parker, William Gropper, and many others watched the "two black hands of the death clock" move inexorably toward twelve midnight. "And then," wrote Gropper, "the clock struck and I heard someone beside me count slowly from one to twelve. He counted, and in that simple count I heard twelve little death songs. And soon on a board near us appeared the words, Sacco, Vanzetti Dead. Then nothing mattered, nothing except the morrow . . . for I knew the workers would remember." [18]

The tension built up during the agonizing last months—which had held together a disparate group of Communists, anarchists, well-meaning old ladies, idealistic students, writers, lawyers, newspapermen, labor officials, liberal Bostonians, and Harvard professors—snapped suddenly after the electrocution, and *The New Masses* began to indulge in some recriminatory post-mortems. The efforts of a "gallant and sincere rabble" of idealists, Egmont Arens wrote, had been no match for the entrenched authority, and now each group relapsed back to its former fatuities. Only the Communists wanted to bind together "these enthusiasts" a little longer. The liberals of *The New Republic* and *The Nation* persuasion, or so it seemed to *The New Masses,* would continue to chide "the influential members of society" for allowing such a miscarriage of justice to occur and do nothing about it. [19]

Arens in his post-mortem of the Sacco-Vanzetti case regretted "the fashion among American intellectuals to despise the Communists" for "always starting a fight." Nor could he condone the Communists "despising the intellectuals, forgetting that the Russian revolution did not spring from unplowed soil." Yet the execution of the two anarchists seemed to justify the Communists' cry: "The intellectuals are soft, flabby, sentimental, unrealistic. They are not to be depended upon, betrayers, defeatists. They are afraid of action. Human freedom can only be won by organized struggle!" For him and his friends, the liberal's trust in what *The New Republic* called "the creative power of human intelligence" and his reluctance to "join either of the blind and fanatical class-conscious sects" smacked of sheer cant. They could not yet appreciate how many of these same liberals had been shocked out of their open-mindedness and could say with the liberal Catholic Shaemas O'Sheel: "Class consciousness, class struggle, have been summoned from the tomb in which they were composing their reluctant limbs; infused with a new blood of rage." [20]

The martyrdom of Sacco and Vanzetti produced a spate of plays, poems, and novels, many of them written by men and women whose radicalism was first kindled by the death of the "dago Christs." John Dos Passos, of all American writers the most passionately engaged in the case, called for writing "so fiery and accurate that it will sear through the pall of numb imbecility that we are again swaddled in after the few moments of sane awakening that followed the shock of the executions." Such writing, passionate and pulsating with indignation, did appear, and with it the less obviously radical but even more destructive sketch by Edmund Wilson in which he sardonically showed how the fate of Sacco and Vanzetti impinged upon the daily lives of well-meaning but self-indulgent and socially irresponsible people.[21] Then, the gush of angry comment momentarily slackened, and the affair of Sacco and Vanzetti seemed to have dropped out of men's minds as news of the fierce strike in Gastonia, North Carolina, began to preoccupy the increasingly class-conscious intellectuals.

But the deaths of Sacco and Vanzetti, as Robert Morss Lovett pointed out in Calverton's *Modern Quarterly,* were not to be a mere dramatic episode—short, hot, and quickly forgotten. Nothing since the disillusionment following World War I, he thought, had "so shaken the Liberal's belief in the working for equal justice of free institutions," or exposed his impotence in the face of organized oppression. The execution of these two "obscure Radicals," Lovett decided, accelerated the desertion of American artists and intellectuals from their old allegiances—a symptom of revolution—and made it impossible "to deny the existence of the Class War in the United States." [22]

Eight years after the agonizing summer of 1927, Malcolm Cowley, whose own radicalism dates from that time, recollected that the "effects of the Sacco-Vanzetti case continued to operate in a subterranean style" before they suddenly came to the surface again with the Depression:

The intelligentsia was "going left"; it was becoming friendly with the Communists; it was discussing the need for a new American revolution. All sorts of people tried to explain this development in all sorts of contradictory fashions, some of which were partly true. Almost nobody mentioned the obvious fact that, whatever else it might be, it was also a sequel to the Sacco-Vanzetti case, a return to united political action. This time, however, the intellectuals had learned that they were powerless by themselves and that they could not accomplish anything unless they made an alliance with the working class.[23]

By 1932 the shades of the "good shoemaker" and the "poor fish peddler" haunted a disunited land, and their last utterances were quoted in leftist circles everywhere. The famous passage in Dos Passos' *U.S.A.* is perhaps the most intense and eloquent pronouncement on the case, catching as it does the upsurge of rage and grief after the execution. Mike Gold was not too far off when he predicted in 1927 that the two men would become a legend, a battle cry, a red flag to workers, peasants, Red soldiers, and Jewish tailors: "That is a beautiful fate, it cheats the grave of darkness, it makes sweet even those last leaping fiery minutes in the electric chair!" [24]

THE DEPRESSION AND THE WRITER

Discussing the militancy of American writers in the summer of 1932, Edwin Seaver compared "this new temper" with the spirit of defeat and despair in 1927. Liberals fought hard to save Sacco and Vanzetti, but "they were handicapped by a terrible sense of inertia, and found themselves unprepared and incompetent to do anything in a crisis whose significance was rapidly achieving world dimensions, even within their own limited sphere of literary activity." In the space of five years, Seaver said, the writer had changed from a passive and defeated observer of society to an active participant. If the "early twenties were a period of self-discovery and self-expression," the early thirties pointed "to a period of social discovery and social expression." No longer was it fashionable to scoff at Main Street; now, writers like Edmund Wilson were trying to understand it. Menckenian "boob-thumping" was yielding to "serious interrogation," and writers, instead of "crying for freedom," were searching for responsibility.[25] What had happened to them to produce this change?

One of the legacies of the Sacco-Vanzetti case was the conviction "widely held by a number of disenchanted writers and intellectuals after 1927" that the "ruling class" would resort to any means, even legal murder, to preserve itself. Whether out of fear or vindictiveness or a misguided reverence for the law, some of the most respected men in American society had "framed" two innocent victims. "It is upon men of your class and position," John Dos Passos declared in an open letter to President A. L. Lowell of Harvard, "that will rest the inevitable decision as to whether the coming struggle for the reorganization of society shall be bloodless and fertile or inconceivably bloody and destructive." [26] Two years after this warning, the economic machine allegedly threatened by the principles of "those Anarchist bastards" sputtered and stalled, and many writers who had come to despise the morality of business now began to doubt its power to function at all.

The stock market crash of October 24, 1929, sounded as sweet to Mike Gold as the crashing banks did to Thoreau in 1857. "Let me admit," he wrote in December, "I enjoyed the recent music of the victim's howls and tears. Too long has one had to submit to the airs of these cockroach capitalists. Every barber was dabbling in Wall Street. Every street-cleaner expanded his chest proudly as he maneuvered his horsedroppings into a can. Wasn't he a partner with Morgan and Rockefeller in American prosperity?" [27] Who could say how long the rotten system would last? It might be ten years or a hundred, but for the moment the crapshooters had lost their shirts.

In the fall of 1929, Gold and his Left Wing friends had no inkling of how sick the economy really was, although Communist theoreticians had predicted the crash. Granville Hicks, who later joined the Communist Party, but was then a liberal assistant professor of English at Rensselaer Polytechnic Institute, remained unperturbed through December, and not until the following summer did it become plain to him that Hoover's optimistic pronouncements about "the resistless, dynamic power of American enterprise" were little more than incantations.[28] The disparity between administration promises and accomplishments evoked a good deal of raucous cynical laughter as well as a kind of desperate nihilism in some quarters, particularly among those who had long abandoned old political loyalties and had not bothered to search for new ones.

A savagely amusing organ for this group was the short-lived magazine *Americana,* edited by Alexander King, George Grosz, and Gilbert Seldes. It appeared in November 1932 with a declaration of war against all political parties in its opening editorial.

We Are Not REPUBLICANS *Because . . .*
the present office holders have dismally failed in leadership and intelligence and because the moneyed oligarchy that runs and ruins this country is animated by stupid and shameless greed best exemplified by the Republican party. As for Mr. Hoover personally, we rest content by presenting the record of his flabbiness and incompetence.

We Are Not DEMOCRATS *Because . . .*
the Democratic party is no less corrupt than the party in power and is simply striving to glut its vicious and insatiable appetite at the public money trough. As for Mr. Roosevelt personally, we consider him a weak and vacillating politician who will be an apt tool in the hands of his powerful backers.

We Are Not SOCIALISTS *Because . . .*
the erstwhile sentimental liberalism of the Socialists has degenerated to the bourgeois mouthings of their spokesman, Norman Thomas.

We Are Not COMMUNISTS *Because . . .*
the American Communist party delegates its emissaries to bite the rear ends of policemen's horses and finds its chief glory in spitting at the doormen of foreign legations. We are also unconditionally opposed to Comrade Stalin and his feudal bureaucracy at Moscow.

We are Americans who believe that our civilization exudes a miasmic stench and that we had better prepare to give it a decent but rapid burial.

We are the laughing morticians of the present.[29]

In addition to the contributions of its editors, it featured the work of Nathanael West, his brother-in-law, S. J. Perelman, and E. E. Cummings.

Cummings, who had taken an irreverent twenty-three day pilgrimage to the U.S.S.R. in the spring of 1931, and had returned from
his adventure with a low opinion of Communism and Communists,[30]
seemed to have little more sympathy for the American capitalists on
the eve of the Presidential election of 1932. "And It Came To
Pass," his sketch of the Presidential election, is not only a good
example of Cummings's angry spoofing, but also catches the spirit of
unorganized and directionless revolt that animated the still politically
uncommitted writer of 1932.

(Scene an eclipse. Enter President HOOSES, disguised as a wolf in
sheep's clothing, walking on water. Everything immediately gets very
dark.)

Hooses (*sheepishly*): Suffer the microphone to come unto me. (*A mike is
suffered.*)—Be of good cheer; it is I. (*Laughter.*) Woe unto ye that laugh
now! for you shall mourn and weep. (*Mourning and weeping.*) Why are
ye fearful, O ye of little faith? Why reason ye, because ye have no
bread? Man shall not live by bread alone. (*Enter, disguised as himself,*
Norman Thomas, *asleep, wearing a halo.*) Get thee behind me, socialism.
Are there not twelve hours in the day? He that hath cheeks to turn, let
him turn. (*Enter Governor* Boosevelt, *disguised as a sheep in wolf's
clothing, swimming in beer.*)

Boosevelt (*wolfishly*): I am the light of the world.

A Voice: Let's go!

Hooses: Blessed are the poor in spirit, for they shall inherit the pot of
gold at the end of every rainbow. Blessed are they that agitate, for they
shall be clubbed. Blessed are the prosperous, for they shall be around
the corner. Blessed are they which do hunger and thirst, for they shall
obtain unemployment. Blessed are the meek, for they shall be filled with
hooey. Blessed are the bull and the bear, for they shall lie down together.
Blessed are the pieceworkers, for they shall be torn piecemeal. Blessed
are they which are persecuted for bonus' sake, for theirs is the kingdom
of tear gas.*

A Voice: We want Waters!

* A reference to the expulsion of the Bonus Army from Washington on
July 25, 1932. Obeying a Presidential directive, General Douglas MacArthur
used tear gas and bayonets to drive out the veterans and destroy their "Hoover
Villas" on Anacostia Flats.

Hooses: Love thine enemas. Bless them that goose you. (*Offering a bayonet*): Take, eat, this is my body.

Norman Thomas (*asleep*): B-r-r-r . . .

Hooses: And now to facts.—The trouble with trouble is, that trouble is troublesome. If trouble were not troublesome, we should not have troublous times. If we should not have troublous times, we did not need to worry. If we did not need to worry, our pockets were not so full.

The Ghost of George Abraham: Full of what?

The voice of Al Capone: Neither do men put new wine in old bottles.

Hooses: Full of hands. Our reconstruction program, involving as it does the ascertainable principle that a depression is the indirect result of direct economic causes, cannot but succeed in seriously mitigating a situation which would otherwise prove ambidextrous to every left-handed right-thinking moron. I therefore sacredly assert, on the one hand, that the time is now ripe for this great nation to evade an issue; and, on the other hand, as an immediate and an eventual solution of this vast country's difficulties, I timidly and confidently propose to fill hands with work by emptying pockets of hands.

A Voice: Burp.

Boosevelt (*taking the mike*): We hold these truths to be self-evident; that all men are created people, and all people are created feeble, and all feeble are created minded, and all minded are created equal. And the sequel to equal being opportunity, it is obvious that opportunity knocks but once and then it boosts. Nothing can really be done unless you and me are willing to fearlessly confront one another with each other; believing, with the common man, that as long as people are men America is the land of opportunity. (*Three Bronx cheers by a common man named Smith.*)

etc. etc.

INVESTIGATIONS AND REPORTS: DREISER

Cummings's burlesque was already a little anachronistic in 1932, for by this time, many of his literary friends and fellow writers, no longer preoccupied with aesthetics or politically neutral, were surveying Depression America with rage and disgust. The attempt of the Alabama authorities to electrocute nine Negro boys for allegedly raping two white girls on a freight gondola in the spring of 1931 had been hotly discussed in the liberal and Communist press.[31] At the same time, bloody strikes flared up in the coal fields of Pennsylvania, Ohio, Indiana, West Virginia, and Illinois, and writers like Theodore Dreiser and Sherwood Anderson, who had paid little attention to the Sacco and Vanzetti case, now accused the operators of crushing the miners by legalized terror.

Since his Russian trip, Dreiser had become more vocal in his criticisms of American capitalism, and by 1931 he could say "quite flatly that my solution for the difficulties of the world, and particularly those in America, is Communism." Trips to the Pittsburgh mining area in June of that year under Communist auspices and his leadership of the so-called "Dreiser Committee," sent down by the Communist-organized National Committee for the Defense of Political Prisoners to investigate conditions in the Harlan County coal fields, only confirmed what he had already been saying and would say again: American workers everywhere were "the economic victims of those giant corporations, still posing as individuals, although they are armed to the teeth with purchased law, hired officials, and over-awed and controlled courts." [32]

Dreiser and his committee of writers, including John Dos Passos, Charles Rumford Walker, Samuel Ornitz, Lester Cohen, and Melvin P. Levy, had gone to Harlan to "test free speech" and to see for themselves whether the reports of intimidation, starvation, and bloodshed were true. The "whole narrative of terror" was even more frightful than they had expected. Under the prodding of the operators, the authorities had dynamited soup kitchens, raided private homes, blacklisted 3,000 miners, jailed hundreds of others, and had deputized gun-toting hooligans. The Dreiser Committee also investigated mines and mining towns in Harlan and Bell counties. They talked to men and women whose "faces were out of early American history" [33] and brought back stories of privation and suffering that re-enforced the Northern stereotype of a savage and benighted South.*

---

* For the next decade or longer—thanks to the brutal tales of Erskine Caldwell and the agitational poetry and prose of the proletarian writers who

Dreiser, "shy, opinionated, sensitive as an old bull elephant," as Dos Passos put it, got himself "into a thorough senatorial scrape," but "there was a sort of massive humaneness about him, a self-dedicated disregard of consequences, a sly sort of dignity that earned him the respect of friend and foe alike." [34] It was this courage and dignity that prompted his old and not always uncritical friend Sherwood Anderson to speak militantly in his defense after Dreiser and several writers who went with him to Kentucky were indicted by a Harlan County local grand jury for criminal syndicalism. Anderson described Dreiser as a "story teller" with "a tremendous searching constant hunger in him to find out about lives." His passion for truth made him resist selling out his talent and drew him down to Harlan —that "little ugly running sore" and symbol of a sick society. Many writers, journalists, academics, and businessmen, Anderson continued, are "speak-easy" radicals who privately confess their heretical views but never dare reveal themselves in public. That is why he rejoiced in the Communists, who, unlike the Socialists, really meant their socialism, and in the bravery of Dreiser and his friends, who dared to speak what millions of Americans thought but left unspoken. Now, Anderson said, he knew what criminal syndicalism was. "I am glad to know. Now I know at last what is the matter with this country. We need less speak-easy citizens and more criminal syndicalists." [35]

The Communists wanted Dos Passos to return to Harlan County to stand trial. He refused: "there was something about the boss communist's sneering tone that made it a little too obvious that he enjoyed making monkeys of the warm-hearted liberals." [36] His friend Edmund Wilson was to have the same feeling of being used after

exploited the Southern jungle, a South took shape in the liberal imagination that resembled in its starkness and simplicity a cartoon by William Gropper. In the South of *The New Masses,* the bodies of Negroes swung from gaunt trees and fat-bellied sheriffs and mean-looking gangsters presided over hellish rites. Their victims, besides the Negroes, were the shabby but clean yeomanry of revolutionary stock who spoke "a pure unmodernized English," and who still retained the American revolutionary fire. This group was to be immortalized in the magnificent photographs taken for the Farm Settlement Administration and in James Agee's memorable *Let Us Now Praise Famous Men* (N.Y., 1941). The Communists cast a lurid light on the South, sometimes distorting it almost beyond recognition and yet highlighting its sores and deformities.

his experience with a second writers' delegation, led by the novelist and critic Waldo Frank, that had ventured into Harlan County in the spring of 1932.

INVESTIGATIONS AND REPORTS: EDMUND WILSON

Like Dos Passos, Wilson had come out of World War I full of disgust for the bourgeoisie and tepid milk-and-water socialism. Throughout the twenties, he had maintained his interest in radical causes even while participating actively in the literary and cultural movements of the day. One gets the impression in reading through Wilson's essays, sketches, poems, and plays written during the twenties that he was not only judging the society in which he lived, but also "intent upon breaking into the real world." [37] But he was trying to settle an internal debate between the old society to which he was attached by class and tradition and the world of revolt, sex, and experience, which troubled and fascinated him. Like his forebears, he had a strong sense of social responsibility, a preference for an integrated community, and a dislike of business anarchism. Outraged ethical feelings drew him and others of a similar background to Communism or fellow traveling. These latter-day Mugwumps, with their family-bred animus toward mere hucksters, tended to see the collapse of business as a moral failure as well as a breakdown in the economic machinery. "We hear a good deal about the romance of big business," Wilson wrote in 1928, "and Americans . . . live much in awe of the rich," but, he went on to say, Nietzsche was certainly right when he said that the only three creators were the scientist, the artist, and the sportsman: "because they play the game for its own sake, they alone may be entirely free from the appetite for power, for money or for the vulgar good opinion of their neighbors." The rich remained clownish and comic "because they have no dignified aims and, except in a very debased sense, no honor: they are funny because, though associates as often as competitors, they are always trying to swindle each other." [38]

Much of the old America he found ridiculous and hopelessly inappropriate to the new, but it provided him with an ethical vision that penetrated the ideological miasmas of Right and Left and kept him intellectually unsubmissive.[39] At a time when many young poets adopted the "Gerontian pose," Wilson urged them to become politicians, bankers, or movie actors. "What is wrong with the younger American poets," he said, "is that they have no stake in society. One does not want them to succumb to society; but one wants them, at least, to have relations to it. If the relation is an uncomfortable or a quarrelsome one, so much, perhaps, the better." [40]

This might have been self-adjuration as well as friendly advice to the disciples of Eliot. Between the time that it was written and October 1930, when Wilson began his series of reports on Depression America, his socialism changed from pink to red, but the Communists, who hoped to capture him for the party in the late twenties, did not yet realize that Wilson's qualified acceptance of the Marxist view of society in no way signified an intention to join them. The Communists then and later were always "they." Wilson observed their tactics and behavior, curiously if not unsympathetically, as they led hunger marches, fought policemen, and organized coal miners. In West Virginia, where he went in June 1931 to report the struggle between the coal operators and the rival unions of Frank Keeney and John L. Lewis, he noted "the gulf between the Keeneyites and the Communists which neither the admiration of the former for the Communists' undoubted guts nor the efforts on the part of the latter to convince the Keeneyites that their present course must lead to Communism, has come anywhere near to bridging." [41] And he observed in a letter to Sherwood Anderson that the Keeneyites were "more valuable radicals than most of the Communists." [42]

Wilson exhibited the same detachment when he arrived in Chattanooga, Tennessee, from West Virginia to cover the Scottsboro case. Obviously in sympathy with the Negroes, he told Anderson he could still understand the apprehension of the whites, outnumbered six to one, and their unwillingness to encourage the Communists. "The Scottsboro case is full of interesting features," he wrote, "but everybody has done so much lying that it is hard to get at the bottom of it." [43]

The double defense by the Communists and the N.A.A.C.P. and "the rupture between the two organizations" always seemed to occur "when Communists and bourgeois liberals attempt to work together." Wilson impartially set down the case for the liberals and their Communist foes. The former accused the latter of "Jesuitical tactics," of diverting defense funds to party propaganda, "of being willing and even eager to make martyrs for their atrocity-mongering press." The Communists, in turn, accused the liberals of timidity, of risking Negro lives in capitalist courts, of dodging the fundamental issues lest they antagonize their rich supporters, and of misleading the proletariat. One suspects, however, from Wilson's published story and from his letter to Anderson that he did not approve of the Communists' belligerent and needlessly antagonistic publicity or of their attempt to make their doctrines "a new and exciting kind of revivalism" for the Negroes.[44]

Wilson's doubts did not keep him from joining Waldo Frank's delegation of writers to Harlan County in February 1932, although at the time he did not realize the expedition was planned and directed by the party. The writers' committee "found life in Pineville like a *New Masses* cartoonist's dream," a town where "the basic antagonisms involved in the industrial system" stood out "in their most acute and naked forms." Arriving with four truckloads of food for the miners, the committee members were treated "as radical interlopers who were bringing communism into the Kentucky coal country." Two committee members were jailed when they tried to speak, and in the evening the Pineville authorities loaded the committee into two cars and drove to the Kentucky-Tennessee border. There, Wilson reported, "we were made to get out of the cars, the lights were turned off and Waldo Frank and Allen Taub [a lawyer] were beaten about the head—apparently with the butts of guns." [45]

Wilson's experience in Pineville, Kentucky, scarcely endeared the capitalist system to him, but his subsequent discovery that he was being "used," and the effort of Allen Taub and his wife to turn a fact-finding expedition into a Communist demonstration convinced him that henceforth he should never affiliate with any organized body.[46]

Edwin Seaver was perhaps too optimistic in charting the leftward surge of writers like Dreiser, Anderson, Wilson, and others. Each continued to embarrass the party, and the last two never fulfilled the high expectations of their Left Wing encouragers, but he was surely right in detecting "a new temper among American writers, a return of the people to a sense of citizenship, to an awareness of social responsibility beyond the literary responsibility merely of a writer to his craft." [47] Rather than support either of the two major political parties in 1932, or cast their votes for what they considered to be a tepid and bourgeois Socialist Party, a number of disgruntled writers, most of them non-Communists, were ready to back the Communist Party presidential ticket.

WRITERS AND POLITICS: 1931-32

Dreiser's trips to the Pennsylvania and Kentucky coal fields encouraged him to put down in greater detail his indictment of American capitalism. *Tragic America* (1932) contained inaccuracies, which Dreiser's critics diligently pointed out, and it was atrociously written. Nonetheless, Edmund Wilson said, it gave a better picture of the current crises than better-written studies. If Dreiser's style is "always collapsing . . . the man behind it remains sound. His prose has a long and steady rhythm which continues to convey his feelings and ideas even when the words don't quite make sense; and his very absurdities have the unmistakably idiosyncratic character of a genuine literary personality." [48]

To the Communists, Dreiser's *Tragic America* marked a step leftward, but *The New Masses* felt bound to criticize Dreiser's ideological errors despite his Communist sympathies. The book was shot through with liberal fallacies. For example, Dreiser advised the national government to adjudicate strikes, forgetting that the corporations owned the government. He knew the churches were counterrevolutionary, since they countenanced resignation, and yet he seemed to "subscribe to the Christian Socialist blather about the need to return to the teachings of Jesus." He dismissed the A. F. of L. officials as "cabbage-heads" instead of denouncing them as misleaders, and he concluded that labor had no leadership, ignoring "the inspiring fights being waged by left-wing unions. . . ." [49]

Yet Dreiser was effective, Wilson pointed out, precisely because he was undoctrinaire. He hailed him as the first major American writer not a Communist to come out for Communism and to translate into American terms "the jargon of the official Communist propaganda." He had taken the curse off the word "Communism" by calling it "equity." Eventually, Wilson thought, "we shall probably . . . have to call it Communism just the same. But it will be a Communism which is less preoccupied with echoing and aping Moscow than American Communism seems to be. It will have back of it the immediate conviction of such unrussianizable Americans as Dreiser." [50]

A year earlier, Wilson had warned "the American radicals and progressives who repudiate the Marxist dogma and the strategy of the Communist Party," that if they expected "to accomplish anything valuable," they would have to "take Communism away from the Communists, and take it without ambiguities, asserting that their ultimate goal is the ownership by the government of the means of production." One might not like the Russian revolution, but it was a successful reality, not an exploded myth and a "formidable fraud" like capitalism. Even the liberals who analyzed the bankruptcy of American economic and political life usually misrepresented the achievements of the U.S.S.R., because they were not able to divest themselves of their old habits and ways of thought. "It's hard for anybody," Wilson said, "but if our professional illuminati can't break through them to some larger grasp of the world which is cracking up around us, we deserve all to be cooked together." [51]

Looking back at the previous decade, and speculating on the fatal tendency of American artists and intellectuals to compromise, Wilson offered a kind of Brooksian explanation for the mediocrity of our national culture. The American thinkers and artists, he said, fell into two categories: "the journalist with an element of genius whose own point of view is close to that of the middle-class world from which he comes and in which he easily finds a large public," and "the intense nonconformist who follows some special line of his own and cuts himself off from the general life altogether." The writer Mark Twain, the painter John Singer Sargent, and the philosopher William James, who belonged in the first category, were cheapened and diluted by their milieu and failed to develop as they should have done; the nonconformists—the writer Herman Melville, the painter Albert Pinkham Ryder, the philosopher C. S. Peirce—were warped and turned inward by their surroundings. Most American writers, with their middle-class biases, had compromised with the "triumphant bourgeoisie" until its collapse, but now that capitalism had run its course, they would have to fall back on America's short but vital pioneer experience, "when we were independent men in a new country." Addressing them with uncharacteristic emotion, Wilson wrote:

So American intelligentsia—scientists, philosophers, artists, engineers—who have been weltering now for so long in a chaos of prostitutions and frustrations: that phase of human life is done! Stagger out of the big office, the big mill—look up and look through those barren walls—look beyond your useless bankrupt fields and pastures! Remember that discovery and freedom which you enjoyed for a little while—the discovery of humanity and the earth has only been begun! . . . What we need now are engineers of ideas as drastic as our practical ones.[52]

Wilson's diagnoses of his country's ills, his blunt assessments of American culture and the intelligentsia's part in creating it, and his call for a drastic retooling of the American political and economic system along Marxian lines reflected not only his own thinking but also the views of the new literary Left. A few of his *New Republic* readers were critical or hostile, like Norman Thomas, the leader of the Socialist Party, and Robert Hallowell, the friend of John Reed.[53] But generally speaking, Wilson's ideas appealed to the writers and intellectuals who were not yet or were never to be Communists but who had no wish to preserve capitalism.

A revealing response came from former Dadaist Matthew Josephson, who implied that even in the feckless twenties, he and his cronies had become socialists at heart. "Then, as prospective men of letters or of professions, we foresaw the most meager stake for ourselves under the heedless capitalist arrangement; so that our interests, quite deterministically, lay behind our indifference and made us secretly or waitingly Marxian." And yet, Josephson said, it was not so much their paltry remuneration that turned the intellectuals against the profit system as it was the "moral nightmares" it gave them. "The moment you are disinterested, as scientist, artist, or teacher, you are hemmed in, jostled and harassed on every side by the stupe-fying principle that determines the whole environment: buy cheap and sell dear." Hence Josephson could appreciate Wilson's "moral anger" and accept his proposal for a wholesale change. He was not blind to the objections of those who feared the threat to individual freedom in collective societies. He, too, had shown how people are regimented in the standardized American society. However, the time had come to stop debating the color of collectivism, to draw up the blueprints, and suppress the "unessential differences among our-selves . . . which delight all the hosts of conservatism." Now was the time for "a bravely dogmatic utterance," an "apocalyptic appeal" that would touch the submerged white-collar class drugged by capi-talist aspirations:

The communist ideal, as Wilson has seen, must be translated into terms of the native, American situation. Far from shunning propaganda we must use it more nobly, more skillfully than our predecessors, and speak through it in the local language and slogans. The idea of "Service" has never seemed wrong in itself; we have suffered largely for the great want of this Christian principle, and for the mockery made of it. Nor do the notions of "drives" or "team spirit," typically American and used toward communal or concerted ends, seem less susceptible of a decent function. The whole aspect of American life in the last decade, under mass-production capitalism, has been intensely gregarious, uniform, herd-like, marked by a vast standardization of human needs and movements. The question of finally consecrating this character of uniformity, through grafting upon it the inspiring collective principle, is one of the new tactics and interpretations. The driving power, as in all great social adventures, must come from the high quantity of moral certainty and moral passion.[54]

AT THE CROSSROADS

The Communists had been listening to the public soliloquies of the Wilsons and the Josephsons with mixed feelings. They had by no means stopped distrusting the intelligentsia, but it was plain that an important segment of them were "not indifferent to the fate of the workers." Even the much-abused H. L. Mencken could reply to a John Reed Club appeal against the persecution of the workers in El

Centro, California: "I am also incurably opposed to denying Communists their constitutional rights." [55] Such expressions, as well as the words and actions of former liberals who were becoming daily more militantly revolutionary, seemed to support the position taken by Egmont Arens in 1929: that in countries where capitalism was still powerful, the "intelligent dissenters against capitalism of all shades of opinion are more valuable to future Communistic action than actual members in the Communist party." Hence, instead of sneering at the middle-class malcontents, the intelligent revolutionaries "ought to go among them, and without ever revealing their purpose, draw them imperceptibly further and further left, just as Lenin's agents did time and time again." [56]

Michael Gold made no effort to conceal his intentions, but after 1929 he spoke out more firmly than ever to the wavering and bewildered liberals who denounced capitalist iniquities but who stopped short of embracing the Communist cause. On occasion he might acknowledge that a writer's work must not be judged "by his private morals or party affiliations," but he kept demanding that the writer "must decide now between two worlds—cooperative or competitive, proletarian or capitalist." Social issues had lost their "beautiful pre-war vagueness." Liberalism, Gold said, was "the art of straddling," a "form of contemporary neuroticism," the philosophy of the lower middle class, "crowded out of its small shop-keeping livelihoods" by "the trustification of the capitalist world." For a long time, liberal economist-philosophers—Veblen, Beard, Dewey, Stuart Chase, to cite a few—had been employing Marxian methodology to undermine the capitalist system, while never daring to admit their debt to Marx or having the courage "to go full route on any idea." [57] Middle-class writers like Dreiser, Lewis, Anderson, and Mencken had mirrored the "defeatism and desperation" of their class without drawing any revolutionary conclusions. Gold professed to be mystified by the refusal of the middle-class intelligentsia to see the import of their own revelations, but he blamed their inbred respectability, their congenital "politeness," their yearning for "compromise"—no matter what the cost.

How did these liberal attributes express themselves? Many years before, in a letter to Upton Sinclair, Gold had paid his respects to

"The Jesus-Thinker," who, like his Master, made no "concessions to the outer world" and might, like a child or a despot, try to fashion the world out of his own fantasies:

Your Jesus is all I have ever suspected the man was like: impractical, unwholesomely sentimental, egotistic and infantile. Such a person roams the streets today: I heard him preach in some of the missions and on that street in Los [Los Angeles] where he had made a little world for himself. He still wears his hair long, and points to his father in the skies. He still believes he can save the world. I talked to him at one of the pentecostal missions in Los, and he tried to convert me from smoking and dance halls and other evils. I have met him in other places—Socialist and Communist locals, occasionally in labor unions. He always gums the works. The masses even the radical masses look upon him as a freak. A revolution is a serious hard-headed practical affair which should be managed by engineers who have a strong human gift of understanding the masses.[58]

Liberals or Jesus-seekers—ethical, fraternal, humanitarian—passed over the brutal instrumentalities of oppression and brooded over "the nobility and purity of their own souls." Mistaking "their own longings for the movement of humanity," they refused to see that a doctor has no thought of ethics as he cuts "some rotten flesh out of the side of a sick man." They desired a fraternal world, but they would not, as Lenin did, face up to the "bloody sacrifices" required to achieve it. In a world, Gold concluded, where millions perished by war and disease, where a "grand edifice of tyranny and woe" was constructed out of human bodies," the masses wanted victory, not purity. "The Russian Bolsheviks will leave the world a better place than Jesus left it." [59]

Almost a decade later, Gold was still striking out against the pussyfooters, against the cult of "good manners" and "politeness," against those who would uphold moderation though a million suffered and died. He denigrated Abraham Lincoln, the perpetual politician, "the perpetual compromiser," and praised the Bolshevik John Brown. If he had to choose, he much preferred "a good old-fashioned God-killer" like Mencken, who had no " 'liberal!' reservations about religion," * to the Jesus-Thinkers; and in 1930 he could write a

---

* Gold called Mencken "our greatest influence in the past decade," but gagged at "the streak of bourgeois paste in him; this bland assumption that

genial reply to his friend Ezra Pound (not one "of these pot-bellied 'free spirits'") when the latter upbraided him for attacking Mussolini's Italy. At least this "free gaudy Elizabethan man-of-letters" was not like "Mr. Steffens," who not only "admired Scarface Mussolini," but, "like Comrade Jesus, has always admired everybody. Oh, this charming trait of tolerance one finds in people who have incomes, and do not have to slave in offices or steel mills!" Steffens, Gold said, belonged to that part of the American intelligentsia "which has always spent the chief part of its time in exposing the sores and leprosies of its uneasy social conscience, and then doing nothing at all." Like most liberals, he was shrewd insofar as his personal affairs were concerned and muddled when it came to dealing with social tragedy. His pose of "the leetle lost cheeild wandering among the social battlefields" typified the liberal who could act at one moment like the disinterested godlike observer and then drag in Jesus "whenever something too tragic and hard happened to distress him in the class struggle." [60]

Ironically, the book that called forth these irate judgments, *The Autobiography of Lincoln Steffens,* was to convince many liberals in the next decade that Communism was the only answer, and Steffens himself became one of the most uncompromising Communist apologists. At the moment, however, Gold did not include Steffens with the handful of bourgeois intellectuals, most notably Edmund Wilson, who were scrambling out of the miasmatic swamp of capitalism onto the clean hard plateau of Communism. Most of them, according to Edwin Seaver, did not yet know what the terms "revolutionary writer" or "bourgeois writer" meant. To them writing was one thing, politics another, and this split in the consciousness of the American writer "between what he conceives to be his function as a social being and his function as a writer" explained his immaturity and his failure to make any impression on American life. Once awakened, they would become fellow travelers, as many of them had already become,

---

capitalism is so firm and inevitable, that it can never be changed. Mencken, despite his sophistication, is always repeating the old platitude: 'you can't change human nature,' when he approaches any social problem. He has as static a concept of human history as any Baptist; he believes the human race has been damned before birth; and nothing can save it." *The New Masses,* VI (Nov. 1930), p. 5.

but they would have to "undergo a revolution within themselves," to learn to think politically and economically, like their European counterparts, before they could shed their bourgeois skins. This took time. But they were already emerging from a self-consciousness of capitalisms's contradictions to an awareness of class consciousness. Said Seaver:

The liberal attitude, to which many of our writers adhere today, is not a way ahead; it is a crossroads from which point it is possible to turn either to the right or to the left, and there can be no doubt that many of our writers will turn to the right as the class struggle grows more intense. But some will just as surely turn to the left.[61]

THE PROCESS OF CONVERSION

Seaver, Gold, Calverton, and other Left Wing writers were not mistaken in their predictions, although the "conversions" which enabled so many critics and novelists to "cast off their middle-class shibboleths" turned out to be less deep-seated and profound than the radicals had hoped. As Floyd Dell had observed perceptively in the mid-twenties, political conversion only touched a part of a person's imagination; the untouched part was likely to remain "under the alien and hostile influences of a bourgeois culture." [62] And so it happened. But in 1932 it seemed to V. F. Calverton that the "radicalization of writers" was "a deep-rooted thing," and not a fad. Heretofore, he thought, the American intellectuals, from Howells on, who had called for a radical change in society had not been in the main stream. Now, with such writers as Theodore Dreiser, Sherwood Anderson, Waldo Frank, Granville Hicks, Newton Arvin, Malcolm Cowley, Clifton Fadiman, Lionel Trilling, Edmund Wilson, Edwin Seaver, and many others swinging leftward, literary radicalism had become "a mainstream affair."

Particularly striking to Calverton was the native revolutionary fervor of the new converts, in most cases "men for whom liberalism in one variety or another was at once both challenge and panacea." Unlike their nineteenth-century prototypes, who "remained optimistic" even as "they were attacking the evils of their society," the pessimism of the new radicals mirrored the resentment of a crumbling class. In a society economically and morally bankrupt, they would have to find a substitute for the old individualism by renewing their faith in the masses.[63]

The summer issue of his magazine in 1932 gave more detailed information about the "impact of economic and social change" on a selected number of American writers who had replied to Calverton's questionnaire, "Whither the American Writer." Seventeen of them [64] made some sort of reply to Calverton's six questions: 1) Is American capitalism "doomed to inevitable failure and collapse" and if not, why "will it not collapse in the next decade"? 2) "What position should the American writer take in the social crisis that confronts him?" Should he keep out of it, participate in it, try to interpret it? 3) "What should be the relationship between a writer's work and the (radical) political party?" Should he try to reconcile his art with propaganda? Should he write as he pleases? 4) Will a writer's work be deepened if he becomes a Communist? Would the same follow if he joined the Socialist Party? 5) Will American literature during the next decade follow the path set by Dos Passos and Gold; Robinson Jeffers and Eugene O'Neill; Thornton Wilder; Cabell and Hergesheimer? 6) Can a proletarian literature develop in America? [65]

Since the writers questioned included a number of conservatives and skeptics along with a number of Left-Wingers, no consensus could be expected, but only two of them had any doubts about the ultimate, if not the immediate, doom of capitalism. Most of the seventeen felt the writer ought to participate in the social crisis and try to interpret it if he felt compelled to; indeed, it was difficult to escape from such a decision. But no one insisted that the writer must, and some believed certain kinds of writers might be well advised, if for literary reasons alone, to remain aloof. In general, the more unequivocally radical (Dos Passos, Seaver, Arvin, Hicks, Cowley) plumped hard for social participation. Even the most radical, however, although denying any fundamental contradiction between art and propaganda, protested against a slavish commitment to a party line. A good many felt that the writer would be truer to his craft, and of more help to the radical cause, if he remained a free agent. Those already sympathetic to Communism naturally believed that

becoming a Communist might benefit the writer, but no one declared
that doing so would automatically improve a writer's work. Significantly, only two out of the twelve who addressed themselves to the
question whether becoming a Socialist would have the same effect
on a writer as becoming a Communist answered in the affirmative.
Joining the Socialist Party, John Dos Passos flippantly observed
"would have just about the same effect on anybody as drinking a
bottle of near-beer," and the other ten dismissed the Socialist Party
as a tepid compromise.[66] The majority hoped or expected the new
trend in American writing to follow the path blazed by Dos Passos
and Gold, but no contributor was willing to prophesy a proletarian
renaissance. "It seems to me," Dos Passos wrote in regard to the
latter point, "that Marxians who attempt to junk the American tradition, that I admit is full of dry-rot as well as sap, like any tradition,
are just cutting themselves off from the continent. Somebody's got
to have the size to Marxianize the American tradition before you
can sell the American worker on the social revolution. Or else
Americanize Marx." [67]

The chronicle of Communism's impact on the literary mind continued in the September 1932 issue of *The New Masses,* in which
Waldo Frank, Clifton Fadiman, Granville Hicks, Sherwood Anderson, Edmund Wilson, and Michael Gold explained explicitly or
guardedly why they had accepted Marx, or turned left, or joined the
Communist Party.

Starting the list of testifiers was Waldo Frank, fresh from Russia
(critically but sympathetically observed) and the experiences of
Harlan, Kentucky. His "movement toward the left," as he wrote to
The New Masses editors, was "a steady, logical evolution." Born in
an upper-middle-class Jewish New York family and a graduate of
Yale, he had little in common with Michael Gold except what Mary
Colum called "that sensuality of mind and intellect which is sometimes a characteristic of the Jew when loosened from his racial
moorings," something akin to the "maudlin sentimentality of the
transplanted Celt." Before Frank discovered Marx, he had rebelled
against the sterility and cruelty of capitalist culture, and as one of
the editors of *The Seven Arts,* he had helped to formulate a revolutionary program in which an aroused proletarian class played no

part. Salvation rested in the hands of "a small band of gallant writers who were to lead the 'multitude'—and who, of course, failed to materialize." America's principal need, he announced in 1919, was to link the aesthetic with the revolutionary.[68]

The novels and travel books Frank wrote in the twenties, sometimes powerful and often misty, were at once lyrical and social. They portrayed slum life, as in *City Block* (1922), or tragedies of racial hatred, as in *Holiday* (1923). His central preoccupation, however, was "the problem of creating a *new world* in our hemisphere," of "overcoming the false individualism that is the essence of our capitalistic order," and of supplanting it with the collective spirit that animated the Spanish, American Indian, and Russian cultures. *Virgin Spain* (1926), *America Hispana* (1931), and *Dawn in Russia* (1932) were written to help Americans understand themselves, but they were treated, except in Latin America, as mere travel books.[69]

Where did Frank stand now, after this slow evolution from "personal revolt against bourgeois society . . . to the discovery of dynamic forces and values in our modern epoch, potential for the creating of a new revolutionary world"? By 1932, he no longer cared to identify himself with bourgeois intellectuals. Without idealizing the worker, he was convinced that the writer must have "faith in the proletarians and farmers who *alone* as a class have not been hopelessly corrupted by the sources and methods of the capitalistic order." Henceforth the writer must co-operate with the masses or "despair and surrender alone," recognize the proletarian class as "the *chief instrument*" for forging the new society; take a "militant part, *as intellectuals*" in the class war; establish a physical solidarity with the people as well as write books; act now "to save mankind from the destruction of capitalist war, and (still worse) from the moral syphilis of capitalistic peace."

Clifton Fadiman's testimony was as down-to-earth as Frank's was lofty. History turned him left as well as a good look at business, "another word for America." Then there were people, perhaps history "disguised as individuals," who put him wise. "Also," he said, "I got a little sour on the sort of stuff I was writing." It did not develop. The point of view was unsatisfactory. Fascism was another possibility, but he was "temperamentally indisposed toward the black shirt." Possibly imitation or "mass compulsion" played a part, historical determinism working again.

Without professing to be a Communist, Sherwood Anderson tried to convey in a few paragraphs why he had deserted capitalism. Actually, his first book, *Why I Believe in Socialism* (torn up after completion), indicated his early sympathies with the Left, and his second novel, *Marching Men,* tried "to get at the every day lives of coal miners in a middle western coal mining town," but Anderson considered his *Winesburg, Ohio,* the most truly revolutionary of his works because it showed that the defeated and unglamorous people were as sensitive to pain and beauty as the rich and successful. Such people as himself, he suggested, should be left free as possible to quarry their stories out of American life, to get the "deeper facts," without resort to propaganda.

The fullest accounts in *The New Masses* symposium of ideological transformation came from Granville Hicks and Gold. The latter had been seasoning his political opinions with autobiographical reminiscences for years. None of his readers needed to be reminded what Gold thought of capitalism, either in its healthy or broken-down state. Most intellectuals, he said, were liberals, namely, incipient fascists; only the working class could introduce socialism; the Anarchists were moribund; the Socialists had swung over to reaction; the "majestic thunder of the Five Year Plan" had "shaken the world"; only the Communist Party could be trusted to establish the just society Gold had been calling for ever since 1914, when he had been booted by a cop during an Anarchist demonstration in Union Square. But Hicks was a new type of recent convert and a heartening indication that American intellectuals of native stock were beginning to see the light.

Hicks had emerged from Harvard as "a fairly typical liberal with a mild interest in socialism, a strong faith in pacifism, and the usual conviction that the desired changes in the social order could be brought about by the dissemination of sound ideas." Throughout the "Coolidge prosperity," he remained vaguely socialist, until the Sacco-Vanzetti case "crushed my faith in liberalism." Still, personal problems and "the myth of prosperity" kept him inactive until the crash, when the rottenness of the capitalist system could no longer be ignored. "Long conversations" with Communist friends destroyed the lingering virus of liberalism and enabled him gradually "to break through the fog of self-deception and confusion." Not until he had begun to study the attitudes of the post-Civil War writers toward industrialism, however, and to read the works of Marx did he understand the implications of the views he had already embraced. Admittedly, he acknowledged, his bourgeois background ill equipped him to take a leading part in the great struggle, but he hoped to make what modest contributions he could on the critical front.[70]

Edmund Wilson's short paragraphs simply stated that since the death of Herbert Croly, editor of *The New Republic,* he had "investigated Marxism and really understood the Marxist position." The story of his discovery he had already published in *The American Jitters,* described by Clifton Fadiman as showing the "educational process by which Mr. Wilson has emerged from his recent absorption in the great values—Culture, Truth, Beauty—into the real world of collapsing American life." [71] In the last chapter of his book, "The Case of the Author," Wilson paid tribute to the acuteness with which Marx foretold the developing contradictions of modern capitalism and the relevance of his theories to an interpretation of American history. The optimism and "hysterical exhilaration" of the twenties had ended and with it the trashy prosperity which had buoyed it up. The crash and ensuing depression proved America was not immune "to the Marxist assumption of the incurable swinishness and inertia of human nature which automatically creates class war." In the face of all the objective evidence of breakdown, the bourgeoisie who had no stake in capitalism stubbornly clung to their economic delusions.

Wilson himself had retained his bourgeois "ideology" even though his World War I experiences had made him a rebel and taught him

that class antagonisms, conflicts, and injustices are real, that they rarely get any publicity, that the class on top virtually controls the organs of publicity, that the capacities of human nature for remaining blind to the consequences of its actions where its comfort and prestige are concerned are so great that it cannot usually be induced even to notice what it is up to without a violent jolt from below, and that there is no hope for general decency and fair play except from a society where classes are abolished.

He had played at being the Menckenian ironist, the old native-stock American, the liberal capitalist, the enthusiast for American energy, the ivory-tower solitary, the mad hedonist. But he came to see that all these roles were variations of compromise with the broken state.

Now, in 1932, he sided with the "cool-headed revolutionists" who looked to Russia. Though still a bourgeois, he shared "certain interests in common with these proletarians," and he reminded other "professional theorists and artists" that they stood to gain more by joining "those elements who will remodel society by the power of imagination and thought" than by trying to adapt themselves to "shabby politicians" and "acquisitive manufacturers." He knew, at last, that science and poetry were not "great independent entities," but are invariably entangled in social institutions, that machines in the classless society would no longer be instruments for human exploitation, that allegedly "precious 'values' cultivated by aristocratic societies" would not be missed "in a society of sound people run for the common good." [72]

FOR FOSTER AND FORD

In September 1932 Wilson and fifty-two other artists and intellectuals, some of them veterans of the two Kentucky expeditions and self-proclaimed converts to Communism and others who would soon become prominent in the Left movement, published an "open letter" to writers, artists, intellectuals, and professional men. The statement denounced the two major parties as "hopelessly corrupt," rejected the Socialists as a do-nothing party, and declared their support for the Communist Party, which also sought to defend the dispossessed classes and establish an equitable society. A month later they organized the League of Professional Writers for Foster and Ford, the Presidential candidates of the Communist Party, and expanded their original declaration into a pamphlet entitled *Culture and Crisis*.[73]

The burden of the pamphlet contained nothing new. Here was the same story of capitalism's fatal contradictions, the lunacy of the administration, the futility of the Socialist Party's "reformist" planning, the threat of fascism, and the fighting program of the Communists, the only party capable of wringing concessions from the ruling class. Its author or authors resorted throughout to the language and imagery of decay, rottenness, breakdown. Roosevelt's election would only prop up the "machine of government" by stuffing the boiler with cotton waste and mending the broken bolts with haywire. "The United States under capitalism" was "like a house rotting away; the roof leaks, the sills and rafters are crumbling." America's plunge into imperialism portended "deep decay." Hoovervilles of tin and paper, the dwellings of the unemployed, were springing up "along the fringes of civilization," part of the wreckage "of nature, of obsolete social patterns and institutions, of human blood and nerve" left by the receding tidal wave of history.

But if the picture of cultural dissolution conjured up by the pamphlet was hardly novel in 1932, the fact that fifty-three writers and artists, many of them well known, were prepared to renounce their bourgeois allegiances, to affiliate as "brain workers" with the only other class they deemed worthy of respect—"the muscle workers"—this was indeed unprecedented in American history. Although speaking for all unemployed America, they addressed themselves specifically to a group most likely to be impressed by the paradox of potential plenty and mass privation, the waste of talent in a country that had "never yet been able to provide its population with a sufficiently large body of trained intellectuals to satisfy its cultural needs." Their Veblenian diagnosis ended with a call to vote Communist:

Very well, we strike hands with our true comrades. We claim our own and we reject the disorder, the lunacy spawned by grabbers, advertisers, traders, speculators, salesmen, the much-adulated, immensely stupid and irresponsible "business men." We claim the right to live and function. It is our business to think and we shall not permit business men to teach us our business. It is also, in the end, our business to act.

We have acted. As responsible intellectual workers we have aligned ourselves with the frankly revolutionary Communist Party, the party of the workers. In this letter, we speak to you of our own class—to the writers, artists, scientists, teachers, engineers, to all honest professional workers—telling you as best we can why we have made this decision and why we think that you too should support the Communist Party or the political campaign now under way.

The signatories of the *Culture and Crisis* pamphlet were, for the most part, independents, not Communists, and a number of them very quickly withdrew from any affiliation with the party. Probably a good many voted Communist, not because they expected or even wanted the Communists to win, but out of protest. This, at any rate, was the reason that Dos Passos subsequently gave. "It certainly wasn't that I wanted the Communists to conduct the revolution in American government which I felt was needed." [74] Yet others, as the Depression deepened, moved closer to the party, uncritically accepted its diagnosis of national and international affairs, battled its intellectual and cultural enemies, and wooed its potential friends.

SEVEN · FROM FREEDOM TO POLITICS

PROBLEMS OF POLICY

THE LEFTWARD TURN of the American intelligentsia between 1928 and 1932 was gratifying to the party veterans who had been agitating without much success only a few years before, but they did not regard the influx of the bourgeois recruits with unqualified satisfaction. *The New Masses* by 1930 was beginning to reflect the policies of the party more consistently than it had in the past, and the cultural directives from abroad presented its editors with a new set of problems. In order to appreciate their delicacy, we must return again to the late twenties and examine the state of affairs of this still-faltering magazine.

The struggle of *The New Masses* to survive between 1926 and 1930 proved that the times were hardly so propitious for radical journalism as they had been in the early days of its namesake. And the amiable conflicts between the liberals and radicals on the magazine foreshadowed some of the deeper and uglier antagonisms to come.

By 1926 the polarizing process that separated the "Reds" from the Bohemian vagabonds or the "playboys" had gone far enough to make the tolerant indiscrimination of *The Masses* impossible. Gold, Gellert, Freeman, and the other radicals still shared some of the gay, obstreperous, bourgeois-shocking inclinations of the liberals, but they were also serious socialists. A number of them had been to Russia.

To them, the "class struggle" was not a romantic phrase, but a term that designated the Passaic strike or the electrocution of Sacco and Vanzetti. They not only believed in the socialist revolution, but they also wanted to recruit revolutionary writers to the movement.

The liberal or non-Communist position and the radical response it provoked emerge clearly in the debates over policy carried on in the early issues of *The New Masses* between John Dos Passos and Ernest Walsh against Michael Gold. At this time, Dos Passos was moving into his most radical phase, but his constitutional aversion to any sort of ideological organization or "imported systems" made him distrust "phrases, badges, opinions, banners, imported from Russia or anywhere else." All "word-slingers," said Dos Passos, shared some of the "functional deformities" of their trade, and in 1926 the radical writers were as far away from reality as the reactionary ones. Yet in "these terribly crucial years," knowing what was going on and being clear-sighted was "a life and death matter." It was the business of *The New Masses* to go on exploring in unexplored places, to bring back uncatalogued specimens, to venture out without fixed preoccupations, to be full of introspection and doubt, to be more disciplined in action than in thought. "The terrible danger to explorers is that they always find what they are looking for. . . . I want an expedition that will find out what it's not looking for." [1]

Gold replied that he could go along most of the way with "friend John," only he preferred to slip "Moscow and revolution . . . into the pilot's compass-box" instead of navigating by "doubt and introspection." The writer, said Gold, can recognize "that Soviet Russia and its revolutionary culture form the spiritual core around which thousands of the younger writers in every land are building their creative selves," yet he denied that young American writers must "take their 'spiritual' commands from Moscow." Humane and sensitive artists needed no promptings from abroad to revolt. The important question was what form this revolt would take. Dos Passos and his vague aesthetic friend John Howard Lawson counseled a bland and impressionistic revolt that could only end in "pessimism, defeatism, and despair." But Dos Passos' own discovery revealed "the world of revolutionary labor," with its "great new themes," its "hopeful unsentimental spirit." Gold hoped that *The New Masses* might be the bridge to this world which "makes great and even cruel demands on its writers" but which "can make them great, in return." *The New Masses* would "not be a magazine of Communism, or Moscow, but a magazine of American experiment." [2]

To Ernest Walsh, publisher of *This Quarter,* Gold's celebration of "revolutionary labor" smacked of cant, and in an open letter to *The New Masses,* he gave his reasons why "organized opinion and emotion never can be right." Gold's basic error, Walsh thought, was the simple black-and-white dichotomy of "good" labor and "bad" capital. No cause or party had a monopoly on virtue; the "unfortunate masses" were not always the "honest masses," and the writer did not create literature by "making a scarecrow out of humanity." Gold was trying to mix the wine of literature with the beer of politics and convert the writer from an outsider into an insider. But the writer had no business tying himself down to a party: "God-almighty, Walt Whitman was a poet, not a laboring man." Walsh concluded with an admonition whose full portent was only belatedly savored. "When you borrow your enemies' weapons you lose the fight. Make your enemies borrow your weapons and be sure they *are* your weapons." [3]

Walsh's death in the fall of 1926 prevented a full-scale answer by Gold, but after paying tribute to Walsh's courage and integrity, he noted that the letter was "typical of the ignorance of history and economics (the social life of man) that afflicts most of our literary men." Nonetheless, Gold said, Walsh expressed "the post-war rebellion of the best elements of the middle-class revolt against all that grand lie compromised under the term of Woodrow Wilsonism. . . ." In time, Walsh might have "plunged into the American mass-life, which creates bigger artists than the cafe cliques of Paris and Italy." [4]

Gold continued to take pot shots at the unorganized idealists in the columns of the magazine, but his tone was always genial and conciliatory, and he managed to recapture some of the bravura of the old *Masses.* His efforts brought compliments from Louis Untermeyer, who wrote in: "Let me join the gang of converts. I, too, as one of the editors of the old *Masses* looked with a mingling of suspicion and foreboding at the first few numbers of the New Masses." From Europe came Ezra Pound's accolade: "For the first time in years I have even gone so far as to think of making a trip to America; so you can take the blame for that if for nothing else." Even Max Eastman overcame his "terrible grouch" after reading the first issues and praised the editors for successfully co-ordinating "your art-theories and sociological pre-occupations to a general standard of excellence." [5]

Unfortunately, the widening differences between the radicals and the liberals made it difficult for the editors to maintain this happy co-ordination of art and politics. Letters came in complaining about the "radical partisanship" of the magazine, while "paragraph writers on the *Daily Worker*" unloaded "columns of sarcasm" against *The New Masses'* discussions of sex and art. At first the editors stuck to their middle ground:

We may as well be frank. We are against dogma, hypocrisy, and rigidity wherever we find it. We are radical, revolutionary, dynamically for change and growth, and we are impatient with liberalism, compromise and reformism. We are as much against the Socialist puritan as we are against the capitalist puritan. We are as much against a labor-union bureaucrat as we are against Mussolini. Smug formulas and complacent institutions we will attack lustily wherever they seem to stand in the way of human freedom. That kind of crusade is lots of fun. The writers and artists and *readers* of the New Masses will not have such a dull time of it. [6]

But it was becoming harder and harder to maintain this tone of amiable independence.

GOLD TAKES OVER

Financial worries continued to harass the editors. Although the magazine (according to Stuart Chase, who went over its books for the Garland Fund in February 1917) was a miracle of efficiency, it ran an $18,000 to $20,000 deficit, and Arens, the managing editor, despaired of raising enough money to keep it going. "The radical groups themselves," he told the fund, "torn as they are in factional warfare, have no money for general causes, and genuine radicalism has gone out of style with the wealthy liberals." Neither the radicals, "impatient of any point of view which is broader than their own," nor the liberals, full of guilt about forsaking a cause "that in their hearts they would like to subscribe to," could be counted upon.[7]

And yet the very conditions that accounted for the magazine's slow and laborious progress proved its need. Its function, Arens declared, was "to point a common direction for all radical factions" and to keep the liberals feeling guilty. If Roger Baldwin, director of the fund, would examine the bound volumes of *The New Masses,* Arens suggested, he would

perhaps understand why the New Masses is welcomed in France and Germany and Russia, in Mexico and South America as the liveliest and most convincing expression of American arts and letters that has come to them. You will see too why the New Masses has become the hope of radicals of all shades of opinion throughout America—why isolated farmers and radical groups in small centers who are out of touch with the main currents of the movement find in this magazine the enthusiasm which keeps alive for them the spark of hope for a better day.

Arens took occasion at this time to correct a rumor gaining currency since the founding of the magazine, namely that it was "more or less a Communist organ." A glance at the executive board, he pointed out, would show that "Communist Party members are in a decided minority." *The New Masses* supported "any live or aggressive radical movement" and was "dedicated to the job of driving together the progressive radical elements, not widening their differences." What he did not acknowledge to Baldwin was the difficulty he was having trying to keep *The New Masses* "a free radical magazine" without being called a counterrevolutionary.[8] He still believed in its value, but by March 1928 he was prepared to liquidate it.

The executive board of *The New Masses,* however, was loathe to give up, and after Ernestine Evans turned down the editorship, Gold and Hugo Gellert volunteered to assume the editorial duties. In a letter to the fund asking for another subsidy of $2,000, Gold and Gellert outlined a new attack. Henceforth, they said, the magazine would seek to build up a group of loyal subscribers. It would "try to be more satirical, literary and artistic, and less directly political." And it would be more modest in its expectations. Would the fund risk another subsidy? If not, the "outgoing managers" wanted "to wind up things at once." [9]

At first the fund refused the request to support a new editorial staff with a new editorial policy. Apparently Baldwin had no confidence in the amateurs, and his doubts may have been abetted by Max Eastman, who wrote to him in April that he could not at this time "identify myself with the New Masses, unless I took it into my own hands entirely—the editorship, I mean—and went into the fight for truth-telling and an intelligent and genuinely American political policy based on the class-struggle. It would mean complete absorption in a political movement—a political-journalistic career." That was out of the question, and he saw no reason "to enter into it half-way." [10]

Once again, however, Freda Kirchwey, who served on the executive board of *The New Masses* as well as on the fund board, came to the rescue. Although she had opposed turning over the management of the magazine to Gold and Gellert, she decided in her capacity as fund member "to allow them to make this desperate attempt." "If the political views of the editors," she wrote to the fund board, "are in question, they are views which have animated the majority of the New Masses board from the beginning. At present they seem to me to offer the one desperate hope the magazine has of surviving—the chance of winning more material and emotional support from the left wing and the Workers' party." [11] The fund agreed to reopen the case, and on October 3, 1928, restored the $2,000—with Baldwin still voting in the negative.

With the assumption of the editorship by Gold, the magazine became what Gold had always wanted it to be: a revolutionary organ dedicated to the working class, smaller in format, and printed on cheaper paper. Let other magazines hunt for "big names," Mike Gold declared. He wanted "the working men, women, and children of America to do most of the writing in the New Masses," no matter how crude. He wanted to print "the raw materials of the workers' art in the New Masses" so that if a "proletarian genius arrives, it will be ready for him." Gold concluded with half-serious extravagance:

WE WANT TO PRINT:
  Confessions—diaries—documents—
  The concrete—
  Letters from hoboes, peddlers, small
town atheists, unfrocked clergymen and
schoolteachers—
  Revelations by rebel chambermaids
and night club waiters—
  The sobs of driven stenographers—
  The poetry of steel workers—
  The wrath of miners—the laughter
of sailors—
  Strike stories, prison stories,
work stories—
  Stories by Communist, I.W.W. and
other revolutionary workers.[12]

The New Masses continued to remain "too damn literary" for the "working stiffs" who filled the magazine's letter columns with tough proletarian sentiments, but under Gold's direction it welcomed eagerly what one studiedly proletarian writer called the "as yet, semi-articulate voices hidden in the mines, textile mills, farms, saw-mills, and lumber-camps." [13]

THE CULT OF THE PROLETARIAN

Long before Michael Gold conjured up his vision of a Shakespeare in overalls, other American intellectuals had from time to time reached out the hand of fellowship to the "swart and sweaty artizan." Even the relatively small number who took up the cause of labor, however, did so in a gingerly, rather than a genial, way. They were more likely to weep over the wrongs of the working class or to raise horrific nightmares of a debased proletariat descending like the Huns on a corrupt plutocracy or to write reproving lectures in which they demonstrated to middle-class readers why the laboring man must not be excluded or neglected.

"Men of literary tastes," Frederick L. Olmsted wrote shortly before the Civil War, "are always apt to overlook the working-classes, and to confine the records they make of their times, in a great degree, to the habits and fortunes of their own associates, or to those of people of superior rank to themselves, of whose sayings and doings their vanity, as well as their curiosity, leads them most carefully to inform themselves. The dumb masses have often been so lost in this shadow of egotisms, that, in later days, it has been impossible to discern the very real influence their character has had on the fortune and fate of nations." [14]

Among the major American authors, only Walt Whitman addressed himself to the workingman without inhibition or restraint, but no writer of stature in nineteenth-century America had written "the Uncle Tom's Cabin of Capitalism" or had ennobled the factory hand or the tenement dweller. Perhaps, predicted Edward Markham in 1901, the "literature of the future" will "discover that the workingman is the prince in disguise." [15]

Most of the nineteenth- and early twentieth-century attempts to deal with the "poor but honest" workingman as a "prince in disguise" failed to convince, because the writers themselves were temperamentally and culturally too far removed from the proletarian's world. Their books were more often than not merely well-intended slumming expeditions from which they returned exalted or depressed. A few neglected and forgotten books did cast some glimmering rays on industrial America; the reports, fictional and otherwise, of men who mingled with tramps and criminals or who spied upon the "People of the Abyss" brought glimpses of a bizarre and exotic underworld to the protected bourgeoisie; but even Sinclair's exposure of the Chicago stockyard jungle and Jack London's emotional and slanted tales of industrial revolt did little to bridge what Francis Hackett called in 1917 "the enormous gap between literate and unliterate America." [16]

The occasion for this comment was Hackett's review of Sherwood Anderson's *Marching Men,* that half-baked yet menacing parable of the sleeping giant, Labor, aroused by a charismatic leader and converted into a kind of prefascist industrial army. Hackett observed in passing that

the proletarian has had small place in American fiction. Under the ban of negligible ugliness, as the eminent novelists see it, comes the great majority of the people. They, the eminent ones, have principally been the children of circumspect parents, Presbyterians or Baptists, middle class in social and moral habits and unlikely to be hospitable to the primordial. Outside their view lies the life of the proletarian except as it impinges on the middle class, and these rawnesses of American existence, so conceived, have as little part in a polite literacy as have peanuts in the poetry of Oscar Wilde. It is not that the facts are seen and rejected. The facts are simply not open to the eminent novelists any more than to social-sentiment workers or bright reporters or class-hyphenates of the sweetest disposition. The proletarians are in a different universe of discourse, and one so unthinkable to eminent novelists that it is promptly ruled out, the way we humane people rule out the superheated hell.[17]

Anderson did not rule out the proletarians, but his collective portrait exaggerated their rawness, cruelty, dumbness, and submissiveness and hardly differed from the inventions of Ignatius Donnally, Edward Bellamy, and Jack London. Anderson's Chicago, furthermore, lacked the verisimilitude of Dreiser's. Yet *Marching Men,* if it was not the "graphic . . . proletarian novel" Hackett declared it to be, did catch the restless mood of the times and prefigured the proletarian myth that very shortly after quickened the imagination of Michael Gold.

Unlike most of the promising radicals who had inevitably "drifted with the tide of the ocean of American middle-class mediocrity" after the first flurry of revolutionary enthusiasm, Gold had remained faithful to the working class and struggled hard to keep the fire of revolution from flickering out during the twenties. No other writer tried more conscientiously to combat Bohemianism or expatriate indifference. "There are only two positive realistic philosophies in America today—" he wrote in 1927, "that of the capitalist imperialists, and that of the Communists," but only the latter had discovered the "technique for capturing the swift powerful movement of the Machine Age." Aristocratic writers found no beauty in geometry, skyscrapers, typewriters, electricity, radio, but the Kremlin had transmuted "vouchers, daybooks and index cards" into poetry, and Gold found " 'beauty' in a pamphlet by Marx, and in Lenin's words roaring and dancing like an earthquake." [18]

Not even the brilliant Trotsky, whose *Literature and Revolution* he had reviewed so rhapsodically, could shake Gold's certainty that an already dawning proletarian culture would make great works of art out of the realities of the Machine Age.

Since the proletarian dictatorship would be quickly supplanted by the classless society, Trotsky had argued, it would disappear before it had time to create a distinct culture of its own. The revolution was less a subject for a new art than a molding force that would create a new classless art.[19] But Gold could not agree:

Even if for only fifty years the proletariat remains in subjection to capitalist society, will there not be some art growing out of this mass of intense, tragic, active human beings? Will they not sing, and need cartoons, plays, novels, like other human beings? Are they not studying, groping, reaching out hungrily for culture? It is not a matter of theory; it is a fact that a proletarian style is emerging in art. It will be as transitory as others styles; but it will have its day.[20]

By 1930 Gold felt his long-sustained agitation in behalf of proletarian literature had been justified and his sardonic critics refuted. Proudly he proclaimed himself "the first American writer to herald the advent of a world proletarian literature as a concomitant to the rise of the world proletariat," and although he acknowledged that his first pronouncements in *The Liberator* had been "rather mystic and intuitive," the "little path" he had blazed in 1920 had become a highroad. To the doubters, he promised a hundred proletarian Shakespeares. A new literary form was evolving, Gold said—he called it "Proletarian Realism"—and he outlined its objectives.

1. Workers, because they are skilled technicians, must write with the technical proficiency of a Hemingway, but not for the purpose of engendering cheap and purposeless thrills.

2. "Proletarian realism deals with the *real conflicts* of men and women." It spurns the sickly, sentimental subtleties of Bohemians, best illustrated by "the spectacle of Proust, master-masturbator of the bourgeois literature." The "suffering of the hungry, persecuted and heroic millions" precludes the inventing of "precious silly little agonies."

3. Proletarian realism is functional; it serves a purpose. "Every poem, every novel and drama, must have a social theme, or it is merely confectionary."

4. It eschews verbal acrobatics: "this is only another form for bourgeois idleness."

5. Proletarians should write about what they know best. "Let the bourgeois writers tell us about their spiritual drunkards and super-refined Parisian emigres . . . that is their world; we must write about our own mud-puddle."

6. "Swift action, clear form, the direct line, cinema in words; this seems to be one of the principles of proletarian realism."

7. "Away with drabness, the bourgeois notion that the Worker's life is sordid, the slummer's disgust and feeling of futility. There *is* horror and drabness in the Worker's life; and we will portray it; but we know this is not the last word; we know that the manure heap is the hope of the future; we know that not pessimism, but revolutionary elan will sweep this mess out of the world forever."

8. "Away with all lies about human nature. We are scientists; we know what a man thinks and feels. Everyone is a mixture of motives; we do not have to lie about our hero in order to win our case."

9. "No straining or melodrama or other effects; life itself is the supreme melodrama. Feel this intensely, and everything becomes poetry—the new poetry of materials, of the so-called 'common man,' the Worker moulding his real world." [21]

Gold did not intend this summary of the proletarian aesthetic to be interpreted as dogma; Marxism, like any other science, he said, grew out of experiment, and its unworkable principles would be discarded. But accepting as given the class nature of contemporary society and the impending decline of the bourgeoisie, he predicted a new proletarian literature, which as yet only *The New Masses* prepared for.[22]

The "new management" that took over the magazine in 1928 succeeded pretty well in making it what Scott Nearing asked it to be: "a real paper—determined, hard-hitting, satirical—full of understanding and sympathy for the class struggle. But it did so at the cost of alienating its more fastidious well-wishers. "What I do not like about the *New Masses*," one of them wrote at the end of 1930, "is the affectation of idealized proletarianism, the monotonous strumming on the hardboiled string, the hostility to ideas on other levels than one, the contempt for modulated writing and criticism, the evasion of discussion. . . ." He was probably referring to a small corps of "worker-writers" who between 1928 and 1930 had been carrying on a "let's-cut-out-the-arty-stuff" campaign in the letter columns and criticizing *The New Masses* for trying to compete with the "pink radical" magazines. Wrote Joseph Kalar from International Falls, Minnesota:

What I would like to see is a *New Masses* that would be read by lumberjacks, hoboes, miners, clerks, sectionhands, machinists, harvesthands, waiters—the people who should count more to us than paid scribblers. It would be interesting to know what percentage of proletarians comprise the subscribers to *New Masses*—if the percentage is low then there is something wrong. Something wrong in the approach. I have found that workers like to read a good snappy article on their line of work—it is like an experience lived over again for them to come upon slang terms peculiar to their occupation. Workers don't write often, they write because if they didn't they would explode. It might be crude stuff—but we're just about done primping before a mirror and powdering our shiny noses. Who are we afraid of? Of the critics? Afraid that they will say the *New Masses* prints terribly ungrammatical stuff? Hell, brother, the newsstands abound with neat packages of grammatical offal.[23]

Kalar, Herman Spector, Martin Russak, Joseph Vogel, H. H. Lewis, and other young revolutionary writers—now virtually forgotten—comprised a new kind of literary coterie, who represented the first proletarian school. Reading their short biographies or autobiographies on the contemporary Left press, we can understand more readily what Mike Gold was getting at when he spoke of the coming proletarian era. The following blurbs are characteristic:

[Joseph Kalar]: . . . age 23 plus; son of iron ore, miner and Slovenian peasant; taught one-room school in homestead district for a year and a half; paper-miller worker and lumber handler; at present, green-lumber scaler. Habitat, wilds of Minnesota. Blacklisted by D.A.R. Indicted by Federal Grand Jury for calling U.S.A. bad names. Contributed to a number of little "free spirit" magazines before his resurrection. Contributed frequently to *Daily Worker*. Aspires to translate bewildered soul of the proletariat articulately, and thus, in a roundabout way, express himself. Contributing editor of *New Masses* and *The Morada*. Now among the unemployed.[24]

[Herman Spector]: Born 1905 in New York City, and has never been farther West than 10th Avenue. Left high school after three years, the loser in a passionate struggle for a vital education, to fulfill the prediction of a pedagogue; you'll turn out to be a ditchdigger or a Bolshevik—. Worked, toward this end, as lumber handler, shipping clerk, truck driver, streetcar conductor, laborer, baker's helper, W.U. "mut," factory hand, butcher boy, envelope addresser, canvasser, soda jerker. Now married, father of a 3-year-old girl, and engaged in writing a novel. Contributed to *Exile, The American Caravan, Free Verse, Anthology of Revolutionary Poetry, Transition, Unrest,* etc. Contributing editor of *New Masses.* Member of the John Reed Club.[25]

[Martin Russak]: . . . was born in 1906. Family for two generations back have been textile workers in Paterson, N.J. and active in the labor movement there. Himself went to work in the mills at the age of 13. During the past two years he has been an organizer for the National Textile Workers Union in Paterson, Pennsylvania and New Bedford. Is a member of the National Executive Board of the Union. His story in this issue is part of a book of a silk weaver's life, on which he works in any odd moments which his job and his activities in the union may permit. . . . Contributing editor to *New Masses.* At present working as a weaver in Paterson.[26]

[H. H. Lewis]: 28 years old. Residence: a farm at Cape Girardeau, Missouri. Former mission stiff and jungle buzzard. Town trade, dishwashing; country specialty, milking Missouri cows; hobby, writing poesie for *New Masses.* His creed: to make words rhyme and syllables come in exact order, to poetically exalt the proletariat out of its misery. His burden: about 2800 lines of radical jingles ready for book publication.[27]

These harsh-sounding "foreign" names and the "unliterary" occupations of the new proletarians grated on the sensibilities of many genteel Americans who did not associate the American muse with "hunkies," "wops," "kikes," and "polacks" of the lower classes. And the manners and language of the upstarts did not reassure them. Mike Gold constantly used metaphors of death and putrescence in describing the "sick" and "rotten" bourgeoisie, but his young proletarians outdid him in picturesque invective.

Joseph Kalar, for example, could not say simply that bourgeois writers were corrupt. He had to contrast the proletarian writer of the future with "the literary vermin that swarm over and gnaw America's literary corpse, who play the scented whore, and for thirty pieces of silver, will do the hootchi-kootchi dance, or wriggle their abdomens in imitation of legendary oriental ladies." Kalar, like so many in his group, could not take his eyes off the fat belly of capitalism. The old Populists had spoken of the "bloated plutocrat," but he extended (or distended) the metaphor: "Capitalism, gorged with booty, beats on its distended belly the death chant to its own inevitable dissolution . . . it breeds countless of sincere writers who bleed at the nose with disillusion and cry in moving anguish." [28]

Images of decay quite properly suggested themselves to the dedicated proletarian writer who wished to convey the idea that capitalism was expiring, but the reiteration of such words as "retch," "vomit," "syphilis," "grease," "rot," "ashcans," "cancerous," and the like in proletarian poetry may have some less obvious significance. Lenin, in "A letter to American Workingmen" (published in *The Liberator* in 1919), had used the language of corruption: "The dead body of bourgeois society cannot simply be put in a coffin and buried. It rots in our midst, poisons the air we breathe, pollutes our lives, clings to the new, the fresh, the living with a thousand threads and tendrils of old customs, of death and decay." The young proletarians preserved the capitalist corpse for their eloquent and sometimes nauseating sermons in prose and verse.[29]

The posturings of the proletarian literary tribunes, their wild claims, their poor taste, their ignorance, their sentimentalism and self-pity, and their primitiveness, their self-conscious toughness made them vulnerable to their better-read critics, who had no trouble demonstrating the absurdities of the "Cult of the Clod" [30] even before the proletarian vogue got under way.

Well-wishers like Kenneth Burke pointed out to the sectarians of the Left that all literature need not aim primarily at the eradication of injustice. The "pamphlet, the political tract, the soap-box oration" might deal "with the specific issues of the day," but the social reformer ought to be glad that so much imaginative literature "is written in defiance of his injunctions." [31]

Eugene Jolas feared that the new school would simply produce "the same old realism with nauseating and boring photography," and the novelist Robert Herrick warned the proletarian writers that their characters must be more than the mere adjuncts of the workers that dominated them. They would have to learn "to surmount the barricades of their own prejudices." Mockery and contempt were not enough.[32]

These and other admonitions rained down upon the proletarian school even after it was dominated by urban intellectuals who had to do "research" on the workers' lives and occupations. In a few years the proletarian aesthetic hardened, the critical controversies over definitions grew more heated, and the myth of the Worker Hero flowered in the novels of social protest during the 1930's. But on the eve of the Great Depression, a small body of brash young radicals had virtual control over the only magazine in the United States sympathetic to their literary and political program; their energy and confidence and crudeness inspired a certain respect and envy in those middle-class writers who no longer wished to be "lonely unicorns."

REVIVING JOHN REED—HERO

Not all of the writers with revolutionary inclinations were good enough to be published in *The New Masses,* and as part of the magazine's program to develop promising artists of the proletariat, it founded the John Reed Club of New York shortly after the stock market crash of 1929.

In announcing "A New Program for Writers," Gold offered the following suggestions for the literary branch of the club: 1) each writer should attach himself to a single industry, study it closely for several years, and make "himself an expert in it," so that he could write about it as "an insider, not like a bourgeois intellectual observer"; 2) he should write publicity for strikes so that he "will have his roots in something real"; 3) if this is done, a "national corps of writers" can become in effect a "staff of industrial correspondents" who will report on the cultural front from all over industrial America; 4) *The New Masses* could then be put "on an industrial basis," and become the tongue of the working class.[33] By no means all of the young radicals supported this particular plan, but a large number were heartened by the idea of affiliating under the aegis of the young martyr buried in the Kremlin.

John Reed in 1929 had already become a legend. The Communist Party exploited him as the model activist intellectual, a Bolshevik Richard Harding Davis whose origins and background controverted the middle-class stereotype of the whiskered, bomb-throwing Red.

To Mike Gold, who had known him personally, Reed was "a cowboy out of the West, six feet high, steady eyes, boyish face; a brave, gay, open-handed young giant," the kind of politically conscious Paul Bunyan that "the pale, rootless intellectuals could never understand." [34] Yet he was an intellectual as much as an activist, and his example did much, Gold thought, to destroy the prejudice against the intellectual in the revolutionary labor movement.

Most revolutionists thought (and still think, Gold implied) that it is somehow unmanly to write a play (as Gold had done) "or discuss the arts," that it was "unworthy for the man of action to be also a man of thought." Reed risked every danger, helped organize the American Communist Party, faced hostile judges with boldness and courage, participated in three important strikes, yet he remained a poet. It was most fitting, therefore, that he should lend his name to an organization of radical artists dedicated to the creation of a new revolutionary culture. He, alone, of the old *Masses* crowd, was worthy of their emulation. Max Eastman had never managed to fuse his careers of poet and revolutionary agitator. Eastman, according to Gold, was "a true artist and scientist," but "he was at heart an aristocrat, an individualist; he could never quite consent to be a part of that collectivist organization he pleads for." And Floyd Dell, so far as Gold was concerned, was "an artistic and moral failure." [35]

CASTING OUT DELL—ANTI-HERO

The assault against Dell as the disagreeable anti-hero, the radical corrupted, was carried on by Gold and the spiritual sons of John Reed with increasing bitterness after 1926. Gold and Dell had sparred with each other in *The Liberator* days when Dell repudiated his anarchistic notions about love and marriage and came out for monogamy and babies.[36] He had also poked barbed fun at Gold's proletarian imago. Yet Dell had not given up his socialist convictions, and in such books as *Intellectual Vagabondage,* in his biography of Upton Sinclair, and in occasional reviews and articles, he continued to voice his radical opinions.

But to the young radicals, Dell was merely paying lip service to ideas he once believed in, and had retired from the class struggle. Reviewing *Love in Greenwich Village* (Dell's nostalgic fictionalized recollections of bittersweet Bohemian days), V. F. Calverton, editor of the Marxist *Modern Quarterly,* accused him of selling out. Dell, Calverton said, ought to be in the vanguard "battling for revolutionary art." Instead, he was devoting himself "to the trifling pastime of writing sexy novels for adolescent Menckenians and jaded bourgeoisie." This was no strategic withdrawal, "a literary N.E.P.," but a fundamental break with his radical past. Calverton held up Dell as a sad object lesson "of the inadequacy and failure of our literary radicals" and an illustration of how the radical who gives up economics for sex can achieve "ineffectuality, sterility, and a place in Who's Who." [37]

Dell wrote Calverton a mild and courteous reply. If he were reviewing himself, he told Calverton, he might very likely have raised the question why a writer so long associated with the socialist movement, tried under the Espionage Act during the war, and now a self-styled Communist should write on "bourgeois themes" and allow "so little (if any) of his political, social, and economic radicalism to be seen." Dell offered the following explanation.

His early radicalism was social revolutionary, rather than Communist, and although he managed to keep a balance between his narcissistic and social impulses, he did not resolve the conflict in favor of the latter until he broke from his Bohemian life. Dell felt no contradiction between his new concern for education, sex, and the family and the realities of the Soviet state. His book, *Intellectual Vagabondage,* signified the repudiation of his Greenwich Village anarchism and by implication his acceptance of Communism. As a realistic novelist writing about contemporary America, he could not tell his story in political terms acceptable to orthodox party leaders, because the Communist movement in the United States represented "necessarily, the rebellious and not the stable impulses." This was America's fault, not his.

His progress from romantic vagabond to "the describer, critic and prophet of the machine-age which he had hitherto been only able to hate" made him "better fit to celebrate in fiction the realistic Communist rule which America had yet to achieve than the present effort to achieve it." From personal experience, he was able to detect "the neurotic origins of much political radicalism," and had he chosen to do so, he might very well have made his reputation as a satirist of the Left. Out of loyalty to the radical cause, he did not take this profitable line, although he sometimes wondered whether or not he had done radicalism a disservice by not doing so. Political satire might have been, finally, instructive to the Communist elite, even if the general public had interpreted it as Dell's repudiation of his radical beliefs. He confessed, in conclusion, that he had not quite concluded the dialogue between his narcissistic and social impulses. If he could finally unite them, make use of the "constructive influences of both the Freudian philosophy and the second Russian revolution," he might write something "more in tune with the critical and destructive literary period now in progress." [38]

The fact that Calverton had borrowed freely from Dell's books, especially *Intellectual Vagabondage,* did not lessen the sting of his attack, but his contemptuous review seemed good-natured when compared to Mike Gold's long reply to Dell's note of resignation from the list of contributing editors of *The New Masses* in May of 1929. In his letter, Dell said that he had wanted to be identified with a magazine representing "a partly Communist and at any rate rebellious literary tendency with which I am in sympathy." Unfortunately, it represented "a neurotic literary and pictorial aestheticism with which I am completely out of sympathy"; [39] hence his resignation.

Gold now spit on his hands, rolled up his sleeves, and wrote a merciless denunciation of his old associate and "apostate" radical. Why did Dell now turn against the magazine? Gold was no "psychoanalyst" like Dell, but he had some explanations. Dell, Gold said, was never a revolutionist and had always "had a distaste for reality, for the strong smells and sounds and confusions of the class struggle. He had none of the contacts with workingmen and strikes and battles that John Reed made." No, Dell was the "Greenwich Village playboy" whose "main interests were centered in the female anatomy." All his great contemporaries he denounced as neurotics: Joyce, Dreiser, Anderson, Hemingway; only he "was thoroughly sane, and completely psychoanalyzed, and therefore a great writer and revolutionist." Although he ended his letter of resignation with Jack London's famous "Yours for the Revolution," he stayed as far away from the class war as possible, refused to agitate on behalf of Sacco and Vanzetti, and wrote cheap articles for the slicks with such titles as "I'd Rob a Bank for My Wife," or "Once I Believed in Free Love, Now I Believe in Marriage." In short, Gold concluded, Dell was no more of a revolutionist than Elinor Glyn. He was "only treading the path of hundreds of other ex-radicals in America." [40]

Gold's attack bristled with implications, although how much aware of them either the executioner or the victim was at the time it is hard to say.

The radicals of *The Masses* had differed from the Marxists of the next decade in their insistence that the writer as *writer* was beyond social criticism; only when he stepped out of his role of poet or novelist and became a social commentator could he be taken to task for holding benighted views. No bona fide Communist in 1929 was willing to grant such latitude, even if a writer like Dell had taken an acceptable line in his articles of opinion. The dual life was no longer possible. Gold and his friends refused to tolerate the personal or ideological vagaries of the pioneers who had prepared the way for a sterner faith. They made no effort to understand why the older radicals found something graceless and unyielding in this new Bolshevik rectitude. Once again, the new generation was rejecting the old.

Dell's subsequent explanation of his quarrel with the hard young proletarians may contain some understandable rationalizations, but it is worth recording. As he "teetered on the edge of the Marxian absurdity," he began to feel that the pervasive radical satire, both literary and pictorial, revealed "a hatred for the human race, mistaken as a hatred for the bourgeoisie," and a too narrow and rigid construction of the revolution. Nor could he respond to Gold's fervent request for a proletarian critic [41] (which was, of course, an idealized self-portrait like Whitman's Poet in the 1855 preface to *Leaves of Grass*), which had thrilled Upton Sinclair. He preferred "the cool, ironic, aesthetic frivolities with which I used to sprinkle the pages of the old Masses and Liberator." Calverton and Gold accused him of being a "sex playboy," but *The New Masses* (Dell observed many years later—and he may have been explaining the phrase in his letter of resignation about neurotic "pictorial aestheticism") never had a good word to say for sex enjoyment or presented women attractively in the cartoons: "The women always had square breasts—which seems to me to denote a puritanism and fanatical hatred of women as the source of pleasure." Gold and Calverton failed to see, Dell said, that sex for him was his "manumission from the bondage of a preoccupation with a Grand Economic Explanation of Everything, which is rigor mortis to the mind." [42]

Dell, said Mike Gold darkly, had "lost his purpose." Yes, Dell replied, but he exchanged "purpose" for "freedom" when he suppressed the latent demagoguery he had always suspected in himself and gave up his monolithic view of art.

Dell, Gold declared, had never been a real revolutionist, and if we accept Koestler's distinction between the "chronically indignant rebel" and "the earnest revolutionary," Gold was right. The former, Koestler observes

is capable of changing causes, the latter is not. The rebel turns his indignation now against this injustice, now against another; the revolutionary is a consistent hater who has invested all his powers of hatred in one object. The rebel always has a touch of the Quixotic; the revolutionary is a bureaucrat of Utopia. The rebel is an enthusiast; the revolutionary, a fanatic. Robespierre, Marx, Lenin were revolutionaries; Danton, Bakunin, Trotsky were rebels.[43]

And so were Mike Gold and, to a degree, Floyd Dell, who concealed the sybarite beneath the blue-flannel proletarian shirts and corduroy trousers. "Under this proletarian exterior," Dell wrote to Freeman, "(like some of the saints in the Middle Ages who wore hair shirts under their elegant attire) I wore silken BVD's—because I liked them, but also, no doubt, as a symbol of the leisure-class part of my nature. I was perhaps the only member of the U.S. armed forces who wore silk underclothing during the entire period of his or her military service—which, to be sure, was only ten days long, at Camp Spartanburg, S.C." Dell had ridiculed the proletarian cult from the start ("My remarks deeply offended some of those who were indulging in that masquerade"), and he remained the "individualist anarchist," constitutionally incapable of becoming slavishly loyal to party organization or joining the party as if it were a church. The conviction that the human race was worth living for and dying for had gripped him before he became a Socialist, "but the idea of Socialism gave a realistic meaning to that conviction, gave it a historical past and a utopian future, and made it a shaping force within one's personality." [44]

Everyone, to be sure, wants to interpret his past behavior as favorably as possible, and Dell may very well have imputed a wisdom to himself in 1926 that did not come until several decades later. Furthermore, what is wisdom to one may be opportunism and cowardice to another. It seems likely that by the mid-twenties, Dell no longer made a sharp dichotomy between good and evil, but saw them hopelessly entangled. In *The Masses* days, the revolution had attached itself to all causes hostile to the established order, but once it had become an orthodoxy, it "tossed the new movements (in army organizations, in agriculture, in industry, in education, in sex relations, in the arts) into the ashcan." Dell concluded later, if he did not in 1926, that Left writers made the mistake of imputing "to the organized aspect of the cause of human freedom virtues which no organization possesses. A political organization wishes to make individual talents of literary and other kinds amenable to its control; it dispenses favors as a way of keeping its victims dependent on it, and it punishes ruthlessly those who try to get out from under its powerful thumb. . . . The political left begins by patronizing and exalting non-political aesthetic 'leftishness' and to the extent that it gets power it liquidates these early adherents and canonizes the literary stuffed shirts." [45]

Dell was not liquidated, but he was attacked with that special brand of billingsgate reserved for the renegades who had been deeply committed to the party. His dismissal from *The New Masses* set the pattern for the more solemn literary executions to come.

CONFERENCE IN KHARKOV

Some months before the Second World Plenum of the International Bureau of Revolutionary Literature convened at Kharkov from November 6 to November 15 in 1930, Joshua Kunitz was in Russia collecting material for a book he was planning to write on Soviet literature. Before the rest of the John Reed Club delegates arrived,* Kunitz had already antagonized the two leading bureaucrats of the all-powerful Russian Association of Proletarian Writers (RAPP), Leopold Averbakh and Serge Dinamov. Not only had he associated with the literary opposition and sharply criticized in the Moscow *News* a play written by a member of the RAPP group; he had also introduced the other American delegates (with the exception of Gold, who arrived late) to the poet and dramatist Serge Tretyakov, leader of the Left Front (LEFS). Before Gold got to the conference, "late as usual," he was intercepted by members of RAPP, who saw to it that he had nothing to do with the Left Front.

Gold was the star of a somewhat confused if not divided American delegation, and judging from his notes printed in *The New Masses* five months later, he had the time of his life.

Damnit, you come from capitalism, you come from the lands where you're a nut, a rebel, an outcast, a lone wolf, a green apple in the belly of things. Your mind has been full of Spartacus on the cross, Shelley, Karl Marx, Tolstoy, John Brown, Lenin, Byron, Gorky, 1905, 1848, 1789, 1870—all of it, the great story. But your body has been kicked around Union Square by a bunch of Tammany cops, or it's been sick with the sight of a million white-collar scissorbills pushing through Nassau Street at lunchtime.

Just so. And then you find yourself in a dimly lit custom house over which waves the Red Flag. A few, casual, sleepy Red soldiers lounge about, and it's Revolution, it's dull, it's normal, it's not a dream, it's the daily bread and cabbage soup of 150 million human beings. "We will not see the Revolution in our lifetime." I've heard this said at least 1000 times. Yet here I am in the U.S.S.R. about to see a big slice of the Revolution in my own lifetime. It comes with a great stab of joy and wonder at first.

What impressed him most about the conference was the solidarity among the delegates from twenty different lands, who bore no re-

---

* Fred Ellis, the cartoonist, Michael Gold, William Gropper, A. B. Magil, Harry Alan Potamkin. Josephine Herbst and her husband, John Herrman, also attended as "sympathetic writers." Of the six official American delegates, only Gropper had been present at the First Plenum in 1927. John Dos Passos was invited but did not come. Kunitz to author in conversation.

semblance to the "peevish, self-centered, jealous and opinionate crew" of literary shopkeepers he met with in America. "Each of us has not come here with a personal world in his head; we have come here as units in a common world. We have a common theory of history, we have shared common experiences. There is a new feeling in life, and it has captured us as its medium." Surely, he felt, this "new universal feeling" meant that "a great new proletarian style in all the arts" was in the making.[46]

In their report, the American delegates noted the important developments in the radical literary front all over the world and the decision of the conference "to adopt a political program of a broader and more concrete character." It would no longer suffice for the revolutionary writer merely to oppose imperialist war and fascism. Now he must actively defend the Soviet fatherland and fight against that "concealed fascism which parades under the mask of 'socialism' —that more insidious type that has come to be known as social-fascism."[47]

The conference also drew up a ten-point "Program of Action" for the United States, which was at once a directive and a criticism. In essence, the program called upon the John Reed Club and *The New Masses* to extend its proletarian base and "to enlist all friendly intellectuals into the ranks of the revolution."[48] The John Reed Club had neglected "cultural activity among the Negro masses" and had paid insufficient attention to Marxist literary criticism; these faults had to be corrected. The Program of Action recommended that the John Reed Club and *The New Masses* organize national federations "of all cultural groups in all languages," establish closer contact with workers, strengthen their contacts with other John Reed Clubs outside of New York and with revolutionary cultural organizations abroad, and sponsor the publication of mass pamphlets and the organizing of "agit prop troupes" of entertainers.

Finally, *The New Masses* was instructed to make itself "in every respect the cultural organ of the class-conscious workers and revolutionary intellectuals of this country."[49]

The John Reed Club, in affiliating with the International Union of Revolutionary Writers (IURW), did not have to reverse any of its policies, but henceforth, as part of an international organization guided and directed from Russia, its future was to depend more upon Soviet political fluctuations than upon American realities.

Three years after the Kharkov Conference, Max Eastman published an article in which he sardonically described how "the American pilgrims" submitted slavishly to "those fervently sophomoric under-Y.M.C.A.-secretaries of Stalin's bureaucratic church of the Dialectic Revolution, who completely bossed the Congress." He denounced Averbakh as "a born organizer whose writings show as much sense as you would expect to find in the complete works of John J. MacGraw," and ridiculed the "crude humiliation of arts and letters, the obsequious and almost obscene lowering of the standards of the creative mind, of which that Kharkov congress and the whole subsequent record of the International Union of Proletarian Writers forms a picture." Eastman paid tribute to the consecration of the dedicated artists "to the cause of communist revolution," but he deplored their gullibility and their subscribing to Averbakh's resolution —"Every proletarian artist must be a dialectic materialist"—when "probably not six creative artists in the world . . . know what dialectic materialism is." With the liquidation of RAPP, he noted, and the substitution in 1932 of "Socialist Realism" for "dialectic materialism," one half-baked theory supplanted another, but the Americans slavishly accepted every directive from Russia, abased themselves when they were spanked for theoretical or tactical derelictions, and renounced their independence in the name of "healthy self-criticism." Eastman concluded that so long as these Left intellectuals belly-crawled, the American masses were "quite right not to trust them. No man possessing the mind and will to revolutionize America will express it by wallowing at the feet of some almost second cousin of the nephew of someone who sat on the knees of a man who helped to revolutionize Russia. . . . Before these young men ever become revolutionists they will have to learn to become rebels." When the revolution comes to America, the "suffering masses" will not expect to find their leader "kowtowing toward Moscow in a position which leaves nothing visible to the American worker but his rump." [50]

Joshua Kunitz's two rejoinders to Eastman's article [51] defended the Kharkov delegates and the John Reed Clubs against Eastman's sneers. The whole point of the conference, Kunitz said, was to unite the revolutionary writers of the world against imperialist war and in defense of the U.S.S.R. Averbakh's "two-line reference to dialectical materialism" was smuggled in to lend prestige to RAPP, but it figured not at all in the deliberations of the conference and made no impression on the Americans—even upon Gold, who sympathized with RAPP more than his fellow delegates did. Kunitz insisted that "there was no regimentation of American writers into any dialectical goose step" at Kharkov, that RAPP was only one of many literary groupings and by no means the dominant one, and that "socialist realism is nothing but the literary equivalent of dialectical materialism."

Kunitz's account of the Kharkov Conference was probably more correct in its details than Eastman's, but he did not make a convincing case against Eastman's charges of the subsequent subserviency of the American revolutionary writers to Soviet directives.

ORGANIZING THE RADICAL WRITERS

Before Kharkov, the John Reed Club had not actively opposed the recruitment of "radicalized intellectuals," but it had been more concerned with discovering and encouraging new proletarian writers and artists. The Kharkov plenum strongly urged a continuance of that policy, but it also warned against "the straightjacket of sectarianism." [52] If the party was to win over the "best elements" among the young intellectuals, it might capture them "not by demanding that they accept our program 100 per cent, but by drawing them into our ranks, guiding them and helping to clarify their social outlook." In his enthusiasm for the new tolerance, Gold now demanded: "Every door must be opened wide to the fellow-travellers. We need them. We must not fear that they will corrupt us with bourgeois ideas. This fear is a form of immaturity. It is as if we doubted our own ability to keep on the main road." [53] Gold was later to have some second thoughts about these "fellow-travellers," but for the moment, they must be saved from the reactionary ideologies that now contested for their minds in a dying culture.

The multiplication of the John Reed Clubs continued after Kharkov, and in May 1932 a conference of the twelve John Reed Clubs of the United States was called at the suggestion of the IURW, with the executive board of the New York club serving as national organizing committee until the election of a national executive board. A draft for a proposed manifesto appeared in *The New Masses* at the time of the conference, full of resounding denunciations of a brutal and decaying capitalist government that drops "the hypocritical mask of democracy, and openly flaunts a fascist face." As "bourgeois culture writhes in a blind alley," the manifesto declared, as unemployment deepens and the imperialists plot a second world war, "the disillusioned middle-class intelligentsia" now see that capitalist culture, as well as its political and economic machinery is bankrupt. "We call upon them to break with bourgeois ideas which seek to conceal the violence and fraud, the corruption and decay of capitalist society." [54]

The thirty-eight delegates [55] who gathered at the Lincoln Center Auditorium in Chicago on May 29 for the first National Conference of the John Reed Clubs first proceeded to elect the presidium: Joseph Freeman (N.Y.), Jan Wittenber (Chicago), Maurice Sugar (Detroit), Conrad Komorowski (Philadelphia), Kenneth Rexroth (San Francisco), Charles Natterstad (Seattle), Harry Carlisle (Hollywood), George Gay (Portland), Carl Carlson (Boston), and Jack Walters (Newark). The delegates nominated as honorary members of the presidium: Maxim Gorky, Romain Rolland, John Dos Passos, Seikichi Fujimori (Japan), Lu Hsün (Chou Shu-jên) (China), Johannes Becker (Germany), Paul Vaillant-Couturier (France), and the American Negro poet Langston Hughes.

The nomination of Louis Aragon was turned down on the grounds that he had openly pleaded poetic license to save himself from a five-year jail sentence for writing a poem in the *Magazine of Revolutionary Literature.*

Michael Gold declined a place as an honorary delegate because "I'm already honored by being a regular delegate here. . . ." Theodore Dreiser, Malcolm Cowley, the Mexican artist D. A. Siqueiros, and several others were nominated but not elected.[56]

Following the nominations and the setting up of the organizational procedure, the conference heard reports from some of the member clubs relating their successes and failures in organizing exhibits of revolutionary drawings, dance and "agit-prop" groups, and "film and photo" leagues; in sponsoring meetings and debates; in establishing workers' schools for art and writing; and in participating in strikes and demonstrations. Oakley Johnson's report of the convention printed in *The New Masses* plays down the sharp disagreements on fundamental policy that were reflected in these unpublished reports and in the exchanges that followed, but behind the minor jealousies and carpings loomed several issues whose significance may not have been clear to many of the delegates.

One had to do with the influence and authority of the parent John Reed Club, criticized explicitly "for its failure to provide effective and responsible leadership to the other clubs throughout the country," [57] and implicitly for trying to dominate the show. As the representatives of the oldest and largest of the John Reed Clubs, the high-powered New York delegation (including three staff members of *The New Masses*) had come to Chicago bringing with them a manifesto as well as plans for organization. Gropper, Gold, and Freeman were old revolutionaries who had spent some time in the fatherland of the Soviets, but the delegation also included an ambitious writer who spoke for a militant clique of the club and who had already tried to wrest the control of *The New Masses* from Mike Gold and convert it into an organ of the John Reed Clubs.[58]

The other issue, not unrelated to the first, as it turned out, hinged on the clubs' position toward the vacillating middle-class intellectuals and in particular on how this consideration was met in the New York delegation's manifesto.

Freeman, who headed the manifesto committee at the convention, conceded that the manifesto was written "in terrific haste," but defended its position in regard to fellow travelers. All nonparty members in the clubs belonged in this category, he pointed out, and many intellectuals still outside the movement had "the same background as members of the John Reed Club and potentially . . . the same future." Certainly the term "fellow-traveller" was not used pejoratively. In attracting such "so-called Marxian critics" as Edmund Wilson and Waldo Frank ("who talk about Marxism which they don't understand very well but actively support the movement"), the John Reed Clubs were not capitulating to the intellectuals; rather, "we are asking intellectuals to adopt our orientation to the Communist Party.

As a member of the manifesto committee, Gold also felt obliged to justify its tone, although he thought it contained too much technical jargon. But Gold detected an unfortunate sectarianism among the delegates who would keep out a distinguished writer like Upton Sinclair because of his ideological deviations. "We are not running a school for young boys," Gold said. "That is another job. . . . We are trying to help the revolutionary movement and bring in forces that can help the movement." Personal feelings had no place. "I may be jealous of Theodore Dreiser, personally. But at the same time, as a revolutionist, I would do a lot of things to keep him in the movement." Gold went on to single out the careerists and petty bureaucrats in the clubs for special attention, "persons who will perhaps never be artists or writers" but who drive away the real artists like Edmund Wilson, John Dos Passos, and Malcolm Cowley: "they won't come to the meetings. They sense mechanization." Gold warned that if the John Reed Clubs became "mechanized bureaucratic structure of any kind, if they are going to hurt the development of revolutionary literature, they will be liquidated":

Since the first day of the organization of the John Reed Club I have been in the minority in saying this club should be organized of the broad middle class intellectual workers. It should be the feeder, the contact organization between these and the Communist movement. It should be the place where radical teachers can first form germs of a teachers' union. . . .

We can't by taking thought produce great writers and great artists. We can only take concerted action. Also we can have very clear political lines. At Kharkov the platform was simple and political. Any writer who subscribed to the political platform was admitted. It should be very clear that no one is asked to change his mental habits. Nothing will be dictated to them. You believe in proletarian writing. Wilson believes in Proustian—I say bring him into the movement, if he is a writer of great influence and great talent. We cannot afford to have aesthetic quarrels.

Clear up the question of fellow travellers. Appeal to the white collar groups in this country who won't come close to the party and for whom the John Reed Clubs can be the first step into the I.L.D. and into the Communist Party.[59]

So spoke a man who not long before had called Proust "the master-masturbator" of the middle class. Gold's remarks already anticipate the program of the broad united front that became official policy three years later.

But some of the "young boys" he was scolding in Chicago were worried that "the artists and writers of distinctly working class origin," who could be "approached on the basis of working class principles" might be lost sight of. Said Harry Carlisle, of the Holly-wood club:

We must not cringe in our approach to these intellectuals. . . . We must teach them that the first thing is to approach an organization on an organizational basis. We must not be short-sighted. Upton Sinclair, who is on the editorial board of *Literature of World Revolution,* is at the same time a perennial candidate on the ticket of the California Socialist Party. He appears on programs in debates with Aimee Semple McPherson. . . . Is our need of Sinclair so great that we can afford to fall down on principles.[60]

Kenneth Rexroth, another California delegate, supported Carlisle. "We are not an organization," he declared, "to bring in big names." Rexroth suspected that it was Gold's tactlessness that estranged Wilson. He saw no reason "to scale down our demand" in order to attract the intellectuals. Nor was Conrad Komorowski, of Philadelphia, content with Gold's elastic definition of the "fellow-traveller." For example, Edmund Wilson's "articles on the literary class war" were only "devious attempts to escape the conclusion that he must join the John Reed Club and the Communist Party." Intellectuals by definition are "part and parcel of the middle class." Comrade Carl-son, of Boston, described the John Reed Club as a "revolutionary workers' club." Its purpose was to absorb the middle class, not to seek its aid.

In answering his critics, Gold once more reminded them of the Kharkov directives and said again that he saw no conflict in the dual task of creating a proletarian literature and winning over the middle-class "revoltees." Because the majority of the proletarian writers lived under difficult conditions and because it would take years before they would "attain the technique and polish of bourgeois writers," it had become "a matter of life and death to attract and bring into the movement revolutionary writers of middle class origin." [61]

WRITERS VERSUS BUREAUCRATS

As Joseph Freeman observed in summing up the debate, the discussion had turned out to be "much broader than a discussion of the Manifesto." Speaking for himself, Freeman asked the delegates not to consider the John Reed Club as a competitor of the Communist Party or to fill the club with nonliterary professionals. His private thoughts on that matter he confined to a memorandum composed shortly before the Chicago conference as a "counter-attack" against the politicians in the New York club "who were fighting to take over the NM and the cultural front."

In his "Memo," Freeman spoke more harshly and more candidly about the club bureaucrats than Gold had done in Chicago. The majority of them, he charged,

are neither intellectuals nor workers nor professional revolutionists. They are not responsible to the traditions of ideas—logic, the rules of evidence, the dialectical method; nor to trade unions; nor to the Party. Most of the people in the writers' group do not write and cannot write; they do not read; they do not know what is going on in the intellectual field and it is impossible to struggle with them on the basis of ideas. This is one of the reasons for the continual turmoil. The moment the struggle is settled on paper, it crops up again; not being Party members, these elements cannot be disciplined by the needs of the economic struggle; not being intellectuals, they cannot be reasoned with. The disrupters are uprooted bohemian elements in the strict sense of the word *bohemian*. A bohemian is not necessarily one who lives in Greenwich Village and gets drunk every night. A bohemian is a person who has broken with his social class; hence he has no social roots; the old ideology is gone and no new ideology has taken its place. As a rule, such persons seek refuge as *hangers on of the art world*. If they become genuine artists, the discipline of their work and the necessity of finding a social base for it would eventually drive them to one camp or the other. Thus we have the revolution in two directions—one toward communism, the other toward fascism. . . . But the more hangers-on, who do not have to write or draw as *work,* who remain suspended, undecided between the old and the new, remain in the strict sense of the word *bohemians.* Unable to express their indecision in *art forms*—as do writers for the liberal journals —they express it in *politics.* They do not enter the political struggle directly because this means to commit themselves to an organization, to cease to be bohemians.

Freeman recommended that the club rid itself "of all elements who are not definitely (a) proletarian; (b) intellectuals, whether Party members or not." People with exclusively political talents should be transferred to the political front.

The writer, Freeman went on to say, was a technician; and what Lenin said of the scientific and technical specialist—that if he came to Communism he would do so not in the same way as an underground worker, agitator, or writer, but "through the portals of his science"—applied to the writer as well. The bureaucrat would not let the writers enter the party through the "portals of their art," hence their resentment, their feeling (even among the best elements) "that only political pressure is being brought to bear upon them." The politicking of the John Reed Club bureaucrats forced the creative intellectuals who happened to be party members to fight back and to be regarded "not as writers but as politicians seeking to force the Party line." [62]

At Chicago, probably only the New York delegates were aware of these background maneuverings, but the conference raised a related issue that in its way was of even greater importance for the future of the Left literary movement than the internal struggle between the creative party people and the uncreative party politicians. Could there ever be a reconciliation, as Gold simply assumed, between the task of training authentic proletarians to create a new kind of literature and the task of converting the susceptible middle-class radicals to Communism?

The party, as we shall see, quite cynically abandoned the first responsibility when it became apparent that it stood to gain more by exploiting the reputations of its "big name" well-wishers and by absorbing the sometimes stubbornly independent John Reed Clubs into an easily controlled united-front organization of writers.

Now, in retrospect, it can be seen that the program of the John

Reed Clubs and *The New Masses* was shot through with contradictions, hopelessly ambitious, constructed on unrealities, and fatally hampered by the restrictions placed upon it by the IURW. While Gold and Freeman and others in their camp were trying desperately to attract the as yet uncommitted middle-class intellectuals with assurances that the party wanted them as writers, not politicians, *The New Masses* humbly acknowledged the charges of the IURW that they were corrupted by "rotten liberalism" (Stalin's elegant phrase) and insufficiently politicized. The editors promised to make a more systematic fight against social fascism, to pay greater attention to the achievements of the U.S.S.R., to attack with greater zeal "imperialist intervention in the USSR," to establish closer contacts with revolutionary movements in Canada and Latin America, to master Marxist-Leninist theory, to root out the "mild and harmless" bourgeois humor, "petty bourgeois passiveness," and "pacifist humanism" in *The New Masses* drawings and cartoons; to integrate their efforts with those of other cultural organizations; to feature more prominently the work and views of prominent writers like Dos Passos, Dreiser, and Sinclair; to define more precisely proletarian literary theory.[63]

The IURW appraisal of *The New Masses'* shortcomings not only displayed an incredible ignorance of the American literary situation and a maddening condescension; it also recommended a course of action that would baffle all but a few of the working-class readers in the United States and alienate the very middle-class radicals the party was so ardently wooing.

Before a Left literary movement could begin to sprout, it was smothered in politics. Had a free and autonomous Communist movement developed in the United States or had *The New Masses* and the John Reed Clubs remained politically unattached, the middle-class malcontents would undoubtedly have entered the Left movement in larger numbers and stayed longer. As it was, some of them, after considerable soul-searching, moved close to the party, some of them joined, some turned to other causes. In most cases one suspects that most of the writers who went Left did so because of the social and political crisis, rather than because of party persuasion.

EIGHT · STATEMENT AND COUNTER-STATEMENT: LITERARY WARS IN THE EARLY THIRTIES

THE RED DECADE

IN HIS *The Red Decade* (1941), the story of the "Stalinist Penetration of America" in the 1930's, Eugene Lyons * drew a picture of an America honeycombed by the open, covert, and unwitting

* Employed by Tass, the Soviet news agency, in the 1920's, a protégé of its aloof and brilliant American director, Kenneth Durant, and friend of Joseph Freeman, Lyons had thrown himself into the campaign to save Sacco and Vanzetti and had written an eloquent book in their memory. Sent to Russia as a U.P. correspondent in 1927, he spent six disillusioning years in the U.S.S.R. (see *Assignment in Utopia*, 1937, and *Moscow Carrousel*, 1935). On his return, already suspect by orthodox party members and fellow travelers, he joined the ever-lengthening list of "renegades" and was ferociously smeared in the Left press. Lyons was understandably soured by this experience, as the sputtering and sarcastic tone of *The Red Decade* bears out. He wrote it as a disenchanted radical, outraged and amazed by the criminal gullibility of Stalin's dupes. His book is full of facts and is indeed a melancholy record of self-delusion and even more reprehensible human failings. It is also a polemic written without charity or understanding and reflects the acrimonious spirit and attitudes of the decade he deplores. The tone of *The Red Decade* is perhaps explained by the self-revelations of *Assignment in Utopia*, a much more impressive and often moving book, in which Lyons reveals his guilt in not acknowledging to himself and to the public his horror of Soviet tyranny. Perhaps his contempt for the blindness of "twittering intellectuals," the apologists for the U.S.S.R., was a way of compensating for his own failure to speak the truth. Lyons, after all, had been there. He knew. The American Utopians relied upon their imaginative inventions.

friends of Soviet Russia. His exposé described how "totalitarian liberals" and "middle-class muddleheads," captivated by their own utopian inventions, were able to inveigle hundreds of thousands of others into the belief that Russia was paradise and America a hell. The writers and artists of "The Red Cultural Renaissance," in particular, were the targets for Lyons's sharpest barbs, for they, he charged, had sold out their intellectual birthrights for a mess of Soviet pottage and invested their emotional lives in an obscene lie.

Lyons somewhat oversimplified the reasons for the leftward turning of artists and writers and pictured it as an indecent rout:

Many of them had been through fashionable types of exhibitionism in the previous decade—dadaism, surrealism, symbolism, lost generation antics and what not. They had climbed into ivory towers fitted out with bars and seductive couches and looked down only to sneer at the madding crowd. They had defied the bourgeoisie with lower-case letters, stuttering sentences and chopped-up female torsos scattered on canvases. All of them now sensed the dissonance between their gin-drinking self-indulgence and the grim Depression world. Besides, mostly they could no longer afford that sort of existence; the bill collectors found them in the loftiest ivory tower.

So, singly and in packs they migrated from the Left Bank of Paris to the political Left of Moscow. They abandoned prosperity bohemianism for proletarian bohemianism. With the egocentric yowling of their species they rushed into intellectual slumming as heatedly as they had gone in for slummy intellectualism. A lot of humdrum novelists and academic grinds joined the general migration.[1]

The turn, as we have seen, was not so automatic, nor were the motives so ignoble. But Lyons's energetic denunciations, oddly similar to the anti-Bohemian salvos in *The New Masses* a decade earlier, were misleading in another respect, for he made it appear as if the Communists bowled over all intellectual opposition and exercised virtual control over literary organs. According to Lyons, the intellectuals passed abruptly to the Left without any soul-searching or misgiving and only "wiggled out" after they discovered they had been harnessed. This view does not square with the facts. Writers joined and left the party, loaned or withdrew their allegiance, for all manner of reasons. And there were, of course, a number of them who remained hostile or critical to Communism, if not always to Communists, throughout "the Red Decade."

HUMANISTS VERSUS LIBERALS

One "philosophy" with political implications if not a political program for a time appeared to present an obstacle to the Marxist theoreticians. At least, they regarded it as important enough to attack. This was Humanism. From the mid-twenties until the end of 1931, when Humanism seemed too dead to bother about, Communist critics and their Left Wing sympathizers paid serious attention to Humanism's oracles, Irving Babbitt and Paul Elmer More, and to their small but aggressive following.

The principles of what became known as Humanism were formulated as early as 1901 by William Crary Brownell ("the Amherst Aristotle") and were not seriously modified by Babbitt and More. In essence, Humanism opposed the naturalistic and romantic strains that by the turn of the century were already beginning to pervade American letters. Its catchwords were "order," "reason," "ethics"; its philosophical origins were Platonic and Aristotelian and Christian; its aesthetic program called for harmony and decorum. Humanism demanded of the artist that he be not only disciplined in his art but also in his personal life. It proclaimed the moral basis of all art. Hence Babbitt and More found the literary innovators of the postwar decades unsatisfactory on many counts and were, in turn, identified by the rebels as genteel and juiceless academics entirely removed from the real concerns of life.

The earliest attacks against "the crepe-clad pundits, the bombastic word-mongers of the *Nation* school" had come from Mencken and, after World War I, from the young modernists. Malcolm Cowley thought the prewar universities were the "seedbeds of Humanism," since the attributes they inculcated—"Good taste, good manners, cleanliness, chastity, gentlemanliness (or niceness), reticence and the spirit of competition in sports," all of them leisure-class values— were matched by the Humanist virtues: *"poise, proportionateness, the imitation of great models, decorum,* the inner check." In 1924 Edmund Wilson referred to Babbitt as an antiromantic scold and to More as a man who by denying "the response to irrational impulse" would "shut off the arts at their source." At the same time, Wilson acknowledged that the generation of Babbitt, Brownell, and More, though less "emancipated" than "our race of writers today," and not so lively, "possessed a sounder culture than we . . . and were better craftsmen." [2]

When Joseph Freeman reviewed current American literary tendencies for the party's theoretical organ, *The Communist,* in 1928, the controversy over Humanism, almost dead since the early twenties, had already flared up again; only now the point at issue was no longer exclusively literary.[3]

Freeman saw in the publication of Gorham Munson's *Destinations* (1928) an explicit rightist political drift in the new Humanism which had only been implicit in the old. The writing of Babbitt and More, bolstered by extensive scholarship, was generally conservative, religious, anti-utopian, lofty and erudite, snobbish. In attacking the Baconian faith in science and Rousseau's humanitarianism, in condemning a philosophy of change and relativity, in opposing not only the sentimental bourgeois reformer but also anyone who upheld "the natural goodness of man" or who made society responsible for human shortcomings, the Humanists were allying themselves with reaction. Both Humanism and Marxism, he conceded, held that art "should stand in vital relation to human nature as a whole" and should not be considered as a form of "play." But Humanism used this social conception of art for reactionary ends. "Consciously or unconsciously," the Humanists, "like Marinetti and his followers in Italy" were "creating an aesthetic fig-leaf for the politics of fascism." [4]

Two years later, Freeman was certain More and Babbitt had provided a philosophy for a new literary movement. The scattered skirmishes of 1928 had developed by 1930 into a full-scale war. Critics, poets, and novelists, Freeman reported to the readers of *The Communist,* were firing articles at one another with the rapidity of machine guns; epithets were exploding with the thunder of high-powered projectiles; the warring literary troops were issuing manifestoes and counter-manifestoes.[5]

What were the issues behind this battle and how did the war start? In reviewing the background, Freeman summarized the changing attitudes in American literary generations since 1912: the superseding of the middle-class Wilsonian liberals, with their "democratic illusions," by the rebellious and emotional bourgeois youth who emerged after Versailles.

Hardened by war, completely cynical as a result of the prosperity . . . this youth no longer pretended to believe in the traditional American values. It was skeptical of democracy, of romance, of Socialism, of humanitarianism in general, and of puritanism in particular. For a long time American writers were preoccupied with the theme of the "younger generation." Needless to say, this "younger generation" did not include the working-class youth, Negro and white. It was the youth of the upper and middle classes, especially the student youth in the universities, which constituted the "problem." This youth alarmed the older bourgeois generation because of its alleged excesses in drinking and love, but above all because it was cynical and without faith. It had no "religion." [6]

Until the fall of 1929, only a few of the young modernists had looked for new values in Moscow or in the philosophy of Humanism. After that date, a number of them realized they would have to decide between "the so-called Humanist movement . . . based on mystical tenets in philosophy, fascism in politics, puritanism in morals, and fixed classical standards in literature," and the socialist movement. Humanism was significant because it compelled "writers and critics of all schools to clarify their positions on fundamental questions"; it forced the liberals to take a stand on social issues they had hitherto avoided.

If they joined the Humanists, the liberals would in effect be supporting a movement that rejected scientific materialism, that endowed man with free will enabling him to exercise an "inner check," that found no virtue in Proust, Joyce, or Gide, that preferred the chaste Wordsworth and Poe to the Unchaste Goethe and Baudelaire, and that discovered the remedy for social ills (as Babbitt put it) in "the moderation and magnanimity of the strong and the successful, and not in any sickly sentimentalizing over the lot of the underdog." The Humanists, in short, envisaged a cultural elite from which the working class was automatically excluded, an elite whose morality was based upon the self-restraint of the well to do.

The liberals put up a "negative form of resistance" to the Humanist assault, Freeman observed, but they responded "without formulating a positive program of their own." [7] And indeed in 1930 only the Communists seemed to offer a systematic answer to the Humanists.

A number of the liberals, however, who struck back at the Humanists for their old-maidishness, snobbishness, and traditionalism, and for their antidemocratic and antiscientific bias, were already moving leftward. Of the thirty-three writers who signed a letter to *The New Republic* demanding to know the name of "a contemporary work of art either produced by an American Humanist or encouraged and approved by one," almost half (Malcolm Cowley, Kenneth Burke, Edward Dahlberg, Granville Hicks, Edmund Wilson, Matthew Josephson, Isidor Schneider, Genevieve Taggard, F. O. Matthiessen, Katharine Anne Porter, John Chamberlain) were already radicals or half radicalized. One could sense a new militancy in Cowley's declaration that Humanism had no validity "for the mill hands of New Bedford and Gastonia, for the beet-toppers of Colorado, for the men who tighten a single screw in the automobiles that march along Mr. Ford's assembly belt." Edmund Wilson, another one of *The New Republic*'s "young lions," leaped on Babbitt's remark that Humanists "should not be moderate in dealing with error," as the traditional view of all inquisitorial councils including the one that sentenced Sacco and Vanzetti. Matthew Josephson charged the "ornate, esthetic cult" of Tory-Humanists with completely misunderstanding their times:

The real power and wealth of this modern world is drawn from its masses and their mass-activities. Human life is ruled more and more imperatively by the most rigid economic consequences (*vide,* mechanism). . . . Its amelioration will be possible only in the terms of its own immediate realities. Yet our classical moralists have their eyes fixed on the past rather than on the irritating present. They have acquired the habit of cursing the tides and the seasons.

Humanism, Newton Arvin announced, "along with its reassertion of many salutary truths," rested fundamentally on a "false conception" of nature, society, the individual, and art.[8]

In time, some of them would take the next step that Freeman was calling for: to understand that "our mechanical civilization" had not only "out-marched its artists" but that it had already "produced a new class whose ways of thinking have their roots in machine civilization and therefore carry the seeds of a new and appropriate art." [9]

THE COMMUNIST OFFENSIVE AGAINST HUMANISM

The managing editor of *The Hound and Horn* might dismiss the battle between the Humanists and anti-Humanists as pretty much "a Tweedledum-Tweedledee affair," and Malcolm Cowley, while not minimizing its implications, see it as an "otherwise absurd and fruitless debate." But to the Communists, the issue was civilization itself, and if they carried on their end of the campaign with unusual pertinacity and virulence, it was because they saw behind the "superstructure" of Humanism the "material basis" of capitalism.

V. F. Calverton contributed the first official blast in *The New Masses* against this "venomous spirit of social reaction." T. S. Eliot and Babbitt he said now had become "the mixed inspirations of our college-boys today" in place of the defunct Mencken, and the intellectuals, no longer lost in the spiritual void of the twenties, had seized upon Humanism as a faith to make them "comfortable in an altogether uncomfortable intellectual world." Denying the importance of external forces and insisting upon the autonomy of the individual, Humanism of necessity was anticollectivist. Because it forced the intellectuals to decide "to be either consistent individualists or consistent collectivists," it simplified the radical's task, but it was "reactionary to the core" and against everything that the Communists stood for. Liberals would have to understand, Calverton concluded, that Humanism was more than a "literary disease." It was a form of intellectual fascism and had to be fought "as a philosophy of *social* reaction." [10]

Editorializing on the same issue, Mike Gold agreed with Calverton that Humanism was "more than a new literary school"; it was "the startling and sly introduction of Fascism into this country." After paying his respects to the " 'humanist' blackshirts" who were trying to undermine the reputations of the Dreisers and the Andersons while producing nothing of value themselves, Gold launched forth at the most eminent representative of these "retreatists" and "necrophiles."

That fairy-like little Anglo-American curate, Thornton Wilder, is about their best specimen writer so far. His novels have the suavity, discretion and flawless rhetoric the "humanists" so prize. Yes, Wilder writes perfect English. But he has nothing to say in that perfect English. He is a beautiful, rouged, combed, well-dressed corpse, lying among the sacred candles and lilies of the past, and sure to stink if exposed to sunlight.[11]

By July, Gold was already writing Humanism's obituary in his characteristically inelegant and hard-boiled style and comically reviewing its rise and fall:

Humanism, seven-day sensation that caused a wagging of waxed moustaches among the more profound and well-tailored of our literary thinkers, can be explained only by the same social analytics. It had been hibernating with Irving Babbitt at Harvard for twenty years, snoring low and mournfully, its pulse feeble, its fat melting away. Then came the Spring. Then came prosperity, a new herd of stock market snobs, a new great mob of *nouveaux riches* needing a gentlemanly philosophy that would go well with their newly-bought antique furniture.

Humanism stumbled out of the caves of Harvard, blinking in the sun. The snobs, young and old, fell down in worship. Here was what they had been looking for. They grovelled at the master's feet. The sick old bear of Humanism was amazed at this sudden adulation. I am sure he has not yet found any explanation for it, and never will. But it was only the economic boom, and American prosperity.

Literature is the camp-follower of Life. In America, the non-literary *nouveaux riches* went in for golf, baggy pants, sophistication, Florida winter tours, duplex apartments, divorce suits, "gentlemanliness," European drinking tours, etc. etc.—all of which no American Babbitt had previously dared to admit into his life.

Their literary camp-followers felt much the same, but found their baggy pants in Humanism.

Then the market crashed; publishers slumped; other sad things happened. There now aren't so many European tourists or antique buyers; and there isn't a tenth as much Humanism as there was a few months ago.

In good times the petty bourgeois feels like an aristocrat and Humanist; he despises the masses. In bad times he feels like a Socialist, reads Dostoievsky, and so takes to thinking about Death and his market losses and the Soul of Man.

So, Humanism will be a dead herring until the stock market comes back (if it ever does). This is our prediction, based on astrological readings of the June stars, the itching in our left corn, and a slight pain in the seat.

Thank God, another bore is dead! Did anyone ever write as boringly as these Humanists? Dull, dull as British ex-Colonels, as American Ph.D.'s, as evangelists and Presidents! A philosophy of dull dignity! And dull literary sons of the vulgar *nouveaux riches* tried to ennoble themselves by adopting this dull dignity. But now money is tight, and people have to work. It's hard to be dignified aristocratic and superior while writing ads for tinted toilet paper in some vulgar non-Humanist's advertising agency! [12]

Behind Gold's flippancy and his unfair "tough guy" jibes at the effeminacy of the "pansy" Humanists lay a serious intention. In his opinion, the effete "youngsters" he satirized lacked humanity and shunned the battlefields; they had no "real philosophy of social progress and change," and "blinded by academic snobbery," they wrote "dull, bloodless, intellectualistic poetry and criticism a la T. S. Eliot, their well-tailored godling." It was easy, Gold said, "to be a 'Humanist' and shelter oneself in the comfortable mausoleums of the past," but it was "better to choose the hard way, to go on living, and to try every day of one's life to write about the living world." [13]

Gold's colleagues on *The New Masses* agreed essentially with his analysis of Humanism's reactionary content, but they were disturbed by the antiliterary tone of his remarks, by his equating "perfect English" with effeminacy, and by the unseemliness of his personal allusions. Joshua Kunitz took occasion to challenge Gold in a review of Upton Sinclair's *Mountain City* and Thornton Wilder's *The Woman of Andros*. Wilder, Kunitz said, was a much better writer than Sinclair even though his novel expressed "humanism par excellence." He saw no reason why proletarian writers might not study Wilder's technique while rejecting his message.[14]

Gold dismissed this distinction as "classroom nonsense." Style and content, he said, cannot be separated "into watertight compartments. 'Technique has made cowards of us all.' There is no 'style'—there is only clarity, force, truth in writing. If a man has something new to say, as all proletarian writers have, he will learn to say it clearly in time: if he writes long enough."

To study a writer's style, Kunitz replied, is not to imitate it. Proletarian writers, as Lenin said, would learn to solve technical problems by studying the masters. "A little less conceit," he admonished Gold, "and a little more perspective." [15]

Joseph Freeman did not comment on this exchange, but he was finally shocked into writing a personal letter to Walt Carmon, then managing editor of *The New Masses* after scanning the letter columns of the magazine. The provoking incident was a letter written by one of Gold's proletarian protégés in answer to a communication from Sinclair Lewis.

Lewis had registered a genial objection to Gold's anti-pansy line. "Listen, Comrade!" he had written, "I met Mike Gold the other night and I think he is a grand guy. But when he said that Walter Pater wrote like a fairy for a fairy, it seemed to me that he was merely doing the humanist idiocy from the opposite angle." In the next issue of *The New Masses,* the young proletarian tried to set Lewis straight. Humanism, he said, was responsible for the flowering of a "fairy literature." Nursing a "mad jealousy" because they had been "deprived of masculine experiences," the Humanists denounced in writing what they secretly envied. "A word like sonovabitch and a good healthy spit in the gutter knocks these men over, but I am sure they would exchange their whole unhealthy stale lives to be able to swear resoundingly and to spit like a man." Humanist literature, exploiting dictionaries instead of life, was "just another disease of capitalism, and if it itches, just a little bed bug poison will offer relief." [16]

This was too much for Freeman. He had criticized the Humanists "as reactionaries in politics, morals, and art," but he was embarrassed by *The New Masses'* tacit approval of "filthy personal abuse." Spitting and swearing had nothing to do with literary criticism. Marxist literature contained plenty "of sharp *political* attack, a battering down of false *ideas,* an exposé of social motives; but no feeble-minded references to other people's personal habits." The private lives of the Humanists were of no concern to the critic, and to accuse them of homosexuality was "as sickly as it was absurd." Inasmuch as the Soviet Union had launched vigorous campaigns against the "manly" habits of swearing and spitting, it did not speak well for a journal of revolutionary criticism to condone them. To do so made it appear "as if we have no *arguments* against reactionary literary schools and gives the New Masses a character which I feel sure it would take no pride in." [17]

Freeman's fears concerning "certain tendencies which unfortunately mark leftwing criticism of a certain kind" did not deter Gold from continuing to give his rough-and-ready opinions to the readers of *The New Masses,* but when Gold reviewed four novels and a volume of plays by Thornton Wilder in the fall literary section of *The New Republic,* the "harsh and scurrilous" tone of his article started a stormy argument in the letter columns of the magazine that continued with mounting heat until the editors called off the controversy several months later "on account of darkness." [18]

In his review, "Wilder: Prophet of the Genteel Christ," Gold made substantially the same case against Wilder as he had done in *The New Masses* six months before. He accused him of peopling a devitalized museum world, "an historic junkshop," with moldy characters, and of brooding over their "little lavender tragedies" with "tender irony." It was not Wilder's desire to restore a religious spirit in American literature that offended Gold: "One can respect any writer in America who sets himself a goal higher than the usual racketeering." What disgusted him was the kind of religion Wilder had in mind:

that newly fashionable literary religion that centers around Jesus Christ, the First British Gentleman. It is a pastel, pastiche, dilettante religion, without the true neurotic blood and fire, a daydream of homosexual figures in graceful gowns moving archaically among the lilies. It is Anglo-Catholicism, that last refuge of the American literary snob.

The falseness of Wilder's thought was mirrored in his "tailor-made rhetoric," the language of death. "Prick it and it will bleed violet ink and *apéritif.*" Both in content and style, his books fitted the needs of a parvenu class that was looking for "a short cut to the aristocratic emotions." In short, Wilder was the laureate of the leisure class with all the virtues "Veblen said this leisure class would demand; the air of good breeding, the decorum, priestliness, glossy high finish as against intrinsic qualities, conspicuous inutility, caste feeling, love of the archaic, etc. . . ." [19]

The tumult of abuse and praise let loose by Gold's article prompted some reflections from Edmund Wilson. He chided Gold for his refusal to acknowledge the dignity of craftsmanship and for failing "to recognize and confess how much he has in common with the author of *The Bridge of San Luis Rey*—sensitiveness to human contacts, a love of picturesque detail, a gift for molding firm prose into short comprehensive units, and even a touch of sentimentality." And yet Wilson could not help but note that although Wilder was "a writer of real originality," he was at the same time a domesticator of Proust, whose exotic themes provided, "as Gold suggests, a sedative for sick Americans." As the attacks against Gold mounted, Wilson decided "that there *was* a class issue involved in the dispute," that "those who defended Wilder protested or pleaded in the tone of persons who had been shocked by the desecration of a dearly beloved thing." * [20]

Very likely, the animus behind the anti-Gold response was inspired as much or more by his manner as by his matter. Some of *The New Republic* readers, especially the lady correspondents, were not accustomed to literary mayhem conducted in the columns of Herbert Croly's magazine. They resented Gold's passion as well as his violent language, resented the very "presence" of this scurrilous and godless radical. And it was not only the Anglo-Catholics who declared him profane and dirty. A rabbi contrasted him disadvantageously to Ludwig Lewisohn, Israel Zangwill, and Abraham Cahan. "Michael," he said, "sees life as a long and endless breadline; he sees human existence through the eyes of bedbugs and epileptic fanatics who style themselves 'Communists' and whose so-called utopian visions spring out of mere brutal envy of others' ways of living." [21]

The emotion aroused by what Hart Crane called "the recent rape of *The Woman of Andros* conducted by Mike Gold" obscured its political meaning. Gold was by no means so guilty of the grosser simplifications as his enemies charged, and in this review, at least, did not defend dogma or propaganda. But he raised certain questions, not necessarily Marxist ones, ordinarily left out of bourgeois literary discussions. Behind the Gold-Wilder fracas was the issue of whether or not a writer had the artistic and moral right to turn his

---

* It is characteristic of Wilson's independence of judgment that he could see merits in both of these writers when each was being so violently assailed. Wilson still believes that Gold was the most naturally gifted of the Communist writers. Wilson to author.

back on his times. Some of the correspondents seemed to think, one of Gold's allies commented caustically, that "the critic should concern himself exclusively with 'style and pattern' . . . and that an author's ideas and feelings about the way people live is none of the critic's damned business." But literature was not "above the social battle," nor could the critic be "disinterested." [22]

Wilder himself was less removed from the social scene than Gold realized, although he understood later why Gold selected him as the target. "In those days didn't I seem very 'humanist'? I was bookish (and how!) and genteel. . . . I was not interested in communism as such—never read Marx; but I had much interest in what was called civil rights, social justice, etc., and had joined a number of organizations that were later blacklisted."

The story of "St. Thornton the Martyr, burned at the stake by the Reds," had its humorous aspects, but to Edmund Wilson, the Gold-Wilder case marked "the eruption of the Marxist issues out of the literary circles of the radicals into the field of general criticism. It has now become plain," he concluded, "that the economic crisis is to be accompanied by a literary one." [23]

A MARXIST SYMPOSIUM

The Humanists as well as the Communists had helped to sweep away the dust of the twenties, to abolish, as a young Marxist named James T. Farrell phrased it, "bohemian isolation of creative effort on a celestial island of pure subjective moodiness." [24] Yet writers, if they were to avoid "an arid intellectualism," had not only to confront the world, but also to comprehend it.

Early in 1932, a number of self-described "bourgeois intellectuals who are working their way to a Marxist position" made plans for a volume of essays on the American social scene; their purpose was to employ the Marxist dialectic to analyze and describe the civilization of the United States. "It is hoped," they declared in a preliminary statement to possible contributors, "we can exclude, on the one hand, those who are contented liberals and, on the other, those who are definitely associated with revolutionary activity. We hope that the book will represent the movement, for the most part fairly recent, of bourgeois intellectuals to a Marxist standard." * Admittedly, few of the contributors knew enough about Marx to apply his theories, but no "rigorous standard of orthodoxy" would be upheld, and each contributor was urged "to familiarize himself, to the best of his ability, with the Marxist method." It was simply assumed "that anyone who contributes to this work is in general sympathy with that method."

The idea was not exactly a new one. In May 1929 V. F. Calverton had made plans for a similar symposium, tentatively called "The New Generation," and had lined up a list of Left-Wingers as possible contributors. Among them were Joshua Kunitz, Harry Elmer Barnes, John Dos Passos, Van Wyck Brooks, Michael Gold, Suzanne La Follette, Robert Wolf, Walter White, J. B. S. Hardman, Lewis Mumford, Waldo Frank, Max Eastman, and Stuart Chase. Mumford, to whom he submitted his list, recommended more women and "a few authentically young people" less "stable and stolid" than Calverton's choices. Mumford had no objections to Communists being included ("there are no vested interests in ideas—even revolutionary ideas— to be protected") and wondered if some who verged "pretty far, by conviction or inertia, to the right" ought not to be included—Edmund Wilson, for example.[25]

By the spring of 1930, the title of the symposium had been changed to "America at the Crossroads," and a number of newcomers attended the planning meetings, among them Sidney Hook, Joseph Freeman, Bernard Smith, Louis Lozowick, Scott Nearing, and Harry Potamkin. For some reason, however, the project never got off the ground, and when Hicks wrote to Calverton in February 1932 offering to abandon his project if it touched too closely upon the symposium, Calverton told him to go ahead.[26]

During the next fifteen months, a lively exchange of letters between archmovers of the new project—Granville Hicks, Bernard Smith, Clifton Fadiman, and Newton Arvin—offered a clue to the temper of the fellow-traveling Left intellectuals. These young radicals had

* Probably written by Granville Hicks, to whom I am indebted for the material relating to this episode. Hicks played the leading role in the attempt to set up the project.

very precise notions about the projected book, "a basic survey of a cultural complex by a homogeneous group," and the politics of the contributors. They should all be told, it was agreed, "that it will *not* be a political document, nor a C.P. Manifesto, nor will it pretend to be an undeviating and strictly orthodox Marxian analysis. It will attempt to be the latter, but it will not claim the achievement." Joseph Freeman had promised to find a competent person who could write an introduction "explaining the Marxian dialectic—its origins, nature and purpose," and keeping "the contributors clear as to what they ought to be and are doing." Clifton Fadiman, John Dos Passos, Newton Arvin, Frank Craven, Edmund Wilson, John Chamberlain, Scott Nearing, Waldo Frank passed muster as possible contributors. One of the planners felt dubious about Lewis Mumford and flatly opposed inviting either Malcolm Cowley or Matthew Josephson. "Both of them are uncertain at the present time in their philosophical and political objectives." [27]

New names and substitutions kept popping up in the multicornered correspondence,* but as the months wore on, the project became more cumbersome, and the men who Hicks and his friends had hoped would be the nucleus, "the men who represented a definite leftward swing of American intellectuals," refused to join, like Wilson, or backed out after first agreeing to participate, like Arvin and Fadiman. Personal problems forced the latter to limit his efforts to business or secretarial assistance, and a job as book reviewer on *The New Yorker* magazine permanently separated him from the young Marxists in 1933. In the meantime, the "Marxist Study of American Culture," which Harcourt, Brace & Company had contracted to publish, languished and died. Only Hicks and Smith had completed their articles and had them approved. And only the bona fide radicals already

---

* The first projected table of contents was as follows: A Preface to Marxism (Sidney Hook); The Social and Economic Scene (Lewis Corey); the Novel (Clifton Fadiman); Poetry (Newton Arvin); Criticism (Bernard Smith); Magazines (Granville Hicks); Philosophy (Sidney Hook); Science (Hyman Rosen) University Education (Howard Doughty, Jr.); Newspapers (Frederick Schuman); Fine Arts (Meyer Schapiro); Sports (Eliot Cohen); Music (Hyman Rosen); Movies (H. A. Potamkin); Theater (John Dos Passos); Radio (James Rorty); Cultural Minorities (Lionel Trilling); The Position of the Intellectual Classes (Herbert Solow). Potamkin, Dos Passos, Rorty, Corey were not definite.

close to the party, the people whom Smith had wished to exclude, seemed to be faithful to the project.

One article of the Marxist study was completed in time to benefit from the comments of the other contributors: Hicks's essay on magazines. These comments give some indication of how his brother radicals applied the Marxist dialectic in 1932:

One correspondent approved of the outline but urged that Hicks make clear "the unity of all bourgeois magazines from the pulps to the slicks, from *Adventure Story Magazine* to the *Atlantic: there is but one ideology.* Whether the periodical be a cheap sex magazine, a popular magazine or a genteel liberal magazine, its point of view toward human conduct and human motives, toward society and social mores, is essentially identical with that of any other bourgeois magazine." Only the readers differed.

Another recommended that Hicks bring out the tie between advertising and editorial matter and show how editors slanted fiction and nonfiction in order to stimulate a buying reaction. Further, Hicks should discuss *Boy's Life* (the organ of the Boy Scouts of America), which subtly inculcated militarism into the minds of hundreds and thousands of tender readers. He also suggested attention should be paid to the influence of bourgeois popular magazines like *The Saturday Evening Post* and *Cosmopolitan* on good writers like Faulkner and Hemingway, who had succumbed to them with disgusting results. Finally, he warned Hicks to be easy on *The Nation* and *The New Republic,* since his readers would come from their subscribers.

A third also had positive thoughts on the question of the liberal magazines. "Distinction should be made between the editorial policies of the Nation and New Republic, which are quite dangerous, and the independent contributions and book reviews, which often contain revolutionary content. To say that the New Republic is a menace to the revolutionary cause is too strong."

A fourth thought Hicks should point out that since the crash, magazines like *The Saturday Evening Post* had featured debunking stories about the idle rich but never criticized the Big Bourgeoisie, the bankers and industrialists. Mary Roberts Rinehart's stories about the police, he noted, never suggested their role as suppressors of the working class. He did not feel that *The New Republic* was important as an organ for the fellow travelers, especially since its editors (Bruce Bliven and George Soule) plugged a policy of "State Capitalism (Fascism)" and since Malcolm Cowley no longer wrote any of the editorial notes. Hicks, he said, should say nothing good about Benjamin Stolberg, an informer and "political assassin." Calverton was another matter. "Whatever Calverton's sins, he had never attacked the party."

The last criticized Hicks's article for its failure to connect the intellectual and professional groups with the middle class. This must be done in order to clarify the various kinds of "reformism favored by liberal journals. The liberal journals do represent the interests of class. The middle-class origin of the intellectuals is all the more important since almost all magazines utilize artists and intellectuals in forming or diffusing specific class ideologies, whether capitalist or middle class."

Read today, these reflections on capitalist culture have a naïveté and primness that may amuse a more cynical generation of readers, but in 1932 such opinions carried a great deal of force. An increasing number of young intellectuals were convinced, as Henry Hazlitt sourly observed, that "bourgeois culture" was merely "a class culture, i.e., an elaborate and colossal system of apologetics; worse, an instrument for class dominance and class oppression," and that the bourgeois critic who failed to recognize this obvious fact simply showed that he was imprisoned in "the walls of his ideological cell." [28] Hazlitt, and a good many other intellectuals throughout the thirties, remained unimpressed and contributed a continuous barrage of counterstatements against literary Marxism.

THE ILLIBERAL AND THE LIBERAL OPPOSITION

As the Marxist symposium was incubating, another convert to the Left, the critic and novelist Robert Cantwell, paid his grudging respect to the editor of *The Criterion* magazine—T. S. Eliot. Eliot, Cantwell conceded, was one of the few conservatives who saw the need for the Tories to articulate their social and political convictions. Although "one of the keenest intellectual apologists for this class," he did not deny "its lack of unifying ideals, its lack of discipline, its intellectual confusion." To defend and preserve it, he had "been making his literary soap-box orations on a union of church and state, and at the same time reserving his praise for those writers who aren't propagandists and aren't concerned with altering things." [29]

Since 1929 this "godling" of the American Humanists had issued a series of well-tempered anti-Communist edicts in his magazine. In sum, Eliot likened Communism to fascism. Both were "perfectly *conventional* ideas," not revolutionary. "A revolutionary idea is one which requires a reorganization of the mind; fascism or communism is now the natural idea for the thoughtless person." He found in both "a combination of statements with unexamined enthusiasms," and their adherents diffused "the emotional element through the theory," thus concealing it from themselves as well as from others, and becoming "the servants, not the masters, of words." Expanding on this theme, Eliot wrote:

Both fascism and communism seem to me to be well-meaning revolts against 'capitalism', but revolts which do not appear to get to the bottom of the matter; so that they are likely to be merely transformations of the present system which will completely satisfy the materialistic interpretation of history. Their economic and political doctrines, which have much in common, are attached to enthusiasms which appear to be contradictory. Fascism supports the Church, Communism would destroy it. But neither attitude seems to me to have any necessary connection: an atheistical fascism, or a devout communism, is theoretically conceivable; but it is quite intelligible that local circumstances should determine the attitude in each place. Fascism is . . . nationalistic, and communism internationalistic: yet it is conceivable that in particular circumstances fascism might make for peace, and communism for war. The objections of fascists and communists to each other are mostly quite irrational. I confess to a preference for fascism in practice, which I dare say most of my readers share; and I will not admit that this preference is itself wholly irrational. I believe that the fascist form of unreason is less remote from my own than is that of the communists.[30]

During the next few years, Eliot's lofty pronouncements began to be taken seriously, as Malcolm Cowley wrote, by "dozens of young men" who followed his example "and called themselves royalists, Catholics and classicists." [31] Eliot was congenial to them for a number of reasons.

1. He did not condone capitalism, which worked imperfectly and was only serviceable, as his friend Ezra Pound had been demonstrating, for usurers and speculators.

2. He remained untouched by what he called "la mystique of economics; the mixture, which may easily be a muddle, of economic theory, humanitarian enthusiasm, and religious fervor," and he distrusted Communism because it produced no art and had no sense of tragedy.

3. Although he did not rule out sociological criticism, which could be employed to show how a degraded society exposed itself in its reading matter, he repudiated the notion that art was determined "by social and economic conditions, that it is wholly relative to these conditions and has no meaning beyond them."

4. Although he respected Trotsky as a first-rate intelligence, he wrote derisively of the primitive young intellectuals in New York who were "turning to Communism, and their communism to literary account." It enabled them to substitute political and social theory for thought. The Christian, Eliot jibed, could read as he chose and even take pleasure from Communist art when it was good, but the Marxist had to forgo these pleasures because he first had to find out what was legitimate or illegitimate in literature before he committed himself:

For this knowledge of literature, he is obliged to apply himself, not to the furtive and facile pleasures of Homer and Virgil—the former a person of doubtful identity and citizenship, the latter a sychophantic supporter of a middle-class imperialist dynasty—but to the arduous study of Ernest Hemingway and John dos Passos; and the end of his precipitous ascent will be an appreciation of the accomplishments of Sam Ornitz, Lester Cohen, and Granville Hicks.

5. He did not conceal his contempt for the deracinated intellectuals of the North, the undesirable "free-thinking Jews," and he openly sided with the Tennessee Agrarians,* justly alarmed, he believed, by

---

* A group of Southern writers, centered in Vanderbilt University, who with other Southern intellectuals published a manifesto, *I'll Take My Stand* (1930), an argument and an outline for an "agrarian" and regional society modeled on the culture of the antibellum South. John Crowe Ransom, Allen Tate, Donald Davidson, Herbert Agar, Robert Penn Warren, and John Gould Fletcher belonged to this group, whose program, in some ways, resembled that of the English "Distributionists"—Hilaire Belloc and G. K. Chesterton.

the industrialization of their section and properly concerned with the central question: What is the good life? "The American intellectual today," Eliot declared, "has almost no chance of continuous development upon his own soil and in the environment which his ancestors, however humble, helped to form. He must be an expatriate: either to languish in a provincial university, or abroad, or, the most complete expatriation of all, in New York." [32]

By no means all of Eliot's American admirers subscribed to his Tory notions or his religious convictions, but his strictures on Marxian aesthetics strengthened their own faith in an art that "aspires to the condition of the timeless" even though it happens to document "the ideas and the sensibility of its epoch." Eliot helped them to formulate their case against the literary Communists and their fellow-traveling allies, who were trying to impose an inflexible orthodoxy on American letters: (a) Communist literary theory, as exemplified in the cruder samples of party-line criticism and in the work of the more intelligent and sophisticated Marxist practitioners, was pernicious; (b) the prophets of the new absolutism, mainly confined to the urban North, were blind to the fundamental metaphysical questions and out of touch with the deeper realities of American life.

Since the Southern Agrarians, Humanists, and other anti-Marxists singled out Edmund Wilson as the chief representative of the economic determinist school, his views on "The Literary Class War," as he called it, must first be considered.[33]

Eliot thought that regionalism in the U.S. could be pushed to ridiculous extremes, but he believed the motives driving Tate and his friends to write *I'll Take My Stand* were "sound and right." The Left critics treated Eliot, and his American traditionalist and classical equivalents, more cautiously and respectfully than they did the muddled liberals, even while attacking their criticism and social *obiter dicta*. An exception was Joseph Koven, who described the Agrarians as the *"Carry them back to Old Virginny"* groups: "(their tar and feather paradise, their heaven of immaculate white virgins and phallic symbols, of faggots and kerosene; where hemp grows on oak trees and charming southern gentlemen sip cooling mint juleps and speak of liberty and progress) *and let the rest of the world* (which is geographically northern, ethnologically black, professionally legal, politically Communistic, racially Semitic, theologically Catholic, by evil addiction, radical and by evil heritage, Yankee) *go to hell*." "The Liberal Legion," *Monthly Review*, I (June 1934), p. 44. Eliot he defined as "A wilting metaphysical amorphophallus, that grotesque specimen of medieval ecclesiastical horticulture set up in the fascist hot-house. Semitic Paraclete's anti-Semitic vicar, conducting poetical services in a celestial men's room. Heil, Father, Son, Holy Ghost and Hitler!" (p. 45).

Wilson's position on "revolutionary literature," "bourgeois art," and "proletarian art" satisfied neither the literary Left nor the literary Right. No other liberal critic at this time (1930-34) discussed with such detachment the fatuities of the pseudo-Marxists and the pedantry of so much Marxist criticism. Marxism and Humanism, he said, erred in the same way. Both were "in the position of trying to gauge the value of works of art on the basis of their literal conformity to a body of fixed dogma." Both were concerned with the question: "Does the work of art contribute toward a certain social end?" Wilson did not deny the validity of the question, but he was impatient with abstract specifications. The Humanist invented a nonexistent past for his theoretical ideal, the Marxist located it in the future; neither understood that "art is something that has to grow out of the actual present substance of life to meet life's immediate needs." It was not enough to see in Joyce and Proust "the morbidity and introversion of bourgeois culture in its decline," and still to undervalue their technical discoveries. Lenin had no qualms about taking over capitalism's technical discoveries, but since the eclipse of Trotsky, the "stupider type of Marxist" refused to see that the Joyces, the Cummingses, the Eliots possessed "the Johannson gauge of consciousness." He merely displayed his incompetence when he failed to understand that "a really first-rate book by an agonizing bourgeois may have more human value, more revolutionary power, than second-rate Marxists who attack it." It was Proust, not "our American Marxist journalists," who made him feel "most overwhelmingly that bourgeois society was ripe for burial." [34]

But if Wilson expressed his contempt for the "wooly and unearthly sounding metaphysical commentary" of the Communist hacks, with their slavish subserviency to Russia and their ridiculous efforts to make Russian conditions apply to the United States,* he had no patience with the catty bourgeois anti-Marxists who talked as if the

---

* Only 4 per cent of Americans were illiterate, he pointed out; there was no unbridgeable gulf between classes, and a nation which produced *Leaves of Grass* and *Huckleberry Finn* had nothing to learn from Russia or from any other country, either in the use of the common language or in the expression of the dignity and the importance of the common man. Our pioneers had created a literature of the common man's escape from bourgeois society long before the Russian masses were beginning to learn to write their names." *NR*, LXVII (Aug. 23, 1933), p. 43.

Communists were bent upon obliterating the culture of the past and compelling every writer to become a propagandist. Let them read the discussions of the Russian intellectuals, and they, as well as their radical opponents, would learn "that the great Communists have been men who fully understood the importance of art." Marx, Engels, Lenin, and Trotsky never claimed that all art must present the world "exclusively from the proletarian point of view," nor did they conceive of proletarian culture as developing independently "of those reserves of knowledge which society worked for under the oppression of capitalism, the landlords, the officials." [35]

Wilson took little stock in the American writers' fear of becoming politically dragooned by Communism. Most of them, he felt, might just as well be writing Communist propaganda as "writing propaganda for capitalism under the impression that they are liberals or disinterested minds, or even when honestly expressing their own ideas and emotions at the cost of going without the capitalist's wages, finding words for points of view which are becoming perforce as time goes on more dreary and muddled and sterile." During revolutionary crises, he thought, works requiring "a more complex vision" had little chance of being written, but at least Communism had created a new literary style, "accurate, impersonal, lucid, compelling" and "stripped of the romantic rhetoric which had obfuscated bourgeois radicalism." Wilson denied that he advocated a proletarian culture or literature. He did believe, however, that socialism could and should profoundly modify American culture "in form and style . . . as well as in point of view," and he took his stand between those who thought that intellectual, moral, and aesthetic activity operated in a social vacuum, and those who thought of human conduct solely in terms of economic appetite.[36]

Communist intellectuals, while regretting Wilson's inability to slough off all of his bourgeois prejudices, applauded his general line. But Joseph Freeman's old classmate Benjamin Ginsburg, who had surrendered to Bolshevism in 1920 while studying philosophy at the Sorbonne and had become disillusioned a few years later, wrote a trenchant critique of the Wilsonian program and the "messianism" of the Left.

Messianism, Ginsburg declared, staked "individual freedom entirely upon a realization of political reform," staked all "on the hope of the future." Hence it was "compelled continually to read its hope into the future in order to support its faith in present action" and to make "a subjective interpretation of reality in its very attempt to be ultra-realistic." Messianic intellectuals, instead of affirming moral and intellectual freedom and defining the goals of society, depreciated themselves and their function in favor of a pragmatic mysticism: the subjecting of culture to social problems. Like Randolph Bourne, he accused the radicals of collaborating so enthusiastically with historical tendency that they were losing touch with the source of their own values. Said Ginsburg:

If we keep in mind the fact that the liberals in America are primarily intellectuals by profession and training, one cannot help wondering whether the preoccupation of intellectuals with political questions is not a pathological reaction to the peculiar cultural conditions existing in America. In no country of the world is there such a tremendous gap between the values recognized by intellectuals and the values that actually govern political and economic realities. And yet in no country is the intellectual so preoccupied with affecting the course of politics to the exclusion of his intellectual interests. The less power he has of determining conditions, the more passionate, it would seem, is his will-o'-the wisp quest of political influence.

It is here that the philosophy of pragmatism is most revealing. Pragmatism has been wrongly called the philosophy of the practical man. It represents rather the anti-intellectualism of the American intellectual, who is over-awed by the practical sweep of American life.

But the true intellectual, Ginsburg concluded, will hold on to his values. He will see socialism as a "regulative ideal," not an absolute dogma, and will support it not as a politician but as a keeper of "the hearth fires of intellectual values, without which intelligent action becomes impossible." It may seem cruel, he acknowledged, to recommend a return to purely intellectual concerns when ten million men were "unemployed," but it was the business of the intellectual to be an intellectual.[87]

Paul Rosenfeld made precisely the same point when he accused American radicals of renouncing their responsibilities as artists, of allowing themselves to be swept "underneath a partisan flag and into the arms of a dogma." Arguing in the same vein as the French essay-

ist Julien Benda, Rosenfeld reminded his fellow intellectuals that it
"never has been and it never will be the function of the artist to
espouse the cause of 'the world' and to defend its special interests
. . . those of power and booty. . . . What he naturally champions
is something the world is not interested in; the use and administration
of material possessions in sympathy with vision." The manifestoes
issued by the Left, Rosenfeld noted, made no plea for culture nor
attempted to win over the Communist leaders "to the side of artistic
workmanship." Indeed, American writers were competing "as to
which could most quickly reconcile himself with the philistinism
which the Communist party shares with every other party." The great
manifesto about "Culture and Crisis" included almost everything in
its denunciation of capitalism "except the meaning of culture," and
the artist-signers who spoke out for the unemployed, the farmer, the
Negro, the trade union, the Chinese people, never realized that writers
"had something to champion and quite as necessary to survival as
the right to eat." Would the American writer, Rosenfeld wondered,
ever be loyal to private experiences, and would the idea that spiritual
satisfactions are important ever be accepted in a country that almost
from the beginning had believed "that, made economically secure and
comfortable, life will automatically grow blessed." [38]

Another version of the "treason" of the intellectuals appeared
about this time in *The Hound and Horn,* described ungraciously by
Granville Hicks as "the semi-official organ of a certain tendency in
American thought, the journal of the young men who accepted the
leadership of T. S. Eliot—the young men who attacked the Humanists for not being humanistic, flirted with Catholicism, and displayed
considerable proficiency in a hard and purely quantitative sort of
criticism." Lawrence Leighton, one of the magazine's "young men,"
criticized Edmund Wilson and the Left intellectuals as a group for
accepting Communism hastily and emotionally as a *pis aller* and
sinking their own unsolved personal problems into a mass movement. Granted that America's mammon culture, as described in
Wilson's *The American Jitters,* was unacceptable. But would not the
artist or writer converted to Communism estrange himself "even
farther from his audience and the source of his material"? Communism, despised by the middle class and the proletariat alike, offered

the writer an "opportunity for vigorous and violent missionary work." Perhaps the "indulgence in heroics, and possible martyrdom" appealed to some artists, but the task of the missionary was "hardly compatible with the more difficult task of being a good critic or a good artist."

Leighton pointed to a road leading to an undiscovered America, a road, he said, Wilson had neglected to explore. The anti-American cult, fashionable in the twenties, had been "sterile and defeatist," and "the self-appointed exiles of an interior decade" now found themselves isolated from the very people "with whom they must work in order to guarantee the worth of what they have to say." Leighton urged the writers and artists to re-examine American traditions.

Patriotism, so regarded, remains one among many modes of emotional and intellectual discipline that can restore the artist or critic to sympathy with his audience and milieu, provide him with material capable of exercising his powers, assist in the solution of his personal problems, and enable him to take part in the direction of American life. The material and sources of that patriotism are not our present concern; their record is largely found in American literature. A revaluation of that literature requiring the employment of both scholarship and criticism is perhaps the great service that could not be performed for the young American writer.[39]

THE CASE AGAINST THE LEFT WRITER SUMMARIZED

Before the "Red" thirties had run out, most of the charges subsequently brought against Marxist writers, Communists, and fellow travelers alike had already been made by the inchoate but numerous body of oppositionists: former radicals, liberals, aesthetes, conservatives, agrarians, socialists, and independents. Communist literary apologists were rarely if ever attacked by their fellow artists and intellectuals as traitors or subversives, but their critics condemned them on moral, aesthetic, and intellectual grounds.

First, their motives for accepting the Communist diagnosis of society were questioned. To the uncommitted, Communism was a mystique, an emotional "debauch," and the young writers converted to its doctrines were motivated, it was said, by the same defective romanticism that had animated the "irresponsibles" of the twenties. "Exploiting the sentimental potentialities of 'social' material," one hostile critic declared, "is not an advance beyond the romanticism that spoke through the hiccuping despair of the twenties; it is merely an extension of that mood to fit a new set of circumstances." "In Marxism," another observed, the writers "for whom politics and economics are not primary concerns . . . find something apparently objective—even revealed, one might say—which they can accept without departing too radically from the romanticism that has hitherto sustained. But a basic romanticism still informs their view; it has merely been united with a doctrine of power and inevitability which assures these writers that the very nature of things is now cooperating with them in what had formerly seemed a solitary revolt against the nature of things." Communist writers, it was often said, not only found religious certainty in the movement, but also an outlet for their power-hunger.[40]

Second, Communism, with its simplistic explanations for social change, its "scientific" illusions, its dogmatism and inflexibility, its narrow pragmatism, was regarded by a number of anti-Marxist critics as completely antithetical to the temperament and function of the creative artist.* The artist, once he involved himself in political affairs, found himself an apologist for the injustices perpetrated by the Right or the Left. He abandoned his proper concern for eternal questions for matters of immediate or transient interest. Only when politics entered deeply into the writer's consciousness, when it was "tacit" rather than "hortatory" and showed in the "bloodstream" of his work, could it be justified. Much too often, however, political convictions stifled aesthetic sensibility and ended as propaganda. Like puritanism and Humanism, Marxism converted art into a weapon instead of judging "aesthetic creation in its own terms" and re-enforced

---

* Especially, the logical consequences of collectivism, the subordination of individuals to masses: "shorn of its altruistic glamour, this collectivist attempt to merge the thinker in the object of thought, and confound the centre with the circumference, will prove its inhumanity . . . one thing is sure—the cup of hemlock (more accurately, a lethal chamber) would await the metaphysical man, homo sapiens, who dared to call his soul his own with that soulless anthill." *transition,* No. 21 (Mar. 1932), p. 121.

the emphasis on the ulterior purposes of literature, the encouragement of "a certain type of morality," [41] that had always been present
in America. To say with Allen Tate "that social problems 'were not
only insoluble but really right to be insoluble forever if we are to
maintain the social tensions which give to a culture its vitality,' "
the critic Richard P. Blackmur commented, in 1934, was bad and
defeatist politically, "but I think it is a sound sentiment for the artist
to make use of in relation to his view of his material; it will help him
both to feel and to represent the drama and conflict that confront
him." *

Third, it was widely held by both strong anti-Communists and
liberal critics of the *status quo* that Communism's theories and program were out of touch with American actualities. By mechanically
applying the Russian experience to the United States, they said, and
by neglecting to account for differences in national character, the
Communists misrepresented the American situation. The absence of
class consciousness in the United States, the tradition of anarchic
individualism, the distrust of American workers and farmers for proposals that attracted the Russian peasantry and proletariat—all mili-
tated against Communist success in America. Large numbers of

* R. P. Blackmur to Malcolm Cowley, April 27, 1934. Consulting Cowley
as a "political outsider" who was "much nearer the proper orthodoxy of our
own age," Blackmur (preparatory to writing a review of Eliot's *After Strange
Gods* and *Exile's Return*), asked: "What I want to know is this, what are
the doctrinaire consequences involved in a writer's becoming a radical. What
is a radical in this sense? I hope you will tell me that radicalism consists in
concentrating the attention with an honest wakeful eye so far as the arts are
concerned, and that a writer ought to be qualitatively aware of the contingent
political and economic problems of the individuals with whom he deals, and
that if he's any good he probably will be. But on the other hand you may
tell me that an artist ought to set his political and economic house in theoretic
order and dress his subjects in those necessarily borrowed and probably ill-
fitting clothes; in that case you will no doubt have a particular theory to
provide. This is a possible view (it is such as Eliot shares; in political economy, distributism, which in his case smells of fascism I think) and it may
be that in life such an absolute committal is inescapable, lest we go naked
and too often afraid. But such a view is a retreat, a hiding into which I
shall not myself rush if I can help it or until the exigence of revolution
compels me. (My metaphors are horribly mixed.)" At this time Blackmur
described himself as "a loose social service statist" and "Still something of
that smelly thing an independent liberal," but he could find no radical leadership to which he wanted to submit.

Americans, to be sure, obviously had lost their belief in the old capitalistic promises; a good many were becoming responsive to "philosophical communism," but the majority of the people neither expected nor wanted a revolution and were quite ready to settle for some necessary reforms.[42] Even the minority of intellectuals who advocated more drastic economic remedies to end the Depression distrusted Communist Party leadership and disagreed with its program for America. Lewis Mumford might be said to represent the radical non-Communist line in 1932.

Writing to Edmund Wilson and Malcolm Cowley in August 1932, in reply to their letter asking him to read the Communist Party platform for the 1932 presidential campaign, Mumford told them that he saw no point "in being tied up even temporarily with a party whose official ideology—dialectical materialism—seems to me as unsound as it is cocky and self-confident, and whose political tactics are so transparently opportunist. We must have something better than the official Communist Party in this country, even if you and I have to take off our shirts and create it." Having spent the past decade trying to work out "the ideological and technical basis for such a party," he was ready to cast his lot with the Communists if they showed any capacity to organize the intelligence of the country. But because the Communist leaders had no program, he found it impossible to support the party ticket, and he suspected their strategy, "with its emphasis upon abstract power and revenge," would more likely "generate a terrific fascist reaction in America, long before they themselves are in a position to apply themselves to the tasks of communism." [43]

One book published in the early thirties summed up the case of the liberal opposition against the Marxians and incorporated most of the anti-Communist arguments already referred to. This was Joseph Wood Krutch's *Was Europe a Success?* (1932), a defense of liberal values and the privileges of intellectual detachment. Krutch, as he later acknowledged to Malcolm Cowley, did not think all Communists held "the extravagant opinions which I attributed, I think correctly, to some very vocal ones," but he could not be on the same side with anyone who could "enthusiastically accept the paradoxical doctrine that the only means of achieving" the "perfect world state" of the future required "for the present the rigid suppression of nearly all specific freedoms." The liberal intellectual, said Krutch, might be ignorant of economics or convinced that the old system would have to go, but even if he accepted the "main contentions" of the "radical radicals," he could not help but deplore their disregard for the "secondary virtues which are commonly implied when we speak of anything or anyone as 'civilized.' " [44]

The Communist's "intense and burning hatred for that urbanity, detachment, and sense of fair play which makes thinking amiable," hardly differed, he thought, from the Fascist's. Both reached "diametrically opposed conclusions by mental processes very similar"; each practiced violence and demanded orthodoxy. If Communism were not a religion, it nonetheless had its bible and its saints; its initiates exhibited all of the classic patterns of conversion in the process of being reborn, and the party-church, having discovered "truth," ruthlessly rooted out the dubious and the heterodox.

No genuine writer, Krutch felt, could submit himself to a political religion that demanded undeviating fidelity to a set of doctrines and that regarded art as a weapon. The Communists in a few years had set back the course of literary freedom so painfully won during the last decades. Crusaders for art of "social significance," the new-Puritans, had subjugated Bohemia, suppressed bourgeois frivolity with Cromwellian ferocity, exiled the individualists, and imposed a kind of Left Babbittry on American culture. Krutch conceded that men are never pure artists. Humanitarian feelings constantly intruded into their novels and pictures. "But man *qua* Artist and man *qua* Reformer are antithetical things, the reformer concerned largely with what he can do to the world, the artist primarily interested in what the world is doing to him." The Communists, Krutch said, saw literature either as a clarion call or an opiate, as propaganda or "dreams." He countered with his own liberal conceptions of art and literature, which he felt were being lost sight of in the decade of convictions. Art, he asserted, "is essentially a form of rationalized and extended Contemplation, designed primarily to render more vivid and assimilable those experiences which are capable of being enjoyed for their own sakes." To communicate an aesthetic experience—the "real business of literature"—demanded "disinterestedness." [45]

THE COMMUNIST REBUTTAL

Replying directly to Krutch, Paul Rosenfeld, and other critics "who could see no difference between fascism and communism" and who accused revolutionary writers of being sterile and of going in "for proletarian religions," Edwin Seaver eloquently made the Communist rebuttal to the liberal plea for "disinterestedness" in literature and explained why so many of the younger writers had become radicals.

"Our conservative, our reactionary critics—that is to say, our liberal critics," Seaver wrote, could not understand the leftward trend in literature. Hence to them, Communism must be a racket or a religion, a new avenue for publicity, a nostrum for literary sterility. In one sense, the liberal critic was right when he spoke of sterile young writers * finding an answer in Communism, but he wrongly interpreted the "revolutionary orientation of the younger writers" as "a sign of their sterility" instead of seeing it as "a sign of rebirth and dedication of creative energies that were in danger of evaporating completely." The writers "in gravest danger of sterility" were not the revolutionists, but those who withdrew from revolution.

During the first three years of this revolutionary decade, Seaver said, many writers and intellectuals embraced Communism not so much for idealistic reasons, but because as a part of the "submerged petty bourgeoisie" they had come to understand "the full meaning of the class war." The masses, they now realized, provided the soil

---

* By "the younger writers," Seaver meant "those writers who are now in their early thirties, who happened to be born around the turn of the century, who encountered the war to end war before they were old enough to know better, and the counterfeit after-the-war-cynicism before they were old enough to realize that one's cynicism is worth as much, and only as much, as the cold cash of experience one has in reserve for security. Morally, spiritually, politically, socially, aesthetically—this generation was bankrupt by the end of the last decade. Sooner or later it would have to be liquidated and make a new start, for ahead lay only complete inanity and despair, only sterility. The utopia of a chicken in every pot may satisfy a Hoover, it cannot satisfy a normal human being." "Sterile Writers and Proletarian Religions," *New Masses,* VIII (May 1933), p. 22. This view of the twenties became a commonplace among Left Wing writers of the thirties and was not seriously challenged until after World War II.

for a real culture; to revolt against "the insanity of poverty in the midst of plenty" was simply common sense. These insights had released their strangled talents, ended their despair: extraversion had replaced introversion, and American literature had been enriched. Seaver advised the critic who saw all of this as "sterility" to take his nose out of the "literary gossip columns"

and go to the Hoovervilles, to the Hard-Luck-on-the-East Rivers, to the deserted mines and the impoverished fields, to the jungles outside our big cities, to the flophouses, to the charity dispensaries, to the empty warehouses where the homeless ones gather by stealth until they are chased out by the law—for it is here, and not in the library, that the strongest elements in our new literature are likely to come from. It is here that you may meet our future Gorkys, and not at your literary teas. It is here that you may meet our future poets and dramatists and novelists, not in the ranks of the cultured riffraff who no longer bother to talk about books.

Having made this tour, the critic could no longer speak of the virtues of detachment or prate about the sacredness of private vision. "What kind of tinker's damn does all your vision amount to," Seaver asked Paul Rosenfeld, "if the innocent Scottsboro boys are to burn? In the face of Alabama justice, of Massachusetts justice, of California justice—in the face, I say, of capitalist justice—what do you suppose William Blake would have considered to be the historic role of the artist? Or Shelley? Or Tolstoy? Or Emerson? Or Thoreau? Or any artist or writer living or dead who is or ever was worthy of the name?"

No, the writer's refusal to take sides, his rant about his sacred obligations to preserve culture simply gave aid to the profiteers and bandits who flourished in a world of poverty and war. Seaver ended his religiously unreligious homily with an impassioned quotation from Romain Rolland:

That unfertile aestheticism which delights in "thought for the sake of thought" is but an inch from the pit. It stinks of the corpse. He only lives who acts. . . . Our age is untamed, cruel, devastating; but it is also energetic, fecund. It destroys and it renews. Now is not the hour to whine and to sulk over our task. Today we have to struggle with old ideas, the dying and murderous gods, and with millions of blind spirits which serve them blindly. It is our task today to create a new vision and a new humanity. We can achieve this only at the expense of energy and unhesitating sacrifice. What we need, what the world needs, is action —and peace, which is the outcome of action.[46]

A somewhat less fervent response to the liberal critics of Communism was made by Granville Hicks, who by 1933 had become one of the recognized Marxist literary spokesmen for *The New Masses*. A Communist convert, although not yet a party member, and familiar with the arguments of the liberal camp from which he had recently deserted, Hicks charged his opponents with setting up and knocking down ideological straw men and of indulging in a sterile and negative kind of faultfinding. He acknowledged the "real weaknesses" that disfigured some Marxist criticism, weaknesses that sometimes justified the "distortions" of the liberals and the "very sharp attacks from critics of intelligence," but he blamed the clumsy Marxist practitioners, not Marxism itself. Calverton, the butt of the liberals, grossly oversimplified when he reduced aesthetic categories to economic ones. Nor could Hicks condone the vulgarians who argued that "if the class struggle is the central fact in life, and if the proletariat not only ought to win but is, historically speaking, certain to win," then the best literature will impell the reader to fight for the toiling masses. Great literature, he acknowledged, had deeper and subtler effects. It could not be judged by its success in making men act.

Yet the Marxists were surely right, Hicks thought, when they showed "the fundamental dependence of literature on the economic organization of society," right in making "class" the key factor in determining variations among groups and explaining "the creation of the individual mind," right in allying themselves with the proletariat the class "most likely to approximate objective truth." Having accepted the Marxist view of history, the Marxist critic had to insist that a book be judged according to its closeness "to the central issues of life," *i.e.,* the class struggle, that it allow the reader to experience vicariously "the lives described whether they are the lives of bourgeois or of proletarians." The author succeeded not by virtue of his technique, but to the degree that he was able to assimilate and understand the experience he was describing. Not only must he make the cause of the proletariat his own; "he should be, or try to make himself, a member of the proletariat." [47]

At this time, Hicks was writing with more assurance than he actually felt. "Marxist criticism is still in its infancy in America," he had written to *International Literature* in January 1933, "and I have had to go my own blundering way." In the next issue of the same magazine, Hicks spelled out the difficulties of being a Marxist critic in America: 1) the difficulty of eradicating bourgeois attitudes; 2) the task of acquiring correct knowledge of Marxism-Leninism; 3) the dangers of making a too-dogmatic application of these principles; 4) the necessity of keeping closely in touch with revolutionary writers and "with the realities of the revolutionary situation." Most of these problems, he thought, could be solved "if the fellow-travelers draw close to the working class." They needed "the discipline of Marxism" and a part in the class struggle. Only by doing so could they "destroy the innumerable survivals of their bourgeois inheritance" and "resolve the conflict between the two sets of interests that are struggling within them." [48] The literary front was highly fluid, with the fellow-traveling writers by no means agreed on Marxist aesthetics and with even the small core of literary Communists quarreling heatedly over the most fundamental issues.

Much of the controversy was lively and stimulating; sometimes it was solemnly ridiculous. Hicks might have cited, for example, the case of the young Marxist critic Philip Rahv, who had been chided by a slightly older Communist, A. B. Magil, when the latter ventured to salvage the Aristotelian idea of Katharsis for proletarian art. Rahv had suggested that "pity" and "terror" might be synthesized by "proletarian militancy." On the contrary, said Magil,

terror is an emotion absolutely alien to the revolutionary proletariat, incompatible with militant class action. One can plausibly conceive of a *capitalist* spectator at a proletarian drama experiencing Rahv's katharsis: he is filled with pity for his fellow-capitalists in the play, and with terror as he sees in their fate the possibility of his own, and consequently is moved to militant action (wage-cuts, speedup, etc.) against the workers in his factory.[49]

The Left Wing magazines bulged with polemical articles in which alleged Marxist critics lambasted the misstatements and simplifications of other alleged Marxist critics. "Of course," Hicks wrote to the Russians, "I have no doubt that the present confusions of the intellectuals will be straightened out," but between 1932 and 1935, the Communist counteroffensive against "the enormous amount of hostile criticism" from the liberal oppositionists lost much of its force because of "existing confusions" in the minds of the Left theoreticians.

MAC LEISH AND THE "SOCIAL MUSE"

Both Seaver and Hicks had reserved some sardonic comments for the poet Archibald MacLeish,* one of the most eloquent, elegant, and talented critics of the literary Left in the early thirties. MacLeish, then as well as later, felt impelled from time to time to make pronouncements about art and society and to serve as a voluntary public advocate for the American Muse. Although he despised the American plutocracy, so unflatteringly presented in his "Frescoes for Mr. Rockefeller's City," he did not try to hide his contempt for the "Soviet of garment workers or Columbia graduate students" who were setting themselves up as the new literary arbiters of the United States.

MacLeish had first publicly referred to these "intellectual terrorists" in a much discussed open letter "To the Young Men of Wall

---

* As a Yale undergraduate, MacLeish had written the elegiac poetry of a romantic and innocently snobbish youth seeking to insulate himself from the raucous world beyond New Haven. He had fought in World War I, obtained a Harvard law degree, and practiced law until 1923. "And then," as Harriet Monroe described it, "a breaking away from tradition at the thrill of a new discovery, a new purpose—that not law but literature was his vocation, not legal oratory but poetry." *Poetry*, XXXVIII, 1931, p. 152. MacLeish expatriated himself to France and stayed there until 1928. During this time, he wrote verse in the vein of Eliot and Pound, contrasted a picturesque and romantically conceived past to a shoddy and mean-spirited present, and proclaimed in rhymed and unrhymed manifestoes the inviolability of the individual spirit. The Depression awakened MacLeish's social sympathies without dulling his suspicions of totalitarianism. From a preoccupation with individual man, "MAN against the stars," he turned to plural man, "MANKIND." During the Spanish war, as will be shown, MacLeish was to become the darling of the Communist literati, but in the early thirties he represented for them the incipient fascism of the well-born intellectual.

Street," the salvageable scions of bankrupt progenitors. Would they abdicate, as their fathers had done? Or would they face the necessity "of giving the economic order shape and structure and human hope" and preserve America from the hate-filled simplifiers eager to replace an admittedly imperfect system with a ruthlessly autocratic one? Speaking "rashly no doubt" for "other American artists," MacLeish declared that artists as artists felt no preference one way or another whether the state was capitalist, Communist, or fascist. In fact, most artists, with a few notable exceptions, confessed their impotence when they forsook art for economics. Their current "proletarian leanings" simply indicated their resentment against the "smug bourgeois majority" who ignored them. But all artists, he said, needed an atmosphere of intellectual freedom to survive. Capitalism, with all its iniquities, provided a more favorable milieu for the artist than Communism or fascism did. Its great weakness was its inflexibility, its reliance upon force, fraud, and charity, its failure to provoke a belief or an emotion comparable to that inspired by Communism. "If you can create an idea of capitalism which men will support with their hope rather than their despair," MacLeish told the young men of Wall Street, "you will inherit the world. If you cannot, you and your children and ourselves with you will vanish from the West." [50]

Naturally, the sentiments expressed in the "Letter" displeased the radicals, but not until *The New Republic* published his "Invocation to the Social Muse" in October 1932 did he become the target for their attacks. In this poem, MacLeish warned the poet to eschew political fashions, to remain estranged and alone:

> Besides, Tovarisch, how to embrace an army?
> How to take to one's chamber a million souls?
> How to conceive in the name of a column of marchers?

His plea met with little approval in *The New Republic*'s letter columns, especially the lines in which he likened the poets to whores who sleep with adherents of various persuasions and are "strictly forbidden to mix in maneuvers." Was the young man who fought at Salamis a whore? asked Allen Tate in a rhymed reply. "The poet is he who fights on the passionate / Side and whoever loses he wins."

"Disliking the political, Mr. MacLeish wrote a political poem," declared another. "If poets *are* whores, then it would follow that the more in bed the merrier." Rolfe Humphries observed that MacLeish's metaphor would have been more precise if he had said poets were not whores, "but kept women (*i.e.*, not proletarians, but bourgeoises)." So long as the "master class" was strong and vital, no disgrace attached to the liaison, but "when your honored lord becomes old and fat, corpulent, senile and queasy, gross and impotent, and you know you can't get away from him, you have very good reasons for locking yourself in your room, throwing tantrums and draining bottles." [51]

Few of MacLeish's fellow bards would agree that the poet should consider himself antisocial; and MacLeish's attempts to answer his critics by insisting once again that the poet's business was simply to be a poet, that it was merely "social cant" to write hymns to dynamos in the vocabulary of Marxism,[52] only heaped coals on the controversy. Both pro- and anti-MacLeish partisans cited evidence to show how political advocacy made or destroyed the literary artist.

The controversy grew more personal after Michael Gold detected symptoms of what he called "the fascist unconscious" in "Frescoes for Mr. Rockefeller's City." Gold's phrase was inaccurate and, in view of MacLeish's high-mindedness and generosity, unfair, but Gold—the celebrator of the proletarian mélange—was quick to detect an "unconscious" animus toward the multicolored "bastards" speaking broken English who had sunk no roots in the American soil. To Gold, MacLeish's use of the "tough land" as a counterpoise to the "Marxists, Jews and those disturbed intellectuals who recently have taken the road to the political left" smacked of a "mystic nationalism," akin to the mythical invocations of Mussolini and Hitler. Gold said:

Mr. MacLeish has no political rights to the Rockies or the landscape. The great magnetic continent belongs to the masses, to the workers. White-collar fascists out of Harvard and Wall Street have less spiritual claim on America than the share-croppers, miners, sailors and gaudy-dancers. Walt Whitman said it once, but it needs to be said again and again; every land belongs to those who fertilize it with their blood and sweat.

MacLeish had ridiculed "Comrade Levine"

> who writes of America
> Most instinctively having in 'seventy-four
> Crossed to the Hoboken side on the Barclay Street Ferry. . . .
> Aindt you read in d'books you are all brudders?

To which Gold replied: "As for us unfortunate Jews who happen to be Communists and annoy Mr. MacLeish so much, we shall go on repeating in our vulgar dialect, despite Hitler and MacLeish, 'Aindt you read in d'books you are all brudders? Aindt you read in d'books you are all brudders?' " [53]

THE STALEMATE

Behind the charges and countercharges lay certain issues that the thirties never resolved. MacLeish himself in the next few years, after skirmishing with such respectful but highly critical adversaries as Malcolm Cowley, made himself more palatable to the Left-Wingers by vigorously attacking fascism in poems and plays and speeches,[54] but a gulf continued to divide those who insisted on separating art and politics and those who indignantly denied MacLeish's contention that the artist's sole motive was "an obscure and personal compulsion." Must the writer engage himself and write polemics? Did the proletariat have a monopoly on all the great themes? Was propagandist art always "a temporary over-simplification of the human predicament"? Was propaganda only what the other fellow writes, and all art propaganda of a sort? Such problems and others were endlessly discussed in hundreds of articles, with neither Communist nor anti-Communist persuading the other.

This literary engagement and the others that erupted periodically between 1929 and 1939 hardly bear out the widely held myth that in the thirties the Communists had captured New York and had "managed to poison the intellectual life of a whole nation." On the contrary, as Granville Hicks has said, "There never was a time when anti-Communism wasn't a vastly easier road to success than Communism, and if Communists engaged in persecution, as they did when they could, they were more often on the receiving end." That the Communists exerted an influence on writers and intellectuals far beyond their numbers is undoubtedly true, but despite their vociferousness and energy, the party failed to attract more than a minority of writers or, more significantly, to hold very many of its intellectual supporters. Its enemies likened the party to a church. If the analogy is appropriate, one must also add that it was a church wracked by heresy, a church whose priestly hierarchy disagreed about basic doctrines and nourished intellectual apostasy.[55]

NINE · "OLD MEN," "NEW MEN," AND THE PARTY

VETERANS AND NEWCOMERS

"COMMUNISM," wrote the author of the article on "Socialism" in the eleventh edition of the *Encyclopaedia Britannica,* "is an idea far more utopian than socialism. Like the idea of a kingdom of heaven or a millennium, it springs often from a spiritual enthusiasm that feels sure of its end, and, at first at least, recks little of the means." This enthusiasm, he went on to say, usually resulted from a conversion experience. Even the advocates of scientific socialism went through some kind of "mental somersault," for "a change of heart, which is also a change of view, is to socialism, as a religion, what economics and political theory is to it as a creed."

The observer begins to see the world of men all over again, throwing from him all the prejudice of his class and abstracting from all classes. This abstraction may be less hard for those who belong to a class that has little, than for those of a class that has much, as religious conversion is held to be easier for the poor. But it is not really easy for any.[1]

To become a Communist at any time was not "easy," but it was probably less easy to join the party and to devote oneself to the revolutionary cause in the twenties than it was during the Depression decade. The "old men," the "romantic rebels" of the post-World War I years, had engaged in a series of losing contests with the strong and confident defenders of the "System." Only their faith sustained them. They had protested in behalf of Tom Mooney, agitated for the Passaic strikers, picketed for Sacco and Vanzetti. They had written poems and tracts about the lynching of Frank Little and the execution of Joe Hill. Although most of them had repudiated the Bohemianism of their youth, the "Wobbly" in them had not been entirely extinguished, and their visions of the socialist millennium resembled (with pagan additions) those of the American nineteenth-century reformers. For the most part they were humanists and pacifists, haters of violence. One can imagine them living quite happily in a utopia that combined the best features of the old Greenwich Village, Bellamy's twenty-first-century cities, a Bolshevik Soviet, a Fourier phalanstery, and a *Masses* editorial meeting.

The older "new men," who came belatedly into the movement after the breakdown of the American economy, had hitherto accepted capitalism as an unchangeable reality even while ridiculing its culture. The Left did not need to insinuate itself into their consciences or to attract them by devious means. On the contrary, a good many of them *"stormed* the offices of the Left magazines and literary groups and begged, pled, wheedled and even *demanded* to be taken in!" The Left provided a refuge, but it demanded less from the "new men" than it had from the "old." Thus, to "go Left" after 1933, the year that the United States recognized Russia, was no longer the daring and rebellious gesture it once had been. Under the New Deal, the reforms fought and suffered for by the "old men" were enacted into law. To champion liberal economic and social legislation was not merely undangerous; it became highly respectable. And after the Communist Party adopted the Popular Front line in 1935, Joseph Freeman observed, one could be simultaneously a Communist and a supporter of F.D.R. and jump on "the sweetest bandwagon in all history."

For now you could be for every kind of social reform here, for the Soviet Union, for the Communist Party, for Proletarian Literature— for everything and anything that was at one time radical, rebellious, subversive, revolutionary and downright quixotic—and in doing so you were on the side of all the political angels of the day; you were on the side of the Roosevelt administration, on the side of Labor, the Negroes, the middle classes; on the side of Hitler's victims, on the side of all the oppressed colonial peoples in the world. In short, this is the only period in all the world's history when you could be at one and the same time an *ardent revolutionary* and an *arch-conservative* backed by the governments of the United States *and* the Soviet Union.[2]

By no means all of the "new men," however, belonged to the group Freeman was alluding to in the above quotation—the writers, teachers, artists, and journalists of his own generation who during the thirties sought him out for ideological injections, who arranged private meetings in cities and college towns to hear him and other literary radicals discourse on Marxism and the arts, and who referred casually in their letters to "coming out" for the "movement." A younger and tougher group of enthusiasts, as we have seen, constituted another contingent of the "new men." Still in their teens or early twenties, they were idealistic and ambitious. Moreover, they considered themselves set apart by age and by cultural affiliations from the older generation of revolutionary writers.

THE YOUNG REDS AND THEIR TEACHERS

Writing in 1934, William Phillips, one of the editors of the newly founded organ of the John Reed Club of New York, *Partisan Review,* carefully distinguished his own "proletarian generation" from his immediate literary forebears. The latter he defined as the "exiles" and *"transition group"* (Hemingway, Cowley, Tate, and company) and the "few confident pioneers" (Freeman, Gold, Kunitz) who, after "several years of partial eclipse," were becoming "the Marxian teachers of the leftward moving writers."

The literary Marxists had been the guides and teachers of the young radicals throughout the dry years. But "the strain and exigencies of pioneering," Phillips thought, "kept them from assimilating the literary spirit of the twenties," which for good or ill was part of the literary heritage of the young radicals. Although his own proletarian group, he said, was tied up in some way with the Communist Party or the labor movement, its literary fathers were writers like Joyce and Eliot (from whose influence not even the most revolutionary writers were immune) and such writers and critics of the twenties as Malcolm Cowley, Hart Crane, Kenneth Burke, and John Dos Passos. The achievements of the "lost generation" may have been overexaggerated; certainly their premises were false; but they left the young radicals "with some impressive judgments and some good writing." To the "proletarians" was left the task of fusing the ideas of the old revolutionaries with the techniques of the nonpolitical experimenters, "to use whatever heritage there is at our disposal for our revolutionary tasks." [3]

Freeman may very well have had Phillips in mind when he reviewed the recent literary history of the Left movement for *The New Masses* in September 1934. Speaking for the handful of old revolutionary writers who before the Depression were ignored by bourgeois publishers and "compelled to propagate their ideas in all the available *ephemeral* forms," he explained why it was they had failed to perfect their craft. How could it be otherwise, he asked, when besides writing articles and reviews for the radical press, they taught classes for workers, ghosted or rewrote other peoples' books, recruited new writers, edited magazines and newspapers, raised money, attended nightly meetings, dug for facts in libraries, and tried to earn a living on the side by turning out various kinds of hack work? "They gave their time and energy without stint and without reward and without intellectual or physical laziness to other writers and to numerous organizations in the hope of developing a widespread movement for revolutionary literature." Freeman knew that more solid work was necessary, but until 1932 the heavy burden of "agitation, education, organization, editing, journalism, speaking" fell on the shoulders of a few trained writers.[4]

In that year, Freeman recalled, he had proposed in his report to the John Reed Club that the members undertake to prepare a number of fundamental books and pamphlets [5] to win over the "fence-sitters," and *"reorganize* the New Masses *from top to bottom"* and *"make it a magazine which a trained mind would listen to with respect and with intellectual profit."* An important part of the American intelligentsia was "swinging to the left," Freeman said. These people would certainly not be won over by "our superficial, crudely humorous expositions of Communism." *The New Masses* would fail in its responsibility to guide the "cultural front" and "raise a new generation of revolutionary writers" until it solved its financial problems and until its editors were released from their excessive organizational tasks and given enough leisure to direct the revolt of the intellectuals. They would also need the aid of the John Reed Clubs and other cultural revolutionary groups.

By 1934, he felt, many of his proposals had been partially realized. Talented new contingents had joined the small body of revolutionary veterans at the cultural barricades. *The New Masses* had been transformed into a hard-hitting weekly. Despite the complaints of certain newcomers against some of *The New Masses* critics,[6] the level of Marxist criticism had clearly improved and the old sectarian attitude of the past had been abandoned. The last was "the most significant change of recent months in our literary movement," Freeman thought, and one to be welcomed, but it also brought with it a danger that he took considerable pains to spell out. Since his comments were at once a recapitulation of the past and a prophecy of what was to come, they deserve careful attention.

THE DANGERS OF LATITUDINARIANISM

During the first years of *The New Masses,* the majority of its editors and contributors wanted the magazine to be "artistic and literary," not political. Founded as a continuation of the old *Masses* and *The Liberator* and at a time when "the proletarian revolution seemed very remote and very unreal," it had no official party connection and it welcomed allegedly "Marxist" critics who "from the very beginning belonged to the enemy camp." Their departure to their white ivory towers after the Garland Fund had been spent induced the saving revolutionary remnant to construct their own red ivory towers of sectarianism. Now that the Depression had undermined both towers, white and red, the unwholesome violation was over. Writers who had spent the past ten years in the movement and those who "during the same period . . . engaged primarily in perfecting their craft" were now working side by side.

But Freeman warned against welcoming under the banners of Communism those recruits who had only recently slandered the party and who showed no evidence of having "really broken with their past." The unreliables fell into the following categories: 1) the Narcissists, the "anemic, sterile heirs of the romantic movement" who were only concerned with self-expression; 2) the counterrevolutionary "revolutionists" whose "pseudo-revolutionary chatter" cannot "conceal from the world their envy, malice, vanity and dilettantism, or their attachment to the bourgeoisie"; 3) the "sincere writers whose immaturity in the movement subjects them to hostile influences and impels them to smuggle in all good faith, but with unfortunate results, middle-class ideas and practices into our ranks." [7] Under the new spirit of Communist *laissez faire,* these elements might misdirect young Left writers into "an exaggerated regard for bourgeois literary fads" and convert the revolutionary press into "an open forum for ill-considered and thoughtless echoes of that bourgeois world which the 'fence-sitters' are presumably seeking to abandon." We must have criticism by all means, Freeman concluded, but criticism that advanced the revolutionary movement, "criticism on an intellectual, political, literary, *Marxist* level." [8]

Freeman's apprehensions turned out to be well-founded. Bourgeois echoes did indeed resound in the revolutionary press; "red" critics did not disagree with comradely forbearance; "sincere" converts to the movement and well-meaning fellow travelers raised all manner of embarrassing issues; and careerists more concerned with their literary reputations than with the advancement of the party did infiltrate into the movement. But Freeman did not anticipate the party's own role in encouraging the infusion of those very unreliable elements that he had warned against.

THE NEW LINE

Inklings of the change in the "line" from a narrow and ultra-Left exclusiveness to a broad and almost indiscriminate inclusiveness were already discernible even before the official announcement of the Popular Front in 1935. The Communist Party, the writer Robert Briffault remarked as late as 1932, "appears to have acquired the reputation of being considerably more exclusive than the Carlton

Club . . . the privilege of admission to its circle is far more difficult than is summary expulsion from it." [9] Not until the sharp turn
from the "hard" policy of the so-called "third period" (1928-35) to
the "soft" policy of collaboration with all enemies of fascism was
agreed upon by the Communist International in the summer of 1935 [10]
did the party officially modify its distrust of intellectuals and let down
the barriers, but the liberal trend could be detected even before the
Moscow Congress.

For example, the party began to take a new interest in organizations of radical writers and artists, and particularly in the leadership
of such groups, but no longer required or even desired the chairman-
ships to be recruited from the loyal "old men" of indifferent reputation no matter how long they had slaved in the vineyards. What it
wanted now was bourgeois sympathizers with "names." New faces
began to appear on the platforms of Communist-sponsored meetings
and forums, often well-known recruits who had recently "come over."
And when the "old-timers" did speak at these gatherings, they might
be instructed by Alexander Trachtenberg, the party's cultural "commissar," to make a liberal talk and wave the flag a little.

In the spirit of the benign and indulgent policy of the united
front, the Communist editors resolved, in the words of the poet-critic
Stanley Burnshaw, "to drive away no one who can be turned into a
friend of the revolutionary movement." The "confusions" of the
"middle-ground" writers often led to incipient fascism, he realized,
but sympathetic guidance was preferable to ferocious attack. Burnshaw had Archibald MacLeish very clearly in mind when he spoke
of the danger of approaching "suspects on political grounds almost
exclusively" and of lumping with fascism the wavering writer still
enamored with the fragments of capitalism. The disorganized writer
could not be driven left by bludgeoning criticism, but he could be
shown during his condition of "creative crisis" why the middle
ground was untenable and why he must logically support Communism. "So long as he is true to himself as a writer," Burnshaw declared, even the incipient fascist is a potential antifascist "honestly
struggling to find a way out of the crisis"; his "very confusion amounts
objectively to quiescence to the process of fascization now going
on." The religious analogy to Burnshaw's dramatic account of damna-

tion and salvation is too obvious to comment upon, but in 1935, such earnest and strenuous reasoning explained why a MacLeish, who had come "dangerously close" to apologizing for World War I and who had mimicked the accents of Jewish workers, had "recently acted on the side of the workers against the exploiters in the Ohrbach Department Store strike." [11]

CONFUSIONS AND UNCERTAINTIES

It was one thing for an eminent writer to be "confused" in 1935 and thereafter, another for a less talented or influential writer with a revolutionary background to be so. Dreiser was so "confused" that he publicly disparaged the Jews, but he received only the mildest of chastisements for his racial pronunciamentos.

Dreiser had never tried to conceal his crude but hardly obsessive anti-Semitism. In 1922, for example, he could describe New York City to his friend Mencken as "a scream—a Kyke's dream of a ghetto. The lost tribe has taken the island." [12] But this was a year when Hitler was so unimportant that the *Daily Worker* misspelled his name. A decade later it did not make that mistake.

In the September 1933 issue of *The American Spectator,* George Jean Nathan, James Branch Cabell, Eugene O'Neill, Ernest Boyd, and Dreiser jocosely slandered the "Chosen People's" manners and culture and facetiously recommended they be settled in Africa or Kansas. This so-called "Editorial Conference" was intended to be conscientiously funny, but Hutchins Hapgood, the old anarchist, was not amused. At a time when the Jews were being persecuted in Germany, he reminded Dreiser, *The Spectator*'s symposium was certainly not "innocent" in its results. Dreiser replied, and Hapgood published the ensuing correspondence under the title "Is Dreiser Anti-Semitic?" [13]

Dreiser retracted nothing. The Jews, he said, avoided the proletarian occupations; they lacked integrity; they were money-minded; and, because of "their cohesion, their race tastes," they were quite capable of overrunning the country. He saw no reason "why a race as gifted, as definite, as religious in its predilections should not be will-

ing to occupy a country of its own." Dreiser denied he wanted to ex-
pel the Jews from America, and he condemned the persecution of
the Jews by the Germans. Nevertheless, he declared, the Jews were
unassimilable, and it would be a good thing for them and for the
world if they were relocated in some Jewish national homeland.[14]

Dreiser's anti-Semitism smacked of the populism of Ignatius Donnelly, not the racist theories of the Nazis; at times, Vachel Lindsay
and Edgar Lee Masters had expressed similar notions about the
Jews. But Dreiser in 1935 was quite insensitive to the implications
of his position and undisturbed by the reports from Germany. That
his hostility to the Nazis was hardly intense is borne out in the letter
to a friend inquiring whether the banning of his books in Germany
"on the ground that they are subversive of morals and character"
was owing to their misapprehension that he was a Jew. He did not
mind if his books were banned "because of their psychologic or
social merits or demerits," but he wanted to know that he was "not
being banned for being racially something that I am not." [15]

Needless to say, Dreiser's views shocked his Communist friends,
and his statement to *The New Masses* that he did not hate the Jews
and had "nothing to do with Hitler or fascism" fell far short of the
"ringing repudiation" that the editors expected from him. He had
hurt "the working masses." And yet the committee who questioned
him, consisting of Corliss Lamont, James W. Ford, John Howard
Lawson, Edwin Seaver, Mike Gold, Joshua Kunitz, Henry Hart, and
Orrick Johns, refused "to believe that it will be impossible for
Theodore Dreiser to regain his traditional place as a fighter for
human liberty." A mollifying editorial to the same effect appeared
in *International Literature*.[16]

Two *New Masses* readers sharply protested against the magazine's
halfhearted rebuke of Dreiser. "Why all the tenderness and solicita-
tion for an individual who is obviously a white guard?" one inquired.
"Honestly now," another asked, "suppose Sinclair Lewis or one of
your other pet aversions had written the infamous Dreiser letters.
Would you have been as eager in his defense as you are in the
defense of Dreiser?" [17]

Only Michael Gold, now speaking for himself, boldly and bitterly
denounced Dreiser in *The New Masses*. He had been his guide and

informant when Dreiser was gathering material for a play about Jews, *The Hand of the Potter,* and had taken Dreiser to meet his mother, who lived in an East Side tenement. "Do you remember," Gold wrote, "the block of tenements I pointed out to you, famous among social workers as having the highest rate of tuberculosis per square foot of any area in the world? Do you remember the ragged children without playgrounds who darted among the street-cars and autos? Do you remember the dark, stinking hallways, the hot congested ant-life, the penny grocery stores?" That, said Gold, was only one of many ghettos spread all over the world. Dreiser's nationalism was fascist, Gold charged flatly, and his foolish words had hurt not the rich Jews, but the Jewish workers. "It is now my belief he can undo this damage only by years of devoted battle against anti-Semitism and fascism." [18]

There is no evidence that the party henceforth made Dreiser toe the mark,[19] but the deviations and confusions of the poet Horace Gregory, one of the founders of the John Reed Club and, in 1935, a self-proclaimed believer in the goals and aims of the Communist Party were carefully scrutinized by Communist critics.

Describing his position for *The New Masses,* Gregory tried to make a case for the pro-Communist writer who still feels it important for his art to remain apolitical and detached from the "heat of conflict." As a writer, he did not understand the sectarian quarrels that split the movement into factions. "The Trotskyites, the Lovestoneites, the Musteites are terms quite meaningless to me," he confessed, whatever their significance in the U.S.S.R. and "in certain sections of New York." Nor could he accommodate himself to shifting "esthetic standards" or to poems celebrating the victories of a people whose culture was too remote from his experiences for him to be able to write convincingly about them. "I am a nationalist," he declared, "not in a political sense but in the sense which you or I describe the inheritance of a culture." Although he recognized its disintegration, he could not write as if the American revolution had already taken place. Let us abandon our "rancorous quarrels," he suggested, and work in a spirit of unity.[20]

Both Edwin Seaver and Meridel Le Sueur, a Midwestern fiction writer, confessed they were confused by Gregory's "confusions." Did

Gregory mean merely that each person must support the party in his own way, and his way was writing poetry? Or was he saying: "All right, I believe in Communism, I'm for the party; now please let me write my poetry in peace." Gregory, Seaver implied, meant the second. Obviously Gregory was not a "true Communist poet," but a poet who happened to be a Communist sympathizer. He had no "integrated philosophy," no vision of the future (hence his inability to write about a victorious Russian worker); his "basic political immaturity" shone through his "naturalist and revisionist cant" about the meaninglessness of splits and schisms; and all of his palaver about "objectivity" became criminal in times of crisis. "The literary honeymoon is over," Seaver said, "and I believe the time is fast approaching when we will no longer classify authors as proletarian writers and fellow-travelers, but as Party writers and non-Party writers." This might not be desirable, but "in time of revolutionary crisis it is inevitable." [21]

Gregory, according to Meridel Le Sueur's diagnosis, suffered from the "middle-class malady" shared by "all of us nourished on rotten bourgeois soil." He revealed the symptoms of "the objective fetish": the fear of joining (as if one "joined" the Communist Party as one "joined" the Rotarians), the infantile notion that the creative worker cannot understand economics or political theory. As for herself, she could "no longer breathe in this maggoty individualism of a merchant society." That is why she hoped to " 'belong' to a communal society, to be a cellular part of that and able to grow and function with others in a living whole." Gregory wanted the advantages of being simultaneously inside and outside. His stand was equivocal and hypocritical —doubly dangerous because of its apparently "frank ideology." [22]

From the Communist point of view, Seaver and Le Sueur correctly deprecated Gregory's uncertainties, but the party's growing tendency to gather in the "big names" while reserving its dialectical scalpel for the less famous could not help but dishearten a number of its literary supporters.

TEN · THE FIRST WRITERS' CONGRESS

THE DEMISE OF THE JOHN REED CLUBS

IN HIS REVIEW of Granville Hicks's fine biography of John Reed, Max Lerner praised Hicks for converting a "deeply rooted" legend into a man. Reed, Lerner believed, had been damned by excessive praise or condescendingly treated as a Faustian "playboy," all heart and no head, whose conversion to Communism could be interpreted as merely another aspect of his generous enthusiasm. Of course the Communists themselves contributed to this romantic legend of Reed, the "pure knight of the revolution, who gave his genius and his blood to set the workers free." By 1930 he had already become, in Joseph Freeman's words, "a fruitful and activizing symbol for American radical literature," the patron saint of a group of young revolutionary writers. "He combined poetry and politics, memorable and transforming words with revolutionary action." [1]

After the national organization of the John Reed Clubs in 1932, active chapters sprang up in a number of smaller towns as well as in the larger cities. They published a number of militant proletarian magazines, featured the work of undiscovered writers and artists, composed and mimeographed leaflets, improvised "skits for mass rallies," wrote "group chants against capitalism," lectured on "art and propaganda, poetry, and revolution, intellectuals and the crisis." [2] Most important of all, perhaps, the John Reed Clubs provided a place where sensitive and socially *déclassé* would-be writers were sympathetically received and warmly encouraged.*

The John Reed Clubs were something quite different from the so-called "innocents' clubs," organized by the party after 1935 as façades behind which the Communists manipulated public opinion. John Reed Club members came in as radicals. Their "innocence," if it can be called such, consisted in their failure to see in the party's promotion of revolutionary literature a "hard-headed, single-minded emphasis on increasing its own power as an organization." [3]

No such notion disturbed the more than forty delegates to the John Reed Clubs conference who gathered in Chicago in September 1934, although the speeches delivered to the representatives of some 1,200 members were not entirely positive. Progress during the past two years had been most gratifying, yet "sectarianism, leftism, right-ism,—the last bourgeois hangovers," pointed to the necessity of adopting "bolder methods." The conference specifically condemned "practices in our work that lead fellow-travelers to think that they must become revolutionary-proletarian writers overnight" and "directed a collective attack against writing which consists of unconvincing, sloganized tracts disguised as poetry and fiction." [4]

One address before the conference was more momentous than most of the delegates realized. Alexander Trachtenberg, speaking "with bolshevist incisiveness and humor," declared the "purpose of the John Reed Clubs" was "to win writers and artists to the revolution." He "stressed the importance of a creative revolutionary literature in the fight against capitalism and joined in denouncing the sectarianism of the cultural movement." And then came the suggestion unanimously endorsed by the conference—that the national committee of

---

* The Negro novelist Richard Wright has described his introduction to the Chicago John Reed Club, which he had (still full of suspicion and hate for white people) cynically visited "in the capacity of an amused spectator." Climbing a dark stairway somewhere in the Loop, Wright entered a dingy and sparsely furnished office. Cigarette butts littered the floor. On the walls hung posters "depicting colossal figures of workers carrying streaming banners. The mouths of the workers gaped in wild cries; their legs were sprawled over cities." Here he met artists and writers who would some day be famous, uncondescending people who treated him as an equal and who were ready to publish his crude poems. *The God That Failed,* ed. by Richard Crossman (N.Y., 1949), pp. 115-20.

the John Reed Clubs be instructed to organize a national congress of writers "within the next six or eight months."

What Trachtenberg really had in mind became clear at a party caucus held in a Chicago hotel. Richard Wright, one among a small group who attended it, was thunderstruck when he learned that since "the People's Front policy was now the correct vision of life," the John Reed Clubs would be dissolved. When he asked what would "become of the young writers whom the Communist Party had implored to join the clubs" but who were excluded from the proposed new organization of established writers, he got no reply, and not a single other person seconded his protest.[5]

Leon Dennen had a similar experience in New York, as he later told Max Eastman:

The real decision to form a League of American Writers . . . was made on the 9th floor of 50 East 13 Street, Earl Browder's headquarters. Alexander Trachtenberg, the Communist Party's cultural commissar, called a few of us together and told us that the John Reed clubs "no longer exist"—henceforth there was to be "a broad organization of American writers." I protested that it was undemocratic to disband an organization without consulting its membership. He replied that first we must carry out the decisions of the party, and then "speak of democracy and what not." I was punished for my protest: although I was a member of the executive committee of the John Reed Club which issued the call for the Writers' Congress, my name did not appear among the dozens signed to the call.

Plans went ahead to mobilize the antifascist writers and to "strike a blow at the growing fascist enemy, the rapidly developing white guard and fascist criticism, and the Roosevelt-fostered national-chauvinist art." [6]

In January 1935 *The New Masses* published the "Call for an American Writers' Congress" with a prefatory endorsement. Granville Hicks, soon to join the party, prepared the first draft, with its confident introduction:

The capitalist system crumbles so rapidly before our eyes that, whereas ten years ago scarcely more than a handful of writers were sufficiently far-sighted and courageous to take a stand for proletarian revolution, today hundreds of poets, novelists, dramatists, critics, short story writers and journalists recognize the necessity of personally helping to accelerate the destruction of capitalism and the establishment of a workers' government.[7]

Two problems concerned the engaged writer, the "Call" continued, one political, the struggle against war and fascism, the other literary, the problem of presenting America in a revolutionary context. The proposed congress, scheduled for May 1, 1935, would bring together the hitherto isolated revolutionary writers "for fundamental discussion." The "Call" invited "all writers who have achieved some standing in their respective fields; who have clearly indicated their sympathy to the revolutionary cause; who do not need to be convinced of the decay of capitalism, of the inevitability of revolution." The main business of the congress would be to "create the League of American Writers" as an affiliate of the International Union of Revolutionary Writers (I.U.R.W.) and to carry out a revolutionary political program.[8]

THE FIRST CONGRESS

Unquestionably, the party's decisions to liquidate the John Reed Clubs, to concentrate on enrolling writers of "some standing," and to promise them immunity from the burdens of "administrative tasks," all indicated a new tack; but it would be a mistake to interpret the proposal of the League as a complete about-face. Its objectives did not differ markedly from the imperatives laid down at Kharkov. Nor was the party quite ready in 1935 to make the first congress as broad and popular as the majority of the organizing committee wanted it to be. Of the sixty-four writers who signed the "Call," a substantial number were trusted members or friends of the party.[9]

At these early organizational meetings, one writer remembers that

there was considerable controversy over how broad the Congress should be. My recollection is that the majority of us who seemed to understand the popular front better than Trachtenberg wanted to make the First Congress as broad as possible. Trachtenberg used a phrase which ultimately became the basis of judgment. He said, "We must count noses." Or perhaps he said, "This is the first time when we count noses." He gave us the impression that the First Congress should consist of those who were trustworthy. And then perhaps we could go on from there.

I think the thing to remember about that time was that all of us believed that people like Trachty had access to secrets which were profoundly true as estimates of the correct way of winning support for the fight against Fascism and for the defense of the Soviet Union. These fellows who had been in it for years walked in an atmosphere of superior knowledge and understanding and experience. They wore Lenin like a halo. Thus, when Trachty said, "This is the time to count noses," he persuaded us that he knew things we couldn't possibly know, and therefore we went along with him.

After Trachtenberg restricted the invitations to the first congress to reliable writers, he arranged preliminary meetings for the purpose of checking the names of the delegates and reading the outlines of the papers to be delivered. The "presiding committee" took charge from the start, thus assuring complete party domination of the League's organization and immediate program. It nominated a nonparty writer, Waldo Frank, "the symbolic leader of the new-era," chairman of the League and saw to it that all on the seventeen-member executive committee were Communists or fellow travelers. Its slate of thirty-nine names for the national council contained many party representatives as well.[10]

There was nothing conspiratorial about the party's domination of the League, nor did it bother to conceal its influence. The writers who came to New York in May for the congress did not need the party to tell them that more than twenty millions were on relief and that the Third Reich menaced the peace of the world. As fellow travelers, many had already worked with members of the party on various issues and felt no hostility to the principles outlined in the League's program. Thus Browder's appearance before the 216 delegates along with Waldo Frank, Joseph Freeman, Friedrich Wolf, Moishe Nadir, Malcolm Cowley, Michael Gold, and Granville Hicks only signified what everyone recognized—the central role of the party in the League. Many writers who heard him, Communist and non-Communist alike, had already "grown accustomed to organization in other fields than our own," [11] and, as individuals, had made known their revolutionary convictions. In one sense, therefore, the League was a culmination of something old as well as a beginning of something new.

Browder's speech to the congress at the opening and only public session was intended to reassure the non-Communist writers that the party had no plan or desire to put them into "uniforms." It simply recognized the necessity of co-operating with "all enemies of reaction in the cultural field"; and although some of its "overzealous" members (especially the recent recruits of nonproletarian origin) might have aroused "certain misgivings about the possibility of fruitful work in this united front," Browder hoped to dispel these misunderstandings by making quite clear the party's position toward writers. It was very simple. The party wanted writers to be good writers, not bad strike leaders. There was no fixed "Party line" about a good or bad work of art. In "the camp of the working class" a free give-and-take prevailed; the ultimate judge was the mass audience. Did the party plan to "politicize" writers by "imposing its pre-conceived ideas of subject matter, treatment and form"? Certainly not. But it did hope to make writers politically conscious, "to open up new worlds to them," and to mobilize a "growing audience" for revolutionary writing. We must dig deep, he told his audience, "into the treasures of our national traditions and cultural heritage" without succumbing to a narrow chauvinism.[12]

In his foreword to the published record of the two-day session of writers, Waldo Frank, the newly elected chairman of the League, spoke of the "heartiness, intellectual solidarity and, above all, youth" of the congress. "Its principal achievement," he continued, "was, perhaps, to integrate elements and forces of American cultural life which, heretofore, have been anarchic, into the beginning of a literary movement, both broad and deep, which springs from an alliance of writers and artists with the working classes." [13] The validity of Frank's observation may be tested by examining now in more detail the papers and reports delivered at the sessions and the backgrounds and beliefs of some of their authors.

AMERICAN WRITERS SPEAK

Of the American authors and writers who spoke at the New York meetings (April 26-27) or whose papers were published in the proceedings, almost all had become by 1935 allies of the party. "You are the American contingent," Freeman told the assembled delegates in his résumé of the revolutionary literary tradition, "of that army of writers all over the world which is militantly fighting for the preservation of culture through the triumph of the working class. . . . We ought to know that we have a revolutionary literary heritage behind us in order that we may transcend it." [14]

Some of the delegates undoubtedly followed the party line. Others, John Dos Passos is only one example, quite obviously did not. A good many of them probably agreed with Malcolm Cowley that the writer stood to gain more from the revolutionary movement than the movement from the writer. And, like Cowley, they may have relished the prospect of a "responsive audience," a "new range of subject matter," a new perspective on themselves, and a chance to abandon a decaying class and to affiliate with a rising class.[15] No speaker, however, confused political correctness with literary talent. More than a few, in fact, seemed to spend as much time belaboring the inanity and sterility of would-be revolutionary writing as in praising or encouraging its producers.

Expressly condemned was the "crude type of dualism" which saw all bourgeois writing as falsification and every "expression of working class life as truth." [16] Waldo Frank called this "over-simplification," the elimination of life by a crude resort to ideological short cuts. His address, "Values of the Revolutionary Writer," clearly showed that in joining the revolutionary movement, he had not renounced his old convictions about the spiritual sickness of America.

Left Wing writers, he charged, had "taken over the philosophy of the American capitalist culture that we are sworn to overthrow." Their lack of self-trust, their disbelief in their own autonomy, made them willing "to take orders" as writers "from political leaders," to borrow and misapply "foreign definitions of values," and to write propaganda instead of "deep revolutionary art." Hence the novels written in newspaper journals and cluttered with stereotypes, the joyless and will-less workers who peopled proletarian fiction and poetry, the unimaginative literary autopsies performed by ignorant critics who turned "Marxism itself into a dogmatically, mechanically *shut* philosophy." All of these strictures bore out Frank's credo, which he never modified: the building of socialism was primarily a "cultural" or "human" problem and only secondarily a political-economic one; the artist must not subordinate himself or his work to the political-economic aspects.[17]

The argument against the "over-politicalized and ideologically schematized" was continued in James T. Farrell's lecture, "The Short Story." His cantankerous and didactic comments on proletarian fiction had already begun to irk some of the Left Wing critics; soon he was to engage in a free-swinging contest with *The New Masses* and ultimately to break with the Stalinists. At the moment, however, he was perhaps the most highly regarded of the younger novelists identified with the movement. Two volumes of his famous Studs Lonigan trilogy were already published, the third on the way. Moreover, unlike the majority of leftist writers, Farrell had really read Marx and was quite prepared to debate the Marxist approach to literature with the party theoreticians.

The burden of his address before the congress was the absence "in many of the new revolutionary short stories . . . of what might be called internal conviction." Erskine Caldwell, Nelson Algren, Ben Field, Langston Hughes, and a few others had succeeded in making revolution a functional part of some of their stories, but most revolutionary writers, Farrell said, simply glued on their radical messages. He missed in their overgeneralized stories the concrete detail that might have edged their accounts of misery, suffering, and oppression and shown them to be "concomitants of a capitalistic civilization." [18]

THE VAGARIES OF KENNETH BURKE

Perhaps the most unusual paper delivered at the congress—at least it provoked most dissent—was Kenneth Burke's talk on "Revolutionary Symbolism in America." Since Burke himself remained such a controversial figure to the Communists, welcomed during this period as an influential ally, yet distrusted because of his ideologically dangerous fondness for paradox, his previous history and his appearance at the congress need further explanation.

Burke belonged to a group of middle-class writers who during the twenties had paid scant attention to revolutionary ideas but who were drawn to the Left after 1929. A high-school classmate of Malcolm Cowley's, a contributor to the little magazines, music editor of the *Dial* between 1927 and 1929, and the recipient of the *Dial* award in 1928 for distinguished service to American letters, Burke had always been skeptical of sociological criticism. Some works, he thought, required historical or philosophical exegesis more than others, but he was no crude environmentalist. One did not explain *Madame Bovary* by studying Flaubert's Rouen.

The Depression made Burke a more explicit critic of capitalism and its culture than he had been in the twenties, but unlike his friends Cowley and Josephson, he retained a good deal of his Bohemian rebelliousness. A chapter in his *Counter-Statement* (1931), advocating a kind of revolutionary aestheticism, contained a program of action as distasteful to Communists as to capitalists.

Burke recommended nothing less than reviving "the earlier bourgeois-Bohemian conflict." The artist, Burke said, could best sabotage the inefficient and ugly industrial system by incarnating and defending inefficiency, negativism, pessimism, dissipation, and bad sportsmanship. "Thus we can defend the aesthetic as antipractical, anti-industrial, anti-machine because the practical, the industrial, the mechanized is so firmly entrenched."

Nor need the artist be overtly political. His aesthetics subsumed his politics. A pastoral poem might very well by implication undermine chain stores. At a time when democracy was besieged by the practical-minded "apostles of hope," the artist ought to support it for its very inefficiency: "for once you postulate human virtue as the foundation of a system, you are a dullard indeed if you can't make a thousand schemes for a good society. A society is sound only if it can prosper on its vices, since virtues are by very definition rare and exceptional." When a society depended for its survival upon the "virtuous-efficient" and could no longer tolerate "shoddy lethargic methods," it was time to junk it. Given the present state of affairs, the artist ought to cultivate "such intellectual vagabondage" as would "constitute a grave interference with the cultural code behind our contemporary economic ambitiousness." [19]

Such frivolous admonitions hardly set well with leftist critics.

Granville Hicks wrote an acidulous review of *Counter-Statement*. Isidor Schneider rapped Burke for "recommending what is little more than a gesture undignified and uncomfortable for the artist, and unserviceable." And Joshua Kunitz castigated Burke's "spitefulness."

His program is essentially an innocuous and petty nihilism; his "negative" aesthetic is the philosophy of the "petit bourgeois gone mad." Inefficiency, indolence, dissipation, vacillation, mockery, distrust, hypochondria, non-conformity, bad sportsmanship, dislike of propaganda, dislike of certainty, treason—these, according to Burke, are the desiderata at the present moment, these are the emphases required to confute the bloated bourgeois, the machine, the efficiency expert, the patrioteer.[20]

Although the Communists found little of value in Burke's anticapitalist reflections, he continued to speculate publicly on "the Nature of Art Under Capitalism" and to move slightly closer to the party's position. Capitalism, Burke declared in 1933, was ethically and socially disastrous, because it provided no outlets for men's predatory drives except ruthless competition and war. Under these conditions of competitive capitalism, Burke said, "Art cannot safely confine itself to merely *using* the values which arise out of a given social texture and integrating their conflicts, as the soundest, 'purist' art will do." Pure art in these circumstances would become a "social menace," a device for "tolerating the intolerable." Therefore, art must for the moment, at least, contain "a large *corrective* or *propaganda* element. . . . It must have a definite hortatory function, an element of suasion and/or inducement of the education variety; it must be partially forensic."

Always the literary tactician and strategist, Burke warned against abandoning "pure" art entirely, since it served an "invaluable psychological end" by making an intolerable world a little more tolerable while it lasts. A certain amount of "acquiescent" or even sentimental writing served popular needs more satisfactorily than a good deal of the harsh proletarian writing,

questionable as propaganda, since it shows us so little of the qualities in mankind worth saving . . . questionable as "pure" art, since by substituting a cult of disaster for a cult of amenities, it "promotes our acquiescence" to sheer dismalness. Too often, alas, it serves as a mere device whereby the neuroses of the decaying bourgeois structure are simply transferred to the symbols of workingmen. Perhaps more of Dickens is needed, even at the risk of excessive tearfulness.[21]

Needless to say, Burke's notions about "pure" art did not coincide with the Communist literary line, but two of his statements composed in 1934 committed him to the Communist solution, even though his attitude toward Marxism, as a *New Masses* reviewer remarked of him later, was "that of a dog gingerly flirting with a porcupine." The first, "On Interpretation," justified the artist's refusal to co-operate with an irrational society. Communism was "the only co-herent and organized movement" because it used resources for the ends of humane living and thus provided the most congenial milieu for art. In the second, "My Approach to Communism," Burke out-lined at some length his rational, ethical, historical, and aesthetic reasons for supporting Communism, likening its aims to "a kind of 'industrial mediaevelism' " that might restore a new equilibrium to a disjointed world. "For our culture," he wrote, "is the adaptation of our spiritual values to external necessities. . . . The language of art thrives best when there is a maximum of stability in our ways of livelihood and in the nature of our expectations." [22]

Implicit in all of Burke's social and aesthetic theorizing was his belief in the autonomy of the artist and the priority of art over politics. His Communism, if you could call it such, was not deeply or religiously felt; rather, it was a strategy, a tactic, a type of organ-ization. His social attitudes, Granville Hicks observed with some justice, were those "of a man who is principally interested in tech-nique," [23] and his talk before the first Writers' Congress in 1935 characteristically dealt with an operational problem—propaganda.

What it came down to was some advice to the Communists on how to manipulate certain myths or symbols in order to win popular sup-port. Confining his remarks to the *"propaganda"* aspect of the sym-bol, Burke urged the substitution of the term "the people" for the term "the masses" because it was "closer to our folkways," suggestive of "the ultimate classless feature which the revolution could bring about," and "richer as a symbol of allegiance." Words like "worker" or "proletarian," negative symbols emphasizing the "temporary an-tagonism," tended to exclude the very elements the Communist propagandist hoped to recruit, whereas "the symbol of 'the people' " contained "connotations both of oppression and of unity." Finally, Burke wished to disassociate "propaganda" from the literal and anti-intellectual application sometimes given it by the strict proletarians and to surround it "with as full a cultural texture" as possible.[24]

His suggestion, Burke acknowledged to his audience, bore "the tell-tale stamp of my class, the petty bourgeoisie" whose allegiance was "vitally important," but whatever the speakers who followed him thought about Burke's class origins, they gave short shrift to his ideas on ideological semantics.

The substitution of "people" for "worker," one critic declared, was "historically associated with demagoguery of the most vicious sort." Hitler, a refugee from Germany observed, used this same device to "supplement his blackjacks and machine guns." Joseph Freeman, who alone seemed to catch the drift of Burke's remarks, defended "the symbol of the 'worker' because of the role which the worker plays in reality." "People" meant something during the bourgeois revolution, when all the people fought against class privileges, but then it took on a reactionary connotation, Freeman thought, "not because of any philosophy of myths, but because it concealed the reality, the actual living antagonism between the social classes." Although only the proletariat could "create a just society for the whole of the people," the progressive intellectual need not feel excluded or fear that the proletariat would deprive him of his culture. Rather, the proletariat salvaged what was best in the old culture and provided leadership for all exploited classes, "including the intellectuals."[25]

Burke refused to be persuaded. The overemphasis of the "worker" symbol, he insisted, helped the reactionaries to divide the workers from the people. But his report of the congress for *The Nation* contained only a good-humored reference to his contretemps with the "party's most demonic orators." He was more concerned with showing how individual divergencies, which sprung from the need of each spokesman to justify "his way of working and seeing," eventually "merged into unity."

I refer to the general feeling that all these writers must somehow enlist themselves in a cultural struggle; that however meager their individual contributions may be, their work must be formed with relation to historic necessities; that what they say, and the way they say it, must involve fundamentally a concept of social responsibility, of *citizenship*.

Although not a party member, Burke attributed the success of the first congress to "the vitality and organizational ability of the Communist Party" and predicted that the League of American Writers formed under its auspices would unite all enemies of fascism and war.[26]

ELEVEN · "THE CENTRE CANNOT HOLD"

POSTSCRIPT TO THE CONGRESS

THE FIRST Writers' Congress had ended on a positive and optimistic note. Harold Rosenberg saw the "decisive clue to the meaning of the Congress" in "the unbreakable connection existing between the course and fate of culture and the art of writing, and the course and fate of society." [1] To John Chamberlain, it signified the end of "the RAPP" period in American literary Communism. The threat of reaction had forced the Left to make common cause with antifascists in other political camps. Happily, said Chamberlain, a new group of "fellow travelers," writers like Henry Hart, Matthew Josephson, and Malcolm Cowley, had provoked "this right-about-face in the Communist ranks," and he was pleased to detect "a diminishing of the terrorist spirit in the literary left," a growing tolerance of differences. Only two or three years before, he observed, the party cast Sidney Hook "into outer darkness" for raising pragmatic objections to the inevitability of Communism. In 1935 two other "revolutionary 'free-willers,' Arminians of the class struggle," Frank and Burke, were not drummed out for ideological heresy.

And yet, Chamberlain had to admit, the absence of well-known antifascists, either by accident or design, raised some doubts about the sincerity of the Popular Front policy. Where were Max Eastman, Charles Beard, Louis Adamic, Louis Hacker, Benjamin Stolberg, Clifton Fadiman, Edmund Wilson? "Trotskyites" had been ignored, he was told, "because of their propensity for reducing all things to a quarrel over the relative merits of Trotsky and Stalin." He was not convinced. If the League kept out antifascist writers simply because they challenged the Communist position, then it would become another " 'innocent club' consisting of communists and supporting writers who just don't talk about radical tactics in politics." A true united-front policy, he felt, would be less inflexible toward political deviations, and as a candidate for the League, he wished to ask "the Communists who called the Congress" why they were so positive they could read the future or know for certain that parliamentarianism was dead.[2]

COMPLAINTS FROM THE LEFT

Chamberlain's misgivings did not prevent him from joining the League in December, but the young proletarians deplored the party's new literary "line" or accepted it without rapture. To be sure, the first congress sounded militant enough. The fight against war and fascism was declared with flourishes of revolutionary rhetoric, and Earl Browder congratulated the writers for taking a position in the "class struggle between capitalists and workers, the two basic forces in American society." But they disapproved of the congress making too many concessions to the petty bourgeois element and to the "hobo bohemians."

Was Edwin Seaver correct in asserting that any treatment of subject matter "from the standpoint and in the interest of the proletariat" made it proletarian? Martin Russak did not think so. The proletarian novel, he said, must deal with the working class alone, not "with the emotions and reactions and values of the upper or middle classes or the *lumpen proletariat*. I don't think the life experiences of hoboes and tramps . . . is legitimate subject matter."

In his reply to Russak, Mike Gold argued for a literature neither petty-bourgeois nor Left-sectarian. The movement was large enough to include both the proletarian and the revolutionary middle-class writers. "So I think," he concluded, "we must stand equally against the idea that proletarian literature has a place only for novels about the working class . . . as well as against the idea that novels about the workers are not important." [3]

Gold's almost overneat solution did not remove the suspicions and resentments that troubled the atmosphere of good feeling at the congress. Ideological quarrels, already perceptible and soon to become irreconcilable, lay behind some of the literary disagreements, but the rivalries were not entirely political. By 1935 the Left literary movement was not only an expression of political intransigence, of social protest; it had also become a school for new writers. To go "Left" might indicate a change of heart. It might also facilitate having one's work published in one of the militant little magazines that fanned the revolutionary fires. No wonder some of the editors of the struggling John Reed Club publications and their contributors worried lest the establishment of the League and the party's apparent desire to foster the "name" writers at the expense of the unknowns choke off the opportunities to see their work in print.

One straw in the wind seemed to bear out these suspicions—an article by Granville Hicks published in *The New Masses* a few months before the first Writers' Congress. Why, Hicks asked, should the revolutionary movement dissipate its talent and money by supporting a spate of mediocre magazines? Of course the more than a dozen radical little "mags" testified to the wide appeal of the revolutionary movement. He could see the point of the John Reed Club magazines printing the literary productions of club members whose work was often not quite appropriate for the "large, varied, and partly hostile audience" of *The New Masses*. But Hicks wanted no other Left magazine to try to duplicate "the principal organ of the revolutionary movement." The old practice of starting a magazine merely because the promoters had a little money and some obliging friends he dismissed sternly as "Bohemian individualism and irresponsibility . . . entirely incompatible with the serious tasks of revolution and the intelligent discipline of revolutionaries." Instead, all literary and financial resources should be used to improve *The New Masses*.[4]

Hicks's plea for "good common sense" went unanswered until Fred R. Miller, the editor of *Blast* ("A Magazine of Proletarian Short Stories" published in New York), replied in the columns of *The Blue Pencil* to Hicks's "big yelp." Employing a tough, breezy, "proletarian" rhetoric, Miller "exposed" the attempt of the monopolistic *New Masses* and *Partisan Review* to freeze out "competition." Sure, he said, this "hand-down from the old *Masses* and *The Liberator* . . . undoubtedly stands first among the cultural organs of the left." But who besides Whittaker Chambers ever got his start there? With the pick of proletarian writers to choose from, they invariably "turned their fiction pages over to Names, as they do even now—bourgeois writers at that, or 'fellow-travelers' with vague revolutionary 'sympathies.' . . . Where was the *New Masses* when the lights went on? It was too busy shooting off, in critical piece after book review, romantic blat about the glorious future of 'proletarian literature' to see good work right under its beezer." Mencken, not *The New Masses,* Miller said, first published Jack Conroy, and the "bumper crop" of young proletarian writers celebrated by Hicks appeared in the "little mags" or bourgeois magazines while "the *New Masses* slumbered on."

As for *Partisan Review,* organ of the New York City John Reed Club, Miller considered it a symptom of the new gentility afflicting the Left. Radical critics and editors, having discovered the puerilities of "soap-box art," now swung too far the other way. "They're off the hackneyed formula stuff (the strike; the worker bunged up by a cop in a street 'riot'; the starving unemployed woman jumping off the cliff) for good. Good!" But now why did *Partisan Review* try to be more respectable than *The Atlantic Monthly,* search for "names" more hungrily than *The New Masses?* "Don't waste your stamps trying to crash the high-toned proletarian mags," he facetiously advised the beginners, "—before you're eligible to their pages you gotta have a rep. Making *The American Mercury* is a damn sight easier and more profitable, and the chances are your story's too revolutionary for the stiff-collar revolutionists anyhow."

Miller was not spoofing, however, when he asked whether the *Partisan Review* editors, in their eagerness to please the bourgeois critics, hadn't "lost all sense of revolutionary direction." Not that it mattered. While *The New Masses* and the *Partisan Review* printed "the soggy stuff of 'revolutionary' dabblers and opportunists," the "mushroom mags" would give a hand to the beginners: "the young jobless men from the proletariat and the lower middle-class coming to literary maturity in this the last depression, young men hard as nails, nobody's fools, knowing the class war from experience, the men fitted to give you the real stuff of proletarian literature." [5]

THE CASE OF THE *Partisan Review*

Had the editors of *Partisan Review* read Miller's diatribe, they might have replied (as Philip Rahv and William Phillips wrote in 1935) that they rejected both "leftism," the "literary counterpart of mechanical materialism," and the Right Wing tendencies of "liberal bourgeois writers." [6] It was not their function to print beginners' stuff, to be belligerently antitraditional, or to substitute political correctness for talent.

Since its first issue (February-March 1934), when it emerged, in Rahv's words, "from the womb of the depression crying for a proletarian literature and a socialist America," it strove "to put forward the best writing then produced by the Left." Ostensibly it was the literary organ of the New York City John Reed Club, but according to Granville Hicks, it printed the work of the "well-established writers" who did not belong to the club instead of encouraging "the less mature members." In short, Hicks thought, it was too much like *The New Masses,* and he wondered whether the movement could afford to support two such magazines. If *Partisan Review* was not to be a publishing outlet for its members, then "it ought to be primarily devoted to long, theoretical critical essays." It ought to consider those "theoretical and practical problems of proletarian culture" too specialized for *The New Masses* readership.[7]

Until it suspended publication in the fall of 1936, Phillips and Rahv noted a decade later, their magazine "on the surface apparently represented the typical Communist position." Yet their criticisms of the party's literary policies began almost immediately and lasted until the break. Their quarrel with the party, they wrote, "may be said to have originated in a protest against the official idea of art as an instrument of political propaganda." To them, Marxism was "a method of analysis." They refused to condone what they called "Party-line notions" governing the "literary movement," the practice of excusing bad writing on the grounds of political expediency. Of all the Marxist literary periodicals, they declared, only *Partisan Review* "resisted the debasements of writing and the rejection of the creative tradition then hailed in many quarters as 'progressive' achievements." [8]

In attempting to unravel the complicated story of this influential magazine from its founding in 1934 until its reappearance in December 1937 as an organ of the party opposition, the historian must rely upon the uncertain memories and contradictory statements of the participants. Did *Partisan Review* have any organizational affiliation after the dissolving of the John Reed Clubs? Was the original magazine started against the opposition of *The New Masses?* Did its editors from the outset hope "to free revolutionary literature from domination by the immediate strategy of a political party"? [9]

Another version of the story adds some interesting additions. It begins in 1932, when "an obscure boy from the Bronx" mailed an essay on Plekhanov to *The New Masses*. Joseph Freeman read it, liked it, and invited its author, Philip Rahv, to send him more. A year or so later, Rahv and his friend William Phillips, both active in the New York City John Reed Club, came to Freeman with the complaint that *The New Masses* was too political. They urged the creation of a literary magazine. Freeman not only agreed, but also helped them to start *Partisan Review* and wrote the opening editorial statement. In substance, the editors promised to publish the best work of the New York John Reed Club members and sympathetic nonmembers; to maintain the viewpoint of the working class, to struggle against war and fascism, and to defend the U.S.S.R.; and to combat "the decadent culture of the exploiting classes," narrow-minded sectarianism, and "debilitating liberalism." [10]

Was *Partisan Review,* then, founded in opposition to *The New Masses?* On the contrary, it has been argued, it never would have appeared without the active support of *The New Masses* editors and writers, some of whom appeared in its pages as late as October 1936. Did Alexander Trachtenberg try to liquidate the review? If he tried and failed, how does this failure square with the alleged control of Left magazines by the party? The important fact is that the review was not suppressed; rather, the argument runs, Rahv and Phillips expropriated the magazine for themselves in 1936 and offered a disingenuous explanation. "Writers in the *Partisan Review* differed with writers in *The New Masses* on literary subjects no more than contributors to *The New Masses* differ among themselves," *The New Masses* editors observed in October 1937, and both groups "agreed on those fundamental political principles which the present Trotskyite editors of the *Partisan Review* attack." [11]

Most of the contributors to *Partisan Review,* the evidence would seem to show, wrote also for *The New Masses,* as Rahv and Phillips did, and raised their voices against "leftism" in other liberal and radical magazines. That *Partisan Review* tried to maintain high standards is undeniably true. That *The New Masses,* as well as many other proletarian magazines, puffed up ineptly written revolutionary books is also true. Yet it is misleading to say that in 1934 and 1935 the party "dominated" leftist critics and required them to make literary evaluations repellent to *Partisan Review*.

Such a conclusion rests upon two faulty assumptions: that the party, then and after, deeply concerned itself with writers and writing, and that radical writers formed a cohesive and malleable group. Naturally, party functionaries hoped to organize writers and to induce them to support policies in line with the official party position, but party leaders like Browder valued writers for their prestige and popularity rather than for the purity of their Marxism or intrinsic literary merit. Mass movements, labor, unemployment—these were the throbbing issues. The writers who believed their work mattered a continental to the "ninth floor" * were deluding themselves; the party distrusted them always as putative defectors and sentimental moralizers. "Oh, we could preach sermons on Sunday," Earl Browder remarked, "but for the intellectuals, every day was Sunday." [12]

As for the writers themselves, their attitude toward the party and party discipline varied considerably. The "old men" had been battling against party Philistinism for years. But they would have regarded it as presumptuous to assert the primacy of the literary act over party policy. Disagreements involving art and politics were to be settled amicably within the family circle, and when party spokesmen interfered in matters of literary policy, the editors of *The New Masses*

* The leaders who occupied the ninth floor of party headquarters.

listened to them but then sometimes went their own way. They certainly did not regard themselves as minions of Stalin.

Not surprisingly, they were sometimes irritated by the "Johnny-come-latelys" who proclaimed the integrity of the artist and their contempt for party hacks. Perhaps the "old men" even envied the freedom of these amateurs and fellow travelers to criticize zealous "leftists" and to minimize political correctness. At any rate, they were both angry and a little puzzled by what seemed to them the needlessly truculent tone taken by certain contributors to *Partisan Review,* and deplored the "uncomradely" habits of "sniping and backbiting" that had been "carried over into the proletarian literary movement" from the "bourgeois literary world." By failing to understand the writer's problems and remaining "almost purely negative," weren't the revolutionary purists in danger of becoming doctrinaires and losing touch with their readers? [13]

Until 1936 the feud (if that term is not too strong) between *The New Masses* and *Partisan Review* remained pretty much a family affair. Then in February of that year, Michael Gold, celebrating the "shotgun wedding" that hitched "that spunky pioneer of midwest proletarian literature" (Jack Conroy's *Anvil*) to *Partisan Review,* "organ of the New York left-wing intellectuals," heaved a few brickbats at the pious sectarians who "carry their Marxian scholarship as though it were a heavy cross." [14] Rahv and Phillips were Gold's undesignated targets, but he specifically singled out James T. Farrell as the worst of the dogmatists.

Farrell's impolite reviews of pro-Communist books had evidently annoyed *The New Masses* editors. Clara Weatherwax's prize-winning *Marching! Marching* (1935), a pastiche of "proletarian" clichés, Robert Briffault's pretentious *Europa* (1935), and Jack Conroy's uneven but by no means unmemorable *The Disinherited* (1933), a harsh novel of the Depression, all fell under Farrell's ax. Now, in *Partisan Review and Anvil,* he executed Clifford Odets, much to Gold's irritation, and dismissed this excessively praised dramatist's *Paradise Lost* as a "burlesque on Mr. Odets' work" and as a play loaded with "dull speeches and swaggering platitudes." These contemptuous strictures only confirmed Gold's opinion that Farrell lacked objectivity and fairness. In answering Josephine Herbst, who had accused him of attacking Farrell no less subjectively than Farrell had reviewed Odets, he confessed he had been moved by "the sharp personal tone" of Farrell's piece. "That kind of mutual slaughter died long ago, with all other sectarianism, and I for one am sore that it should be revived." [15]

A few months later, Alan Calmer replied for *Partisan Review and Anvil* in a eulogistic review of Farrell's *A Note on Literary Criticism* (1936), the latter's most sustained assault against the alleged "leftism" of *The New Masses* group.

This essay, as Calmer pointed out, was far from being a "mere 'note' on literary criticism." Farrell was trying once and for all to demolish "the vulgar practices of 'leftism,' " [16] typified, according to Farrell, by the "revolutionary sentimentalism" of Michael Gold (whose "Marxmanship" he ridiculed) and the "mechanically" determined Marxism of Granville Hicks. By the time he was finished, Farrell had accused the would-be Marxist critics, Russian and American, of committing every sin in the book. They had introduced extraliterary considerations; separated aesthetic from social implications; ignored the "persistence-value" of art, which endures long after the conditions that reproduced it have disappeared; oversimplified criticism by introducing Procrustean measurements; confused art and propaganda; stigmatized individualism; and, in general, made foolish or irrelevant judgments because they did not take their Marxism seriously. "How often for instance, have we not read in the *New Masses* a book review three-quarters of which was devoted to the reviewer's statement that the crisis is sharpening, with a final quarter devoted to the implications that the reviewer was a better revolutionary and a better Marxist than the author!"

The critic who called himself a Marxist must not only learn to absorb ideas "instead of using them as labels pasted on other ideas—"; he must also combine his Marxism "with actual and theoretical information concerning American politics." The critic helped neither "humanity or the proletariat," when he expressed—"perhaps in blatant bold-face—a few political slogans he learned yesterday." [17]

Farrell's book won commendations from quarters as far apart as Edmund Wilson and the Catholic Book Club, but *The New Masses'* critics, quite naturally, received it less enthusiastically. Grudgingly they acknowledged that he performed "some valuable services" by summarizing "the vitiating and constricting elements in our Marxist literary criticism." What made his book unsatisfactory finally was his refusal to "see so-called Sectarianism in its historic context," to see it as an unfortunate but excusable reaction to the aestheticism of the bourgeois critics who had rejected "working class experience" as "a fit subject for literature" and who had "ignored the capitalist nature and its class basis." Farrell's "central ideas" were not "anti-Marxist," Hicks conceded, but he reprimanded him for exaggerating the obvious, for being neither clear nor comprehensive, and for allowing his "personal grudges" to becloud the issues.

It seemed more than coincidental to *The New Masses* group that Farrell's book had been so enthusiastically welcomed by anti-Marxists. Does a busy creative writer, Isidor Schneider asked, drop his work and take on an assignment in criticism unless he feels urgently impelled to do so? Wasn't Farrell speaking for other writers who felt similar "dissatisfactions and disappointments?" Farrell would hardly have written his antileftist polemic unless he were assured of substantial support. Therefore his book indicated "a new crisis in revolutionary literature." [18]

Plainly, Farrell's comrades-in-arms were the *Partisan Review and Anvil* editors, always cited with respect in his book. Still a loyal minority in 1936 and not yet ready to defend Leon Trotsky (whom Farrell never mentioned in *A Note on Literary Criticism,* although he frequently referred to less formidable Soviet theorists), this rebellious coterie would soon find valid political reasons to justify what began as a literary *démarche*. Their crusade against "leftism" started too late, for, as Calverton gleefully observed, Stalinist critics in the post-RAPP period no longer had to minimize aesthetic values. That was why "Mr. Hicks and Mr. Schneider today can actually stand up on their hind legs, with their ears at half mast, and woof-woof away Mr. Farrell's stridulous bark." When a reorganized and anti-Stalinist *Partisan Review* began publication in December 1937, however, the editors and Farrell were free to attack the politics as well as the aesthetics of the official party line. Celebrating the rebirth of *Partisan Review,* Farrell contemptuously dismissed *The New Masses'* charge that the new editorial board had stolen the name of the old magazine, and he summed up the results of "the insane leftist tendencies continuously exemplified in *New Masses*."

The left wing cultural movement which was so noisily proclaimed a few years ago is bankrupt. Its theaters are closed. The new generation of young writers is not being heard from. Most of the emphases which were made . . . with such aggressive and intolerant assurance are forgotten like a bad dream. They are pulled forth only as a kind of false glory to serve the purposes of casting unfounded insinuations of the attempt of others to establish an independent and skeptical literary magazine. For the rest, it is forgotten.[19]

BETWEEN CONGRESSES

Farrell wrote these words after the second Writers' Congress, which he had not bothered to attend. He had turned down an invitation to become a member of the League's executive committee in October 1936 and had written an "Interim Report" on the dismal record of the young proletarian writers hailed two years before as the vanguard "of a new literature in America and a new generation." [20] His blunt and spiteful summary of literary unfulfillment appeared on the eve of the second Writers' Congress scheduled for June 4, 1937.

If the League had failed to boost the qualitative and quantitative output of its membership, as Farrell asserted, what had it done as an organization between April 1935 and June 1937 besides sponsor a few protests and investigations? Three of these "protests" or "investigations" are worth looking into.

On June 17, 1935, the League, with *The New Masses* and the National Committee for the Defense of Political Prisoners, organized a protest meeting on behalf of League member Granville Hicks, recently dropped from the faculty of Rensselaer Polytechnic Institute on the grounds of "retrenchment." The meeting produced no results; Hicks was not rehired.

In the same month, the League sponsored a mission to Cuba, led by Clifford Odets, the "Golden Boy" of the Left theater. The fifteen-man delegation planned to investigate prisons, visit "famous Realingo 18—the first Soviet in America," already reported on by Josephine Herbst, and inquire into "the role of the American Ambassador in the internal affairs on the island." Before the party could disembark, the police of the Mendieta-Batista government boarded the ship, detained the delegation overnight in a stinking jail, and deported them the next day "at the point of scores of rifles and sub-machine guns." Not even the boisterous welcome tendered to them on their return, the protest of Archibald MacLeish to Cordell Hull, or a mass meeting could transform the expedition into a triumph.[21]

A few weeks later, a small group of writers, including Jack Conroy and Emmett Green, ventured into the wilds of Alabama to test "the notorious Downs' law," a Birmingham city ordinance making it a crime punishable by a maximum fine of $100 and six months in jail to possess more than one copy of any radical periodical. The committee distributed copies of *The Nation, The New Republic, The New Masses,* and the *Daily Worker,* among other radical publications, but were not arrested. They were merely seized by detectives, pushed into the City Hall, fingerprinted and photographed. Montgomery was to be the next stop on their itinerary. There they hoped to obtain an audience with Governor Bibb Graves and ask him to veto a state antisedition bill. Sixty-three miles south of Birmingham, however, some vigilantes driving a roadster drew up to them and fired shots into their car. Denied police protection, they abandoned their automobile and escaped to Tennessee via taxi, bus, and train.[22]

It is easy to smile at these inglorious exploits, so daring in design, so futile in consequence. American literary men seldom took such physical risks for political reasons before or after the 1930's, and it is no longer fashionable for delegations of writers to poke their noses into forbidden territory. It was different then. When would-be revolutionary writers faced the real perils of Cuba and Alabama or the lesser hazards of the picket line in front of Ohrbach's department store, they were demonstrating their own readiness to share the "experiences of the disinherited" and their willingness to enlist as literary foot soldiers in the "war of the classes." Their exposure to strikes and riots produced few masterpieces. Often it led, as Joseph Freeman wrote in his introduction to *Proletarian Literature in the United States* (1935), to bad proletarian art. The bourgeois converts who were beaten up by Harlan County deputies or who demanded the release of Tom Mooney and the Scottsboro boys "retained the umbilical cord which bound them to bourgeois culture." But in the year of the first Writers' Congress, thanks to the assault upon the artistic conscience by a society in upheaval, "the dichotomy between poetry and politics had vanished, and art and life were fused." [23]

As part of its campaign to safeguard culture "from the menace of fascism and war," the League sent Michael Gold and Waldo Frank to the first International Congress of Writers for the Defense of Culture, convening in Paris in June 1935.

Attending, Gold reported to *The New Masses,* were "a galaxy of distinguished authors that any American publisher would give his eye teeth to have in his catalogue (that is, if the bankers have left him a solitary molar)." André Gide, André Malraux, Louis Aragon, and others represented France; Boris Pasternak, Isaac Babel, Ilya Ehrenburg, Alexis Tolstoy spoke for Russia; Heinrich Mann, Lion Feuchtwanger, Anna Seghers, Ernst Toller, Bertolt Brecht, and others made up the German delegation of exiles. From England came E. M. Forster and Aldous Huxley. Apart from a small group of "Trotskyite . . . pathologues living in a self-centered world and helpful only to the enemy," Gold found the atmosphere at the congress harmonious. It was a "glorious thing" to find writers, those "engineers of the human soul," as Stalin phrased it, "accepting the challenge and taking their place among the leaders of humanity." In Paris, Gold exulted, the united front really worked. Socialist and Communist rallied against the fascists, and the whole city seemed to him a kind of Gallic soviet, a "deep, serious, and passionate" city that bore no likeness to the Paris of the bourgeois escapists.

Gold wrote of his discussions with Babel, writer and "manager of a big horse-breeding collective." ("In the Soviet Union," he told Gold, "one forgets one is a Jew.") He met his boyhood hero, Martin Andersen Nexö, author of *Pelle the Conqueror,* and with the British delegates Ralph Fox and James Hanley, helped to celebrate the Danish novelist's sixty-fifth birthday. He heard Malraux ("lean, intense, and young, the restless aviator type") and observed Aldous Huxley ("lanky, pale, boyish, shy . . . more like some of our own intellectuals"). He said nothing at all about his fellow delegate, Waldo Frank, or of Frank's address to the congress in which the chairman of the League of American Writers once more reiterated in smoky language his plea for an organic view of life.[24]

About 300 people came to hear Gold's report on the Paris meeting, with Cowley presiding and Quincy Howe talking on the political situation. The receipts came to forty dollars, just enough to pay the League's office rent and telephone bills. Shortly after, the League's executive committee endorsed Granville Hicks's idea to honor John Reed. Edwin Seaver thought the League should set up a joint committee with the Friends of the Soviet Union to sponsor a meeting that, in Genevieve Taggard's words, would "recarve the picture of John Reed in the minds of Americans" and "banish if possible that sentimentalized conception that the 20's fostered." The committee hoped to draw Dos Passos and Van Wyck Brooks into the proceedings and perhaps one radical student from Harvard.

A more ambitious League undertaking was a lecture series: "The Mind of America," delivered in the winter and spring of 1935-36. These talks on "intellectual currents in the United States today" not only made money for the League, but also enabled it "to affect several thousand people seeking information on 'left' tendencies in culture."

From the spring of 1936 until the end of the year, however, League activities slackened. Waldo Frank proved an indifferent chairman, and the majority of League members hardly bestirred themselves. The League *Bulletin* of October 1936 reported that of the forty-five members participating in the Presidential campaign, thirty-six backed Earl Browder, six favored Norman Thomas, and two supported Roosevelt. It contained no news about writers in picket lines or revolutionary new programs.[25]

Out in California, however, 250 writers from west of the Rockies gathered in San Francisco on November 13. For three days the assembled columnists, poets, novelists, playwrights, movie writers, professors, and newsmen attended public sessions and discussed such copies as "The Writers in a Changing World," "Fascist Trends," "Writing and Propaganda." Upton Sinclair recalled the days when Fremont Older, George Sterling, Jack London, and Lincoln Steffens gave distinction to San Francisco. Mike Gold, temporarily back in his old haunts, told "the inheritors of the great democratic tradition of Mark Twain and Jack London" about the Paris Writers' Congress; Harry Bridges, leader of the longshoremen, spoke, as did "the beloved California poet" Sara Bard Field and Charles Erskine Scott Wood (who "stole the show"). John Steinbeck came, and William Saroyan, recently returned from the Soviet Union and regarded by the sober-minded of the Left as flip and irreverent.* Ella Winter, Lincoln Steffens's widow, instructed interested delegates on California strikes, jails, and vigilante groups. From Hollywood came Donald Ogden Stewart (Ella Winter married him the next year); Sam Ornitz, author of *Haunch, Paunch, and Jowl;* Guy Endore, author of *Babouk* (1934), a violent story of the Santo Domingo slave insurrection; Budd Schulberg, of Dartmouth College; Irwin Shaw, whose antiwar play "Bury the Dead" † had buoyed up the Left theater; and the most talented writer of them all, Nathanael West, who spoke on "Makers of Mass Neuroses."

The Western Writers' Congress was not the first regional meeting since the formation of the League of American Writers in 1935. A conference of Midwestern writers had met in Chicago in the spring of 1936, not in the spirit of "reactionary regionalism," Meridel Le Sueur made clear, but out of "the strong necessity to build that consciousness in our own region, to create stronger and richer roots for the growth of the creative personality, a rich and wide audience." The isolated writer need no longer feel alone. "Such conferences of writers and artists are the living glowing nuclei of a new life within the maggoty body of a social corpse." The congress in California,

---

* Characteristic "Saroyanisms": "I have the idea that the Communists now being held in jail here are rather fine Americans and perhaps the most genuinely patriotic individuals in the city. I'm not sure, though, and I wouldn't be willing to go to jail for the theory, because I have a lot of writing to do and don't like writing in jail. . . ." *The New Republic,* Vol. LXXX (August 29, 1934), pp. 77-78. "I honestly believe writers for the most part are rats, but I know there is nothing you can do about it. The kind I hate worse are the kind who think they belong to some special tribe of humanity, and maybe they do, I'm not saying maybe they don't, but this tribe gripes me very much because I have an idea that a writer is exactly as important as the fellow who sweeps up horse-manure and dumps it into a can, and sometimes a lot less interesting." The last appeared in *International Literature,* No. 9 (Sept. 1935), p. 110. One wonders how the editors regarded this uncomradely outburst. Saroyan's political philosophy at this time seemed to be: "What the hell, people are alike everywhere"—an attitude somewhat more latitudinarian than the Communist Party's.

† Originally entitled, "Bury the Dead, They Stink." George Sklar, who produced the play for the theater union, removed the last two words. Conversation with author.

however, turned out to be a more ambitious affair, and the League officers in New York were eager to have the Western writers affiliate with what they regarded as the parent body.[26]

The link between the two groups was the novelist and journalist Harry Carlisle, executive secretary of the Western Writers' Congress and a staunch Marxist. Carlisle and other members of his committee agreed with Malcolm Cowley on the advantages of a national organization of writers, but at first they hesitated to affiliate directly with the League. They had deliberately made their platform as broad as possible in order to win wide support, and they wondered if the League program were not "a bit too left for our immediate purposes." [27] California writers still feared the Red label.

After the Western conference, Carlisle and his friends were less apprehensive and agreed to take part in the second Writers' Congress already shaping up in New York. The San Francisco meetings had gone smoothly. "We had a Trotsky rash here," Carlisle wrote to Cowley. "It eliminated itself early in the preparatory stages, and was practically absent during the congress." [28] Since then, writers' groups had been formed in Berkeley, Palo Alto, San Francisco, Hollywood, and Seattle.

Back east, the League suddenly came to life. The outbreak of the Civil War in Spain in the summer of 1936 presented a cause all anti-fascists, for the moment at least, could unqualifiedly support. A small number of writers joined the Abraham Lincoln Brigade; the majority who remained home suffered the pangs of sensitive men who felt they belonged on the battlefields.

The solidarity engendered in the Left movement by Spain's anguish, however, was shaken by the sensational Moscow trials, reports of which filled the American press for the next two years. At the moment when the party seemed to have succeeded brilliantly in its united-front campaign, the arraignment and execution of the old Bolsheviks blurred the sharp distinction between Communism and fascism the party had been so assiduously fostering. By transforming Trotsky from a disappointed oppositionist into a malevolent and diabolical plotter conspiring with fascist leaders to destroy the U.S.S.R., the Comintern at one stroke alienated a large number of its American allies and obliged its still-loyal adherents to defend an insupportable position.

PART THREE

·

DISENCHANTMENT

AND

WITHDRAWAL

Can the serious writer ever reconcile his art with activist politics, continue to write while serving in the ranks of a revolutionary party or any party?

Most American writers did not have to face that question. Before 1935 the American Communist leaders showed little interest in writers; after 1935 the party preferred to concentrate on the popular literary figures whose sympathy, even if qualified, they could exploit for publicity purposes. At no time, however, were writers completely trusted. They constantly threatened to kick over the traces and become an embarrassment; and the "big names"—Dreiser, Sinclair, Steinbeck, Hemingway, MacLeish, Wolfe—were the most uncertain and unreliable of all. The writers who worked more closely with the party rarely did so with the uncritical enthusiasm of the "Jimmy Higgins's." As one former party member, a well-known woman, observed, they refused to shut up or to take discipline. They wanted to rewrite the petitions they were asked to sign. She herself concluded, after trying to write a novel from the party point of view, that she was handicapped by being a writer and a Communist, that one could not be good at both.[1]

Yet these writers did not leave the movement because they were dictated to. Very few of them were hauled over the coals and forced to recant. Rather, it seems to have been boredom that repelled them and killed their zeal, the rituals of meetings where nothing of importance was discussed, the discovery that one's comrades, among the leaders and the rank and file, were ignorant or vulgarly ambitious or unpleasant. Thus, in 1928 a disgruntled radical wrote to a friend:

One of the bitternesses of human relations is that one gets inspiration and passes it on only to another. Once I got it from Floyd Dell and Max Eastman, people that now seem to me to have such feet of clay, and from two or three women you don't know—now I get it from people mostly dead, Stendhal and Proust, and Joyce. —In the mess of cynicism, of hackwork, of lies and prostitution that so quickly come to surround the kernel of truth, one forgets sometimes the rewards for choosing a way of life that originates at least in honesty.

It occurred to this man, as it must have occurred to many radicals before and since, that the artist's problems remained no matter what the society: "the truth is that it is not we who are out of joint, but the times as well. I read Blake last night at the library, and have no illusions that the world will ever seem a happy place to certain kinds of people, —his problems, his panics were so like mine, and so, I suppose, were King Akhnaton's sculptor's if one only knew." [2]

The depth and intenseness of a writer's disillusionment, of course, depended upon the motives that first drew him into the movement, the length of time he stayed in, and the extent of his involvement. The radicals of the twenties had embraced Communism when it offered no prestige, no tangible rewards. The latecomers, although they may have turned left for the same reasons as the pioneers—"experience of social injustice or degradation; a sense of insecurity bred by slumps and social crises; and the craving for a great ideal or purpose, or for a reliable intellectual guide through the shaky labyrinth of modern society" [3]—were less likely to have experienced the full emotional impact of "the great Idea."

This was especially true, in all likelihood, for the majority of fellow-traveling liberals whose rejection of bourgeois society and capitalism was less thoroughgoing than they had imagined and who, perhaps unconsciously, yearned to be reabsorbed into the America they had denounced. Never having broken with their class, they could slip back into their old ways and their old thoughts without having to make any serious readjustment; but to a Joseph Freeman, a Granville Hicks, a Richard Wright, if not to a Howard Fast,* the retreat from Communism was not so deftly managed.

Why did some remain in the party even though they harbored doubts and resentments? "There is the powerful drug of habit," Joseph Freeman has pointed out. "But there is also loyalty—to an idea, a Party, individuals. Unlike periods of relative social peace, a revolutionary situation fuses political and private life into one burning existence inspired by a common goal which is also your personal goal. And your fellow Christians, Jacobins or Communists are also— and with that as an indispensable basis—your personal friends. The cumulative revolutionary tradition is not only one of liberty and quality, but of *fraternity*. Besides, outside the fold there is no salvation. To leave is to be damned by your former comrades and friends —and your own conscience." [4]

A number of writers renounced their allegiance to the party only after the alternative, the condoning of policies and practices that violated the very principles the party allegedly stood for, became impossible. There was a time or an occasion for each, a "last straw" situation, an "ideological boiling point," [5] after which the writer renounced his allegiance. The final act of rejection was usually preceded by an extended period of uncertainty during which he stifled his doubts, extenuated or rationalized away unpleasant facts, or simply refused to contemplate them.† To the anarchists and the

---

* Critics of Howard Fast have not questioned the sincerity of his public and unabashed anguish (see *The Naked God,* N.Y., 1957), but his switch from Stalin Prize winner to Hollywood scenarist, the "now-it-can-be-told" air in which he relates his round trip into and out of the Communist pit, his calculated vagueness when writing of his own thoughts and practices between 1943 and 1956, and the moral complacency and egotism that shine steadily throughout his revelations (Faust is saved at last) are irritating components of a sometimes interesting book. The novelist or romancer constantly stands in the way of the autobiographer. As a result, *The Naked God* conceals more than it reveals. It is Fast's "White Paper," not a Koestlerian self-exploration; it is a forged *propusk* granting the author permission to re-enter the capitalist world. See the exchange between Fast and Eugene Lyons, *The New Leader,* Vol. XXXIX (July 9, 1956), pp. 6-8; (July 30, 1956), pp. 16-20, and R. G. Davis's perceptive review of *The Naked God, ibid.,* Vol. XLI (Feb. 3, 1958), pp. 22-24.

† According to Michael Blankfort, no one broke with the party over a single issue. The final break was a culmination of a series of emotional and

social revolutionaries of the October revolution, disaffection might have started with the Soviets' bloody suppression of the sailor rebels at the Kronstadt naval base in 1921. Alexander Berkman broke with the Bolsheviks over the handling of that insurrection, and a series of succeeding "Kronstadts," as Louis Fischer called them,[6] provided occasions for other disillusioned Communists and sympathizers to separate themselves once and for all from the Great Cause.

Whether the particular issues happened to be momentous ones, like the expulsion of the anti-Stalin opposition in 1927 and the exile and deporting of Trotsky, the forced collectivization of the peasants which began in 1929, the mass treason trials of 1936-38, Stalin's savage persecution of his own nationals who had been sent to aid the Spanish Loyalists, or the Nazi-Soviet pact of 1939; or whether the "Kronstadts" were of lesser consequence, like the suicide of Trotsky's daughter in 1933, or the Madison Square Garden riot in 1934, the consequences were the same. In anger or sorrow, or sometimes with a sense of relief, the writer quietly slipped away from the party or noisily took his leave. Some waited to be thrown out for intellectual deviations, refusing at the last moment to yield or to recant.

The careers of many writers might have served as characteristic episodes in this story of disenchantment, but I have narrowed the number to six. Two, Joseph Freeman and Granville Hicks, had been at one time or another members of the Communist Party. Two, Max Eastman and V. F. Calverton, had been for many years critical but

---

intellectual blows. Blankfort, for example, was disturbed by the Franco-Soviet pact of 1934. How could a Communist country make a pact with a capitalist one? Then he was told, and then everything became clear—until another crisis occurred. The "straightening-out process" was carried out as follows: "You meet with six comrades. You don't openly criticize the USSR but you raise certain questions, suggest certain doubts. The others explain and you take it. The meeting breaks up. Four people walk home together; the conversation changes a little as doubts are more frankly confessed and the opinions become more personal. Two more drop off and your final conversation may be with the one other person who shares your misgivings. This conversation is the frankest of all." The first duty of any good Communist, according to Blankfort, was loyalty to the U.S.S.R., and all else followed from this initial premise, whether it pertained to domestic or foreign affairs. The people who believed in the primacy of the U.S.S.R. had no difficulty following any party decision. But very few, he feels, took this unequivocal stand. Most people had doubts. Conversation with author, November 1958.

unfaltering supporters of the Communist regime in Russia, and two, Malcolm Cowley and John Dos Passos, could be described each in his own way as passionate fellow travelers. None broke at the same time, and each had his special grievances. Their collective political experience between 1920 and 1940 provides a record of the meanness and nobility of the radical cause, "Innocence and infamy, spiritual depravity and fair repute." [7]

TWELVE · THE LONE REBEL OF CROTON

FEW "RENEGADES" of Communism were denounced with so much fury or variety as Max Eastman once he had taken his stand with the Trotskyist opposition. From the time he published Lenin's Testament until his "unmasking" in the Moscow treason trial of March 1938 as the paid agent for British and Japanese Intelligence, he invariably appeared as an enemy of the U.S.S.R. in the Soviet press. Stalin himself branded him as a "notorious crook" and a "gangster of the pen," the only American writer to obtain that distinction.

Like his friend Trotsky, Eastman denounced the ruling circle in the Kremlin as the betrayers of socialism. He did so as the public advocate of the Soviet Union, the "honest Bolshevik critic" who, until at least the mid-thirties, simultaneously defended the Russian revolution against its capitalist critics and condemned the bigoted and bureaucratic betrayers of Lenin. He learned very soon that party leaders hated such well-intentioned critics as himself more than they did their "real enemies" and scornfully rejected his efforts "toward socialist construction." [1]

Eastman had come back to the United States in the spring of 1927 eager to tell the Americans about his Russian experiences. During his long sojourn abroad, however, he had lost touch with his public; lecture bureaus and publishers did not seem to be interested in his views. Short of money, he gladly accepted an invitation to write three popular articles on the Bolsheviks for a curious and short-lived magazine called *The Smokers Companion,* edited by a lyrical admirer of Mussolini. The anti-Communist editor, nevertheless, introduced Eastman as "that great socialist and philosopher" who would "at last" tell the truth about Soviet Russia.

Eastman, chatty, reassuring, and folksy, revealed the "truth" about the great experiment in precisely the style and tone the party might have used (but seldom did until 1935) in all its communications to the bourgeois world. The Bolshevik, he said, was not "some kind of long-haired animal that loves to drink human blood," but a scientific engineer with a method and a goal. Bolsheviks' ideas resembled our own, but they analyzed society in a different way. The party itself was not a political party so much as a scientific or professional association. It might be likened instead to an army or to a consecrated brotherhood, something between "the Knights of the Round Table" and "the Jesuit Fathers." Eastman made the theory and processes of Bolshevism as American as Rotary. There was "very little mysticism or sentimental bunk about it." The Russian leaders reminded him of "the big, forceful, clear-headed American captains of industry." [2]

His domestication of the Bolsheviks, however, did not impress the American Communist Party, and even his old *Masses* associate and Croton neighbor Robert Minor snubbed him. But his former literary compatriots on *The New Masses* remained friendly for a time. He had sent them from France two stories by Isaac Babel, and now the editors asked him to join the executive board. Eastman served in that capacity until his resignation in January 1928.

How and why did the rupture occur? Eastman blamed the "officialdom of the Workers Party" for putting pressure on the editors of the allegedly independent magazine. An article on Lenin "in which I advanced some slightly unorthodox views of his treatment of the sacred dogmas of Marxism" with some hints "for a revolutionary revision of those dogmas" apparently touched off the attack against him in the *Daily Worker. The New Masses* editors "ordered all such heresies to cease," and he was asked to confine his contributions henceforth to literary reviews. Shortly after, they turned down his proposal to write a short article from the standpoint of the opposition on the expulsion of Trotsky and Zinoviev. According to Eastman, they preferred to take no sides on this issue of supreme interest to their readers in order to stay in favor with the party and at the same time maintain the fiction of independence. In his letter of resignation, he accused the magazine of being neither free nor revolutionary: "a better name for it would be the 'Yellow Masses.'" [3]

The editors of *The New Masses* did not print Eastman's letter, but Mike Gold, whom Eastman singled out for special censure, made a mild and amiable reply in *The Nation*. According to Gold, he did not dominate the fifteen-man board of editors, "that den of ravenous liberal tigers." They voted against Eastman's Trotsky article because the magazine "was not intended to be anything but an experimental place for the young social writers and satirists of America." Neither he nor most of *The New Masses* artists and writers were Trotskyists, but "none used the magazine for stating his position." Gold concluded: "All social idealism has been destroyed in young America. It has been killed by Mencken, the stock market, prohibition, and other well known causes. We are fighting this new bourgeois nihilism. It is enough to work for one poverty-stricken little magazine." [4]

Today it seems paradoxical and almost quixotic that a man who could lament in prose and verse * the corruption of the Bolshevik dream under Stalin should at the same time describe himself as "actively engaged in defending the Soviet Union in public lectures all over the country." [5] Yet this was Trotsky's position until he died and

---

* For example, his sonnet "Eleventh Anniversary," published in *The Nation*, Vol. CXXVII (Nov. 14, 1928), p. 522.

> Trotsky is banished; Lenin lies in state.
> The sword, flung off, still flickers in the sod;
> The god-destroyer, dead, becomes a god.
> A fog of worshipers, where shone the great,
> Worms in to darken and to desecrate,
> A troupe of crude farce actors tread the boards
> Where trod the chiefs of the real battle hordes
> Of the exploited, storming the forts of fate.
> Thousands then in that day spoke boldly, find
> Rash the straight word, imprudent the clear mind,
> Undisciplined the will that states: *We can.*
> Oh, what a quickly shifting ear is man!
> Speak if you have no deed; the truth is great.
> They rot to earth who only stand and wait.

the position of many former Stalinists after the Moscow trials of 1936-38. Eastman's views, though not unique, alienated orthodox Communists and hardly satisfied the chronic Red-haters who despised both pro- and anti-Stalinist radicals. Even Trotsky, whose history of the Russian revolution Eastman so brilliantly translated, was impatient with his literary agent's revisionist theorizings,[6] and the Trotskyists with whom he was in touch after 1928 valued him principally as an anti-Stalin polemicist—not as a political thinker.

A literary portrait done in 1935 by Haakon Chevalier described him as a many-sided man—revolutionist, philosopher, and scientist —yet somehow incomplete. The brilliant parts remained isolated from each other. A born rebel and a lively and incisive writer, his approach was "always either an attack on, or a defense of, a man or a theory." He had a passion for leadership and a strong wish to identify himself with a group, yet he was so egotistical that he would not remain in a group. Lenin haunted him. Did he dream of becoming America's Lenin?

Yet look at the two men: Lenin—compact as a bullet, singleminded, undramatic to the point of self-effacement; uncompromising and relentlessly steering a straight course through the mad chaos of the world in upheaval; the whole wealth of his genius harnessed to a single purpose; a man without a personal life, the living incarnation of the *will* of a whole people. Max Eastman—genial, easy-going, wayward, passionately individualistic, with a colorful life full of personal emotions and adventures, his gifts flowing out in many directions; a dramatic figure, a Bohemian, a free soul, whose center of gravity is always in himself.

This irresponsible knight-errant, Chevalier concluded, this mixture of Charlie Chaplin, "the pathetic child-man," and Sir Galahad, rode "blithe and debonair upon his prancing charger, through a magic leafy forest, full of spells and dragons . . . singing 'Tire-lire, tire-lire' in quest of revolution." [7] In short, Eastman remained a party of one, alternately scolding and praising the Soviet Union but growing colder and colder toward "the great experiment" as crowds of writers and intellectuals were "coming over" to socialism and rallying "with extreme emotion to the 'defence of the USSR.'" [8]

Until 1933 the Stalinists regarded Eastman principally as a nuisance or as a belated Greenwich Villager; they treated him less indulgently after he denounced his old comrades in *Artists in Uniform* (1934). And he, in turn, began to see the conspiratorial hand of Moscow behind every attack against him and his books. The "sly boys of the propaganda squad," he firmly believed, were out to get him; it was imperative that he "launch a statement of my true position into the *main stream*." [9]

The bitter denunciation of *Artists in Uniform* and its small sale of less than 500 copies led Eastman with some reason to suspect the handiwork of literary saboteurs. Another less sinister and more plausible explanation may simply be that Eastman was bucking a strong leftward current. At that time, no one rejected the back-slider more fiercely than the recent convert. Why did Eastman not attack the iniquitous capitalists in his own country? his critics asked. Why did he attack his opponents personally? And why didn't he go to Russia "to learn what the Russians can teach us, to the end that we may get out of our uniforms?" [10] Was not his anti-Soviet tirade inspired by his "vaulting EGO! God, these intellectuals who write books and articles against the Soviets for years, and never breathe a word against capitalism, at least not with the fire used against the only workers' state in this sorry world. And they call themselves revolutionists, these psychological misfits of the petty bourgeois, with their elements of 'enduring values in the tradition of liberalism.' " [11] Only Eastman's fellow oppositionists subscribed to his claim that in Russia the writer either capitulated to the state and accepted its perquisites or courted "social misery and literary death."

To his former friends and protégés, such sentiments constituted the basest betrayal of the revolution, and destroyed the remnants of their friendship. "I have never turned away from a friend who lost his path through drink, disease, or personal weakness," wrote Michael Gold in the *Daily Worker*. "But Max Eastman, former friend, you have sunk beneath all tolerance! You are a filthy and deliberate liar! When you charge the Gorkys and Faydeyeffs of the Soviet Union with being cheap American pen-prostitutes, you have aligned yourself with the white guards who say the same thing. Nay, you are worse, since you yourself were once the Bolshevik leader of a generation of young intellectuals. The world has always loathed the Judases more than it did the Pontius Pilates." [12] Kunitz dismissed

Eastman as a Philistine and hypocrite ("how he does manage to befoul everything he touches!") and proudly accepted the designation of artist in uniform. "Yes, we are artists in uniform. We are Leninists, Communists, Bolsheviks. As to Eastman, his one time pink uniform has faded. It is white now, whiter indeed than the uniforms of the White Russian generals." [13]

Stung by the insults of his old comrades, Eastman wrote a thirteen-page reply, more to satisfy himself than to convince the unconvincibles (he never bothered to publish it), and turned for the moment to nonpolitical writing. Not until some time later did he acknowledge to himself that he had not been nearly so detached in writing *Artists in Uniform* as he had thought and that he was much closer to the complete rejection of Soviet Communism in 1934 than he had at first realized. From now on, he could no longer act as the anti-Stalinist defender of Soviet Russia. The Moscow trials following shortly convinced him that the "battle for socialism" in the U.S.S.R. was "definitely lost." Reactionary decrees in the spheres of education, sex and family relations, prison reform, and labor had undone the work of the revolution. By abandoning the internationalism of Lenin and cultivating a mystique of "the Fatherland," Stalin had helped to establish Hitler's power; by shooting the old Bolsheviks and converting his parliament into "a clump of puppets," he had assured his own.[14] "Anybody who can't see now," he wrote to Calverton, "that Stalin's zig-zags are going straight as a zig-zag can, back to capitalism—or the rule of an economically privileged caste, is either wilfully an ass or congenitally a god damned fool." [15]

On March 7, 1938, Eastman saw his name blazened on the front page of the *Daily Worker* as an accomplice of the Trotskyist conspiracy. His old friend of the Genoa days, Christian Rakovsky, introduced his name into the last of the Moscow trials. It was Eastman, Rakovsky testified, who put him in touch with British Intelligence agents in 1925 and cleared the way to his becoming ambassador to England by assuring the Secret Service that Rakovsky was in league with Trotsky. On Carlo Tresca's advice, Eastman sued the *Daily Worker* for libel, not because he wanted a retraction of this ridiculous story, but to protect himself. Tresca had advised this move, Eastman says, to circumvent any assassination attempt by the vindictive Stalin's gunmen. By calling attention to himself as an anti-Stalinist, he could use the publicity as a shield. The newspaper settled for $1,500, and Stalin, having already assassinated his character, was content to leave his body unriddled. Eastman had reached the end of his "ideological journey." In 1940 he renounced the whole socialist idea.

AS EASTMAN'S RIFT with the party widened, the only radical magazine he felt he could write for was V. F. Calverton's *Modern Quarterly*. His long and friendly association with the ebullient editor began in 1928. Eastman's theoretical study, *Marx and Lenin,* had been set upon by party spokesmen and by a very self-confident and articulate student of John Dewey, Sidney Hook, at that time a fellow-traveling Marxist who would himself veer off from the party line a few years later. Calverton gave Eastman space for a reply, and the Hook-Eastman controversy simmered and boiled in the magazine until 1933, when the tactful editor, who admired both of the contestants but who deplored the degeneration of the controversy into "a personal-accusation contest," called a halt.[1]

Throughout his short life (1900-40), Victor Francis Calverton constantly found himself involved in the imbroglios of warring parties, and although he survived longer than most in an ideological no man's land, sectarian partisanship hampered and finally killed his experiment of conducting an independent magazine open to radicals of all opinions—a kind of intellectual brokerage house for revolution.

Born plain George Goetz, in Baltimore, Maryland, of German-American parentage, Calverton toyed with the notion of becoming a professional baseball player and of studying for the Lutheran ministry before deciding on a career as a man of letters. According to his own account, he came of age politically with the outbreak of World War I. After attending the Baltimore public schools, he "got a job as a timekeeper with Bethlehem Steel, stole enough time from the company to read a book a day and saved enough money to go to Johns Hopkins University," where, he said, "I was miseducated by the professors but succeeded in educating myself by reading twelve books a week for several years." [2]

In 1923, with a few friends, Calverton reorganized a small university publication, founded a year earlier, into *The Modern Quarterly,* and adopted the pen name V. F. Calverton lest he jeopardize his job in the Baltimore public schools. The magazine's manifesto denied the distinction between intellectual and worker and between pure art and propaganda, committed the magazine to Socialism, and attacked "liberal" programs and the "liberal" magazines that espoused them. From then until he died, this "constant heretic," "colossus of left-wing literature," "ebullient Marxist editor," "Peter Pan of piquant paganism," "plagiarist of the intellectual atmosphere," and "ideological racketeer," as he was variously described by his friends and enemies, remained true to his ideal. He wrote or edited seventeen books, traveled and lectured in forty-five states in addition to Europe and Canada, served as editor and scout for several publishing houses, sponsored numerous causes, literary, political, and social, contributed articles and reviews to almost every important big magazine and a good many little ones, carried on an enormous correspondence with the great and the obscure all over the world, and edited *The Modern Quarterly* (later *The Modern Monthly*) almost by the skin of his teeth. Baltimore remained his home base, but from 1928 he kept a residence in Greenwich Village, to which a steady flow of writers and intellectuals repaired for argument and entertainment. Until the early thirties they included radicals of all persuasions. With the advent of the third period in Communism in 1928-29 and the heightened intolerance of the party, Calverton's evenings were boycotted by most of the followers of the party line.[3]

Although eager to play the neutral and hoping to weld all of the warring groups into a genuine united front against capitalism and fascism, Calverton did take sides and sometimes violated his alleged detachment. These lapses, however, were less disturbing to his friends than his almost excessive open-mindedness. Starting in the twenties as an independent Marxist, friendly to adherents of any political persuasion and as fascinated by psychology, sex, anthropology, the Negro, art, history, literary criticism, and fiction as he was by revolutionary politics, he found out, after the political issues had hardened, that his contributors and friends were more single-minded and less tolerant than he was. Could a man interested in so many things and sympathetic to so many points of view be serious enough about any one of them? "I approve of Mr. Calverton's free-ranging appetite for ideas," Gorham Munson observed. "I object to his bolting them." [4]

Often he antagonized those he was most eager to please and had to address placating letters to ruffled comrades who charged him with irresponsibility, inconsistency, superficiality, and egotism. Editors and contributors to his magazine constantly threatened to resign for personal or ideological reasons. His old friend and coeditor, Samuel D. Schmalhausen, quit in a moment of pique. It was the result, he wrote to Calverton, "of this apparently uncontrollable tendency of your brain to use every one who crosses your path for purposes of ego-aggrandizement. . . . I suppose the key is simply that infinitely egocentric narcissism, hitched to an infinite energy of personal ambition." [5] Had his interests been less far-flung, had he held fewer opinions more firmly and systematically, and had he been less driven by ambition, his life would not have been so frenetic, or, perhaps, so remarkable.

Calverton's career is almost a one-man history of the American radical movement between 1920 and 1940. A full-fledged radical at twenty-three and editor and publisher of a magazine which became his private organ, he quickly launched himself into the radical intellectual world and established himself in some circles as a sort of *Wunderkind* of American letters.* His own boast that he printed "almost every left-wing liberal and radical who had artistic aspirations" is very nearly true. His contributors ranged all along the entire

---

* "Say George, to me you are an amazing psychological phenomenon: Publisher, Editor, Critic, Sociologist, Psychologist, Anthropologist, Rebel Fighter, Lover, and now—Creative Artist! Hell and damnation—I'm envious of you! Your tireless energy and versatility are enough to drive any normal, plodding, phlegmatic guy like myself to despair. What gets me is that you are so damned good in everything you tackle." Joshua Kunitz to V. F. Calverton, Dec. 18, 1929 (VFC).

spectrum of the Left, including such names as Earl Browder, Michael Gold, Max Eastman, Granville Hicks, Bertram Wolfe, Leon Trotsky, Isidor Schneider, Sidney Hook, W.E.B. Du Bois, Newton Arvin, Upton Sinclair, and Edmund Wilson. But the time of their appearance in his magazine coincided with his own ideological position and the flexibility of the party line.

Between 1922 and 1929 it was still possible for all radical camps to co-operate on many issues. "American Communism," wrote Lillian Symes, "had emerged from its first frenzies of underground romanticism," and "intra-radical warfare was at a comparatively low ebb." Thus the independent or nonpartisan journal of socialist opinion could enjoy some degree of support from a number of radical groups.[6]

Calverton started out as a militant socialist, moved close to the Communist Party (Workers Party of America) in 1925, shifted toward the Opposition in 1929 after the *Daily Worker* thwacked him for some of his deviations, and settled down in the anti-Stalinist camp following the polemic against him in *The New Masses* in January 1933. Even so, he refused to indulge in public mudslinging and did his best to keep the lines of communication open between the rival political armies. He continued to believe that the health of the revolutionary movement depended upon every radical writer, no matter what his political affiliation, writing the truth as he saw it.

The party made its overture to Calverton in the spring of 1925 after the appearance of his first book, a collection of socio-literary essays called *The Newer Spirit,* in which he mechanically demonstrated the dependence of literary substance and form upon the material conditions of the society. Michael Gold hailed the achievement in a letter to Calverton which suggests Emerson's rapturous welcome of Whitman.

"I believe you are at the beginning of an interesting and perhaps great intellectual career," Gold wrote, "—that is, if you don't get scared of your own bold thoughts and turn liberal and soft." Compared to him, Gold continued, the scholars on the old *Masses* and *The Liberator* were "rather dilletante." Eastman had

a fine mind, but he was a thorough bourgeois in his aesthetics, for which I always fought him. Also I suspect he really liked the Platonic version of life better than the Darwinian. Floyd Dell has become the historian of the phallic hunting girls of Greenwich Village. Who else was there with guts and Marxian wisdom to write for American revolutionists? The Communist Party has some good fighters and some good pamphleteers, but not a real scholar and critic like yourself.

Confessing that he had "always felt displaced in America," had "always disliked nearly every critic I ever read," Gold hailed Calverton as the "young master of the new world and the newer spirit" who would redeem "this stuffy bourgeois country." [7]

Gold warmly praised *The Newer Spirit* in the *Daily Worker*,[8] and through Gold the news about the young luminary reached Upton Sinclair, William F. Dunne, William Z. Foster, and Earl Browder. When Calverton then proposed to analyze the work of Plekhanov and Trotsky, Foster encouraged him but added some cautionary provisos. The former's place, wrote Foster, was "already well established in the revolutionary movement," his "genuine contributions" assessed, and his Menshevist weaknesses understood; but Trotsky was a harder nut to crack. "His part has been a much more subtle one to analyze. One can easily break his political neck on the Trotsky issue." Foster went on to say that Trotsky had performed valuable services for the revolution but that his talents were less suitable in the time of reconstruction. Eastman, he said, had "killed himself in the movement by his treatment of the Trotsky question," and Foster urged Calverton to study the subject carefully before writing. "I hope you won't take offense at this advice," he wrote, "carrying as it does the covert suggestion that possibly you write on subjects without giving them careful consideration." [9]

As it turned out, Calverton did break his political neck on the Trotsky question, inadvertently if not deliberately, but for several more years he remained on good terms with some of the party leaders. He contributed several pieces to *The Communist*, the theoretical organ of the party, wrote a column for the *Daily Worker*, and appeared in *The New Masses*. William F. Dunne, editor of the former, regarded him in 1926 as the most promising of the Marxist critics. "I think," he wrote to Calverton, "you should consider, if you are not a member of our party, making application and getting in touch with the Central Executive Committee. If you carry your Marxian knowledge into other fields of activity, then you belong in the Communist Party." [10]

With the encouragement of Foster and others, Calverton visited Russia in the summer of 1927, after being warned by a friend that he chose a critical moment and to mind his p's and q's. Warmly received in Moscow, he returned to America, he told one of his persistent critics on the *Daily Worker,* "with the great inspiration of their work still vivid in my mind and the cordial greetings I got from the comrades there still a splendid memory." [11]

But now the party theoreticians discovered Trotskyist and "social fascist" impurities in his writings, even while his articles were appearing in the Soviet press. The *Daily Worker* "exposed" *The Modern Quarterly* as a "Trotskyite" organ, much to Calverton's chagrin, and when the *Worker* refused to publish his denial, he appealed in February 1929 to the party functionary Jay Lovestone, "in hopes that you may be able to see that it is printed." There was no basis for the charge, he insisted. He had made his pro-Stalin position clear to another influential Communist, Bertram Wolfe, and taken the Stalin side in a debate with Isaac Don Levine. He pointed to Louis Fischer's anti-Trotsky article in the current issue of the *Quarterly.* [12]

But these reassurances did not reassure. The invitations from Moscow ceased, and a volume of American criticism he was coediting with Serge Dinamov "suddenly wouldn't be brought out because of 'shortage of paper.'" Foster denounced him as a fascist in *The Communist,* and another heavy gun in the same magazine called him a petty-bourgeois revisionist and a co-operator with the Japanese Government. And then *The New Masses,* which had closed its columns to Calverton but had not openly assaulted him, was censured by Moscow for its laxness: "the journal," admonished A. Elistratova in *International Literature,* "should begin a ruthless exposure of the social-fascist spokesmen, not contenting itself with merely keeping silent about them as in the case of Calverton and Max Eastman." *The New Masses* obliged with the already mentioned "encyclopaedic" attack in January 1933. [13]

Since Calverton must have known the party's hostility toward the Left splinter groups, his expectation to keep in the good graces of Moscow and at the same time to associate with the Opposition seems unbelievably naïve. James Oneal, editor of the socialist *New Leader,* had rebuked him in 1926 for contributing to the *Daily Worker,* "the filthiest thing that ever appeared in the United States." It would be impossible, Oneal warned, "to keep on good terms with two movements fundamentally apart and indulge in a critical attack on one or the other." Another close friend of *The Modern Quarterly,* Hiam Kantorovitch, kept up a steady barrage against the Communists during Calverton's pro-Communist period. "I do not think," he wrote, "that any religious sect, the Catholic Church of the dark ages included, has ever been so intolerant of other peoples' ideas, as these 'fighters for liberty' are." Calverton and others like him, according to Kantorovitch, regarded socialism as "an intellectual affair, a thing to write about, an idea, but not a practical movement, not something for which one must fight and sacrifice." Much as he liked Calverton personally, he and his friends intended to fight him as an exponent of an intolerant faith. Calverton refused to accept this view of Communism until *The New Masses* experience convinced him that close literary associations and friendships snapped under the tension of political pressures.[14]

To be sure, the writers jumped less quickly to the crack of the party whip than the politicians did. Although he had been criticized at a John Reed Club meeting in August 1932 for his remarks on superorthodoxy and his writing for *The Modern Quarterly,* Joseph Freeman had been friendly. It pained him, Joshua Kunitz assured Calverton, to have to fight him on the ideological front, since he had always found him kind, considerate, and "genuinely comradely." The critical reference to him in *The New Masses,* he said, had been delivered at the John Reed Club meeting. He had been attacking Kenneth Burke's conception of Marxism when Burke blurted: "I got it from Calverton." Everybody laughed, but under the circumstances, Kunitz had to correct the source of the error. Such forbearance, unfortunately, did not last much longer. Mike Gold, whose letters to Calverton until 1933 had been warm and genial, finally found it necessary to break off relations after Calverton published Max Eastman and that other "notorious renegade," Charles Yale Harrison.[15]

Gold confessed he had erred for the past two years. Calverton, he knew, "had some ordinary complexes that afflict literary men when they come into contact with a proletarian movement," but he believed in his "good-will" and thought "that in time he would adjust himself." Gold recollected how the party leaders encouraged Calverton, how a "prominent Soviet critic" introduced his works into the U.S.S.R., and how Gold himself favorably reviewed Calverton's first collection of essays, *The Newer Spirit.* "Nobody hounded him because of his 'deviations,' all criticism of him was friendly." Gold opposed the long anti-Calverton critique in *The New Masses,* he said, because he thought it was silly to pay so much attention to one man's mistake. But now he could no longer defend him as the "mere eclectic" trying to maintain a broad program and to "reconcile all tendencies." He had cast his lot with the recently expelled Lovestone group and the Trotskyites. "The New York woods," Gold remarked, "are full of glib intellectuals, who can tear a novel, a poem or a political movement to pieces, but are themselves as incapable as Hamlet of deed or decision." These "intellectual Hamlets go through enormous sweaty tragedies" but they usually "drift contentedly" into the capitalist world where they serve as "a kind of intellectual Bomb Squad." Calverton and his journal were beginning to perform this function by befouling the "living revolution." [16]

Gold's pronouncement coincided with other repudiations of Calverton and his Oppositionist views by former friends and by fellow-traveling contributors to his magazine. "I don't see the use of using any intermediate terms in the political vocabulary now," Robert Briffault wrote from Paris. "If you're not a communist you're a fascist. Nothing else matters."

Newton Arvin and Granville Hicks stopped writing for the magazine, as did Stanley Burnshaw, the poet, who only a few months before had congratulated Calverton on the "shellacking" he had handed *The New Masses.* Kyle Crichton resigned as a contributor. Nathaniel Weyl broke off personal relations in an angry letter. Edwin Seaver worried about the petty-bourgeois aspects of Calverton's position and acknowledged his adherence to the party line "although not a party member." It seemed to him "sound and constructive and tried by much experience." Obed Brooks, the pen name for Robert Gorham Davis, whose column, "The Literary Front," had been a feature in Calverton's magazine for almost a year, appeared for the last time in the August 1933 issue.

The cruelest cut for Calverton was the friendly but firm leave-taking by Michael Blankfort, one of his gifted protégés, who resigned as associate editor over the Trotsky issue in the summer of 1933. Calverton warned him that he was lining himself up "with all of the most vicious elements, at least as I see them in the Communist ranks, which are tending to destroy rather than build up the possibilities of a future Communist world," but the two men stayed friends.[17]

From 1933 until his death seven years later, Calverton continued to edit his ostensibly independent journal, "a forum of radical opinion." Himself a victim of "the self-devouring internecine warfare which now prevails among the parties of the left," he had hoped to unite all the Left Wing groups into a genuine united front. But as Bertram Wolfe pointed out to him in 1934, he did not differentiate clearly enough between his own views, decidedly anti-Stalinist, and the editorial policy of the magazine. As a result, his readers and contributors were sometimes puzzled and often disturbed by the magazine's stand on Trotsky, Stalin, and the U.S.S.R.

Corliss Lamont, one of Calverton's few financial supporters, thought Russia ought to be criticized but not excessively; no consistently anti-Soviet magazine, he said, could get very far in the labor movement. Scott Nearing wrote in that *The Modern Monthly* "contained an overdose of Trotsky," a man he liked personally but considered a political menace, and a number of others urged Calverton to abide by his editorial declarations, to eliminate mudslinging, and to attempt to merge the factions. "I know you have been making gestures for collaboration," wrote Haakon Chevalier, "but through these gestures intense animosities are all too visible. The fault I know is on both sides, but the bigger you are the more generous you can afford to be." [18]

The "intense animosities" radiating from *The Modern Monthly* were generated by the writings of a group who did not share the editor's conception of the magazine as a neutral forum and who were not entirely at ease with one another. Sidney Hook described himself as an unaffiliated Communist "without dogmas." Max Eastman had no party affiliations either, but he was decidedly not a Hookian. He and Edmund Wilson joined Calverton's editorial board in March 1934, and all three of them—Hook, Eastman, and Wilson—were highly critical from time to time of Calverton's editorial practices. Calverton had to use all his blandishments to keep them from quitting.

Wilson, for example, questioned a proposal Calverton had drawn up calling for an autonomous revolutionary party which would avoid the mistakes of the Communist and Socialist parties and tailor itself to American conditions. He approved the aim but questioned the wisdom "of having the magazine itself take so definitely hostile a stand toward the Socialists and official Communists." Should it not try "to persuade Socialists and Communists as well as other people and even have them contribute to the paper?" He advised Calverton to omit the name of Marx from his statement, since the contributors need not be Marxists "and the very labelling of anything as Marxist seems to produce a theological odor." Some time later he was ready to resign over the inclusion of a John Sloan drawing, illustrating Eastman's article "Bunk About Bohemia," which depicted "my old friend Mike Gold in a chamber pot." Neither he nor Eastman wanted to assume editorial responsibility in what seemed like a one-man operation. Eastman was particularly irritated by Calverton's breezy irresponsibility and by his habit of writing blurbs for his own work.[19]

Calverton certainly "cared enormously whether his books were noticed and ignored, and whether reviews were favorable or unfavorable," but he did not sacrifice himself to his magazine for seventeen exhaustive years simply to promote his own works. He had dedicated it to socialism in 1923; he remained a socialist despite his disillusionment with the radical movement that had insulted him and excluded him from its organizations. He could accept the criticisms and the diatribes of his political enemies with his customary aplomb, but the decline of his magazine's influence after the mid-thirties gnawed "like a cancer." He was "losing everything bit by bit. No more authority or influence anywhere." The endless lecture tours exhausted him and brought in little money. Finally, in the fall of 1938, *The Modern Monthly* once more became a quarterly, for reasons that Calverton made clear in an editorial:

The consolidation of the New Deal and the consequent changes in attitude of . . . many thousands of individuals who had formerly considered themselves part of the left-wing movement, has seriously curtailed
the field of active supporters for an independent radical journal. . . .
On the other hand, a number of splinter groupings representing a con-
glomerate of left viewpoints have come into existence. Each claiming
justification as the "true" bearer of social wisdom and revolutionary
honor, they have scattered dogma and reaped the barren fruits of sectarianism.[20]

For the last two years of his life, Calverton spoke out against New
Deal reformism and particularly against the radical sectarians who
ignored American realities. "I am disgusted with the run of Marxists
who try to fit America into the Marxist pattern," he wrote to Van
Wyck Brooks in 1939. "It won't fit. We do, indeed, need a new
terminology, adopted to the American outlook. The only reason I
continue to identify myself with Marxism at all is because I feel that
originally I owe such a debt to Marx, and that a certain number
of his theses hold true today." [21]

At the same time that he was calling for "a thorough re-examina-
tion of radical doctrine," [22] Calverton was completing the last of his
seventeen books, *Where Angels Dared to Tread,* a study of American
communitarian movements. Before he finished it, he had signed a
contract to write his autobiography and, characteristically, spent the
advance.

He died with only a few pages of the autobiography completed,
but it might have been, as his friend George Britt advised Calverton's
publisher, a remarkable history of the radical generation. "I can't
think of anyone so well equipped as George Calverton," he wrote,
"to portray in sympathetic but critical tones the history of the aspiring radical intellectualism of the post-war years." Calverton epitomized and brought "to luxurious development a type of urban radical
scholastic" who flourished in the decades between the wars. He and
his friends belonged to the jazz age; in their own way, they were
"just as completely hopped-up, voracious, irresponsible and self-
confident." Money meant less to them than it did to their acquisitive
and apolitical contemporaries; they did not want to sell bonds and
marry the boss's daughter. But they were just as competitive and
just as eager to achieve their own kind of influence and power.

Britt described Calverton as a "notable contactman" among the literary set. "Sensitive and alert to new ideas and new people, he has pursued them unblushingly and made friends." [23] No fad or vogue or movement, political or intellectual, escaped him, and he rushed to set down "new" ideas about sex and marriage, Freudianism, romantic proletarianism, American history, or literary criticism before he had taken the time to assimilate them. His overhospitable mind was crammed with facts from a dozen disciplines, with original and borrowed thoughts that never coalesced into a philosophy. Unsuited by temperament to become a doctrinaire anything, much less a disciplined member of the Communist Party, he correctly defined himself as a "Calvertonian."

Like other radicals of his generation, Calverton presented himself as an unsentimental scientist, an unswerving rationalist. Yet those who knew him well detected a utopian and even a mystical bent to his thought and an obsession with death.[24] His best piece of fiction, *The Man Inside* (1936), is in effect an essay, masked by a sensational plot, on the inner cosmos of the human mind, a trans-scientific world. The "man inside" is terrified and energized by his fear of annihilation. Only by de-individualizing himself, by dissolving himself in the matrix of the race, Calverton argued, as the transcendentalist Edward Bellamy had before him, could men escape from this paralyzing fear. "Socialism, the negation of individualism, will give birth to a new man, a man freed of the illusion of individuality, who, unhampered, can explore the life-force within the man inside." [25]

But who could assist mankind in this act of self-liberation? That was a question posed by George Santayana, to whom Calverton had sent a copy of his book. If the Hitlers of the world were to be the instruments, "who shall unhypnotize the hypnotizers." [26] Who does the hypnotizing, Calverton replied, depended upon who controlled "the socially-hypnotic mechanisms," namely, the press, radio, religion, education, for "the human mind in general, with but rare exceptions, is far more susceptible to suggestion than logic." [27] Once the economic problems of the "man outside" had been solved through socialism, it would be possible to reach the man inside.

FOURTEEN · COWLEY'S RETURN

THE INTELLIGENTSIA who turned against the party before Malcolm Cowley did singled him out as the classical "horrid example" of the "Stalinist" stooge or muddled pseudo-Marxist, and they attributed the intellectual confusion of *The New Republic* and *The Nation* to men of his stamp.

In the twenties, according to the sharp-tongued Lillian Symes, these "two liberal weeklies" had taken "their revolution vicariously." They had scolded, advised, and applauded the radicals "at a safe distance." In contrast to the "capitalist" and to the "frankly revolutionary press," however, their efforts to report the facts honestly and to keep their intellectual independence gave them an influence "out of all proportion to their circulations." But with the Depression, an army of "politically uneducated but highly articulate intellectuals" offered their pens and voices to the cause. For every knowledgeable volunteer, dozens "passed directly through the experience of emotional conversion into the orbit of Communist activity, surrendering their souls in an ecstasy of self-abasement to the high priests of the new proletarian culture." Only a few dared to join the party. The majority camped on the "intellectual outskirts" of Communism as friendly neutrals protected by their liberal labels and functioning as the conscious or unconscious auxiliaries "in those numerous committees, groups, leagues against this and that which constitute the party periphery and which permit the leftward liberal to dabble safely in the class struggle."

Cowley, in her opinion, belonged to the large contingent of enthusiastic innocents. His appointment to *The New Republic* after the departure of Edmund Wilson turned the columns of this weekly into "a playground of the proletarian artists and critics." Editorially, the magazine was still "liberal," but its allegedly nonpartisan position, she said, was a pretense: *"The New Republic* 'line' was, for the most part, a polite echo of the party 'line,'" and, despite its occasional wavering, more consistently Stalinist than even *The Nation.*[1]

Cowley's "conversion" to the Left was not so sudden or unpremeditated as Lillian Symes implied, nor did his appearance on *The New Republic* signal the left turn. Although his interest in the Soviet Union had been aroused as early as 1927, he did not begin to take revolutionary ideas very seriously until his trip to Kentucky with Waldo Frank's delegation in 1932. In Harlan County, he went into the miners' miserable shacks and talked to a people without food and without hope. He contrasted them to the strong and smiling workers stunningly photographed in the Soviet publication *USSR in Construction,* which deeply impressed him in 1931;[2] the sad Kentuckians symbolized for him the sickness of the capitalist economy. His membership on the National Committee for the Defense of Political Prisoners, founded in the fall of 1931, brought him into close contact with party people[3] and radical writers, as did his association with the League of Professional Groups, but the party still considered Cowley unreliable as late as 1932.

Until 1939, when he left the movement, Cowley quite consciously but somewhat uneasily allowed himself to be used as a front man by the party. He spoke for it, defended it, encouraged its writers, yet he never gave himself completely to it. Reviewing his articles between 1932 and 1939, one suspects he only half believed his own adjuration to artists to take part in the class struggle. He believed in it objectively but not religiously. Cowley never wrote as a "convert." His rebelliousness, nurtured in the twenties, took on a social character in the Depression; yet for all of his talk of the working class offering "a sense of comradeship and participation in a historical process vastly bigger than the individual,"[4] he and his friends hugged their individuality.

Politically, he usually followed the party line. He agreed that the

Soviet Union was the only genuinely antifascist power. He disliked the Trotskyists for personal as much as ideological reasons and carried on a private war against *Partisan Review* for doing precisely what they had accused *The New Masses* of having done—meddling in politics. If *The New Masses,* he wrote in 1938, published second- and third-rate writers and printed nothing that might offend an ally or comfort an enemy, *Partisan Review* carried on "a grand anti-Russian campaign under the infra-red banner of the Fourth International," and committed "all the literary crimes they charged against their opponents." [5] In a letter to Edmund Wilson, who had chided him for being sneering and supercilious,* Cowley accused "the Partisans" of calling themselves Marxists and revolutionists when in reality they were merely practicing the "book reviewer's trade." How could one have faith in revolutionists who took no risks; who had repudiated Lenin as well as Stalin? These Trotskyists, he remarked to Wilson, have become "such extreme and uncompromising revolutionaries that they don't have to work with other people, and in fact don't have to work at all, except for writing just enough to prove their moral superiority." [6] Cowley's dislike of the Trotskyists, it should be noted, never led him to condone the intolerance and fanaticism of the Communists or to connect political correctness with literary talent.

"Is a Revolution good or bad for writers?" he asked. It might be both. The political crises preceding every major revolution were periods of literary experimentation and ferment. The successful revolution produced a momentary intoxication and perhaps a few great poems; but writing did not flourish in the period of disenchantment which inevitably concluded every great expenditure of idealism. During the revolution, the writer felt compelled to engage in non-literary pursuits. He suffered from a censorship he was "too weary or disillusioned to fight." Nevertheless, the revolution might ultimately

---

* "You're a great guy to talk about the value of a non-partisan literary review after the way you've been plugging the damned old Stalinist line, which gets more and more cockeyed by the minute (did you see the interview with Stalin in Liberty, in which he invokes Peter the Great, Napoleon and even Napoleon the Third, washes his hands of Spain and China, and returns a non-committal answer to a question about an alliance with Hitler?)" Wilson to Cowley, Oct. 20, 1938.

have a liberating influence, especially on the literature of other countries. If it did "not justify those sentimental radicals who call for a revolution at any price and trust that their literary problems will be washed away in other people's blood," neither did it justify the apprehensions of the timid. Cowley wasted no sympathy on the beneficiaries of the American and French revolutions proclaiming "the utter wickedness and futility of all revolutions." [7]

He had in mind, of course, the Russian revolution, and he devoted a good deal of time defending, sometimes overingeniously, its bloody aftermath to his readers, to his friends, and, very probably, to himself. Cowley expressed his views on the U.S.S.R. and its critics most succinctly in a reply to Edmund Wilson's "complaints" about the literary Left. Two sharply contradictory attitudes toward the Soviet Union, Cowley said, divided progressives everywhere. One group saw the revolution endangered from within by a dictatorial faction, the other and larger group, although often critical of much that was taking place in Russia, believed the real threat to the revolution came from the enemies outside. Extremists among the former were so convinced of Stalin's diabolism—his cruelty, stupidity, and unmitigated evil—that they were prepared to co-operate with Czarist insurrectionists. Cowley disclaimed any sympathy with extremists blindly loyal to Stalin and his policies and extremists who transformed him into a devil incarnate. He sided with the moderates who held "the personal character of Stalin" to be "relatively unimportant" and who thought that the security of the world depended upon the strengthening of Russia's "industrial and military resources . . . in the face of an international fascist alliance." [8]

His strategy of moderation, accepted by many fellow travelers during the middle thirties, sounded reasonable enough, but many liberals found it impossible to reconcile the internal and external policies of the U.S.S.R., to believe, for example, that the Moscow trials of 1936, 1937, and 1938 struck at the outside aggressors and prevented a world war.[9] Cowley's comments on the trials appearing in *The New Republic* between 1936 and 1938 painfully illustrate the dilemma of a man of good will straining to preserve an illusion and parading his uncertainties and unfirm convictions.

Trotsky obviously did not appeal to him as a person ("I have never liked the big-city intellectuals of his type, with their reduction of every human question to a bald syllogism in which they are always right at every point . . . and their opponents always stupid and beneath contempt"),[10] and Cowley seems to have accepted the confessions at face value. At least this was the gist of a letter he wrote to Wilson in May 1937:

I went so dead on the Moscow trials that I can't get around to answering your letter. One weakness of your point of view is that it doesn't visualize what sort of "opposition to the regime" the defendants in these last trials are guilty of. I think that their confessions can be explained only on the hypothesis that most of them were guilty almost exactly as charged. With that guilt as a start, they could be made to confess still other things if that seemed desirable. But I have noticed that Trotsky himself walks on eggs when it comes to discussing the guilt of the accused. To the best of my knowledge, he has never said that they were innocent. He leaves that to his followers.[11]

Yet he could not absolve Stalin of all blame even though he considered his policies wiser "than those advocated by his enemies," and he deplored the cult of Stalin-worship. Had more democracy obtained in the U.S.S.R., the opposition might not have been goaded into committing treasonable acts. Was it possible, he wondered in 1938, "whether certain types of power do not inevitably corrupt the men who hold it"? * From time to time, this doubt and others crept into his defense of the first two trials and weakened his extenuations. By the third, he was prepared, despite his warning to American radicals that they keep their perspective, to swallow his misgivings and sign his name, along with other Soviet apologists, to a statement

---

* *New Republic*, XCV (May 25, 1938), p. 79. The trials suggested the same thought to the old radical Scott Nearing, who was upset by the failure of the defendants to "stand up and fight back" and by the possibility that the U.S.S.R. was the old Russia still, "with its secret police, its little father, its red-tape-ridden bureaucracy; and its huge military establishment as a facade behind which individuals scheme and plot in secret—because there is no legally recognized way to oppose." An even more disturbing thought occurred to him. Perhaps socialism, in its finished form, was the servile state. Does socialism necessarily involve spies, conspiracies, "a drastic regimentation within a bureaucratic military set-up"? If the victory of socialism meant the loss of "all our freedoms—are we paying an excessive price"? The rise of national socialism and the Moscow trials engendered these gloomy thoughts. "It needs a lot of re-thinking. The history of the past 20 years has made mincemeat of more than the outstanding theories of K. Marx." Nearing to V. F. Calverton, March 13, 1938 (VFC).

declaring the trial a positive good. His letter to Wilson in the fall of 1938, however, still indicated a degree of uncertainty:

What is my own position? Generally pro-Russian, pro-Communist, but with important reservations. I think that the Communists have done marvelous work for the American labor unions, but sometimes they spoilt it by getting their union mixed up in international politics. I think that Russia is still the great hope for socialism. If it is attacked by Germany and Japan, and beaten with the financial help from England, there won't be any socialism in our time. But I don't like a lot of things that are happening in Russia, for example in the arts. The Moscow trials revealed a widespread hatred of Stalin, especially among the old Bolsheviks. I think that the plot against him grew out of the industrial mess in 1930 and the famine in 1932, when it seemed as if the whole system might go to smash. Bukharin's policy at that time might have been wiser than either Stalin's or Trotsky's. What Stalin did was largely determined by the fear of foreign attack; he thought that a huge war industry had to be built up at all costs. The foreign situation is something you tend to discount when discussing Russian affairs. But nobody can say that life is perfect in a country that let two or three million of its own citizens starve to death.[12]

If Cowley had made up his mind once and for all about Communism, if he had closed his ears and eyes to the skeptics and to passionate anti-Stalinists like Edmund Wilson, he might have remained in the movement a little longer. Hamilton Basso interpreted his friend's "longing for 'order'" as a religious manifestation, but Basso knew his friend well enough to see that this desire was modified by Cowley's almost biological need to retain his right to criticize. For every Isidor Schneider writing him optimistic letters from Moscow describing the Soviet peoples' enormous relief after the extermination of the "Trotskyite" wreckers, there were the letters of Basso, Allen Tate, Edmund Wilson, and Kenneth Rexroth challenging his pro-Communist assertions or encouraging his misgivings. Since his friends usually couched their objections to Communism in aesthetic as well as moral terms, and since Cowley found the Philistinism of the party harder to stomach than its politics, he was not deaf to their arguments.[13]

Tate, for example, informed Cowley that he disliked Marxian poets as well as capitalist poets, and for the same reason. Each rejected anyone who opposed his own conception of the good society or who was indifferent to it. Tate claimed he had "frequently attacked certain capitalist defects more vehemently" than Cowley had. "From my point of view . . . you and the other Marxians are not revolutionary enough: you want to keep capitalism with the capitalism left out." In principle, he said, Communism was no better than Mesmerism or Fourierism or Hitlerism or Fascism. And as for poets,

all poets are automatically revolutionary: if they are genuine poets. They exhibit every idea they handle at the moment of its disintegration; they are the perpetual foes of abstraction. What you demand is that they reject the Capitalist abstractions and accept the Communist. By assuming the world a poet merely assumes that the present moment offers all the elements for a full statement of the human situation.

From his own "Agrarian" vantage point, Cowley's radicalism was simply disguised defeatism based upon a false belief in Communism's inevitability. Much as he disliked capitalism, Tate saw not "the slightest chance of a worker's dictatorship now or ever in this country." A fascist or capitalist dictatorship was far more likely.[14]

Basso also rejected Communism as just another mental absolute. Wasn't the world built on doubt? "The reason I'm against all kinds of dictatorship," he wrote to Cowley, "is because I don't want the freedom to doubt to be extinguished. I can't accept Marx as a Bible, as infallible, when I know goddamn well he *is* fallible." Marxism professed to be scientific, but science dared not "invoke causality without many reservations." Even Edmund Wilson, said Basso, tied himself up "into dialectic knots" by ignoring "the physicist's principle of *indetermination*." Cowley could talk as much as he liked about "Comradeship within a party—decisions arrived at and then obeyed—a strengthening of one's individual purpose by the feel that it is shared . . . in these times of crisis." What was this but Jesuitism, a rationalization for another kind of toe-kissing. More and more it seemed to Basso that the Communist orthodoxy, like the Catholic Church, presumed "the necessity of an all-wise hierarchy to tell people what to do and whose toe to kiss."[15]

Kenneth Rexroth, an "I.W.W." since his picaresque youth,* ap-

---

* Born in 1905, in South Bend, Indiana. Some members of his father's family, Ohio German, belonged to a communistic religious sect, and Owenites could be found on both sides. The son of a "passive socialist" wholesale druggist, Rexroth joined the Wobblies when he was a precocious teen-ager. As an

proved of the party "on the whole," certainly more than he approved "of their improvers," but, as a former insider, he had sardonic things to say about literary politicians. The poets who turned Communist "to move their souls," he told Cowley, soon found out "that the 3rd or any International" cared little whether they lived or died. A writer might stick to his knitting and still identify himself with the masses, but he could not be a politician-writer. No politician dared to permit a concern for the good and the beautiful to impair his efficiency; no poet could write an ode to Governor Lehman and keep his senses. Rexroth was willing to leave the problem of means and ends to the modern logicians, but what, "pray tell," he asked Cowley, "is all this to Earl Browder"? What was it to a V. J. Jerome busy splitting the party factions in the League of American Writers over the issue of whether or not John Dewey was to be attacked as an agent of the Mikado? [16]

Gradually and reluctantly under the impact of events, Cowley began to modify his views. Uneasiness about his fellow-traveling role, probably intensified by the troublesome questions raised by his friends outside of the movement and by his colleagues on *The New Republic,* dampened his radical convictions. The Russian-German pact of August 1939 proved what he already knew: that the American Communist Party was too closely linked to Soviet Russia's foreign policy.

"inveterate hitch-hiker," he worked as a fruit and grain harvester, in the forest service in Washington and Montana, and at one time or another, according to his own testimony, passed through almost every incorporated town in the country. Rexroth talked to I.W.W. men, carnival performers, criminals, front men, female impersonators, and anarchists. His first poems appeared in *Blues.* Besides his activities in the unemployed councils, the John Reed Club, and other party organizations during the "third Period," Rexroth painted a mural for a Public Works art project and worked on one of the federal writers' projects. "I believe the time will come soon," he wrote to Cowley, *circa* 1938, "if not interrupted by Fascism when every working stiff will be lots eruditer than E. Pound if he cares to be and folks will read Dante's Canzoni often for fun. I write that kind of poetry because I think it important and beautiful. I also think that unless a few intellectuals get busy and shake the farts out of their drawers and write things people, real people, busy and harnessed here and now, are going to understand and read, they are going to be dead, and the working stiff mentioned above isn't going to be able to read at all. And by farts I mean funny ideas about what Marx should of thought about Wallace Stevens. . . ." (MC)

More disheartening to him was the degeneration of the radicals themselves. Why did a movement starting "with such purpose and dreams of a better society" end so shabbily? He refused to believe that the "Communists I saw working hard and sacrificing themselves are really without a single exception unprincipled careerists," yet the intellectuals had made a mess of things. He confessed as much to Edmund Wilson in February 1940:

I am left standing pretty much alone, in the air, unsupported, a situation that is much more uncomfortable for me than it would be for you, since my normal instinct is toward cooperation. For the moment I want to get out of every God damned thing. These quarrels leave me with a sense of having touched something unclean. . . . It makes me wonder what the world would be like if it were ruled by the intellectuals. Some of them we know are admirable people, humble and conscientious, but intellectuals in the mass are not like that. A world run by them would be a very unpleasant place, considering all the naked egos that would be continually wounding and getting wounded, all the gossip, the spies at cocktail parties, the informers, the careerists, the turncoats. Remember too that the character assassinations now so much in vogue (and even you are succumbing to the fashion, with your open letters to the NR) are nothing less than symbolic murders. They would be real murders if the intellectuals controlled the state apparatus. Maybe that is part of the trouble in Russia.

Yet Cowley did not intend to renounce the saving remnant. Not every radical intellectual entered the movement to make a career for himself, and those who did were "damned fools because there are much brighter and easier careers to be found elsewhere." No, the best started out "with a willingness to sacrifice themselves—and even when they betray their ideals, I tend to forgive them in their bastardy."

Cowley concluded his letter to Wilson with a stanza from a poem he had once written "addressed to the people of tomorrow."

> Think back on us, the martyrs and the traitors,
> Of cowards even, swept by the same flood
> Of passion toward the morning that is yours:
> O children born from, nourished with our blood.[17]

FIFTEEN · THE ADVENTURES OF
JOHN DOS PASSOS

UNTIL HIS REVIEW of *The Adventures of a Young Man,* Cowley
had been one of the most intelligent and appreciative critics of John
Dos Passos. He had read each volume of his trilogy *U.S.A.* with
sympathetic attention although the bleakness of Dos Passos's "final
message" clashed with Cowley's mid-thirties optimism about the outcome of the class struggle. "For all their scope and richness," Cowley
wrote, "they fail to express one side of contemporary life—the will
to struggle ahead, the comradeship in struggle, the consciousness of
new man and new forces continually rising. Although we may be a
beaten nation, the fight is not over." [1] Nevertheless, he ranked Dos
Passos among the few serious novelists of the times.

Three years later, only a few months before Cowley himself would
break with the movement, he pronounced Dos Passos's novel of the
Spanish Civil War his weakest book since *One Man's Initiation*
(1921). This judgment, he confessed, "may have been affected by
disagreement with his political ideas," but he found the novel tired
and derivative as well as factually unreliable and its conception of
human motives low and mean-spirited. [2]

In the summer of 1939, the Spanish Civil War was already a
bitter memory, but for a few months it had been the one conflict on
which Left radicals of almost every persuasion could agree. It touched
"people of my sort," Cowley wrote, more deeply than "any other
international event since the World War and the Russian revolution."

To him, as to most American intellectuals, Communist and non-Communist, it seemed to lay bare without ambiguity "two systems of life": Landlords, the Church, the Military and Finance representing class privilege and intolerance; and the aspiring workers and peasants, artists and poets guiding "a poverty-stricken people toward more knowledge, more freedom, more of everything." If the Republican government lost to the Franco-Hitler-Mussolini coalition, then fascist-inspired insurrections "might be repeated in Czechoslovakia, in France, in all the free nations of Europe." [3]

Cowley's pro-Loyalist fervor had been quickened by a visit to Spain in July 1937 as a delegate to an international writers' congress held in Valencia. He went absolutely convinced of the party's correctness in opposing the anarchosyndicalist elements in Spain (denounced as "uncontrollables" or "Trotskyites") and found his views confirmed by the Propaganda Ministry in Barcelona. He gave no credence whatsoever to the reports emanating from Spain since the early summer, and publicized in the antiparty press, of the brutal repressions carried out against antifascist anarchists and socialists by the Stalin-dominated government. [4] The kindest explanation he could offer for Dos Passos's acceptance of such charges was his anger and remorse over the death of a friend executed (understandably, in Cowley's opinion) by the Spanish Government.*

The hero of *The Adventures of a Young Man* is not John Dos Passos, but his career and the author's are symbolically parallel. Glenn Spotswood joins the Communist Party because ostensibly it fights for better social order. He works as an organizer in Harlan County until he discovers the party exploiting the strike to enhance its own prestige rather than to save the miners. Glenn's refusal to follow the twists and turns of the party line makes him a renegade

---

* According to Cowley, Hemingway, after interceding for José Robles, the friend of Dos Passos, "with the highest officials of the Spanish government, became convinced of his guilt. Dos Passos continued to believe he was innocent, even after learning that he had been convicted and shot." *NR*, XCIX (June 14, 1937), p. 163. Replying to Cowley (*ibid.*, pp. 308-09), Dos Passos gave his opinion that his old friend and translator had been murdered by the Communist controlled "special section," because "Russian secret agents felt that Robles knew too much about the relations between the Spanish war ministry and the Kremlin and was not, from their very special point of view, politically reliable."

in the eyes of the party leaders, and their vindictiveness dogs him in Spain after he joins the International Brigade. Persecuted as a Trotskyist and jailed, he is released only to be sent on a mission which is nothing less than an unofficial death sentence.

Dos Passos, an observer rather than a joiner, never belonged to the Communist Party, never organized a strike, never fought in Spain, but he watched these events with his own eyes. The death of Glenn Spotswood signified the end of Dos Passos's turbulent affiliation with the radical movement. His Spanish war novel must not be read as a sectarian tract or what a *New Masses* critic called "a crude piece of Trotskyist agit-prop." Rather, as Farrell rightly said, it describes "a dead-end of a historic movement—the Communist Party." [5]

The beginning of his radical adventures dates back at least as far as 1916, his last year at Harvard, and possibly earlier. During his undergraduate years, he was conscientiously rejecting all the "truths" he had previously taken for granted. He smashed no idols, but symptoms of incipient rebellion crept into the favorable reviews of John Reed's *Insurgent Mexico* (1914) and *War in Western Europe* (1916) that he wrote for the *Harvard Monthly*.[6] He particularly liked Reed's impressionistic style, the happy combination of the factual and the personal, which Dos Passos later incorporated into his own pungent brand of "reportage." *

After graduation and on the eve of his embarkation for France as a "gentleman volunteer" ambulance driver, Dos Passos's letters almost exploded with rebellion.

I have been spending my time of late going to pacifist meetings and being dispersed by the police. I am getting quite experienced in the cossack tactics of the New York police force. I've been in a mysterious police raid, too; nearly piled into a black maria—Every day I become more red—My one ambition is to be able to sing the *international*—. . . .

---

* Nathan Asch described Dos Passos in 1934 as a kind of artist-reporter: "The usually vague distinction between the artist and the reporter become pronounced here and consists in the artist's having more depth and comprehension and sympathy, maybe more love for humans living. He has many functions, but when he re-creates something that really happens he does a better job than would an apparently cold, objective, will-not-take-sides reporter. Events in his hand become significant, have a meaning, acquire direction, become a part of life, and place themselves in time's duration." *NR,* LXXVIII (May 9, 1934), pp. 370-71.

I think we are all of us a pretty milky lot,—don't you? with our tea-table convictions and our radicalism that keeps so consistently within the bounds of decorum—Damn it, why couldn't one of us have refused to register and gone to jail and made a general ass of himself? I should have had more hope for Harvard.

All the thrust and advance and courage in the country now lies in the East Side Jews and in a few of the isolated "foreigners" whose opinions so shock the New York Times. They're so much more real and alive than we are anyway—I'd like to annihilate these stupid colleges of ours, and all the nice young men, therein, instillers of stodginess—every form of bastard culture, middle class snobism.

And what are we fit for when they turn us out of Harvard? We're too intelligent to be successful business men and we haven't the sand or the energy to be anything else.

Until Widener is blown up and A. Lawrence Lowell assassinated and the Business School destroyed and its site sowed with salt—no good will come out of Cambridge.

Or again, still bloody and facetious:

I've decided my only hope is in revolution—in wholesale assassination of all statesmen, capitalists, war-mongers, jingoists, inventors, scientists—in the destruction of all the machinery of the industrial world, equally barren in destruction and construction.

My only refuge from the deepest depression is in dreams of vengeful guillotines.

His distrust for Wilsonian platitudes antedated his war experiences, but his protests were high-spirited and gay. Eastbound on the U.S.S. *Chicago* in June 1917, he professed huge delight at the presence of five Socialists and poked fun at "Archie" Roosevelt and other patrician officers, bloodthirsty imperialists to a man. Were he back at Harvard, he wrote to Arthur McComb, he would be attacking conscription, the daily press, and "the intellectual classes." After a month's spell in a French training camp, his mood darkened:

Politically, I've given up hope entirely—the capitalists have the world so in their clutches—I mean the elderly swag bellied gentlemen who control all destinies—that I don't see how it can ever escape. There are too many who go singing to the sacrifice—who throw themselves gladly, abjectly beneath the Juggernaut. It's rather a comfort to have given up hope entirely.

Although it was a relief to escape into "a pleasantly cynical sullenness" and "stride away from the human race," he knew that in time he would feel the twinges of conscience and "take up again my self-inflicted burden."

During the summer and fall of 1917, he caught the full blast of the war, later recorded ingloriously in his *Three Soldiers:* the mutilated bodies, the horses choking to death in poison gas, the drunken troops. He found it hideous and absurd. Wasn't it time, he asked, to stop crying over the dead or over a probably mythical liberty? "Like the Jews at their wailing place, the Liberals cover their heads with their robes of integrity and wail, wail, wail—God, I'm tired of wailing. I want to assassinate." Only one thought consoled him. At least the poison gas of trench warfare was better than the miasma of lies that enshrouded the world, and if the war could not be stopped, one might still "heave 'arf a brick into the Temple of Moloch if nothing else" and "disturb with laughter the religious halo of the holocaust." He still saw the ridiculousness of Richard Norton, surrounded by fat officers, addressing the Norton-Harjes Ambulance Unit: "and as gentlemen volunteers you enlisted in this service, as gentlemen volunteers I bid you farewell."

From August 1917 until the summer of 1918, when he was sent back to the States because of his antimilitary views, he lived the life of a vagabond ambulance driver, first in France, then in Italy, finding the agony and the misery of Europe preferable to the American "orgy of patriotic bunk." With Robert Hillyer, he repaired broken engines, scavenged for wine and omelets, and collaborated on a novel. At this time, too, he saw a good deal of another "gentleman volunteer," a "certain Jack Lawson, a dramatist smoking a pipe of unexampled stench," busily engaged in writing "a future Broadway success."

Back in the States in the fall of 1918, he waited to find out whether he would be discharged on account of his bad eyes or assigned to another ambulance unit. The organization of army life appalled him. "Organization," he declared, "is death." And yet he did not want to be anywhere else. "I'm glad I'm here," he wrote to McComb, "even if I seem to grumble. I've always wanted to divest myself of class and the monied background—the army seemed the best way—From the bottom—thought I, one can see clear—So, though I might have escaped behind my sacred eyes, I walked with the other cattle into the branding pen—" Dos Passos enlisted in the medical corps, but he saw no more active service.[7]

He emerged from the war an independent-radical seeker, filled with the mission (as he said of the Spanish novelist Pío Baroja) "to put the acid test to existing institutions, to strip them of their veils." [8] Before his discharge, he spent the spring of 1919 in Paris observing the Peace Conference with Hillyer, Lawson, and other friends, and sniffing happily the radical winds of doctrine blowing in from the east. "We knew that the world was a lousy pesthouse of idiocy and corruption," he wrote later, "but it was spring. We knew that in all the ornate buildings, under the crystal chandeliers, under the brocaded hangings the politicians and diplomats were brewing poison, fuddled old men festering like tentcaterpillars in a tangle of red tape and gold braid," but the caterpillars could be burned.[9] Discovering the drawings of George Grosz at this time seemed to Dos Passos like "finding a brilliant new weapon" or "hearing a well-imagined and properly balanced string of cusswords." They mirrored the corruption that Dos Passos was setting down in words, and he may very well have patterned his corrosive satire after Grosz's visual images.*

The radicalism of Dos Passos simmered in the early twenties, boiled furiously between 1927 and 1932, and began to cool thereafter. At no time did he consider joining the Communist Party, but he supported it during his fellow-traveling stage as the successor to the I.W.W. and as the "arch-enemy" of privilege. In the public eye, however, if not his own, his association with *The New Masses* and with the radical writers of the New Playwrights Theatre from 1927 to 1929, linked him with the revolutionary movement; and his own *Airways, Inc.* (1928)—packed with suicides, frame-ups, electrocutions—was a horrendous diatribe against capitalist institutions. He obviously intended it to illustrate what he was calling at this time,

---

* "A satirist is a man whose flesh creeps so at ugly and savage and incongruous aspects of society that he has to express them as brutally and nakedly as possible to get relief. He seeks to put into expressive forms his grisly obsessions the way a bacteriologist seeks to isolate a virus or a dangerous micro-organism. . . . Looking at Grosz's drawings you are more likely to feel a grin of pain than to burst out laughing. Instead of letting you be the superior bystander laughing in an olympian way at somebody absurd, Grosz makes you identify yourself with the sordid and pitiful object." Introduction to Grosz's *Interregnum* (N.Y., 1936), p. 18.

"socially creative ideas . . . the new myth that's got to be created to replace the imperialist prosperity myth if the machinery of American life is ever to be gotten under social control." [10]

In creating this new myth, however, Dos Passos seemed to subordinate people to conditions, to be concentrating on the disaster rather than on the people concerned. Edmund Wilson, a good friend and his most astute critic, wondered if Dos Passos's hatred of capitalist society was not becoming a "distaste for all the beings who compose it." In *Manhattan Transfer* (1925), his first collective novel, humanity "came off badly"; unintentionally Dos Passos had damned "the sufferers along with the disease." In *Airways, Inc.,* the sufferers were inconceivably hideous. Dos Passos did not distinguish capitalism's official representatives from the unprotesting multitudes unfortunate enough to have been born under the system and too stupid to oppose it. Such an impossible society of yahoos impelled Wilson "to rush to the defense of even the American bathroom, even the Ford car—which, after all, one begins to reflect, have perhaps done as much to save the people from the helplessness, ignorance, and squalor as the prophets of revolution have done." When a gifted and intelligent man like Dos Passos resorted to such flat dichotomies of good and evil, when he martyred his "good guys" and made "the wrong side" invariably repulsive, he was betraying an inward sentimentality "of which his misapplied resentments are merely the aggressive side." Dos Passos brought his own political ideas under suspicion "because we suspect the processes by which he arrived at them." [11]

If Wilson deprecated his friend's "infatuation" with social revolution, the Communists did not. They held up Dos Passos to the wavering or timid literati as the prime example of a man who had saved himself and strengthened his work by seeing "the promise of a dynamic tradition in the new social order that is slowly emerging today. . . ." True enough they could not applaud his preference for political independence or agree with his advice to middle-class liberals (namely, "everybody who isn't forced by his position in the economic structure of society to be pro-worker or anti-worker") to try to mitigate the ferocity of the class struggle, but they took pride in his revolutionary temper and in his growing reputation in the Soviet Union. All signs pointed to his closer union with the party.[12]

But future events proved what some party spokesman already

suspected: Dos Passos's "psychological orientation" was "not revolutionary," [13] at least not to the extent of endorsing all party practices. *The New Masses* was grieved early in 1934 when it found the name John Dos Passos among the signers of "an Open Letter to the Communist Party" protesting against "the disruptive action of the Communists which led to the breaking up of the meeting called by the Socialist Party in Madison Square Garden of February 16th."

The Socialist Party had called the mass meeting to honor the Socialist victims of Chancellor Dollfuss, whose soldiers had shot down Viennese workers and bombarded their apartment houses. In their efforts to take over the meeting, Communist "goon" squads provoked a riot. "Instead of working class unity," the signers declared, "factional warfare ruled. Speakers were howled down, fists flew, chairs were hurled, scores were injured." The riot dishonored the antifascist cause, and although the signers opposed the Socialist leadership here and abroad, they nevertheless held the Communists culpable.[14]

Communist spokesmen, blaming the Socialists for the fracas, expected the "nauseatingly distorted" accounts perpetrated by the "scribes" and "lackeys" of the capitalist press, but Dos Passos was a comrade, a contributor to *The New Masses,* a man whose "books have helped mold a challenging attitude toward capitalism and its concomitant evils," a "literary guide and inspiration." What was he doing in this "queer company" of "revolutionary butterflies"? Dos Passos replied that he signed the letter because he feared for the future of the American radical movement, "of which the Communist Party in this country is politically the most advanced outpost."

What happened in Madison Square Garden was shocking to me because it indicated the growth of unintelligent fanaticism that, in my opinion, can only end in the division of the conscious elements of the exploited classes into impotent brawling sects, and in the ruin for our time of the effort towards a sanely organized society.[15]

From the party point of view, Comrade Dos Passos's answer obviously showed he was confused; he mistook Bolshevik firmness for "unintelligent fanaticism." But reviewers in *The New Masses* continued to speak of him as America's first novelist, and Hemingway's

superior, until he returned from Spain disenchanted. Only then did
the once-neglected Hemingway, who had written only a few pieces
for *The New Masses* and had kept his individuality inviolate, become
in 1937 and 1938 the party's favorite literary name. Dos Passos in
the summer of 1937 was well on his way to becoming a class enemy.

Herbert Solow, tracing the shifting literary reputations of Dos
Passos and Hemingway, explained the causes for Dos Passos's de-
valuation. In Spain,

Dos Passos found bombs horrifying, bloodshed gruesome, anarchists
hounded by a Stalinist camarilla, the People's Front conceding to Anglo-
French imperialism and suppressing socialism. He consequently criticized the Stalinists to his companion.

Hemingway found bombs intriguing, bloodshed exciting, anarchists "treasonable," the People's Front noble, socialism nonsense. He consequently
denounced his companion.

Back from Spain,

Dos Passos published articles criticizing the Communist International,
defended the honor of the Spanish anarchists, supported the Trotsky
Defense Committee, opposed collective security.

Hemingway performed at the Communist Party's Writers Congress,
joined sixteen C.P.-controlled committees, wrote a play "exposing" the
"Fifth Column," fished tarpon at Key West, and socked Max Eastman.[16]

The party critics still were unwilling to abandon Dos Passos, but
his retreat to middle-class liberalism, his new confidence in an America cut off from Europe's ruling cliques by a friendly Atlantic, his
revived interest in the American democratic heritage seemed a
"strange metamorphosis." [17] And his published "Conversation" with
Theodore Dreiser, surely one of the oddest and wooliest political
discussions ever carried on between two distinguished novelists, must
have seemed even stranger.

It took place in Dreiser's apartment, December 17, 1937. From
a rather uncertain exchange on the political situation in New York
City, the conversation veered to Upton Sinclair, Quakerism, and
W.P.A. writers to the subject of Russia:

Dos Passos: Five years ago, a great many Americans pretended to be
very hopeful about Russia. I think now because of this terrific terror,

because of the fact that the terror has to keep on, and keeps going on, people feel that something is not working there.

Dreiser: Well, I was strong for Russia and for Stalin and the whole program, but in the last year, I have begun to think that maybe it won't be any better than anything else.

Dos Passos: Well, though, look at the achievements of the French Revolution, a great many survived through the period following Napoleon. I think a great many of its achievements are still going on.

Dreiser: Yes, and a great many achievements of the Russian Revolution are right here with us. We're indebted to them for a lot of things—40 hour week, W.P.A.—I mean for public works—the dole, because they had the dole over there from the first. Wages and laws, control of farming. This bill that's up now. That would never come in this country except for Russia in 1917, at least not in our day.

Dos Passos: No, I think all the great achievements of the Russian Revolution have been made, and that's absorbed into history. And I still don't understand what's happening there. It sounds like . . .

Dreiser: And damned if I do. They claim that they give the Russians a liberal education, you know, a technical education from farming and dairying up. They also give them training in the arts, pertaining to the theatre, the libraries, and gymnastics, health, diet—all that's supposed to go with being a Russian. But what seems to be lacking is the question of ideology, of what they are to think. And they *are* to think that any other form of government is insane and that everybody outside Russia is worse off than they are, that they are less miserable than anybody else. I know that to be a fact. Still, that may be a temporary condition, an attempt to achieve cohesion and unity. It has been how many years now? Twenty years, and they have done that much, but it's just a question in my mind whether they'll do more, or whether Russia will be liberalized. Maybe they do want to have a little religion, or greater class differences, or a little more money—less standardization in life, you know.

Dos Passos: Yes.

When asked by Dreiser if he would like to "Russianize" America if he could, Dos Passos said he would not. Although he agreed with Dreiser that the situation was very bad, America still had a chance: it was "probably the country where the average guy has got the better break." Nationalize the monopolies, yes, but find a way to instill the spirit of "the New England town meeting into bureaucratic industry." [18]

A few months after the "Conversation," Mike Gold passed judgment on Dos Passos in the *Daily Worker*. Arnold Gingrich, publisher of *Esquire,* had sent Gold a copy of *U.S.A.,* the separate volumes of which Gold had read and praised, asking him if he did not think it was "the greatest book written in modern America." Gold disliked sitting "in 'esthetic' judgment" on the book of a writer infected with the lunacy of Trotskyism. Once, he admitted, he had praised Dos Passos enthusiastically, as many other American and Soviet critics had done, because he was "going somewhere." And rightly so: "we recognized in him a powerful if bewildered talent" and "tried to help him free that talent from the muck of bourgeois nihilism." On rereading the trilogy, Gold was struck by the pervasiveness of the word "merde," symptomatic of Dos Passos's disgust with the world and his hatred of humanity. "Like the Frenchman Céline, Dos Passos hates Communists because organically he hates the human race." [19]

Other critics not so passionately involved in the movement would later assess Dos Passos's disaffection more clinically than Mike Gold did, seeing his chronic rebelliousness, his dogged search for a satisfying faith, and his stubborn libertarianism as a manifestation of latent hostility to his father and a consequence of adolescent frustrations. Whatever its origin, however, it seems clear enough now, as it seemed to some of his contemporaries in the thirties, that Dos Passos never found any form of collectivism congenial. And when the party, speaking for the oppressed, became itself in his eyes an agency of the oppressor, he repudiated it. His change of heart was already apparent in *The Big Money,* the third volume of his trilogy, in which the revolutionary leaders appeared, according to Isidor Schneider, as dehumanized robots, and in which Dos Passos's concern extended only to the lone individual.

"My sympathies," he wrote in 1939, "lie with the private in the front line against the brass hat; with the hodcarrier against the strawboss, or the walking delegate for that matter; with the laboratory worker against the stuffed shirt in a mortarboard; with the criminal against the cop."

Several decades later, this chronic oppositionist and foe of organization was still conducting a one-man campaign against universal Bureaucracy. [20]

SIXTEEN · THE ARRIVAL AND DEPARTURE OF GRANVILLE HICKS

THE TROUBLE with Dos Passos, Granville Hicks decided in 1938, was his excessive detachment or inability "to write about the revolution from the inside." That was why he remained primarily an observer, a writer who used his eyes but not his mind; and that was why he shied away from conclusions and commitments. He came close to Communism for a few years without ever daring to study Marxism closely; he "only partly subdued his passion for aloofness." Politically, as his talk with Dreiser so painfully showed, he was "capable of any kind of preposterous vagary." [1]

If Dos Passos could not make up his mind, Hicks could and did, although he did not actually join the Communist Party until 1935. Before 1930, Hicks considered himself a nominal socialist (he voted for Al Smith in 1928, however) and he knew little about the Communist movement until 1931. The group to which he belonged, for the most part young teachers and writers scattered around New England, regarded *The Nation* and *The New Republic* as their organs, not *The New Masses*. But the Depression quickened their interest in politics and in Communism, which they discovered largely through their reading rather than through direct contact with the party. That came later.

Like his close friends Newton Arvin and Robert Gorham Davis, Hicks came from middle-class, old-stock America, the child of frugal hard-working parents who cheerfully scrimped to assure his Harvard education. After taking his degree in 1923, he spent two years at Harvard Theological School, taught for three years in the Bible and the English departments at Smith College, and returned to Harvard in 1928 to obtain a master's degree in English. From there he went to Rensselaer Polytechnic Institute as a member of the English Department and remained until he was "dropped" in 1935. During this interim, he had undergone certain experiences that produced "the phenomenon known as the alienation of the intellectuals."

In Northampton, Massachusetts, an audience of hostile townsmen packed a mass meeting held in behalf of Sacco and Vanzetti and shouted down a resolution he proposed to send to Governor Fuller. That was two years before the Depression caught him and his friends intellectually and morally unprepared, for they, also, had been enjoying their own kind of spiritual self-indulgence even though it had not taken the form of money-chasing. Observing the effects of the economic earthquake, he recalled his feelings in Northampton "when my diplomatic little resolution—so tactfully, so politely, so meechingly worded—had been roared down." Dos Passos was right. There were "two nations," and the "other nation" could not be fooled "with careful words" and "noble sentiments." [2] He was ready now to substitute a headier brew for the "near-beer" doled out by the Socialist Party.

Hicks later observed that in his case, as well as with others, "conversion" did not "come overnight" or through a process of "pure logic." He was influenced by John Reed and Lincoln Steffens, impressed by the articles of George Soule in *The New Republic* which analyzed a collapsing capitalism, and attracted to the amiable Communists like Gold, Freeman, and Calverton who wrote him flattering letters and asked for literary contributions. Hicks and Arvin nosed around the party in 1931 "a little furtively, a little frightened of what we were letting ourselves in for," but they still distinguished Communism from the Communist Party and approved of Edmund Wilson's recommendation to take Communism away from the Communists. They pictured party members as spending their time passing out leaflets on the water front or standing outside of subway entrances. Hicks and his friends did not intend to stop being intellectuals; for a short time they were content to operate as an independent cadre on the fringe of the party.

Not many months had passed, however, before Hicks realized that if he really wanted Communism, "the practical thing to do was to work with the Communists." They were not only devoted people; they also had an organization, and so it seemed quite natural for him to join "a rather impressive number of intellectuals" in endorsing the candidacies of Foster and Ford. During the next three years, while some of the 1932 enthusiasts lost their radical zeal or affiliated with the Trotskyists, Hicks moved closer to the party.[3]

A letter he wrote to *International Literature* in January 1933 reveals his state of mind at this time. "Literary conditions" in America, he begins, are "in something of a mess." He detects a falling off of interest in Communism since the manifesto of the League of Professional Groups. "Edmund Wilson's articles on Trotsky in *The New Republic* . . . reveal not only a rather lamentable tendency, but an extraordinary naivete." Apparently Wilson does not realize he is taking a "definitely anti-CP stand." Clifton Fadiman "is also wavering," and it seems to Hicks "that Malcolm Cowley and Waldo Frank though loyal enough to the party, have not carefully enough thought out their position. Newton Arvin is all right but not doing much work." Finally he complains of "the dogmatism of certain party members and associates of the John Reed type, who cannot disagree with a man's ideas without denouncing him as a social fascist. This dogmatism not only repels sympathizers but also gives ammunition to their enemies among the bourgeois critics." [4]

Despite these misgivings, Hicks became an editor of *The New Masses* in 1934 and finally a party member in 1935, the year the Seventh World Congress of the Communist International met in August of 1935 and inaugurated the Popular Front.

Since 1935 Hicks had regarded fascism as the quintessence of barbarism and decadent capitalism. The party's crusade against Socialist "social fascists," exemplified so unpleasantly by the Madison Square Garden riot, had made him "heartsick," even though he sternly disapproved of the public protestations of the Dos Passos group, some of whom, he felt, were hostile or indifferent to the party. "Public criticism, then, could only aid those whose faults seemed to me worse than the party's, and I had to content myself with private protest." The new line, he believed, brought the strategy of the party closer to American realities and lessened the intellectual and emotional strain generated by the sectarianism of the old Bolshevik fundamentalists. It made fascism the "chief enemy," and it permitted the Communists "to cooperate with the insurgent forces in the labor movement and with the progressives in the New Deal." [5] Hicks, in the role of the Yankee Protestant American, could serve the party as a classic illustration of Browder's Popular Front maxim, "Communism is twentieth century Americanism."

I Like America (1938), his only book the party made a serious effort to circulate, indicates how easily he took to the "new vocabulary" of moderation and patriotism. Read today, with a few of the pro-Russian passages excised, it seems about as revolutionary as Bellamy's *Looking Backward*. Clear, persuasive, undogmatic, it contains not a trace of sectarian jargon or logic. Businessmen are not excoriated as exploiters but shown as decent people forced by an unfeeling and obsolescent economic system to engage in practices personally offensive to them. Communism, far from crushing individualism, is the only system that guarantees "the majority of individuals" the opportunity to develop. "I am a Communist," he tells the reader, "and I want the same things you do."

Let us work together for them. If you prove to be right, that settles the matter, for it would be quite impossible to do away with capitalism if the masses of the people were prosperous. If you're wrong—well, I don't believe you will stand by and let Fascism stamp its economy of scarcity upon us.[6]

Here is no manifesto demanding a "dictatorship of the proletariat" for the "toiling masses," no declaration of war against a "ruthless capitalist class," no program to establish "soviets" and "Red Guards" and a Negro state in the South. *I Like America,* instead, is a soft-spoken and amiable declaration of independence in the old reformist vein; it is grass-roots Marxism, an argument for the progressive verities: justice, equality, opportunity.

The subdued evangelical tone pervading *I Like America,* particularly in the pages where Hicks described the reasons why he became a Communist, suggests his prior religious orientation. Behind the perfectly rational reasons for preferring what seemed to be a workable economy over an unworkable one lay the serene faith in the inevitability of socialism. "There is nothing more comforting," Hicks wrote some years after, "especially for minorities, than the belief that God is on your side, and, sensitive as we were to the cruelties both of capitalism and revolution, we needed comfort." One of the participants in Hicks's first book, a fictional symposium called *Eight Ways of Looking at Christianity* (1926), spoke of Christianity as "good news." A little more than a decade later, Hicks testified from his *New Masses* pulpit:

Communism is good news. Once understood, once believed in, it holds out hope to all but capitalism's pampered few. If one accepts the Marxist analysis of history, one believes that the establishment of a classless society is not only possible but inevitable.

To be sure, Communists did not claim Utopia would be ushered in without pain, that perfection automatically followed from revolution, but a faith in Communism, if it worked no miracles, "inspired a confidence that is capable of changing human lives."

I have seen among intellectuals, confusion and weakness yield to clarity and strength. I have seen a baffled and desperate day laborer transformed into a militant, capable leader of labor. I have seen men and women, working together for their class, transcend the pettiness and frailty observable in the conduct of each as an individual. There is nothing miraculous about this; it results quite simply from an insight that is confirmed alike by logic and action.[7]

If to be "confused," a word current in Left circles during the thirties, meant among other things a loss of faith in the Communist millennium, then Hicks was never confused; he knew exactly where he stood. His faith was strong enough, at any rate, to carry him over the "hurdle of the trials" and to prevent his private suspicion that they might be "complete frame-ups" from undermining his belief in the righteousness of the antifascist crusade. It also allowed him to take for granted the party's covert control of the League of American Writers. "In discussions held by the party fraction in the League," he wrote in *Where We Came Out,* "I frequently protested against tactics that seemed to me ineffectual or obvious, but I would have been as shocked as the next one at any suggestion that the party might relinquish its control." [8]

Hicks had written the first draft of the "Call" for the Writers' Congress in 1935 and had been active in its deliberations. By the time of the second congress in 1937, the party felt it expedient to push aside open Communists like Freeman, Gold, and Hicks in favor of illustrious fellow travelers whose appearance would dramatize the Popular Front. Alarmed by this calculated discrimination, Hicks wrote to the League secretary and received a reassuring reply: "I don't think we meant to exclude Communists as such; our main emphasis was on getting new people to read papers. However, as it turns out, Ella Winter is going to do one paper, and there are enough others who are sufficiently left, I think, to more or less fill the bill. I am thinking of Arvin, Cowley, Burke, Rukeyser, Holmes and Lawson." Many Communists got on the commissions, she added, "but that was more or less accidental too, since we were trying to pick people who we thought would be most competent for the subjects." [9]

Accidental or not, the Communist fraction dominated the 1937 Congress as thoroughly as it had the first, even though some non-Communists sat in the spotlight. International fascism, Spain, the impudence and wickedness of Trotskyists, the triumphant surge of the Popular Front—these were the themes reiterated throughout the speeches in Carnegie Hall and in the closed discussions. The planners, as might be expected, did not urge the attendance of the "renegade" defenders of Trotsky, and although Waldo Frank, technically still chairman of the League, had signed the "Call" for the Second Writers' Congress in May,[10] his open letter in the same month asking for an international commission of Socialists and Communists "to study the evidence of the Moscow trials and of Trotsky's counter charges" obviously disqualified him from further service.[11] Ostensibly the League welcomed all antifascist writers of "professional standing," but as Dwight Macdonald explained in a letter to *The Nation,* "the Congress assumed an a priori agreement on Stalinist policies." The attempts of a few oppositionists to raise embarrassing issues hardly disturbed the proceedings. "Several Trotskyites present," *The New Masses* commented, "who did not participate in the creative discussions, attacked the Soviet Union and the people's front in Spain. Their conduct in an atmosphere of full and free discussion convinced the doubtful that Trotskyism is sterile, destructive, and reactionary." [12]

Only a few of the literary luminaries who addressed the convention tried to answer the Trotskyist insinuations. The largely non-Communist audience agreed with Ernest Hemingway, the star of the congress, when he ironically disposed of the schismatics and logic-choppers. It was more comfortable, he said, to cling to undangerous ideological positions, "positions to be held by the typewriter and consolidated with the fountain pen," but that was no way to fight fascism—"a lie told by bullies." They cheered Archibald MacLeish, now very much in favor with the party, when he lashed out at "the man who refused to defend his convictions for fear he may defend them in the wrong company." Earl Browder's blunt declaration that writers have no sacred right "to go free-lancing in the field of sharpest political struggles without accountability to anyone," his plea for "discipline," not regimentation, and his rebuke to the "sentimentalists and muddle-heads" (read Waldo Frank) who inadvertently helped the fascists, all harmonized with the music of the Popular Front. Hicks's speech, "The Writer Faces the Future," clashed with none of these assumptions, but he did not try to play down the pre-eminence of the Communist Party in the antifascist movement.

Let us disagree, if we will, on literary or political matters, Hicks told the delegates, but "our differences cannot be allowed to interfere with our work for the ends on which we agree." Here he was implicitly criticizing the Trotskyists (as Joseph Freeman did more directly in one of the discussions) and taking the party line that the Trotskyists' intransigence at home and in Spain disrupted the fight against the fascists. Communists, he said, "have been the most active workers in the literary united front" because Communism attracts "the most determined and the most self-sacrificing members of a group." He reproved those Communists who minimized the Communist contributions out of deference to the squeamishness of the liberals and called upon them to win the liberals by demonstrating their devotion: "they are less afraid of Communism than they are of us." [13]

Hicks's address was the last paper delivered at the congress, which closed harmoniously with the election of Donald Ogden Stewart, humorist and screen writer, as national chairman of the League.[14] Franklin Folsom, the new executive secretary, injected fresh life into the League's activities during the next two years. Under his energetic leadership, regional League chapters were organized, and League members set up schools for writers, held literary forums, and arranged meetings to raise money for the Spanish Republicans. In the fall of 1937, Ludwig Renn and Ralph Bates, both serving in the International Brigade, toured the country under League auspices, and in the same year the League published the proceedings of the second congress under the title of *The Writer in the Changing World.*

Necessarily Hicks found himself involved in these matters and other League affairs and was frequently asked by Folsom for guidance and support.

What, for example, could be done with a mulish writer like Dreiser who agreed to attend an international peace conference in Paris for the League and yet who refused to join it? Dreiser, ordinarily a trustworthy ally of the party, had strange notions about the Spanish embargo. His "emphasis" was "not in lifting it but enforcing it. . . ." Naturally Folsom and his fellow League members got worried. They arranged a dinner for him shortly before he was to sail for Europe and brought Ralph Bates to give "the old dope a great harangue about Spain." Cowley again urged him to join the League, and Dreiser, Folsom reported to Hicks, "did read our aims and said he approved of them. But with enormous stubbornness he refused to join. The boat was to sail the following morning and we capitulated." [15]

Folsom brought other less nerve-racking matters to Hicks's attention. Could Hicks come down to Washington and debate Floyd Dell, "this erstwhile friend of proletarian literature," and help out the new League chapter there? "Dell has refused to join the League, and he is apparently making cracks about writers having to choose between real literature and proletarian literature." Folsom doubted if the chapter could pay Hicks anything. Did Hicks agree that Heinrich Mann should be the League's candidate for the next Nobel Prize in literature? The New York fraction had tentatively decided on Mann, "who was called to our attention by the European campaign for him, news of which reached us through party channels though the ninth floor apparently has no news of it and I do not know whether the party over there supports the campaign." Folsom sent Hicks a list of the past and present contributors to *Partisan Review* and the names of the Trotsky defense committee as well as briefing him on battle reports from the literary front which related to the less monumental concerns of the party literary coterie in the thirties.[16]

Hicks, living in the comparative isolation of Grafton, New York, and preoccupied with his own work as a publisher's reader and *New Masses* editor, did not belong to the party's inner circle. But he conscientiously and ably carried out his duties as a Communist intellectual in a bourgeois world, whether at Harvard University, where he spent the 1938-39 term as Counsellor in American Civilization, or in the columns of the radical and liberal press, or on public lecture platforms speaking to indifferent and hostile [17] as well as friendly audiences. His Marxist survey of American literature, *The Great Tradition,* published in 1933 and revised in 1935, received wide if not always friendly attention,[18] and his fine biography of John Reed became the definitive book on this Communist saint. His growing literary reputation, his engaging and un-Bolshevik-like demeanor, and his earnestness and candor made him much sought after as a lecturer. The party considered him one of its most trustworthy spokesmen and particularly valuable as a plausible interpreter of the revolutionary movement to the liberal wing of the middle class. In 1939 he was speaking three or four times a week.

Yet in the spring of that year, one half of him yearned to get out of the movement. He turned down the assignment of educational director for the party, because he did not want to depend upon it for his livelihood. And despite Folsom's urging, he did not bother to attend the third writers' congress June 2-4; the party's policy of keeping its own followers in the background antagonized him (Freeman, already in disgrace, was the one exception, and the "ninth floor" regarded his inclusion as a blunder). As yet, however, he had no overt quarrel with the League or the party. It cost him no more qualms to back F.D.R., support the white-collar unions, boycott Japan, and advocate collective security. The doubts and misgivings he had suppressed only welled up after the announcement of the nonaggression and trade pacts between the Soviet Union and the German Government on August 23, 1939. Sickened by the news, Hicks hesitated for a few weeks and talked with party leaders before he decided to resign. Browder urged him to take his time but warned him that he would have to defend the pact on the party's terms. "If you do stay," he added, "you'd better be prepared for worse shocks to come." [19]

Hicks offered a reasoned and even-tempered explanation for his departure from the Communist Party in a letter he sent to *The New Republic*. It betrayed no anguish; it was not eloquent or denunciatory. Hicks was not even prepared at this time "to condemn the pact and its consequences." History, he said, might ultimately justify the Soviet strategy, and although he could understand "those who have been made bitter by a sense of betrayal," he himself felt "no impulse to denounce the Soviet Union." [20] Even socialist commonwealths could err. Apparently in October, Hicks still adhered to at least portions of the statement he and some 400 writers and artists signed on August 10, repudiating the aspersion that the U.S.S.R. resembled every other totalitarian state. [21]

But the pact disclosed the incompetence and disingenuousness of the American Communist Party, whose leaders were totally unprepared for the announcement. Their apologetics, "completely devoid of clarity and logic," pointed to only one conclusion: "if the party leaders could not defend the Soviet Union intelligently, they would defend it stupidly." Had they been less ignorant, they might have prepared the American people for the new development. Their failure to do so not only destroyed "the democratic-front line" but also convinced many of its defenders, Hicks included, not to "accept a change that is dictated by the exigencies of Soviet foreign policy." Hicks still considered it imperative to aid Russia, but no longer as a party member. He had joined the party because he thought it was effective; "I am resigning," he said, "because it is no longer an organization in which I can be effective." [22]

Hicks's distress at leaving the party at a moment "when it is in extreme peril" and his promise to do his best to defend it ("no progressive movement is safe if the party is suppressed") did not propitiate the editors of *The New Masses*. In their chilly acknowledgment of his defection, they placed him among the people "who have incompletely grasped the implications of their philosophy, or who are susceptible to the current of demoralization with which the enemy seeks to divide progressives in crucial periods." He was breaking away from "the great tradition" and turning his back on the "future" that John Reed saw and Lincoln Steffens confirmed.[23]

SEVENTEEN · "NEVER CALL RETREAT"

OF THE WRITERS discussed thus far who withdrew from the movement, none was able to analyze his experiences in autobiography or fiction with the philosophic insight of a Silone, a Koestler, or a Malraux, a Mannes Sperber or a Victor Serge. Was it because American writers were not "close to situations in which the ideological conflict makes for genuine *human* tragedy"? Were these "ideological matters" entertained as abstractions merely and not passionately felt? [1]

Joseph Freeman is an exception. His novel *Never Call Retreat* (1943), published four years after his "departure," is on one level a summing up of his experience in a revolutionary political movement, a kind of sequel to *An American Testament*. Essentially, however, it is a philosophical prose poem on the never-ending betrayal and rediscovery of the democratic vision. Not only is it free of the rancor and bitterness of most confessions written by former Communists; it is also the work of a writer who could say with Whitman, "I am the man, I suffer'd, I was there."

Freeman belonged to that small number of dedicated intellectuals enamored of the dream of socialism. Most of the American writers who went Left simply acted as extras in the great movie of revolution. They wrote reviews, poems, novels, plays, critical essays while the radical mood possessed them and then passed on to other intellectual passions. But for a few literary Communists, the "Cause" was life itself; their existence almost depended upon the presence and approbation of the party fellowship, and they yielded themselves to the movement without restraint or calculation. The prophecy of a classless society which had banished poverty, ignorance, and war and had given free play to human capacities seemed irresistibly appealing to them.

Freeman never renounced this vision, but he came to realize that many practical revolutionaries and many politicians of the party did not conceive of socialism in these idealistic terms. In 1927, while attending the plenum as interpreter for the American and English delegations, he heard Stalin define socialism as "correct economic relations." The idea of socialism which Freeman shared—universal freedom, equality, truth, and justice—Stalin dismissed as a "petit bourgeois dream." [2]

Subsequent events confirmed the antihumanist implications of Stalin's words, but for the time being Freeman was ready to accept the hard leadership and discipline the times demanded. In the twenties and early thirties, the Bolsheviks looked like "very honest people and their enemies liars, bastards and a menace to mankind." [3] Besides, the holy wars and the terror were still ahead. Literature was not yet a "weapon." It was still possible to write and speak irreverently about politics and personalities.

From the thirties on, however, the party did not treat poetic intransigence so leniently as it had done in the days of Lenin and Trotsky. It also made greater demands upon its trusted writers. Freeman found himself involved in a network of cultural clubs, associations, congresses, theater groups, magazines, and leagues. At such a time, who could afford to be "subjective"? During these crowded months, the Cause absorbed him completely. In 1931 he left the Tass news agency and worked for the Soviet Amtorg Trading Corporation in New York; from 1932 to 1934 and again from 1936 to 1937, he edited *The New Masses,* turning out dozens of articles and speeches, writing poetry when he got the chance, and publishing prefaces, pamphlets, and full-length books. [4] In between these regular chores of writing and editing, Freeman spent hours in committees and conferences. He addressed mass meetings, lectured on everything from imperialism to poetry before a variety of groups, debated enemies of the U.S.S.R. like Isaac Don Levine, and tried to settle the factional disputes in the John Reed Club and *The New Masses*. He reorganized the California John Reed Club at the party's behest in 1933, and in the same year, without waiting for the party's permission and at a time when the party and its press were silent on Hitler's seizure of power, he and Ella Winter set up the first anti-Nazi committee in the United States. To Chicago, Detroit, Boston, and other cities he traveled with Henri Barbusse and Henry Wadsworth Longfellow Dana on behalf of the League Against War and Fascism. He was a key figure at the Midwest conference of the John Reed Clubs. He made it possible for Margaret Bourke-White to get into Russia, the first of the American photographers to be received there. He escorted the insouciant Russian writer Boris Pilnyak to Hollywood in 1931, where the two of them wrote a script for Irving Thalberg.

Freeman was one of the founders of the Theatre Union and wrote captions for Russian movies. He met his friend Sergei Eisenstein when the great Russian film director arrived in America, and he observed the fierce and involved controversy between Eisenstein and Upton Sinclair over the making and the mutilation of Eisenstein's unfinished film "Que Viva Mexico." [5] In 1937 he was again in California—already the mecca for talented radicals still hot for the movement but uneasy about their large salaries—in order to raise money for *The New Masses*.

All of these activities, in addition to an intense personal and social life, kept Freeman and others like him in a whirl of perpetual motion. The thirties turned college professors into union leaders, philosophers into politicians, novelists into agitators, poets into public speakers. Writers felt they could both write and lead the active life because what they thought and did were related—especially during the early days of the united front. The crusade against fascism and war, the sense of being soldiers in the socialist revolution, gave them a spiritual elation and unlimited energy.

Unfortunately for the movement, the radicals fought among themselves as well as against the forces of darkness. Old friends turned on each other in print, introducing into literary discussions the tone and the terminology of Russian party wars.* Controversies of this

---

* The "Communist literary men" in America, as Edmund Wilson noted in 1937, had begun to play "at living in a world in which their group has seized power and can excommunicate and suppress." Wilson protested that "Party

sort sickened Freeman, who preferred to argue over issues, not personalities. But, as he made clear in his introduction to *Proletarian Literature in the United States,* he did not side with those who declared the poet to be above the party. Too often, he wrote, "this noble gesture of neutrality led, in practice, straight to the camp of reaction," [6] and in this 1935 preface, he explicitly rejected the notion of Communism as unchangeable dogma fixed by infallible leaders.

Freeman was struggling not only against social reaction and economic depression and against the antiparty militants; he was also contending "against doubts that were smoldering under the great light of faith," [7] doubts that flickered in the memoirs he began to write in the summer of 1934. Published two years later, *An American Testament* got enthusiastic notices in the bourgeois and party press, and the Workers' Book Shop planned to distribute a large number of copies. A few months after its appearance, however, and just after Freeman had scheduled a lecture tour to speak on his book, Browder summoned him to his office and told him that his book had been condemned in Moscow. As Freeman was to learn shortly, Moscow did not read his book as personal or social history. He had made the criminal mistake of referring to Trotsky as a person—not as a murderer or class enemy. Only the influence of Browder, who was present at the Comintern conference chaired by Georgi Dimitroff and attended by other party notables, prevented a public denunciation.

At Browder's request, the American party was given the responsibility of handling Freeman in its own way. Freeman was told to kill his own book. Although this directive came as a shock, Freeman behaved like a good Communist. He asked the Workers' Book Shop to cancel its large order, which it did. His publishers never discovered why this happened until many years later. Freeman then

---

lines in literature are nonsense! Literature will get along quite well without the interference or guidance of even the most brilliant politician." Not even a world crisis, he declared, justified Louis Kronenberger's contention that social values superseded literary values when the enemy was at the gate. Literature was not, in other words, a weapon. "There is no sense in pursuing a literary career under the impression that one is operating a bombing plane." *The Shores of Light,* pp. 646-50. Wilson was referring to Kronenberger's article "Criticism in Transition," *Partisan Review,* III (Oct. 1936), pp. 5-7.

called off his lecture tour, forbade any reference to *An American Testament* in *The New Masses,* and refused to take any advertising in the magazine for his book. These moves choked off circulation, and a potential best seller sold about 4,000 copies.[8]

Freeman was in a dilemma. The only way he could restore himself to favor, Browder told him, was to be a good Communist. But what did that mean? He had written a well-intentioned book; it had provoked an ominous reaction in high places. He still believed in his revolutionary ideals, but he no longer believed in a Soviet holy land, for by the spring of 1937, the first and second of the Moscow "show" trials had already been held, and many of his old Russian comrades had perished or disappeared. He suspected the trials were rigged. Joshua Kunitz, just back from the Soviet Union, where he had covered the first trial for *The New Masses,* had told him as much. Yet he could understand why the sixteen Bolshevik veterans might be involved in some attempt to overthrow the Stalin government. How else could an opposition remonstrate against a dictatorial one-party state? In his articles, Kunitz had justified the Stalinists, but his account of the crimes of the sixteen defendants was insufficiently vehement for Moscow. The Soviet Government refused the magazine permission to report the second trial, which began in January 1937.

Freeman, then in Mexico as a delegate (with Waldo Frank) to the International Congress of Culture, was much more shaken by the second trial than he had been by the first, because the accusations brought against the new batch of Stalin's victims—their alleged conspiracy to yield Soviet territory to the fascist powers—had obviously been trumped up. When the party cabled him to come home immediately and cover the trial, Freeman refused. The cables kept coming while Freeman stayed in Mexico three or four more weeks. Finally he returned to New York by boat, the slowest way, and by the time he arrived, the trial was over.

Freeman had compromised himself in the eyes of the party, and for the next two years it slowly and inexorably made clear its displeasure. The growing coolness of old associates coincided with personal sorrows that all but overwhelmed him. His father died; his close friend Ernst Toller, a refugee writer from Hitler's Germany, hanged himself; and Alexander Gumberg,* whose support and friendship had always meant so much to him, died shortly after. The Nazi-Soviet pact was still some months away, but already, perhaps beginning with the collapse of the Spanish Republic, the literary Left seemed to be disintegrating. Isidor Schneider, back from Russia, reported that Soviet literature and criticism were on a very low level. The fires of idealism had died down, and men who once poured into the Communist amphitheater now discreetly looked for the exits.

Freeman, knowing the ax would fall sooner or later, waited for the stroke. His hundred-page booklet on Left Wing criticism in the United States reached the galley stage but never was published. V. J. Jerome and Robert Minor found it full of deviations. He had been much too kind to Eastman; he had not mentioned, they said, the $50,000 Eastman got from the British Secret Service. Moreover, he grievously erred in naming Floyd Dell as the first literary critic to predict the Depression instead of naming Stalin. Freeman tore up the galleys. He knew the essay would never be published.

In 1939 Freeman had taken a job with the Soviet pavilion at the New York World's Fair. When the Russian heads of the office were tipped off that his status was precarious, their friendliness changed to coldness and finally to hostility. Very likely their suspicions and the suspicions of Moscow were quickened by gossip about Freeman's alleged disloyalty. He had been summoned to party headquarters and confronted with a recent issue of the Trotskyist organ *The Militant*. On the first page, in a box headed "Rumor" appeared a story that Freeman was getting ready to denounce the Soviet Union and quit the movement. Freeman denied the rumor vigorously, but, on the advice of a top party leader, did not bother to reply to *The Militant*.

Then in the August issue of *The Communist International,* the

* Described by G. F. Kennan "as a middleman in the unfolding pattern of Soviet-American relations," Gumberg's extraordinary career is described in Kennan's *Soviet-American Relations* (Princeton, 1956-8), 2 vols., and in W. A. Williams, *American-Russian Relations, 1781-1947* (N.Y., 1952). According to the latter, Gumberg "played a crucial role in the movement for recognition" (p. 202). Gumberg represented the All-Russian Textile Syndicate in New York and worked closely with Senator Borah and Dwight Morrow in the long campaign for United States recognition of the U.S.S.R. Freeman knew him as a kindly and skeptical friend and adviser.

Comintern spoke in the voice of one P. Dengel, who reprimanded the *Daily Worker* both in New York and London for recommending *An American Testament* to their readers. The vicious role of "the spy Trotsky and his outfit" as fascist agents, Dengel noted, was already well known when Freeman's book appeared, yet throughout Freeman portrayed him sympathetically. His book did "not arouse any hatred for the vile Trotskyite enemies of the working class and the anti-fascist movement"; it was nothing more than "an underhanded defense of the Trotskyites," and yet "two large Communist papers" recommended "this filth to their readers."

Freeman was now out of the movement, assiduously avoided by comrades who still liked him personally but who respected the party ban. The door was not slammed tight. He might restore himself, he was told, by writing acceptable articles for *The New Masses*. But Freeman did not want to return under those or any conditions. He was ready to face the penalties of exclusion, the ostracism by the party and the distrust of the people who never could have understood why a writer should want to join the Left in the first place. The movement had been an international home, a church, a way of life. He had often criticized it to himself and to his friends, but his doubts were the doubts of a believer—quite a different attitude "from the faith of the doubter." [9] While he stayed in the movement, he believed in it without reserve. Despite Stalin's crimes, Russia was still the bastion of socialism besieged by fascist barbarians.

In the months that followed, Freeman sought to retrace his path and to discover the old base from which he had started his "long pursuit" of the socialist vision. Having given seventeen years to the movement, he had been denounced, expelled, and abandoned. But he learned to thank his persecutors for freeing him from an illusion without destroying his socialist vision and for inadvertently restoring him to literature. Thanks to Browder, the American party press did not reprint "the ukase" of his excommunication pronounced in *The Communist*. Freeman never attacked the party in print, which made the anti-Communist literati doubt his sincerity.

Freeman had abandoned politics. Henceforth, if he spoke, it would be through his poetry and fiction. Once "Comrade Freeman," as Kenneth Rexroth observed to Malcolm Cowley, "up until a few years ago the only American who could quote Marx and Racine with equal facility, wrote his best poems about the pain of the loss of friendship and the unreliable nature of uncritical love, and that in the days when he was majordomo of the Proletcult Rampant." [10] After 1939 Freeman was able to write about matters close to his heart without fear of losing himself in what Rexroth called "a maze of class angles."

"You talk as if all history were contemporary history," a French professor remarks to Paul Schuman, the hero of *Never Call Retreat* (1943). Like Schuman, Freeman preferred to apprehend the meaning of "living forms" by "historic analogy." Instead of literally retelling the story of his life, he invented a Viennese scholar of *Kulturgeschichte,* a modern Saint Augustine, through whom he could comment on 5,000 years of human experience as well as his own.

Schuman's childhood and adolescence are spent in Vienna during the brief intellectual and artistic resurgence immediately preceding the assassination at Sarajevo. He is old enough to fight in the last stages of the war, and after he returns to his shattered city, he studies history at the university and thereafter at the Sorbonne, where he writes a dissertation on Condorcet. Back in Vienna, he observes the growing disorders, the mounting power of the Nazis, the dogged sectarianism of the antifascist parties who refuse to join forces against "the brown menace." Schuman, now a professor of history, is well aware of the sinister tendencies, but like so many other Viennese intellectuals, he will take no responsibility for the state of society. Only after his English-born wife is killed in Spain, his father shot down by the Heimwehr, his Communist friends imprisoned, Austria absorbed into the Third Reich, and he himself tortured in a concentration camp does he really become engaged.

Schuman finally escapes with the help of the Underground and ends up in America, a patient of a psychiatrist to whom he relates the story of his life, but the details of Freeman's complicated story, replete with sensational incident and crowded with characters, are less relevant than the reflections of his protagonist on the fascinating variations of Freeman's theme.

The theme is stated in a number of different ways and dramatically reiterated in the action: All revolutions are betrayed but never entirely obliterated; "the letter killeth"; knowledge and power without love can only end in catastrophe; evil is not in the external world but in ourselves; "All men are equal, not in capacity but in value." The articulators or exemplars of these beliefs are Condorcet, a young Communist poet, a fourth-century Christian scribe, and finally Schuman himself.

He is fascinated by the French Revolution, by its swift course from the *Social Contract* to Fouché's police. But he is especially drawn to Condorcet, too republican for the constitutionalists, too indulgent for the Jacobins, a man of no party at last but dedicated to the revolutionary ideals of those who would destroy him. Condorcet, writing his history on the progress of the human spirit while hiding from his Jacobin persecutors becomes the symbol of the poet-revolutionary martyr, dear to Schuman and to Schuman's inventor.

Condorcet's contemporary embodiment is the Communist poet, Kurt, whose execution by the Nazi commandant in the concentration camp is less tragic than his treatment at the hands of his fellow Communists in the prison. Their leader and his idol, a courageous but terrible simplifier, excommunicates him after first warning him to stick to his "nice harmless pastime," and to leave matters of serious import to those who are better qualified. "If you insist on nosing into things you don't understand, which are no concern of yours," the "Commissar" tells the "Poet," "we'll break your head." Kurt appreciates the necessity for discipline, for unswerving obedience to the party, but he is a poet who cannot transfer his hatred of capitalism as a system to its adherents, and much as he loves his comrades in the party, he knows they are fallible men. "Where there is no love," he tells his prison mates before he is beheaded, "there can be no freedom, security, or good life." At first Schuman is skeptical of this gospel, but he finally identifies himself with this hounded innocent.

Schuman's last alter ego is a vividly conceived figment of a dream. Before his incarceration, Schuman is given a mutilated manuscript written in an obscure fourth-century Umbrian dialect. The author is one Eusebius. Schuman never translates the manuscript, but Eusebius invades his dreams in the guise of a Christian revolutionary who once again bears witness to Saint Augustine's comment: "The wicked persecute the good with the blindness of the passion that animates them, while the good pursue the wicked with a wise discretion." It is not the Romans who hound the pure and guileless Eusebius, but the Christian sectarians who adhere to the letter of the church and hate their enemies. Like Condorcet, Eusebius is caught between the Girondists and the Jacobins of the early Christian era, and his eschewing of power and his tolerance are interpreted by his envious colleagues as criminal heresy.

Anyone who reads *Never Call Retreat* in the light of Communist Party history and Freeman's own experiences will have no difficulty detecting pertinent analogies. Change the party labels, change the names of the issues dividing liberals, Communists, and Socialists, Stalinists and Trotskyists, change the terms signifying orthodoxy and deviation, and the episodes he writes about might have occurred in Moscow or New York between 1917 and 1939. At the party's request, Kurt removes from circulation one of his poems no longer in tune with the current party line. Freeman's memoirs are attacked on the same grounds that Eusebius's teachings are assailed by his orthodox comrades: he "portrays the spy Trotsky and his outfit in a sympathetic manner throughout"; he does "not arouse hatred for the vile Trotskyite enemies of the working class"; he attempts "to arouse sympathy for them as people who 'erred.'"

Freeman did not write this parable on dream and reality, contemplation and action, spirit and authority, justice and power, the poet and the commissar as a way of calling attention to his own difficulties, nor could his book by any stretch of the imagination be dismissed as it was by a reviewer in *The New Masses* as "another anti-Red Testament by an ex-Red." [11] His purpose in writing it was to understand, not to blame, to assert mankind's complicity in every earthly tragedy, and to review his own life in the light of history. Far from constituting a break with his past, *Never Call Retreat* was a non-Marxian restatement of the ideals that had first drawn him into the radical movement: the ethic of the prophets, the Sermon on the Mount, the poetry of Dante, Milton, and Blake.

Freeman had made what Charles Péguy called "the second break." Many examples, Péguy wrote, could be found of people who had sacrificed their interests and past associations for the "true" cause. It required courage to make the break, but at least they were sustained by friends and partisans who shared their half of the world. But, if still enamored by the elusive truth, they broke a second time, if they discovered the party they had joined was "absolutely identical with all other parties," vulgar, gross, unjust, false, then they experienced the woe of real solitude. Only a "superbrave man" dared to make this second break.

And yet, the life of an honest man must be an apostasy and a perpetual desertion. The honest man must be a perpetual renegade, the life of an honest man must be a perpetual infidelity. For the man who wishes to remain faithful to truth must make himself continually unfaithful to all the continual, successive, indefatigable renascent errors. And the man who wishes to remain faithful to justice must make himself continually unfaithful to inexhaustibly triumphant injustices.[12]

EIGHTEEN · "THINK BACK ON US"

BY NO MEANS all of the letters sent to Granville Hicks after he announced his resignation from the Communist Party were congratulatory. Some old and tried believers like Henry Wadsworth Longfellow Dana reviled him; Anna Louise Strong, whose faith in the Soviet Union survived the test of the pact and even a subsequent expulsion from the U.S.S.R., scorned his want of faith. "When your wife is reported as seen in suspicious circumstances, do you 'reserve judgment,' or do you say: 'She'll have a good reason, I absolutely trust my wife.' " [1] Other correspondents regretfully banished Hicks to that undiscovered country from whose bourn no fellow traveler returns.

Yet the many letters he received from friends and well-wishers during the autumn of 1939 commending him for his stand encouraged him to feel that he had not stepped "into a void of impotence and loneliness" [2] supposedly awaiting all renegades. Might not this be the historical moment to found an independent Left Wing party and to reconstitute a new non-Communist united front? On October 15, a small group of disenchanted intellectuals met at the house of Max Lerner, among them Richard Rovere, Paul Sweezey, and Robert Lynd, to discuss this possibility,[3] and in the next months Matthew Josephson, I. F. Stone, and Malcolm Cowley were invited to explore "the possibilities of forming a new organization, mainly educational in character, of progressive elements on the left." [4] Hicks, on his part, printed and mailed to a select list of friends some six issues of a private bulletin which he hoped might serve as a clearinghouse for different opinions about the proposed new movement.

The plan foundered, and given the confusion and the uncertainties after the Nazi invasion of Poland, it is not hard to see why. Some writers, like Cowley, simply did not wish to become involved again in political organizations. Others, although contemptuous of the American Communist Party, were not yet prepared to equate Russian Communism with the Third Reich. Animosities between the former Stalinists and the Trotskyists still rankled although both groups, to their mutual discomfort, were inadvertently allied on some points. But the most divisive issue was World War II.

The Marxists of the independent Left diagnosed it as a struggle between imperialist powers and took a strong noninterventionist position. Once again, said Dwight Macdonald, the "war intellectuals" who since 1917 had idealized imperialistic wars when they broke out and debunked them only when they were over, who believed "in the power of verbal formulae to sweeten the ghastliest realities" were off on a moral spree.[5]

Not so, replied the interventionists. Now the declared foes of reactionary and radical isolationists alike, they called for massive resistance to fascism and for all-out aid to the Western powers. MacLeish, Lewis Mumford, and Waldo Frank were among the most fervent advocates of this policy.

Each of these three writers had rubbed shoulders with the party in the early thirties, and each responded violently to the Hitlerian menace, especially after August 1939. MacLeish indicted his own literary generation (not excusing himself) for educating their juniors "to believe that all declarations, all beliefs are fraudulent." His "irresponsibles" were the scholars and the creative artists, made impotent by objectivity and insulated from the political and social realities of their time. Only their science and their craft seemed to matter to them. Mumford extended the indictment of intellectuals and liberals to Americans in general and to the materialistic culture that made them fat and helpless. In *Men Must Act* (1939) and *Faith for the Living* (1940), he outlined a program to resist the spread of fascism: first, nonintercourse with the fascist bloc no matter what the consequences, and second, the "re-fortification of democracy," which entailed the restoration of the family, the return to the land, and "the growth of the person." Waldo Frank's *Chart for Rough Water* (1940) carried on the assault against American materialism, shallow liberalism, and fallible intellectuals. In the last category, Granville Hicks, Sherwood Anderson, Edmund Wilson, and John Dos Passos served as the horrid examples. Frank called for a return to the "Great Tradition," the awareness of the divine in man.[6]

The repudiation of Communism, the U.S.S.R., and the pact by former party members and sympathizers (the retreat from Moscow by the intellectuals seemed to be motorized) embarrassed the party stalwarts but hardly left them speechless. The class origins and personal make-up of the "migratory intellectuals," as Mike Gold called them three years before the pact, made them putative renegades. They had been passing in and out of the movement since the twenties, offering their "pompous and formal schemes" to the practical doers, worrying about the Communist line, but ignoring the bread-and-butter realities. Never before, however, not even after the Moscow trials, had the "coffee-pot" intellectuals departed in such wholesale numbers.[7]

In order to explain the widespread disaffection and to bolster the faith of the wavering, party spokesmen examined the motives of Hicks, Cowley, Frank, Ralph Bates, MacLeish, Mumford, and other "laureates of betrayal." How could former allies end up as slanderers of the U.S.S.R.? Why did they allow themselves to become the "ideological Fifth Column for capitalism"?

Because, said V. J. Jerome, these "pseudo Marxists," never really understood the working-class movement to which they came only a few years before "like arrogant slummers." They misconstrued the meaning of "the Democratic Front tactic" and tied the Communist Party to the tail of the Democratic kite instead of correctly interpreting the Popular Front as a maneuver of the proletariat to build up its strength until the time when it would take the offensive under party guidance. Open fascism they recognized, but not the fascist sword of the bourgeoisie concealed in the scabbard of democracy. To the MacLeishes and the Mumfords, fascism was not degenerate capitalism, but a force at once hostile to the ruling class and the proletariat. This delusion prevented them from seeing the pact in its true light, as a victory for peace, the removal of one sixth of the globe from the imperialistic war, the defeat of the Chamberlain-Hitler "complot."

Marx demonstrated, Jerome asserted, how "conceptive ideologues" throughout history had functioned as the apologists for the *status quo* and how they invariably failed in crises. Fortunately, in 1939 the majority were not Hamlets or Don Quixotes, philosophical idealists, and hirelings of capitalism. For every Granville Hicks, Ralph Bates, or Vincent Sheean, there were "hundreds of decent, modest intellectuals who stand guard at their posts despite reaction's offensive." [8]

Notwithstanding their display of official confidence, *The New Masses'* critics kept up a fierce fusillade against the growing number of defectors they variously categorized as "warmongers," "deserters," "fascist mystics," "Utopians," "navel-contemplators," "canting apologists" for "Big Business" and "the British Empire," "authors of surrender," "half-baked eclectics," "intellectual jingoists," "Imperialists," and "irrationals." [9] For ideological ammunition, they resurrected Randolph Bourne, whose name had not occurred to them during the period of collective security but whose attacks against the false "clerks" of 1917 and particularly his castigation of John Dewey now seemed providentially apropos. The League of American Writers presented the Randolph Bourne Memorial Award to the outspokenly isolationist and anti-British Theodore Dreiser in 1941. Samuel Sillen confronted the "penitents" engaged in "the weekly struggle with the specter of Karl Marx" with their rejected convictions,[10] and V. J. Jerome savagely ridiculed the crusaders for the preservation of capitalist civilization:

Let us sing the glory of "civilization as we know it"! The joyous leisure of men without jobs, the inner harmonies of chain-gangs, the essential dignity of prostitution, the superb solitude of the untended sick, the twilight in the eyes of workers discarded at forty, the shining wings of youth beating against the barred doors of factories and offices, the infinite Wanderlust of the evicted, the rhythmic machine-gunning of strikers, the spiritual ecstasy of lynchers, the flaming beauty of war! . . .[11]

None of these pamphleteers, however, could match the veteran of a dozen literary campaigns, Michael Gold, in spirited invective.

Throughout the people's-front period, his proletarianism had gone out of fashion, and Gold hardly figured in the writers' congresses of 1937 and 1939. In the latter congress, even his old antagonist Thornton Wilder took precedence over him at one of the public meetings. But with the collapse of the people's front and the desertion of the liberals, whose sincerity had never impressed him very deeply, Gold emerged again to defend the slandered revolution.

In a series of articles which first appeared in the *Daily Worker* and then shortly after were published in expanded form as *The Hollow Men* (1941), Gold laid into the renegades who had turned to the party in the early years of the Depression and who had then befouled "the great tradition." Gold's explanations for the "betrayal" were predictably orthodox, but he brought to his task a fervor and a violent humor that made the diatribes of Jerome and Sillen seem tepid by contrast. He had a threefold purpose in writing what Malcolm Cowley was to call "The Michael Golden Legend": [12] 1) To justify the 1930's as one of the greatest creative decades in the history of American culture; 2) to demonstrate that this artistic burgeoning was largely inspired by the Communist Party, which had disclosed to the demoralized artists and intellectuals the class nature of their morally and financially bankrupt society; 3) to show that the "cynicism," "climberism," and "mental prostitution" of bourgeois intellectuals really sprang from their hatred of "the People."

Gold wrote as a passionate partisan, not as an objective historian; his pamphlet was an angry reminder to those ex-radicals, eagerly repudiating their former party connections, that they, too, had once seen Depression America through Communist eyes. He was most effective when he relied on ridicule, when he described Edmund Wilson ascending "the proletarian 'band wagon' with the arrogance of a myopic, high-bosomed Beacon Hill matron entering a common street-car," or farcically presented the Yankee *Blut und Boden* program demanded by "Mahatma Lewis Mumford" to compete with the yahoo religion of the Nazis. He was weakest when he relied on logic, when he accused the "war intellectuals" of being capitalist lackeys and of distorting history. He fatally invalidated his polemic by neglecting to mention the Nazi-Soviet pact or the Finnish invasion and by brushing away the Moscow trials. [13]

THE UNWELCOME PRODIGALS

Had the prodigals, former Communists and fellow travelers, been readmitted to "the human race" without recrimination or discrimination, their political and social adjustment might have proceeded more smoothly than it did. Unfortunately for them, they had to bear not only the harsh but expected retaliations from the party spokesmen but also the jibes of the Left-opposition splinter groups and the gloating "I-told-you-so's" of the radical travelers who had gotten off the Red Special several stations before. The former Communist could expect "a reception committee of assorted gloaters and skeptics ready to present him with the key to the doghouse." [14] Bygones, he discovered, were never bygones. His sincerity might be questioned if he publicly testified to a change of heart; his anti-Communism might be suspect if he remained silent.

> Once you've held a belief like communism and given it up [an agonized apostate says in Granville Hicks's novel *Only One Storm*], there's no hope for you. If you were right before, people say, you must be wrong now. And if you're wrong before, they say, the chances are you're wrong again. I can't even have the satisfaction of explaining my mistakes, for I never admitted publicly that I was a communist. In the eyes of the world I'm the silliest thing there is—a fellow-traveler who couldn't stand the pace.[15]

James T. Farrell might be considered one of the most outspoken members, if not the chairman, of the "reception committee" which greeted the belated train-jumpers. At this time he fully shared what he called Trotsky's "capacity for contempt," and, like Trotsky again, "knew how to despise these liberal intellectuals who behind a set of pretentious gestures, invariably reflected the hypocrisy of bourgeois public opinion." The former fellow travelers had "not satisfactorily explained their sudden change of mind," and he brushed aside John Chamberlain's invitation to the prepact and postpact disavowers of the Kremlin to "call off the dogs" and work together.

There were no "sincerometers," said Farrell, paraphrasing Lenin, to gauge a man's personal sincerity, but he offered some "objective reasons why many of the fellow-travelers went off the reservation." Since their largely bourgeois audience could no longer swallow the party line after the Hitler-Stalin agreement, practical considerations forced them to shift their allegiance. "It was good for their careers." But it took "a historic earthquake" to arouse them from their ideological stupor, not the Trials or the other crimes of Stalin, and Farrell detected in their "intellectually shabby" explanations and extenuations traces of the same Stalinism they had ostensibly rejected. "No," he concluded, "these intellectuals have not assimilated their 'mistakes.' One seeks in vain for an analytical and principled statement which will reveal why they lacked foresight and then suddenly possessed such remarkable hindsight." [16]

Leon Dennen, who came into the movement before Farrell did and who broke with the party after the Moscow trials, was as stoutly anti-Communist as Farrell, but somewhat more detached in his analysis of the radical intelligentsia. The behavior of the intellectuals throughout the thirties, Dennen declared, demonstrated once again "that in time of crisis the intellectual is the first one to become frightened . . . and to crumble morally." The trait all intellectuals have in common is the tendency to vacillate, to change sides. Dennen distinguished "the sincere and able practitioners" who created a powerful social literature during the thirties from the "Stalinist hacks" or from the fellow travelers seeking "the romance of the revolution without any of its responsibilities," but both the honest and the phony groped in a liberal fog. Ever since the pact, the liberal literati, especially the recently disillusioned, continued to berate one another with "literary and philosophical curse-words." Not one had a "definite socio-political philosophy" or had in mind an organized group through which his vague proposals could be realized. Few dared to take a clear stand on the war.[17]

Like John Chamberlain, Dennen wanted all honest socialists, no matter what their previous allegiances, to join in a genuine united front, yet his own paper, *The New Leader,* was as ungracious as *Time* in its comments about Malcolm Cowley. When Cowley announced his withdrawal from the League of American Writers after the failure of his plan to wrest control of the organization from the Communist faction, it referred to him as "that political axe-wielder."

His resignation, it said, vindicated "the critics of red totalitarianism and all its Stalinoid fronts" but it did not eliminate "the memory of his facile vituperation. . . ." [18]

Time, which had gaily reported "The Revolt of the Intellectuals" in January 1941, carried one year later a story about a new volume of poems, *The Dry Season,* by Malcolm Cowley. According to *Time,* Cowley, recently appointed chief information analyst of the Office of Facts and Figures, had been accused by Congressman Martin Dies of having "seventy-two connections . . . with the Communist Party and its front organizations." The review (which appeared in the political news section of the magazine, not the literary) quoted snatches of a few revolutionary poems Cowley had written in the early thirties in such a way as to make them seem like the recent pronouncements of a devout Communist. Cowley's reply to *Time* placed the poems in their proper context and suggested that the country found "graver dangers" than a *Putsch* "by a determined rabble of poets and literary editors."

Time cheerfully conceded that Cowley was "no danger to his country," but the story cost him his job. Having undergone the ordeal experienced by many politically tainted intellectuals—the combined attack by Communists and congressmen—Cowley decided the less he had to do with governmental agencies the better.[19]

Joseph Freeman, dead to his friends in the Communist world, was also having employment problems about the same time Cowley was forced to resign from the O.F.F. He had just turned in the manuscript of *Never Call Retreat* to his publishers and was looking around for work when the Luce publications asked him to write a 5,000-word piece on twenty-five years of the Russian revolution. Two months later, he turned in a 30,000-word article which Henry Luce liked so much that he had it printed as a separate pamphlet and mailed to every congressman, state governor, and top military and business leader of the country. On the strength of this historical sketch, Joseph Davies, the United States Ambassador to Russia, offered him a position as his special assistant, which Freeman refused, but he welcomed the invitation to work for Time, Inc. Because of his Communist background, however, he had to be screened, and the "screener" happened to be Whittaker Chambers, whom Freeman had first met in 1928 and who joined him on the staff of *The New Masses* in 1931.

Eased from his editorial job on the *Daily Worker,* Chambers had dropped out of the party although still technically a member. His story "You Can Make Out Their Voices," published in the March 1931 issue of *The New Masses,* became almost overnight a Communist classic, and by the time International Publishers issued it as a pamphlet (*Can You Hear Their Voices*) and Hallie Flanagan produced it as a play at Vassar College, Chambers had become a literary proletarian luminary. This story and three others, all about Communists, were highly praised by that eminent Russian authority of American literature, the rosy-cheeked A. Elistratova.

Chambers's fiction also induced Joseph Freeman and Michael Gold to offer him an editorship on *The New Masses* in place of Walt Carmon, and after straightening out his differences with the party, Chambers took over his editorial duties. But only for a short time. He "disappeared" in the summer of 1932 after editing a few issues of the magazine. Freeman, on leave during this interim, simply assumed that Chambers "had disappeared in a fit of bohemianism."

The interview occurred after this long interval. Chambers, grim and unfriendly, bore little resemblance to the young poet who had improvised Whitmanesque chants in the alcoholic twenties. He made no mention of the days he later referred to briefly in *Witness* and made it plain that he did not want Freeman as an associate.[20] Needless to say, Freeman flunked his "screen test."

Not all of the returning "prodigals" had to run the gauntlet of criticism. Most of them, after all, had only loaned their names and occasionally their pens to the Cause and never considered themselves under party discipline. As sympathizers they could enjoy all of the psychic satisfactions of belonging to a revolutionary movement without sharing its hazards.[21] When the party went bankrupt, only the long-term depositors lost their life savings, not the transients, with their small checking accounts. The relatively small number of writers and intellectuals who had impulsively joined the party in the mid-thirties and as impulsively resigned from it a year or two later might never have been reminded of their careless gesture had not the congressional archaeologists brought it to their attention in the early fifties.

"SUCH A RESULT SO SOON
AND FROM SUCH A BEGINNING!"

The Communist literary movement ceased to have much importance after 1940 even though the party recovered some of its lost prestige with the beginning of the German offensive against the Soviet Union on June 22, 1941.

Many members of the League of American Writers had resigned, unable to stomach either the party's pacifist line of the preinvasion period or the superpatriotic fervor with which it supported the Soviet-American alliance.[22] Some of the familiar names responded to the call for the fourth writers' congress, held in New York from June 6 to 8, 1941, several weeks before Hitler's invasion of Russia again compelled an abrupt about-face in the line, but few celebrities attended what turned out to be the last League convention.

Theodore Dreiser came, of course, and Richard Wright, who brought news to the congress of "the dogged reluctance" of the American Negroes to believe in F.D.R.'s propaganda. Dashiell Hammett spoke sarcastically of "our national defense effort against civil liberties." Donald Ogden Stewart played some variations on a theme of writers dashing madly toward "Nearest Exits," and Genevieve Taggard once more summoned the ghosts of Emerson, Thoreau, Whitman, Garrison, Phillips, and Mark Twain to combat "the sweet and flaccid sentiments of our present pro-war columnists." But the journalists, Hollywood writers, and the scattering of novelists and poets who represented "literature" at the congress already seemed a more peripheral and less-gifted group than the previous membership. The demise of the League in the fall of 1942 provoked slight comment, and no comparable organization arose in its place.[23]

The literary spokesmen of the party remained officially optimistic during and immediately after the war years. None of *The New Masses* editors conceded in print that the literary movement had been injured by the mass of defections. It was "good riddance to bad rubbish" so far as they were concerned, and they predicted the emergence of a new and more dedicated group of "proletarian writers." In the meantime, the party relied on Howard Fast and the Hollywood contingent of screen writers and novelists to carry on the revolutionary literary tradition: Dalton Trumbo, whose anti-war novel, *Johnny Got His Gun* (1939), was serialized in the *Daily Worker* in "The Yanks Are Not Coming" period; John Howard Lawson, now a resolute Marxist, who in 1934 had deprecated his failure "to serve the revolutionary working class either in my writing or my practical activity"; [24] and Albert Maltz, who suffered a serious ideological collapse but was nursed back to regularity by solicitous comrades.

Maltz's controversial answer to the question "What Shall We Ask of Writers?" had been prompted by a thoughtful and almost wistful article written by Isidor Schneider some months before. Throughout the summer of 1943, editors and friends of *The New Masses* had been discussing the work of the magazine, and reluctantly, according to Schneider, had agreed on the following points: 1) "no formulated Marxist criticism" existed comparable to *Capital* or *State and Revolution;* 2) "the social criticism of the Left" during the middle thirties, "its most influential period," did not come directly from Marxist sources, but from bourgeois critics like Taine, Brandes, and Parrington; 3) in their social criticism, overenthusiastic "critics of the Left" resorted to moral epithets like "escapist," "ivory tower," and "decadent," thereby diverting Left criticism "from its main direction into culturally reactionary by-paths." These clichés prevented them from appreciating "the brilliant work of Kenneth Burke" as well as the "vast contributions of James Joyce."

Schneider did not say in so many words that writers should be writers first, not labor organizers or newspaper propagandists. The writer, he said, who withdrew completely from the labor movement injured himself as grievously as the one who obliterated "his literary self in the role of organizer"; the work of Reed, Myakovsky, and Ehrenburg proved that reporting could reach "classic stature." But writers weakened their novels or poems or plays when they sacrificed reality to political expediencies. "No writer," he declared, "need worry about being politically correct if his work is faithful to reality." [25]

Maltz welcomed this "frank and earnest article" (which after all merely repeated what Freeman, Gold, and Kunitz had been saying off and on for years) and then somewhat guardedly but with unmistakable feeling proceeded to illustrate his own notions of leftist shallowness produced *"by the intellectual atmosphere of the left wing."*

For example, the slogan "art is a weapon" had been vulgarized to the point where its original meaning—art reflects or attacks social values—had been lost. In practice, it had come to mean "that *unless* art is a weapon like a leaflet, serving immediate political ends, necessities, and programs, it is worthless or escapist or vicious." Why, he asked, was Lillian Hellman's play *Watch on the Rhine* attacked in *The New Masses* in 1940 and praised as a film in 1942? Because, he answered, events had occurred during the interval "calling for a different political program." Citing Engels as his source, Maltz criticized the practice of making the "canons of immediate utility . . . the primary values of judgment." Even politically unreliable writers like Steinbeck or Farrell had made significant contributions to the Left movement. He saw no reason why they should be judged by the committees they belonged to. "There is not always a commanding relationship between the way an artist votes and any particular work he writes." Nor did a writer's political retrogression, Maltz went on to say, automatically signify a degeneration of his talent. He concluded with a contemptuous dismissal of the writer who would misuse his art and betray the "great humanistic tradition of culture" by serving "an immediate political purpose." [26]

Maltz's article bristled with heresies. Had he written it during the united-front days of 1935-39 or in the war years of Soviet-American co-operation, when everybody from Monsignor Fulton Sheen to Captain Eddie Rickenbacker had kind words for the Stalin regime,[27] it might have slipped by without official censure. It appeared, however, well after the famous Jacques Duclos letter of May 1945 presaged the end of peaceful collaboration between the United States and the Soviet Union and the bankruptcy of "Browderism." William Z. Foster now headed a reorganized Communist Party, which

Browder had dissolved in May 1944 and had reconstituted as the Communist Political Association. A week before the publication of Maltz's article, Browder, once hailed as "the beloved leader of our movement," was expelled from the party as a "social imperialist." Maltz, in his innocence, had expressed his scorn for a historian he knew of who after reading the Duclos letter felt obliged "to revise completely the book he was engaged upon." But Howard Fast did not agree with him, nor did Joseph North, Alvah Bessie, Mike Gold, John Howard Lawson, Samuel Sillen, or William Z. Foster, each of whom sharply reprimanded Maltz for his dangerous "revisionism."

Maltz's article, it seemed, was "liquidationist," "anti-progressive," and "reactionary." In effect, he argued for a split between the citizen and the writer in saying that art and politics don't mix. Were this true, the Communist Party, the most political of movements, would be the most detrimental to the writer. In fact his description of the Duclos letter as another "headline," and his plea that writers place human experience above politics, simply invited the writer to dispense with the party altogether. Most reprehensible to his critics was Maltz's conception of the self-contained writer, who irrespective of his social views might produce a work of true literary value.[28]

These counterarguments were advanced firmly and sometimes harshly by fellow writers, but no one was more anti-Maltzian than Maltz himself when he acknowledged his errors a few months later in the party press.

His "one-sided, non-dialectical approach," he confessed, had been revisionist in the worst sense. "For what is revisionism?" he asked. "It is distorted Marxism, turning half-truths into total untruths, splitting ideology from its class base, denying the existence of the class struggle in society, converting Marxism from a science of society and struggle into apologetics for monopoly exploitation." Because of his mistaken zeal, the enemies of the Left had once more been able to raise the cry of "artists in uniform." Clearly his "fundamental errors" indicated a "failure to break deeply old habits of thought." He had "severed the organic connection between art and ideology." He should have explained, as the histories of Céline, Farrell, and Dos Passos did so well, how "a poisoned ideology and an increasingly sick soul can sap the talent and wreck the living fibre of a man's work." Although he thought his article better suited to the slanderous social-democratic *New Leader* than to *The New Masses,* he saw at least one merit in its publication: the intense answers it provoked marked a return to sound Marxist principles, which under the mis-leadership of Browder had been abandoned. Unable to attend a *New Masses* symposium on the subject of "Art As a Weapon," at which his mistaken ideas were once again dissected, he sent a mes-sage of congratulation from California.[29]

Foster, who spoke at the symposium, had already pronounced the last words on the Maltz case in *The New Masses.* The evil genius, he said, was really Browder. Just as his "imperialistic theories" set the party "to tailing after the capitalists in the field of politics," so Maltz accepted the "bourgeois propaganda to the effect that art is 'free' and has nothing to do with the class struggle." His views, said Foster, "happily being corrected by Maltz himself," would "make the artist merely an appendage and servant of the decadent capitalist system and its sterile art." Of course the party did not want to "regi-ment the artists," but Maltz's incorrect assumptions "had to be discussed with all the sharpness necessary to achieve theoretical clarity." [30]

If Foster's tone was benevolent, his words indicated plainly enough what the party expected from its artists. Isidor Schneider notwith-standing, political correctness was more important than being "faith-ful to reality." The novelist and Spanish Civil War veteran Alvah Bessie expressed Foster's mind faithfully when he told Maltz: "We need writers who will joyfully impose upon themselves the discipline of understanding and acting upon working-class-theory." Fosterism in 1946 doomed any hopes that Schneider and other *New Masses* editors may have entertained about the liberalizing of Left culture. "Political tactics" *were* elevated "into political principles," and the "emergency mindedness and crude political determinism of the past," deprecated by Schneider, once again pervaded Left criticism.[31]

Between the ouster of Browder and the Khrushchev "revelations" in 1956, the party rode herd on its dwindling corps of writers, as Howard Fast luridly described it in *The Naked God,* but Com-munism as a cultural movement continued to slacken.

Mainstream, a literary quarterly giving its "allegiance to the Marxist science of history, culture, and human progress," [32] began bravely in the winter of 1947 and suspended publication after four issues. *The New Masses,* which had changed its format and refurbished its staff in 1946, folded in January 1948. The successor to both, *Masses & Mainstream,* came out in March 1948 as a monthly. It is still in existence, but its writers are virtually unnoticed, its circulation under 6,000. Only its readers know of the Left Wing books it reviews, books published by obscure firms and unjustly ignored by the bourgeois press.

Many were asking with Howard Fast in 1949: "Where are the great ones of the 'thirties, the whole school of talented progressive writers who arose out of the unemployed struggles led by the Communist Party . . . ?" [33] Most of them were still alive, but they were dead to the movement.

A BACKWARD GLANCE

The Communists longingly looked back to the thirties as the time when Left literature counted for something, when writers and artists willingly collaborated with the party and the working class. They predicted with more vehemence than conviction another proletarian renaissance after the conclusion of the war. Most of their former allies, however, had renounced the old dreams of revolution and by 1940 were already beginning to take stock of themselves and the revolutionary cause they had resolutely or tentatively supported. What happened to American intellectual life in the thirties, Granville Hicks wrote in 1943, "already seems mysterious, even to many who were party members." [34]

Between "Black Thursday," 1929, and the Russian-German pact almost ten years later, the mood of the literary Left had passed from angry elation to disillusionment. Writers who once had marched in May Day parades, picketed department stores, and bled inwardly (and sometimes outwardly) for Spain now wondered why they had given themselves so impetuously to an idea. How could they have been so certain of capitalism's doom? Why had they rapturously identified themselves with the "toiling masses" and thrilled when they met real "workers"? What had led them to expect a dazzling explosion of proletarian culture? Why had Russia become for so many of them the holy land?

Some of those who disparaged their recent enthusiasm or who publicly lamented their gullibility at being "taken in" by the Communists or led astray by ideological chimeras either forgot or chose to ignore the by no means reprehensible motives which first attracted most of them to the party. They did not come into the movement because they were broke or because publishing houses were failing. They became radicals because they thought the economic system had gone kaput, because they saw too many hungry and desperate people, and because men and ideas they detested seemed in the ascendant. Marxism offered a convincing explanation why these conditions obtained as well as a program for changing the world; the party satisfied their latent religiosity and made them feel useful.

The writer who joined the Communist Party, who believed in its doctrines, or who associated in some manner with Communist-controlled organizations was not necessarily simple-minded, easily beguiled, or unworldly. Not every radical writer was neurotic or hungering for a secular religion or on the make. Obviously, many of the intellectuals who went left did so out of some deep-seated personal need; happy, "adjusted" people usually don't join political parties whose acknowledged purpose is the destruction of the old social system and the formation of a new one. But not all literary Communists or fellow travelers were maladjusted by any means, nor did they regard the support of the Left as a violent or a desperate act.

To see the Communist movement "simply as the sum total of the pathologies of its members," or to call the intellectuals' "real revulsion from real lacks in our life a flight from reality," Leslie Fiedler has rightly observed, "is utterly misleading." [35]

The Depression *and* the Communist Party, it has been argued, gave focus to the unformulated radicalism of the 1930's and influenced, directly or indirectly, almost every American writer of any importance. And according to Lionel Trilling, the Left literary movement gave "a large and important part of the intellectual middle class . . . 'something to live for,' a point of view, an object for contempt, a direction for anger, a code of excited humanitarianism" which could not be "wholly reprobated." Influence of this kind is hard to measure, but even if the literary impress of Communism was not so extensive or so labyrinthine as some former Communists would have it, it was certainly considerable.[36]

The Communist Party cannot take sole credit for the W.P.A. writers' projects, although Communists undoubtedly had a great deal to do with the tone and content of some of the writing published under W.P.A. auspices.[37] If it was not alone responsible for the vigorous Left Wing theater which stirred New York audiences in the thirties, it is hard to imagine this theater apart from such names as Clifford Odets, Alfred Hayes, Albert Maltz, George Sklar, Irwin Shaw, Paul Peters, John Howard Lawson, Harold Clurman, Herbert Biberman, Michael Blankfort, Mark Blitzstein, Sidney Howard, and others, all friends or members of the party at one time or another. By no means all of the realistic novels published during the thirties were inspired by Communism, yet its doctrines contributed to the prevailing radical spirit which lifted many writers out of their small and mean preoccupations and lent some dignity to even the most amateurish of literary productions.

But if politics and social questions agitated the literary mind in a wholesome sense and "drew the literary imagination closer to social reality," they tended under party influence to become ends in themselves and to distract the younger writers in particular from equally important aesthetic considerations. What started out as a liberating doctrine developed into a constricting one as dream hardened into dogma and the new and the idiosyncratic into ritual. Politics in itself, as Philip Rahv wrote in 1939, is neither good nor bad for the writer. "The real question is more specific: what is the artist actually doing in politics? What is he *doing with it* and what is it *doing to him?* How does his political faith affect him as a craftsman, what influence does it exercise on the moral qualities and on the sensibility of his work?"[38]

The strongest writers of the thirties used politics and were not used by it. The party could not have dictated to a Dos Passos, a Hemingway, a Lewis, a Dreiser, a Steinbeck, a Wolfe even if it had tried to do so. But the Left writer, in and out of the party, faced something more insidious than party pressure: his own compulsion to subordinate the problems of his craft and deeply felt intellectual concerns to political policy. He willingly enrolled or inadvertently found himself in the corps of literary shock troops. He attended conventions and wrote resounding manifestoes and signed petitions and protests. He became a spokesman or a partisan in the literary wars, and he accommodated himself too easily to the Philistinism of the party.

The Communist writer under party discipline was expected to take on the literary assignments that would be most immediately beneficial to the revolutionary cause. The primary needs of the party were not poems or novels or critical essays; first and foremost, the party needed journalists for its press. And so, inadvertently, it became a devourer of talent (as militant parties or churches often become), transforming would-be poets and historians and novelists into producers of journalistic ephemera. Those who had acquired a stock of intellectual capital before enlisting as literary shock troops survived the ordeal better than did those who entered the movement without ever having undergone the apprenticeship of study and reflection, but even they did not escape unscathed. Party work, however inspiring it may have been in many respects, was hardly conducive to literary creation or careful scholarship. But because the party inspired selfless devotion and because the Communist vision made personal ambition seem mean and inconsequential, dedicated revolutionaries quite willingly sacrificed their artistic ambitions for the good of humanity. It is surely no accident that, with a few important exceptions, most of the enduring "proletarian" or radical literature was written by fellow travelers not involved in party journalism or by former party members, who, rid of their multitudinous duties, could at last give themselves to literature.

This is not to say that writers ought to have remained politically autonomous, although some of them might have done better work if they had. Nor was the sin of the Left writer, if you can call it such, to think politically. They impoverished themselves not because they were disgusted with capitalism or because they damned social iniquity, but because they were unable or forbidden to enter into the world of their adversaries and retain what F. Scott Fitzgerald called the "double vision," the "ability to hold two opposed ideas in the mind, at the same time, and still retain the ability to function."

The literary "giants" glorified by the party after it decided officially to graft the twig of Marxian revolution on the Washington Elm and the Charter Oak—Whitman, Emerson, Thoreau, and Mark Twain, among others—retained this "double vision." Political and social issues touched them deeply, but they were seldom beguiled into making foolish public statements, and, what is more important, they did not stoop to attacking their fellow writers who disagreed with them.

One of the saddest aspects of the thirties was the willingness of so many writers not only to submit to the chastisements or admonishings of their political mentors but to assist them in whipping other writers. The writers who condoned Stalin's "liquidations" or who conducted their own trials and heresy hunts were shortly to be tried and symbolically murdered by American inquisitors.

That was the prediction of the friend and mentor of Jack Reed, the wise old Indian fighter, poet, lawyer, and satirist Colonel Charles Erskine Scott Wood, who, rebuked by Earl Browder and the *Daily Worker* for allowing his name to appear on the Trotsky Defense Committee,[39] read them a lecture on the imprudence of American Communists brushing aside constitutional safeguards. "You may need them sometime," he warned them. Trotsky might be guilty, but as yet he had not been proved so; he had not yet received "his day in court."

"Shall be confronted with the witnesses against him." Is that plain? Can you really comprehend its meaning? It is not schoolboy oratory. It is not only our own "Supreme Law." It is the crystallization of the thought of centuries, crystallized in revolutionary combat with tyrants and autocratic governments, and not to be lightly erased to suit the convenience of Moscow and the emotions of the young American acolytes. Please use your brains.

Wood could write these words in 1936 when he was still the warm supporter of Russia and what he called "the Russian idea of economic equality," but he did not regard "the Stalin government as *Russia,* nor as the sole repository of the Russian idea." That, he said, would "live long after Stalin and Trotsky are gone. I do not regard the

Russian government as infallible and not to be questioned. . . ."
He would have approved the remark Proudhon made to Marx in
1846: "Because we stand in the van of a new movement, let us not
act like apostles of a new religion, even if it be a religion of logic,
a religion of reason." [40]

The party of Marx disregarded this suggestion as completely as
the master himself, and although the overwhelming majority of its
priesthood and laity did not commit acts of treason in the McCarthy
sense of the word, they did in Julien Benda's sense: that is to say,
they "divinized politics," organized "political hatreds," put party
ahead of art, and yielded themselves to historical tendency. [41]

During and after the war years, the thirties came to be looked
upon by many men and women who had lived through them as a
time of "smelly orthodoxies" when the intellectuals took refuge in
closed systems of belief. The "irresponsible" twenties looked much
better after ten years of intense social consciousness, and, as Granville Hicks predicted, the abandoned ivory towers began to be re-
claimed. With the cold war and the crusade of Senator McCarthy,
the books and issues of the thirties were considered dangerous as
well as dated. The official exhumations of the Red Decade and the
memoirs of former Communists (some of them as doctrinaire in their
anti-Communism as they had been when they ferreted out class
enemies for the party) bathed the decade in a lurid light.

In their excavations of the radical past, the historians have dug
up little but fragments and ruins. Yet surely a movement which
involved so many intelligent and generous men and women cannot
be barren of significance. Communism, it has been said, contributed
nothing of permanent value to American literature; but even if the
poems, plays, novels, criticism, and reportage composed under party
sponsorship or written by writers whose social sympathies had been
quickened by party agitation were worthless (which is simply not
true), no writer who lived through the revolutionary interlude either
as advocate or critic remained unaffected. If his agonizing over the
working class, his debates over the nature of art and politics, his
temptations, his doubts, despairs, ecstasies, meant little to Browder
or Foster (one influential trade-union leader was worth more to

them than five dozen writers), they were of immense importance to the writer himself. The strong impact of Communism's program upon even those writers who opposed it must be reckoned with. So must the vitalizing influence of the Left Wing intellectuals who stirred up controversies, discovered new novelists and playwrights, opened up hitherto neglected areas of American life, and broke down the barriers that had isolated many writers from the great issues of their times.

We who precariously survive in the sixties can regret their inadequacies and failures, their romanticism, their capacity for self-deception, their shrillness, their self-righteousness. It is less easy to scorn their efforts, however blundering and ineffective, to change the world.

A NOTE ON SOURCES · NOTES · INDEX

A NOTE ON SOURCES

In preparing this volume, I have relied upon the following sources of information:

1) Secondary material: histories, biographies, and articles dealing with the period between 1912 and 1946. These works are cited in the notes.

2) A number of autobiographies or memoirs, some of them unpublished, of men and women who have recorded their part in some of the episodes I take up in this book. Mr. Joseph Freeman has kindly turned over to me some unpublished sections of his *An American Testament,* a book which I have drawn on extensively. Mr. Max Eastman has kindly allowed me to see the soon-to-be-published continuation of his autobiography. His working title is "Journey Through an Epoch." I have shortened it in my notes to "Journey."

3) Radical, liberal, and conservative magazines and newspapers. I am particularly indebted to Mr. Jack Conroy for loaning me samples of his fine collection of proletarian literary magazines. Mr. Granville Hicks, Mr. Leon Dennen, and Mr. B. C. Hagglund have also allowed me to consult some of the rare "little magazines" in their private collections.

4) Letters and memoranda in special library collections or in the possession of individual owners. The most important for my purposes were a file of correspondence addressed to Mr. Malcolm Cowley, the V. F. Calverton papers, the Upton Sinclair papers, the Randolph Bourne papers, a collection of letters owned by Mr. Granville Hicks, and a sequence of letters written by Mr. John Dos Passos.

5) Letters written to me by some of the chief participants of my story. The most numerous and valuable were the letters of Mr. Joseph Freeman, a brilliant interpreter of these years.

6) Pamphlets, mimeographed minutes of meetings, and published and unpublished reports of writers' congresses.

7) Personal interviews with a good many of the writers who played major or minor roles in the Left literary movement.

Every quotation is documented in the notes, but I have often placed the number at the end of a paragraph and summarized the citations in paragraphs. The notes could also be described in some cases as extended commentary on the ideas, issues, and events discussed in the body of the text.

NOTES

PART ONE · PATTERNS OF REBELLION

1. The first quotation in the paragraph is from William Phillips, "The Intellectuals' Tradition," in *The Partisan Reader,* ed. by W. Phillips and P. Rahv (N. Y., 1946), pp. 489-90; the second is Van Wyck Brooks quoting Alfred Stieglitz. Brooks added that American literary movements, unlike those in England and the Continent, move back and forth and never incorporate what has already been accomplished. "What constitutes a generation in literature is, no doubt, the emergence and the dominance of one writer, of two or three writers perhaps powerful enough to impose their ideas upon the mass." We do not have these great writers, Brooks said, and we lack the wisdom to discern them. "Nothing takes root or germinates in our literary soil." *F,* IV (Nov. 9, 1921), p. 214.

2. Perry Miller, *The Transcendentalists: An Anthology* (Cambridge, Mass., 1950), p. 10.

CHAPTER ONE • THE REBELS

1. *L*, IV (March 1921), p. 8.
2. Orrick Johns, *Time of Our Lives: The Story of My Father and Myself* (N. Y., 1937), pp. 128-29.
3. Art Young, *On My Way* (N. Y., 1928), p. 178.
4. The quotations from Untermeyer, Eastman, and Oppenheim are all taken from *The Young Idea* (N. Y., 1917), compiled and edited by Lloyd R. Morris, pp. 75, 17, 68.
5. Van Wyck Brooks, *America's Coming of Age* (N. Y., 1915), p. 80. Socialists and Communists claimed Whitman without being precisely sure what he really thought of capitalism and trade unions. It was enough that he believed in the future and "affirmed." Leslie Fiedler points out that one of Whitman's most characteristic masks was the revolutionist and that Whitman was among the first of the American writers to be translated by the Soviet Government. *Leaves of Grass One Hundred Years After*, ed. by Milton Hindus (Stanford, Calif., 1955). Coincidentally with the decline of the revolutionary spirit in the 1920's, Whitman's reputation sank. For Paul Elmer More, T. S. Eliot, Ezra Pound, Yvor Winters, and others, he was or became the poet of disorder. Revived as a socialist master in the thirties (see Newton Arvin's *Whitman*, N. Y., 1938), he tumbled again after 1946 and is once more being rehabilitated by the formalist critics.
6. *SA*, II (Sept. 1917), p. 633.
7. *NR*, XVI (Aug. 17, 1918), pp. 84-86. The Puritan remained a symbol of reaction and oppression for the next thirty years, a target for the intellectual Bolsheviks and the foes of Stuart P. Sherman, Paul Elmer More, and other humanists.
8. Quoted in H. M. Jones, *The Bright Medusa* (Urbana, Ill., 1952), p. 83.
9. H. F. May, *The End of American Innocence: The First Years of Our Own Time, 1912-1917* (N. Y., 1959), p. 303.
10. "Change," *The Pagan*, I (Sept. 1916), pp. 27-28.
11. The first quotation is from Norman Foerster, *The Dial*, LIV (Jan. 1, 1913), p. 4. The quotation from Shaw is in Johns, *op. cit.*, pp. 177-78.
12. Brooks's first quotation is in *America's Coming of Age*, pp. 98-99, his second in *F*, II (Jan. 12, 1921), p. 431.
13. Van Wyck Brooks, *Letters and Leadership* (N. Y., 1918), pp. 44-45.
14. Floyd Dell, *Love in Greenwich Village* (N. Y., 1926), pp. 34-35.
15. *The Dial*, LVII (Oct. 1, 1914), pp. 239-41.
16. Granville Hicks, *John Reed: The Making of a Revolutionary* (N. Y., 1936), p. 394.
17. *SA*, I (Dec. 1916), p. 158.
18. The quotation from Freeman is in his *An American Testament: A Narrative of Rebels and Romantics* (N. Y., 1936), p. 284; Art Young's remark is in his *On My Way*, p. 129.
19. All quotations in this paragraph were taken from Daniel Bell, "Marxian Socialism in the United States," in Donald Egbert *et al.*, *Socialism and American Life* (Princeton, 1952), I, pp. 287, 288, 257.
20. Max Eastman, *Venture* (N. Y., 1927), p. 25.
21. Louis C. Fraina, "The Social Significance of Futurism," *The New Review*, I (Dec. 1913), pp. 964-70. See also his article on Cubism in *Reedy's Mirror*, May 16, 1913.
22. "Speculations, or Post-Impressionism in Prose," *Arts and Decorations*, III (March 1913), pp. 172-74.

23. In a letter to a conservative, she wrote: "You accuse us of being a set of anarchists because we do not linger contentedly over the deposits of past achievement. This is as true of us as it is of any moderns who have ever concerned themselves with the hitherto 'unknown.' But we claim it as our special virtue that we *want* to know more and that our minds are open to new manifestations. . . . The outline around many of the old forms must be admitted as too hard and too narrow. Its inelasticity constitutes its defeat. Recognized definitions no longer enclose the whole truth, and the first qualification of a definition is that there shall be nothing left over. There is so much left over, in many cases, that the important constituents are now mostly on the outside. And that is our area—the outside—that is where we have our being—it is our element and our native air, and the name we give to it is the universal consciousness . . . today we are out in the untried—feeling our way towards the truth of tomorrow." Mabel Dodge Luhan, *Movers and Shakers* (N. Y., 1936), p. 94.

24. *Ibid.*, p. 88.

25. Eastman, *Venture*, p. 210.

26. *Ibid.*, pp. 210-11.

27. The three quotations in this paragraph appear in Hicks, *John Reed*, pp. 102-03, and Grace Potter, "Max Eastman's Two Books," *The New Review*, I (1913), p. 795. For a less rapturous account by one of the participants, see Elizabeth Gurley Flynn, *I Speak My Own Piece* (N. Y., 1955), pp. 154-56.

28. *The Comrade*, I (Oct. 1901), p. 12.

29. Quoted in *The Comrade*, I (Oct. 1901), p. 14.

30. Walter B. Rideout, *The Radical Novel in the United States, 1900-1954* (Cambridge, Mass., 1956), pp. 23-24.

31. Tom Quelch, "The New Paganism," *The New Review*, I (June 1913), pp. 503-05. Founded in 1913, this magazine included on its editorial board two editors of *The Masses*, Dell and Eastman, and one *Masses* contributor, Arturo Giovannitti, revolutionary poet.

32. Theodore Draper, *The Roots of American Communism* (N. Y., 1957), p. 48.

33. This account of *The Masses* is taken partly from Hicks, *John Reed*, pp. 92, 94.

34. The quotations in this paragraph are in Eastman, *Enjoyment of Living* (N. Y., 1948), p. 421.

35. They constituted a kind of "Who's Who of artistic and literary America for the next two or more decades." Draper, *op. cit.*, p. 49. The following artists and writers appeared in *The Masses* and its immediate successor, *The Liberator*: Franklin P. Adams, Sherwood Anderson, Roger Baldwin, John Barber, Cornelia Barnes, Djuna Barnes, Carleton Beals, Maurice Becker, S. N. Behrman, George Bellows, William Rose Benét, Alexander Berkman, Konrad Berkovici, Francis Biddle, Maxwell Bodenheim, Frank Bohn, Howard Brubaker, Arthur Bullard, Gelett Burgess, Witter Bynner, K. R. Chamberlain, Stuart Chase, Sarah T. Cleghorn, Elizabeth Coatsworth, Glenn O. Coleman, George Creel, Olive T. Darton, Randall Davey, Jo Davidson, Arthur B. Davies, Stuart Davis, Floyd Dell, Babette Deutsch, Mabel Dodge, John Dos Passos, Finley P. Dunne, Joseph Freeman, Lewis Gannett, Inez H. Gillmore, Arturo Giovannitti, Susan Glaspell, H. J. Glintenkamp, Oliver Herford, Eugene Higgins, James Hopper, Helen R. Hull, Leslie N. Jennings, James Weldon Johnson, Ellis O. Jones, Morris Kantor, Helen Keller, Harry Kemp, Freda Kirchwey, J. J. Lankes, William Ellery Leonard, Vachel Lindsay, Philip Littel, Amy Lowell, Claude McKay, Edna St. Vincent Millay, Alice Duer Miller, Robert Minor, David Morton, James Oppenheim, Ernest Poole, Arthur Ransome, John Reed, Elmer Rice, Boardman Robinson, Romain Rolland, Bertrand Russell, Carl Sandburg, Siegfried Sassoon, Evelyn Scott, G. Bernard Shaw, Upton Sinclair, John Sloan, Wilbur D. Steele, Maurice Sterne, Ruth Suckow, Horace Traubel, William Troy, H. J. Turner, Louis Untermeyer, Mary Heaton Vorse, Abraham Walkowitz, William E. Walling, Clive Weed, Elinor Wylie, William Carlos Williams,

Edmund Wilson, Horatio Winslow, Charles A. and Alice Beach Winter, Frances Winwar, Eugene Wood, Art Young, Marya Zaturenska.

36. The quotations in this paragraph are in *Enjoyment of Living*, pp. 416, 558-59, 420, 548. The reference to *"mere* Bohemianism" is in Eastman, "Bunk About Bohemia," *MM*, VIII (May 1934), p. 201.
37. *Enjoyment of Living*, p. 475.
38. Eastman's words and Freeman's recollection of them are mentioned in *An American Testament*, p. 61. Eastman does not remember saying this. "To whom was I laying down this law? I was no Savanarola." Eastman to author.
39. Eastman's remarks on prudery and *The Masses* are in *Enjoyment of Living*, p. 479. Hapgood's review appeared in the *NR*, LXXVII (Nov. 29, 1933), p. 80. Malcolm Cowley came to the same conclusion, *NR*, LXII (April 30, 1930), pp. 304-05. See Eastman, *Venture*, p. 69, for passage on "futuristical artists."
40. Floyd Dell, *Intellectual Vagabondage: An Apology for the Intelligentsia* (N. Y., 1926), pp. 113-14.
41. Eastman to author, April 3, 1957.
42. *NR*, XXI (Dec. 24, 1919), pp. 122-23.
43. *SA*, I (Nov. 1916), p. 73.
44. Brooks, *Letters and Leadership*, p. 126.
45. Paul Rosenfeld, *NR*, XLI (Dec. 10, 1924), p. 13.
46. Brooks, *America's Coming of Age*, p. 105.
47. *NR*, XVI (Sept. 28, 1918), pp. 261-62.
48. "The Inner Hermit," *The New Review*, I (Jan.-Feb. 1913), p. 64.
49. "The Dreiser Bugaboo," *SA*, II (Aug. 1917), pp. 514-15.
50. Dell, *Intellectual Vagabondage*, p. 241.

CHAPTER TWO • FOUR RADICALS

1. Eastman, *Enjoyment of Living*, p. 586.
2. *Ibid.*, p. 118.
3. *Ibid.*, p. 387.
4. For Eastman's fictional portrait of the socialist-reformer type, see *Venture*, pp. 98-99. He is described as a man who advocates the class struggle while repudiating class hate, who thought of the I.W.W. as "an association of western cut-throats who had somehow got themselves mixed up in the public mind with socialism, and brought the thing to a stand-still when it was just on the point of sweeping the country."
5. See Eastman, *Enjoyment of Living*, pp. 423-24.
6. *Ibid.*, p. 432.
7. The quotations in the succeeding paragraphs are taken from *ibid.*, pp. 432, 355, 402, 437.
8. In December 1913, the Associated Press brought suit for libel against Eastman and Art Young for slander. Eastman's hot editorial lambasting of the A.P. for coloring the news "with poisonous intentions" and selling it "to the highest bidder" had been accompanied by Young's cartoon showing the president of the A.P. "pouring 'lies' out of a bottle marked POISON into a reservoir which supplied 'NEWS' to a city with the American flag flying over it." *Ibid.*, p. 464. The A.P. finally dropped the suit, fearing, Eastman suspects, a full-dress hearing on the suppression of news.
9. *Ibid.*, p. 452.
10. Morris, *The Young Idea*, pp. 16-17.
11. Max Eastman, "Journey Through an Epoch" (unpublished manuscript).
12. Max Eastman, *Understanding Germany: The Only Way to End the War and Other Essays* (N. Y., 1916), p. 142.
13. Eastman, "Journey."
14. Emma Goldman, *Anarchism and Other Essays* (N. Y., 1911), p. 175.

15. See Floyd Dell's autobiography, *Homecoming* (N. Y., 1933), p. 293, and Freeman's *An American Testament,* p. 101.
16. Written by Joseph Bell, and quoted in *An American Testament,* p. 101.

> Emma Goldman and Alexander Berkman
> Are in prison tonight,
> But they have made themselves elemental forces,
> Like water that climbs down rocks,
> Like wind in the leaves:
> Like the gentle night that holds us:
> They are working on our destinies:
> They are forging the love of nations.

17. The quotations from Dell are in *Homecoming,* pp. 315-17. For other accounts of the first trial, see Floyd Dell, "The Story of a Trial," *L,* I (June 1918), pp. 17-18. Speeches delivered at the "Victory Dinner" are printed in the same issue (pp. 19-23). See also Hicks, *John Reed,* pp. 304-05, Freeman, *An American Testament,* pp. 101, 163-64, Young, *On My Way,* pp. 293-99, and Morris Hillquit, *Loose Leaves from a Busy Life* (N. Y., 1934), pp. 222-33.
18. For the reference to London as "Rover boy," see Bell, *op. cit.,* p. 295; Dell's remark is in *Homecoming,* p. 283. For London's attitude toward the war, see P. S. Foner, *Jack London, American Rebel* (N. Y., 1947), p. 126.
19. Hicks's *John Reed,* although written when the author was still a member of the Communist Party, is an objective biography and the best introduction to Reed. It should be supplemented by the pages on Reed in Draper's *The Roots of American Communism,* Max Eastman's *Heroes I Have Known* (N. Y., 1942), and G. F. Kennan, *Soviet-American Relations, 1917-1920,* I, *Russia Leaves the War* (Princeton, 1956-58), pp. 67-69, 359-60, 405-11. Browder's comment on Reed may be found in *NM,* XXXVII (Oct. 29, 1940), p. 7. The quote from Untermeyer is in his *From Another World* (N. Y., 1939), p. 58. Lippmann's portrait of Reed appeared in *NR,* I (Dec. 26, 1914), p. 15.
20. Hicks, *John Reed,* p. 246.
21. Reed's reports on the war on the eastern front were published as *The War in Eastern Europe* (N. Y., 1916). The book was well received in both the radical and the bourgeois press. John Dos Passos, who some years later would be reporting a different set of wars, reviewed it favorably for *The Harvard Monthly.* For Lippmann's quote, see *NR,* I (Dec. 26, 1914), p. 15.
22. "Small on the huge bench sits a wasted man with untidy white hair, an emaciated face in which two burning eyes are set like jewels, parchment skin split by a crack for a mouth; the face of Andrew Jackson three years dead. This is Judge Kenesaw Mountain Landis." *L,* I (Sept. 1918), p. 20.
23. John Reed, *Daughter of the Revolution,* ed. by Floyd Dell (N. Y., 1927).
24. Hicks, *John Reed,* p. 244.
25. *Ibid.,* p. 296; Draper, *op. cit.,* pp. 120, 417-18.
26. For the favorable impression, see Johns, *op. cit.,* p. 236; for the critical, Hiam Kantorovitch, "Rise and Decline of Neo-Communism," *MQ,* I (Spring 1924), p. 22.
27. *L,* I (June 1918), p. 26.
28. Eastman, "Journey."
29. Eastman's remark on bigoted Marxism is in his "Journey." Mother Jones is quoted in *NR,* II (Feb. 20, 1915), pp. 73-74. For a colorful if not always accurate story of the life of Mary Harris ("Mother") Jones, see *Autobiography of Mother Jones* (Chicago, 1925). Born in Cork, Ireland, she died in her hundredth year (1930). After losing her husband and four children in a yellow-fever epidemic in Memphis, Tennessee, she became one of the most colorful labor organizers and spokesmen in the United States. Between 1877 and 1923, hardly a major strike took place without the presence of this remarkable woman. Her passionate dedication to the rights of labor as well as her pic-

turesque speech endeared her to thousands of workingmen and even to many of the men who opposed her.

30. Lenin's pamphlet helped to convert Whittaker Chambers to Communism when he read it in 1925. See Chambers, *Witness* (N. Y., 1952), p. 194. For the influence of this pamphlet, see Draper, *op. cit.*, pp. 107-08, 415. The quotations in this paragraph and the next are taken from Eastman, "Journey."

31. Hicks, *John Reed*, pp. 312-13.

32. Both quotations in this paragraph are in Dell, *Homecoming*, pp. 326-27.

33. *Max Eastman's Address to the Jury in the Second Masses Trial* (N. Y., 1919), pp. 42, 18.

34. Dell, *Homecoming*, p. 327.

35. Beulah Amidon to Alyse Gregory, Oct. 14, 1948 (RB).

36. The first quotation in this paragraph is Bourne to Simon Pelham Barr, Jan. 19, 1914, the second, Bourne to Alyse Gregory, Nov. 19, 1916 (RB).

37. My sources for Bourne's career are Louis Filler, *Randolph Bourne* (Washington, D. C., 1943), pp. 40-42, and A. F. Beringause, "The Double Martyrdom of Randolph Bourne," *Journal of the History of Ideas*, XVIII (Oct. 1957), p. 594. Beringause agrees that Bourne had become a socialist at twenty-one. His precollege experience of working for a manufacturer of piano rolls, his reading of Henry George, and his attempt to blend Christianity with economics, and his own crippled state encouraged him to find the reasons for inequality and injustice. Bourne's impressions of England and the quotation on American traits are in his letter to H. W. Elsasser, Oct. 10, 1913 (RB).

38. For Bourne's remarks on American writers, see Bourne to Alyse Gregory, Jan. 5, 1914; on Romain, in Bourne to Carl Zigrosser, March 6, 1914 (RB). The quotation on Germany is quoted in Filler, *op. cit.*, pp. 52-53.

39. Bourne to Carl Zigrosser, May 20, 1914 (RB).

40. The quotation on religion and politics is taken from Beringause, *op. cit.*, p. 599. A letter to Bourne from Carl Zigrosser, March 23, 1914 (RB), links Bourne with his other idealistic contemporaries: "Speaking about being on the lookout for sociological art, do you ever see the *Masses?* It certainly is the livest paper in the country; it just sparkles with wit and telling stabs, and its art is sincere and vital." Bourne first met Eastman in the winter of 1916 in Madison, Wisconsin: "Max Eastman was also there all the time, making his usual commotion in the University by getting the University buildings closed against him as a 'propagandist.' This was my first chance to get acquainted with him, our Village lines never having crossed." Bourne to Alyse Gregory, n.d. (RB). Bourne's comment on pragmatism is in *NR*, II (March 13, 1915), p. 154. His revolt against Dewey is discussed in Sidney Kaplan, "Social Engineers as Saviors: Effects of World War I on Some American Liberals," *Journal of the History of Ideas*, XVII (June 1956), pp. 347-69. His attack against liberals is taken from his *Untimely Papers* (N. Y., 1919), pp. 124-25, and his criticisms of *New Republic* liberals in a letter to Brooks, March 27, 1918 (RB).

41. See Bourne to Elizabeth S. Sergeant, Oct. 10, 1915, and to Everett Benjamin, Nov. 26, 1917, for the quotations on his alleged pro-Germanism and his opinions of the Bolsheviks (RB). Waldo Frank's remarks appear in his *Our America* (N. Y., 1919), pp. 199-200, 227-28. For the last quotation in the paragraph, see Freeman, *An American Testament*, p. 167.

42. *L*, I (Dec. 1918), pp. 45-46.

43. See Freeman, *An American Testament*, p. 167, and Eastman, "Journey."

44. The Rolland-Eastman controversy is printed in *L*, II (Dec. 1919), pp. 23-24, and III (March 1920), p. 25.

45. For the Clarté discussion, see *L*, III (April 1920), pp. 40-42.

46. Quoted in Eastman, "Clarifying the Light," *L*, IV (June 1921), p. 5.

47. *Ibid.*, pp. 5-7.

48. Freeman, unpublished chapter of *An American Testament*.

49. *F*, III (June 29, 1921), p. 385. On the other hand, the historian Alexander Kaun supported Eastman. He, too, believed that the intelligentsia should leave propaganda to the professionals and concentrate on education. Clarté's program of meetings, books, brochures, tracts, journals he classed as propaganda. "The role of the educationist is to generate ideas, to create new concepts, new needs, new aspirations." The artist's function was to oppose Philistinism, which stood "for narrowly selfish interests, for uncritical acceptance of traditions and conventions, for enjoying mediocrity because of its safety, and for adherence to things-as-they-are because of fear of novelty." "The Role of the Intellectuals," *F*, V (March 1922), pp. 57-58.

50. Dell's comments are in *L*, II (Dec. 1919), pp. 41-42.

51. *L*, III (Jan. 1920), p. 46.

52. *L*, III (April 1920), pp. 15-19.

53. And elsewhere, too. Reviewing a book by G. K. Chesterton in 1918, Dell wrote sympathetically of Chesterton's antideterministic radicalism, his anarcho-syndicalism (which he shared with Thoreau, Emerson, Whitman, Bakunin) that regarded the state with "suspicion, contempt, or overt hostility—in contrast to the determinists who were busy trying to use the State for their own purposes." See Dell, *Looking at Life* (N. Y., 1924), pp. 134-35. Dell noted the charge that Chesterton and Belloc were reactionaries wanting to reverse history (a similar charge was brought against their American "Distributivist" followers in the 1930's), but Dell in 1918 felt that the revolutionary movement could learn from them.

54. *L*, III (May 1920), pp. 10-14.

55. "Soviet Russia—1920," *N*, CXI (July 31, 1920), pp. 121-26; (Aug. 7, 1920), pp. 152-54.

56. *Ibid.* (Aug. 7, 1920), p. 153.

57. *L*, III (Aug. 1920), p. 27.

58. *L*, III (Sept. 1920), pp. 55-57.

59. *L*, III (Sept. 1920), p. 7, and IV (Aug. 1921), pp. 5-6.

60. *L*, IV (May 1921), p. 7.

61. *L*, III (May 1920), p. 15.

62. *L*, III (June 1920), p. 22.

63. *L*, IV (Aug. 1921), pp. 5-6.

64. The quotations in this paragraph appear in the following: Rebecca West, "The Barbarians," *NR*, I (Jan. 9, 1915), p. 20; Rose Pastor Stokes, *L*, III (June 1920), p. 22; James Oppenheim, *SA*, II (July 1917), pp. 340-43; *L*, I (Dec. 1918), p. 32, II (June 1919), pp. 11-18.

65. Eastman, *Education and Art in Soviet Russia*, p. 7.

66. Dell's review appeared in *L*, II (May 1919), p. 45. The following quotation is in *The Dial*, LXVI (March 22, 1919), p. 302.

67. Reed to Upton Sinclair, Nov. 6, 1918 (US).

68. The whole issue has been judiciously assessed by Draper, *op. cit.*, pp. 284-93. For a Communist version, see Michael Gold, "John Reed: He Loved the People," *NM*, XXXVII (Oct. 22, 1940), pp. 8-11.

69. *F*, II (Nov. 3, 1920), p. 181.

CHAPTER THREE · EXPATRIATES AND RADICALS

1. Joshua Kunitz, another Russian-born literary radical, had a similar kind of experience. As a boy in Russia, he and his comrades read the works of Cooper, Irving, H. B. Stowe, and Mark Twain in Hebrew. When he came to America, he was in love with its history and traditions (he had surreptitiously read a biography of Washington written by some nineteenth-century Russian author), and he paid a visit to Irving's birthplace. Conversation, Oct. 26, 1956.

2. Freeman, *An American Testament*, p. 25.

3. *Ibid.*, p. 47.
4. *Ibid.*, p. 104.
5. *Ibid.*, p. 105.
6. *Ibid.*, p. 125. Besides Brown, other writers and intellectuals, some of them future Left sympathizers, served with the American Ambulance Service and the Norton-Harjes unit under French control or with the Red Cross services on the Italian front. Among them were John Dos Passos, Ernest Hemingway, Malcolm Cowley, E. E. Cummings, John Howard Lawson, Robert Hillyer, Sidney Howard, Louis Bromfield, and William Seabrook. Freeman's war experiences are contained in a letter from him to the author, July 16, 1958.
7. All quotations in the last three paragraphs are from Freeman, *An American Testament*, pp. 112, 156, 162, 172-73.
8. For Freeman's quotation, see *ibid.*, p. 180; the last quotation in the paragraph is from Malcolm Cowley, *Exile's Return* (N. Y., 1934), p. 91.
9. "The oldest contributor was fifty-eight and the youngest over thirty. . . . Nevertheless, they were referred to as 'young intellectuals,' and the term obtained currency . . . it came to be used loosely as a designation for anyone not specifically identified with the stand pat tradition. . . . All the writers in *The Dial, New Republic, Nation, Freeman* and *Survey* became 'young intellectuals,' even if they had numerous grandchildren." Burton Rascoe, *A Bookman's Daybook* (N. Y., 1929), p. 264.
10. Harold Stearns, "What Can a Young Man Do," *F*, I (Aug. 4, 1920), p. 489. Great opportunities existed for fraud, business, science, politics, Stearns continued, but for the artist, who wishes to escape a humdrum middle-class existence, Europe was the only haven. Before the war, the big cities offered an escape from the "rural horrors," but now, he said, the Big Town had become the small town writ large. *Ibid.*, pp. 488-91. A fellow Harvardian, reviewing Stearns's *America and the Young Intellectual* (N. Y., 1922), enthusiastically agreed with this view. "Was there ever a society in which the man of thought as such, stood in less esteem than in contemporary America?" Newton Arvin asked. "Was there ever a society in which the life of meditation was more wantonly unprovided for, or the claims of the creative life more brutally ignored?" *F*, IV (Jan. 18, 1922), p. 450.
11. *NR*, XXX (March 8, 1922), pp. 54-57.
12. *The Dial*, LXXII (June 1922), p. 562.
13. Cowley, *Exile's Return*, p. 82.
14. *NR*, XXX (March 15, 1921), pp. 76-77.
15. "The Migratory Artist," *F*, II (March 9, 1921), p. 607.
16. Cowley, *Exile's Return*, pp. 138-39.
17. *Ibid.*, p. 159. See also Vincent O'Sullivan's report in *F*, IV (Feb. 8, 1922), pp. 518-19. He declared the movement sterile and unproductive, bloodless, hysterical, vindictive, cruel. "Some middle-aged young men persist in believing that Dada is still alive," he wrote from Paris, "and holding up the corpse by the arm-pits, they drag it through certain magazines and reviews in England and America." But the young men knew it was dead. He acknowledged, however, that it produced a few good writers: Aragon, Breton, Soupault, and a few others.
18. Edmund Wilson, *NR*, XXXVIII (April 9, 1924), pp. 181-82. Burton Rascoe's account of an interview with Josephson in 1923 suggests that Wilson's burlesque was hardly exaggerated. After dismissing Anatole France, Hardy, Conrad, Sherwood Anderson, Sinclair Lewis, Willa Cather as obsolete and bad, he praised a Heinz soup ad as "really marvelous . . . vibrant and alive" and enthusiastically spoke of familiarizing the American people with such geniuses as Charlie Chaplin, Al Jolson, Fanny Brice, Ring Lardner, Joe Cook, and other stars he had just discovered, through the agency of his magazine, *Broom*, with its 1,500 circulation. Rascoe commented on the paradox of the American intellectuals roaming the "cultural capitals of Europe" while the European

intellectuals found American jazz, architecture, and billboard advertisements thrilling. Rascoe, *op. cit.*, pp. 138-41.

19. *1924*, No. 3 (1924) and No. 4 (1924), pp. 73, 74, 141-42.
20. Louis Untermeyer, "The New Patricians," *NR*, XXXIII (Dec. 6, 1922), p. 41.
21. Brooks's comments are taken from *F*, VII (Aug. 8, 1923), p. 527, (July 11, 1923), p. 431.
22. Van Wyck Brooks, *Three Essays on America* (N. Y., 1934), p. 211.
23. Burke's criticism of Brooks appears in *The Dial*, LXXXIV (Jan. 1928), pp. 56-59; Hyman's parody is in *NR*, XXXVIII (April 30, 1924), pp. 249-54; Watson's comment is in *The Dial*, LXX (May 1921), pp. 562-68, Cowley's in *NR*, LXXIX (Aug. 8, 1934), p. 350.
24. Watson, *op. cit.*
25. Untermeyer, "The New Patricians," pp. 41-42.
26. Freeman, *An American Testament*, p. 182.
27. *Ibid.*, pp. 186, 197-98, 213. The Gorham Munson quotation is from *NR*, XXXIV (April 18, 1923), p. 220.
28. *F*, I (Aug. 11, 1920), p. 527.
29. The reference to Freeman is in *L*, V (July 1922), p. 27. Some of the contributors to *The Liberator* were Randolph Bourne, John Dos Passos, Edmund Wilson, Carl Sandburg, Elmer Rice, Rolfe Humphries, S. N. Behrman, Sherwood Anderson, Louise Bogan, Amy Lowell, Elinor Wylie, William Carlos Williams, Djuna Barnes, Vachel Lindsay, George Bellows, Stuart Davis, Jo Davidson, Arthur B. Davies, Morris Kantor, and many others. For the criticism of *The Liberator*, see Richel North (A. D. Emmart), "The Limitations of American Magazines," *MQ*, I (July 1923), p. 24.
30. Eastman, "Journey."
31. *Ibid.*
32. Quoted in letter from Freeman to author, July 12, 1958.
33. Gold had used other pen names, but Michael Gold stuck. The original was Corporal Michael Gold, a Civil War veteran and the father of his friend Leroy Gold. He first began to use Michael Gold as a pen name during the days of the Mitchell Palmer raids. The quotations about the East Side are in Michael Gold, *Jews Without Money* (N. Y., 1930) and *L*, III (July 1920), pp. 30-31. Dorothy Day's reminiscence is in her autobiography, *The Long Loneliness* (N. Y., 1952), p. 71.
34. "Certain enemies have spread the slander that I once attended Harvard College. This is a lie. I worked on a garbage dump in Boston, city of Harvard. But that is all." Michael Gold, *120 Million* (N. Y., 1929), p. 123. Gold finds the subject too painful to discuss even today and chooses to recall very little of his experience. He told me that he and a group of his friends (among them Henry Hazlitt, Herbert Feis, and Lewis Mumford) used to go to Staten Island together. Feis was working in an advertising office, and it was he who urged Gold to go to Harvard. Gold scraped together the money and took the plunge. He worked for a Boston newspaper part time, shared a bed with a fellow student, and enjoyed a course in biology given by Professor George H. Parker. He studied under Bliss Perry, also, but did not think much of him. Conversation with author.
35. Carleton Beals, *Glass Houses: Ten Years of Free-Lancing* (N. Y., 1938), pp. 35-36.
36. Eastman's description of Gold is in "Journey"; Freeman's in *An American Testament*, p. 257.
37. Freeman, unpublished chapter of *An American Testament*.
38. *L*, IV (Feb. 1921), pp. 20-21.
39. *Ibid.*, pp. 22-24.
40. Gold, "Thoughts of a Great Thinker," *L*, V (April 1922), p. 24.
41. Gold, "Prize-Fights vs. Color Organs," *L*, V (March 1922), p. 26.
42. *Ibid.*, pp. 26-27.

CHAPTER FOUR • FROM BOHEMIA TO REVOLUTION

1. *The Liberator* as the reflector of Village life is discussed by Freeman in *An American Testament*, p. 257; Gold is quoted in Eastman's "Journey"; Wilson's story appeared in *L*, IV (May 1921), pp. 25-26, 28. See Freeman, *op. cit.*, p. 250, for the quote on *The Liberator*'s coverage.

2. Claude McKay, *A Long Way from Home* (N. Y., 1937), pp. 139-40.

3. *L*, V (June 1922), pp. 25-26.

4. Eden and Cedar Paul, *Proletcult* (N. Y., 1921), pp. 23, 93. See also Edward J. Brown, *The Proletarian Episode in Russian Literature, 1928-1932* (N. Y., 1953), pp. 6-10. The publication of the Pauls' book coincided with an increased interest in workers' education in America. By 1924, Freeman was teaching in the Workers' School, founded by the Communist Party in 1923; and in 1925, the Moscow-organized Proletarian Artists and Writers League asked a number of American writers to join its National Executive Committee. The sponsoring American group who sent out the invitations to leading American writers included John Dos Passos, John Howard Lawson, Mary Heaton Vorse, Genevieve Taggard, Robert Wolf, Michael Gold, Joseph Freeman, Louis Lozowick, Simon Felshin, and Hugo Gellert. The proposed function of the American group was to organize journalists, translate foreign literature, co-ordinate workers' colleges and cultural groups, and start a magazine. As Freeman suggests in his account of the P.A.W.L., the group made the mistake of Clarté and attempted too much. It "died within a few months." Freeman, *An American Testament*, pp. 372-74; Freeman to author, June 8, 1958.

5. Paul, *op. cit.*, p. 20.

6. The following letter is a comment on the party's attitude toward intellectuals: "A party leader in Detroit, an economist, recently referred, casually, to my having my 'hobby' for after-hours activity. He was referring to my writing poetry and stories. I should not like to think that was increasingly the Communist point of view." *L*, VII (June 1924), p. 24. Freeman's observation is in *An American Testament*, p. 323. In regard to the disposition of *The Liberator*, so Floyd Dell told Freeman, Eastman before leaving for Europe "left *written* instructions to the staff that they should keep the magazine going at all costs; but if they could not keep it going, then they should NOT let it die; they should turn it over to the C.P." Freeman to author, fall 1958.

7. Gold, "O Californians! O Ladies and Gentlemen!" *Gently, Brother*, II (March 1924).

8. Freeman to author, Sept. 21, 1958. *The Liberator* merged with *The Labor Herald* and *Soviet Russia Pictorial* in October 1924, and became *The Workers Monthly*, the official party organ edited by Earl Browder.

9. All quotations from Gold are contained in a series of undated letters to Upton Sinclair in US. Internal evidence in some cases indicates the approximate time of their composition.

10. All quotations in this paragraph are taken from the correspondence in GF: John Dos Passos to Maurice Becker, Feb. 1925; Susan Glaspell to Maurice Becker, Feb. 26, 1925.

11. Freeman to Elizabeth Gurley Flynn, Dec. 10, 1925 (GF).

12. See Granville Hicks, "The Liberals Who Haven't Learned," *Commentary*, II (April 1951), pp. 319-29.

13. Prospectus sent to the American Fund for Public Service, March 23, 1925 (GF).

14. The details of the fund's grant to the magazine are in the following letters: Helen Black to Freda Kirchwey, May 27, 1925; Freda Kirchwey to Elizabeth Gurley Flynn, Oct. 22, 1925; Joseph Freeman to Elizabeth Gurley Flynn, Feb. 2, 1926 (GF). Some of the comments on the proposed magazine were: "I believe *The New Masses* will bear the same relationship to the commercial press

as the experimental theatre does to Broadway. My blessing and lustiest cheers!" (Eugene O'Neill); "The people you have with you insure life. The old *Masses* cut across the whole consciousness of America. No one knew what it had meant until it was gone. If you can do all what it did, be as bold, fun-loving, full, satirical—everyone will bless you" (Sherwood Anderson); "I am delighted to hear the *Masses* is to be revived. . . . It is needed badly today. The United States still wallows idiotically in Rotary and Coolidgism. Lay on! And good luck to you!" (H. L. Mencken); "I don't know whether I agree with you people, but I do want to see you express yourselves. Get it off your chests. . . . Go to it, you bums, and may the devil give you his blessing along with these fair ten bucks" (William Allen White).

15. Freeman, unpublished chapter of *An American Testament.*
16. Dell, *L,* V (Jan. 1922), p. 26.
17. This series, "Literature and the Machine Age," was published later as *Intellectual Vagabondage.* The following references are taken from this very important and neglected essay.
18. Compare the following story of the poet Park Barnitz (as recorded by Dell's friend Edna Kenton) with Cowley's story of Harry Crosby in *Exile's Return:*

    "Born 1877; died 1902. Son of Dutch Reformed clergyman, of Kansas. Went to various schools in the state, and, after several expulsions, went to Boulder, Colo., and at the university there found for the first time great stimulation. Later he attended Harvard Graduate School. Had a remarkable knowledge of the art history of the world, and of musical history, and of all literatures. Snapped up all the languages, and knew much of the philosophies. Was a favorite pupil of Barrett Wendell and of William James. Was at Harvard in 1898-99. Returned then to Kansas.

    "Was addicted to all drugs, and had a background of extraordinary experiences. Held the curious pose of an aristocratic man of the world, combined with all his bizarre and decadent predilections and desires.

    "Was six feet . . . inches tall, and extremely thin—weighed only one hundred and fifteen pounds. Delighted to wear evening clothes and high hat without an overcoat. Died at his Kansas home, a victim of drugs and resulting ill-health. Except for the Manuscript of 'Chave,' as yet unpublished, 'The Book of Jade' is his only work."

    The Book of Jade, dedicated to Baudelaire, contained poems entitled "Ashtoreth," "Parfait Amour," "Ennui," "Sonnet of the Instruments of Death," "The Grotesques," "Dead Dialogue," and others. In the last, a number of corpses discuss the meaning of life and decide it is only death.

    > "Just for this end
    > Hideously propagated evermore." (Pp. 214-16.)

19. Several decades later, Cummings wrote: "When you confuse art with propaganda, you confuse an act of God with something which can be turned on and off like the hot water faucet. If 'God' means nothing to you (or less than nothing) I'll cheerfully substitute one of your own favorite words, 'freedom.' Let me, incidentally, opine that absolute tyranny is what most of you are really after; that your so-called ideal isn't America at all and never was America at all: that you'll never be satisfied until what Father Abraham called 'a new nation, conceived in liberty' becomes just another sub-human superstate (like the 'great freedom-loving democracy' of Comrade Stalin) where an artist—or any other human being—either does as he's told or turns into fertilizer." Quoted in Charles Norman, *The Magic-Maker, E. E. Cummings* (N. Y., 1958), p. 336.
20. Not according to C. Hartley Gratton. Dell's intellectuals, he wrote in a review, were "sapheads" who "conducted themselves like idiots." "Frankly, I do not believe that Mr. Dell's book is of much value as a defense of the intelligentsia. Most of the genuinely important members of the group would avoid the types he portrays like the plague." *NR,* XLVII (June 23, 1926), p. 145. Ernest Boyd, in *The Independent,* CXVI (April 3, 1926), p. 397, stated that Dell's book did

not speak for the young intellectuals of the 1920's although it may have applied to Dell's particular circle.

21. "He has done the one thing that is more popular even than lynching socialists and Negroes; he has plastered a Professor with—you have no doubt read the passage in question—cow manure." *L*, II (Dec. 1919), p. 42.

22. Paul Simon, "A Medal for Mencken," *L*, VI (March 1923), p. 27.

23. Elsa Bloch, "The Arrow-Collar Menace," *L*, VII (June 1924), p. 32.

24. H. L. Mencken, "Meditation in E Minor," *NR*, XXIV (Sept. 8, 1920), pp. 38-40.

25. *NR*, XXVII (June 1, 1921), pp. 10-13.

26. "No one can accept the proposition that Mr. Mencken's audience in the heyday of his glory consisted of a lewd pack of decadent bourgeois cynics. You couldn't throw a stone into a Communist Party mass meeting without hitting someone who, one time in the past, heartily agreed with Mr. Mencken's bitter assault on everything that was typically bourgeois." Letter to *NM*, XXI (Nov. 17, 1936), p. 19. See C. B. Cowing, "H. L. Mencken: The Case of the 'Curdled' Progressive," *Ethics*, LXIX (July 1959), pp. 255-67, for a perceptive analysis of Mencken's "waning progressivism."

27. Dell, *Intellectual Vagabondage*, p. 259.

28. *The Dial*, LXXXIII (Nov. 1927), pp. 434-38.

29. Writer, newspaperman, diplomat, soldier. Educated at Princeton and Harvard Law School, he entered the diplomatic service and served in Russia, Mexico, Holland, Colombia, and Chile. For a while, he was a foreign correspondent for the A.P., *Leslie's Weekly*, and the Chicago *Tribune*. After the war, in which he served as a captain, he became secretary for the Russian Committee of the Near East Relief. Hibben's deep sympathy for the Russian revolution brought charges of disloyalty against him, but he was acquitted. He published his own account of the Russian famine and angered Herbert Hoover by retaining his own committee for the relief of Russian children. As might have been predicted of one who had renounced all attachments to his family and class, he picketed for Sacco and Vanzetti and was arrested with some other well-born protestors. When he died in December 1928, the largest gathering of radicals since the death of Randolph Bourne attended his funeral. With Bourne, he is enshrined in Dos Passos's *U.S.A.* See *NR*, LVII (Dec. 19, 1928), p. 130.

30. The quotation of Williams is from his article "The Voyage of the Mayflower," *The Transatlantic Review*, II (July 1924), p. 51; for Westcott's remark, see *ibid.*, II (Oct. 1924), p. 447; Lewisohn's description of America is in *transition*, No. 1 (April 1927), pp. 86-87.

31. The references to Kay Boyle and Gertrude Stein are in *transition*, No. 14 (Fall 1928), pp. 103, 97-98; for Cummings, see Norman, *op. cit.*, p. 212; the remark about America's want of cultural facilities is in *transition*, No. 14, p. 98.

32. The poem is quoted in *transition*, No. 13 (Summer 1928), p. 86. The questions are in *transition*, No. 14 (Fall 1928), p. 97. The European view of America's contribution to culture is reflected in answers to the question: How is the influence of America manifesting itself in Europe? Here are a few extracts:

"Through the most emphatic garbage, the ignoble sense of money, the indigence of ideas, the savage hypocrisy in morals, and altogether, through a loathsome swinishness pushed to the point of paroxism" (p. 250).

"The influence of americanism is so enormous, because it is analogous in certain tendencies with other currents forming the young German today: Marxism, the materialistic philosophy of history, the purely animalistic social doctrine, Communism, whose common attacks are directed against the individualistic and the metaphysical being" (p. 252).

"I consider America responsible for that shame of our age: *the glorification of work,* that stupid ideology which has engendered the idea of *material progress,* the disdain of every utopia or poetry tending toward the perfection of the human soul . . ." (p. 252).

"Only a valiant minority—Mencken, Lewis, Frank, *The Nation, The New Republic,* trying to keep America from becoming an enormous Main Street devoted to self-adoration or the cult of the God-dollar and good prey for the charlatans" (p. 265).

33. *transition*, No. 14 (Fall 1928), p. 183. Jolas's war against Philistines and Philistine culture was actually closer to the kind of protest of *The Masses* group and *The Seven Arts* than to the "new patricians" of the twenties, and he stood for "visionary and magical things of life." The following outburst from his "Revolt Against the Philistines," in *transition*, No. 6 (Sept. 1927), pp. 176-77, is rather characteristic:

"He is not interested in the arts, save in their scandals. . . . Our mechanical epoch is the incubator of a new and more violent philistinism. Rooted in his consciousness of superiority, because of the mechanical efficiency of his life's arrangements, the good citizen has become a mere zoological number. Tear down the frontiers and you will find him everywhere, with the same love for money, for steamheat, for electricity, for aviation, for autos, for radio. . . . To him the industrialization of the arts is the ideal he can understand. Afraid of the unrest that a striving for some vision has as consequence, he clings to the banal illusion of mechanical progress, the imbecility of his clubs, the re-masticated idea of his newspapers." So Emerson or Thoreau might have written about the Philistines of their own generation.

34. *transition*, No. 14 (Fall 1928), p. 57.

35. The "collectivities," he argued, "whether American or Bolshevist" were "implacably against" the pure artists, and he speculated on how artists would be used in the "millennium" when they were published in book-club editions of five million. Clearly they would have to be less *"peripheral,"* more concerned with "values" than with methodology. So he gathered from the declaration of Soviet cultural commissars, which he had been reading "with much curiosity." *Ibid.*, p. 62.

36. *Ibid.*, pp. 56-64. "The dissent of such a type may be just, morally; but its lack of any positive sources of strength alienates my sympathy. An army of such cohorts makes poor timber for any leadership. And yet they must be lumped with the rest to form the dissenting and oppressed 'proletariat' of the age, the spearhead of which is the type: artist" (p. 60).

37. *Ibid.*, No. 13 (Summer 1928), p. 275.

38. See Ezra Pound, *Patria Mia* (Chicago, 1950), p. 77 and *The Dial,* LXXIV (March 1923), p. 280.

39. *The Dial,* LXXIV (March 1923), pp. 278-80.

40. *Exile,* No. 4 (1928), pp. 116-17.

41. *Ibid.*, p. 6.

42. *Ibid.*, No. 3 (1928), pp. 108, 102, and No. 4 (1928), pp. 5, 6, 11.

43. *transition*, No. 13 (Summer 1928), pp. 155-56.

44. *Ibid.*

45. *Ibid.*, Nos. 16-17 (June 1929), p. 122.

46. Robert Sage, "Mr. Gold's Spring Model," *ibid.*, No. 15 (Feb. 1929), pp. 184-88.

CHAPTER FIVE • RUSSIA WITH (WITHOUT) RAPTURE

1. *L,* III (Feb. 1929), p. 5.

2. See R. K. Murray, *Red Scare: A Study in National Hysteria, 1919-1920* (Minneapolis, Minn., 1955), pp. 190-209.

3. Charles and Mary Beard, *The Rise of American Civilization* (N. Y., 1930), II, p. 640.

4. Eastman, "Journey." See also Gold's satire on the reformist attitude, "On to Harding and Home Again," *L,* V (Jan. 1922), pp. 14-20.

5. Eastman acknowledged later that he had forgotten that Lenin in his twenty-one points had called for the organization of an illegal as well as a legal party in all countries. The issue of the underground party against an open legal party is discussed in Draper, *op. cit.*, pp. 333-34.

6. Eastman, "Journey."
7. "Theosophy on the High Seas," *L*, V (April 1922), p. 11.
8. See E. H. Carr, *The Bolshevik Revolution, 1917-1923* (N. Y., 1953), III, pp. 355-82, and Louis Fischer, *The Soviets in World Affairs* (London, 1930), I, Chap. IX.
9. Eastman, "Down the Coast from Genoa," *L*, V (June 1922), pp. 6-8.
10. *L*, V (July 1922), p. 27.
11. Eastman, "Journey." He came to believe that the Russians are biologically on the upswing.
12. Charles Recht, who attended the November 7th celebration in Moscow with Eastman, Gregory Weinstein, Meyer Bloomfield, and Albert Rhys Williams, reported: "We also started a dispute with the redoubtable Max on a fine point in Russian grammar, in the course of which he succeeded in showing his superiority. They say that he will soon be able to conjugate 'I love' in Russian as he did in Italian at Genoa." "An American in Moscow," *Soviet Russia Pictorial*, VIII (March 1923), p. 48. Writing in *L*, VII (July 1923), p. 23, Eastman declared admiringly: "Trotsky's voice is so powerful that you rest when he talks. And his thought is so powerful that you rest when he is thinking. He is a born and inevitable leader of men. There is mature restraint and wisdom in his speech, and yet there is young and overflowing boldness." Eastman's "portrait" came out as *Leon Trotsky: The Portrait of a Youth* (N. Y., 1925), an admirable little book and a most perceptive diagnosis of this great man. Eastman's sympathetic identification with "the old party workers," this "noble order," this "selected stock of men and women who could be relied upon to be heroic, like a Knight of the Round Table or the Samurai" (p. 108) was at this time spontaneous and unqualified. For a retrospective view, see his *Reflections on the Failure of Socialism* (N. Y., 1955), p. 11.
13. The reference to Soviet Communism as holy writ is in Eastman, *Reflections*, pp. 11, 12, and "Journey."
14. Eastman, *Heroes I Have Known*, p. 257.
15. See Eastman's introduction to Trotsky's *The Real Situation in Russia* (N. Y., 1928), pp. iii-xvii. This volume, translated by Eastman, was a collection of speeches and documents written by Trotsky and forming the case of the Opposition members of the Central Committee to Stalin's majority. Stalin suppressed the "Opposition Platform" and jailed or exiled its formulators.
16. For the quotations in this paragraph, see Eastman, *Heroes I Have Known*, p. 243, "Journey," *Reflections*, p. 15. Theodore Draper, *American Communism and Soviet Russia* (N. Y., 1960), p. 360, and Eastman, *Since Lenin Died* (N. Y., 1925), p. 106, are also apposite. Eastman slightly exaggerated his ostracism. The real break came a few years later. Claude McKay, who had been lionized in Russia, praised him for aiding the proletarian movement. "You are lifting the clumsy hand of Moscow off it." Eastman, "Journey."
17. *The Autobiography of Lincoln Steffens* (N. Y., 1931), pp. 741-63, 790-802, 806-07.
18. "Journey."
19. The sources for this paragraph are Steffens, *Autobiography*, pp. 807, 823; *The Letters of Lincoln Steffens* (N. Y., 1938), II, pp. 682, 739; "Journey." For a destructive analysis of Steffens as a shoddy thinker and confused dogmatist, see A. B. Rollins, Jr., "The Heart of Lincoln Steffens," *South Atlantic Quarterly*, LIX (Spring 1960), pp. 239-50. Granville Hicks in "Lincoln Steffens: He Covered the Future," *Commentary*, XIII (Feb. 1952), pp. 147-55, sees Steffens as the prototype of the fellow traveler whose "quest for certainty" turned him into a rigid believer in Soviet Communism.
20. Steffens, *Letters*, II, pp. 685, 724.
21. *Letters*, I, p. 463, and *Autobiography*, p. 797.
22. *Letters*, II, p. 545.
23. *Ibid.*, p. 693.
24. *Ibid.*, II, p. 669, and Lincoln Steffens, *Moses in Red* (N. Y., 1926), p. 30.
25. *Letters*, II, p. 880.
26. Freeman, *An American Testament*, p. 415.

27. Freeman to author, June 18, 1958. Tass, at Moscow's request, worked assiduously to keep the American press from referring to the U.S.S.R. as "Russia,"
and in the twenties the A.P. and the U.P. complied. Today, the Soviet regime
accepts the designation "Russia," with its implications of intense nationalism.
Freeman thinks the drift to nationalism "began subtly with 'socialism in one
country' in 1927 and quickened during World War II under Stalin," when
the state became "less and less the Soviet Union of Lenin, and more and more
the Russia of Ivan the Terrible."

28. Freeman, *An American Testament*, p. 336.

29. *Ibid.*, p. 405. The quotations which follow may be found on pp. 455, 459, 505,
506, 547, 533, 543, 544, 527.

30. Freeman to author, June 22, 1958.

31. *Ibid.*, June 6, 1958.

32. All quotations after note 31 are taken from Freeman's June 6, 1958 letter to
the author. The quotation from Freeman's *An American Testament* is on p. 623.

33. Freeman, *An American Testament*, p. 623, and Freeman to author, July 19, 1958.

34. Hofmannsthal's article appeared in *The Dial*, LXXIV (March 1923), pp. 281-
88; Mann's in the same magazine, LXXXIII (July 1927), pp. 53-59.

35. *NR*, XLIV (Oct. 28, 1925), pp. 246-48, (Nov. 11, 1925), pp. 301-03.

36. B. D. Allison, "From the Cultural Front in Russia," *The Dial*, LXXXV (Sept.
1928), pp. 239-45. Almost at the same moment, Theodore Dreiser (who had
spent eleven weeks in Russia in the late fall and early winter of 1927) was
reporting that in the new Russia, "Zane Grey, James Oliver Curwood, Rex
Beach, Ethel M. Dell, as well as Jack London, Fanny Hurst, Edna Ferber, are as
popular and more so than even Tolstoi or Gogol or Dostoievsky could hope to
be." *Dreiser Looks at Russia* (N. Y., 1928), p. 35.

37. "The Bolshevik Religion," *NR*, LIV (April 11, 1928), pp. 250-51.

38. The sources for the quotations in this paragraph are, in order, *The Dial*, LXXX
(April 1926), p. 314, and LXXXIII (Dec. 1927), pp. 503-04; *transition*, No. 13
(Summer 1928), p. 101, and No. 14 (Fall 1928), pp. 141-42.

39. *Dreiser Looks at Russia*.

40. *Ibid.*, pp. 9, 115, 10-11, 19. Dreiser's unsuccessful attempt to see Trotsky
prompted the following comment: "I was told that it was quite impossible,
that the mere seeking of such an interview by me would do harm not only to
myself but to Trotsky. Already he was being watched and anything he had to
say intercepted and censored or destroyed. So anything that I might possibly
obtain from him would also be examined and censored" (pp. 123-24).

41. *Letters of Theodore Dreiser*, ed. by R. H. Elias (N. Y., 1959), II, p. 466.

42. Dos Passos, "The Caucasus Under the Soviets," *L*, V (Aug. 1922), pp. 6-7.

43. Dos Passos, *In All Countries* (N. Y., 1934), pp. 6, 57, 72.

44. *NM*, II (Nov. 1926), p. 5.

45. Gold to Sinclair, n.d. (US).

46. *NM*, II (Nov. 1926), p. 5.

47. Gold, "America Needs a Critic," *NM*, I (Oct. 1926), p. 7.

48. Edward J. Brown, *op. cit.*, pp. 238-39.

49. "The Eastern Bogey," *NM*, II (Nov. 1926), p. 13.

50. Freeman, "Poetry and Common Sense," *NM*, III (May 1927), p. 9.

51. See Trotsky, *Literature and Revolution* (N. Y., 1926), pp. 48, 60.

52. Gold, "America Needs a Critic," p. 7.

53. Freeman, "Poetry and Common Sense," p. 10.

54. Robert Wolf, "They Also Dance," *NM*, III (April 1928), p. 21.

PART TWO · THE APPEAL OF COMMUNISM

1. Cowley, *Exile's Return*, pp. 293, 299.

2. William James, *The Varieties of Religious Experience* (Modern Library), p. 181.

Cowley's epilogue also reveals other hallmarks of conversion: the loss of worry, "the sense of perceiving truths not known before," the new look of the objective world. Cowley, *Exile's Return*, pp. 242-43.

3. Cowley, *Exile's Return*, pp. 300, 302, 203. Cowley later developed the religion-Communism analogy in "Faith and the Future," *Whose Revolution?* ed. by I. D. Talmadge (N. Y., 1941).

4. Nathaniel Hawthorne, *The Blithedale Romance* (The Norton Library, 1958), pp. 46, 247, 38-39.

5. Margaret Marshall, *NR*, CXXX (May 31, 1954), pp. 18-19. "The loftier the goal, the dirtier the means; first, because there is so much at stake; secondly, because a goal disguised in moral terms frees the conscience and with it all the repressed aggressions and hatred of the moral individual." Freeman, "Notes on the Psychology of Revolution" (manuscript).

6. John Gates, *The Story of an American Communist* (N. Y., 1958), p. 13.

7. *Ibid.*, p. 23.

8. *Ibid.*, pp. 112-14.

9. *Front*, I (April 1931), pp. 271-73.

10. Koestler, *Arrow in the Blue* (N. Y., 1952), p. 278.

11. *NM*, VI (Nov. 1930), p. 14.

12. *NM*, XVI (Sept. 3, 1935), p. 21.

13. *NR*, LXXI (July 20, 1932), p. 256.

14. *NR*, LXXIII (Jan. 18, 1933), p. 272.

15. *NF*, II (Nov. 19, 1930), pp. 225-27.

16. Schneider reported his experience in *International Literature*, No. 3 (March 1937), p. 110; Josephson's account is in *NR*, LXXIX (June 6, 1934), pp. 90-93.

17. *International Literature*, No. 12 (1937), p. 110.

18. See *DW*, March 25, 1933. Freeman's manifesto appeared in *NM*, VIII (April 1933), pp. 3-9.

19. *NM*, VIII (April 1933), pp. 10-13.

20. Norman H. Pearson, "The Nazi-Soviet Pact and the End of a Dream," in *America in Crisis*, ed. by D. Aaron (N. Y., 1952), p. 336.

21. *NM*, VIII (April 1933), p. 11.

22. Freeman to author, June 15, 1958.

23. Oscar Jaszi, "Socialism" in *The Encyclopedia of the Social Sciences*, XIV, p. 210.

24. Koestler, *Arrow in the Blue*, pp. 280, 275.

25. "The Fetish of Being Outside," *NM*, XIV (Feb. 26, 1935), p. 23.

26. Johns, *Time of Our Lives*, pp. 333, 326. Johns (1887-1946), onetime associate editor of *The New Masses*, one of the organizers of the first Writers' Congress and the League of American Writers, and director of the New York City Federal Writers' Project (1935-1936), had joined the party in San Francisco early in 1932 after participating in a demonstration for the unemployed. "I had seen demonstrations of workers before," he wrote, "but I had never dreamed of joining with them. It was a moment of decision—of impulsive decision— but I realized that it culminated a long and logical progress of reasoning, fed by many books and articles and by the news of what was going on in the country" (p. 320). See also Edward A. Shils's penetrating *The Torments of Secrecy* (N. Y., 1956), pp. 126-35.

27. One writer relates that after requesting permission to join the party, much to the surprise of his Communist acquaintances, he was taken to a union meeting, a seaman's branch in the Village, and was thrilled by what he felt to be a Dostoevskian atmosphere. Another commented upon the sharp distinction the party made between proletariat and petit bourgeois, and noted that more than one writer wore a workman's shirt when they were on the staff of the *Daily Worker*. Since the majority of the New York City Communists were not proletarian during this period, the authentic worker, for some intellectuals, acquired a romantic glamour.

CHAPTER SIX · "GO LEFT, YOUNG WRITERS"

1. Robert Wolf, *NM*, VIII (Feb. 1928), p. 18. See Rideout, *op. cit.*, p. 130, for a criticism of Wolf's explanations.
2. Theodore Draper says that in 1929 the party numbered approximately 9,500. Of these, he says, one third were English speaking. *American Communism and Soviet Russia*, pp. 188-89.
3. *Ibid.* The metaphor of literary prostitution was constantly employed in radical circles. A typical comment is the following: "After all, in a country where it matters not at all what one *is,* and what one *has* is all that counts, why not don the red kimono, put an automatic piano in the study to provide the proper atmosphere, spring to our typewriters when our publishers call out 'gentlemen calling; ladies in the parlor please.' " Jack Woodward, "A Writer's Apologia," *NM*, IX (Feb. 1929), p. 14. When Archibald MacLeish likened the poet to a whore in 1932, he caused an uproar among liberals and Communists alike.
4. The quotations in this paragraph are from M. H. Hedges, "The War of Cultures," *NM*, I (May 1926), p. 20, and Joseph Freeman, "Sherwood Anderson's Confusion," *NM*, IV (Feb. 1929), p. 6. Hedges was the author of several labor novels and edited the official organ of the electrical workers' union. For an analysis of his work, see Rideout, *op. cit.*, pp. 120-22.
5. Wolf described him in 1928 as "more or less the official poet of the Communist movement in America. Controversies about Mike Gold are dangerous and difficult to avoid—I shall only say that in my opinion he is a vigorous, robust, and often far too verbose and sentimental writer, and that his ideology is far more Anarchist than Communist. His best poem, *A Strange Funeral in Braddock,* is very fine. Mike hates the industrial system, which hurt him cruelly in his youth, as it hurts many slum-proletarians, and when he tries rather self-consciously to love it, he loves it for all the wrong things—for its dirt, noise, smoke, disorder—rather than for its efficiency, speed, abundance, cleanliness, ease. Mike's ideal is a green pasture in the midst of rivers, and when his conscience tells him that this is incorrect, he returns only to take refuge in the mouths of smokestacks that belch smoke but turn no wheels." Wolf, *op. cit.,* p. 20. For Gold's remark on Communists and intellectuals, see *NM*, IV (Sept. 1928), p. 14.
6. Gold, "Notes on Art, Life, Crap-Shooting, Etc.," *NM*, V (Sept. 1929), pp. 10-11. By the "intellectual mob," Gold meant the American disciples of George Gurdjieff (among them Waldo Frank, Jean Toomer, Gorham Munson, Jane Heap, Lincoln Steffens); the Neo-Catholics (T. S. Eliot, Wyndham Lewis, etc.); the bourgeois pessimists ("A small mob of faded lilies" under leaders like Joseph Wood Krutch); the Primitive Bunk-ists (D. H. Lawrence, Sherwood Anderson).
7. The quotation ending "by their commanders" is from *NM*, IV (Sept. 1928), p. 13; the one ending "and corruption" from *NM*, V (Sept. 1929), p. 12; the one ending with "Fascist discipline," *NM*, IV (Sept. 1928), p. 14. His tentative approval of *transition* was shared by Bernard Smith, who noted the escapist and mystical qualities in a collection of *transition* stories but at the same time acknowledged the editor's (Eugene Jolas) "sincerely rebellious understanding of the forces which are degrading art and rendering the artist impotent today. The two tendencies obviously reflect the conflict that must disturb every sensitive intellectual who is still under the influence of old ideologies but conscious of the economic and social movements that are transforming our environment. Their mysticism may be ignored. The awareness of 'chaos' is significant. There is ferment. It is still submerged beneath 'bourgeois forms of literature,' but it must inevitably arise to the surface." *NM*, V (April 1929), p. 16. Lincoln Kirstein, who edited the "esthetic" *Hound and Horn,* like Gold and Smith, found *transition* "more interesting as the mirror of a state of mind than a re-

pository in which to find valuable artistic endeavor. Its sociological implications overbalance its aesthetic, and the consequent style that frames the magazine comes from this fact." *Hound and Horn,* II (Jan.-Mar. 1929), p. 198.

8. Gold, "Go Left, Young Writers," *NM,* IV (Jan. 1929), pp. 3-4.

9. Gold, "American Jungle Notes," *NM,* V (Dec. 1929), pp. 9-10.

10. Harbor Allen, Bruce Barton, Van Wyck Brooks, Heywood Broun, Stuart Chase, Babette Deutsch, Waldo Frank, Robinson Jeffers, Joseph Wood Krutch, Llewelyn Powys, Edwin Seaver, Upton Sinclair, Genevieve Taggard, Edmund Wilson— an odd lot.

11. *NM,* II (Jan. 1927), pp. 5-9.

12. "The Ruskinian Boys See Red," *NM,* III (July 1927), p. 18. This was a review of the Machine Age Exposition held on May 16-18, 1927, in New York City. Her crack at the Ruskinian boy and girl anarchists drew a sharp rejoinder from Lewis Mumford in a later issue. The "revolutionary boys and girls," he said, "are tired and bored; they must worship something: so they worship the Machine: they must believe in something: so they believe in the Machine Age." Veblen or their own eyes should have taught them that the Machine Age is a product of the business system and that their "chief fetish"—the skyscraper— is "merely a by-product of congestion." Mumford pointed out that bonds, Babbitts, and installment buying went along with the beauties of the Machine and were "equally the marks of a servile plutocracy." Machines were good or bad, Mumford thought, depending upon their helpfulness or indifference to human life. In her reply to Mumford, Genevieve Taggard disclaimed any wish to imply that the Machine Age was "good or perfect"; she simply thought it "false and literary" to like it and pretend that we don't. We talk about the enslavement to the machine, but what we principally dislike is work of any sort. "The yell is a leisure class yell and not a Social Philosophy." The proletariat knows it has to work, but the "literary boys and girls don't know how to work, even at their literary tasks. They go from mental golf-club to golf-club, because they belong to a class, emotionally, that has no structural or functional or whatever you like, connection with this going concern of a world." *NM,* III (Sept. 1927), pp. 23-24. See Edward O'Brien, *The Dance of the Machines* (N. Y., 1929) for a full-scale commentary on the mechanization of American men and American culture. O'Brien discusses, among other things, the Soviet proletcult and the machine.

13. "Are Artists People?" *NM,* II (Jan. 1927), pp. 5-9.

14. *Ibid.,* p. 6.

15. *L,* IV (June 1921), p. 36.

16. Eugene Lyons, *Assignment in Utopia* (N. Y., 1937), p. 31. The most detailed account of the Sacco-Vanzetti case is G. L. Joughin and E. M. Morgan, *The Legacy of Sacco and Vanzetti* (N. Y., 1948). R. K. Murray in *Red Scare* places the episode in the context of the Mitchell Palmer raids and the anti-Bolshevik hysteria. Other accounts of particular interest are John Dos Passos, *Facing the Chair* (N. Y., 1927), Felix Frankfurter, *The Case of Sacco and Vanzetti* (Boston, 1927), and a short chapter in F. J. Hoffman, *The Twenties* (N. Y., 1955). Upton Sinclair's *Boston* (N. Y., 1928) is perhaps the best-known fictional account of the affair.

17. Gold, "Lynchers in Frockcoats," *NM,* III (Sept. 1927), p. 6.

18. "Sacco-Vanzetti—A Symposium," *NM,* III (Oct. 1927), p. 9.

19. *NM,* III (Oct. 1927), p. 3.

20. Arens's comments are in *ibid.* The quotation ending "class-conscious sects" is in *NR,* LII (Sept. 7, 1927), p. 58; for O'Sheel's words, see *ibid.,* p. 61.

21. The phrase "dago Christ" is from Malcolm Cowley's "For St. Bartholomew's Day," published in *N,* CXXVII (Aug. 22, 1928), p. 175. *America Arraigned!* ed. by Lucia Trent and Ralph Cheney (N. Y., 1928), is an anthology of poetry about Sacco and Vanzetti. Poems by Edna St. Vincent Millay, Dos Passos, Babette Deutsch, and many others appeared in the liberal press. See Hoffman,

op. cit., pp. 360-61. The source of Dos Passos's comment is *NM,* III (Nov. 1927), p. 25. Wilson's sketches are "A Preface to Persius," *NR,* LII (Oct. 19, 1927), pp. 237-39, and "The Men from Rumpelmayer," in *The American Earthquake* (N. Y., 1958), pp. 152-60. In the last, the agony of Sacco and Vanzetti forms a leitmotiv for a lobster dinner. One of the two attractive and sympathetic girls shows as much concern for the lobsters about to be boiled alive as for Vanzetti, who must be innocent because, as she says, anyone who could say, " 'I am innocent of these two harms' . . . couldn't have done anything really bad . . ." (p. 154).

22. "Liberalism and the Class War," *MQ,* IV (Nov. 1927-Feb. 1928), pp. 191-94. Lovett, with Glenn Frank and David Starr Jordan, had organized the Citizens' National Committee for Sacco and Vanzetti. His conclusion was backed by a correspondent to *The New Republic* who wrote: "The class struggle is on, and the day of the liberals is past. The 'socially important mediating minds,' as you so naively call them, have all taken their stations alongside their pocketbooks, and from now on they mean, not merely to fingerprint all the wops and hang all the anarchists, but to crack the skulls of all the young intelligentsia who try to use the streets for purposes of social protest. . . ." *NR,* LII (Oct. 26, 1927), p. 247.

23. "Echoes of a Crime," *NR,* LXXXIV (Aug. 28, 1935), p. 79.

24. *NM,* III (Oct. 1927), p. 7.

25. "American Writers and Kentucky," *NM,* VII (June 1932), p. 9.

26. *N,* CXXV (Aug. 24, 1927), p. 176.

27. "American Jungle Notes," *op. cit.,* p. 8.

28. Granville Hicks, *I Like America* (N. Y., 1938), pp. 97-98.

29. *Americana,* I (Nov. 1932).

30. Once, in the twenties, Cummings had watched some Parisian policemen break up a Communist demonstration, and noted in one of his poems how they picked themselves up, brushed off the dirt, spit blood and teeth:

> "the Communists have (very) fine eyes
> (which strill hither and thither through the
> evening in bruised narrow questioning faces)"

(quoted in Norman, *op. cit.,* p. 202). In Russia, he translated, as an act of friendship, Louis Aragon's "The Red Front," a long revolutionary poem, which he later destructively analyzed in *Eimi* (N. Y., 1933), an account of his short visit to the U.S.S.R. in 1931. From then on, Cummings carried on a sniping war against the Communists. In *No Thanks* (N. Y., 1935), a volume of poems, Cummings attacked the "kumrads" as haters of life and fearers of love who danced to the pipes of Moscow.

31. For an account of the Scottsboro case, see *Letters of Theodore Dreiser,* II, pp. 535-36. Irving Howe and Lewis Coser, *The American Communist Party* (Boston, 1957), pp. 213-16, succinctly relate the long-drawn-out struggle to save the defendants and the role of the Communist Party in the case between 1931 and 1935, when a compromise was reached and four of the accused were released. Communist tactics, they conclude, might well have saved the boys from death, but the party "exploited" the case for its own ends and won a considerable Negro following "through hard work . . . partly through lack of scruples; partly through the default of others" (p. 216).

32. For the first quotation in this paragraph, see *Letters of Theodore Dreiser,* II, p. 513; for the concluding one, Dreiser, "Individualism and the Jungle," *NM,* VII (Jan. 1932), p. 4. On January 9, 1932, Dreiser wrote to Ralph Holmes, "I believe capitalism, with its mighty stock market, so highly manipulated for speculation, with its monopolies depriving citizens of their livelihood, with its waste, and its general cut-throat and by-force methods, is a menace that absolutely must not be doctored or dickered with. . . . A new method must be evolved, and for that method one must look to Russia." *Letters of Theodore Dreiser,* II, pp. 572-73. Dreiser did not join the Communist Party until 1945,

but according to Earl Browder (conversation with author, July 6, 1956), Dreiser sought and was denied admission much earlier. Browder personally opposed his admission and doubted his Communism. Dreiser was accepted after Browder's expulsion.

33. Dos Passos, *The Theme Is Freedom* (N. Y., 1956), p. 81. An early and slightly different account of the Harlan episode can be found in his *In All Countries*, pp. 191-98. For additional information, see C. R. Walker, "We Went to Harlan," *NM*, VII (Dec. 1931), p. 3, and Sam Ornitz, "Miners & Mules," *ibid.*, p. 4. The full report of the investigation is *Harlan Miners Speak, Report on Terrorism in the Kentucky Coal Fields Prepared by Members of the National Committee for the Defense of Political Prisoners* (N. Y., 1932).

34. Dos Passos, *The Theme Is Freedom*, p. 74.

35. The occasion was a meeting of the National Committee for the Defense of Political Prisoners in New York City on Dec. 7, 1931. Dos Passos, one of the indicted writers, gave a one-sentence speech "saying that conditions in Harlan are typical of the whole coal industry, and that something's got to be done about it." New York *Herald Tribune*, Dec. 7, 1931. Anderson's speech was printed as "Let's Have More Criminal Syndicalism" in *NM*, VII (Feb. 1932), pp. 3-6.

36. Writing in 1956, Dos Passos declared that in 1931 he already felt that Communists were using the plight of the Harlan miners for their own ends, scorning "sincere I.W.W. and A.F. of L. men" and "denying help to men who wouldn't play their game." Nevertheless, he still felt they were the only ones who seemed to have the revolutionary dedication. He edited the reports of the Dreiser Committee, "but I was a little more wary in my dealings with them after that." *The Theme Is Freedom*, pp. 86-87.

37. Delmore Schwarz, "The Writing of Edmund Wilson," *Accent*, II (Spring 1942), p. 183. See also Stanley Hyman, *The Armed Vision* (N. Y., 1948), pp. 37-39.

38. *NR*, LIV (April 4, 1928), p. 226.

39. Three plays, collected in *This Room and This Gin and These Sandwiches* (N. Y., 1937), represent, in Wilson's words, "three successive stages of the artistic and moral revolt" after World War I. They may also be clues to his private struggle.

The first, "The Crime in the Whistler Room," produced by the Provincetown Players in 1924, dramatizes the clash between the old and the new America. Miss Clara Streetfield, a maidenly genteel do-gooder has rescued a waitress named Bill (short for Elizabeth). Like Daisy, the heroine of Wilson's first novel, *I Thought of Daisy* (N. Y., 1929), Bill is a commoner from Pittsburgh. She is in love with Simon Delacy, a wild Middle Western F. Scott Fitzgerald and author of a notorious novel, "The Ruins of the Ritz." Delacy is dissipated but innocent, an *enfant terrible* filled with boundless confidence. He fights with waiters and goes to parties thrown by bootleggers. The Streetfields represent the decayed gentility of the past, the decade of Whistler and Thomas Bailey Aldrich. There is a long dream sequence in which Clara's bachelor brother, in whose weak degenerate face can be seen the remnants of his powerful forebears, makes a defense for his supplanted class. Simon recognizes that Mr. Streetfield had genuine temperament but that he was betrayed by his generation just as Simon is by his. (Wilson himself, one suspects, is drawn to this defunct world which he is rejecting. He, too, must have read Saint-Simon and Jane Austen and retained, and retains, a partiality for order, elegance, tradition.) But whereas the older man succumbed, like the heroes of Edith Wharton or J. Alfred Prufrock, Simon reclaims his simple, honest, frankly sensual, but innocent sweetheart. He says to her: "You and I have the same ideas! I've told the whole of America where to get off! And you've never been bounced by it! You have rejected both the drudgery of the slaves and the dismal salvation of the masters! You and I stand apart from this race! We must found a race of our own" (p. 83). The future, he tells her, belongs to them. This is the declaration of independence of the twenties, and when it turns to dust and ashes, Marxism will succeed it, and the new generation, in the name of Marx, will say that the future belongs to them.

"A Winter in Beech Street" must have been written around 1931–32. There are references to the Coolidge election, but part of the action is related to the "Payson" (Paterson) strike and hints of the possibility of the Beech Street Theatre doing a dramatization of the strike. The comments on anarchism, the Reds, and labor reminds us of the old *Masses* group, but the play really belongs to the period when Greenwich Village unity was breaking down. The central character, Arthur, is a kind of stuffed shirt. He is saved by his connection with the theater group of Bohemians, and he finally gets Sally, the pretty actress, to marry him. She is something like Daisy, something like Bill, but she is less simple and more of an intellectual. Arthur does not lose all of his prissyness; he is still a little prim and vindictive, lacking the open-heartedness and spontaneity of the artists. Yet he has the reserve and firmness which keeps him from becoming a boozer. He has learned to unbend, to repudiate his genteel past, to resign from his club, buy drinks for his friends, enjoy the slovenly intimacy of a rumpled bed; but he does not yield to Bohemia. Rather, he tempers it with prudence and responsibility. Politics is more insistent in this play, the struggle for survival more bitter than in "The Crime in the Whistler Room," the references to revolution more pervasive.

"Beppo and Beth" is frankly a Depression play, written after the Crash. It ends with a discouraged Beppo deciding to remarry Beth after an evening of farce and terror.

40. Wilson, "The Muses Out of Work," *NR*, L (May 11, 1927), p. 321.
41. Wilson, *The American Earthquake*, p. 321. Wilson's reports were published as *The American Jitters: A Year of the Slump* (N. Y., 1932). They are reprinted in *The American Earthquake*.
42. Wilson to Sherwood Anderson, June 23, 1931 (Anderson Papers, Newberry Library).
43. *Ibid.*
44. The source of the first and second quotations in this paragraph is Wilson, *The American Earthquake*, p. 342. For the last, see Wilson to Anderson, *op. cit.*
45. The quotation ending with "naked forms" is from Wilson, "Class War Exhibits," *NM*, VII (April 1932), p. 7. Besides Wilson and Frank, the writers' committee also included Malcolm Cowley, Mary Heaton Vorse, Polly Boyden, Benjamin Lieder, Dr. Elsa Reed Mitchell, John Henry Hammond, Jr., Liston M. Oak, Quincy Howe, A. M. Max, and Harold Hickerson. The quotation ending with "coal country" is from M. A. Hallgren, *Seeds of Revolt* (N. Y., 1933), p. 65; the one ending with "butts of guns" is from Wilson's "Class War Exhibits," p. 7. For a full account of the episode, see the minutes of "A Hearing in Washington," in which Frank, Taub, and C. R. Walker reported to a Senate committee on the situation in Kentucky, in *Harlan Miners Speak*, pp. 313-48. Malcolm Cowley reported his version of the episode in "Kentucky Coal Town," *NR*, LXX (March 2, 1932), pp. 67-70.
46. Conversation with author.
47. "American Writers and Kentucky," p. 9.
48. *NR*, LXX (March 30, 1932), p. 185.
49. *NM*, VII (May 1932), p. 24.
50. *NR*, LXX (March 30, 1932), p. 186. " 'Equity,' " wrote John Dos Passos, "was the word Dreiser used continually. He wanted equity. Like so many words it was a hard one to corner. I had trouble getting a sharp meaning out of it. It led him, strangely, into a communist camp in later years. I already had a suspicion that this equity meant taking away everything the rich had. We were an ill-educated lot but I had already acquired enough political sophistication to know that wouldn't make the poor any richer. We had to learn our way as we went. American writers were babes in the woods in those days." *The Theme Is Freedom*, p. 87. Although Wilson did not know it at the time, Dreiser

had made a similar comment about the connotations of the word "Communism" for Americans. As he wrote to a correspondent in April 1932: "The Communists are usually met with bitterness if not bullets, but I am convinced that the reason for that lies in the fact that the American temperament will not accept Communism as practiced by the Russians. But I believe that Communism as practiced by the Russians, or, at least, some part if not most of it, can certainly be made palatable to the average American if it is properly explained to him and if the title Communism is removed." *Letters of Theodore Dreiser*, II, p. 576. Dreiser and Wilson were both following a line of reasoning set forth in the 1890's by Edward Bellamy, who substituted "Nationalism" for "Socialism," a term, he said, that smacked of infidelity, free love, and brimstone.

51. The quotations in this paragraph are taken respectively from "An Appeal to Progressives," reprinted in Edmund Wilson, *The Shores of Light* (N. Y., 1952), p. 532; *NR*, LXVIII (Nov. 11, 1931), pp. 344-45; and "What Do the Liberals Hope For?" *NR*, LXIX (Feb. 10, 1932), p. 348. Commenting on this article, Lincoln Steffens harped on his favorite theme of liberal squeamishness and the futility of the old democratic shibboleths of majority rule and free speech: "My [our] victory in Russia did take some of the fight out of me. The growing success over there made all progressive movements and liberal programs seem superficial, long and rather hopeless. And to start out again at the bottom to plan to search deeper toward the roots for a revolution—that looks like a long, hard course to take for an old, habituated Menshevik with only a thin skin of Bolshevism on his hardened arteries." *NR*, LXX (Feb. 17, 1932), p. 15.

52. "Brokers and Pioneers," *NR*, LXX (March 23, 1932), p. 145.

53. Thomas noted that if Wilson merely wanted to change the personnel of Communism, that was one thing. But if he wanted Socialism without the paraphernalia of dictatorship, if he did not believe that that was inevitable, then his "Communism" would not be "Communism" and he would join the Socialist Party. *NR*, LXV (Feb. 11, 1931), p. 354. Hallowell, disturbed by Wilson's readiness to give up traditional democracy and capitalism, argued that the country only needed to be true to its abandoned principles. Neither racketeering capitalism nor Communism would do. America needed to experiment intelligently with regulated capitalism, not to meddle with revolution. The old machine was still workable. Only the liberals stood between the old free America and the unfree America that would certainly emerge if the views of the liberals were ignored. *NR*, LXV (Feb. 4, 1931), pp. 324-26.

54. Josephson, "The Road of Indignation," *NR*, LXVI (Feb. 18, 1931), pp. 13-15.

55. Mencken's reply is quoted in Helen Black, "Inciting to Revolution—," *NM*, VI (June 1930), p. 9. Other declarations of support came from John Sloan, Genevieve Taggard, Edmund Wilson, Upton Sinclair, Carl Van Doren, Waldo Frank, Harriet Munroe, Isidor Schneider, Stark Young, and others.

56. *NM*, V (Feb. 1929), p. 29.

57. The quotations ending with "party affiliations," "art of straddling," "capitalist world" and "any idea" are taken from *NM*, V (Dec. 1929), p. 20, (April 1930), p. 3, VI (Aug. 1930), p. 3, and p. 4.

58. Gold to Sinclair, n.d. (US).

59. "The Jesus-Thinkers," *L*, V (Sept. 1922), pp. 11-12.

60. The quotations ending with "compromiser," "man-of-letters," and "class struggle" are in *NM*, VI (Oct. 1930), p. 2, VII (June 1931), p. 5, and V (April 1930), pp. 4-5.

61. "Literature at the Crossroads," *NM*, VII (April 1932), p. 12.

62. *The Workers Monthly,* IV (May 1925), p. 362.

63. "Leftward Ho!" *MM*, VI (Summer 1932), pp. 26-32.

64. John Dos Passos, Sherwood Anderson, Ernest Sutherland Bates, Henry S. Canby, Floyd Dell, C. Hartley Grattan, Edwin Seaver, Henry Hazlitt, John Chamberlain, Rudolph Fisher, Malcolm Cowley, Percy H. Boynton, Pierre Loving, Edmund Wilson, Newton Arvin, Granville Hicks, Clifton P. Fadiman.

65. "Whither the American Writer," *MQ*, VI (Summer 1932), p. 11.
66. The Communists, of course, spoke of the Socialists with contempt. Hicks, a recent convert in 1932, dismissed the philosophy of socialism as a futile and dishonest compromise with the petty bourgeois. "Being a Socialist—like being a liberal—means that the writer is not really thinking and feeling in terms of the class struggle, that he is not really allying himself with the proletariat." Socialism, in short, was middle-class, respectable, lukewarm, "too deeply implicated in the capitalist outlook to provide firm *direction*" (Grattan). Socialism accepted anyone, from "a fake bohemian to a lawyer for the oil trust" (Seaver), and it did not question the writer's imagination (Cowley) or demand an abandonment of a writer's class attitudes (Arvin). "Whither the American Writer," pp. 11-19. Matthew Josephson spoke for a large segment of the Left writers when he contrasted the "mildly rebellious" Socialist Party, with its "vaguely generalized appeal for a *partial* collectivism," to the militant Communist Party: "Where the Communists, with their principles of direct action, live in a revolutionary ferment, or give themselves to revolutionary planning, the Socialists have for a long time passed their days as little capitalists, putting on their red bonnets at night to preach their variety of non-militant socialism. How can those who spend most of their time adjusting themselves to a powerful and complex economic order hope to overthrow it by using persuasion in their leisure time?" *NR*, LXXII (Aug. 17, 1932), p. 22.
67. "Whither the American Writer," p. 11.
68. The quotation ending with "evolution" is in "How I Came to Communism," *NM*, VIII (Sept. 1932), p. 6. Mary Colum's comment appeared in *F*, III (Oct. 17, 1923), p. 140. She described Frank's style as "often gaudy and unsubtle; so unsubtle that, at times, it seems as if he intended it to be written in letters of smoke a mile high, rather than in the pages of a book." *Ibid.* The quotation ending with "materialize" is in "How I Came to Communism," p. 6. Frank's *Our America* announced his demand for art and revolution.
69. "How I Came to Communism," p. 7.
70. *Ibid.*, p. 8.
71. *MQ*, VI (Summer 1932), p. 112.
72. Wilson, *The American Jitters*, pp. 297-313.
73. *Culture and Crisis: An Open Letter to the Writers, Artists, Teachers, Physicians, Engineers, Scientists and Other Professional Workers of America* (League of Professional Groups for Foster and Ford, 1932). The other signers were Leonie Adams, Sherwood Anderson, Newton Arvin, Em Jo Basshe, Maurice Becker, Slater Brown, Fielding Burke, Erskine Caldwell, Robert Cantwell, W. L. Chappell, Lester Cohen, Louis Colman, Lewis Corey (Fraina), Henry Cowell, Malcolm Cowley, Bruce Crawford, K. C. Crichton, Countee Cullen, H. W. L. Dana, Adolf Dehn, John Dos Passos, H. N. Doughty, M. A. de Ford, Waldo Frank, Alfred Frueh, Murray Godwin, Eugene Gordon, Horace Gregory, Louis Grudin, John Herrman, Granville Hicks, Sidney Hook, Sidney Howard, Langston Hughes, Orrick Johns, W. N. Jones, Matthew Josephson, Alfred Kreymborg, Louis Lozowick, Grace Lumpkin, Felix Morrow, Samuel Ornitz, James Rorty, Isidor Schneider, F. L. Schuman, Edwin Seaver, Herman Simpson, Lincoln Steffens, Charles R. Walker, Robert Whitaker, Edmund Wilson, Ella Winter.
74. Dos Passos, *The Theme Is Freedom*, p. 101.

CHAPTER SEVEN · FROM FREEDOM TO POLITICS

1. "The New Masses I'd Like," *NM*, I (June 1926), p. 20.
2. Gold, "Let It Be Really New!" *NM*, I (June 1926), p. 20.
3. *NM*, I (Dec. 1926), p. 23.
4. *Ibid.*

5. The letters of Pound and Eastman are in *NM*, I (Dec. 1926), p. 3; of Untermeyer, in *ibid.*, II (Jan. 1927), p. 3.

6. "On Being Radical," *NM*, III (May 1927), p. 3.

7. Egmont Arens to the American Fund for Public Service (GF).

8. Arens to Roger Baldwin, Jan. 31, 1928 (GF).

9. Michael Gold and Hugo Gellert to the American Fund for Public Service, March 23, 1928 (GF).

10. Eastman to Roger Baldwin, Feb. 4, 1928 (GF).

11. Freda Kirchwey to Anna Marnitz, April 3, 1928 (GF).

12. *NM*, IV (July 1928), p. 2.

13. *NM*, V (Nov. 1929), p. 22. A year later, a German revolutionary writer congratulated *The New Masses* on ridding itself of "vacillating elements." The magazine, he noted, "still manifests vestiges of an expressionism which does not always harmonize with the true-to-reality writing of its contributors. But of late a change seems to be impending here as well." *NM*, VI (Oct. 1930), p. 23.

14. Frederick L. Olmsted, *A Journey in the Seaboard Slave States in the Years 1853-1854* (N. Y. and London, 1904 edition), I, p. 240.

15. See Edward and Eleanor Marx Aveling, *The Working-Class Movement in America* (London, 2nd edition, 1891), pp. 17-18, and John Swinton, *A Momentous Question* (N. Y., 1895), p. 185. For a good summary of the writers who did concern themselves with what the Marxists called "the innermost depths of the modern inferno," see Rideout, *op. cit.* Markham's remark is in *The Comrade*, I (Oct. 1901), p. 11.

16. *NR*, XII (Sept. 29, 1917), p. 249.

17. *Ibid.*, pp. 249-50.

18. The sources of the quotations for this paragraph are: *F*, IV (Nov. 9, 1921), p. 209; *NM*, II (March 1927), pp. 5-6; *ibid.* Some 155 years before, an American, Thomas Odiorne, had argued along the same lines as *The New Masses* writer in his *The Progress of Refinement* (1792). The frontiersmen who chopped down the forests, Odiorne said in creaking blank verse, were not "idle clowns."
    "And all, performing their allotted part,
    Became shrewd artists at their work, expert,
    Exact. . . ."
Quoted in Merle Curti, *The Growth of American Thought* (N. Y. and London, 2nd ed., 1951), p. 178.

19. At this time, Earl Browder agreed: "At the same time I am more inclined to Trotsky's view on the question of whether proletarian culture is possible of development. We have got so far to go before we make use of even a considerable portion of what has already been created that I seriously doubt the capacity of the working class to create a new system of culture during the period of struggle. Without a doubt we will witness a tremendous release of creative forces and the proletariat will establish the lines within which the future developments must come, but that the distinct class character will be woven thru the contents of the culture of the future, seems doubtful to me." Browder to V. F. Calverton, Oct. 29, 1925 (VFC).

20. *NM*, I (Oct. 1926), p. 8.

21. *NM*, VI (Sept. 1930), pp. 4-5.

22. Gold acidly remarked that no publishing house concerned itself with proletarian literature. Even International Publishers took "a rather academic approach to economics" and was as "stodgy and unenterprising in its Communist way as the Yale University Press was in its way." *Ibid.*, p. 5.

23. Nearing's letter is in *NM*, IV (July 1928), p. 2; the "well-wisher's" letter (Newton Arvin) is in *NM*, VI (Dec. 1930), p. 22; Kalar's letter is in *NM*, V (Sept. 1929), p. 22.

24. *Front*, I (April 1931), pp. 193-94.

25. *Ibid.*, p. 194.

26. *NM*, VI (Nov. 1930), p. 22.

27. *NM*, V (Nov. 1929), p. 22.

28. *The Morada*, No. 3 (May 15, 1930), pp. 91-93.

29. Lenin's letter is in *L*, I (Jan. 1919), p. 10. A former proletarian novelist, Edward Dahlberg, concluded (after he had renounced Communism) that the proletarian writer's "necrophilism, the bitter corpse-lust," was really a projection of his own self-revulsion. The *"People"* became "the ritual bull that must be killed and eaten so that society, the cadaver-flesh of the masses can be reborn!" Socialism, barren of myths of rebirth, lacking "cosmognal mystery," must seek its purgation through the dismemberment of the worker. *Do These Bones Live* (N. Y., 1941), pp. 59-62. Howard Fast was an expert practitioner of the decay-and-disease school of Communist polemic. He could write of Ezra Pound's Bollingen Award: "Like a foul fistula, overloaded with pus, this corruption exploded in the presentation of the Bollingen-Library of Congress award to the fascist poet, Ezra Pound." *Literature and Reality* (N. Y., 1950), p. 18.

30. Dudley Fitts in *The Hound and Horn*, IV (July-Sept. 1931), p. 636.

31. "Re-definitions: II," *NR*, LXVIII (Aug. 26, 1931), pp. 46-47.

32. For Jolas's quotation, see *transition*, No. 15 (Sept. 1929), p. 188; for Herrick's, *NR*, LXXX (Oct. 17, 1934), p. 261.

33. *NM*, V (Jan. 1930), p. 21. Joseph Kalar did not completely agree with Gold. He observed that a roving observer could do a better job in catching the essence of a particular industry than one who was immersed in it. *NM*, V (April 1930), p. 21. Ralph Cheyney wrote that poems of industry were composed in retrospect. *NM*, V (Feb. 1930), p. 21.

34. Gold, "John Reed and the Real Thing," *NM*, III (Nov. 1927), p. 7. Gold at this time chided the party for its Philistinism: "The word 'intellectual' became a synonym for the word 'bastard,' and in the American Communist movement there is some of this feeling." *Ibid.*

35. Gold, "Floyd Dell Resigns," *NM*, V (July 1929), p. 10.

36. Dell, *Homecoming*, p. 350.

37. *NM*, I (Oct. 1926), p. 28.

38. Dell to Calverton, Oct. 17, 1926 (VFC).

39. "Floyd Dell Resigns," p. 11.

40. *Ibid.*

41. "O Life, send America a great literary critic. The generation of writers is going to seed again. Some of them started well, but are beginning to live fat and high, and have forgotten the ardors of their generous youth. This generation of writers is corrupted by all the money floating around everywhere. It is unfashionable to believe in human progress any longer. It is unfashionable to work for a better world. . . . Send us a critic. Send us a giant who can shame our writers back to their task of civilizing America. Send us a soldier who has studied history. Send a strong poet who loves the masses, and their future. Send us someone who doesn't give a damn about money. Send one who is not a pompous liberal, but a man of the street. Send no mystics—they give us Americans the willies. Send no coward. Send no pedant. Send us a man fit to stand up to skyscrapers. A man of art who can match the purposeful deeds of Henry Ford. Send us a joker in overalls. Send no saint. Send an artist. Send a scientist. Send a Bolshevik. . . ." Gold, "America Needs a Critic," *NM*, I (Oct. 1926), p. 9.

42. From the correspondence of Floyd Dell.

43. Koestler, *Arrow in the Blue*, p. 272.

44. From the correspondence of Floyd Dell.

45. *Ibid.*

46. Gold, "Notes from Kharkov," *NM*, VI (March 1931), p. 4.

47. "The Charkov Conference of Revolutionary Writers," *NM*, VI (Feb. 1931), p. 7.

48. "Notes from Kharkov," p. 5.

49. "The Charkov Conference," p. 7.

50. "Artists in Uniform," *MM*, VII (Aug. 1933), pp. 347-404.

51. *NM*, VIII (Aug. 1933), pp. 14-15, VIII (Sept. 1933), pp. 13-15.
52. "The Charkov Conference," p. 8.
53. "Notes from Kharkov," p. 5.
54. "Draft Manifesto of John Reed Clubs," *NM*, VII (June 1932), pp. 3-4.
55. Representing ten John Reed Clubs with a claimed membership of 800 writers and artists: Portland, Oregon, 1; Detroit, 9; Boston, 2; Philadelphia, 1; Newark, N. J., 2; San Francisco, 3; Hollywood, Calif., 1; Seattle, 1; Chicago, 8; New York, 10. The Washington, D. C., and Cleveland John Reed Clubs were not represented. Each club was entitled to elect one member to the presidium.
56. *Minutes of the First National Conference of the John Reed Clubs* (mimeographed version in possession of author).
57. "The John Reed Club Convention," *NM*, VIII (July 1932), pp. 14-15.
58. Freeman to author, July 3, 1958.
59. *Minutes*.
60. "The John Reed Club Convention," p. 14.
61. *Minutes*.
62. Freeman to author, July 3, 1958.
63. For charges against *The New Masses*, see A. Elistratova, "New Masses," *International Literature*, No. 1 (1932), pp. 107-14. The chief "social fascists," of course, were Max Eastman and V. F. Calverton. The *mea culpa* of *The New Masses* editors is in *NM*, VIII (Sept. 1932), p. 20.

CHAPTER EIGHT • STATEMENT AND COUNTERSTATEMENT

1. Eugene Lyons, *The Red Decade: The Stalinist Penetration of America* (Indianapolis and N. Y., 1941), p. 129.
2. For further background on the Humanist controversy, see Hoffman, *The Twenties*, pp. 142-43; Cowley, *Exile's Return*, p. 37; Wilson, *The Shores of Light*, pp. 143, 245.
3. Hoffman, *The Twenties*, p. 143.
4. "Notes on American Literature," *The Communist*, VII (Sept. 1928), pp. 570-78.
5. Freeman was referring to a pro-Humanist symposium, *Humanism and America* (N. Y., 1930), ed. by Norman Foerster, and a reply by a group of militant anti-Humanists, *The Critique of Humanism: A Symposium* (N. Y., 1930), ed. by C. Hartley Grattan. Among the leaders of Humanism's cohorts were, besides Babbitt, More, and Foerster, Gorham Munson, Robert Shafer, P. S. Frye, and Seward Collins. Malcolm Cowley, Edmund Wilson, Newton Arvin, Kenneth Burke, Allen Tate, R. P. Blackmur, and Lewis Mumford were some of their formidable opponents.
6. Freeman, "Social Trends in American Literature," *The Communist*, IX (July 1930), pp. 641-51.
7. *Ibid.*, p. 648.
8. The letter from the thirty-three appeared in *NR*, LXII (March 26, 1930), p. 153. For Cowley's attack, see *NR*, LXII (April 9, 1930), p. 208. Wilson's comment on Babbitt is reprinted in *The Shores of Light*, pp. 455-56. Josephson's remark on the Tory-Humanists is in *NR*, LXII (April 16, 1930), pp. 250-51. For Arvin's quotation, see *NF*, I (March 29, 1930), p. 68.
9. Freeman, "Social Trends," p. 651.
10. The editor of *The Hound and Horn* was Alan M. Strook. His comment appeared in *NF*, I (June 18, 1930), p. 348; Cowley's is taken from *Exile's Return*, p. 234. The quotations from Calverton are taken from "Humanism: Literary Fascism," *NM*, V (April 1930), pp. 9-10.
11. Calverton, *NM*, V (April 1930), p. 4.
12. *NM*, VI (July 1930), p. 4.
13. *NM*, VI (July 1930), p. 5.
14. *NM*, V (May 1930), p. 18.

15. Gold's reply to Kunitz and Kunitz's rejoinder are in *NM*, VI (June 1930), p. 22, and (July 1930), p. 23.
16. For Lewis's letter, see *NM*, VI (July 1930), p. 22; for the reply, *NM*, VI (Aug. 1930), p. 22.
17. Quoted in letter from Freeman to author, June 30, 1958.
18. Wilson, *The Shores of Light*, p. 500, describes the controversy; the editorial decision to call off the battle is in *NR*, LXV (Dec. 17, 1930), p. 141.
19. *NR*, LXIV (Oct. 22, 1930), p. 267.
20. Wilson, *The Shores of Light*, pp. 502-03, 500.
21. The "scurrilous and godless" comment is in *NM*, VI (Jan. 1931), pp. 4-6; the rabbi's letter in *NR*, LXV (Dec. 17, 1930), p. 141.
22. Crane's allusion to the controversy is in *The Letters of Hart Crane*, ed. by Brom Weber (N. Y., 1952), p. 357; Smith's remark in *NR*, LXV (Dec. 10, 1930), p. 104.
23. Wilder's comment on the affair is taken from a card to the author, March 25, 1959; the reference to St. Thornton is in a letter from Harry Hansen to V. F. Calverton, n.d. (VFC); Wilson's summary is in *The Shores of Light*, p. 539.
24. J. T. Farrell, "Thirty and Under," *NF*, I (July 2, 1930), pp. 373-74.
25. Calverton's plans are contained in a letter to Lewis Mumford, May 6, 1929 (VFC); Mumford replied on May 8, 1929 (VFC).
26. The new title is suggested by Calverton in a letter to Dos Passos, July 8, 1930 (VFC). Hicks wrote to Calverton, Jan. 15, 1932 (VFC).
27. Like his friends Hicks and Arvin, Smith, to quote his own *Forces in American Criticism* (N. Y., 1939), "found the adjustment to Marxist ideas relatively easy" (p. 374). He remained an orthodox fellow traveler throughout the thirties. His ideas at this time and those of his friends are reflected in a sequence of letters in the possession of Granville Hicks, who kindly permitted me to see them.
28. Hazlitt, "Literature and the Class War," *N*, CXXXV (Oct. 19, 1932), p. 361.
29. *NR*, LXXII (Sept. 14, 1932), p. 133.
30. *The Criterion*, VIII (July 1929), pp. 682-91.
31. Cowley, *Exile's Return*, p. 239.
32. The quotation ending with "religious fervor" is in *The Criterion*, XI (April 1932), p. 467; the one ending with "beyond them" in *ibid.*, pp. 690-91; the one ending with "Granville Hicks," in *ibid.*, XII (Jan. 1933), pp. 244-49. The reference to "free-thinking Jews" is in T. S. Eliot, *After Strange Gods* (N. Y., 1934), p. 20. The quotation ending the paragraph is in *The Criterion*, X (April 1931), pp. 484-85.
33. The quotation ending with "its epoch" is also Eliot's. See *The Criterion*, XII (Jan. 1933), p. 248. Constance Rourke, for example, was one who could chide the Marxists on extrapolitical grounds. Calverton and Hicks, she felt, underestimated the role of sections and made too much of industrial nationalism and the class struggle in their interpretations of American literature. Decentralization had prevented the possibility of a deep collective life developing. This explained why American literature, "with a number of magnificent beginnings," had few sequences and why each of these had been "associated with regions or sections." *NR*, LXXVI (Sept. 20, 1933), p. 150. E. W. Parks cited Calverton's *The Liberation of American Literature* as the worst example of the "noisy turbulence" that signified so much of Left Wing criticism. Communism was plainly a flop, he said, but "literary racketeers" continued to capitalize "on the 'revolutionary cause,' until that cause can be bled no longer." *NR*, LXXV (Aug. 9, 1933), pp. 343-44. Throughout the thirties, a good many writers and critics continued to find fault with the literary Communists on these and other grounds. Thus Allen Tate could single out Edmund Wilson as a critic "in the direct line of descent from the crudely moralistic allegory of the Renaissance. The notion that all art is primarily an apology for institutions and classes, though it is now the weapon of the Marxists against 'capitalist' literature, has been explicit in our intellectual outlook since the time of Buckle in England, and Taine and Michelet in France. It is an article of faith in the 'capitalist' and

utilitarian dogma that literature, like everything else, must be primarily and solely, an expression of the will." *NR*, LXXVIII (March 28, 1934), p. 182. See also Seward Collins, *The Bookman*, LXXII (Oct. 1930), pp. 162, 209-17, for a more detailed attack on Wilson and his criticism.

34. *NR*, LXX (May 4, 1932), pp. 319-23.
35. For the quotation ending with "commentary," see *ibid.*, p. 349; for the other quotations, *NR*, LXXVI (Aug. 23, 1933), p. 43.
36. See *NR*, LXX (May 11, 1932), p. 348, and LXXVI (Aug. 23, 1933), p. 43.
37. *NR*, LXVI (Feb. 18, 1931), pp. 15-17.
38. Paul Rosenfeld, "The Authors and Politics," *Scribner's Magazine*, XCIII (May 1933), pp. 318-20.
39. Hicks's comment is in *NR*, LXX (April 20, 1932), p. 278. Leighton's opinions are in *The Hound and Horn*, VI (Jan.-March 1933), pp. 324-29.
40. Both hostile critics were writing in *The Examiner*, I (Winter 1938), p. 104, and I (Fall 1938), p. 385. The view that Communist writers were power-hungry derived considerable support from Max Nomad's *Rebels and Renegades* (N. Y., 1932). This book incorporated the ideas of the Polish revolutionist Waclaw Machajski. In 1899 Machajski advanced the theory that all political and economic revolutions were directed by a radical intelligentsia whose conscious or unwitting purpose was to supplant the capitalist class with the help of the proletariat and to become themselves the new rulers. See Daniel Bell, *The End of Ideology* (Glencoe, Ill., 1960), pp. 335-46.
41. H. B. Parkes, "The Limitations of Marxism," *The Hound and Horn*, VII (July-Sept. 1934), p. 566. Parkes conceded that the writer as citizen might side with the working class, but he warned the writer to make this "an alliance . . . not an identity of interests. The intellectual, qua intellectual is not a partisan but a spectator." If he wrote about the class struggle "with the purpose not of understanding it but idealizing one side or the other, falsifying or sentimentalizing the crude realities," it ceased to be literature and became propaganda (pp. 565-81). This essay and other relevant comment later appeared in Parkes's *The Pragmatic Test: Essays on the History of Ideas* (N. Y., 1941). R. P. Blackmur in *The Hound and Horn*, VII (July-Sept. 1934), pp. 725-26, also spoke against superficial politicizing.
42. See M. E. Werner, "American Anarchy and Russian Communism," *The Hound and Horn*, VI (Oct.-Dec. 1932), pp. 5-16.
43. Mumford to Edmund Wilson and Malcolm Cowley, Aug. 17, 1932 (MC). During the twenties, Mumford, deeply influenced by his master, Patrick Geddes, had shown no interest in party politics. Even in the thirties, his "socialism" was Platonic rather than Marxist-Leninist, and he was criticized by orthodox Marxists as a Thoreauvian individualist, and for his unwillingness to jump on the "Red Special." Mumford has correctly observed that the moving idea in the thirties was not a socialist transformation of American society but a desire, especially on the part of middle-class intellectuals and professional people, to cure a desperately sick economy. For a short time, they were ready to try any system or program that promised to restore economic and political democracy and correct injustice.
44. See Krutch to Cowley, Jan. 3, 1935, and Krutch, *Was Europe a Success?* (N. Y., 1934), p. 29.
45. Krutch, *Was Europe a Success?* pp. 32, 61, 63, 75.
46. Seaver's remarks on the new Gorkys and the "cultured riffraff" is in *NM*, VIII (May 1933), p. 23; his quotation of Rolland is in *NM*, VIII (June 1933), p. 13.
47. Hicks, "The Crisis in American Criticism," *NM*, VIII (Feb. 1933), p. 5. The liberal critics Hicks had in mind were Krutch, Henry Hazlitt, Elmer Davis, H. L. Mencken, Henry Seidel Canby, M. R. Werner, and Archibald MacLeish. "The sneers and the denunciations in the daily press" by such journalists as Henry Hansen, Isobel Patterson, and William Soskin he did not think merited replies. Hicks became a *New Masses* editor in 1934 but did not join the party until a year later.

48. *International Literature,* No. 2 (1933), p. 125, No. 3 (1933), p. 109.
49. Rahv's essay appeared in *NM,* VIII (Aug. 1932), pp. 7-10. Magil's critique in *NM,* VIII (Dec. 1932), pp. 16-19.
50. *SRL,* VIII (Jan. 16, 1932), pp. 453-54. MacLeish developed the theme of this article more fully in "Preface to an American Manifesto," *Forum,* XCI (April 1934), pp. 195-98. His line at this time inspired the following thumbnail sketch of him by a Left writer: "Basso cantante in the lumpen intellectuals' oratorio to Beatific Big Business, fascist patron saint and deity." Joseph Koven, "The Liberal Literary Legion," *Monthly Review,* I (June 1934), p. 44.
51. For the quotation from MacLeish's "Invocation," see *Collected Poems, 1917-1952* (N. Y., 1952), pp. 93-94. For the replies, see *NR,* LXXIII (Dec. 14, 1932), pp. 125 and 348.
52. "The Social Cant," *NR,* LXXIII (Dec. 21, 1932), pp. 156-58.
53. The lines from "Comrade Levine" are in MacLeish, *Collected Poems,* pp. 76-77. Gold's attack, "Out of the Fascist Unconscious," appeared in *NR,* LXXV (July 26, 1933), pp. 295-96. The debate did not end here. MacLeish, Carl Sandburg maintained, had merely indulged in the "genial custom" of imitating brogues and dialects. *NR,* LXXVI (Sept. 30, 1933), p. 157. Gold replied that MacLeish's reference to Jews was not "a genial accident." This was not the first time MacLeish had exhibited his bias, he said, and, "at the risk of appearing hypersensitive," he would continue to protest "when the monster of race prejudice lifts its head." Sandburg, Gold said, "never wrote poems in phony Yiddish dialect to make a joke of the idea that men were brothers." *Ibid.,* p. 158. In a later communication, MacLeish referred to Gold as "an intelligent but badly frightened young man whose defensiveness about his politics, his race and his literary career amounts to an obsession." Gold, he said, was hurt "by my ridicule of a well known New York literary type (to which, I may add, he does *not* belong)." *Ibid.,* p. 215. In his final rejoinder, Gold admitted he was frightened of fascism: "We are willing to be the harsh and unpleasant and sometimes faulty alarm bells of this fear." *NR,* LXXVII (Jan. 3, 1934), p. 228. Summing up the affair in 1938, Arthur Mizener said: "Because he knew how unimportant the anti-semitism was to the real point of the satire, and because he did not want his poem misunderstood again as Gold had misunderstood it, MacLeish quietly changed 'Levine' to 'Devine' when the 'Frescoes' was republished in *Poems.* Perhaps, too, he was beginning to examine more closely that feeling of his about Jew and Nigger—not this Jew or that Nigger, but the idea of each as a group to which his traditional feeling was attached—and to realize that this unexamined feeling in him was emotionally illogical—and, once [it] got beyond the poet's use of poetry, dangerous." *Sewanee Review,* XLVI (Oct.-Dec. 1938), p. 517.
54. Namely, *Panic, a Play in Verse* (Boston and N. Y., 1935), *The Fall of the City* (N. Y., 1937), and *The Land of the Free* (N. Y., 1938). Reviewing *Panic,* Malcolm Cowley observed that MacLeish had "obviously come down from his ivory tower" and chosen "to write about the life of his own time." *NR,* LXXXII (March 27, 1935), p. 90. *The New Masses* no longer referred to "Der Schöne Archibald" as Hitler's poet laureate. After 1939, however, the old vendetta against him was resumed.
55. The remark about Communism's poisoning the nation is John Chamberlain's, quoted by Granville Hicks in *Where We Came Out* (N. Y., 1954), pp. 51-52. For Hicks's answer, see *ibid.,* p. 51.

CHAPTER NINE · "OLD MEN," "NEW MEN," AND THE PARTY

1. James Bonar, Vol. XXV (1911), p. 302.
2. The quotations are taken from letters of Joseph Freeman to the author, June 16 and June 28, 1958. "In the Twenties," Freeman notes further, "communism was envisioned as the ideal society of the *future* that would liberate us from

the horrors of capitalism; in the Thirties, communism according to the CP slogans—was 20th century Americanism: ie. communism was 20th century capitalism—and never was a truer word spoken or a truer slogan launched, tho few people realized it at the time." *Ibid.*, July 16, 1958.

3. William Phelps (Phillips), "Three Generations," *PR*, I (Sept.-Oct. 1934), p. 51.

4. Freeman, "Ivory Towers—White and Red," *NM*, XII (Sept. 11, 1934), pp. 20-24. This important essay was inspired by an article by the novelist Albert Halper in the *Daily Worker* in which Halper accused Marxian critics of being "intellectually lazy" and of failing to defend their position against reactionary reviewers.

5. Freeman's recommended titles should be compared with the topics listed in the Marxist symposium discussed earlier: "Politics and Poetry" (the relation of art to socioeconomic forces, especially in America); "The Bankruptcy of Liberalism" (in economics, politics, philosophy, literature, with a plan for a "way out"); "Class Justice" (a study of the Sacco-Vanzetti, Mooney, Scottsboro, and other cases); "Painting and Politics" (a study of the Mexican art movement and the relation of art to politics); "American Philosophy" from the Marxist viewpoint; "Marxist Essays" (on such writers as Sinclair Lewis, Sherwood Anderson, H. L. Mencken, Mike Gold, Ezra Pound, John Dos Passos, Floyd Dell, T. S. Eliot); and studies on the American film and press; a critique of various "planning schemes" to save America; the American working class (labor conditions in the U.S.); American imperialism; Latin America today. "Ivory Towers," p. 21.

6. Freeman referred to "A Symposium of Marxist Criticism," sponsored by *The New Masses* ("Author's Field Day," XII, July 3, 1934, pp. 27-36), in which Erskine Caldwell, Robert Cantwell, Jack Conroy, Edward Dahlberg, James T. Farrell, Josephine Herbst, John Howard Lawson, Myra Page, and others paid their disrespects to Granville Hicks and his fellow staff critics for lapses in judgment and taste in their articles and reviews. Many of the comments of the author-critics were harsh and unfriendly. Freeman observed that these captious writers "were remote from our movement until recently" and that they knew "nothing about our work or the problems it involves." "Ivory Towers," p. 23.

7. "Ivory Towers," p. 23. Compare Freeman's classification of the concealed enemies with the dramatist Michael Blankfort's categories invented circa 1931: 1) the "anarcho-cynicist" (the rebel without party or platform, the incipient "Trotskyists," the antiorganizational type); 2) the "Little Napoleon" (the careerist and man of action enamored with "revolution," ferocious foe of deviationists, the "bloodhound of the Revolution" who drifts into anarcho-cynicism when the barricades don't materialize on Broadway; 3) "intellectual purgatories" (cut off from the masses, preoccupied with theory, unable to submit to party discipline, often brilliant and sincere, but dangerous to party unity). Of the three types, only the third deserves sympathy, but he is also the most threatening to a minority party that cannot afford to be magnanimous and "must fight with every means at its command, scurrilous, personal, vindictive, against anyone who would embarrass it momentarily. It must be ever aware of even the slightest deviation on the part of an influential intellectual. . . ." Blankfort, "Little Napoleon and Other Americans" (unpublished manuscript).

8. Freeman, "Ivory Towers," p. 24.

9. *MQ*, VI (Summer 1932), pp. 52-53. At the same time, Briffault sympathized with the party's distrust of intellectuals. If it let down the barriers, it would be inundated with crackpots and "speedily converted into a lunatic asylum for demented sociologists."

10. The Seventh World Congress of the Communist International was held in Moscow, July 25 to August 20, 1935. Georgi Dimitroff's speech that spelled out the tactics of the "Popular Front" approach can be read in a pamphlet, *The United Front Against Fascism and War* (Workers Library Publishers, 1935). See Bell, *op. cit.*, pp. 355-56.

11. Burnshaw, " 'Middle-Ground' Writers," *NM*, XV (April 30, 1935), pp. 19-21.
12. *Letters of Theodore Dreiser*, II, p. 405.
13. *N*, CXL (April 17, 1935), pp. 436-38.
14. *Letters of Theodore Dreiser*, II, pp. 651-52, 658-69.
15. *Ibid.*, pp. 714-15.
16. See *NM*, XV (April 30, 1935), pp. 10-11, and *International Literature*, No. 6 (June 1935), pp. 100-01.
17. *NM*, XV (May 14, 1935), p. 21.
18. "The Gun Is Loaded, Dreiser," *NM*, XV (May 7, 1935), pp. 14-15.
19. Dreiser never did make a convincing retraction, nor was Archibald MacLeish, whose aroused social conscience and militant antifascism delighted the party after 1935, ever criticized again for the alleged anti-Semitism of the "Frescoes." Freeman acidly commented on the anti-Semitic stereotypes in Thomas Wolfe's *Of Time and the River*. "How careless of Dreiser to write his infantile opinions about the Jews to Hutchins Hapgood! Why did he speak directly, 'critically,' in his own name, and rouse the ire of the Jews, the liberals, the radicals? If he had only placed those opinions in the mouth of a 'character,' " as Wolfe had done, no one would have complained. *PR*, II (July-Aug. 1935), p. 6. Three years later, Robert Forsythe (Kyle Crichton), in a tribute to Wolfe, dismissed this "contempt for the Jews" as a passing phase and praised him as a man who could have been and was becoming a "great radical writer." *NM*, XXIX (Sept. 27, 1938), p. 14. By this time, a writer's reputation and prestige carried more weight with the party than his ideological deviations.
20. *NM*, XIV (Feb. 12, 1935), pp. 20-21.
21. *NM*, XIV (Feb. 19, 1935), pp. 21-22.
22. *NM*, XIV (Feb. 26, 1935), pp. 22-23.

CHAPTER TEN • THE FIRST WRITERS' CONGRESS

1. Lerner's review appeared in *N*, CXLII (April 29, 1936), pp. 552-53. Although widely praised in the United States, Hicks's *John Reed* outraged the Russians because, among other things, Hicks mentioned Trotsky's name twenty-seven times. Hicks, incidentally, never showed the manuscript of his book to any party functionary. Conversation with author. The reference to Reed as the "pure knight" is in Gold's article in *NM*, VI (Oct. 1930), p. 5. Freeman's tribute is in *NM*, XIX (June 16, 1936), p. 23.
2. Alan Calmer, "Portrait of the Artist as a Proletarian," *SRL*, XVI (July 31, 1937), p. 3. The most important proletarian magazines were *The Partisan Review* (New York) and *The Anvil* (edited by the proletarian novelist Jack Conroy in Moberly, Missouri); they merged briefly in 1936. Others were *Leftward* (Boston), *Partisan* (Hollywood), *Cauldron* (Grand Rapids), *Left Front* (Chicago), *Left Review* (Philadelphia), *New Force* (Detroit), *The Hammer* (Hartford). By January 1934 nearly thirty clubs had been formed.
3. Philip Selznick, *The Organizational Weapon: A Study of Bolshevik Strategy and Tactics* (N. Y., 1952), p. 125.
4. The first quotation in this paragraph is in Orrick Johns, "The John Reed Clubs Meet," *NM*, XIII (Oct. 30, 1934), p. 25; the second in *PR*, I (Nov.-Dec. 1934), pp. 60-61.
5. *The God That Failed*, ed. by Richard Crossman (N. Y., 1949), p. 136.
6. Dennen's letter is quoted in Max Eastman, *Heroes I Have Known*, p. 203. The quotation ending with "chauvinist art" is in Johns, "The John Reed Clubs Meet," p. 26. Johns was elected national secretary. For his career as a Communist, see his autobiography, *Time of Our Lives*.
7. *NM*, XIV (Jan. 22, 1935), p. 20.
8. Consisting of the following objectives: 1) "Fight against imperialist war, defend the Soviet Union against Capitalist aggression"; 2) "against Fascism, whether

open or concealed"; 3) "for the development and strengthening of the revolutionary labor movement"; 4) "against white chauvinism (against all forms of Negro discrimination or persecution) and against the persecution of minority groups and of the foreign-born; solidarity with colonial people in their struggles for freedom"; 5) "against the imprisonment of revolutionary writers and artists, as well as other class-war prisoners throughout the world." *PR*, II (Jan.-Feb. 1935), p. 96.

9. The organizing committee consisted of Malcolm Cowley, Henry Hart, Michael Blankfort, Edwin Seaver, and Orrick Johns. Some of the important friends or members of the party were Earl Browder, Ben Field, Alan Calmer, Lester Cohen, Jack Conroy, Edwin Dahlberg, Joseph Freeman, Michael Gold, Orrick Johns, Joshua Kunitz, John Howard Lawson, Louis Lozowick, Edward Newhouse, Joseph North, Moissaye Olgin, Paul Peters, Isidor Schneider, Edwin Seaver, Alexander Trachtenberg, Ella Winter, Richard Wright. Such writers as James T. Farrell, Erskine Caldwell, Nelson Algren, Robert Cantwell, Malcolm Cowley, and Nathanael West had already clearly demonstrated their revolutionary sympathies, and the same was true for such well-established names as Waldo Frank, Theodore Dreiser, and Lincoln Steffens.

10. Conversation between author and Hicks.

11. *NM*, XIV (Jan. 29, 1935), p. 21.

12. *The American Writers' Congress*, ed. by Henry Hart (N. Y., 1935), pp. 66-70. Browder's mention of "uniforms" was clearly a reference to Max Eastman's *Artists in Uniform* (N. Y., 1934), whose publication was followed by heated retaliations by party spokesmen.

13. *The American Writers' Congress*, p. v.

14. *Ibid.*, p. 58.

15. *Ibid.*, pp. 60-62.

16. *Ibid.*, p. 95.

17. *Ibid.*, pp. 71-78.

18. *Ibid.*, pp. 103, 107-08. A few months after the congress, Lionel Trilling took Farrell to task on the same grounds that Farrell had earlier used to criticize Jack Conroy's novel *The Disinherited* and the revolutionary short-story writers. Reviewing *The Guillotine Party*, he complained that Farrell only gave the surface reality of modern life. His vision of society, Trilling wrote, "aids our understanding" but "it does not sufficiently give the sense of principle behind complexity in modern life." This weakness was less evident in Farrell's novels, where "'over-expansion of detail may pass for complexity," but Trilling thought that it fatally impaired Farrell's short stories. *N*, CXLI (Oct. 23, 1935), pp. 484-85.

19. Kenneth Burke, *Counter-Statement* (N. Y., 1931), pp. 136-55.

20. See *NR*, LXIX (Dec. 2, 1931), pp. 75-76; New York *Herald Tribune Books*, Dec. 13, 1931, p. 4; *NM*, VI (April 1931), pp. 16-20.

21. "The Nature of Art Under Capitalism," *N*, CXXXVII (Dec. 13, 1933), pp. 675-78.

22. The comment of the reviewer is in *NM*, XXIV (Aug. 10, 1937), p. 26. Burke's first statement appeared in his essay "On Interpretation," *The Plowshare*, Feb. 1934, the second in *NM*, X (March 20, 1934), pp. 16, 18-20.

23. *NR*, LXIX (Dec. 9, 1931), p. 101.

24. *The American Writers' Congress*, pp. 87-94.

25. *Ibid.*, pp. 168-71.

26. *N*, CXL (May 15, 1935), p. 571.

CHAPTER ELEVEN • "THE CENTRE CANNOT HOLD"

1. *Poetry*, XLVI (July 1935), p. 224.

2. *SRL*, XII (May 4, 1935), p. 4; May 11, pp. 3-4, 17-18.

3. The statements of Browder, Seaver, and Gold are in *The American Writers' Congress*, pp. 66, 165, 166.

4. *NM*, XIII (Dec. 18, 1934), pp. 22-23.
5. "The New Masses and Who Else," *The Blue Pencil*, II (Feb. 1935), pp. 4-5.
6. *Proletarian Literature in the United States*, ed. by Hicks *et al*. (N. Y., 1935), pp. 370-71.
7. The passage by Rahv is in William Phillips and Philip Rahv, "In Retrospect: Ten Years of Partisan Review" in *The Partisan Reader*, pp. 679-80. The original editorial board consisted of Nathan Adler, Edward Dahlberg, Joseph Freeman, Sender Garlin, Alfred Hayes, Milton Howard, Joshua Kunitz, Louis Lozowick, Leonard Mins, Wallace Phelps, Philip Rahv, Edwin Rolfe. Other editors up to 1936 included Leon Dennen, Kenneth Fearing, Edwin Seaver, Alan Calmer, Ben Field. Between February and October 1936, the magazine affiliated with *Anvil*, Jack Conroy's magazine, and came out as a literary monthly, *Partisan Review and Anvil*. The last issue was edited by Calmer, Phillips, and Rahv. For Hicks's strictures, see "Our Magazines and Their Function," *NM*, XIII (Dec. 18, 1934), pp. 22-23.
8. *The Partisan Reader*, pp. 680-81.
9. Letter of Phillips and Rahv in *NM*, XXV (Oct. 19, 1937), p. 21.
10. *PR*, I (Feb.-March 1934), p. 2.
11. *NM*, XXV (Oct. 19, 1937), p. 21.
12. Conversation with author, July 6, 1956.
13. Quoted from Hicks's comments on a critical essay by Phelps (Phillips) and Rahv, *PR*, II (April-May 1935), p. 29.
14. *NM*, XVIII (Feb. 18, 1936), p. 22. Gold quoted with approval Newton Arvin's comment on the scholasticism of Phillips and Rahv. Arvin saw no reason why Marxist criticism had "to be drily expository or prosaically analytical, or why it can only be written from the eyebrows up."
15. Farrell's review of Odets is in *Partisan Review and Anvil*, III (Feb. 1936), pp. 28-29; Gold's review of *Paradise Lost* in *NM*, XVIII (Feb. 18, 1936), pp. 22-23. Josephine Herbst's letter and Gold's reply are in *NM*, XVIII (March 10, 1936), p. 20.
16. "Down with 'Leftism,'" *Partisan Review and Anvil*, III (June 1936), p. 8.
17. James T. Farrell, *A Note on Literary Criticism*, pp. 24, 78, 201, 155.
18. "Sectarianism on the Right," *NM*, XIX (June 23, 1936), pp. 23-24. The debate did not end here. Farrell rebutted at length (Aug. 18) in *The New Masses*; Schneider replied in the same issue, as did Morris U. Schappes, who accused "the left-wing literary movement" of coddling Farrell (p. 23). V. F. Calverton, another of Farrell's "vulgarians," entered the fray by announcing that Farrell suffered "from the well-known disease of educating himself in public." His "orthodox book" suffered mainly from a slavish adherence to Marx, a thinker who might "enlighten critics as to the nature of historical processes" but who provided no aesthetic tools. Farrell, said Calverton, confused Marxist criticism with Stalinist criticism, "which is Marxism corrupted and vitiated." See *MM*, IX (Aug. 1936), pp. 16-18, 31, and IX (Oct. 1936), pp. 15-17. Edmund Wilson conceded that Farrell's book suffered from his "characteristic faults." It was diffuse, badly organized, and unclear. Nonetheless, Farrell intelligently demonstrated that most Marxist critics did not understand dialectical materialism, that Marxism had nothing important to say about the goodness or badness of a work of art, that Marx and Engels appreciated literary values far more than did their epigoni, that "social-economic pigeon-holes . . . do not constitute 'categories of value,'" and that the significance of great art does not lie in its function as a class weapon. *N*, CXLII (June 24, 1936), pp. 808-09.
19. For Calverton's gibe, see *NM*, IX (Oct. 1936), p. 16. Farrell wrote his attack against *The New Masses* in the *Socialist Call*, Sept. 18, 1937, p. 5. See also *PR*, IV (Dec. 1937), pp. 3-4, 74-76.
20. Farrell listed such hopefuls as Erskine Caldwell, Robert Cantwell, Jack Conroy, Ben Field, Michael Gold, Albert Maltz, Edwin Seaver, and other contributors to *Proletarian Literature in the United States* who had either stopped writing or produced "slapdash," "miserable," or "pretentious" work. How was it that

writers with "fresh sensibility," living in an exciting period of history, and working with unhackneyed materials should have created so little? He concluded: "What, in brief, have they been doing?" *SRL,* XVI (June 5, 1937), pp. 10, 14.

21. See *NM,* XVI (July 2, 1935), p. 46, (July 16), p. 10; *DW,* July 4, 1935, pp. 1-2, July 12, p. 2. The fullest account is in a pamphlet written by Carleton Beals and Clifford Odets, *Rifle Rule in Cuba* (N. Y., 1935), pp. 3-31.

22. This account has been taken from *NM,* XVI (Aug. 13, 1935), p. 4; *N,* CXLI (Sept. 18, 1935), pp. 319-20; *DW,* July 18 and 31, 1935.

23. *Proletarian Literature in the United States,* pp. 20, 28.

24. Gold's reports of the International Congress appeared in *NM,* XVI (July 30, 1935), pp. 9-11, (Aug. 6), pp. 13-15, (Aug. 13), pp. 18-21. Frank's speech was published in *Partisan Review and Anvil,* III (Feb. 1936), pp. 14-17. Cowley's article on the congress appeared in *NR,* LXXXIII (July 31, 1935), p. 339, and Oakley Johnson's in *International Literature,* No. 8 (Aug. 1935), pp. 72-74. Recently expelled from a university teaching post for his Communist opinions, Johnson was then living in Moscow and writing a book on education.

25. Accounts of the League's activities are contained in letters from Katharine Buckles to Granville Hicks. The memorial meeting for Reed was held on October 18, 1935, at the Civic Repertory Theater. It was sponsored finally by the League of American Writers and the John Reed Club. Alfred Kreymborg read Reed's poem "America, 1918." Other speakers included Granville Hicks, Carlo Tresca, and Robert M. Lovett. The comment on the effect of the lecture series is taken from Ellen Blake's letter to Hicks, Sept. 22, 1936. In November 1935 the League membership was about 135. "Applications for membership," Isidor Schneider wrote, "flow in but the standard is kept high, membership is granted only to creative writers whose published work entitles them to a professional status." *The Publishers' Weekly,* CXXVIII (Nov. 2, 1935), p. 1656.

26. For Gold's talk, see *PW,* V (Nov. 9, 1936), p. 308. The description of West's talk is in *PW,* V (Nov. 30, 1936), pp. 345-46. Meridel Le Sueur is quoted in *PW,* V (Nov. 16, 1936), p. 124.

27. Barbara Chevalier to Malcolm Cowley, Oct. 14, 1936 (MC). Besides Carlisle, the other officers of the Western Writers' Congress were as follows: President: Charles Erskine Scott Wood; Vice-Presidents: J. D. Barry, Donald Ogden Stewart, Harold Eby; Council Secretary, Haakon M. Chevalier.

28. Jan. 27, 1937 (MC). Carlisle did have some trouble with Colonel Wood and Sara Bard Field, his wife. Both had signed a petition requesting asylum for Trotsky, and despite the pressure of Carlisle and his friends, the two stuck to what they called their "constitutional" point of view. They did agree, however, "to protest any use of their name as construing an attack on the Soviet Union and general policies."

PART THREE · DISENCHANTMENT
AND WITHDRAWAL

1. Transcript of interviews in possession of author. The novelist Budd Schulberg arrived at the same conclusion. His leftist sympathies quickened by a summer in Moscow, in 1934, where he attended the first Soviet Writers' Congress and met many distinguished Soviet writers, Schulberg later broke with his Communist associates over his refusal to submit his work to the scrutiny of the members in his "youth group." According to his account, Schulberg was accused of being a "literary 'deviationist'" and "gravely lacking in social responsibility." Believing that *"any* conception so long as it is one's own and gives unity to the work" outweighed "a bushel of solemn tracts on Soviet Realism," Schulberg went his own way. See his "Collision with the Party Line," *SRL,* XXXV (Aug. 30, 1952), pp. 6-7, 31-37. He gave a fuller account of his experiences with party spokesman V. J. Jerome and with John Howard Lawson

in his testimony before the Committee on Un-American Activities. See "Communist Infiltration of Hollywood Motion-Picture Industry—Part 3," *Hearings Before the Committee on Un-American Activities,* 82nd Congress, 1st Session, May 23, 1951, pp. 581-624.

2. Quoted in letter from Dr. Leslie Adams to Malcolm Cowley, March 23, 1934 (MC).

3. Isaac Deutscher, *Russia in Transition and Other Essays* (N. Y., 1957), p. 205.

4. Manuscripts in possession of author.

5. Louis Fischer in *The God That Failed,* p. 222.

6. *Ibid.,* p. 204.

7. Herman Melville, *Billy Budd and Other Prose Pieces,* ed. by R. W. Weaver (London, 1924), XIII, p. 112.

CHAPTER TWELVE · THE LONE REBEL OF CROTON

1. Eastman, *Artists in Uniform,* pp. vii-viii.

2. *The Smokers Companion,* I (June 1927), pp. 42-43, 90, 92, (July 1927), pp. 42-43, 99, (Aug. 1927), pp. 30-31, 103.

3. *N,* CXXVIII (May 1, 1929), p. 533.

4. *N,* CXXVIII (May 15, 1929), p. 585. For further details about Eastman's relations to *The Masses* and *The New Masses,* see his "Bunk About Bohemia," *MM,* VIII (May 1934), pp. 200-08.

5. *N,* CXXVIII (Feb. 27, 1929), p. 257.

6. "But as soon as Eastman attempts to translate Marxian dialectics into the language of vulgar empiricism, his work provokes in me a feeling which is the direct opposite of thankfulness." *MM,* VII (May 1933), p. 212.

7. "Max Eastman. The White-Headed Boy," *PW,* II (Feb. 22, 1935), pp. 88-89. Chevalier, who apparently retained his own brand of romantic revolutionism long after Eastman's disenchantment, underplayed Eastman's toughness and common sense, which usually anchored his fancies, but others have also noted the "wise-child" aspect of Eastman, his "over-sensitiveness," "vanity," and "spitefulness" intermingling with his candor, magnanimity, and generosity.

8. Max Eastman, *The End of Socialism in Russia* (N. Y., 1937), p. 3.

9. Eastman to Calverton, June 24, 1934 (VFC). As evidence of Moscow's plot to "get" him, Eastman interpreted a *New Masses'* review of Albert Perry's *Garrets and Pretenders* (VIII, May 1933, pp. 18-20) as a covert attempt to "liquidate" him by presenting him as a Bohemian aesthete. Robert Carlton Brown's amusing if inaccurate reminiscence about the old *Masses,* "Them Asses," *American Mercury,* XXX (Dec. 1933), pp. 403-11, inadvertently, he felt, assisted Moscow's vendetta against him. The Stalinists, he suggested in a letter to *The New Republic,* had first "inoculated" the magazine's readers against *Artists in Uniform* with Matthew Josephson's article on Russian literary politics and then "trotted out" Lincoln Steffens to impugn his motives and obfuscate the issue. See Josephson, "The Literary Life in Russia," *NR,* LXXIX (June 6, 1934), pp. 90-93, and Eastman's letter, *ibid.,* pp. 321-22.

10. Lincoln Steffens, "Swatting Flies in Russia," *NR,* LXXIX (June 20, 1934), pp. 161-62. Alexander Kaun, who read Eastman's book in manuscript, had praised it and even cited additional examples of literary persecution in the U.S.S.R., but he reversed himself when he came to write a review of the book: "Why should Max Eastman," he asked, "worry his fine head about 'artists in uniform'? Genuine artists will not suffer from any uniform as is demonstrated amply by Soviet writers, painters, composers. Perhaps they manage to take their uniform with a sense of humor." *PW,* IV (Feb. 10, 1936), p. 71.

11. E.G.S. to V. F. Calverton, Aug. 2, 1934 (VFC).

12. *DW,* Feb. 16, 1934.

13. *NM,* XI (May 8, 1934), pp. 24-26.

14. Eastman, *The End of Socialism in Russia*, pp. 20, 45.
15. Eastman to Calverton, June 11, 1936 (VFC).

CHAPTER THIRTEEN · THE RADICAL IMPRESARIO

1. Hook's initial attack appeared in *MQ*, IV (May-Aug. 1927), pp. 388-94; Calverton's remonstrance in *MQ*, VII (Sept. 1933), pp. 511-12. The two men obeyed Calverton's call for a truce for a while, but in September 1934 the battle flared up again. Hook, in an open letter to Lincoln Steffens about *Artists in Uniform*, conceded that Eastman "may have invented a few details to fill out the picture" but that his account of the "intellectual pogrom" was essentially true. *MM*, VIII (Sept. 1934), p. 486. Eastman interpreted this "defense" as a slur and insisted that every fact had been double checked. Eastman to Calverton, Sept. 25, 1934 (VFC). Hook made no effort to conceal his poor opinion of Eastman at this time, but by 1937 he paid tribute to Eastman's courageous and lonely fight "against the spoliators of the revolutionary tradition." See Eastman, "Journey."
2. Calverton's "own account" is "Between Two Wars," *MQ*, XI (Fall 1940), pp. 5-6. One of his grandfathers had been a German "Forty-Eighter." His father's denunciation of the Spanish-American War as a "blot on the American flag," he wrote, "had a profound influence upon me and led me to view society from a radical point of view which has dominated all my literary work." Quoted by George Britt, *MQ*, XI (Fall 1940), p. 10. Britt's article and S. J. Kunitz and H. Haycraft, *Twentieth Century Authors* (N. Y., 1952), p. 240, are the sources of information about Calverton's education.
3. For a sympathetic picture of Calverton's Baltimore background and the literary circle at his Pratt Street residence, see Vera Fulton, "2110," *MQ*, VII (Fall 1940), pp. 33-35. Lillian Symes, "V. F. Calverton, Socialist," *ibid.*, pp. 21-22 is the source for Calverton's relation with the party. Possibly she exaggerates the "boycott."
4. *New English Weekly* (Aug. 3, 1933), pp. 383-84.
5. Schmalhausen to Calverton, Jan. 10, 1933 (VFC). "Part-time literary critic, psychoanalyst and sexologist, defender and debunker of Communism, Schmalhausen moved through the pages of the *Quarterly* with the gusto of a whirlwind. His articles were bitter, iconoclastic, sometimes in questionable taste, but always hilariously provocative." So Herman Singer wrote in *MQ*, XI (Fall 1940), pp. 18-19. Other estimates of Schmalhausen's writing and influence on the magazine were less kindly. "Above all things," a friend wrote to Calverton, "don't succumb to the smart alec style as your friend Schmalhausen has. You have no idea how that diluted Menckenism, Plain-Talk-backwash, subway-tempo stuff sets on edge the teeth of scholars and gentlemen, like myself. And it's as impermanent as anything can be, as jazz will be, let's say." Grant Knight to Calverton, April 28, 1930 (VFC).
6. The source for Calverton's publishing claims is Kunitz and Haycraft, *op. cit.*; the quotation from Symes is in Symes, *op. cit.*, p. 21.
7. Gold to Calverton, May 4, 1925 (VFC).
8. "His book, to the best of my knowledge, is the first serious attempt in this country to apply the touchstone of Marxian interpretation to every phase of human thought." *DW*, May 30, 1925. Other critics reviewed it less ecstatically than Gold. Mencken, one of Calverton's targets, observed that the author, like all socialists, was excited by facts "known to all the rest of us since childhood." Had Calverton been "sound on the open shop, the Dawes plan and the Coolidge idealism," Mencken observed, he might have wangled a Harvard chair for himself, but now he would get only a "few superior sniffs." *American Mercury*, V (June 1925), p. 252. Waldo Frank made Calverton out to be a clumsy popularizer whose work demonstrated "the intellectual and spiritual bankruptcy of

our revolutionary labor movement. . . . Beneath Mr. Calverton's preference for works of art 'exalting the workingman' is hidden an undifferentiated love of power." *NR,* XLIII (June 24, 1925), p. 132. The best review was Kenneth Burke's in the New York *Herald Tribune,* May 10, 1925. Burke admitted the deficiency of the purely aesthetic approach to art but insisted, as he brilliantly continued to insist during his Marxist period, that sociology was no substitute for aesthetic considerations. The most hostile notice was H. M. Wicks's review in the *DW,* Sept. 24, 1925. Wicks flatly contradicted Gold and dismissed Calverton as a vulgar Philistine and anti-Marxist. Browder wrote to Calverton that he disapproved of "the spirit and method" of Wicks's attack, since it contributed nothing to the discussion, but he did side with Wicks and Trotsky against Calverton "on the question of whether proletarian culture is possible of development. We have got so far to go before we make use of even a considerable portion of what has already been created that I seriously doubt the capacity of the working class to create a new system of culture during the period of struggle. Without a doubt we will witness a tremendous release of creative forces and the proletariat will establish the lines within which the future developments must come, but that the distinct class character will be woven thru the contents of the culture of the future, seems quite doubtful to me." Browder to Calverton, Oct. 29, 1925 (VFC).

9. W. Z. Foster to Calverton, Sept. 8, 1925 (VFC).
10. William F. Dunne to Calverton, Oct. 3, 1925 (VFC).
11. Calverton to H. M. Wicks, Sept. 22, 1927 (VFC).
12. *DW,* Jan. 12, 1929, contained the "exposure" of *The Modern Quarterly.* Calverton wrote to Jay Lovestone, Feb. 16, 1929 (VFC). The details of his self-defense are taken from a carbon copy of a letter addressed to the *DW,* Jan. 17, 1929 (VFC).
13. Calverton discussed the "paper shortage" in *MM,* VII (March 1933), p. 111. Calverton and Dinamov continued to correspond until as late as 1933. In that year, Dinamov chided Calverton for not replying to his long letter. "If you are angry with me, don't forget that we Russians consider self-criticism as the best method of growth and development." Dinamov to Calverton, Jan. 19, 1933 (VFC). Dinamov disappeared in the great purges. Foster's and the other party critic's attack appeared in *The Communist,* X (Feb. 1931), pp. 107-11, 851-64, (Nov. 1931), pp. 941-59. For Elistratova's attack, see *International Literature,* No. 1 (1932), p. 107. Leon Dennen, who met the author of this terrifying directive to *The New Masses* in Moscow shortly after her article appeared, was startled to discover a twenty-year-old apple-cheeked girl who knew English imperfectly and absolutely nothing about the United States. Conversation with author. For Calverton's response to his official condemnation, see V. F. Calverton, "An Open Letter to the New Masses," *MM,* VII (March 1933), pp. 110-14, 127-28.
14. See Oneal to Calverton, May 12, 1927, Hiam Kantorovitch to Calverton, Nov. 13, 1926, and another letter with no date (VFC). There is a useful account of Kantorovitch in the *American Socialist Quarterly,* V (Oct. 1936), pp. 2-5, (Dec. 1936), pp. 39-40.
15. Sidney Hook had written to him about the John Reed Club meeting, Aug. 19, 1932 (VFC). Kunitz wrote to him April 11, 1932 (VFC). Harrison, a former editor of *The New Masses* and author of a novel called *Generals Die in Bed* (N. Y., 1930), broke with the party in 1933. See *NM,* VIII (Feb. 1933), pp. 24-25; *MM,* VII (May 1933), p. 313; *N,* CXXXVI (March 22, 1933), pp. 321-22. Harrison's novel *Meet Me at the Barricades* (N. Y., 1938), written after he broke with the party, contains malicious portraits of Gold and Browder.
16. *DW,* Nov. 6, 1933.
17. Briffault to Calverton, April 7, 1933 (VFC); Seaver to Calverton, Feb. 17, 1933 (VFC). Davis, introduced to *The Modern Monthly* by Granville Hicks, his close friend and collaborator, had suggested to Calverton "a monthly polemic department" to answer such critics as Hazlitt, Krutch, Canby, and Hansen "when

they venture out of the safe fields of impression and eclecticism to attack the Marxists" (Davis to Calverton, Nov. 20 and 28, 1932), and he had established such a department. Then the party came down on Calverton, and Hicks and Davis were in a dilemma. Hicks had told Calverton that although he felt fellow travelers should be neutral in factional disputes, if compelled to do so, he would side with the party and disassociate himself from an Opposition journal. Hicks to Calverton, Jan. 9, 1933. Davis sympathized with the Opposition and found the role of the fellow traveler a very precarious one. Should he support the party, "refusing however to be guilty of their intellectual limitations and errors," or fight for correct principles? The second course was particularly tempting to a former bourgeois liberal. "And if you are not ready to support the party, why not attack them, not of course as communists or Stalinists, but on particular formulations, as on this Social-Fascist business? It would give no particular comfort to the bourgeois; it would be revolutionary theoretic united front, but at the same time a struggle for correct principles. . . ." Davis to Calverton, Jan. 9, 1933. Yet he was not quite ready to attack the party as Calverton wanted him to do, even though he felt the "Social Fascism business is something that should be attacked" along with the party's position on the Negro question. "To hasten the revolutionary movement in America today," he added, "is impossible through the existing agency of the Communist Party." *Ibid.,* Jan. 15, 1933. By February, he declared that the Third International had "capitulated to Fascism," and in April he still was willing to string along with *The Modern Monthly* so long as it kept to its present policy. From then on, all communication with Calverton ceased. Calverton's letter to Blankfort, n.d., is in VFC.

18. The reference to internecine warfare is in *MM,* VIII (May 1934), p. 197. For the other quotations and references in this paragraph, see Wolfe to Calverton, Aug. 6, 1934; Lamont to Calverton, Jan. 6, 1934; Nearing to Calverton, March 2, 1933; and Chevalier to Calverton, July 13, 1934 (VFC).

19. Hook's definition of his political position is taken from his article "Why I Am a Communist," *MM,* VIII (April 1934), p. 143. Wilson's theoretical views at this time are expressed in a letter to Calverton, Nov. 4, 1933 (VFC). His complaint about the lampooning of Gold is in a letter to Calverton, June 2, 1934 (VFC). A memorandum in the Calverton Papers referring to Wilson's disagreement with Calverton's policies is as follows: "However, he is willing to write a letter saying he will continue to contribute to it and approve of it in policy. We tried to dissuade him on the basis of the fight that is going on and the fact that the CP will distort the statements. Also Wilson believes he is more a Marxist than Hook, Eastman and Bates with whom he disagrees."

20. Calverton's remark about the reviews of his own books is taken from *MQ,* XI (Fall 1940), p. 48. His expression of despair about his influence is in a letter to Nina Melville, n.d. (VFC). His editorial is quoted in *MQ,* XI (Fall 1940), p. 23.

21. Calverton to Brooks, Dec. 27, 1939 (VFC).

22. *MQ,* XI (Fall 1940), p. 23.

23. Memorandum in the Calverton papers.

24. See S. L. Solon, "V. F. Calverton's Quest for Utopia," *American Mercury,* (LII, May 1941), pp. 625-30, and "Calverton—Between Two Worlds," *MQ,* XI (Fall 1940), pp. 25-28.

25. V. F. Calverton, *The Man Inside* (N. Y., 1936), p. 182.

26. Santayana to Calverton, Nov. 2, 1936 (VFC).

27. Calverton to Santayana, Nov. 25, 1936.

CHAPTER FOURTEEN · COWLEY'S RETURN

1. "Our Liberal Weeklies," *MM,* X (Oct. 1936), pp. 7-10. In 1932, Granville Hicks in his unpublished essay "The Magazine in America" on American maga-

zines had also described *The New Republic* as the "journal of muddled liberalism," but made different recommendations: "When in the issue of January 14, 1931," he wrote, "Edmund Wilson published his 'Appeal to Progressives,' the *New Republic* became the principle vehicle of expression of what are now called the fellow-travelers of Communism. Not that the magazine went over to Communism; it has, on the contrary, vigorously repudiated such a stand. But it opened its columns to those liberals who were moving leftward, and thus took advantage of one of the vital moments of the current era. At the same time it devoted a considerable amount of space to the question of social planning, the chief subject of interest for liberals who have remained in the capitalist camp. . . . Its career almost perfectly reflects the course of liberalism in the past two decades: from confidence through disillusionment and confusion to division and new alignments." Both *The Nation* and *The New Republic* were "confused" because their editorial policies clashed with the views of their Communist and fellow-traveling contributors. "One does not question their high-mindedness; one simply forsees that they must eventually accept the logic of their position."

2. Conversation with author.
3. The N.C.D.P.P. was an organization of writers, artists, and other professional people of all races, creeds, and political affiliations who were dedicated "to a militant defense of 'all persons prosecuted or persecuted on charges basically political, and economic in nature.' " Ostensibly independent and unaffiliated, the N.C.D.P.P. was in effect controlled by the Communist membership. Nonparty members who attempted to initiate actions not acceptable to the party (such as the resolution of Herbert Solow and James Rorty to organize a united front of all antifascist organizations before the party had decided to do so) were voted down and criticized. In May 1933 a group of antiparty dissidents (among them Herbert Solow, Lionel Trilling, Anita Brenner, and Eliot Cohen) resigned in protest against "the sectarian attitude and bullying factional tactics" of the N.C.D.P.P. officials. Letter from H. Solow *et al.* to Joshua Kunitz, May 8, 1933. Solow's group founded the Provisional Committee for Non-Partisan Labor Defense. Two years later, another group, including Edmund Wilson and Adelaide Walker, resigned over the failure of the N.C.D.P.P. to support "cases other than those assumed by the ILD [International Labor Defense] or those endorsed by the Communist Party." It particularly criticized the committee's refusal to protest against the arrest and trial of Russian revolutionaries accused of plotting Kirov's assassination. "A resolution demanding such open trials so that the workers of the world should not remain in the dark about their enemies, was voted down after a barrage of abuse, with name-calling and mud-slinging." Adelaide Walker *et al.* to N.D.C.P.P., Jan. 25, 1935. Horace Kallen, Suzanne La Follette, Mark Van Doren, Newton Arvin, Clifton Fadiman, and Frank Boas also resigned in 1935.
4. Cowley, *Exile's Return*, p. 302.
5. *NR*, XC (Oct. 19, 1938), p. 313.
6. Cowley to Wilson, Oct. 31, 1938.
7. *NR*, LXXXIX (Dec. 2, 1936), pp. 147-48.
8. *NR*, LXXXIX (Jan. 20, 1937), pp. 348-50.
9. "For there can be no question that the entire world would already be at war had this and the preceding trials not taken place." Henry Hart in *Direction*, I (June 1938), p. 28
10. *NR*, XC (April 7, 1937), p. 267.
11. Cowley to Wilson, May 14, 1937.
12. Cowley to Wilson, Oct. 31, 1938. See also Cowley to Betty Cox, Sept. 16, 1960.
13. See Basso to Cowley, July 17, 1939 (MC). "The average citizen here," Schneider wrote in his letter, "thinks nothing is impossible and looks for Soviet airmen to capture all the world records and Soviet scientists to do all the impossibilities. The general faith in endless marvels is astounding. Therefore the wiping out of anti-Soviet elements is reacted to with a greater sense of secur-

ity. It would be as if an engineering commission in New York were to announce that land under the foundations of the Brooklyn Bridge was sifting away and that new concrete foundations were being laid, and that the strata under all the other bridges were similarly being examined. The citizens of New York would be grateful for that and feel all the securer. So here the trials and all that has followed has been met with gratitude and an increased sense of security and this is possible because the capitalist encirclement is felt as a reality here and the trotskyite plots are realities and because the people has a confidence in the leadership that is impossible to understand anywhere else." Schneider to Cowley, n.d. (MC). Schneider later denounced the machinations of the American Trotskyites in his novel *The Judas Time* (N. Y., 1947).

14. Tate to Cowley, Dec. 19, 1930, May 19, 1934, Dec. 17, 1934, Dec. 19, 1934 (MC). The only chance to overthrow finance capitalism, Tate believed, was to back the program of the Southern Agrarians, which did not, as the Left Wing critics argued, seek to restore the past. Rather, said Tate, it took a hint from the past and sought to "create a decent society in terms of American history." Tate to Cowley, April 6, 1936 (MC).

15. Basso to Cowley, Aug. 12, 1937, July 17, 1939, and three undated letters (MC).

16. Rexroth to Cowley, n.d. (MC).

17. Cowley to Wilson, Feb. 1940.

CHAPTER FIFTEEN • THE ADVENTURES OF JOHN DOS PASSOS

1. *NR*, LXXXIII (Sept. 9, 1936), p. 132. Lionel Trilling took issue with this view in a first-rate essay, "The America of John Dos Passos," *PR*, IV (April 1938), pp. 26-32.

2. *NR*, XCIX (June 14, 1939), p. 163. In his review of *The Adventures of a Young Man*, Farrell interpreted the largely unfavorable criticism of the book as "a warning to writers not to stray off the reservations of the Stalinist-controlled League of American Writers to which more than one of the critics belong." Farrell had hard things to say about Cowley, Louis Kronenberger, and Alfred Kazin. See *American Mercury*, XVII (Aug. 1939), pp. 489-94.

3. *NR*, XCII (Oct. 6, 1937), p. 237. *Writers Take Sides* (N. Y., 1938), a collection of statements by American authors on the Spanish Civil War, demonstrates the overwhelming support given to the Spanish Republican government by American writers. Of the 418 American writers who gave their views on the Spanish war, 410 strongly favored the Loyalists, seven took no positive stand, and one author (Gertrude Atherton) sided with Franco. Besides Communists and party sympathizers, the list included names like Thornton Wilder, Edgar Lee Masters, Fanny Hurst, Maxwell Anderson, John Steinbeck, Hemingway, and many others.

4. Cowley reported his experiences in five articles for *NR*, XCII (Aug. 25-Oct. 6, 1937), pp. 62, 93, 152, 179, 233, and one for *NM*, XXIV (Aug. 10, 1937), p. 16. Other American delegates to the Writers' International Association for the Defense of Culture were Anna Louise Strong, Louis Fischer (already there), and Langston Hughes, who did not make it. The most painstaking summary of Stalinist repressions in Spain was Anita Brenner's in *MM*, X (Sept. 1937), pp. 4-27.

5. See *NM*, XXXII (July 4, 1939), p. 21 for the party view of Dos Passos's novel. For Farrell's comment, see *American Mercury, op. cit.*, p. 490.

6. *Harvard Monthly*, LX (Nov. 1914), p. 67, LXII (July 1916), p. 149.

7. Dos Passos's letters quoted here were all written to his friend Arthur McComb. Two are undated. The others were written on June 28, 1917, Aug. 27, 1917, Sept. 12, 1917, July 31, 1917, Aug. 10, 1917, Sept. 12, 1917, Oct. 5, 1918. I am indebted to Mr. Dos Passos for permission to quote these letters. According to Dos Passos, Hillyer left before their collaborative novel was finished. Each author was supposed to write alternate chapters. Finishing the book, Dos Passos

wrote, "made me discharge a shocking bit of ammunition prematurely." Dos Passos to McComb, Dec. 31, 1917.

8. Dos Passos, *F*, II (Oct. 20, 1920), p. 133.

9. Introduction to George Grosz's *Interregnum* (N. Y., 1936), pp. 14-15.

10. Dos Passos, *NR*, LXVI (April 1, 1931), p. 175. John Howard Lawson, Mike Gold, Em Jo Basshe were his associates in the New Playwrights Theatre. Persuaded by Mike Gold, the philanthropist Otto Kahn donated $30,000 to finance the group ("dubbed the 'revolting playwrights' by Alexander Woollcott," according to Harold Clurman), and then proceeded to produce a half-dozen much-criticized plays. References to the group can be found in Clurman's *The Fervent Years* (N. Y., 1945) and in *NM*, III (Jan. 1928), p. 27, (March 1928), p. 23, (April 1928), p. 27. Dos Passos's remarks on the New Playwrights and his observations on the problems and possibilities of the revolutionary theater are stated in his introduction to his *Three Plays* (N. Y., 1934), pp. xi-xxii, and in *NM*, IV (Aug. 1929), p. 13, III (Dec. 1927), p. 20. By "revolutionary," he meant a theater that had broken with the current theatrical practices, not the theatrical tradition: "It must draw its life and ideas from the conscious sections of the industrial and white collar working classes which are out to get control of the great flabby mass of capitalist society and mould it to their own purpose. In an ideal state it might be possible for a group to be alive and have no subversive political tendency. At present it is not possible." *NM*, III (Dec. 1927), p. 20. Dos Passos's highly jaundiced afterthoughts about his New Playwright friends and Lawson in particular are contained in his rather mediocre novel *Most Likely to Succeed* (N. Y., 1954).

11. Wilson's critique of Dos Passos is in *NR*, LVIII (April 17, 1929), pp. 256-57. See also Padraic Colum's review in *The Dial*, LXXXVI (May 1929), p. 442, for a similar comment.

12. The quotation ending "emerging today" is by Alan Calmer in *NR*, LXXI (July 20, 1932), p. 264. Commenting on Hart Crane's death, Calmer remarked that had Crane been born a decade later, he might have been saved by Communism. Dos Passos's advice to middle-class liberals is in his article "Back to Red Hysteria!" *NR*, LXIII (July 2, 1930), p. 169. See also his "Wanted: An Ivy Lee for Liberals," *NR*, LXIII (Aug. 13, 1930), pp. 371-72, and his "Intellectuals in America," *NM*, VI (Aug. 1930), p. 8, with a reply by Robert Evans (Joseph Freeman), pp. 8-9. The theme running through all these articles was the importance of attracting the ideologically salvageable elements of the middle class for the revolution. Dos Passos, with his Veblenian bent, felt they could be found among "the engineers, scientists, independent manual craftsmen, writers, artists, actors, technicians of one sort or another." Freeman acknowledged that such people under "the pressure of economic depression" might swing to the working class, but the writer himself must not waste his time by "seeking impossible middle roads." He must use his talents to paint the horrors of capitalism.

For evidence of Soviet interest in Dos Passos's work, see issues of *International Literature*, especially between 1932 and 1934. Two writers ask him in an open letter to come out in the press against imperialism (Nos. 2 and 3, 1932, p. 109). A report of an organized discussion of his work held in Moscow in the spring of 1933 contains friendly criticisms and high praise: "What's good in Dos Passos? That he is seeking. That he is active and hates the old world. That he has experienced in his own skin the meaning of peace and war (capitalistic). That he is broad. That he is candid. That he is simple (*cries of*—'Yes! yes!')" (No. 5, 1933-1934, p. 108). A review of two Soviet productions of *Fortune Heights* (running simultaneously in Moscow) by David Mirsky (No. 3, 1934, pp. 152-54).

13. Isidor Schneider, *PR*, I (June-July 1934), p. 54.

14. See *NM*, X (March 6, 1934), p. 8. The New York *Times* gave full coverage to the story (Feb. 16, 1934), and the episode was widely reported. *The Modern*

Monthly, VIII (March 1934), pp. 87-92, printed "An Open Letter to American Intellectuals" pointing out that the Communist Party through its organized hooliganism had destroyed the chance to build a genuine united-front protest on behalf of the Austrian workers and to dramatize the meaning of fascism to American labor. The letter called upon American intellectuals "sympathetic with the revolutionary movement" to resign from the party if they were members and from any "auxilliary organizations, well-described as 'innocents clubs.'" The Communist position was defended in some detail by Oakley Johnson in *The Monthly Review*, I (June 1934), pp. 12-16. The riot received extended treatment in James T. Farrell's *roman à clef, Yet Other Waters* (N. Y., 1952), pp. 267-312. "The Communists," declares the hero, "have disgraced themselves permanently in the American radical movement after this disgusting spectacle" (p. 276).

15. For the Communist comment on the affair and their appeal to Dos Passos to detach himself from the "revolutionary butterflies," see *NM*, X (Feb. 27, 1934), pp. 8-10, X (March 6, 1934), pp. 8-9. By the "queer company," *The New Masses* editors meant the group of early defectors from the party position who had before been the chief contributors to *The Manorah Journal* (Eliot Cohen, Anita Brenner, Lionel Trilling, and others). Isidor Schneider placed them among "the intellectuals who have turned left in the last few years and have since turned right, and further left and roundabout." Some of the signers of the letter, he noted, had been members of the National Committee for the Defense of Political Prisoners but had resigned to set up a rival committee. *NM*, X Feb. 27, 1934), p. 24. For Dos Passos's reply, see *ibid.*, p. 6.

16. "Substitution, at Left Tackle: Hemingway for Dos Passos," *PR*, IV (April 1938), p. 63. See also David Sanders, "Ernest Hemingway's Spanish Civil War Experience," *American Quarterly*, XII (Summer 1960), pp. 133-43.

17. Dos Passos's "metamorphosis" was noted in *NM*, XXIV (July 6, 1937), p. 13. He spelled out his pessimistic conclusions about Europe and his new thoughts about America in *Journeys Between Wars* (N. Y., 1938). Matthew Josephson thought it odd that the man who described the "dread fate which overtakes innocent bewildered, middle-class liberals" should now represent an attitude he once condemned. *NR*, LXXXXIV (April 27, 1938), p. 365.

18. "A Conversation. Theodore Dreiser and John Dos Passos," *Direction*, I (Jan. 1938), pp. 2-3, 28.

19. *DW*, Feb. 26, 1938.

20. The psychoanalytic explanation for Dos Passos's radicalism is offered by Martin Kallich in *The Antioch Review*, X (March 1950), pp. 99-106. Kallich suggests that the hatred of his father "may have contributed to his distrust of all forms of authority that can possibly invade the individual's right" (p. 102). It should be noted, however, that his father, a successful and rich corporation lawyer, displayed his own kind of intransigence. The allegedly "Tory" Dos Passos, now living in Westmoreland County, Virginia, is still no "defender of vested interests." See Granville Hicks, "The Politics of John Dos Passos," *The Antioch Review*, X (March 1950), p. 97. Schneider's review is in *NM*, XX (Aug. 11, 1936), pp. 40-41. For Dos Passos's 1939 credo, see *PR*, VI (Summer 1939), p. 27.

CHAPTER SIXTEEN • THE ARRIVAL AND DEPARTURE OF GRANVILLE HICKS

1. *NM*, XXVII (April 26, 1938), p. 22.

2. For the story of his being fired, see *NM*, XV (June 4, 1935), pp. 9-10. He tells of his "alienation" in *Where We Came Out*, p. 28. The Northampton incident is told in Hicks, *Small Town* (N. Y., 1946), pp. 220, 34-35. See also "Com-

munism and the American Intellectuals," in *Whose Revolution?* ed. by I. D. Talmadge (N. Y., 1941), p. 80.

3. The account of his leftward progress is taken from "Communism and the American Intellectuals," p. 80, *Where We Came Out,* p. 38, and *Small Town,* p. 222. See also *Hearings Before the Committee on Un-American Activities,* 53rd Congress, 1st Session, Feb. 26, 1953, pp. 95-115.

4. *International Literature,* No. 2 (1933), p. 129. In the same letter, Hicks disclosed that he would not write for Calverton's magazine any more "unless my mind or its policy changes." The next year he contributed to an *International Literature* symposium entitled "Where We Stand," in which he still expressed anxiety about apostate intellectuals. No. 3 (1934), p. 90. Other American contributors to the symposium were Theodore Dreiser, Joseph Freeman, Louis Adamic, Isidor Schneider, Corliss Lamont, Joseph Kalar, and James Steele.

5. See "Communism and the American Intellectuals," pp. 93, 94.

6. Granville Hicks, *I Like America* (N. Y., 1938), pp. 149, 147.

7. The quotations in order are from "Communism and the American Intellectuals," pp. 86-87, and *NM, XXV* (Sept. 28, 1937), p. 22.

8. See "Communism and the American Intellectuals," pp. 97, 45.

9. Hicks's views on the second congress were obtained in conversation. The reply of the League secretary is in a letter, Ellen Blake to Granville Hicks, May 20, 1937.

10. The "renegades" were James T. Farrell, Edmund Wilson, V. F. Calverton, John Chamberlain, Charles E. S. Wood, Charles Y. Harrison, Mary McCarthy, Dwight Macdonald, Lionel Trilling, William Ellery Leonard, John B. Wheelwright, Joseph Wood Krutch, and others, all affiliated with the American Committee for the Defense of Leon Trotsky. Among the other signers of the "Call" for the second writers' congress were Newton Arvin, Van Wyck Brooks, Erskine Caldwell, Marc Connelly, Langston Hughes, James Weldon Johnson, Paul de Kruif, John Howard Lawson, Robert Morss Lovett, Archibald MacLeish, Claude McKay, Lewis Mumford, Clifford Odets, Vincent Sheean, Upton Sinclair, Donald Ogden Stewart, Genevieve Taggard, Jean Starr Untermeyer, Carl Van Doren, Ella Winter.

11. Frank's open letter was published in *NR, LXXXI* (May 12, 1937), pp. 19-20. Two years before, Frank had addressed an open letter to the Soviet ambassador in Washington asking for clarification about the 1935 trials. It, too, was friendly, moderate, concessive. He professed reluctance "to sit in judgment against the political decisions of Moscow" but feared the "weakening effect" of the trials "upon the Union's champions in America and elsewhere." The U.S.S.R.'s position as " 'fatherland' of all true revolutionaries, the world over" made it imperative for the Soviet leaders to clarify ambiguities. *NR, LXXXII* (Feb. 27, 1935), p. 77. Frank's second letter revealed the same faith in the Soviet leaders and the same concern for the "countless sincere people throughout the world whose *morale* is indispensable to the revolutionary movement at this hour . . ." (p. 19). Speaking for himself, Frank declared that Trotsky's charges of a frame-up seemed unreasonable. Frank's letter could in no way be interpreted as a hostile attack against the U.S.S.R., but so far as the party was concerned, it automatically placed him in the enemy camp.

12. For the Macdonald letter, see *N, CXLIV* (June 19, 1937), p. 714. For the Stalinist comment on the oppositionists, see *NM, XXIII* (June 15, 1937), pp. 8-9. The several Trotskyists referred to were Harry Roskolenko, Dwight Macdonald, and a few others. The questions *not* discussed had to do with the freedom of the socialist critics to "comment on Soviet arts and letters, the relationship of the writer to political parties, the attitude of writers who accept the people's front in politics toward revolutionary literature—must they shift their allegiance to liberal democratic literature?—and the reason why left-wing literature today has not come to more impressive fruition." Macdonald, *op. cit.,* p. 714. In other words, pretty important questions.

13. The quotations in the last two paragraphs are in *The Writer and the Changing World*, ed. by Henry Hart (N. Y., 1937), pp. 73, 57, 50-53, 237, 189.

14. According to Stewart, Joseph Freeman had phoned Ella Winter to report Waldo Frank's refusal to accept the chairmanship of the L.A.W., and to get some suggestions for Frank's successor. Stewart described himself as a political innocent at this time, but he accepted. Conversation with author.

15. Folsom to Hicks, July 27, 1938. One week later, Dreiser wrote the following to his secretary: "Here is how it happened. Last Sunday wires from the League of American Writers and The American League for Peace & Democracy began to arrive asking me to attend—all costs paid—the International Convention for International Peace to be held in Paris July 21-22-23. All I had to do was to go and I represented them and that I believe in peace. That seemed easy, so, since I needed a lot of peace just then, I decided to do it. So here I am in the gaudiest candy box ever set afloat." Dreiser to Yvette Szekely, July 14, 1938.

16. They dealt with, for example, gossip; the deviations, Left and Right, of writers in the movement; the promising candidates.

17. This writer, then a graduate student at Harvard University and a fellow Counsellor, vividly remembers the debate between Hicks and Father Curran of the Brooklyn *Tablet* held in Mechanics Hall, Boston, in the spring of 1939. The hall was packed with hysterical followers of Father Coughlin. They drowned out Hicks's attempts to speak with screams and catcalls and behaved as if they were perfectly capable of lynching him. It took great courage to face that howling mass.

18. Cowley found much to praise but criticized Hicks for his overharsh judgments, his simplistic dichotomies, and his too literal application of economic determinism. *NR*, LXXVI (Nov. 8, 1933), pp. 368-69. Hicks indignantly denied these charges. Hicks to Cowley, Nov. 7, 1933 (MC). James T. Farrell, who had been quarreling with Hicks off and on for several years, wrote a slashing review of *The Great Tradition* in *The American Spectator*, IV (April 1936), pp. 21-26; Clifton Fadiman called it "brilliant" and recommended it especially to those who did not share the author's political convictions. *N*, CXXXVII (Oct. 18, 1933), pp. 449-50. Harry Levin called the first edition "an able defense of a challenging thesis" but condemned the new chapter added to the second edition, because it "jeopardized his thesis and threw the whole subject out of scale. Having successfully pointed out the defects of Henry Adams and Edith Wharton, he now celebrated the merits of B. Traven and Clara Weatherwax." "The Twilight of Marxist Criticism" (unpublished manuscript).

19. Conversation with author. See also "Communism and the American Intellectuals," p. 96.

20. *NR*, C (Oct. 4, 1939), pp. 244-45.

21. *N*, CXLIX (Aug. 26, 1939), p. 228. The manifesto was intended to combat an appeal to non-Communist writers and artists made shortly before by the League for Cultural Freedom and Socialism, organized and directed by Dwight Macdonald and other writers associated with *Partisan Review*. See *PR*, VI (Summer 1939), pp. 125-27 for the statement of the L.C.F.S. The pro-Soviet signers stressed "ten basic points in which Soviet socialism differs from totalitarian fascism." 1) The U.S.S.R. was and continues to be "a bulwark against war and aggression"; 2) it has alienated anti-Semitism and other minority restrictions; 3) established public ownership of the means of production; 4) raised living standards and ended unemployment; 5) organized almost twenty-four million workers into trade unions; 6) emancipated women; 7) "effected one of the most far-reaching cultural and educational advances in all history"; 8) substituted science for superstition in every phase of life; 9) demonstrated that its dictatorship is only transitional by "its epoch-making new constitution"; 10) and shown that it is advancing by different paths to the same goals desired by America.

22. *NR*, C (Oct. 4, 1939), p. 244.

23. *NM*, XXXIII (Oct. 3, 1939), p. 21.

CHAPTER SEVENTEEN · "NEVER CALL RETREAT"

1. "Communism and the American Writer. A Report on the Tenth Newberry Library Conference on American Studies," *The Newberry Library Bulletin*, V (Aug. 1959), pp. 105-06.
2. Freeman to author, June 16, 1958.
3. *Ibid.*, June 8, 1958.
4. Joseph Freeman, *Voices of October* (N. Y., 1930); *The Soviet Worker* (N. Y., 1932); *The Background of German Fascism* (N. Y., 1933), a pamphlet; preface to *Proletarian Literature in the United States* (N. Y., 1935), and *An American Testament* (N. Y., 1936).
5. An extensive literature has grown up about this much-debated incident. For the view that Sinclair destroyed "The Greatest Thing Done On This Side of the Atlantic," by Seymour Stern and Sinclair's reply, see *MM*, VII (Oct. 1933), pp. 525-32, 575-76. The best summaries are Ivor Montagu, "The Sinclair Tragedy," *New Statesman and Nation*, VII (1934), pp. 85-86; Edmund Wilson, "Eisenstein in Hollywood," in *The American Earthquake*, pp. 397-413; and Marie Seton, *Sergei M. Eisenstein* (N. Y., 1960), pp. 156-244, 513-16. With liberals and radicals almost universally pro-Eisenstein, Sinclair felt impelled to appeal directly to Stalin, who cabled his support November 21, 1931: "Eisenstein loose [*sic*] his comrades confidence in Soviet Union stop He is thought to be a deserter who broke with his own country stop Am afraid the people here would have no interest in him stop." The message concluded with an invitation to visit the U.S.S.R. (US). Sinclair proudly told this writer that he was the only American private citizen to whom Stalin sent a direct communication. Stalin's message may be found in US. According to Marie Seton, *The New Masses* did not publish a thirty-page letter sent by Eisenstein giving his side of the story since the magazine had already announced its support of Sinclair's candidacy for governor of California. Seton, *op. cit.*, p. 282.
6. Joseph Freeman in *Proletarian Literature in the United States*, p. 22.
7. Freeman to author, June 17, 1958.
8. Rinehart sold the rights of Freeman's book to Victor Gollancz, the English publisher of the Left Book Club, for $1,000. *An American Testament* was even more highly regarded in England than in America and sold extremely well. The English edition is a cut version of the American.
9. Freeman to author, April 8, 1960.
10. Rexroth to Cowley, n.d. (MC).
11. *NM*, XLVI (May 4, 1943), p. 26.
12. Charles Péguy, *Basic Verities: Prose and Poetry* (N. Y., 1943), p. 51.

CHAPTER EIGHTEEN · "THINK BACK ON US"

1. Anna Louise Strong to Hicks, Sept. 29, 1939.
2. Hicks, *Where We Came Out*, p. 74.
3. Hicks to author.
4. Max Lerner to Malcolm Cowley, Oct. 19, 1939 (MC).
5. *PR*, VI (Spring 1939), p. 8.
6. MacLeish's pronouncements are taken from *NR*, CII (June 10, 1940), p. 790, and *A Time to Speak* (N. Y., 1940), pp. 116-18.
7. Charles Yale Harrison quipped about the motorized intellectuals in the *NL*, Nov. 11, 1939, p. 8. Gold's comments are in *NM*, XXI (Dec. 15, 1936), pp. 27-29.
8. V. J. Jerome, *Intellectuals and the War* (N. Y., 1940), pp. 5-23. Portions of this pamphlet first appeared in *NM*, XXXVII (Sept. 24, 1940), pp. 14-15, and

(Oct. 1, 1940), pp. 17-18. Jerome came into the movement in the late twenties and emerged in the early thirties as the party functionary in charge of the intellectuals. Apparently he never commanded the complete admiration or respect of his subordinates and had very little influence on the intellectuals.

9. Epithets coined by Samuel Sillen, Isidor Schneider, Ruth McKenney, V. J. Jerome, and others. See *NM*, XXXIII (Sept. 26, 1939) to XXXVII (Oct. 29, 1940).

10. *NM*, XXXVII (Oct. 8, 1940), p. 4.

11. Jerome, *op. cit.*, p. 59.

12. *Decision*, II (July 1941), pp. 40-45.

13. Michael Gold, *The Hollow Men* (N. Y., 1941), pp. 68, 99-102.

14. Daniel Lang, "It's Hard to Recant," *Twice a Year*, V-VI (Fall-Winter 1940, Spring-Summer, 1941), p. 492.

15. Granville Hicks, *Only One Storm* (N. Y., 1942), p. 396.

16. For Farrell's comments, see *PR*, VII (Sept.-Oct. 1940), pp. 390, 141. Chamberlain made his plea in *NR*, CII (Jan. 22, 1940), p. 118.

17. Dennen's unusual background gave him important advantages over most of the young radicals associated with *The New Masses* and *Partisan Review* in the early thirties. Born in the United States, he returned with his parents to Russia shortly before the 1917 revolution and remained there until the early twenties. His literary career as critic, essayist, and translator began when he was still in his teens, and his knowledge of Russian enabled him to anticipate the switches in Soviet literary theory and politics well ahead of his colleagues. In 1932 he returned to the U.S.S.R. for a year's stay. *Where the Ghetto Ends* (N. Y., 1934) was his report on the situation of the Jews in the Soviet Union, the one aspect of Russian life that Dennen could write about with qualified enthusiasm. As a reporter for the Moscow *Daily News*, he caught disturbing glimpses of government repression, but he swallowed his doubts. Never a docile or acquiescent follower even when he was in the movement (counterrevolutionary charges were twice brought against him in the John Reed Club), Dennen became a "notorious class enemy" in 1938 when he began to write for the social-democratic *New Leader*. He could not stomach the trials, and the doubt that "constantly gnawed at my conscience" finally forced him to break. The "Munich betrayal" convinced him "that a showdown between the forces of fascism and democracy" was imminent and that the socialist movement needed moral restoration. The great crime committed by the Communists, Dennen thought, was to banish truth from the socialist movement. See *NL*, July 27, Aug. 6, Aug. 17, 1940.

18. *NL*, Aug. 17, 1940.

19. Sample bits from "The Revolt of the Intellectuals": "with the exception of Granville Hicks, probably none of these people [Newton Arvin, John Dos Passos, John Steinbeck, Malcolm Cowley, and others] was a Communist. They were fellow-travelers who wanted to help fight fascism. How should they know that Lenin was the first fascist and that they were cooperating with the party from which the Nazis had borrowed all of their important methods and ideas?" Or again: "The literary intellectuals might be slow, lazy, self-important, unpractical, fussy or funny, but they had reached their convictions 'not without years in the wilderness and days of blindness.' Above all they were articulate." *Time*, XXXVII (Jan. 6, 1941), pp. 58-59. The review of *The Dry Season* appeared in *Time*, XXXIX (Feb. 16, 1942), pp. 13-14. For Cowley's letter and *Time*'s reply, see *ibid.* (March 16, 1942), p. 6.

20. Chambers's meager account of his literary activities is in *Witness*, p. 264. Freeman's account is taken from his letters to author, July 6, 1958, July 1, 1958.

21. For a masterful portrait of the committed fellow traveler, see Lionel Trilling, *The Middle of the Journey* (N. Y., 1947).

22. See Cowley's "In Memoriam," *NR*, CIII (Aug. 12, 1940), pp. 219-20, containing his resignation from the League and his letter (*ibid.*, p. 280) in reply to a letter from the National Board of the L.A.W. A copy of Oliver La Farge's

letter of resignation to Franklin Folsom, July 17, 1940, charging that the League's policy was directed by the Communist Party, may be found in MC. See also Hicks, *Where We Came Out*, p. 77.

23. Richard Wright, *NM*, XXXIX (June 17, 1941), pp. 8-12. The quotations from Hammett, Stewart, and Taggard are taken from mimeographed copies of their speeches delivered at the congress.
24. *NM*, XI (April 17, 1934), p. 29.
25. *NM*, LVII (Oct. 23, 1945), p. 22.
26. *NM*, LVII (Feb. 12, 1946), pp. 19-20.
27. Howe and Coser, *op. cit.*, p. 433. Russia was domesticated for American readers of the bourgeois press. *Life*, in its March 29, 1943 issue, entirely devoted to Soviet-U.S. co-operation, described the Russians as "one hell of a people" who "look like Americans, dress like Americans, and think like Americans." The N.K.V.D., according to the *Life* editors, was comparable to the F.B.I. and was set up to track down traitors. Harrison Salisbury, in *Colliers*, described a Russian boss of the Urals as "built like a Golden Gloves champ . . . tough as one of Zane Grey's Texas gunmen . . . could stand up and slug it out toe to toe with such American pioneers as Jim Hill, Jay Gould or Jim Fiske." Quoted from Paul Willen, "Who 'Collaborated' With Russia?" *Antioch Review*, XIV (Fall 1954), pp. 259-83.
28. See *NM*, LVIII (Feb. 26, 1946), pp. 6-10, (March 19), pp. 18-20. Samuel Sillen's critique ran for six issues of the *DW*, Feb. 11 through Feb. 16, 1946. For Foster's reflections on the episode, see *NM*, LIX (April 23, 1946), p. 2. An account of the Duclos letter and its consequences is given by David A. Shannon, *The Decline of American Communism* (N. Y., 1959), Chap. I.
29. Maltz's apology appeared in *NM*, LIX (April 9, 1946), pp. 21-22; his message to the symposium in *DW*, April 18 and 19, 1946.
30. *NM*, LIX (April 25, 1946), pp. 6-9.
31. *NM*, LIX (March 12, 1946), p. 10, (Feb. 12, 1946), pp. 24-25.
32. *Mainstream*, I (Winter 1947), p. 7.
33. Howard Fast, *Intellectuals in the Fight for Peace* (N. Y., 1949), p. 14.
34. *NR*, CVIII (May 10, 1943), p. 614.
35. *Commentary*, XX (Sept. 1955), p. 285.
36. See Hicks, "The Fighting Decade," *SRL*, XXII (July 6, 1940), p. 17. Trilling's comments are in *PR*, VI (Fall 1939), p. 109.
37. For a fictional account of Communists in the writers' projects, see Norman MacLeod's *You Get What You Ask For* (N. Y., 1939).
38. Rahv, *PR*, VI (Summer 1939), pp. 7-8.
39. The original proposal to investigate the Soviet charges of Trotsky's alleged dealings with fascist terrorists came from the Socialist Party in August 1936. Three months later, a letter signed by Norman Thomas, Devere Allen, John Dewey, Horace Kallen, Freda Kirchwey, and Joseph Wood Krutch, the "Provisional American Committee for the Defense of Leon Trotsky," appealed to liberals to investigate these charges. *The New Masses* denounced the committee, as did *Soviet Russia Today*, a monthly published by the American Friends of the Soviet Union. In March 1937 the latter carried an open letter warning liberals not to permit themselves to be dupes of the Trotskyists or to lend support "to Fascist forces which are attacking democracy in Spain and throughout the world." One need not approve of "all the means" employed by the Soviet Government to improve the conditions of its people, the letter went on to say, but it should be allowed to protect itself from its internal and external foes. The party kept up its barrage against the committee, headed by John Dewey, which conducted an inquiry into Trotsky's case in Coyoacán, Mexico, where Trotsky was then residing. Corliss Lamont unpersuasively attempted to refute the findings of the Dewey commission, and other party spokesmen sought to discredit the commission's report (*Not Guilty*, 1938) as well as the manifesto of the Committee for Cultural Freedom, which drew uncomfortable analogies

between Soviet, German, Italian, and Japanese totalitarianism. See Peggy E. Gilder, "American Intellectuals and the Moscow Trials," honors thesis, Smith College, 1960. The anti-Trotsky argument is presented in *NM*, XXI (Nov. 10, 1936), p. 20; *Soviet Russia Today*, VI (March 1937), p. 14, VI (Jan. 1938), p. 14; *NR*, XCIII (Dec. 22, 1937), p. 181; *DW*, Aug. 14, 1939. Eugene Lyons describes the episode, replete with names of fellow-traveling and party letter signers in his *The Red Decade*, pp. 251-52. See also the New York *Times*, Dec. 14, 1937, p. 10, and *N*, CXLVIII (May 27, 1939), p. 626.

40. The quotations from Wood are taken from a typescript copy of an unpublished letter to the *Daily Worker* in reply to an attack against him in the Dec. 17, 1936 issue of that paper. I am indebted to Mr. Herbert Solow for showing me this letter. The quotation from Proudhon is from Martin Buber, *Paths to Utopia* (London, 1949), pp. 11-12.

41. Julien Benda, *The Betrayal of the Intellectuals* (Boston, paperback edition, 1955), pp. 86, 21.

INDEX